Financial Market Risk

What is financial market risk? How is it measured and analyzed? Is all financial market risk dangerous? If not, which risk is hedgeable?

These questions, and more, are answered in this comprehensive book written by **Cornelis A. Los**. The text covers such issues as:

- competing financial market hypotheses;
- degree of persistence of financial market risk;
- time–frequency and time–scale analysis of financial market risk;
- chaos and other nonunique equilibrium processes;
- consequences for term structure analysis.

This important book challenges the conventional statistical ergodicity paradigm of global financial market risk analysis. As such it will be of great interest to students, academics and researchers involved in financial economics, international finance and business. It will also appeal to professionals in international banking institutions.

Cornelis A. Los is Associate Professor of Finance at Kent State University, USA. In the past he has been a Senior Economist of the Federal Reserve Bank of New York and Nomura Research Institute (America), Inc., and Chief Economist of ING Bank, New York. He has also been a Professor of Finance at Nanyang Technological University in Singapore and at Adelaide and Deakin Universities in Australia. His PhD is from Columbia University in the City of New York.

Routledge International Studies in Money and Banking

Financial Market Risk

Measurement and analysis

Cornelis A. Los

Routledge
Taylor & Francis Group

LONDON AND NEW YORK

First published 2003
by Routledge
2 Park Square, Milton Park, Abingdon, Oxon, OX14 4RN

Simultaneously published in the USA and Canada
by Routledge
270 Madison Ave, New York NY 10016

Routledge is an imprint of the Taylor & Francis Group

Transferred to Digital Printing 2005

Typeset in Times New Roman by
Newgen Imaging Systems (P) Ltd, Chennai, India

British Library Cataloguing in Publication Data
A catalogue record for this book is available from the British Library

Library of Congress Cataloging in Publication Data
Los, Cornelis Albertus, 1951-
    Financial market risk : measurement & analysis / Cornelis A. Los.
        p. cm. – (Routledge international studies in money and banking ; 24)
    Includes bibliographical references and index.
    1. Hedging (Finance) 2. Risk management. I. Title. II. Series.

HG6024.A3L67 2003
332'.01'5195–dc21   2003040924

ISBN 0–415–27866–X

Printed and bound by Antony Rowe Ltd, Eastbourne

To
Janie and Klaas Los, Saba and Leopold Haubenstock, and P. Köhne

with
Gratitude for life, liberty and the pursuit of happiness

Contents

Figures

Tables

Preface

In the spring semester of 2000, I was asked to teach a new course on Risk Theory III for 15 third- and fourth-year undergraduate students and 2 postgraduate Masters students at the School of Economics of Adelaide University, in Adelaide, South Australia.[1] I could have chosen an existing textbook on *Risk Theory* for actuarialists,[2] and that would have saved me countless hours of research and writing, but, instead, I decided to be courageous and develop a new course from scratch and to focus on (1) the measurement, and (2) the analysis of financial market risk, and, perhaps, to discuss some of the implications for financial portfolio management.

Previous professional experiences had widened my perception of financial market risk, both of financial crises and of financial turbulence, when I was a Senior Economist for Nomura Research Institute (America), Inc. between the years of 1987 and 1990. An example of this being the following event: on November 19, 1987, the Dow Jones Industrial Average plunged 508.32 points, losing 22.6 percent of its total value. That drawdown far surpassed the one-day loss of 12.9 percent that began the great stock market crash of 1929 and foreshadowed the Great Depression. The Dow's 1987 plunge also triggered panic selling and similar drops in stock markets worldwide. But the US stock market recovered, after the Fed first pumped in a massive amount of liquidity and then drained it two weeks later in a classic monetary action, that prevented an already persistent, and now rapidly becoming illiquid, stockmarket to grind to a screeching halt. Although this was a massive market failure, it was a financial crisis without many consequences thanks to the rapid successful monetary engineering action by the Fed (in contrast to the Fed's bungling in the 1930s!).

On Friday January 20, 1990, as a Senior Economist of Nomura Research Institute (America), Inc., the research arm of the Japanese global securities firm Nomura Securities, Inc., I predicted on CNBC TV, in response to a question by the Chief Economist of *Business Week*, that the Tokyo stock market would decline by 40 + percent. I stated that, because the Japanese stock market was an "administered" market, it would happen in carefully controlled phases, in the first- and third quarter of that year. This would happen in response to a slight tightening of the money supply by the Bank of Japan in December 1989, which attempted to deflate Japan's asset "bubble." The Japanese stock market actually lost 69 percent of its value in 1990, in the respective predicted quarters. Until now, it never fully recovered from that financial crisis, because Japan's banks were determined not to restructure and to write off any book value of their financial institutions. These financial institutions obstructed the free working of the market system and became "zombies," or "living dead," which continued to destroy global capital for more than a decade thereafter. For more than ten years, Japan's financial system operated as a black hole for capital flows, retarding global economic development. Even the availability of free money (= money available at zero interest) did not induce any domestic activity in what had become a pure Keynesian liquidity gap. The Bank of Japan was pushing on a string. Why the difference between the US stock market and the Japanese stock market?

In 1991–1993, as Chief Economist of ING Bank, Inc., later ING Capital, Inc., in New York City, I became familiar with the trading of distressed debt of the Latin American and domestic US markets, resulting from the collapses of credit worthiness and the increases in the respective country and regional risk premia. At that time I wrote sales revenue generating country risk reports on Latin American emerging markets, e.g., my report on Mexico, in July 1993, generated $21 million in sales of Mexican distressed debt for ING Bank with one week.[3] In 1992–1993, I also monitored the European Financial Crisis, when the European Monetary System became undone and accelerated the rush into the overvalued Euro, which subsequently after January 1, 1999 depreciated by more than 15 percent in value versus the US dollar. It's only recently that the Euro is returning to par with the US dollar.

Finally, in 1995–1999, when I was an Associate Professor in Banking and Finance at the Nanyang Business School of the Nanyang Technological University (NTU), from my vantage point in Singapore, I closely monitored the Asian Financial Crisis in 1997, i.e., the collapse of the Asian bank loan, stock and currency markets, closely followed by the Russian Financial Crisis of 1998, i.e., the default of Russian government debt, which led, via the implosion of the German bond market to the $500 billion collapse – and subsequent bail-out by the Fed – of Long Term Capital Management, Inc.[4]

Primarily in reaction to the Asian Financial Crisis of 1997–1998, I designed and supervised a Masters thesis research project on the Wavelet Multiresolution Analysis (MRA) of Asian foreign exchange markets (Karuppiah and Los, 2000), to demonstrate that most of the Asian currency markets were antipersistent and had continued their regular trading. There was a sharp discontinuity in the Thai baht on July 2, 1997, the day after the handover of Hong Kong back to the People's Republic of China, followed by considerable financial turbulence. But there was no collapse of the other Asian FX markets, which continued to function properly, as shown by our analysis.[5] In fact, for the first time we could measure the differences in the degrees of persistence of the various Asian FX markets and show that some markets operated faster and more efficiently than others.

I had become deeply involved in that fascinating Asian FX project and, with the assistance of Dr Er Meng Hwa's Center for Signal Processing at NTU, I became convinced that financial market risk should not only be measured in terms of its frequency distributions, as the conventional Markowitz'–Jorion Value-at-Risk approach suggested, but that it should be completely analyzed in terms of its long-term time dependencies, preferably in the all-encompassing time–frequency domain.

The fundamental characteristic of financial time series, such as FX rates or asset returns, is that they are nonstationary (stationarity is a precondition for classical correlation, spectral and harmonic analysis) and singular (non-singularity is still a precondition for Gábor's Windowed Fourier analysis). This insight was reinforced when I learned from signal processing engineers about the technological advance made by Mallat's wavelet multiresolution analysis (MRA) in 1989. It demonstrated that time–frequency visualization and analysis of non-differentiable, singular, nonstationary and non-ergodic financial time series is possible by wavelet MRA. Simultaneous analysis of many frequency and time dependencies is made possible because the new wavelet MRA operates as a gigantic data microscope that can be fine-tuned to any level of analytic resolution one wants to use for research.

I obtained further inspiration in Adelaide from the provocative 1994 book *Fractal Market Analysis* of Edgar Peters, Manager of PanAgora Management, who substitutes his Fractal Market Hypothesis (FMH) for the 1970 Efficient Market Hypothesis (EMH) of Eugene Fama. A foray into the rapidly expanding field of parametric stable distributions brought me in contact with Nolan's clear explanations of their Zolotarev parametrization. In October 2000, at an international conference at the University of Konstanz, I noted that some of my European colleagues had also made progress in that direction, in the context of the emerging Extreme Value Theory.

All these efforts helped me to sort out the confusing array of critical exponents in Chapter 4. Additional reading of Benoit Mandelbrot's awe-inspiring 1982 monograph, *The Fractal Geometry of Nature*, and the compilations of his articles in his recent books, on *Fractals and Scaling in Finance* and *Multifractals and 1/f Noise*, immeasurably influenced the direction of my research. They also stimulated many of the computer graphics and other illustrations of this book.

Finally, a relearning, and drastic upgrading, of my rudimentary secondary school knowledge of fluid dynamics at Adelaide University, supported my original "hydrological " or "meteorological" interpretation of global cash flow dynamics and the measurement and modeling of financial turbulence and of financial crises.[6] Of course, there exists the well-known historical precedent of an economist applying hydrological concepts to Economics. In the 1950s, in the basement of the London School of Economics (LSE), the New Zealand economist A. W. Phillips, of elusive Phillips curve fame, engineered an actual water flow model of the National Income Accounts of an economy.[7] Many introductory textbooks of Economics still refer to this model by way of National Income flow diagrams. Also in Finance, the dynamic cash flow theory finds some resonance. For example, James van Horne of Stanford University has a (5th) edition introductory finance textbook on *Financial Market Rates and Flows*.

However, following Mandelbrot, my book applies hydrological concepts to Finance, in particular to the identification from inexact data of models for stable financial risk, financial turbulence and financial crises, that can quantitatively assist in the time–frequency analysis and optimal management of such financial market risks.

I thank Dean Colin Rogers and Professors Jonathan Pincus, Kym Anderson and Richard Pomfret in the School of Economics of Adelaide University in South Australia, for providing me with a rustic, but productive research environment in the year 2000 to develop a series of three new courses in Finance: (1) "Computational Finance: A Scientific Perspective," which resulted in my eponymous book published in 2001 by the World Scientific Publishing Co. in Singapore; (2) "Financial Risk: Measurement and Management," which forms the basis for this book published by Routledge; and (3) "Dynamic Valuation and Hedging," which is used for parts of courses in the new Master of Science in Financial Engineering program at Kent State University and which may develop further into a third book. My Honors students at Adelaide University provided the necessary stimulus, raised lots of questions, produced self-correcting feedback and did helpful library research and computations during my series of lectures.

In the southern hemisphere Fall Semester of 2001, Dean Garry Carnegie and Professors Jonathan Batten and Stewart Jones of Deakin University in Burwood, a suburb of Melbourne, Victoria, Australia, provided me a second place to work on this book, while, as a Visiting Associate Professor of Finance, I taught a course on Business Finance Decision Making and tutored students on the finer points of Finance and Financial Markets.

My employment as a tenure-track Associate Professor of Finance by Kent State University in Ohio allowed me to finish this book and to ready it for production. In particular, I would like to express my deepest thanks to Dean George Stevens and Associate Dean Rick Schroath, who both have been unwavering in their support of my tenuous position in Kent State's Business School. At Kent State, I interacted with and enjoyed the excellent services of the library and I received the highly desirable computational assistance and error corrections of my postgraduate students Kyaw Nyonyo from Burma, Joanna Lipka from Poland, Kang Zhixing (Richard), Zong Sijing and Chen Xiaoying from the People's Republic of China, Rossitsa Yalamova from Bulgaria, who found new relevant articles and checked a large number of bibliographic references, and Sutthisit Jamdee from Thailand, who worked with me to produce a movie of a colorized dynamic scalogram for real-time high frequency financial data. Doctoral candidates Kyaw and Zong prepared the scalograms and scalegrams of the Financial Crises in Mexico, Brazil and Chile in Chapter 8, using interactive software available on the web. All these students actively participated in my doctoral seminars on Research in Finance in the Fall terms of 2001 and 2002.

I also enjoyed the exchanges about my research with Mohammed Kazim Khan and Chuck Gartland, both Professors of Mathematics, Richard Kent, Professor of Economics, Jim Boyd, Associate Professor of Finance, who hired me, and my colleague Mark Holder, Assistant Professor of Finance and Director of Kent State's new Master of Science in Financial Engineering program, which we together helped to give birth to. This program is one of 38 such programs in the world and the only one devoted to derivatives, in particular, energy and weather derivatives.

It's also high time that I acknowledge a lifelong debt of intellectual trust and encouragement to the late Mr P. Köhne, the Head of the Nicolaas Beets School, a no longer existent elementary school in Heiloo, North-Holland, The Netherlands, who in the early 1960s, conducted a unique socio-economic experiment with four boys and four girls. Mr Köhne selected two boys and two girls from poor to low moderate socio-economic background (I was one of them) and two boys and two girls from high-moderate to high socio-economic background and gave them a dedicated preparation for the entrance exam to the Gymnasium, the former Dutch prep school for university level education, to prove that meritorious education and not socio-economic background mattered for individual success. He proved to be right: all eight boys and girls passed their entrance exam and successfully completed their Gymnasium education. Later on, all eight students received university degrees and became very successful in their respective professions, unfortunately, after Mr Köhne had already passed away.

I dedicate this book to Mr Köhne, and I dedicate it also to my parents and my mother-in-law and (now late) father-in-law for maintaining their faith in me throughout my life, but in particular during the past critical six years, when I was an Associate Professor of Banking and Finance in the Australasian region. The coming years may be just as turbulent, but, hopefully, not as catastrophic as the Asian Financial Crisis of 1997, which originally inspired this book.

Finally, I want to acknowledge my debt to Robert Langham, Editor – Economics of Routledge, who invited me to publish this book in Routledge's International Studies in Money and Banking; to Terry Clague, his Editorial Assistant, who kept me on track when we moved back to the States and when my wife underwent her lung cancer operation; to Moira Eminton, Editor for Taylor & Francis Books, who kept this and many other projects on track during a merger by her publisher, and who had to move from London to New York; and to Vincent Antony, project manager of Newgen Imaging Systems (P) Ltd., in India, who was able to accomodate my math and figures in a beautiful typesetting.

As always, I'm very grateful to my beautiful and very dapper wife Rosie, who prevents me from making the most serious grammatical errors and who, despite major setbacks, continues to brighten my days with love and laughter.

Cornelis A. Los
Kent State University

Notes

1 That is, in the spring semester of 2000 in the northern hemisphere, which was the actual Fall semester for Australia in the southern hemisphere.
2 Such as Bühlmann, Hans (1970) *Mathematical Methods in Risk Theory*, Springer-Verlag, New York, NY.
3 That was *before* the Mexican Financial Crisis of 1994!

4 Cf. Jorion (1999) "How Long-Term Lost Its Capital," *RISK*, September, and Dunbar, N. (2000) *Inventing Money: The Story of Long-Term Capital Management and the Legends Behind It*, John Wiley & Sons, Chichester, UK.
5 The Asian Financial Crisis did not originate in the antipersistent Asian FX markets, but in the non-transparent and persistent Asian bank loan markets and in the government controlled, illiquid and persistent Asian stock markets.
6 Contained in my Dutch Doctorandus (= MPhil) thesis of 1976.
7 I was a Research Student at the University of London in 1975–1976, when I first learned about system identification and control theory and about Phillips' interesting hydrodynamic contraption.

Introduction

Probabilitatem Non Esse Delendam, Esse Deducendam[1]

This book covers the latest theories and empirical findings of financial market risk, its measurement, analysis and management, and its applications in finance, e.g., for dynamic asset valuation, derivatives pricing and for hedging and portfolio management. A special and rather unique part of this book is devoted to measuring when financial turbulence can occur and when financial catastrophes are probable.

To gain a basic understanding of financial market risk, we must ask at least four fundamental questions:

(1) What is financial market risk?
(2) How do we measure financial market risk? For example, which frequency and timing distributions of financial market risk do we actually measure?
(3) Is all financial market risk dangerous or can we distinguish between "safe" financial market risk and "dangerous" financial market risk? For example, which financial market risk is diversifiable, which is hedgeable and which is non-diversifiable and non-hedgeable?
(4) How can we manage financial market risk to our advantage? For example, how much financial market risk is hedgeable?

These four questions will be answered, or at least discussed in technical detail, in the four consecutive Parts of this book.

In Part I on Risk Processes, we discuss the four different concepts of measuring risk, such as uncertainty, randomness, irregularity and probability. We discuss risk invariants, in particular, against time and frequency, called self-similarity, or, more precisely, self-affinity. We highlight the statistical invariants of stationarity and time–frequency scaling and provide various descriptors of serial time dependence, of discontinuity and of concentration. Our objective is to determine the periodicity, aperiodic cyclicity, turbulence, intermittence and arrhythmias of the financial time series currently produced in great abundance by the global financial markets.

This detailed analysis of financial time series helps us to determine what is the best way of measuring financial market risk. In this book, we find that the best way of measuring risk is as a residual, unexplained *irregularity*. For that purpose we analyze the fractality, or self-affinity, of speculative and cash market pricing, and propose various forms of measurement and visualization of long-term dependence, in particular, of market persistence or antipersistence, using wavelet Multiresolution Analysis (MRA). As Yves Meyer comments in his interesting series of lecture notes: "The study of profound problems is often influences by the available instruments and techniques."[2] We put these concepts of financial risk within the context of two major market hypotheses: the Efficient Market Hypothesis of Eugene Fama and the Fractal Market Hypothesis of Benoit Mandelbrot and Edgar Peters.

In Part II on Risk Measurement we discuss the various ways of measuring financial market risk in both its time and frequency, c.q., scale, dimensions. The basic tool for such inexact model identification of financial market risk is "correlation" or, slightly more specific, "convolution." Thus, in this book, we compute the "resonance" coefficients both for Fourier Transforms and for Wavelet Transforms. For the measurement of the irregularity of financial time series, we compute critical Lipschitz–Hölder exponents, in particular the Hurst Exponent, and the Lévy Stability Alpha, and relate them to Hoskings fractional difference operators, e.g., the Fractional Brownian Motion model, which will be our benchmark model.

We use three techniques of nonstationary time series analysis to measuring time-varying financial market risk: Range/Scale analysis, windowed Fourier analysis, and wavelet MRA, and we mathematically relate these powerful analytic techniques to classical Box–Jenkins time series analysis and Pearson's spectral frequency analysis, which both rely on the assumption of stationarity and ergodicity. By empirical examples, we demonstrate the superiority of these advanced techniques, which can deal with the occurrence of non-stationarity and non-ergodicity. The modeling focus will be again on Hoskings' fractionally differenced time series, in particular, on Fractional Brownian Motion.

Part III on Term Structure Dynamics is the most adventurous part of the book, delving into the transient phenomena of chaotic risk and of financial turbulence. It defines financial chaos and demonstrates how such chaos can develop in financial markets. For the first time, we develop a theory of dynamic cash flow analysis, which allows the modeling of the transient phenomena of financial chaos and of turbulence within an adapted financial framework of term structure analysis and which allows the measurement of such phenomena by wavelet MRA.

Financial turbulence is not necessarily a bad phenomenon. We learn that it is actually an efficiency enhancing phenomenon that only occurs in the antipersistent, most liquid anchor currency markets. Financial turbulence should, therefore, be sharply distinguished from the real bogey of financial managers: financial catastrophe or crisis. A financial crisis is measured as a discontinuity or singularity in a persistent financial time series. It is unpredictable and occurs only in persistent financial markets with low liquidity.

Now, some financial crises are more dangerous than others. For example, it may not be dangerous to speed up the trading and price formation activity in a financial market and encounter a crisis, because the financial market may move through a so-called safe financial crisis. Whereas slowing down trading and price formation may lead to an unsafe financial "blue sky catastrophe." It may cause a financial crisis in which the pricing system close to an attractor suddenly heads for the attractor at infinity: the market pricing process breaks down and can't recover.

Thus, ultimately, this Part III is laying the groundwork for an ongoing, but not yet completed, search for integrity measures for financial markets, to quantify the margin of safety between a financial market's attractor and the fractal boundary of its safety basin. The Lipschitz α_L and the Hurst H-exponent discussed in Part II can be viewed as such an integrity measures. I've already observed that these measures change very dramatically by basin erosion at a point on the solution path at which a realistic, inexact financial pricing system is liable to escape. This is now known by system safety engineers as the "Dover cliff" effect. However, a complete quantification of the margin of safety for financial markets is not covered by this book. It will probably have to wait for still more detailed empirical and theoretical research.

Still, we find that the statistician's averaging spectral decomposition, which is based on the ergodic stationarity assumption, has inhibited and slowed down scientific progress regarding the investigation of transient structures, such as turbulence vortices in financial markets. It is also clear that financial analysis is currently shifting from the study of the steady-state solutions of financial markets to the study of their transient behavior. This book is intended to help this transition in finance (and economics) along and to speed it up.

For the first time in financial-economic analysis, we are looking to measure and engineer the true empirical conditions that ensure the safe and continuous working of our financial market pricing systems *time locally* and not *on (time) average*. Financial market systems are the complex institutional arrangements that guarantee the optimal allocation and most effective and efficient use of our scarce financial resources. They are crucial for the proper projection, adoption and integration of new financial technology and thereby for the growth in productivity that raises the living standards of all humankind.

Part IV contains one chapter on Financial Risk Management: the stable kind, the cyclical kind, the turbulent kind and the critical kind. It discusses Extreme Value Theory and some consequences for the popular Value-at-Risk approach to portfolio and bank management. Insurers try to reduce financial risk at a cost, by diversification, using fund management portfolios to reduce the unsystematic risk and by hedging to reduce the systematic risk.

But sometimes financial market risk cannot be reduced because of its peculiar empirical characteristics of long-term time-dependence and non-stationarity, a phenomenon already studied in the 1960s by Fama and by Samuelson, a winner of the Nobel Memorial Prize in Economics. Sometimes, we want to have more financial market risk, because we speculate that more financial risk may lead to higher average returns on our investments. Thus, financial risk management is not only about reducing risk!

Indeed, the Chinese pictograph for *risk* in the following Figure 1 consist of two symbols: the first Chinese symbol "Wei" represents danger, the second symbol "Ji" stands for opportunity.[3] Thus, the Chinese define risk as a combination of danger

Figure 1 Risk = Danger (Wei) + Opportunity (Ji).

and opportunity. Greater risk, according to the Chinese, means we have greater opportunity to do well, but also greater danger of doing badly. Interestingly, we will see that Fourier analysis mathematically teaches us that, in a similar fashion:

> **risk = volatility = energy = power**

We'll use Value-at-Risk (VaR) as an initial organizing paradigm for financial risk management, contrast it with a few alternative risk paradigms and trace the implications of L-stable, heavy tail distributions of market pricing for portfolio risk management. We also show the importance of long-term time dependence for Value-at-Risk and for modern portfolio management and relate our findings to the latest results in Extreme Value Theory. This properly measured approach to financial risk is of crucial interest to senior financial risk managers of global banks, insurance and pension funds.

Much of the illustrative material throughout this book has been drawn from rather recent research papers in economics, finance, physics and signal processing. It is a feature of advanced financial market risk measurement and analysis – probably more than in most branches of finance – that the details of rather simply specified topics – like the cash flow dynamics or the frequency of trading in the financial markets – are complex and still imperfectly understood. It has been my personal experience that I've had difficulty in convincing postgraduate students that some topics I proposed to them have not been fully explained decades ago. It is thus often appropriate to use even for introductory purposes (e.g. Chapters 1–2) topics that are still the subject of research. This attractive feature of an only partially explored subject also makes it easier for this book to serve both as a (challenging) senior undergraduate text in economics and finance and as a source of relevant technical information for postgraduate financial researchers and practising professionals in the financial services industry.

The descriptions of the figures often contain details that are intended for the more advanced reader who wants to know the particular conditions to which the data refer. I hope they are detailed enough to convey something of the flavor of empirical financial market risk measurement and analysis. The book is fully referenced. Some of the references indicate sources of material – of illustrations or ideas. Other references have been included for the reader who will use the book as an information source and wishes to follow up a topic in detail. No attempt at completeness of references has been made, since that would involve far too many references. I've tried to give appropriate entries into the literature of the various topics, more often a recent review or significant paper, but also sometimes the pioneering research paper, because it was so well written.

Since the primary purpose of this book is to be pedagogical, in the Chapter Exercises readers can prepare different cases of financial market risk and loss, catastrophe and disaster, and trace the implications for their respective management. All Exercises are preceded by short suggestions of the most appropriate software for the measurement of financial risk. All Exercises were tested by senior, master and doctoral students in Tutorials in the School of Economics of Adelaide University and in the Graduate School of Management of Kent State University. Together with graduate students Melin Kassabov and Rossitsa Yalamora I've prepared a solutions manual for all these Chapter Exercises which will be made available via a web site. We have included in Appendix B a simple data set based on daily prices of the S&P500 stock market index for 1988. Other data sets can easily be downloaded from the Internet. For example, on his web site, John Hull of the University of Toronto has made available the daily prices of the TSE300, S&P500, FTSE100, CAC40 and Nikkei225 stock market indices for the period July 5, 1994–July 10, 1998.

The combined theoretical and practical approach of this book helps the readers (1) to select relevant frameworks for analysis, concepts, tools and techniques applied to real financial market data, and (2) to distinguish between information, knowledge and wisdom in this rapidly adjusting domain of new knowledge.

Notes

1 *Latin translated:* "Probability should not be deleted, it should be deduced." The Latin phrase was formulated by Dr Rudolf E. Kalman, when, on May 3, 1993, he delivered his lecture on "Stochastic Modeling Without Probability" at the Sixth International Symposium on Applied Stochastic Models and Data Analysis at the University in Chania, Crete, Greece. There Dr Kalman proved that there is very little, if any, scientific basis for Haavelmo's 1944 presumption of the *empirical* existence of Kolmogorov probability. Such an empirical existence has to be deduced from the data to be established as a scientific fact. Kolmogorov's probability theory is still only a theory and has not yet a scientifically established support in empirical reality. Science cannot accept Plato's dichotomy between "true reality" and the world we perceive, because if it did, it would become quickly a religion. True science accepts Aristotles' objectivist epistemology.

2 Meyer, Yves (1993) *Wavelets: Algorithms & Applications* (Translated and revised by Robert D. Ryan), Society for Industrial and Applied Mathematics (SIAM), Philadelphia, PA, p. 119)

3 As I was informed by two of my MBA students at Kent State University: Kang Zhixing (Richard), who was one of my Research Assistants, and Wang Zhengjun.

Part I
Financial risk processes

1 Risk – asset class, horizon and time

1.1 Introduction

1.1.1 Classical market returns assumptions

Most investors, portfolio managers, corporate financial analysts, investment bankers, commercial bank loan officers, security analysts and bond-rating agencies are concerned about the uncertainty of the returns on their investment assets, caused by the variability in speculative market prices (market risk) and the instability of business performance (credit risk) (Alexander, 1999).[1]

Derivative instruments have made hedging of such risks possible. Hedging allows the selling of such risks by the *hedgers*, or suppliers of risk, to the *speculators*, or buyers of risk, but only when such risks are systematic, i.e., when they show a certain form of inertia or stability. Indeed, the current derivative markets are regular markets where "stable," i.e., systematic risk is bought and sold.

Unfortunately, all these financial markets suffer from three major deficiencies:

(1) Risk is insufficiently measured by the conventional second-order moments (variances and standard deviations). Often one thinks it to be sufficient to measure risk by only second-order moments, because of the facile, but erroneous, assumption of normality (or Gaussianness) of the price distributions produced by the market processes of shifting demand and supply curves.
(2) Risk is assumed to be stable and all distribution moments are assumed to be invariant, i.e., the distributions are assumed to be stationary.
(3) Pricing observations are assumed to exhibit only serial dependencies, which can be simply removed by appropriate transformations, like the well-known Random Walk, Markov and ARIMA, or (G)ARCH models.

Based on these simplifying assumptions, investment analysis and portfolio theory have conventionally described financial market risk as a function of asset class only (Greer, 1997; Haugen, 2001, pp. 178–184). In a simplifying representation:

> **portfolio return volatility** $\sigma_{pp} = f(\text{asset class } \omega)$

Figure 1.1 shows the familiar presentation of risk as a function of asset class by Ibbotson and Sinquefield, who have collected annual rates of return as far back

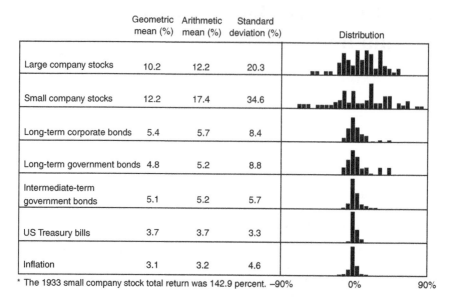

	Geometric mean (%)	Arithmetic mean (%)	Standard deviation (%)	Distribution
Large company stocks	10.2	12.2	20.3	
Small company stocks	12.2	17.4	34.6	
Long-term corporate bonds	5.4	5.7	8.4	
Long-term government bonds	4.8	5.2	8.8	
Intermediate-term government bonds	5.1	5.2	5.7	
US Treasury bills	3.7	3.7	3.3	
Inflation	3.1	3.2	4.6	

* The 1933 small company stock total return was 142.9 percent.   −90%   0%   90%

Figure 1.1 Historical average annual returns and return volatility, 1926–1995.

Source: *Stocks, Bonds, Bills and Inflation 1996 Yearbook*,™ Ibbotson Associates, Chicago (annually updates work by Roger G. Ibbotson and Rex A. Sinquefield). Used with permission. All rights reserved.

as 1926 (Ibbotson and Sinquefield, 1999). The dispersion of the return distributions, measured by the respective standard deviations, differs by six different asset classes:

(1) common stocks of large companies;
(2) common stocks of small firms;
(3) long-term corporate bonds;
(4) long-term US government bonds;
(5) intermediate-term US government bonds;
(6) US Treasury bills.

When an investor wants a higher return combined with more risk, he invests in small stocks. When he wants less risk and accepts a lower return, he is advised to invest in cash.

For example, Tobin (1958) made two strong assumptions, which were believed to be true by many followers: first, that the distributions of portfolio returns are all normally distributed and, second, that the relationship between the investors' portfolio wealth and the utility they derive it from is quadratic of form.[2] Under these two conditions, Tobin proves that investors were allowed to choose between portfolios solely on the basis of expected return and variance. Moreover, his liquidity preference theory, shows that any investment risk level (as defined by the second moment of asset returns) can be attained by a linear combination of the market portfolio and cash, combined with the ability to hold short (borrow) and to hold long (invest). The market portfolio contains all the non-diversifiable systematic risk, while the cash represents the "risk-free" asset, of which the return compensates for depreciation of value caused by inflation. The linear combination of the market portfolio and cash can create any average return and any risk-premium one wants or needs, under the assumption that the distributions of these investment returns are mutually independent over time.

1.1.2 What's empirically wrong?

Regrettably, there are many things wrong with this oversimplified conceptualization and modeling of the financial markets and one has now become alarmingly obvious. Financial disasters are much more common and occur with much higher frequencies than they should be according to the classical assumptions. An incomplete but rather convincing listing of financial disasters can be found in Kindleberger (1996). Bernstein (1996) and Bassi *et al.* (1998) mention many additional instances.

The world's financial markets exhibit longer term pricing dependencies, which show, in aggregated and low frequency trading observations, devastating, but essentially unpredictable aperiodic cyclicity, like the Plagues of the Old Testament or sharp and disastrous discontinuities, like Noah's Flood. On the other hand, they show, in high frequency trading frequencies, turbulence structures and "eddie" like condensation and rarefaction patterns. Analysts are now applying highly sophisticated mathematical measurement methods from particle physics to identify such empirical structures. In fact, quite a few finance articles regarding this topic have recently appeared in physics journals, such as *Nature* (Potters *et al.*, 1998; Kondor and Kertesz, 1999; Mantegna and Stanley, 2000).

First, we'll quickly learn that the uncertainty of the investment returns is a much wider concept than just the volatility of the prices as measured by second-order moments. Higher order moments, like *skewness* and *kurtosis*, play an underestimated, but a very important role. For example, the distributions of investment returns exhibit positive biases, because of the termination of nonperforming businesses and the continuing life of performing ones. There is a financial need to succeed and not to fail. Thus, the return distributions are positively skewed. In addition, the tails of the rate of return distribution returns are fatter, i.e., the outlying returns are more prevalent, than normally expected.

Second, we will observe that the stationarity of the investment returns cannot be so easily assumed, since we empirically observed that the distributions of investment returns change over time. Overwhelming empirical evidence has now accumulated that volatility, i.e., the standard deviation of price or rate of return changes, which in Modern Portfolio Theory (MPT) measures the risk of assets and portfolios, is not time-invariant. Even worse, it also does not exhibit trends or any form of stability! As Peters (1994, pp. 143–158) shows: both realized and implied volatilities are *antipersistent*. An antipersistent time series reverses itself more often than a normal or neutral time series.[3] This phenomenon may occur because markets develop their institutional frameworks and mature, thereby changing the constraints of their financial pricing processes. These cash flow constraints determine the behavioral regimes of the dynamic pricing processes of which the volatilities become turbulent.

Third, we find that intertemporal dependencies cannot easily be filtered out of the observed pricing series by simple serial correlation (ARIMA) models. The random pricing processes cannot be so easily reduced to independent white noise series, since financial pricing series exhibit global dependencies, due to an intricate pattern of widely differing investment horizons of financial institution. For example, do long-term or short-term bonds have the largest variance of return? The answer to this question depends on the time horizon of investors. Commercial banks have short-term liabilities in the form of deposits. These institutions minimize risk by matching these liabilities with short-term investments. On the other hand, pension funds and life insurance companies have long-term liabilities. If they are concerned at all about their survival, they will immunize their portfolios and view investments in long-term bonds as less risky than short-term investments (Haugen, 2001, pp. 358–359). Such scaling patterns of differing investment horizons introduce long-term dependencies among the rates of return of the various asset classes.

Consequently, Mann and Wald's (1943) conventional econometric assumption of serial dependence for time series can be shown to be empirically false. Global, long-term dependence plays a pervasive and important role. Thus, it is more comprehensive and justifiable to present financial market risk, in a simplifying representation, as follows.

$$\text{asset return distribution } P = f(\text{asset class } \omega, \text{ horizon } \tau, \text{ time } t)$$

Not only is the rate of return distribution produced by speculative markets dependent on the asset classes and on the time horizons τ of the investors, but this distribution function may be time-varying, as indicated by the time t-argument. This empirical reality, which only now starts to become properly modeled (Bouchaud and Potters, 2000), has serious consequences for portfolio management and investment analysis. Tobin's (1958) liquidity preference theory is clearly too simple to adequately reflect all these dimensions of risk. The simple, static, 2-dimensional return-risk tradeoff, on which classical MPT is based, will have to be replaced by multidimensional and dynamic return-risk tradeoffs, as was earlier suggested in Los (1998, 2000b).

Example 1 *A fine example of the time-dependence of price distributions is the well-documented strong time-dependence of the standard deviation or* volatility *of stock price changes (Schwert, 1989).*

This first chapter contains many concepts and definitions to acquire a proper analytic and technical lingo for the remainder of this book, and to review basic statistical analysis. It forms the *prolegomena* of the main body of our discussion. In particular, we'll review Kolmogorov's axiomatic (set-theoretic) definition of probability and of random processes, the real world definition of frequency distributions and of observed time series, and the summarizing characterization of these time series by their moments and cumulants.

1.2 Uncertainty

There is no doubt in the mind of physicists that uncertainty, like relativity, is of an absolutely fundamental nature, that admits no exceptions. The world could not even physically exist without uncertainty:

> One of the fundamental consequences of uncertainty is the very size of atoms, which, without it, would collapse to an infinitesimal point.
>
> (Schroeder, 1991, p. 113)

In mathematics, the theory of Hilbert bases and (linear) operator algebra led to the formulation of the Uncertainty Principle (Meyer, 1985), which we judiciously and fruitfully exploited in our preceding book on *Computational Finance: A Scientific Perspective* (Los, 2001). But for the development of financial risk theory we may need a somewhat broader definition.

According to Webster's *New Universal Unabridged Dictionary* (Deluxe Second Edition, Dorset and Baber, 1983, p. 1990):

un·cĕr 'tain·ty=the quality or state of being uncertain; lack of certainty; doubt

and

un·cĕr 'tain
(1) not certainly known; questionable; problematical;
(2) vague; not definite or determined;
(3) doubtful; not having certain knowledge; not sure;
(4) ambiguous;
(5) not steady or constant; varying;
(6) liable to change or vary; not dependable or reliable.

Similarly, in modern risk theory, we distinguish three different, but closely related concepts: randomness, chaos and probability.[4] Let's explain what each of these concepts mean and discuss their limitations.

1.2.1 Randomness = irregularity

Essentially, from Webster's Dictionary, we have the following informal definition for randomness:[5]

randomness = the state of being haphazard, not unique, irregular

Thus, these definitions are based on the regular use of the word "randomness" in the English language (cf. Bernstein, 1996).

1.2.1.1   *Degree of irregularity*

What is regular is defined and fixed and clearly determined. But how irregular is the absence of determinedness? Recently, Pincus and Singer (1996) asked the question: what is the degree of irregularity and how do we measure it? One extreme is the certainty of being fixed, of being unique, a constant, and having thus no spectrum at all. The other extreme, the ultimate state of irregularity, is when something is indistinguishable from background noise, that has no spectral features, i.e., noise that covers the whole spectrum.

For example, white noise has a *flat* spectrum. Thus, it exhibits a specific, distinguished spectral feature and, therefore, cannot be called irregular or random background noise. In between these two extremes we find degrees of irregularity that can be described by variously shaped spectra. Each irregular series has its own spectrum, be it a Fourier spectrum for a stationary series; or a changing spectrum for a nonstationary series, to be analyzed by either windowed Fourier Transforms or by Wavelet Transforms, depending on how fast the changes occur. One now computes even a singularity spectrum for observational series, which show many discontinuities or jumps, as we will discuss in Chapter 8.

1.2.1.2   *Measures of sequential irregularity*

In financial risk theory we are not interested in irregularity *per se*, but in dynamic irregularity, i.e., in irregularity as it manifests itself over time. For example, how irregular are the prices produced by a market pricing mechanism over time? Figure 1.2 provides some examples of financial market price series and their rates of return (Mittnik *et al.*, 1998, p. 84):

(1) the daily AMEX Composite index from September 1, 1988 to July 28, 1994, with $T = 1,810$ observations;
(2) the daily AMEX OIL Composite index from September 1, 1988 to July 28, 1994, with $T = 1,810$ observations; and
(3) the daily DEM/USD Exchange Rate from January 2, 1973 to July 28, 1994 with $T = 5,401$ observations.

For the past hundred years, since Bachelier's PhD thesis of 1900, in which he described speculative price formation as a Random Walk, people have attempted to describe the degree of irregularity of market pricing and of related investment returns (Bachelier, 1900). The currently best known rational measures of such irregularity are the Lipschitz exponents (such as the Hölder–Hurst exponents), which will be discussed in Chapter 4.

1.2.2   *Pseudorandomness versus genuine randomness*

People working with computers often sloppily talk about their system's "random number generator" and the "random numbers" it produces. But numbers calculated by a computer through a deterministic process, cannot, by definition, be random. Given knowledge of the algorithm used to create the numbers and its original

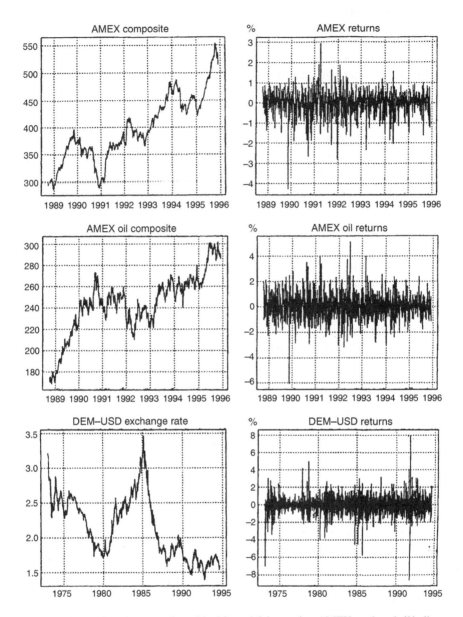

Figure 1.2 Levels and returns of empirical financial time series: AMEX stock and oil indices and DEM–USD exchange rate.

state or *seed*, you can predict all the numbers returned by subsequent calls to the algorithm, whereas with genuinely random numbers, knowledge of one number or of an arbitrarily long sequence of numbers is of no use whatsoever in predicting the next number to be generated.

Computer-generated "random" numbers are more properly referred to as *pseudorandom* numbers, and pseudorandom sequences of such numbers (Goldreich, 1999). A variety of clever algorithms have been developed that gener-ate sequences of numbers which pass every statistical test used to distinguish ran-dom sequences from those containing some pattern or internal order. A high-quality pseudorandom sequence generator generates data that are indistinguishable from a sequence of bytes chosen at random. Indistinguishable, but not genuinely random!

We no longer have to use pseudorandom number generators. There are now systems to collect *genuine random numbers*, generated by a process fundamentally governed by the inherent uncertainty in the quantum mechanical laws of nature, directly to your computer in a variety of forms.

Example 2   Hotbits *are random numbers generated by timing successive pairs of radioactive decay electrons or beta particles. These particles are produced by the spontaneous transformation of neutrons (with charge 0) in the nucleus of Krypton-85 into pairs of protons (with charge +1) and free electrons (= beta particles with charge −1). The free electrons, or "beta rays," are then detected by a Geiger–Müller tube in a simple radiation monitor (Figure 1.3) interfaced to a computer. The unstable nucleus of the radioactive Krypton-85 (the 85 means there are a total of 85 protons and neutrons in the atom) spontaneously turns into the stable nucleus of the non-radioactive Rubidium-85, which still has a sum of 85 protons and neutrons, and a beta particle is emitted with an energy of 687 kiloelectron volts (keV), resulting in no net difference in charge:*

$$^{85}\mathrm{Kr} \longrightarrow {}^{85}\mathrm{Rb} + \beta^- + \gamma \tag{1.1}$$

In this case, a gamma ray is also emitted with an energy of 514 keV, carrying away some of the energy. "Gamma rays" are nothing other than photons – particles of light, just carrying a lot more energy than visible light. Krypton-85 has a half-life of 10.73 years. This is called its half-life, since every 10.73 years half of a very large number of Krypton-85 nuclei present at the start of the period have decayed into Rubidium-85. But there is no way, even in principle, to predict when a given atom of Krypton-85 will decay into Rubidium-85. It has a 50/50 chance of doing so in the next 10.73 years, but that's all we can say. The inherent uncertainty of such decay time is genuinely random. Since the time of any given decay is random, the interval between two consecutive decays is also genuinely random (not unlike between two financial transactions). Using the Geiger teller, we can now measure the lengths of the uncertain intervals after the fact and thus collect genuinely random numbers. We measure a pair of these intervals, and emit a zero or one bit based on the relative length of the two intervals. To create each random bit, we wait until the first count occurs, then measure the time, T_1, until the next. We

Monitor 5 – radiation monitor
• **Detect: Alpha, Beta, Gamma, X-rays**
Features: Easy to read analog meters, red light count, anti-saturation circuitry and audible beeper
Specifications:
Ranges: ×1, ×10, ×100 and BATT (battery check)
Power: One 9 volt alkaline battery provides up to 2,000 hours of operation at normal background levels
Temperature: −20°C to +50°C
Detector: Uncompensated halogen-quenched with 1.5–2.0 mg/cm² mica end window
Energy sensitivity: Detects Alpha down to 2.5 MeV through the end window; typical efficiency at 3.6 MeV is greater than 80%. Detects 50 KeV Beta at 35% typical efficiency; 150 KeV is typically 75%. Detects Gamma and X-rays down to 10 KeV through the end window, 40 KeV minimum through the case.
Meter reading: 0–50 mR/hr and 0–50,000 CPM, or 0–500 uSv/hr and 0–50 mR/hr

Monitor 5 Meter	C31,475	$299.00

Figure 1.3 Simple and relatively inexpensive radiation monitor.

then wait for a third pulse and measure T_2, yielding a pair of durations. If they're the same, we throw away the measurement and try again. Otherwise if T_1 is less than T_2 we emit a zero bit; if T_1 is greater than T_2, a one bit. In practice, to avoid any residual bias resulting from nonrandom systematic errors in the apparatus or measuring process consistently favoring one state, the sense of the comparison between T_1 and T_2 is reversed for consecutive bits.

1.2.3   Chaos = deterministic dynamic nonuniqueness

Chaos is a special form of irregularity. It means that at a certain time something, that was certain and unique, suddenly can become nonunique, although it remains very well determined. The dynamic system can have more than one equilibrium state to be in, because of equilibrium state *bifurcations* (Lorenz, 2001). How many times the system "orbits" or "jumps" through a set of equilibrium states depends on the nonlinear constraints imposed on the dynamic system. However, these separate equilibrium states of the same system can be perfectly well identified, determined and described, like H_2O molecules orbiting through the two coexisting equilibrium states of ice floating in liquid water. The molecule is either in the "ice" state, or in the "water" state, and it orbits through these two states as time progresses (Prigogine, 1997).

> **chaos** = deterministic dynamic nonuniqueness

Even more precisely, complete chaos is the coexistence of an infinite number of unstable deterministic equilibrium orbits, through which the dynamic system cycles. Chaos is a form of "inexactness," since there is clearly *nonuniqueness* or *aperiodic cyclicity*.[6] But it is not pseudorandomness, since there coexist more than one equilibrium state of being at the same time, while with pseudorandomness there is only one equilibrium state of being at the same time. However, chaos is deterministic, since there is no doubt what these distinct, but coexisting equilibrium orbit states are: they are perfectly well determined. The set of such distinct but coexisting aperiodic equilibrium states is called the *strange attractor*. Already more than a decade ago, chaos is asserted to have been observed in speculative market prices on the trading floor (Savit, 1988, 1994). For a way of visualizing the distinction between a chaotic financial time series and a truly random or irregular one, cf. Chapter 9.

1.2.4   Probability = complete set of relative frequencies

Probability is a very well defined and constraint form of randomness. In mathematics, probability is the ratio of the chances favoring a certain state to all the chances for and against it. Thus, probability is a *rational measure:* it measures *relative frequencies*. It counts the number of times of being in state *A* relative to the total number of states, i.e., the sum of the number of times of being in state *A* relative to the number of times of being in the *A* and *non-A* states.

Thus, the basic problem of using a probability measure to describe a degree of uncertainty is that one has to know the complete universe of states that may occur to compute the relative frequency or probability of a particular event. But the definition of the concept of uncertainty already indicates that we're doubtful or ignorant of what may happen. In other words, the very fact that we cannot completely know the extent of the universe from which the event is drawn precludes the use of probability measures in most of real life. Probability only plays a role in games that have completely predefined rules. Most real life situations are not like well-defined games. Often we don't know which gaming rules in a particular situation apply or what possibly such rules may be. Science deals with attempting to discover such gaming rules and the relative frequencies by which particular events occur. In other words, the probability distribution of a particular event is itself a phenomenon that science tries to discover and identify. It is pseudoscience to presume and predefine such probability distributions before the finite empirical data sets have been analyzed.

Remark 3   *Earlier financial analysts claimed that probability is a necessary concept for the pricing of derivatives and that the broader concept of uncertainty would not do. Nowadays it is acknowledged that probability is not needed for the pricing of options, because the prices of derivatives can be replicated by the linear combinations of the prices of portfolios of fundamental assets. The prices of such fundamental assets are uncertain and not probabilistic, as this book demonstrates. Even bond prices are uncertain, when discontinuous credit or default risk is taken into account. However, one can always give an ex post probabilistic interpretation* *to the prices of derivatives, once they have been priced on the basis of replication portfolios consisting of fundamental assets.*

1.2.4.1 Kolmogorov's axiomatic probability

In 1933, the Russian mathematician Kolmogorov provided one particular axiomatic definition of probability, using set theory (Kolmogorov, 1933; cf. also Papoulis, 1984, for a complete treatment). Since Kolmogorov, particular non-Kolmogorovian definitions of probability have been discovered, *inter alia*, by the Italian mathematician Luigi Accardi, a student of Kolmogorov and now Professor of Mathematics at the University of Rome. Thus, currently, at least two definitions of probability coexist. The definition of probability is no longer unique! However, we will still discuss Kolmogorov's set-theoretic definition of probability, since it is the most familiar. But it is also a somewhat misleading representation of real world "randomness," since it is based on simple integer counting of events within a preselected or presumed "universe." This discussion assists with making the connection to the modern approach to randomness, i.e., to our broader concept of randomness as uncountable "irregularity."

To provide the axiomatic definition of probability in the proper context of set theory, we assume some familiarity with the Boolean notions of *sets, complements, intersections* and *unions*, as well as with the notion of *function*. The following presentation by a series of definitions sequentially building on each other, beginning with the fundamental set definitions, follows an earlier tutorial exposition prepared for the Federal Reserve Bank of New York by Los (1982) (cf. also Chow and Teicher, 1978).

Definition 4 *A space Ω is a nonempty set which serves as the ultimate reference set, or the "universe."*

Definition 5 *A nonempty family of subsets, say $\mathcal{A}$, is said to be an* algebra, *or* field, *if for $A_1, A_2 \in \mathcal{A}, \bar{A}_i \in \mathcal{A}, i = 1, 2$ and $A_1 \cup A_2 \in \mathcal{A}$, i.e., $\mathcal{A}$ is closed under the Boolean set operations of* complements *and* unions.

Here $\bar{A}_i$ means non-A_i, i.e., the complement of A_i.

Definition 6 *Let $\mathcal{A}$ be an algebra defined on Ω, then if for $A_i \in \mathcal{A}$*

$$\bigcup_{i=1}^{\infty} A_i \in \mathcal{A} \tag{1.2}$$

$\mathcal{A}$ is said to be a σ-algebra (or Borel-field*).*

Thus, $\mathcal{A}$ is closed under Boolean set operations and sequential limits.

Definition 7 *Let Ω be a space and $\mathcal{A}$ a σ-algebra relative to Ω. Then, the set $(\Omega, \mathcal{A})$ is said to be a* measurable space *and the set of $\mathcal{A}$ is said to be a* measurable set.

Definition 8 *Let Ω be a space and $\mathcal{A}$ a nonempty class of subsets of Ω. A set function μ on $\mathcal{A}$ is a real valued function on $\mathcal{A}$, i.e., if $A_1 \in \mathcal{A}$, then $\mu(A_1)$ is a real number.*

Definition 9 *Let μ be a set function on $\mathcal{A}$. Let $A \in \mathcal{A} \subset \Omega$ and $\{A_i : i = 1, 2, \ldots\}$ is a collection of disjoint sets such that*

$$A = \bigcup_{i=1}^{\infty} A_i \tag{1.3}$$

and

$$\mu(A) = \sum_{i=1}^{\infty} \mu(A_i) \tag{1.4}$$

then μ is said to be σ-additive, or countably additive.

Definition 10 *A nonnegative, σ-additive set function μ, defined on a class $\mathcal{A}$, which contains the empty set $\emptyset$, such that*

$$\mu(\emptyset) = 0 \tag{1.5}$$

is said to be a measure. *If μ is a measure on a σ-algebra of subsets of Ω, the triplet $(\Omega, \mathcal{A}, \mu)$ is said to be a* measure space. *If, in addition,*

$$\mu(\Omega) = 1 \tag{1.6}$$

then the triplet $(\Omega, \mathcal{A}, \mu)$ is said to be a probability space, *and is denoted $(\Omega, \mathcal{A}, P)$, where P is the* probability measure, *which maps $\mathcal{A}$ to the real numbers between 0 and 1.*

Definition 11 *Let $(\Omega, \mathcal{A}, P)$ be a probability space. An* event *is simply a set $A \in \mathcal{A}$. The real number $P(A)$ is said to be the probability (-measure) attached to the event A, or, for short, the* probability *of A. Events A of probability zero, i.e., such that*

$$P(A) = 0 \tag{1.7}$$

are called null events, *or* null sets.

Remark 12 *The monotone property of a measure ensures that*

$$0 = P\{\emptyset\} \leq P\{A\} \leq P\{\Omega\} = 1 \tag{1.8}$$

Definition 13 *The probability space $(\Omega, \mathcal{A}, P)$ is said to be* complete, *if any subset of a set in G with $P(A) = 0$ also belongs to $\mathcal{A}$.*

Any probability space $(\Omega, \mathcal{A}, P)$ can always be completed!

Definition 14   *A property is said to hold* almost certainly *(a.c.) [also: almost surely (a.s.), almost everywhere (a.e.), or with probability one (w.p.1)], if it holds everywhere, except possibly on a null set A, i.e., a set A such that $P(A) = 0$.*

After so many preparatory definitions, we have finally arrived at the classical, Kolmogorov's, axiomatic definition of a random variable (r.v.).

Definition 15   *Let $(\Omega, \mathcal{A}, P)$ be a complete probability space. A measurable function $X: \Omega \to \mathbb{R}$ (where $\mathbb{R}$ is the real line) is said to be a r.v. if*

$$P(A) = 0, A = \{t: |X(t)| = \infty\} \qquad (1.9)$$

Surprisingly, perhaps, Kolmogorov's apparently innocuous definition of r.v. excludes a lot of irregular events, e.g., all singularities and discontinuities. Thus, nowadays, Kolmogorov's definition is considered deficient by sophisticated real world mathematicians, such as Mandelbrot (1982), Pincus, Kalman and Singer (Kalman, 1996; Pincus and Singer, 1996; Pincus and Kalman, 1997). For example, we can observe and measure (= count the frequency of) special irregular events, called "singularities." The occurrence of singularities is a frequent occurrence in the real world and not all singularities are alike. Thus, in Chapter 8 we will discuss the concept of a "singularity spectrum" and how we can measure it. Therefore, we need a new non-Kolmogorov concept of a "random variable," which effectively asserts

$$P(A) \geq 0, A = \{t: |X(t)| = \infty\} \qquad (1.10)$$

1.2.4.2   Empirical real world: relative frequency

In the empirical world, we determine the probability of an irregular event by measuring how relatively often it occurs. We measure its relative frequency of occurrence. We do NOT require that the absolute measure of that event is finite. Thus, for empirical simplicity, as long as we set the total number of measured events (= the measured "universe" equal to unity), we can *always* define:

> **probability** = relative frequency of events

Based on the preceding discussion of why probability measures a very specialized form of randomness, we categorically state that it is more in agreement with the empirical world to define:

> **randomness** = irregularity

and not to bound the describing and measuring functions of such irregularity, in contrast to what Kolmogorov's probability axioms require. In fact, we can now measure the degree of randomness of a price or rate of return process, by measuring the *degree of irregularity* of such a process (Pincus and Singer, 1996).

1.2.5   *The Ellsberg Paradox*

Peters (1999) uses the Ellsberg Paradox to illustrate the essential difference between uncertainty and probabilistic risk.[7] In the Ellsberg Paradox, you are shown an urn that contains 90 balls. Of these, 30 balls are red, and the remaining 60 balls are an *unknown* mixture of white and blue balls. One ball is to be drawn from the urn, and you are paid an amount of money if a particular color ball is chosen. You are given two payoff options to choose from as in Table 1.1.

Look over Options 1 and 2 in Table 1.1 and decide which you would choose and keep your choice in mind. Most people choose Option 1 for the set of payoffs in Table 1.1. We will soon see why.

Next, turn to the two other options that are offered in Table 1.2. The drawing will be of the same urn, with the same mixture of red, white and blue balls, as before.

Which of these two new options would you now choose? Be honest! Most people choose Option 4 for the second set in Table 1.2. But why?

In Option 1, you know for certain that you have a $\frac{1}{3}$ probability of winning. But you have no idea of the probability of winning in Option 2. It could be anywhere between zero and $\frac{2}{3}$, i.e., it could be zero or higher than the $\frac{1}{3}$ of red. This demonstrates that most people prefer to go with the odds they know, instead of to choose for uncertainty.

Option 4 is chosen for the same reason. You know that Option 4 has a $\frac{2}{3}$ probability, because 60 of the 90 balls are either white or blue, but you do not know the odds of finding a red *or* a blue ball, which can be anywhere between $\frac{1}{3}$ and 1. Again, most people prefer to go with the odds they know, instead of to confront or deal with uncertainty.

Now, by itself, each choice appears rational. Remember, though, that you chose *both* Options 1 and 4. Here is where the Paradox comes into play. Choosing Option 1 over Option 2 means that you *believe* that a red ball is more likely to be drawn than a white ball. However, choosing Option 4 over Option 3 implies that you

Table 1.1 Ellsberg Paradox payoffs: Options 1 and 2

	Red ($)	White ($)	Blue ($)
Option 1	100	0	0
Option 2	0	100	0

Table 1.2 Ellsberg Paradox payoffs: Options 3 and 4

	Red ($)	White ($)	Blue ($)
Option 3	100	0	100
Option 4	0	100	100

believe that "white or blue" is more likely than "red or blue" and thus you *believe* that white is more likely than red when choosing Option 4. Consequently, choosing both Option 4 and Option 1 under the same conditions is inconsistent, since the two beliefs supporting the respective choices are in conflict with each other, according to the tenets of subjective probability, so loved by "rational" Bayesian statisticians.

Why do the majority of people choose Options 1 and 4? Because, when faced with true uncertainty, we are more comfortable with what we know, than what we don't know. Thus, uncertainty is very different from probabilistic risk, which is known. Probabilistic risk depends on the concept of known odds. The odds are known and calculable for probabilistic games like throwing dice, turning a wheel of fortune, or playing a hand of cards. Uncertainty is more dangerous than low-but-known odds, since, essentially,

> **uncertainty** = our ignorance

We hate being ignorant! It is this hate for ignorance that drives scientists to look for certain and unique mathematical models to explain the structure of natural phenomena. Once such a mathematical model is found, e.g., DNA's double helix, there is no longer uncertainty, even though the measurement precision is not perfect! (cf. Los, 2001, chapter 1). Mathematicians often confuse uncertainty with measurement imprecision.

1.3 Nonparametric and parametric distributions

Let's introduce a few additional classical measurement definitions to enable the frequency analysis in the following chapters. An important concept for the following discussion is the distribution function.

Definition 16 *Let X be a random variable defined on the probability space $(\Omega, \mathcal{A}, P)$. Then the distribution function (d.f.) of X is defined by the probability (= relative frequency) P such that*

$$F_X(x) = P\{t: X(t) < x, x \in [-\infty, \infty)\} \tag{1.11}$$

Remark 17 *From the preceding discussion it is clear that the frequency d.f. has the following properties:*

(i) F_X *is nondecreasing* $\hspace{3cm}$ (1.12)

(ii) F_X *is left continuous:* $\lim\limits_{\substack{y<x \\ y\to x}} F(y) = F(x), \quad x \in \mathbb{R}$ $\hspace{1cm}$ (1.13)

(iii) $F_X(\infty) = \lim\limits_{x\to\infty} F_X(x) = 1$

$\hspace{2.5cm} F_X(-\infty) = \lim\limits_{x\to\infty} F_X(-x) = 0$ $\hspace{2cm}$ (1.14)

One of the greatest scientific challenges still is to identify the true frequency distribution of a particular measured event from a finite set of time series data. However, it is also clear that this challenge is even surpassed in difficulty, when simultaneously the distribution of these events over time has to be taken into account. We will have to look at the complete 2-dimensional frequency-time-distribution picture.

1.3.1   Moment and cumulant generation

The complete description of empirical frequency distributions requires infinite knowledge, which we, humans, don't possess. Therefore, we try to summarize distributions by using a limited number of characterizing *summary statistics*. We will discuss the definitions and properties of moments and cumulants of the first four orders of distributions. Moments and cumulants are useful semi-invariant summary statistics of distributions. First, we give the definition of a joint characteristic or moment-generating function.

Definition 18   *For one continuous random variable X with density $f(x)$, the char-acteristic function is the Fourier Transform of the density function $f(x)$ defined by*

$$\Phi(\omega) = E\left\{e^{j\omega x}\right\} = \int_{-\infty}^{+\infty} e^{j\omega x} f(x) dx \tag{1.15}$$

The characteristic function completely determines the distribution of X and has many useful mathematical properties. $E\{\cdot\}$ denotes the expectation operation, the number $e = \lim_{m\to\infty}(1 + (1/m))^m = 2.71828,\ldots$, and j is the imaginary number $j = \sqrt{-1}$ (or $j^2 = -1$).

The Fourier Transform will be discussed in greater detail in Chapter 5.

Definition 19   *Given a set of n real random variables $\{x(1), x(2), \ldots, x(n)\}$, their* joint moments *of order $r = k_1 + k_2 + \cdots + k_n$ are given by the partial derivatives of the characteristic function evaluated at zero frequencies ω_i, $i = 1, 2, \ldots, n$ (Papoulis, 1984):*

$$\text{Mom}[x^{k_1}(1), x^{k_2}(2), \ldots, x^{k_n}(n)] = E[x^{k_1}(1) \cdot x^{k_2}(2) \cdots x^{k_n}(n)]$$

$$= (-j)^r \frac{\partial^r \Phi(\omega_1, \omega_2, \ldots, \omega_n)}{\partial \omega_1^{k_1} \partial \omega_2^{k_2} \ldots \partial \omega_n^{k_n}}\bigg|_{\omega_1 = \omega_2 = \cdots \omega_n = 0} \tag{1.16}$$

where

$$\Phi(\omega_1, \omega_2, \ldots, \omega_n) = E\left\{e^{j(\omega_1 x(1) + \omega_2 x(2) + \cdots + \omega_n x(n))}\right\} \tag{1.17}$$

is their joint characteristic function.

For example, for two joint random variables $\{x(1), x(2)\}$, we have the second-order integer moments

$$\text{Mom}[x(1), x(2)] = E\{x(1) \cdot x(2)\} \tag{1.18}$$

$$\text{Mom}[x^2(1)] = E\{x^2(1)\} \quad \text{and} \tag{1.19}$$

$$\text{Mom}[x^2(2)] = E\{x^2(2)\} \tag{1.20}$$

However, often in signal processing, instead of using moments, cumulants are used, because of their ability to suppress noise, when it is additive Gaussian, and their usefulness for estimating frequencies. Let's first define these cumulants.

Definition 20   *The joint cumulants of order* $r = k_1 + k_2 + \cdots + k_n$ *of a set of random variables* $\{x(1), x(2), \ldots, x(n)\}$ *are defined as the coefficients in the Taylor expansion of the natural logarithm of the characteristic function about zero, i.e.,*

$$\text{Cum}[x^{k_1}(1), x^{k_2}(2), \ldots, x^{k_n}(n)]$$

$$= (-j)^r \frac{\partial^r \ln[\Phi(\omega_1, \omega_2, \ldots, \omega_n)]}{\partial \omega_1^{k_1} \partial \omega_2^{k_2} \cdots \partial \omega_n^{k_n}} \bigg|_{\omega_1 = \omega_2 = \cdots \omega_n = 0} \tag{1.21}$$

In this book we will not discuss multivariate joint distributions of the set of random variables $\{x(1), x(2), \ldots, x(n)\}$, but only distributions of a single random variable x. In that case their are no cross moments, and the moments m_r can be simply computed by

$$m_{\mathrm{r}} = E\{x^r\} = \int_{-\infty}^{+\infty} x^r f(x) dx \tag{1.22}$$

where $f(x)$ is the *probability density function* (p.d.f.).

For example, the first four integer moments of x are simply

$$m_1 = \text{Mom}[x] = E\{x\} \tag{1.23}$$

$$m_2 = \text{Mom}[x \cdot x] = E\{x^2\} \tag{1.24}$$

$$m_3 = \text{Mom}[x \cdot x \cdot x] = E\{x^3\} \tag{1.25}$$

$$m_4 = \text{Mom}[x \cdot x \cdot x \cdot x] = E\{x^4\} \tag{1.26}$$

and the first four integer cumulants of x are related to these moments, as follows:

$$c_1 = \text{Cum}[x] = m_1 \tag{1.27}$$

$$c_2 = \text{Cum}[x \cdot x] = m_2 - m_1^2 \tag{1.28}$$

$$c_3 = \text{Cum}[x \cdot x \cdot x] = m_3 - 3m_2 m_1 + 2m_1^3 \tag{1.29}$$

$$c_4 = \text{Cum}[x \cdot x \cdot x \cdot x] = m_4 - 4m_3 m_1 - 3m_2^2 + 12 m_2 m_1^2 - 6 m_1^4 \tag{1.30}$$

These relationships between the moments and cumulants can be verified by substituting the Taylor expansion into the preceding general definitions for joint moments and cumulants and working out the differentiations about zero.[8] Notice that if the first moment (mean) $m_1 = c_1 = 0$, there is considerable simplifications, since it follows that $c_2 = m_2$, $c_3 = m_3$, and $c_4 = m_4 - 3m_2^2$.

Remark 21 *Interestingly, the classical literature only presents integer moments. As Chapter 3 will show, the recent spate of articles and books on stable distributions in finance has considerably expanded our concept of moments. It now includes* fractional moments, *related to fractal distributions.*

1.3.1.1 Moments of parametric distributions

Figures 1.4 and 1.5 are borrowed from Nikias and Petropulu (1993), pp. 10 and 11. Figure 1.4 illustrates the first four order moments and cumulants of the p.d.fs for three symmetric parametric distributions: the *Laplace, Gaussian* and *Uniform* distributions. Note that for symmetric p.d.fs all m_n and c_n for odd n are identical to zero and that for the Gaussian distribution all cumulants c_n of order greater than second ($n > 2$) are also zero. Thus, second-order statistics $c_2 = m_2 = \sigma^2$, the variance, are sufficient to characterize a Gaussian distribution, since then $c_1 = m_1 = c_3 = m_3 = c_4 = 0$ so that $m_4 = 3m_2^2 = 3\sigma^4$.

In contrast, Figure 1.5 illustrates three nonsymmetric parametric distributions: the *Exponential, Rayleigh* and so-called K-distributions. It is clear that these distributions require all four order of moments or cumulants to completely describe these distributions.

However, moments and cumulants of any order $r > 0$ can be computed for any type of empirical and theoretical distribution, parametric or nonparametric. The fundamental research problem of identification of frequency distributions of finite empirical financial observations, like speculative stock, bond or foreign exchange prices or their increments, is that we do not know a priori how many orders of statistics are sufficient to completely describe such distributions. What can be proven is that, in general, *the computation of joint cumulants of order r requires knowledge of all moments up to order r* (Nikias and Petropulu, 1993).

Furthermore, if a set of variables $\{x(1), x(2), \ldots, x(n)\}$ is jointly Gaussian, then all the information about their distribution is contained in the moments of order $r \leq 2$. Therefore, all moments of order greater than two ($r > 2$) have no new information to provide. This leads to the fact that all joint cumulants of order $r > 2$ are identical to zero for Gaussian vectors. Hence, the cumulants of order greater than two, in some sense, measure the non-Gaussianness (non-normality) of a distribution. Furthermore, it is always possible to compute the empirical moments and cumulants and then check how close such empirical distributions are to various known parametric distributions. But such approximations by theoretical distributions can never lead to a unique identification of an empirical distribution. There will always be a subjective degree of confidence in the resulting distributional fit.

What do the various moments measure?

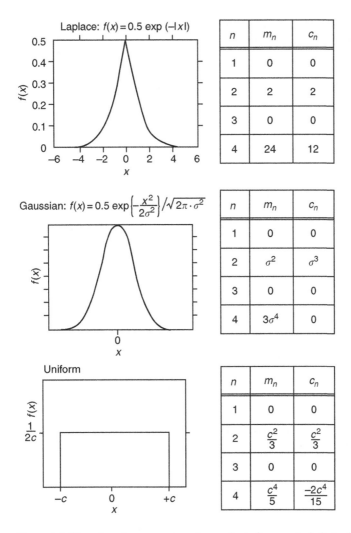

Figure 1.4 The nth-order moments and cumulants for $n = 1, 2, 3, 4$ of the Laplace, Gaussian and Uniform p.d.fs.

Definition 22 *The* location *of a distribution is measured by the first-order statistic, the mean, or average,*

$$c_1 = m_1 = E\{x\} \tag{1.31}$$

It is easy to *laterally shift* a distribution so that $c_1 = m_1 = 0$ to achieve considerable simplification, by computing deviations from the mean $\varepsilon = x - m_1 = x - E\{x\}$, since then the first-order statistic of such deviations ε, $m_1(\varepsilon) = c_1(\varepsilon) = 0$.

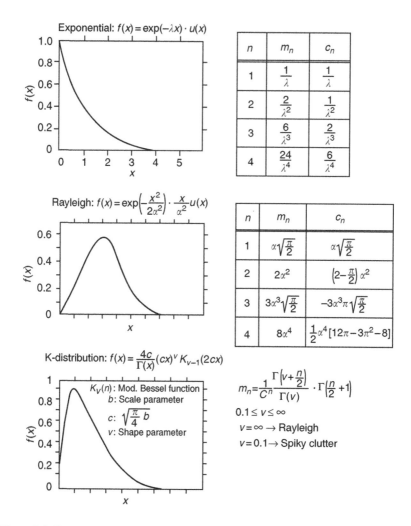

Figure 1.5 The nth-order moments and cumulants for $n = 1, 2, 3, 4$ of Exponential, Rayleigh and K-distribution p.d.fs.

Therefore, it is strongly advised that all empirical data are computed as deviations from their means, so that $c_1 = m_1 = 0$.

Definition 23 *The* scale, dispersion, *or* variance *of a distribution is measured by the second-order statistic*

$$c_2 = m_2 \ (\textit{since} \ m_1(\varepsilon) = 0) \tag{1.32}$$

Distributions can always be scaled or reduced to normalize distributions, by dividing by the scale. Usually this is done in combination with the lateral shift.[9] Thus, the standardized variable $z = \varepsilon/m_2$, so that $c_1(z) = m_1(z) = 0$ and $m_2(z) = c_2(z) = 1$.

Definition 24 *The* skewness *of a distribution is measured by its third-order statistic*

$$m_3 = c_3 \ (\text{since } m_1(\varepsilon) = 0) \tag{1.33}$$

For example, notice in Figure 1.5 that the third-order statistics of symmetric distributions equal zero, $m_3(\varepsilon) = c_3(\varepsilon) = 0$, while those of asymmetric distributions are unequal zero, $m_3(\varepsilon) = c_3(\varepsilon) \neq 0$ (since $m_1(\varepsilon) = 0$). In fact, when $m_3(\varepsilon) = c_3(\varepsilon) < 0$ the distribution is *negatively skewed* and when $m_3(\varepsilon) = c_3(\varepsilon) > 0$, the distribution is *positively skewed.*

Definition 25 *The* kurtosis, *or degree of peakedness, of a distribution is measured by its fourth-order statistic*

$$c_4 = m_4 - 3m_2^2 \tag{1.34}$$

Usually the comparison is made with the Gaussian distribution, which has $m_2 = \sigma^2$, so that we conventionally measure the normalized kurtosis.

Definition 26 *Normalized kurtosis is measured by*

$$\begin{aligned} \kappa_{\text{normalized}} &= \frac{m_4}{m_2^2} \\ &= \frac{c_4}{m_2^2} + 3 \\ &= \frac{c_4}{\sigma^4} + 3 \end{aligned} \tag{1.35}$$

When the kurtosis is the same as that of a Gaussian distribution, $c_4 = 0$, and thus normalized kurtosis equals $m_4/m_2^2 = 3$, we speak of *meso-kurtosis.* When $c_4 > 0$, i.e., normalized kurtosis $m_4/m_2^2 > 3$, the distribution exhibits large kurtosis, or *lepto-kurtosis*: the frequency distribution is more heavily concentrated around the mean than the Gaussian distribution. When $c_4 < 0$ and normalized kurtosis $m_4/m_2^2 < 3$, the distribution exhibits low kurtosis, or *platy-kurtosis*: the frequency distribution is less heavily concentrated about the mean than the Gaussian distribution.

Example 27 *Figure 1.6 shows how such an empirical distribution is constructed in the left panel (sideways) using a number of bins into which the time series values of particular ranges are collected (Frisch, 1995, p. 29). Notice how binning gathers*

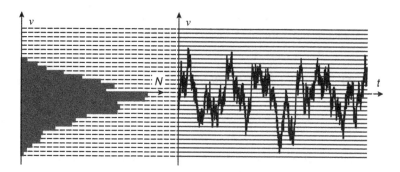

Figure 1.6 Construction of the histogram of a time series by binning.

the distributional or frequency information of the time series, but loses the time-dependence information of the series. Until recently, statisticians have paid more attention to the distributional information of time series, while signal processing engineers have paid more attention to their dependence on time. In this book we'll discuss both the frequency and time-dependence information, first separately and consecutively, and then simultaneously.

Example 28   *Figure 1.7 shows the raw and transformed daily returns of the DAX index in Frankfurt for the period after Black Monday, November 1987–August 1998. The histograms on the right show the relative frequencies of the returns in the same scale (Ormoneit and Neumeier, 2000, p. 49).*

Example 29   *Figure 1.8 shows the empirical histogram of the minute-by-minute logarithmic increments of the Japanese Yen (JPY) for the month of June 1997 compared with the theoretical Gaussian distribution (curved line), with the same variance. The distribution of these logarithmic increments is clearly leptokurtic: notice the extreme "peakedness" of the histogram, indicating the higher than normal occurrence of small movements, and the "fat" tails, indicating the higher than normal occurrence of "outliers." There is also a clearly noticeable dearth of intermediate movements. Notice also that in particular bins (the 6th bin to the right and the 4th bin to the left of the mode) no observations exist. Thus, empirical distribution is incomplete. It clearly contains* null events A, *so that* $P(A) = 0$.

Example 30   *A similar phenomenon as in the preceding example has been discussed in the financial literature regarding* foreign currency options *(cf. Hull, 2001, pp. 286–288). The* volatility smile, *which relates option volatility* σ *to the strike price X, is used by traders for empirically pricing of foreign currency options. It has the general form in Figure 1.9. The volatility smile is relatively low for at-the-money*

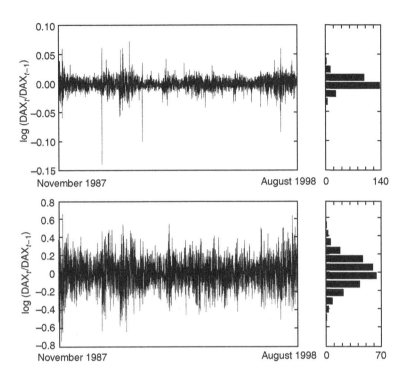

Figure 1.7 Raw and transformed daily returns of the DAX. The histograms on the right show the relative frequencies of the returns in the same scale.

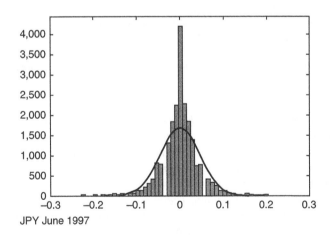

Figure 1.8 Empirical histogram of minute-by-minute log-increments of the JPY in June 1997.

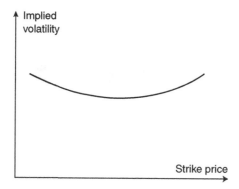

Figure 1.9 Volatility smile of foreign currrency options.

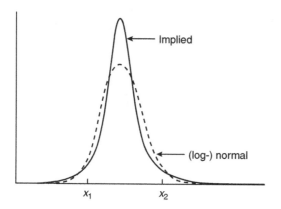

Figure 1.10 Implied distribution and (log-) normal distribution of foreign currency options.

options. It corresponds to the (Black–Scholes) implied distribution in Figure 1.10, which has higher kurtosis than the corresponding lognormal distribution with the same mean and standard deviation. Figures 1.9 and 1.10 are consistent with each other. Consider first a deep-out-of-the-money call option with a high strike price of X_2. The relative occurrence of this event is higher for the implied distribution than for the lognormal distribution. Therefore, we expect the implied distribution to give a relatively high price for the option. A relatively high option price leads to a relatively high implied volatility. Which is exactly what is empirically observed in Figure 1.9. A similar reasoning applies for a deep-out-of-the-money put option with a low strike price of X_1. Thus, the lognormal distribution of foreign currency prices understates the relative occurrence of extreme movements in exchange rates. Based on the measurement of daily movements in 12 different exchange rates over *a 10-year period, Hull and White (1998) found that daily changes exceeded three standard deviations on 1.34 percent of days, while he lognormal model predicts that this should happen on only 0.27 percent of days. Daily changes exceed four, five and six deviations on 0.29, 0.08 and 0.03 percent of days, respectively. The lognormal model predicts that we should hardly ever observe this happening. The two reasons for this empirical phenomenon mentioned by Hull and White (1998) are nonconstant volatilities and the impact of jumps (discontinuities) in the exchange rates, often in response to the actions of central banks.*

Example 31   *The traders who empirically price equity options use a* volatility skew, *as in Figure 1.11. The volatility σ decreases when the strike price increases (Macbeth and Merville, 1979; Lauterbach and Schultz, 1990; Rubinstein, 1994; Jackwerth and Rubinstein, 1996). The volatility used to price a low strike price option is significantly higher than that used to price a high strike price option. This volatility skew corresponds to the skewed and leptokurtic implied distribution in Figure 1.12. It has a fatter left tail and a thinner right tail than the lognormal distribution. For example a deep-out-of-the-money call with a strike price of X_2 has a lower price when the implied distribution is used than when the lognormal distribution is used. A relatively low price leads to a relatively low implied distribution. One possible explanation for this volatility skew in equity options is financial leverage. As a company's equity declines in market value, the company's financial leverage increases. Its equity becomes more risky and its volatility σ increases and vice versa (Hull, 2001, p. 290). Thus, we can expect the volatility of equity to be a decreasing function of price, consistent with Figures 1.11 and 1.12, and implying that it is time-dependent. Interestingly, prior to the October 19, 1987 stock market crash*

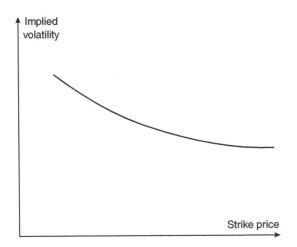

Figure 1.11 Skewed volatility smile of equities.

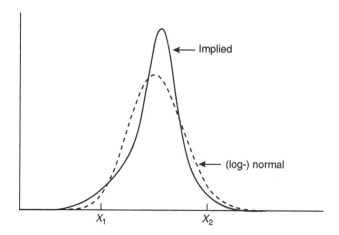

Figure 1.12 Implied distribution and (log-) normal distribution.

Table 1.3 First four moments of FX returns: USD/DEM and USP/JPY

FX rate	Interval τ	Mean	Variance	Skewness	Kurtosis
USD/DEM	30 minutes	-1.40×10^{-6}	7.53×10^{-7}	0.60	46.10
	6 hours	-1.68×10^{-5}	8.42×10^{-6}	0.27	11.75
	24 hours	-6.62×10^{-5}	3.48×10^{-5}	0.12	6.04
	1 week	-4.65×10^{-4}	2.41×10^{-4}	0.17	4.24
USD/JPY	30 minutes	-2.20×10^{-6}	7.16×10^{-7}	−0.05	24.02
	6 hours	-2.65×10^{-5}	7.98×10^{-6}	−0.17	11.64
	24 hours	-1.06×10^{-4}	3.13×10^{-5}	−0.16	7.06
	1 week	-7.57×10^{-4}	2.22×10^{-4}	−0.23	4.29

implied volatilities were much less dependent on strike prices. Rubinstein (1994, p. 784) suggests that one reason for the pattern in Figure 1.12 may be "crash-o-phobia." Traders are concerned about the possibility of another crash similar to the one of October 19, 1987, and they price options accordingly. It appears that the implied distribution for a stock price has fatter left tails than the distribution calculated from empirical data on stock market returns. Also the volatility skew became more pronounced after the October 1997 and August 1998 declines.

Example 32   *Table 1.3 provides the first four moments of the return distributions at different time intervals for the German* Deutschemark *(DEM) and the JPY against the* US *dollar (USD). The period of observation is January 1, 1987 to June 30, 1996. The data for the USD/DEM and USD/JPY in this Table 1.3 are selected from table 2 in Müller et al. (1998), p. 73, which contains similar data for* *three additional currencies: GBP/USD, USD/CHF, and USD/FRF. The distribution of foreign exchange (FX) returns is computed from the bid (= intention to buy) and offer (= intention to sell) price quotations of the market maker through the logarithmic middle price*

$$x(t) = \frac{\ln X_{\text{bid},t} + \ln X_{\text{offer},t}}{2} \tag{1.36}$$

and the return $r(t)$ is measured over a fixed time interval τ as

$$r(t) = x(t) - x(t - \tau) \tag{1.37}$$

where $x(t)$ is the sequence of logarithmic middle prices spaced equally in Greenwich Mean Time (GMT). The standard deviations are about twice as large as the means and the absolute values of the skewness are mostly significantly smaller than one. From these facts we conclude that the empirical distributions are almost symmetric. The mean values are slightly negative, since during the period of observation there was an overall increase in the value of the USD versus the DEM and versus the JPY (less USD per DEM and JPY, means relatively higher USD value). But comparing these four empirical moments with the theoretical moments of the theoretical distributions of Figures 1.4 and 1.5, we notice that for the shortest time intervals, the measured kurtosis of these empirical distributions is higher than normal ($\gg 3$). Interestingly, all rates show the same general characteristics: a decreasing kurtosis with increasing time intervals. In other words, the shapes of the distributions depend on the time horizon τ. At intervals of about one week, the kurtosis is rather close to the Gaussian value. This argues against scaling in the FX markets for time intervals of one week and larger. The topic of scaling we'll discuss further in Chapter 3.

Example 33 *Table 1.4 provides the first four moments of the return distributions at different time intervals for the short-term cash interest rates from the interbank money market for the US, Germany, and Japan. The period of observation is January 2, 1979 to June 30, 1996. The data in this Table 1.4 are selected from table 3 in Müller et al. (1998), p. 74, which contains similar data for two additional countries, Great Britain and Switzerland. Compare once more these empirical moments with the theoretical moments of the theoretical distributions of Figures 1.4 and 1.5 and notice that these empirical distributions are again not Gaussian, mainly because of their much higher than normal kurtosis ($\gg 3$), but also because of their skewness.*

Example 34 *In Figure 1.13 three empirical frequency distributions are plotted for the USD/DEM and two for the USD 6 month cash interest rate (This is figure 2 in Müller et al. (1998), p. 62). The cumulative frequency is on the scale of the cumulative Gaussian probability function. Gaussian distributions have the form of a straight line in this representation. Notice that this is approximately the case*

Table 1.4 First four moments of FX returns by time interval

Interest rate	Interval τ	Mean	Variance	Skewness	Kurtosis
USD 3 months	24 hours	-1.27×10^{-5}	2.41×10^{-6}	-0.16	24.72
	1 week	-8.88×10^{-5}	2.20×10^{-5}	-0.53	14.98
USD 6 months	24 hours	-1.04×10^{-5}	1.98×10^{-6}	-0.20	20.49
	1 week	-7.33×10^{-5}	1.71×10^{-5}	-0.82	14.48
DEM 3 months	24 hours	-1.72×10^{-7}	7.93×10^{-7}	0.39	28.68
	1 week	-7.35×10^{-7}	5.62×10^{-6}	0.22	18.80
DEM 6 months	24 hours	-4.76×10^{-7}	7.80×10^{-7}	0.22	33.52
	1 week	-3.99×10^{-6}	5.35×10^{-6}	0.10	11.90
JPY 3 months	24 hours	6.06×10^{-7}	1.28×10^{-6}	1.23	43.74
	1 week	4.24×10^{-6}	7.65×10^{-6}	2.80	36.97
JPY 6 months	24 hours	-2.47×10^{-6}	9.94×10^{-7}	0.50	46.29
	1 week	-1.73×10^{-5}	6.22×10^{-6}	2.42	28.04

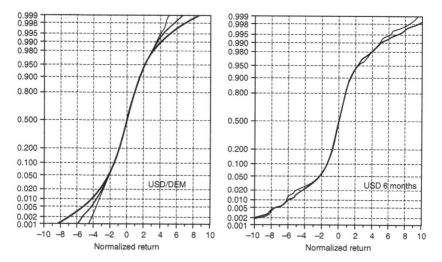

Figure 1.13 The empirical cumulative distributions for USD/DEM and USD 6 months cash interest rate, shown for different time horizons τ: 30 minutes, 1 day and 1 week for USD/DEM and 1 day and 1 week for USD 6 months. The fat lines are the shortest time intervals.

for the cumulative distribution of weekly returns, whose kurtosis is only slightly higher than normal. In contrast, the distributions of 30-minute and 24-hour returns are distinctly fat-tailed and their kurtosis values are very high. Again, the shape of the FX distribution is not preserved under time aggregation as was the case for the cotton prices in Mandelbrot (1963a). It is clear that the distributions of FX rates depend on the time horizon τ. Only in the case of the USD 6 month interest rates, both distributions for the 1-day and 1-week interval look remarkably alike. For these interest rates it is therefore not possible to reject the hypothesis of their distribution being stable under time aggregation. The kurtosis, which is high for the 1-day interval, remains high for the 1-week interval. Also the cumulative distribution for the interest rates is more fat-tailed than for the FX rates, as we can see by comparing Tables 1.3 and 1.4. Of course, the empirical distributions of the interest rates are more noisy than for the FX rates, due to both their lower precision of quotation and their lower frequency.

1.3.2   Heavy-tailed stable distributions

Stable distributions (or L-stable distributions) are a class of distributions that allow for skewness and heavy tails, like we found in the preceding examples of the cash interest rates. This class of distributions was characterized by Lévy (1937, 2nd edn, 1954) in his study of sums of independent, identically distributed (i.i.d.) variables. The general stable distribution is described by four parameters, similar to the moments:

(1)   an index of stability, or *characteristic exponent*, $\alpha_Z \in (0, 2]$, which describes the degree of kurtosis;
(2)   a *skewness parameter* $\beta \in [-1, 1]$;
(3)   a *scale parameter* $\gamma > 0$, similar (but not equivalent) to the second distribution moment; and
(4)   a *location parameter* $\delta \in \mathbb{R}$ (a real number).

Only a few stable distributions have closed formulas for densities and distribution functions, such as the Gaussian, Cauchy and Lévy distributions. There are three reasons to use these stable frequency distributions:

(1)   There are solid theoretical reasons to expect that real world phenomena exhibit non-Gaussian stable distributions, like in the case of Fractional Brownian Motion.
(2)   The Generalized Central Limit Theorem states that the only possible non-trivial limit of normalized sums of i.i.d. variables is stable (and that may be even true for non-i.i.d. variables too (cf. Kalman, 1994, 1995)).
(3)   Empirically, many large data sets exhibit skewness and heavy tails and are poorly described by the Gaussian distribution or by lognormal distributions.

Examples of such stable distributions in finance and economics are given in Mandelbrot (1963a,b, 1966), Fama (1963, 1965), McCulloch (1996), Bassi *et al.* (1998). We will define and discuss the theory of stable distributions and several theoretical and empirical examples of stable distributions in Chapter 3.

1.4   Random processes and time series

Thus far, we have discussed frequency distributions *per se*, without taking account of the time-dependence of dynamic financial random processes and of financial time series. In this section we introduce this important time dimension, since most dynamic phenomena exhibit time-dependence characteristics. Of course, we need both a frequency and a time-dependence analysis of any financial time series, preferably simultaneously, before we can properly model its frequency and dependence characteristics. It is astonishing to observe, how many statisticians, signal processing engineers, and other empirical researchers analyze each of these two characteristics – frequency or time dependence – in isolation or independently from each other, and how often they ignore the either one of these two characteristics.

First, we'll give the formal definitions of a random process and of a time series, which are surprisingly restrictive. Then we discuss some of the peculiar empirical characteristics of financial time series.

Let $(\Omega, \mathcal{A}, P)$ be a probability space and let T be the ordered set of real numbers corresponding to the times at which the *sequential observations* are carried out

Definition 35   *A monotonically decreasing family of σ-algebras $\{\mathcal{A}_t : t \in T\}$ on a given probability space $(\Omega, \mathcal{A}, P)$ such that $\mathcal{A}_0 \subset \mathcal{A}_1 \subset \cdots \subset \mathcal{A}_{t-1} \subset \mathcal{A}_t \subset \mathcal{A}$, where $\mathcal{A}_0$ is the trivial algebra $\mathcal{A}_0 = \{\emptyset, \Omega\}$, is called a* current of σ-algebras.

Definition 36   *The sequence of random variables (r.v.s) $\{X(t), \mathcal{A}_t : t \in T\}$ denotes an object of a current of σ-algebras $\{\mathcal{A}_t : t \in T\}$ on the measurable space $(\Omega, \mathcal{A})$, and the sequence of r.vs $\{X(t) : t \in T\}$, where the r.vs $X(t)$ are $\mathcal{A}_t$-measurable for all $t \in T$, is called a* random, *or* stochastic process.

Definition 37   *The sequence of r.vs $\{X(t) : t \in T\}$ is $\{\mathcal{A}_t\}$*-predictable *if $X(t) \in \mathcal{A}_{t-1} \subset \mathcal{A}_t$ for all $t \in T$.*

As we will see in the following chapters, some financial series are predictable and some are unpredictable. However, the predictability of a series of observations is not determined by its being random or deterministic, as this Boolean definition shows. Predictability has to do with the form of *dynamic inertia*. An event is only predictable, according to this definition, if it lies within the *historical information set* or *set of historical experiences*. For example, there exist deterministic, but unpredictable time series, called chaotic series, to be discussed in Chapter 9.

There is a more specific and complete Kolmogorovian definition of a *dynamic system*, which generalizes the concept of time shift, or *time horizon* τ, and which is less restrictive than the classical current of σ-algebras definition, which led to ARIMA or Markov type process definitions with unique equilibria. This new concept of a dynamic system is more open-ended, since it allows for bifurcations and the simultaneous coexistence of nonunique equilibria. This less restrictive definition of an abstract dynamic system we'll encounter again when we discuss the iterative degeneration of such a system into chaos in Chapter 9, which come about because of the simultaneous coexistence of more than one nonunique equilibria.

Definition 38   *A* dynamic system *is a quadruplet $(\Omega, \mathcal{A}, P, L)$. The set Ω is the universal space. $\mathcal{A}$ is a σ-algebra of Ω. P is the probability measure, which maps*

A to the real numbers between 0 and 1 and which satisfies the three axioms of Kolmogorov

$$(1) \quad P(A) \quad \geq 0 \quad \text{for all } A \in \mathcal{A}, \quad \text{non-negativity} \tag{1.38}$$

$$(2) \quad P(\cup_i A_i) = \sum_i P(A_i), \quad \text{additivity} \tag{1.39}$$

$$(3) \quad P(\Omega) \quad = 1, \quad \text{completeness} \tag{1.40}$$

where A_i is any countable set of disjoint sets $\in \mathcal{A}$. The time shifts, L_i, are a family of operators depending on a variable time $t \geq 0$, which can be either continuous or discrete. The time shifts L_is satisfy the semi-group property

$$L_0 = 1, \quad L_t L_\tau = L_{t+\tau} \tag{1.41}$$

and conserve the probability

$$P(G_t^{-1} A) = P(A), \quad \text{for all } t \geq 0 \text{ and all } A \in \mathcal{A} \tag{1.42}$$

By definition, dynamic systems represent temporal end/or spatial evolutions or diffusions of a set of particles, like the original Brownian motion, but with the possibility of nonunique pathways. Dynamic systems are represented by a set of state variables and a specification of the (stochastic) processes they follow, as their values are observed from moment to moment. These processes implicitly specify the densities governing the values of the state variables at future times.

1.4.1 Stationarity and serial dependence

We will now introduce two essential concepts for time series analysis: *stationarity* and *time dependence*. These two concepts have been more or less ignored by financial economists and financial analysts, who traditionally, but erroneously, have assumed that all empirical financial and economic time series are stationary and that their increments are mutually independent.

1.4.1.1 Stationary processes

Definition 39 *A random process $\{X(t), \mathcal{A}_t : t \in T\}$ is said to be* stationary in the strict sense *(distribution stationary, or strongly stationary), if*

$$P\{X(1), X(2), \ldots, X(t)\} = P\{X(1+\tau), X(2+\tau), \ldots, X(t+\tau)\} \text{ a.c.} \tag{1.43}$$

for all t and $t + \tau \in T$.

Notice that under stationarity in the strict sense, the *whole* joint probability distribution does not change over time. This is not easy to check empirically, as we will see, since we will have to measure all characteristic, integer and fractional, moments of the distributions. Regrettably, we can't know a priori how many moments are required to characterize an empirical distribution. Thus, pragmatically, only the moments are computed that one is interested in.

Definition 40   *A random process $\{X(t), \mathcal{A}_t : t \in T\}$ is said to be* stationary in the wide sense *(covariance stationary, or weakly stationary) if*

$$E|X^2(t)| < \infty \tag{1.44}$$

and

$$E\{X(t)X(t - \tau)\} = h(|t - \tau|) \tag{1.45}$$

i.e., the covariance is a function only of the absolute time period $|t - \tau|$.

Stationarity in the wide sense is empirically much easier to check, since it restricts the checking to second-order integer moments only.

Remark 41   *The stationarity of random process is equivalent to the property of identically distributiveness (i.d.) of r.v. in classical (non-dynamic) statistics.*

In finance, this has meant until recently that only the first two integer moments of return distributions are computed. For example, Black (1976) looked at stock price volatility (second moment) and how it changes over time, while Ilmanen (1995) looked at the expected returns (first moment) in international bond markets and found them to be nonstationary, c.q., time-varying. Recently, empirical financial researchers have become more aware of the non-Gaussianness of such rate of return distributions and have begun to compute their third, fourth and even higher moments, moving beyond the pragmatic checking of stationarity in the wide sense and in the direction of the rather elusive goal of checking for stationarity in the strict sense.

Example 42   *Stationarity in the wide sense is required for classical optimal hedging, since the use of the minimum variance hedge ratio assumes that the future standard deviations of and the correlation between the changes in the spot and futures prices remain unchanged (Stulz, 1984). The minimum variance hedge ratio is:*

$$h^* = \rho \frac{\sigma_S}{\sigma_F} \tag{1.46}$$

where σ_S = standard deviations of the changes in the spot price; σ_F = standard deviation of the changes in the futures price; σ_{SF} = covariance between the changes in the spot price and the futures prices, respectively; and

$\rho = (\sigma_{SF})/(\sigma_S \sigma_F)$ *correlation between spot S and futures F prices. The use of* h^* *assumes that* σ_S, σ_F *and* ρ *remain constant over time:*

$$\sigma_S, \sigma_F, \rho = constant \, for \, all \, t \tag{1.47}$$

However, the futures and spot markets show little stationarity in the wide sense and, in this context, several questions had already been raised some decades ago about their hedging performance (Ederington, 1979; Franckle, 1980). These research questions have been insufficiently addressed in the finance literature.

Example 43   *The Black–Scholes and the binomial option pricing models also assume that the variance of the rates of return of the underlying asset is constant throughout the life of the option (Haugen, 2001, p. 472). In contrast, the constant elasticity of variance option pricing model of Cox (1996) assumes that the variance of the rate of return is parametrically dependent on the level of z_t the underlying price. A reduction in the market value of common stock reflects an erosion in the firm's equity base. Or, a reduction in the value of equity relative to the value of the firm's debt means an increase in stockholder risk. Such a dependency can be modeled by a so-called financial "single-index" model, where the systematic component of the stock's variance equals the product of the stock's squared β and the variance of the index, as follows:*

$$r_t = E\{r_t\} + b_t z_t \tag{1.48}$$

where

$$b_t = a_1 S_t^{(a_2-2)/2} \quad and \quad z_t \sim N(0,1) \tag{1.49}$$

The increment in the rate of return is equal to the product of (1) an index z_t associated with the individual stock and (2) a coefficient b_t, which relates the returns on the stock to the factor z_t. Let's look at three different situations: (1) If $a_2 = 2$, then $b_t = a_1$, and $\sigma_{rr} = b_t^2 \sigma_{zz} = a_1^2$. This is the special case assumed in the Black–Scholes framework. (2) If $a_2 = 4$, then $b_t = a_1 S_t$, and $\sigma_{rr} = b_t^2 \sigma_{zz} = a_1^2 S_t^2$. When $a_2 > 2$, the variance of the rate of return becomes larger as the stock price becomes larger. This positive dependence of the variance on the level of the stock price is contrary to both theory and empirical evidence. (3) If $a_2 = 0$, then $b_t = a_1 S_t^{-1} = a_1/S_t$, and $\sigma_{rr} = b_t^2 \sigma_{zz} = a_1^2/S_t^2$. When $a_2 < 2$, the variance of the rate of return becomes larger as the stock price becomes smaller. Such a negative dependence of the variance on the level of the stock price conforms to both theory and empirical evidence (MacBeth and Merville, 1979, 1980; Emanuel and Macbeth, 1982).

It now appears also that, for more complete financial risk measurement, analysis and management, we need to compute at least the first four moments of wide sense stationary processes. Some researchers argue even in favor of the computation of several more moments. Next, we must check which of these moments are time-invariant and which are time-varying (Priestley, 1988; Cizeau *et al.*, 1997). It will be observed in the Exercises of Chapter 2 that the first four moments of a simple stock market index series like the S&P500 index are all time-varying and that consequently its distribution is non-stationary in the strict sense. One may try to discover how the time-varying moments systematically relate to either the time series or to additional, so-called *exogenous* variables.

Example 44   *A striking example of a non-stationary foreign exchange rate distribution, where the non-stationarity is in the form of an institutional discontinuity, is given in Figure 1.14. This figure portrays the two semi-annual cumulative distributions of one-minute changes of the Thai baht (THB) relative to the USD in 1997. THB abruptly fell on July 2, 1997 and the Asian Financial Crisis followed. The distribution of the first half year January–June 1997 in blue is significantly more concentrated than the distribution of the second half year. The small insert chart with differential spectra include data points in both halves corresponding to percentile increments of 10 percent. Thus, the 10, 20, 30 percent, . . . , data values for the second half year are plotted against this in the first half year. Using a 45° line to indicate equality between the two half years, the extremely large deviation from the 45° line was tested against both halves, and indicated a significant difference (Los, 1999, p. 275; also in Abu-Mostafa* et al., *2000, p. 237). In comparison, the shape of the distribution of the DEM, an anchor currency, measured over the same semi-annual periods, remained remarkably stationary in 1997, with the exception of a few outliers, as shown in Figure 1.15. (Los, 1999, p. 276; also Abu-Mostafa* et al., *2000, p. 238).*

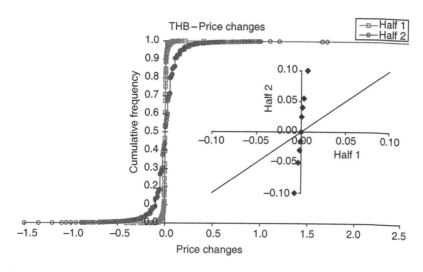

Figure 1.14 Semi-annual cumulative distributions of THB–FX increments, January–December 1997.

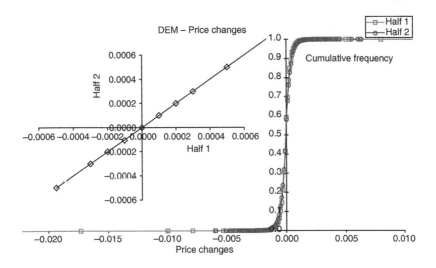

Figure 1.15 Semi-annual cumulative distributions of DEM–FX increments, January–December 1997.

1.4.1.1.1 MOMENTS AND CUMULANTS OF WIDE SENSE STATIONARY PROCESSES

The definitions of the cumulants and moments of wide sense stationary processes are straightforward, although not always simple, e.g., the fourth-order cumulant is a complex expression.

Definition 45 *The first-order cumulant, or* mean value:

$$c_1 = m_1 = E\{X(t)\} \tag{1.50}$$

Definition 46 *Second-order cumulant or* covariance sequence:

$$
\begin{aligned}
c_2(\tau_1) &= m_2(\tau_1) - m_1^2 \\
&= m_2(-\tau_1) - m_1^2 \\
&= c_2(-\tau_1)
\end{aligned}
\tag{1.51}
$$

where $m_2(\tau_1)$ is the autocorrelation function dependent on the time horizon τ_1 of time series 1.

Notice that covariance sequences are symmetric in time. The time interval is τ_1.

Remark 47 *When $m_1 = 0$, the covariance sequence simplifies to*

$$c_2(\tau_1) = m_2(\tau_1) \tag{1.52}$$

Definition 48   Third-order cumulant

$$c_3(\tau_1, \tau_2) = m_3(\tau_1, \tau_2) - m_1[m_2(\tau_1) + m_2(\tau_2) + m_2(\tau_2 - \tau_1)] + 2m_1^3 \quad (1.53)$$

Remark 49   *When $m_1 = 0$, this simplifies to*

$$c_3(\tau_1, \tau_2) = m_3(\tau_1, \tau_2) \quad (1.54)$$

Definition 50   Fourth-order cumulant

$$
\begin{aligned}
c_4(\tau_1, \tau_2, \tau_3) = {} & m_4(\tau_1, \tau_2, \tau_3) - m_2(\tau_1) \cdot m_2(\tau_3 - \tau_2) \\
& - m_2(\tau_2) \cdot m_2(\tau_3 - \tau_1) \\
& - m_2(\tau_3) \cdot m_2(\tau_2 - \tau_1) - m_1[m_3(\tau_2 - \tau_1, \tau_3 - \tau_1) \\
& + m_3(\tau_2, \tau_3) + m_3(\tau_2, \tau_4) + m_3(\tau_1, \tau_2)] \\
& + (m_1)^2[m_2(\tau_1) + m_2(\tau_2) + m_2(\tau_3) + m_2(\tau_3 - \tau_1) \\
& + m_2(\tau_3 - \tau_2) + m_2(\tau_2 - \tau_1)] - 6(m_1)^4 \quad (1.55)
\end{aligned}
$$

Remark 51   *When $m_1 = 0$, this expression simplifies to*

$$
\begin{aligned}
c_4(\tau_1, \tau_2, \tau_3) = {} & m_4(\tau_1, \tau_2, \tau_3) - m_2(\tau_1) \cdot m_2(\tau_3 - \tau_2) \\
& - m_2(\tau_2) \cdot m_2(\tau_3 - \tau_1) - m_2(\tau_3) \cdot m_2(\tau_2 - \tau_1) \quad (1.56)
\end{aligned}
$$

If the random process is zero mean ($m_1 = 0$) (and we can always make it so, if and when the mean is a constant, by analyzing the deviations from the mean), it follows that the second- and third-order cumulants are again identical to the second- and third-order moments, respectively. However, to generate the fourth-order cumulant, we still need knowledge of the fourth- and second-order moments.

1.4.1.2   Conditional probability

The study of random processes would not have progressed without the concept of conditional probabilities, which led to the *Bayesian* interpretations based on Bayes Theorem.

Definition 52   *The conditional probability is*

$$P(A \mid B) = \frac{P(A \cap B)}{P(B)} \quad (1.57)$$

which is implicit in Bayes Theorem (Bayes, 1763):

Theorem 53   (Bayes)

$$P(A \mid B)P(B) = P(B \mid A)P(A) = P(A \cap B) \quad (1.58)$$

Definition 54 *The* conditional expectation *of a random variable* $\{X(t): t \in T\}$ *given the* σ*-algebra* $\mathcal{A}_t$ *is itself the random variable*

$$E\{X(t) \mid \mathcal{A}_t\} \tag{1.59}$$

measurable with respect to the information set $\mathcal{A}_t$ *and satisfying the equality*

$$\int_A X(t) dP_0 = \int_A E\{X(t) \mid \mathcal{A}_t\} dP_0 \tag{1.60}$$

Examples of wide sense stationary random processes with serial dependence are Markov processes, Geometric Brownian motion, Random Walks (– arithmetic Brownian motion), and non-stationary (G)ARCH processes, to be discussed in greater detail in Chapter 5. All these processes are used for conditional forecasting (e.g. French and Roll, 1986).

1.4.1.3 Markov process

Definition 55 *The random process* $\{X(t): t \in T\}$, *defined on the probability space* (Ω, G, P), *is said to be a* Markov process in the strict sense, *or to possess the Markov distribution property, if and only if*

$$P\{X(t) \mid X(1), \dots, X(t-1)\} = P\{X(t) \mid X(t-1)\} \, a.c. \tag{1.61}$$

Definition 56 *A random process* $\{X(t): t \in T\}$ *is said to be a* Markov process in the wide sense *if*

$$E\left\{|X(t)|^2\right\} < \infty \tag{1.62}$$

and

$$E\{X(t) \mid X(1), \dots, X(t-1)\} = E\{X(t) \mid X(t-1)\} \, a.c. \tag{1.63}$$

Remark 57 *In general, for a time series, of course*

$$E\{X(t) \mid X(t-1)\} \neq X(t-1) \tag{1.64}$$

Thus, a Markov process in the wide sense need not be a martingale (see Chapter 2 for the definition of a martingale). A Markov process in the strict sense involves a stronger restriction than a martingale, since the Markov property involves whole distributions, rather than just the expectations implied by these distributions.

1.4.2 Ergodicity

A crucial, but often misunderstood, or more precisely, ignored, concept for the classical ensemble approach to time series – which, ideally, considers one historical realization of a time series as only one element of the set, or *ensemble*, of many possible realizations – is Birkhoff's ergodicity (cf. Halmos, 1956).

Theorem 58 (Birkhoff's ergodicity) *Let* $\{X(t)\}$ *be a random process, i.e., a measurable, or more specifically, an integrable function defined in the interval* $[0, 1]$. *Then the expected value* $E\{\cdot\}$ *(also called the ensemble average) can be replaced by a (limiting) time average, since*

$$\lim_{T \to \infty} \frac{1}{T} \sum_{t=0}^{T} \{X(t) \cdot X(t + \tau_1), \ldots, X(t + \tau_{r-1})\}$$

$$= \int_0^1 \{X(t) \cdot X(t + \tau_1), \ldots, X(t + \tau_{r-1})\} \tag{1.65}$$

$$= E\{X(t) \cdot X(t + \tau_1), \ldots, X(t + \tau_{r-1})\} \text{ a.c.} \tag{1.66}$$

If a random process is (Birkhoff) *ergodic* in the most general form, a.c., all its moments can be determined from a single set of observations. Thus, Birkhoff's Theorem allows us to replace time averages over one time interval or orbit by ensemble averages. Clearly, a particular random process might be ergodic for certain higher order moments, but not for others. In practice, when we are given a finite length realization of an ergodic process, we cannot compute the infinite limit, but only the approximating finite estimate

$$\frac{1}{T} \sum_{t=0}^{T} X(t) \cdot X(t + \tau_1), \ldots, X(t + \tau_{r-1})$$

Remark 59 *Birkhoff's Theorem is the crux of the statistician's frequency oriented approach to time series. It's very controversial and is obviously not accepted by signal engineers, on physical grounds. I have not yet seen an empirical scientific test or check for this ideal property of ergodicity, other than the exact computations based on the wavelet scalograms, to be discussed in Chapter 7. Based on the empirical observations thus far, it would be very surprising if this equality empirically exists in financial time series and if the assumption such an empirical equality can ever be checked (Los, 2001). After all, such a scientific check presumes the existence of an ensemble of infinitely many possible parallel worlds. But we have only available for scientific analysis one finite length realization, or, at best, a limited number of finite length time realization of a particular dynamic process. The right-hand side of the ergodicity equation is based on infinite or complete set of frequencies and the left-hand side on an infinite or complete set of observations. Most empirical invariance properties only hold within limited ranges of finite frequencies and of finite time intervals. Moreover, the Heisenberg Theorem is in direct conflict with the completeness assumptions of Birkhoff's ergodicity.*

1.4.3   Global dependence and long-term memory

The *global dependence*, also known as *long-term dependence*, of random processes and time series, is much harder to define than *serial*, or *short-term dependence*, such as the wide sense Markov process, since the correlations are not serial or even overlapping. Global dependence is not of the nature of a conditional martingale or a Markov nature, since it is not conditional on the whole past, as in the case of martingales, or on the immediately preceding period, as in the case of the Markov property. In fact, global dependence may occur even when serial correlations are close to zero! Global dependence shows correlations only at transient or varying frequencies.

Therefore such dependencies can better be described in the combined time-frequency domain than in either the time domain or the frequency domain and they can best be analyzed in a multi-scale fashion (Moody and Yang, 2000). The frequency domain *per se* is useful only for characterization of stationary processes. For an early documentation of the usefulness of multi-scale decomposition in hydrology, see Mandelbrot and Wallis (1969). The global dependence of the time series of asset returns is a central theme of this book and therefore its characteristics will be discussed in almost all following Chapters.

1.5   Software

The computations of the following Exercises can be executed in Microsoft EXCEL spreadsheets using its built-in functions, or by using the MATLAB® Statistics Toolbox available from The MathWorks, Inc., 24 Prime Park Way Natick, MA 01760-1500, USA. Tel (508) 647-7000; Fax (508) 647-7001; http://www.mathworks.com/products/wavelettbx.shtml.

1.6   Exercises

Exercise 60   *Using EXCEL spreadsheet functions and the data from the S&P500 daily data for the year 1998 found in the data set in Appendix B, compute the (logarithmic) rates of total return, and the first differences (= increments or innovations) of both the price series and of the total rates of return. Make sure that you save these and other results in an EXCEL Workbook, and, preferably, back them also up on a CD or a diskette.*

Exercise 61   *Plot the four series $X(t), \Delta X(t), x(t) = \Delta \ln x(t)$ and $\Delta x(t)$ created in the first Exercise against time.*

Exercise 62   *Produce scatter plots of the four series $x(t)$ against $x(t-1)$, then $x(t)$ against $x(t-10), x(t-20), x(t-30), x(t-40), x(t-50), x(t-100)$, and against $x(t-200)$, respectively.*

Exercise 63   *Compute the first four moments and cumulants of the four series and determine their mean, variance (or standard deviation), skewness and kurtosis.*

Exercise 64   *Using the statistics produced in the fourth Exercise, can you answer if any of these series exhibit serial dependence or global dependence? Why or why not?*

Exercise 65   *Run MATLAB® Help, Examples and Demos, Toolboxes, Statistics: Run Probability: have a close look at the p.d.f. (= probability density function) and c.d.f. (= cumulative density function) of all available theoretical statistical distributions. Compare the continuous with the discrete distributions, the centric with the noncentric distributions, and the symmetric with the asymmetric distributions.*

Exercise 66   *Run MATLAB® Help, Examples and Demos, Toolboxes, Statistics: Interactive Contour Plots: interpret this colored 2D image of a 3D function.*

Notes

1 With little loss of generality, in this book we mean by asset returns or investment returns: total returns = sum of cash payments and capital gains. All dividend payments are assumed to be reinvested in the assets.

2 Tobin's (1958) argument that portfolio returns are usually normally distributed, even when the security returns are not, is based on an application of the central limit theorem, which requires that the returns on the securities combined in the portfolio are uncorrelated. But security returns are always correlated to some degree and therefore the classical i.i.d. central limit theorem does not apply.

3 The term antipersistent will be explained in greater detail in Chapter 4. The commonly used term mean-reverting implies that both the mean and the variance are stable: volatility has an average value toward which it tends to move and it reverses itself constantly, trying to reestablish its equilibrium value. That is not true with an antipersistent time series. Financial market volatility is unstable like a turbulent flow: it has no trends, but will frequently reverse itself in an uneven fashion. A large increase in volatility has a high probability of being followed by a decrease of unknown magnitude.

4 Surprisingly, these crucial distinctions were already made in 1921 in a non-mathematical form by two economists, Frank Knight (1885–1972) and John Maynard Keynes (1883–1946), who disliked each other intensely. In particular, the Chicago economist Frank Knight made sharp distinctions between uncertainty, randomness and probability (Knight, 1964, original 1921). The commonsensical Knight would have appreciated the modern concept of randomness as irregularity, which we adopt as the most rational, although, perhaps, not the exact measurement of it. The rather elitist Cambridge, UK, economist Keynes distinguished between historical probability = relative frequency and subjective probability (Keynes, 1921). Keynes personally appreciated the irrational probability concepts developed by the eighteenth century enigmatic, nonconformist minister Thomas Bayes (1701–1761), a Fellow of the Royal Society, in Bayes' posthumously published "Essay Towards Solving A Problem In The Doctrine of Chances" in *Philosophical Transactions* (Bayes, 1763).

5 John Stuart Mill (1806–1873), the great nineteenth-century English philosopher and economist demanded in his influential pamphlet *On Liberty* (1859), in which he relentlessly attacked conformity and timidity, that we accept uncertainty or randomness as the necessary human condition. He wanted us to live, as his modern disciple Isaiah Berlin might say, with the assumption that life is neither stationary nor easily understood. In this context, it is significant that in his first major work, *A System of Logic*, Mill analyzed the epistemological principles underlying empiricism (Mill, 1843).

6 Chaos, why and how it occurs – by the process of *period-doubling* – is discussed in great detail in Chapter 10.
7 This section is borrowed, with slight alterations, from Peters (1999, pp. 22–24). Dr Daniel Ellsberg is, indeed, the one of Pentagon Papers' fame.
8 This treatment can easily be expanded into a multivariate framework (Stein, 1981).
9 Lateral shifting and scaling are the two defining operations of wavelet analysis, to be discussed in Chapter 7.

Bibliography

Abu-Mostafa, Yaser S., Blake LeBaron, Andrew W. Lo and Andreas S. Weigend (2000) *Computational Finance 1999*, The MIT Press, Cambridge, MA.

Alexander, Carol (Ed.) (1999) *Risk Management and Analysis, Volume 1: Measuring and Modelling Financial Risk*, John Wiley and Sons, New York, NY.

Bachelier, L. (1900) "Théorie de la Spéculation," (Doctoral dissertation in Mathematical Sciences, Faculté des Sciences de Paris, defended March 29, 1900), *Annales de l' École Normale Supérieure*, 3(17), 21–86. Translated, with permission of Gauthier-Villars, Paris, France, as chapter 2 in Cootner, Paul H. (Ed.) (1964) *The Random Character of Stock Market Prices*, The MIT Press, Cambridge, MA, pp. 17–78.

Bassi, Franco, Paul Embrechts and Maria Kafetzaki (1998) "Risk Management and Quantile Estimation," in Adler, Robert J., Raisa E. Feldman and Murad S. Taqqu (Eds) *A Practical Guide to Heavy Tails: Statistical Techniques and Applications*, Birkhäuser, Boston, MA, pp. 111–130.

Bayes, Thomas (1763) "An Essay Toward Solving a Problem in the Doctrine of Chances," *Philosophical Transactions*, Essay **LII**, 370–418. Also in Kendall and Plackett (1977), pp. 134–150.

Bernstein, Peter L. (1996) *Against the Gods: The Remarkable Story of Risk*, John Wiley and Sons, Inc., New York, NY.

Black, Fischer (1976) "Studies in Stock Price Volatility Changes," *Proceedings of the 1976 Business Meeting of the Business and Economics Statistics Section*, American Statistical Association, pp. 177–181.

Bouchaud, Jean-Philippe, and Marc Potters (2000) *Theory of Financial Risks: From Statistical Physics to Risk Management*, Cambridge University Press, Cambridge, UK.

Chow, Yuan Shih, and Henry Teicher (1978) *Probability Theory: Independence, Interchangeability, Martingales*, Springer Verlag, New York, NY.

Cizeau, P., Y. Liu, M. Meyer, C.-K. Peng and H. Eugene Stanley (1997) "Volatility Distribution in the S&P500 Stock Index," *Physica*, A, **245**(3/4), 441–445.

Cowles III, Alfred (1933) "Can Stock Market Forecasters Forecast?," *Econometrica*, **1**(3), 309–324.

Cox, John (1996) "The Constant Elasticity of Variance Option Pricing Model," *Journal of Portfolio Management*, **23**(1) (Special Issue), 15–17.

Ederington, L. G. (1979) "The Hedging Performance of the New Futures Market," *Journal of Finance*, **34**(1), 157–170.

Emanual, D., and J. MacBeth (1982) "Further Results on Constant Elasticity of Variance Call Option Model," *Journal of Financial and Quantitative Analysis*, **17**(4), 533–554.

Fama, Eugene F. (1963) "Mandelbrot and the Stable Paretian Hypothesis," *The Journal of Business*, **36**(4), 420–429. Reprinted as chapter 14 in Cootner, Paul H. (Ed.) (1964) *The Random Character of Stock Market Prices*, The MIT Press, Cambridge, MA, pp. 297–306.

Fama, Eugene F. (1965) "The Behavior of Stock-Market Prices," *The Journal of Business*, **38**(1), 34–105.

Franckle, C. T. (1980) "The Hedging Performance of the New Futures Market: Comment," *Journal of Finance*, **35**(5), 1273–1279.

French, K., and R. Roll (1986) "Stock Return Variances: The Arrival of Information and the Reaction of Traders," *Journal of Financial Economics*, **17**(1), 5–26.

Frisch, Uriel (1995) *Turbulence: The Legacy of A. N. Kolmogorov*, Cambridge University Press, Cambridge, UK.

Goldreich, Oded (1999) "Pseudo-Randomness," *Notices of the American Mathematical Society*, **46**(10), 1209–1216.

Greer, R. (1997) "What is an Asset Class Anyway?," *Journal of Portfolio Management*, **24**(1), 86–91.

Halmos, P. R. (1956) *Lectures on Ergodic Theory*, Chelsea, New York, NY.

Haugen, Robert A. (2001) *Modern Investment Theory*, 5th edn, Prentice Hall, Upper Saddle River, NJ.

Hull, J. C. (2001) *Fundamentals of Options and Futures Markets*, Prentice Hall, Upper Saddle River, NJ.

Hull, J. C., and A. White (1998) "Value at Risk When Daily Changes in Market Variables Are Not Normally Distributed," *Journal of Derivatives*, **5**(3), 9–19.

Ibbotson, Roger G., and Rex A. Sinquefield (1999) *Stocks, Bonds, Bills, and Inflation: 1998 Yearbook (1926–1998)*, Dow Jones-Irwin, Chicago, IL.

Ilmanen, A. (1995) "Time-Varying Expected Returns in International Bond Markets," *Journal of Finance*, **50**(2), 481–506.

Jackwerth, J. C., and M. Rubinstein (1996) "Recovering Probability Distributions from Option Prices," *Journal of Finance*, **51**(5), 1611–1631.

Kalman, Rudolf E. (1994) "Randomness Reexamined," *Modeling, Identification and Control*, **15**(3), 141–151.

Kalman, R. E. (1995) "Randomness and Probability," *Mathematica Japonica*, **41**(1), 41–58, and "Addendum," **41**(2), 463.

Kalman, Rudolf E. (1996) "Probability in the Real World as a System Attribute," *CWI Quarterly*, **9**(3), 181–204.

Kendall, Maurice G., and R. L. Plackett (Eds) (1977) *Studies in the History of Statistics and Probability*, Vol. II, Macmillan, New York, NY.

Keynes, John Maynard (1921) *A Treatise on Probability*, Macmillan, London, UK.

Kindleberger, Charles P. (1996) *Manias, Panics, and Crashes: A History of Financial Crises*, John Wiley and Sons, New York, NY.

Knight, Frank H. (1964) *Risk, Uncertainty and Profit*, Century Press, New York, NY (original 1921).

Kolmogorov, A. N. (1933) *Grundbegriffe der Wahrscheinlichkeitsrechnung*, Springer, Berlin (Translated by Nathan Morrison: *Foundations of Probability*, Chelsea, New York, NY, 1950).

Kondor, I., and J. Kertesz (Eds) (1999) *Econophysics: An Emerging Science*, Kluwer, Dordrecht, The Netherlands.

Lauterbach, B., and P. Schultz (1990) "Pricing Warrants: An Empirical Study of the Black–Scholes Model and Its Alternatives," *Journal of Finance*, **44**(4), 1181–1210.

Lévy, Paul (1954) *Théorie de l'Addition des Variables Aléatoires (Theory of the Summation of Random Variables)*, 2nd edn, Gauthier-Villars, Paris, France (original 1937).

Lorenz, Edward N. (2001) *The Essence of Chaos*, University of Washington Press, Seattle, WA (original 1993).

Los, Cornelis A. (1982) "Discrete-Time Martingale Convergence Results and Nonlinear Estimation Using Time-Series Data," Research Paper No: 8222, Federal Reserve Bank of New York, New York, 107 pages.

Los, Cornelis A. (1998) "Optimal Multi-Currency Investment Strategies With Exact Attribution in Three Asian Countries," *Journal of Multinational Financial Management*, **8**(2/3), 169–198.

Los, Cornelis A. (1999) "Nonparametric Testing of the High-Frequency Efficiency of the 1997 Asian Foreign Exchange Markets," *Journal of Multinational Financial Management*, **9**(3/4), 265–289.

Los, Cornelis A. (2000a) "Nonparametric Efficiency Testing of Asian Stock Markets, Using Weekly Data," in Fomby, Thomas, B., and R. Carter Hill (Eds), *Advances in Econometrics: Applying Kernel and Nonparametric Estimation to Economic Topics*, **14**, JAI Press, Inc., pp. 329–363.

Los, Cornelis A. (2000b) "Frequency and Time Dependence of Financial Risk," *The Journal of Performance Measurement*, **5**(1), 72–73.

Los, Cornelis A. (2001) *Computational Finance: A Scientific Perspective*, World Scientific Publishing, Co., Singapore.

Macbeth, J. D., and L. J. Merville (1979) "An Empirical Examination of the Black–Scholes Call Option Pricing Model," *Journal of Finance*, **34**(5), 1173–1186.

Macbeth, J. D., and L. J. Merville (1980) "Tests of the Black–Scholes and Cox Option Valuation Models," *Journal of Finance*, **35**(2), 285–301.

McCulloch, J. Huston (1996) "Financial Applications of Stable Distributions," in Maddala, G. S., and C. R. Rao (Eds), *Statistical Methods in Finance* (*Handbook of Statistics*, **14**, Elsevier, Amsterdam, The Netherlands, pp. 393–425).

Mandelbrot, Benoit B. (1963a) "New Methods in Statistical Economics," *Journal of Political Economy*, **71**(5), 421–440.

Mandelbrot, Benoit B. (1963b) "The Variation of Certain Speculative Prices," *The Journal of Business*, **36**(4), 394–419, and **45**, 1972, 542–543.

Mandelbrot, Benoit B. (1966) "Forecasts of Future Prices, Unbiased Markets and Martingale Models," *The Journal of Business*, **39**(1), (Special Supplement), 242–255.

Mandelbrot, Benoit B. (1982) *The Fractal Geometry of Nature*, W. H. Freeman, New York, NY.

Mandelbrot, Benoit B. (1997) *Fractals and Scaling in Finance: Discontinuity, Concentration, Risk*, Springer Verlag, New York, NY.

Mandelbrot, Benoit B., and J. R. Wallis (1969) "Some Long-Run Properties of Geophysical Records," *Water Resources Research*, **5**(2), 321–340.

Mann, H. B., and A. Wald (1943) "On the Statistical Treatment of Linear Stochastic Difference Equations," *Econometrica*, **11**(3/4), 173–220.

Mantegna, R. N., (Ed.) (1999) *Proceedings of the International Workshop on Europhysics and Statistical Finance, Physica*, A, **269** (Special Issue).

Mantegna, R. N., and H. Eugene Stanley (2000) *An Introduction to Econophysics: Correlations and Complexity in Finance*, Cambridge University Press, Cambridge, UK.

Merton, Robert C. (1999) *Continuous Time Finance*, rev. ed., Basil Blackwell, Oxford, UK.

Meyer, Yves (1985) "Principe d'Incertitude, Bases Hilbertienne et Algèbres d'Opérateurs" ("Uncertainty Principle, Hilbert Bases and Operator Algebra"), in *Séminaire Bourbaki*, **145–146**, 209–223, Astérisque, Paris.

Mill, John Stuart (2000) *A System of Logic, Ratiocinative and Inductive, Being a connected view of the Principles of Evidence, and the Methods of Scientific Investigation* (*Collected Works of John Stuart Mill, 2 volumes*), Classic Books, New York, NY (original 1843).

Mittnik, Stefan, Svetlozar T. Rachev and Marc S. Paolella (1998) "Stable Paretian Modeling in Finance," in Adler, Robert J., Raisa E. Feldman and Murad S. Taqqu (Eds) (1998) *A Practical Guide to Heavy Tails: Statistical Techniques and Applications*, Birkhäuser, Boston, MA, pp. 79–110.

Moody, John, and Howard Yang (2000) "Term Structure of International Foreign Exchange Rates," in Abu-Mostafa, Yasaer S., Blake LeBaron, Andrew W. Lo and Andreas S. Weigend, *Computational Finance 1999*, MIT Press, Cambridge, MA, pp. 247–265.

Müller, Ulrich A., Michel A. Dacorogna and Olivier V. Pictet (1998) "Heavy Tails in High-Frequency Financial Data," in Adler, Robert J., Raisa E. Feldman and Murad S. Taqqu (Eds) *A Practical Guide to Heavy Tails: Statistical Techniques and Applications*, Birkhäuser, Boston, MA, pp. 55–77.

Nikias, Chrysostomos L., and Athina P. Petropulu (1993) *Higher-Order Spectra Analysis: A Nonlinear Signal Processing Framework*, Prentice Hall, Englewood Cliffs, NJ.

Ormoneit, Dirk, and Ralph Neumeier (2000) "Conditional Value at Risk," in Abu-Mostafa, Yasaer S., Blake LeBaron, Andrew W. Lo and Andreas S. Weigend, *Computational Finance 1999*, MIT Press, Cambridge, MA, pp. 41–52.

Papoulis, A. (1984) *Probability, Random Variables and Stochastic Processes*, McGraw-Hill, New York, NY.

Peters, Edgar E. (1994) *Fractal Market Analysis*, John Wiley and Sons, New York, NY.

Peters, Edgar E. (1999) *Patterns in the Dark: Understanding Risk and Financial Crisis with Complexity Theory*, John Wiley and Sons, New York, NY.

Pincus, Steve, and Burt H. Singer (1996) "Randomness and Degrees of Irregularity," *Proceedings of the National Academy of Sciences (USA)*, **93**, 2083–2088.

Pincus, Steve, and Rudolf E. Kalman (1997) "Not All (Possibly) 'Random' Sequences Are Created Equal," *Proceedings of the National Academy of Sciences (USA)*, **94**, April, 3513–3518.

Potters, M. R. Cont, and J.-P. Bouchaud (1998) "Financial Markets as Adaptive Ecosytems," *Europhysics Letters*, **41**, 239–242.

Priestley, M. (1988) *Non-Linear and Non-Stationary Time Series Analysis*, Academic Press, San Diego, CA.

Prigogine, Ilya (1997) *The End of Certainty: Time, Chaos and the New Laws of Nature*, The Free Press, New York, NY.

Rubinstein, M. (1994) "Implied Binomial Trees," *Journal of Finance*, **49**(3), 771–818.

Savit, Robert (1988) "When Random is Not Random: An Introduction to Chaos in Market Prices," *Journal of Futures Markets*, **8**, 271.

Savit, Robert (1994) "Chaos on the Trading Floor," Chapter 14 in Hall, Nina (Ed.) *Exploring Chaos: A Guide to the New Science of Disorder*, W. W. Norton and Company, New York, NY, 174–183.

Schroeder, Manfred (1991) *Fractals, Chaos, Power Laws: Minutes from an Infinite Paradise*, W. H. Freeman and Co., New York, NY.

Schwert, G. W. (1989) "Why Does Stock Market Volatility Change over Time?," *Journal of Finance*, **44**(5), 1115–1153.

Stein, C. (1981) "Estimation of the Mean of a Multivariate Normal Distribution," *Annals of Statistics*, **9**(6), 1135–1151.

Stulz, R. M. (1984) "Optimal Hedging Policies," *Journal of Financial and Quantitative Analysis*, **19**(2), 127–140.

Tobin, James (1958) "Liquidity Preference as Behavior Towards Risk," *Review of Economic Studies*, **25**(2), 65–85.

Webster, Noah (1983) *New Universal Unabridged Dictionary* (DeLuxe Second Edition, edited by Jean L. McKechnie), Dorset and Baber, New York, NY.

2   Competing financial market hypotheses

2.1   Introduction

Since Fama's (1970) martingale formulation of the Efficient Market Hypothesis (EMH), most textbooks in finance have blindly adopted this theoretical idealization of financial markets. However, the problem, in which a theoretical random process accurately describes the changes in the logarithm of a price in a financial market, is still open. Several competing models have been proposed to explain at least the following two stylized facts of observation:

(i) there is empirical evidence that the tails of measured distributions are fatter than expected for the classical Geometric Brownian Motion (GBM).
(ii) there is empirical evidence that the second moments of the relative price changes vary over time, i.e., that there is wide sense non-stationarity.

Eugene Fama himself was well aware of competing financial market hypotheses. In the 1960s, he had reviewed and criticized the work on fractal market pricing theory, or the Fractal Market Hypothesis (FMH), by Mandelbrot, which emphasizes the empirically observable and well-corroborated self-similarity of power laws of financial pricing, in particular in stock markets (Fama, 1965). Such time-dependent self-similarity of empirical financial pricing laws contradicts the EMH based on martingale theory, as explained in this chapter.

While theoreticians have favored Fama's martingale based EMH, and Fama continues to support the martingale based EMH (Fama, 1991), more than twenty years of empirical research results assiduously compiled by Peters (1994) tend to support the FMH.[1] In this book we will present new methods of empirical analysis to corroborate and refine those FMH results.

2.2   EMH: martingale theory

2.2.1   *Martingales and fair games*

Before we follow Fama (1970) and interpret the efficiency of financial markets in terms of martingales, it may be wise to obtain first an intuitive understanding of what martingales are. Martingales are very useful concepts for when time series observations are dependent, since they usually are! Examples are abundant, like

(1) when the observations result from feedback processes;
(2) when the estimation situation is nonlinear; and
(3) when the information sets are increasing, because of accumulation of observations.

Intuitively, a discrete martingale can be understood as a sequence of values of conditional (pricing) events, which is as likely to go up as to go down, in each of a series of consecutive time instants.

Definition 67   *For the sequence* $\{X(t): t = 1, 2, \ldots\}$, *if*

$$E\{X(t+1) \mid X(1), X(2), \ldots, X(t)\} = X(t) \tag{2.1}$$

then the sequence $\{X(t)\}$ *is called a* martingale.

For example, if $X(t)$ represents the stake in a game at time t held by one of two gamblers, the game between the two gamblers is fair if and only if the martingale property holds. Martingales are one of the simplest kinds of random processes for which a number of convergence results and central limit theorems (CLTs) are available (Chow and Teicher, 1978; Los, 1982). For estimation theory, however, the martingale-difference (MD) property is more fundamental, since this property lies in between the properties of independence and uncorrelatedness, respectively. Martingales are the partial sums of MDs, which we will define shortly.

To do so, we need, first, the following definitions of sub- and supermartingales, as follows.

Definition 68   *A random process* $\{X(t), \mathcal{A}_t: t \in T\}$ *is called a* submartingale *if*

$$E\{|X(t)|\} \leq \infty \tag{2.2}$$

and

$$E\{X(t) \mid \mathcal{A}_s\} \geq X_s \ a.c., \quad s < t; s, t \in T \tag{2.3}$$

The random process is called a supermartingale *if, instead,*

$$E\{X(t) \mid \mathcal{A}_s\} \leq X_s \ a.c., \quad s < t; s, t \in T \tag{2.4}$$

The random process is a martingale, *if the process is both a submartingale and a supermartingale.*

Remark 69   *Sub- and supermartingales are also called* semi-martingales.

We can now easily define the more relevant concept of a MD.

Definition 70   *A random process* $\{X(t), \mathcal{A}_t: t \in T\}$ *is called a* MD *if*

$$X(t) = \Delta Y(t) = Y(t) - Y(t-1), \quad X(1) = Y(1) \tag{2.5}$$

where the random process $\{Y(t), \mathcal{A}_t: t \in T\}$ *is a martingale.*

Since for an MD

$$E\{X(t) \mid \mathcal{A}_{t-1}\} = E\{Y(t) - Y(t-1) \mid \mathcal{A}_{t-1}\}$$
$$= E\{Y(t) \mid \mathcal{A}_{t-1}\} - E\{Y(t-1) \mid \mathcal{A}_{t-1}\}$$
$$= Y(t-1) - Y(t-1) = 0 \tag{2.6}$$

the MD process is often defined by the conditional expectation:

$$E\{X(t) \mid \mathcal{A}_{t-1}\} = 0 \tag{2.7}$$

Thus, a martingale is conditional on all preceding information or experience contained in the historical information set $\mathcal{A}_{t-1}$. In particular, MDs have a history! They are *not* mutually independent!

2.2.2 Independence and uncorrelatedness

Compare now this definition of the MD-property with the following classical definitions of independent and uncorrelated random variables (r.vs), to see why the martingale property is different from both and why it is more general.

Definition 71 *Let* $\{X(t): t \in T\}$ *be a sequence of r.vs on a given probability space* $(\Omega, \mathcal{A}, P)$ *with*

$$E\{X(t)\} = 0 \tag{2.8}$$

and $\{\mathcal{A}_t: t \in T\}$ *a current of σ-algebras on the measurable space* $(\Omega, \mathcal{A})$. *Then* $\{X(t)\}$ *is a sequence of* independent *r.v. with respect to* $\{\mathcal{A}_t\}$ *if $X(t)$ is measurable with respect to $\mathcal{A}_t$ and is independent of $\mathcal{A}_{t-1}$ for all $t \in T$.*

Thus, independent r.vs have no history! They are immeasurable using past historical information. Otherwise stated, they are only measurable with respect to current information.

Remark 72 *Only the outcome of a throw of the theoretical ideal fair die is an independent r.v. Such a complete system situation never occurs in the real world, as Fama (1970) understood, based on his earlier observations (Fama, 1965). Even a real world so-called randomized experiment can never be the equivalent of the theoretical ideal fair die, in contrast to what statisticians appear to believe. The physical, finite constraints of the real world prevent that from happening. The system is never complete. Even computerized randomization will not result in this theoretical equivalence, since computers have finite memory registers.*

Empirical data are virtually never independent. Only the physical process of atomic decay leads to pure random "bits." In empirical reality there is always some form of historical conditionality, some constraint, some form of dependence on the past, even with a so-called "fair" die (Kalman 1994, 1995, 1996). Thus, the fundamental scientific research questions should be: what kind of dependence is that? Is that dependence serial ("short term") or global ("long term")? What is uncorrelatedness? Is it similar to independence, or is it more restricted? This last question we can answer: it is more restricted.

Definition 73 *Let* $\{X(t): t \in T\}$ *be a sequence of r.vs on a given probability space* $(\Omega, \mathcal{A}, P)$ *with* $E\{X(t)\} = 0$ *and* $\{\mathcal{B}_t: t \in T\}$ *a current of* linear *spaces* $\mathcal{B}_t \supset \mathcal{B}_{t-1}$ *on the measurable space* $(\Omega, \mathcal{B})$. *Then* $X(t)$ *is a sequence of* uncorrelated *r.vs with respect to* $\{\mathcal{B}_t\}$ *if* $X(t) \in \mathcal{B}_t$ *and is uncorrelated with all elements of* $\mathcal{B}_{t-1}$ *for all* $t \in T$.

The crucial part of this definition of uncorrelatedness is the *linearity* of the independent information sets, which we'll discuss in detail in Chapter 3. Uncorrelatedness is linear independence. A random process of increments can be uncorrelated = linearly independent, but nonlinearly dependent. In contrast, martingales allow for nonlinearity, i.e., for both general dependence and for the more restricted correlatedness. But, depending on whether the current of data spaces on which they are defined is nonlinear or linear, MDs are independent or even uncorrelated, respectively (Mantegna, 1997).

2.2.3   *Random Walk and GBM*

We'll need some additional definitions to expand the arsenal of our analytic tools, to sharpen our analytic concepts and make them more specific and detailed, since there is quite some sloppiness in this field of research (cf. Osborne, 1959, 1962). First, we'll define a Random Walk and its sibling, the GBM. Both are currently the most popular time series models in finance.

Definition 74 *A Random Walk, or* Arithmetic Brownian Motion (ABM) *is a particular wide sense Markov process with independent, identically distributed (i.i.d.) (= stationary) innovations*

$$X(t) - X(t - 1) = \varepsilon(t), \ where \ \varepsilon(t) \sim i.i.d. \tag{2.9}$$

Definition 75 *A GBM is a Random Walk of the natural logarithm of the original process* $X(t)$. *Thus, first we define*

$$\ln \frac{X(t)}{X(t-1)} = \ln X(t) - \ln X(t-1)$$

$$= \Delta \ln X(t)$$

$$= x(t) \tag{2.10}$$

so that we have the ratio

$$\frac{X(t)}{X(t-1)} = e^{x(t)} = e^{x(t-1)+\varepsilon(t)} \tag{2.11}$$

or, equivalently, after taking natural logarithms,

$$x(t) = x(t-1) + \varepsilon(t), \quad where \; \varepsilon(t) \sim i.i.d. \tag{2.12}$$

Consequently, we can also state, simply

$$\Delta x(t) = x(t) - x(t-1)$$
$$= \varepsilon(t), \quad where \; \varepsilon(t) \sim i.i.d. \tag{2.13}$$

The *innovations* $c(t)$ of such a logarithmic Random Walk or GBM are identically distributed in the wide sense = wide sense stationary (= with constant mean and variance), and they are mutually independent.

Quite a few of the classical probability theory and estimation results are derived from the CLT of Lindeberg-Lévy, which formulates the convergence in distribution to a standard normal distribution of normalized and centered sums of i.i.d. random variables (Lévy, 1937; see also Dhrymes, 1974; Chow and Teicher, 1978). The usual approach to prove these asymptotic CLT-based results is to apply an ergodic theorem, which assumes that the ensemble- and time-averages are identical. But, as we now understand, this ergodic approach requires such considerable (Platonic) idealization of the empirical situation, that it is unrealizable. It just does not apply to the finite, empirically observable world. Worse, such idealization leads to considerable distortions and hinders future progress in our scientific understanding of the world.

In finance, one usually assumes a sequence of i.i.d. observations. In reality, this assumption of independence is violated because of financial feedback and adaptation processes: financial investors and traders learn from their valuation and trading mistakes. Further, an indispensable condition for the application of an ergodic theorem is that the probability measure must converge almost certainly (a.c.). To achieve convergence a.c., strict stationarity of the observations is assumed. But this assumption can never be checked completely against the data. Thus, we've come full circle.

The fundamental empirical problem is that the idealizing assumption of ergodicity, which is based on the unrealistic assumption of an idealized ensemble set, is uncheckable on the basis of a single historical realization of the random process, i.e., on a single historical set of time series data. We should check the complete ensemble, but we can't. We assume it theoretically exists, while we can't check that it empirically exists. Such uncheckable assumptions don't belong in *science* (Los, 2001).

2.2.4 *Dependence-allowing efficiency*

Samuelson (1965) and, in particular, Fama (1970) used the martingale (difference) property to define *efficient market pricing*, so that market efficiency no longer depends on the conventional

$$\boxed{\text{i.i.d.} = \text{independence} + \text{stationarity}} \qquad (2.14)$$

assumption of the innovation series that drives the speculative pricing process as modeled by, say, the original Random Walk of Bachelier (1900; see also Cootner, 1964), or the GBM. Thus, from now on, in this book, when we talk about efficiency, we distinguish a particular degree of efficiency: the Samuelson–Fama efficiency. That is the compact definition of market efficiency, which allows for other, in particular, nonlinear forms of market efficiency than the one defined by i.i.d. innovations. There are clearly other degrees of efficiency.

Definition 76   *A market is* Samuelson–Fama-efficient, *when the random market pricing process is a martingale.*

It's important to realize that this degree of market pricing efficiency allows for a particular kind of dependence over time and that other kinds of dependence are possible. In fact, as Mandelbrot (1966, 1971) showed, martingales and MDs are too restrictive to describe efficient empirical speculative markets, since they don't allow for *singularities* in the empirical time series, i.e., the discontinuities and sharp breaks which are observed in empirically efficient speculative markets. Martingales require that:

$$E\{|X(t)|\} \leq \infty \qquad (2.15)$$

Mandelbrot demonstrated that there are random speculative pricing processes, for example, sequences of price singularities, like the incremental changes in FX quotations, which have infinite variances, so that:

$$E\{|X(t)|\} = \infty \qquad (2.16)$$

Therefore, they falsify the classical statistical assumption of ergodicity, as we discussed in Chapter 1.

Fortunately, we can still empirically measure the risk in those singular markets, but not by using conditional expectations and martingales. Consequently, the efficient convergence to a limiting, dynamic (time-varying) equilibrium distribution is now viewed to be dependent not on the classical i.i.d. r.v. assumption, but on a particular class of dependent r.v. assumption. Such efficient convergence towards a dynamic equilibrium is dependent on either stable distributions or on even more transient phenomena, like the spectrum of singularities of the speculative price series, as in the case of empirical FX quotations. We'll discuss the measurement and analysis of such singularity spectra in Chapter 8.

2.3 FMH: fractal theory

2.3.1 *Importance of investment horizons*

Why do we need a different concept of time-dependence than the serial time-dependence favored by classical time series analysis? Because of the simultaneous existence of a variety of investment horizons τ_i in the financial markets. To demonstrate the importance of the various investment horizons in market pricing processes, Holton (1992) contrasts the immateriality of these horizons in the idealized Random Walk process with the empirically measured materiality of such horizons for speculative pricing series. His simple graphs clearly demonstrate the incorrectness of the Random Walk model, even as an approximation, for such empirical pricing processes, since the Random Walk assumes stationarity of the volatility of the innovations. Before we discuss the details of this new view, we introduce the formal definition of a total rate of return on an investment, as used in this book.

Definition 77 *The* total rate of return on an investment X *made at time* $t - 1$ *is represented in various forms, as*

$$
\begin{aligned}
x(t) &= \frac{\Delta X(t)}{X(t-1)} \\
&= \frac{X(t) - X(t-1)}{X(t-1)} \\
&= \frac{X(t)}{X(t-1)} - 1 \\
&\approx \ln\left(\frac{X(t)}{X(t-1)}\right) \quad \text{for relatively small numbers} \\
&= \ln X(t) - \ln X(t-1) \\
&= \Delta \ln(X(t))
\end{aligned}
\tag{2.17}
$$

Definition 78 *In finance, the* volatility *of $x(t)$ observed at appropriate moments in time (e.g. in minutes, hours, days, weeks, months, years, etc.) is measured in period τ_i by the standard deviation, measured by using time-averages:*

$$
\begin{aligned}
\sigma_{\tau_i} &= [E_{\tau_i}\{[x(t) - E_{\tau_i}\{x(t)\}]^2\}]^{0.5} \\
&= \left[\frac{1}{\tau_i} \sum_{t=1}^{t=\tau_i} \left[x(t) - \frac{1}{\tau_i} \sum_{t=1}^{t=\tau_i} x(t) \right]^2 \right]^{0.5}
\end{aligned}
\tag{2.18}
$$

What are the specific consequences of the assumptions of stationarity and independence (i.e., the conventional combined i.i.d. assumption), discussed in Chapter 1? Let's spell them out beforehand, so that we can find the stark discrepancies and clashes between these theoretical assumptions and empirically observed reality. Under the assumptions of wide sense stationarity, the means are constant, thus

$$E_{\tau_i}\{x(t)\} = \frac{1}{\tau_i} \sum_{t=1}^{t=\tau_i} x(t)$$

$$= \frac{1}{\tau_j} \sum_{t=1}^{t=\tau_j} x(t)$$

$$= E_{\tau_j}\{x(t)\}$$

$$= \text{constant}, \quad \text{where } \tau_i, \tau_j \in T \tag{2.19}$$

and the volatilities are also constant

$$\sigma_{\tau_i} = \sigma_{\tau_j} = \sigma_\tau, \quad \text{where } \tau_i, \tau_j \in T \tag{2.20}$$

In addition, it is assumed that there is complete independence between periods, implying that there is also uncorrelatedness = linear independence between periods. Thus, all cross-covariances between periods are implicitly assumed to be zero and are, consequently, ignored

$$\sigma_{\tau_i \tau_j} = \left[\frac{1}{\tau_i + \tau_j} \sum_{t=1}^{t=\tau_i+\tau_j} [x(t) - E_{\tau_i}\{x(t)\}][x(t - \tau_i - \tau_j) \right.$$

$$\left. - E_{\tau_j}\{x(t - \tau_i - \tau_j)\}] \right]^{0.5} = 0 \quad \text{where } \tau_i, \tau_j \in T \tag{2.21}$$

The result is that the squared volatility (= variance) of the whole observation period $T = \tau_1 + \tau_2 + \cdots + \tau_n$ is measured by the sum of the constant squared volatilities in each of the subperiods:

$$(\sigma_T)^2 = \sum_{t=1}^{T} (\sigma_\tau)^2 = T(\sigma_\tau)^2 \tag{2.22}$$

Thus, one reaches the conclusion that the volatility of the whole observation period is an exponential function of time, with an exponent equal to 0.5:

$$\sigma_T = \sigma_\tau T^{0.5} \tag{2.23}$$

Therefore, Random Walk volatility, which relies on the combination of the two assumptions of stationarity and independence, behaves as a square root function of time. When we normalize these theoretical volatilities by the square root of their time horizon, all normalized volatilities equal the same constant volatility.

When the time periods of observation are equal to each other and $\tau_i = \tau$ for all i, the observation period is proportional $T = n\tau$. For given $T = $ length of the set of observations, when the time periods τ of observation become smaller, i.e., when the scale of time observation becomes smaller and is reduced to $\tau \rightarrow 1$, the fundamental time unit of observation increases, $n \rightarrow T$, and we observe relative smaller risks.

Definition 79 Normalized Random Walk volatility *is*

$$\sigma_\tau = \sigma_T (n\tau)^{-0.5} = \sigma_T T^{-0.5} \quad for \ \tau = 1 \tag{2.24}$$

Thus, under the simplifying Random Walk assumption, we only have to compute the volatility of an asset class once over the complete time period T as in Figure 1.1, and then we can extrapolate all other time horizon volatilities for these asset classes by appropriate scaling adjustments. On a normalized basis, still each asset class has its own constant volatility, as in Figure 2.1. This is what we mean by the financial market risk being dependent only on the asset class ω, since there is only one fundamental theoretical frequency $\omega = 1/\tau$.

Remark 80 *This i.i.d. assumption implies* self-similarity of the risk, *since the risk σ_T over the horizon T, is similar to the risk σ_τ of the base observation period τ, except for the* Fickian scaling factor $T^{0.5}$.

But is this Random Walk property empirically true? Figure 2.2 shows the empirically observed reality of normalized volatility, i.e., of the empirically measured volatility for each maturity τ is normalized by dividing it by $T^{0.5}$. Figure 2.2 shows that empirical financial market risk is not only dependent on asset class ω, but also on the investment horizon τ. The normalized volatility of currencies increases over

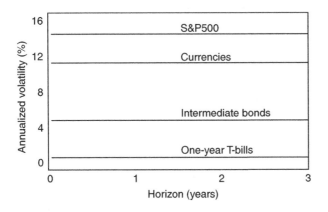

Figure 2.1 Annualized volatility of theoretical Random Walk model of constant, normalized, asset return volatilities.

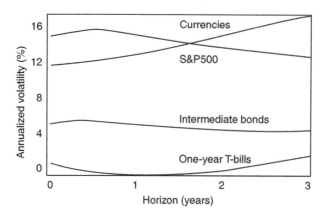

Figure 2.2 Empirical annualized volatility of financial market returns: financial market
risk is a function of horizon: time-dependent, standardized, asset return
volatilities.

time. The volatility of the rates of return of the S&P500 index increases within the
horizon of one year, but then declines the longer the horizon. Similar behavior can
be observed for the intermediate bonds, except that the initial horizon is about a
quarter of a year. The volatility of the rates of return of one-year T-bills declines
within a year, is zero at the horizon of one year, and thereafter it increases again.

Thus, when Holton varies the time horizons and computes for each horizon separately the corresponding empirical volatility, it appears that these volatilities are
not constant, but time-dependent. This is a clear refutation of the i.i.d. assumptions
of the Random Walk model of risk. We have to conclude that time-dependence
plays a much more important role in the financial markets than financial analysts
have accounted for. Thus, there is not one fundamental, homogeneous time horizon τ in the financial markets but there exists a whole set of heterogeneous time
horizons τ_i. The term *horizon analysis* is currently used in the empirical financial
markets for the analysis of such time-dependencies of financial risk.[2]

2.3.2   *Fractal Market Hypothesis*

We can now also provide a simple definition of the FMH of Mandelbrot (1982)
and Peters (1994). This definition will provide us with an analytic framework, that
will be refined and made more precise in the following chapters of this book.

Definition 81   FMH: *The magnitude of a risky (= random) market asset pricing
process is both frequency-(= asset class ω) dependent and horizon τ_i-dependent
and shows global dependencies via its fractality, i.e., via its self-similarities in the
frequency and time domains. Such a process can be homogeneous = mono-fractal
(= exhibiting one form of self-similarity), or non-homogeneous = multi-fractal
(= exhibiting many coexisting self-similarities).*

We have not yet provided a precise definition of the term fractal in the FMH. Here it is:

Definition 82 *A geometric object is* fractal *when it has a fractional dimension D.*

Contrast this definition with that of the well-known Euclidean objects, with which we've become so familiar because of the classical mathematics education of our childhood.

Definition 83 Euclidean *geometric objects have discrete integer dimensions, such as D(point) = 0, D(straight line) = 1, D(plane) = 2, D(cube) = 3.*

Euclidean geometry is the study of points, lines, planes and other geometric figures, using a modified version of the assumptions of Euclid.[3] In contrast, a *fractal* geometric object has a fractional dimension. Such a fractal dimension indicates the extent to which the fractal object fills the Euclidean dimension in which it is embedded. For example, the random process $x(t)$ of rates of return process on the S&P500 stock price index has the measured fractional dimension $D = 1.4$ within the 2-dimensional (2D) (x, t) data plane.

Such fractional dimensions can be measured by various methods, such as Range–Scale (R/S) analysis, Roughness–Length (RL) analysis, Variograms, Spectrograms (based on Fourier Transforms) and Scalograms (based on Wavelet Transforms), as we will discuss in the coming chapters (cf. in particular Chapters 5–8).

Fractal geometry describes objects that are *self-similar* (Mandelbrot, 1982). This means that when such objects are magnified, their parts are seen to bear an exact resemblance to the whole, the likeness continuing with the parts of the parts and so on to infinity, as in the Figure 2.3 of the famous Julia set.[4]

Mandelbrot's Julia set resembles the empirical breaking-wave patterns in clear-air turbulence, due to changes in the wind within and around the jet stream, in Figure 2.4 (Perry, 2000, p. 40). Such empirical turbulence measurements have been made possible by a burst of recent research in technologies for real-time detection of turbulence in all its varieties, like the onboard Doppler laser radar, or lidar, used to produce the multicolored graph in Figure 2.4, predicting various persistence and anti-persistence phenomena, such as thunderstorms and tornadoes, respectively.

Inspired by this real time technology and these visualization results, a major research question of this book on financial market risk is: are such fractal patterns also observable in financial time series, such as the rate of return data in various asset markets and in foreign exchange markets? In Chapter 10, we'll show evidence for an affirmative answer.

It is important to emphasize that fractal processes have two important properties:

(1) Fractals are *scale-symmetric* (= self-similar): the fractal process can be magnified, but keeps the same shape. In financial risk-theoretic terms, a marginal distribution of a fractal speculative pricing process maintains its shape when

observations are taken at different time intervals, although the size of these shapes (= their *amplitude*) can change.

(2) Fractals are *translational-asymmetric*: the fractal process does not keep the same shape when shifted. Fractals are devoid of translational symmetry, i.e., they don't exhibit the smoothness associated with Euclidean lines, planes and spheres. Instead, a rough, jagged quality is maintained at every scale at which an object can be examined (cf. Figure 2.3).

Keep in mind that there are both upper and lower limits to the size range over which empirical fractal objects are self-similar. Above and below that size range, the shapes are either rough (but not self-similar), or smooth, i.e., conventionally Euclidean. In financial risk-theoretic terms, a fractal rate of return process is aperiodic, although it does show a form of cyclicity over a particular time range, because of the observed scale-symmetry.[5]

The risk inherent in a market pricing process depends on the different lengths of the investment horizons of the various market participants, who neither have uniform investment horizons, nor have investment horizons than can be easily normalized. In addition, the financial risk depends also on the particular frequency distribution ($\approx$ asset class ω), as usual.

Fractal, computer-generated image

Figure 2.3 Mandelbrot's Julia set. This set's major element of stability is a budlike shape.

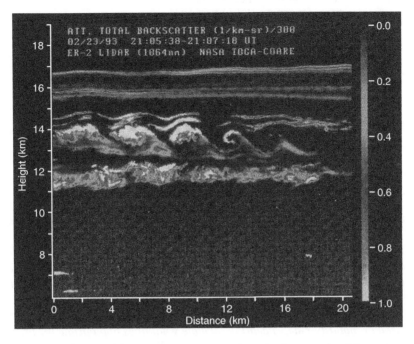

Figure 2.4 Clear-air turbulence, in which air currents move in strong breaking-wave patterns, shows up starkly in this image observed with a downward-looking Doppler laser radar, or lidar, aboard the NASA ER-2 high-altitude research aircraft.

Using this broader definition of financial market risk, generally expressed in probability distribution terms, we define such "financial risk" as the shape of the frequency distribution of the investment returns. This distribution function P can be used to provide a wider definition of financial risk:

$$\boxed{\text{financial risk} = P(\omega, \tau, t)} \tag{2.25}$$

where ω (for frequency) categorizes the asset class, τ represents the particular investment horizon or its *maturity*, and t indicates the important dependence of this frequency distribution on time. Empirically measured financial risk is notoriously time-scaling *and* time-varying.

The importance of volatility research is most acutely experienced in option markets, where Black and Scholes considered their tests of market efficiency in response to Fama's martingale definition of efficiency and debated how options should be valued. This debate is far from settled, despite Nobel Memorial Prize winning Black–Scholes formulas (Black and Scholes, 1972; cf. also Galai, 1977; Chiras and Manaster, 1978; Hull and White, 1987, 1988; Figlewski, 1989).

Table 2.1 Volatility matrix of European option prices for various strike prices and expiration dates

Maturity τ	Strike price X				
	0.90	0.95	1.00	1.05	1.10
1 month	14.2	13.0	12.0	13.1	14.5
3 month	14.0	13.0	12.0	13.1	14.2
6 month	14.1	13.3	12.5	13.4	14.3
1 year	14.7	14.0	13.5	14.0	14.8
2 year	15.0	14.4	14.0	14.5	15.1
5 year	14.8	14.6	14.4	14.7	15.0

Example 84 *Sophisticated financial market participants are fully cognizant of the phenomenon that financial risk is frequency ω-, horizon τ-, and time t-dependent (Harvey and Whaley, 1991, 1992). Currently option market traders use the* volatility term structure *when pricing options. They recognize that the volatility used to price an at-the-money option depends on the maturity τ of the option. They use so-called* volatility matrices, *which combine volatility smiles (which are frequency ω-dependent) with the volatility term structure (which is horizon or maturity τ-dependent) to tabulate volatilities appropriate for pricing an option with any strike price and any maturity. Table 2.1 provides an example of such a volatility matrix, which forms a contour plot of the options volatility, and, via the Black–Scholes model, of the options price (Hull, 2001, p. 291). Volatility tends to be an increasing function of maturity τ, when, at a particular time t, short-dated volatilities are historically low. This is because then there is the expectation that volatilities will increase. Similarly, volatility tends to be a decreasing function of maturity τ, when, historically at a particular time t, short-dated volatilities are high. Then there is the expectation that volatilities will decrease. Thus, the changing term structure of volatilities reflects a nonlinear feedback mechanism in the financial markets based on adjusting expectations (cf. Chapters 10 and 11).*

Example 85 *Recently more empirical research has been done on the intraday and intraweek volatility patterns of various stock and futures market indices. Also this research shows the time-dependence of market volatility. Usually one tests the null hypothesis of arbitrage equality of the cost-of-carry model between the futures and spot markets, H_0: $\sigma_f = \sigma_s$, which is almost always rejected, against one of two alternative hypotheses based on information asymmetry in the markets: (1) the "wait-to-trade" hypothesis, H_1: $\sigma_f > \sigma_s$, or (2) the "noise-traders" hypothesis, H_1: $\sigma_f < \sigma_s$. Using 15-minute data covering July 1, 1994 to June 28, 1996, Tang and Lui (2001), who provide also a comprehensive literature survey on these issues, find that the first alternative hypothesis is true for all weekdays in Hong Kong: interday data for the Hang Seng Index Futures (HSIF) are more volatile than those of the*

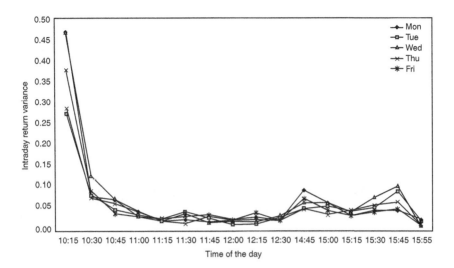

Figure 2.5 Intraday return variance of the HSI by weekdays based on data for July 1, 1994 to June 28, 1996.

Hang Seng Index (HSI). However, for the intraday returns, the HSI is significantly more volatile than the HSIF for the first 15–20 minutes after the markets open on all weekdays, except on Mondays. Intraday and intraweek volatility patterns exist for both markets. Figure 2.5 shows the variation of the intraday variance of the HSI by weekdays and Figure 2.6 does the same for the HSIF.

Example 86 *Not all results for the valuation of derivatives are sensitive to the time-variation of risk. The* put-call parity *is true for any set of distributive assumptions, since it is based on simple arbitrage. It does not depend on the lognormal assumption underlying the Black–Scholes model. The put-call parity holds true even when the underlying distribution is time-varying, because at a particular moment t the financial risk of a put option, $P(\omega, \tau, t)$, is the same as that of a corresponding call option with the same maturity τ written on the same underlying asset class ω (Klemkosky and Resnick, 1979).*

Contrast this new time-dependent definition of financial market risk with the more narrow definition of financial risk, expressed exclusively in terms of a time-invariant term structure of volatility (= second-order moments), as used, for example, in Müller *et al.* (1995), Dumas *et al.* (1998) and Batten *et al.* (1999):

$$\sigma_\tau = g(\omega, \tau) \tag{2.26}$$

This definition allows invariant volatility scaling in the financial markets. This second-order definition of financial market risk is dependent on the asset class ω and on the investment horizon τ, but not on time t.

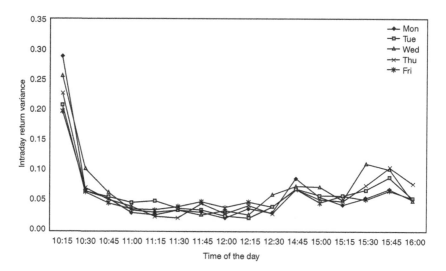

Figure 2.6 Intraday return variance of the HSIF by weekdays based on data for July 1, 1994 to June 28, 1996.

The even older, and, as currently considered, very unrealistic i.i.d. definition of financial market risk is expressed by the exceedingly simple expression, which continues to be erroneously taught as being "true" to undergraduate students:

$$\sigma = \text{constant} \tag{2.27}$$

In other words, this older definition assumes strict stationarity of the asset return distributions. Amin and Morton (1994) investigated many functional forms of implied volatility considered up to 1994 and rejected all of them.

Notice that our newest definition of financial risk $= P(\omega, \tau, t)$ encompasses both preceding functional definitions of financial market risk, but that it is a much broader definition of risk since it is focusing on the shape and time dependence of the whole frequency distribution and not only on the functional form of its dispersion measure or second moment.

The following two examples show that the empirically measured financial risk in the term structure of interest rates at various maturities τ is, indeed, dependent on time t, or is *time varying*.

Example 87   *Figure 2.7 shows the one-month Eurodollar yield $x_\tau(t)$, where $\tau = $ one month, together with its volatility $\sigma_\tau(t)$. The following stylized facts emerge: (1) This short-rate series is a* persistent *time series. It spends long, consecutive periods above and below the (sample estimate of) the unconditional, or long-run mean. (2) In the 1979–1982 period, the average level and volatility of the short rate was substantially higher than for other years in the 1971–2000 period.*

(a) Volatility (annual %)

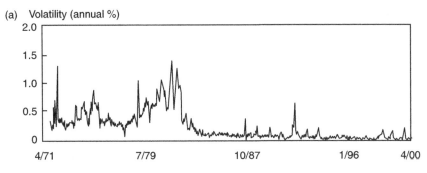

(b) Level (annual %)

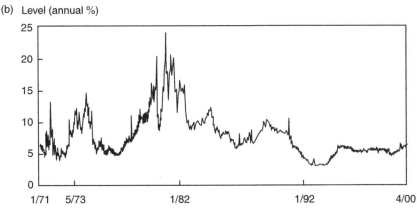

Figure 2.7 One-month Eurodollar yield and time-varying (a) turbulent volatility and (b) daily data, April 1971 to April 2000.

(3) The volatility of the short-rate level appears to be both time varying and show long-term dependence (Chapman and Pearson, 2001, pp. 78–79). Of course, a more precise and definite measurement of the degree of long-term dependence should be executed by the more sophisticated technology discussed in Chapters 6 and 7.

Example 88 *Figure 2.8 plots the level $x_\tau(t)$ (panel (a)) and volatility $\sigma_\tau(t)$ (panel (b)) of the τ = five-year, constant-maturity treasury (CMT) yield from January 1962 through April 2000. This longer maturity series has a lower mean and volatility than the short rate in Figure 2.7, the overall movements in levels and volatility are qualitatively similar. In particular, the five-year rate appears also to be a long-term dependent series, and the 1979–1982 period was characterized by substantially higher yield levels and volatility than any other years in the data set. These observations appear to be also true for CMT yields of maturities from 1 to 30 years (Chapman and Pearson, 2001, pp. 78 and 80).*

(a) Volatility (annual %)

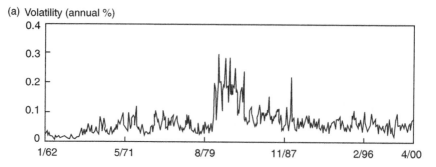

(b) Level (annual %)

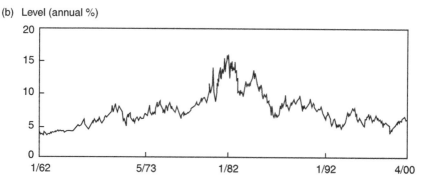

Figure 2.8 Five-year CMT yield and time-varying (a) turbulent volatility and (b) daily data,
January 1962 to April 2000.

The lower panels in Figures 2.7 and 2.8 show the variability of the volatility of
the yields of these two financial instruments, which reminded Mandelbrot (1972)
of the variability of energy (= volatility = risk) dissipation in a turbulent fluid,
which he modeled by multifractal diffusion models, to be discussed in Chapters 8
and 11. This shows the deep link between the uses of the fractal approach in the
study of turbulence and of finance.

Example 89   *Based on the recognition that some volatilities are time varying and
not constant, a recent innovation in the swap markets is the so-called* volatility
swap *(cf. Hull, 2001, p. 407). Just like a* vanilla swap *exchange floating for fixed
payments, a* volatility swap *exchanges varying volatility or financial risk for fixed
volatility or financial risk. Suppose the nominal principal is* S_0. *On each payment
date, one side in the volatility swap pays* $S_0 \sigma_\tau$, *where* σ_τ *is the historical volatility
measured in the usual way, by taking daily observations on the underlaying asset
during the immediately preceding accrual period, or horizon* τ, *and the other
side pays* $S_0 \sigma_K$, *where* σ_K *is a pre-specified constant volatility.* Variance swaps,
correlation swaps, *and* covariance swaps *are defined similarly.*

2.4 Importance of identifying the degree of market efficiency

The identification of the degree of market efficiency is important not only for the accurate measurement, analysis and management of market risk, but also for the correct and accurate valuation and pricing of both fundamental and derivative financial instruments. In particular, it is an important research topic in the derivatives markets, which exists specifically to value and price risk. The following discussion borrows from Hull (2001, pp. 27–28 and 64–66) and Johnson (1960).[6]

2.4.1 Speculators' forecasts and normal backwardation in futures markets

The issue was initially raised as a scientific research question by Cowles (1933), who asked if forecasters could predict the stock market, but it took until Houthakker (1957), before the individual commodity markets were empirically analyzed. Houthakker looked at empirical futures prices for wheat, cotton and corn in the period 1937–1957 and he found significant market inefficiencies. He showed that significant profits could be earned by taking long futures positions, suggesting that an investment in an asset has positive systematic risk and consequently the present futures price F_0 systematically under-predicts the expected future spot price of the asset $E\{S_T\}$ at the time of maturity T, as follows. Finance theory tells us that the present value of the expected cash flows of a risky investment to the speculator, who takes a long position in the futures market, consists of the sum of a certain cash outflow and a, certainty equivalent, expected cash inflow:

$$-S_0 + E\{S_T\}e^{-xT} = -F_0e^{-rT} + E\{S_T\}e^{-xT} \tag{2.28}$$

where r is the risk free rate of return and x is the discount rate appropriate for the risky investment, i.e., the expected return required by investors on the risky investment, which depends on the systematic risk of the investment.[7] Assuming that all investment opportunities in a free, competitive securities markets have zero net present value, we have

$$-F_0e^{-rT} + E\{S_T\}e^{-xT} = 0, \quad \text{or}$$

$$F_0 = E\{S_T\}e^{(r-x)T}$$

$$< E\{S_T\} \quad \text{when } x > r \tag{2.29}$$

Both economists John Maynard Keynes (1930) and John Hicks (1939) had already discussed this situation in theoretical terms under the term of *normal backwardation*, when the speculators tend to hold long positions and the hedgers tend to hold short positions. This occurs because speculators require compensation for the systematic market risks they are bearing. While the hedgers lose money on average, they accept this situation and pay that "insurance premium," because the futures contract reduces their risks.

Theoretically, there are two other cases possible. First, the case of *unbiased prediction* by futures prices, which would indicate that the futures markets are efficient. If the spot price S_T would be uncorrelated with the level of the stock market, the investment would have zero systematic risk, in which case $x = r$ and $F_0 = E\{S_T\}$. Second, the case where S_T would be negatively correlated with the level of the stock market and the investment would have negative systematic risk. In this case $x < r$, and $F_0 > E\{S_T\}$. In this case, called *cotango* by Keynes and Hicks, it would be profitable for hedgers to hold long positions and speculators to hold short positions.

Telser (1958) appeared to have found the first case of unbiased prediction. He studied the period from 1926 to 1950 for cotton and from 1927 to 1954 for wheat and found no significant profits for traders taking either long or short positions. His results are corroborated by Gray (1961), who looked at corn futures prices during the period 1921–1959, and by Dusak (1973), who studied more recent data on corn, wheat and soybeans in the period 1952–1967.

Dusak calculated directly the correlation of the movements in the commodity prices with movements in the S&P500 and found little or no systematic risk, lending support to the hypotheses of unbiasedness and of efficiency. However, from the current perspective, Dusak's study suffers from the prejudice to look only at linear correlations and to ignore nonlinear dependencies. Moreover, his unidirectional projection method of regression, strongly biased his correlation results downwards, since the level of uncertainty in his data is high.[8] More recent work by Chang (1985), using data on the same commodities but with more advanced statistical techniques, supports the normal backwardation hypothesis, $F_0 < E\{S_T\}$.

Other shortcomings of most of these earlier studies are that they assume that the market return distributions are Gaussian, i.e., symmetric and time invariant, and that they are stationary, so that linear correlation studies can be applied. The empirical market reality differs from both these assumptions and these conventional correlation studies can now be shown to be scientifically deficient.

2.4.2 *Measurement of degrees of market efficiency and persistence*

Overall, our own conclusion is that since, empirically, more asset prices are positively correlated with the levels of the market indices than negatively correlated, normal backwardation should be expected to be prevalent in the futures markets. Therefore, the current research questions discussed in this book are: what is the character and degree of dependence in the markets – in other words, what is the degree of efficiency in the various markets – and what is the degree of the resulting prediction bias? These research issues remain important for the derivatives markets, as testified by the research of, for example, Rendleman and Carabini (1979), Bhattacharya (1983), Klemkosky and Lasser (1985) and Harvey and Whaley (1992).

In the following chapters, we will first expand on the issue of how to identify the degree of market efficiency. First, we'll discuss how to make the frequency distributions of the various asset classes more realistic than the usual Gaussian assumption, i.e., approximating closer to empirical reality. We do this by introducing non-Gaussian, in particular skewed and heavy-tailed stable distributions. It will be emphasized that even this elegant statistical approximation approach has substantial scientific shortcomings. Next, we discuss in more detail the various investment horizon (maturity) dependencies of these frequency distributions and how we can possibly analyze them in a scientific, non-approximation fashion. Then, our analysis will move from the (assumed) stationary investment return processes of, say, classical option pricing, via the nonstationary rate of return processes, to the transient rate of return processes. Ultimately, in Chapter 8 we will focus on series and spectra of singularities, which are not necessarily evenly spaced throughout time and which represent essentially unpredictable, but still "characterizable" market risks. Some of these possible return innovation series can even be characterized as Cantor "dust," as Mandelbrot does (Mandelbrot, 1982).

2.5 Software

The computations of the following Exercises can be executed in Microsoft EXCEL spreadsheets using its built-in functions, or by using the MATLAB® Statistics Toolbox available from The MathWorks, Inc., 24 Prime Park Way Natick, MA 01760-1500, USA. Tel (508) 647-7000; Fax (508) 647-7001; http://www.mathworks.com/products/wavelettbx.shtml.

2.6 Exercises

Exercise 90 *Produce frequency histograms of the four main series of the first Exercise in Chapter 1, based on the S&P500 daily data for the year 1988: $X(t)$, $\Delta X(t)$, $x(t) = \Delta \ln X(t)$ and $\Delta x(t)$, to get a rough idea of the shape of their probability density functions (p.d.fs). Use the FREQUENCY function in a Windows EXCEL spreadsheet and plot the resulting p.d.fs.*

Exercise 91 *Test for stationarity of the four series of the preceding Exercise by computing the windowed first four moments and by plotting them. How many observations should each observation window contain?*

Notes

1 This support has a different focus from, but is in line with the evidence compiled by Haugen (1995). Haugen emphasizes the inefficiency of the stock markets and supplies the evidence for their persistence. However, Haugen ignores the ultra-efficiency of the foreign exchange markets and, therefore, provides no evidence for their anti-persistence. The signal processing terms persistence and anti-persistence can be roughly translated into the financial-economic terms of inefficiency and ultra-efficiency. Of course, neutral persistence = martingale increments = Fama efficiency.
2 For an empirical example of such *horizon analysis*, cf. Los, 2001, pp. 217–220.
3 Euclid is, perhaps, the most famous scientist of all time, who worked in Hellenistic Alexandria around 300 BC. His *Elements of Geometry* was a standard mathematical text for more than 2000 years (Euclid, 1956).
4 Fractional dimensions were not discussed until 1919, when the German mathematician Felix Hausdorff launched the idea in connection with the small-scale structure of mathematical shapes. Other mathematicians of the time considered such shapes as "pathologies" that had no empirical significance. This attitude persisted until the mid-twentieth century and the work of Polish-born French mathematician Benoit Mandelbrot (1924–present),

who developed fractal geometry. Mandelbrot's 1961 study of similarities in large- and small-scale fluctuations of the stock market was followed by work on phenomena involving nonstandard scaling, including the turbulent motion of fluids and the distribution of galaxies in the universe. By 1975, Mandelbrot had developed a complete theory of fractals, and publications by him and others made fractal geometry accessible to a wider audience and the subject began to gain importance in the sciences.

With an MS in aeronautics (1948) from the California Institute of Technology, Mandelbrot served in the French air force, then earned a PhD in mathematics (1952) from the University of Paris. Moving to the United States in 1958 to work at IBM's Watson Research Center, he joined Yale University in 1974, where he is now a full time Professor in Mathematics.

5 The terms *periodicity* and *cyclicity*, and the differences between them, are explained in Chapter 4.

6 Figlewski (1986) is a good general source for theoretical and empirical issues of hedging with futures.

7 According to the celebrated Capital Asset Pricing Model (CAPM). But that relationship is more uncertain than is often assumed (Los, 1999).

8 For a strong, logical and scientific critique of the prejudices of the unique choice projection direction implied by regression and the resulting downward bias of the correlation results, cf. Los, 2001, chapters 4 and 5.

Bibliography

Amin, K. I., and A. J. Morton (1994) "Implied Volatility Functions in Arbitrage-Free Term Structure Models," *Journal of Financial Economics*, **35**(2), 141–180.

Bachelier, L. (1900) "Théorie de la spéculation," (Doctoral dissetation in Mathematical Sciences, Faculté des Sciences de Paris, defended March 29, 1900), *Annales de l' École Normale Supérieure*, **3**(17), 21–86. Translated, with permission of Gauthier–Villars, Paris, France, as chapter 2 in Cootner, Paul H. (Ed.) (1964) *The Random Character of Stock Market Prices*, The MIT Press, Cambridge, MA, pp. 17–18.

Batten, Jonathan, Craig Ellis and Robert Mellor (1999) "Scaling Laws and Variance as a Measure of Long-Term Dependence," *International Review of Financial Analysis*, **8**(2), 123–139.

Bhattacharya, M. (1983) "Transaction Data Tests of Efficiency of the Chicago Board Options Exchange," *Journal of Financial Economics*, **12**(2), 161–185.

Black, F., and M. Scholes (1972) "The Valuation of Option Contracts and a Test of Market Efficiency," *Journal of Finance*, **27**(2), 399–418.

Chang, E. C. (1985) "Returns to Speculators and the Theory of Normal Backwardation," *Journal of Finance*, **40**(1), 193–208.

Chapman, David A., and Neil D. Pearson (2001) "Recent Advances in Estimating Term-Structure Models," *Financial Analysts Journal*, **57**(4), 77–95.

Chiras, D., and S. Manaster (1978) "The Information Content of Option Prices and a Test of Market Efficiency," *Journal of Financial Economics*, **6**(2/3), 213–234.

Chow, Yuan Shih, and Henry Teicher (1978) *Probability Theory: Independence, Interchangeability, Martingales*, Springer Verlag, New York, NY.

Cootner, P. H. (Ed.) (1964) *The Random Character of Stock Market Prices*, The MIT Press, Cambridge, MA.

Cowles III, Alfred (1933) "Can Stock Market Forecasters Forecast?," *Econometrica*, **1**(3), 309–324.

Dhrymes, Phoebus (1974) *Econometrics: Statistical Foundations and Applications*, Springer Verlag, New York, NY.

Dumas, B., J. Fleming and R. E. Whaley (1998) "Implied Volatility Functions: Empirical Tests," *Journal of Finance*, **53**(6), 2059–2106.

Dusak, K. (1973) "Futures Trading and Investor Returns: An Investigation of Commodity Risk Premiums," *Journal of Political Economy*, **81**(6), 1387–1406.

Euclid (Thomas L. Heath, Ed.) (1956) *The Thirteen Books of Euclid's Elements*, Dover Publications, New York, NY.

Fama, Eugene F. (1965) "The Behavior of Stock-Market Prices," *Journal of Business*, **38**(1), 34–105.

Fama, Eugene F. (1970) "Efficient Capital Markets: A Review of Theory and Empirical Work," *Journal of Finance*, **25**(2), 383–417.

Fama, Eugene F. (1991) "Efficient Capital Markets: II," *Journal of Finance*, **46**(5), 1575–1617.

Figlewski, S. (1986) *Hedging with Financial Futures for Institutional Investors*, Ballinger, Cambridge, MA.

Figlewski, S. (1989) "Options Arbitrage in Imperfect Markets," *Journal of Finance*, **44**, 1289–1311.

Galai, D. (1977) "Tests of Market Efficiency and the Chicago Board Options Exchange," *Journal of Business*, **50**(2), 167–197.

Gray, R. V. (1961) "The Search for a Risk Premium," *Journal of Political Economy*, **69**(3), 250–260.

Harvey, C. R., and R. E. Whaley (1991) "S&P100 Index Option Volatility," *Journal of Finance*, **46**(4), 1551–1561.

Harvey, C. R., and R. E. Whaley (1992) "Market Volatility Prediction and the Efficiency of the S&P100 Index Options Market," *Journal of Financial Economics*, **31**(1), 43–73.

Haugen, Robert A. (1995) *The New Finance: The Case Against Efficient Markets*, Prentice Hall, Englewood Cliffs, NJ.

Hicks, John R. (1939) *Value and Capital*, Clarendon Press, Oxford, UK.

Holton, Glyn A. (1992) "Time: The Second Dimension of Risk," *Financial Analysts Journal*, **48**(6), 38–45.

Houthakker, H. S. (1957) "Can Speculators Forecast Prices?," *Review of Economics and Statistics*, **39**(2), 143–151.

Hull, J. C., (2001) *Fundamentals of Options and Futures Markets*, Prentice Hall, Upper Saddle River, NJ.

Hull, J. C., and A. White (1987) "The Pricing of Options on Assets with Stochastic Volatilities," *Journal of Finance*, **42**(2), 281–300.

Hull, J. C., and A. White (1988) "An Analysis of the Bias in Option Pricing Caused by Stochastic Volatility," *Advances in Futures and Options Research*, **3**, 27–61.

Johnson, L. L. (1960) "The Theory of Hedging and Speculation in Commodity Futures Markets," *Review of Economics Studies*, **27**(3), 139–151.

Kalman, Rudolf E. (1994) "Randomness Reexamined," *Modeling, Identification and Control*, **15**(3), 141–151.

Kalman, Rudolf E. (1995) "Randomness and Probability," *Mathematica Japonica*, **41**(1), 41–58 and "Addendum," **41**(2), 463.

Kalman, Rudolf E. (1996) "Probability in the Real World as a System Attribute," *CWI Quarterly*, **9**(3), 181–204.

Keynes, John Maynard (1930) *A Treatise on Money*, Macmillan, London, UK.

Klemkosky, R. C., and D. J. Lasser (1985) "An Efficiency Analysis of the T-Bond Futures Market," *Journal of Futures Markets*, **5**(4), 607–620.

Klemkosky, R. C., and B. G. Resnick (1979) "Put-Call Parity and Market Efficiency," *Journal of Finance*, **34**(5), 1141–1155.

Lévy, Paul (1954) *Théorie de l'Addition des Variables Aléatoires* (*Theory of the Summation of Random Variables*), 2nd edn, Gauthier-Villars, Paris, France (original 1937).

Los, Cornelis A. (1982) "Discrete-Time Martingale Convergence Results and Nonlinear Estimation Using Time-Series Data," Research Paper No. 8222, Federal Reserve Bank of New York, July, 107 pages.

Los, Cornelis A. (1999) "Galton's Error and the Under-Representation of Systematic Risk," *Journal of Banking and Finance*, **23**(12), December, 1793–1829.

Los, Cornelis A. (2001) *Computational Finance: A Scientific Perspective*, World Scientific Publishing Co., Singapore.

Mandelbrot, Benoit B. (1966) "Forecasts of Future Prices, Unbiased Markets and Martingale Models," *The Journal of Business*, **39**, January (Special Supplement), 242–255. Reprinted as Chapter E19 "Nonlinear Forecasts, Rational Bubbles, and Martingales," with annotations and corrections, in (1997) *Fractals and Scaling in Finance: Discontinuity, Concentration, Risk*, Springer Verlag, New York, NY, pp. 471–491.

Mandelbrot, Benoit B. (1971) "When Can Price Be Arbitraged Efficiently? A Limit to the Validity of the Random Walk and Martingale Models," *The Review of Economics and Statistics*, **53**(3), 225–236.

Mandelbrot, Benoit B. (1972) "Possible Refinement of the Lognormal Hypothesis Concerning the Distribution of Energy Dissipation in Intermittent Turbulence," in Rosenblatt, M., and C. Van Atta (Eds) *Statistical Models and Turbulence*, Lecture Notes in Physics, 12, Springer Verlag, New York, NY, pp. 333–351.

Mandelbrot, Benoit B. (1982) *The Fractal Geometry of Nature*, W. H. Freeman, New York, NY.

Mantegna, R. N. (1997) "Degree of Correlation Inside a Financial Market," in Kadtke, J. B., and A. Bulsara (Eds) *Applied Nonlinear Dynamics and Stochastic Systems near the Millennium*, AIP Press, New York, NY, pp. 197–202.

Müller, U. A., M. M. Dacorogna, R. D. Davé, R. B. Olsen, O. V. Pictet and J. E. von Weizsäcker (1995) "Volatilities of Different Time Resolutions – Analyzing the Dynamics of Market Components, " *Journal of Empirical Finance*, **4**(2–3), 213–240.

Osborne, M. F. M. (1959) "Brownian Motion in the Stock Market," *Operations Research*, **7**, March–April, 145–173. Reprinted as chapter 4 in Cootner, Paul H. (Ed.) (1964) *The Random Character of Stock Market Prices*, The MIT Press, Cambridge, MA, pp. 100–128.

Osborne, M. F. M. (1962) "Periodic Structure in the Brownian Motion of Stock Prices," *Operational Research*, **10**, 345–379. Reprinted as chapter 13 in Cootner, Paul H. (Ed.) (1964) *The Random Character of Stock Market Prices*, The MIT Press, Cambridge, MA, pp. 262–296.

Perry, Tekla S. (2000) "Tracking Weather's Flight Path," *IEEE Spectrum*, **37**(9), 38–45.

Peters, Edgar E. (1989) "Fractal Structure in the Capital Markets," *Financial Analysts Journal*, **45**(4), 32–37.

Peters, Edgar E. (1994) *Fractal Market Analysis*, John Wiley and Sons, New York, NY.

Rendleman, R., and C. Carabini (1979) "The Efficiency of the Treasury Bill Futures Markets," *Journal of Finance*, **34**(4), 895–914.

Samuelson, Paul A. (1965) "Proof That Properly Anticipated Prices Fluctuate Randomly," *Industrial Management Review*, **6**, 41–49.

Tang, Gordon Y. N. and David T. W. Lui (2001) "Intraday and Intraweek Volatility Patterns of Hang Seng Index and Index Futures and a test of the Wait-to-Trade Hypothesis," paper presented at the FMA International Meetings in Toronto, Canada, October 19.

Telser, L. G. (1958) "Futures Trading and the Storage of Cotton and Wheat," *Journal of Political Economy*, **66**(3), 233–255.

3 Stable scaling distributions in finance

3.1 Introduction

As we discussed in Chapter 1, the distributional form of financial asset returns has important implications for theoretical and empirical analyses in economics and finance. For example, asset, portfolio and option pricing theories are typically based on the shape of these distributions, which some researchers have tried to recover from financial market prices, as, for example, recently Jackwerth and Rubinstein (1996) and Melick and Thomas (1997) did for the options markets.

In particular, stable distributions are currently *en vogue* again for risk valuation, asset and option pricing and portfolio management, long after having been in fashion for a short-lived period in the 1960s. They provide more realistic financial risk profiles, in particular in the high frequency antipersistent FX markets, where excess kurtosis is found, but also in the persistent stock markets (Hsu *et al.*, 1974; Mittnik and Rachev, 1993a,b; Chobanov *et al.*, 1996; McCulloch, 1996; Cont *et al.*, 1997; Gopikrishnan *et al.*, 1998; Müller *et al.*, 1998; Los, 2000).

The scientific debate – about what kind of distributions best represent financial time series – is not yet settled, and maybe never will. Some authors claim the financial market return distributions to be close to Paretian stable (Mandelbrot, 1962, 1963a–c, 1966; Fama, 1963, 1965a,b; McFarland *et al.*, 1982; Rachev and Mittnik, 2000); others that they are close to Student-*t* distributions (Boothe and Glasserman, 1987). Still others reject any single distribution (Caldéron-Rossel and Ben-Horim, 1982). However, everybody agrees on two empirical observations: FX and cash return rates are fat-tailed. Extreme values are more prevalent than the conventional Gaussian distribution suggests, i.e., extreme risks are *abnormally frequent*.

Thus, the main motivation for studying stable distributions is the need to evaluate *extreme risks* in the financial markets. Regrettably, most of the current models for assessing such risks are still based on the assumption that financial market returns are distributed according to the Gaussian distribution. With the Gaussian distribution the evaluation of extreme risks is directly related to the volatility σ, as we noted in Chapter 1, but in the case of fat-tailed distributions this is no longer the case.

A new controversy has arisen in the financial research community as to whether the second moment of the distribution of rates of returns exists, i.e., whether it converges to a (time-normalized) constant, or not. As emphasized by Müller *et al.* (1998), this question is central to computational finance, since financial models heavily rely on the existence of the volatility of returns, σ (Los, 2001). Some empirical financial distributions, such as the rates of return of the S&P500 Index exhibit such non-existent, i.e., non-convergent volatilities. Their variances are not only nonstationary, they are essentially unpredictable!

As we observed in Chapter 1, financial market risk has been associated with this volatility of returns σ, ever since in the 1950s Markowitz attempted to put portfolio theory on a scientific footing (Markowitz, 1952, 1991). From the Sharpe ratio for measuring the portfolio performance of mutual funds (Sharpe, 1966) to dynamic fundamental asset and derivative pricing models, the risk constant σ is always present. Of course, for full-scale global multi-currency, multi-asset investment portfolio valuation, one investigates the whole covariance matrix Σ, instead of only independent variances σ^2.

To broaden the set of our theoretical distributional benchmarks, in this chapter we focus on the statistical theory of stable marginal distributions of investment returns, in particular, on the theory of their Paretian scaling distributions, *irrespective of the structure of their temporal dependence*. We want to have a theoretical concept of statistical frequency distribution that exhibits the property of self-similarity and to show how that property is related to certain time intervals via stable scaling laws of time aggregation. Later on we will establish a (not yet specified) connection between the frequency of occurrence and the timing of occurrence of certain risky events.

In this chapter, we explain, first, the difference between linear and affine relations and time series. Then some invariant properties of stable distributions are defined, like those of weighted mixtures, choice maximization and aggregation, closely following Mandelbrot (1962, 1963b). Next, we focus on the particular parametrizations of stable distributions of Zolotarev, following the explanation by Nolan (1999a,b) and Rachev and Mittnik (2000). The chapter concludes with some examples of empirical financial research, which use this new theory of stable distributions, and discuss some of the essential weaknesses of the statistical approach to identify these distributions from inexact and irregular data.

3.2 Affine traces of speculative prices

Although, in Chapter 1, we stated that correlation was a form of linear dependence, we have not yet defined linearity, nor time-invariance, or time-dependence. In this section, we will define linearity, affinity, time-invariance and time-dependence, all within the context of a financial system by using simple operator algebra.[1]

3.2.1   Linearity versus affinity

3.2.1.1   System transformations

Let's first define what is meant by such a crucial concept as a *system*.

Definition 92   *A system is a mathematical model of a physical process that relates the input function (or source) to the output function (or response). Thus, a system can be considered a mapping of an input $X_i(t)$ into an output $X_o(t)$. Using the symbol f to symbolize this mapping, we have*

$$X_o(t) = f\{X_i(t)\} \tag{3.1}$$

and f is the system *operator, which transforms the inputs $X_i(t)$ into outputs $X_o(t)$.*

f may be a linear or a nonlinear system operator.

Definition 93   *A system is* invertible *when*

$$X_i(t) = f^{-1}X_o(t) \tag{3.2}$$

Thus, the output can just as well be the input, and *vice versa.*

Definition 94   *A system is* time-invariant *when*

$$X_o(t + \tau) = f\{X_i(t + \tau)\} \tag{3.3}$$

where τ is an arbitrary constant, representing a time interval.

Time intervals have no influence on the output of a time-invariant system, since the system does not change within such time intervals.

Definition 95   *L is called the* linear operator *and the system represented by L is called a* linear system*, if the operator L satisfies the following two conditions of additivity and homogeneity:*

$$L\{X_{i1}(t) + X_{i2}(t)\} = L\{X_{i1}(t)\} + L\{X_{i2}(t)\}$$
$$= X_{o1}(t) + X_{o2}(t) \quad \text{(additivity)} \tag{3.4}$$

$$L\{cX_i(t)\} = cL\{X_i(t)\}$$
$$= cX_o(t) \quad \text{(homogeneity)} \tag{3.5}$$

For example, the time lag-operator L which delays the input by one period is linear, as can be easily checked, since it satisfies these two properties of linearity. Notice that

$$X_{t-\tau} = L^\tau X_t \tag{3.6}$$

Multiple period lags consist of a geometric series of linear one-period lag operators.

Remark 96   *Note that the* first difference operator Δ *can be derived from the time lag-operator, since*

$$\Delta = 1 - L \tag{3.7}$$

This is easy to check, since

$$\begin{aligned}
\Delta X(t) &= X(t) - X(t-1) \\
&= X(t) - LX(t) \\
&= (1 - L)X(t)
\end{aligned} \tag{3.8}$$

Now we see also why the Geometric Brownian Motion (GBM) can be written as

$$\begin{aligned}
\Delta x(t) &= (1 - L)x(t) \\
&= \varepsilon(t), \quad \text{with } \varepsilon(t) \sim i.i.d.
\end{aligned} \tag{3.9}$$

with $x(t) = \Delta \ln X(t)$.

Since the lag operator is linear, the first difference operator is also linear. *Higher-order difference operators* can be expressed as products of the first difference operator:

$$\Delta^d = (1 - L)^d \tag{3.10}$$

for any $d \in \mathbb{R}$. These higher-order difference operators play an increasingly important role in empirical financial research, as we will observe in the following chapters.

Example 97   *The Random Walk in Chapter 2 can be viewed as a linear system, when we focus on the first price differences* $\Delta X(t)$, *since we can write*

$$\Delta X(t) = (1 - L)X(t) = \varepsilon(t), \quad \text{with } \varepsilon(t) \sim i.i.d. \tag{3.11}$$

In this model conception, the series of time-dependent prices $\{X(t)\}$ is linearly transformed, or *filtered*, into innovations, which are assumed to be i.i.d. Consequently, to empirically test this Random Walk model, we compute the first differences of such price series and then test if the resulting series of innovations is, indeed, stationary and independent. If not, the price series cannot be described by the Random Walk model. Recently we executed non-parametric stationarity and independence tests on high-frequency, minute-by-minute Asian FX series in Los (1999), which are nonstationary and not independent, and on weekly Asian stock market returns in Los (2000), which show a fair amount of stationarity, but do not show independence.

However, the order of financial system differentiation is often empirically measured to be a fraction and not an integer.

Definition 98   *A fractional difference operator is* $\Delta^d = (1 - L)^d$ *for* $d = $ *non-integer* $\in \mathbb{R}$.

We'll meet these empirically important fractional difference operators again in Chapter 4, where we discuss Fractional Brownian Motion (FBM), which can better explain the observed simultaneous phenomena of non-stationarity and long-term time dependence.

In Chapter 4, we will discuss the two major types of their time dependence: serial (short-term) dependence, modelled by integer difference operators or global (long-term) dependence, modelled by fractional difference operators.

3.2.1.2 Affine transformations

Definition 99 *M is called the* affine operator *when*

$$X_o(t) = M\{X_i(t)\}$$
$$= cX_i(t) + d \tag{3.12}$$

where c and d are amplifying *and vertical* frame shifting *constants, respectively.*

The affine operator is clearly nonlinear, since, first, it is not additive:

$$M\{X_1(t)\} + M\{X_2(t)\} = c[X_1(t) + X_2(t)] + 2d$$
$$\neq M\{X_1(t) + X_2(t)\}$$
$$= c[X_1(t) + X_2(t)] + d \tag{3.13}$$

and, second, it is not homogeneous, since

$$M\{cX(t)\} = cX(t) + d$$
$$\neq cM\{X(t)\}$$
$$= cX(t) + cd \tag{3.14}$$

However, we can always transform an affine data series into a linear data series by taking *deviations from the mean*, since

$$x_o(t) = \left[X_o(t) - \frac{1}{T} \sum_{t=1}^{T} X_o(t) \right]$$

$$= [cX_i(t) + d] - \left[\frac{c}{T} \sum_{t=1}^{T} X_i(t) + \frac{1}{T} \sum_{t=1}^{T} d \right]$$

$$= c \left[X_i(t) - \frac{1}{T} \sum_{t=1}^{T} X_i(t) \right] + d - d$$

$$= c \left[X_i(t) - \frac{1}{T} \sum_{t=1}^{T} X_i(t) \right]$$

$$= cx_i(t) \tag{3.15}$$

which is clearly additive and homogeneous, and thus linear. Thus, we've found a second reason to compute deviations from the mean, before we analyze a financial time series, such as rates of return.

3.3   Invariant properties: stationarity versus scaling

We learned in Chapter 1 that stationarity in the wide sense (weak stationarity) is defined by constant, invariant risk:

$$\sigma_t = \sigma_s, \quad \text{with } t, s \in T \tag{3.16}$$

We learned also that a Random Walk has invariant normalized risk. As long as the scaling factor remains invariant or stable, we can transform any horizon risk linearly into normalized risk by proper scaling. By scaling we normalize the horizon risk of an asset to its own invariant asset risk class. In the case of the Random Walk, we use Fickian scaling. The Random Walk risk scales *self-similarity* according to the number of periods n, where the total time of observation is $T = n\tau$, since we can express the self-similarity of the horizon risk of the Random Walk within the horizon τ as follows:

$$\sigma_\tau = \frac{1}{n^{0.5}} \sigma_T$$
$$= \left(\frac{\tau}{T}\right)^{0.5} \sigma_T \tag{3.17}$$

or, in inverse form,

$$\sigma_T = \sigma_\tau n^\lambda$$
$$= \sigma_\tau n^{0.5} \tag{3.18}$$

But there are distributions which have different scaling exponents than the *Fickian scaling exponent* $\lambda = 0.5$ of a Random Walk or ABM (on the basis of the market prices $X(t)$), or of a GBM (on the basis of the investment return $x(t) = \ln(X(t)/X(t-1))$. It appears that these *non-Fickian scaling exponents*, $\lambda \neq 0.5$, are prevalent in empirical finance. A subgroup of such statistical scaling distributions are the Pareto–Lévy power laws.[2]

Definition 100   *A (Pareto–Lévy) scaling distribution (or power law) is a frequency distribution $P(X(\tau) > x)$ of independent random variables $X(\tau)$ with a scaling factor σ_T, which is dependent on the frequency of (observed) occurrence, such that*

$$P(X(t) > x) \sim \sigma_T = \sigma_\tau n^\lambda \tag{3.19}$$

where λ is the scaling exponent, the total time of observation is $T = n\tau$ and τ is the minimal time period of observation, or horizon, e.g., a minute, an hour, a day, a month or a year, etc.

The essence of power laws is the inherent *self-similarity* over n: no matter what the size of n, the power law will have the same shape. The shape of the power law is determined by the exponent λ. The size of the distributional shape is determined by n and the *fundamental volatility* σ_τ.

Remark 101 *Notice that we make a distinction between the observation, or trading time τ and actual time t. Thus, only when the trading time is the same as the actual time we have $\tau = 1, T = n$, and the power law can be expressed in terms of the total time of observation:*

$$P(X(t) > x) \sim \sigma_T = \sigma_\tau T^\lambda \tag{3.20}$$

For some financial time series, we must distinguish between trading time and observation time, like for FX series, where the tick-by-tick trading is often more frequent than the recording of transaction prices by commercial bank quotations. Researchers have often only access to the regularly spaced price quotations and not to the more frequent and irregularly spaced tick-by-tick transaction prices.

A power law can be written in logarithmic form as an affine relation:

$$\ln \sigma_T = \lambda \ln n + \ln \sigma_\tau \tag{3.21}$$

so that, in principle, the exponent λ can be found from the expression:

$$\lambda = \frac{\ln \sigma_T - \ln \sigma_\tau}{\ln n} \tag{3.22}$$

In terms of financial risk theory, Peters (1994, pp. 27–37) appropriately calls this relationship the *term structure of volatility*.

How easy is it to compute the invariant scaling exponent λ from the observations? Not as easy as it appears, since, a priori, we do not know σ_τ, the basic standard deviation (risk) of the unit of observation, that is, the observation "noise." This has to be measured first, somehow, or at least simultaneously. We will discuss this epistemological issue in greater detail in Chapter 4. The relevance of this issue for portfolio risk management and Value-at-Risk issues will be discussed in Chapter 12.

3.4 Invariances of (Pareto–Lévy) scaling distributions

Many objects that come in different sizes have self-similar power law distributions of their relative abundance over large size ranges, of the form:

$$f(x) \sim x^{1/\alpha} \tag{3.23}$$

A recent example of the application of the scaling laws of financial volatility to the analysis of financial long-term dependence is Batten *et al.* (1999). The only prerequisite for such a self-similar law to prevail in a given size range is the absence of an inherent size scale. Thus, invariance of scaling results from the fact that homogeneous power laws lack natural scales: they do not harbor a characteristic unit (such as a unit length, a unit time or a unit mass).

Remark 102 *Real-world data are never completely scale-invariant because of "end effects." For example, no living village has fewer than 1 inhabitant or more than 100 million inhabitants – except the proverbial "global village," which is more of a simile, than a reality.*

Mandelbrot (1962, 1963b) discusses three invariances of scaling, or self-similarities, of stable Pareto–Lévy power law distributions:

(1) invariance of scaling under weighted mixture (= weighted linear combination);
(2) invariance of scaling under choice maximization (minimization); and
(3) invariance of scaling under aggregation.

More invariances are possible, as Figure 3.1 shows, but they are all related to the three invariances defined by Mandelbrot, which we'll now discuss in the following three sections.

3.4.1 Weighted mixtures

Suppose that the random variable X_W is a weighted mixture of the independent random variables $X(\tau)$, and denote by p_τ the probability that X_W is identical

Scheme	Stability property[a]
Summation	$X_1 \overset{d}{=} a_n(X_1 + \cdots + X_n) + b_n$
Maximum	$X_1 \overset{d}{=} a_n \max_{1 \le i \le n} X_i + b_n$
Minimum	$X_1 \overset{d}{=} a_n \min_{1 \le i \le n} X_i + b_n$
Multiplication	$X_1 \overset{d}{=} A_n(X_1 X_2 \cdots X_n)^{C_n}$
Geometric summation	$X_1 \overset{d}{=} a(p)(X_1 + \cdots + X_{T(p)}) + b(p)$
Geometric maximum	$X_1 \overset{d}{=} a(p) \max_{1 \le i \le T(p)} X_i + b(p)$
Geometric minimum	$X_1 \overset{d}{=} a(p) \min_{1 \le i \le T(p)} X_i + b(p)$
Geometric multiplication	$X_1 \overset{d}{=} A(p)(X_1 X_2 \cdots X_{T(p)})^{C(p)}$

Figure 3.1 Stable probabilistic schemes.

Note
a Notation "$X_1 \overset{d}{=}$" stands for "equality in distribution."

to $X(\tau)$. Since

$$P(X_W > x) = \sum_\tau p_\tau P(X(\tau) > x)$$

$$\sim \sum_\tau p_\tau \sigma_\tau n^\lambda$$

$$= \sigma_W n^\lambda \tag{3.24}$$

we see that X_W is also scaling and the scale parameter $\sigma_W = \sum p_\tau \sigma_\tau$ is a *weighted average* of the separate scale parameters σ_τ. (The sign $\sim$ means "is proportional to.") Thus, scaling is invariant under weighted mixture (= weighted linear combination) of the random variables.

3.4.2   Choice maximization

Ex post, when the values of $X(\tau)$ are known, let X_M be the largest value. This X_M is also scaling with the scale parameter $\sigma_M = \sum \sigma_\tau$, since, in order that X_M is the largest, i.e., $X_M \leq x$, where x is a value, it is both necessary and sufficient that $X_\tau \leq x$ for every τ. Hence we have the product

$$P(X_M \leq x) = \prod_\tau P(X_\tau \leq x) \tag{3.25}$$

Consequently

$$P(X_M > x) = 1 - P(X_M \leq x)$$

$$= 1 - \prod_\tau P(X_\tau \leq x)$$

$$= 1 - \prod_\tau (1 - P(X_\tau > x))$$

$$\sim 1 - \prod_\tau (1 - \sigma_\tau n^\lambda)$$

$$\sim \sum \sigma_\tau n^\lambda = \sigma_M n^\lambda \tag{3.26}$$

for sufficiently small σ_τ, where $\sigma_M = \sum \sigma_\tau$.

3.4.3   Aggregation

Let X_A be the sum of the random variables X_τ. The *aggregate* X_A is also scaling, with a scale parameter that is again the sum of the separate weights $\sigma_A = \sum \sigma_\tau$.

Using a similar argument as for weighted mixtures

$$P(X_A > x) = \sum_{\tau} P(X_\tau > x)$$

$$\sim \sum_{\tau} \sigma_\tau n^\lambda$$

$$= \sigma_A n^\lambda \tag{3.27}$$

where $\sigma_A = \sum \sigma_\tau$. Mixtures combined with aggregation leave the scaling distribution invariant – up-to-scale.

3.5   Zolotarev parametrization of stable distributions

We will now discuss stable distributions in general, by following closely Nolan's (1999a,b) admirably clear theoretical presentation, and we will see where the Pareto–Lévy scaling laws of Mandelbrot, which exhibit infinite variance in the limit, fit in. Interestingly, the study of general stable distributions was begun by Paul Lévy in 1924 in his study of normalized sums of i.i.d. variables. Stable distributions are a class of distributions, that includes the Gaussian and Cauchy distributions in a family that allows skewness and heavy tails (= excess kurtosis). Distributions with heavy tails are regularly observed in economics, finance, insurance, telecommunications and physics.

Remark 103   *In finance, the interest in the skewness of return distributions has primarily emerged in the context of the discussion about the empirical truthfulness of the Capital Asset Pricing Model (CAPM), which is based on Markowitz Mean– Variance Analysis. That model assumes normal distributions and/or quadratic wealth-utility preference functions, which don't include preferences for skewness and kurtosis. However, the moment a certain degree of skewness is preferred by the investors, the conventional CAPM is no longer a model of market efficiency (Kraus and Litzenberger, 1976; Friend and Westerfield, 1980). In other words, the empirically observed skewness implies that the CAPM cannot represent an efficient market model.*

Some people have objected against the use of stable distributions with infinite variance, because empirical data supposedly exhibit only bounded ranges. However, the rates of return of the S&P500 Index have indeterminate (= "infinite") variance! Still, bounded data sets are routinely modeled by Gaussian distributions which have infinite support. Thus the epistemological question is, why would distributions with infinite support with bounded ranges be methodologically acceptable, while distributions with finite support and unbounded ranges would not be? After all, we're primarily interested in the *shape* of the distributions.

It appears that the shape characteristics of stable distributions, other than the Gaussian, are more conform to the frequency distributions we empirically observe, in particular in finance (Rachev and Mittnik, 2000). Stable distributions provide a realistic fit with very parsimonious parametrizations. Furthermore, infinite variances is not something restricted to stable distributions. If a distribution has asymptotic power decay on its tails, then the number of moments is limited. If the exponent of the power decay is less than 2, then the distribution will have infinite variance, as we will see in Chapter 4.

We turn now to Zolotarev's definition and parametrization of stable distributions, since that is currently the most popular theoretical representation (Zolotarev, 1986; Adler *et al.*, 1998).

3.5.1 Definitions of stable distributions

Definition 104   (Original definition of stable distribution): *A random variable X is stable, or stable in the wide sense, if for X_1 and X_2 independent copies of X and for any positive constants a and b,*

$$aX_1 + bX_2 \stackrel{d}{=} cX + d \tag{3.28}$$

for all choices of a and b and for some nonnegative $c \geq 0$ and some $d \in \mathbb{R}$. Thus, if the weighted sum of X_1 and X_2 equals in distribution an affine relationship.

The symbol $\stackrel{d}{=}$ means equality in distribution, i.e., both expressions have the same probability law, although the size of the distribution is indeterminate.

Definition 105   *The random variable X is* strictly stable *or* stable in the narrow sense *if this relationship holds with the "intercept" $d = 0$, thus if their weighted sum equals in distribution a linear relationship.*

Definition 106   *A random variable is* symmetrically stable *if it is stable and symmetrically distributed around 0, e.g.,*

$$X \stackrel{d}{=} -X \tag{3.29}$$

In other words, the equation

$$aX_1 + bX_2 \stackrel{d}{=} cX + d \tag{3.30}$$

states that the shape of the distribution of X is preserved up to scale c and shift d under addition. For *scaling distributions*, which are a subset of stable distributions, this is, of course, equivalent to the invariances under weight mixture and aggregation of Mandelbrot's (1963a) Pareto–Lévy distributions. The word stable is used because the shape of the distribution is stable or unchanged under sums of this additive type. As already mentioned, there are not only additive stable, but also max-stable, min-stable and geometrically stable distributions, that preserve stability under choice maximization, choice minimization, etc.

There are other equivalent definitions of stable random variables. Here is a variation of the original definition of an (additive) stable distribution:

Definition 107 (Variation of the definition of a stable distribution) *X is stable (in the wide sense) if and only if for all $n > 1$ there exist constants c_n and $d_n \in \mathbb{R}$ such that*

$$X_1 + X_2 + \cdots + X_n \stackrel{d}{=} c_n X + d_n \tag{3.31}$$

where $X_1, \ldots, X_n$ are independent, identical copies of X.

It appears that the only possible choice for c_n is $c_n = n^{(1/\alpha_Z)}$. X is again strictly stable if and only if $d_n = 0$ for all n. Thus, a defining invariance property of stable distributions is that linear combinations of stable random variables are also stable.

The most concrete way to describe all possible stable distributions is through their characteristic functions, or Fourier transforms (cf. Chapters 1 and 4), which is what we will do next. All stable distributions are scale and location shifts of standardized stable distributions, just like any Gaussian $X \sim N(\mu, \sigma^2)$ is the scale and location shift affine transform $X = \sigma Z + \mu$ of the standardized Gaussian $Z \sim N(0, 1)$, for which standardized probability tables exist.

Following Nolan, we will present the popular *standardized* or *reduced* parametrization of stable distributions of Zolotarev.[3] This standardization of stable distributions uses the sign (or modified Heaviside) function, which is defined as:

$$\text{sign}(\omega) = \begin{cases} -1 & \text{for } \omega < 0 \\ 0 & \text{for } \omega = 0 \\ +1 & \text{for } \omega > 0 \end{cases} \tag{3.32}$$

Theorem 108 (Zolotarev, 1986, standardized parametrization of a stable distribution) *A random variable X is stable if and only if $X \stackrel{d}{=} cZ + d$, with $c \geq 0, d \in \mathbb{R}$, and $Z = (\alpha_Z, \beta)$ is a random variable with the following characteristic function, where $0 < \alpha_Z \leq 2, -1 \leq \beta \leq 1$,*

$$E\{e^{j\omega z}\} = \int_{-\infty}^{+\infty} e^{j\omega z} dG(z)$$

$$= \begin{cases} e^{(-|\omega|^{\alpha_Z}[1+j\beta \tan(\pi\alpha_Z/2)\,\text{sign}(\omega)(|\omega|^{1-\alpha_Z}-1)])} & \text{if } \alpha_Z \neq 1 \\ e^{(-|\omega|[1+j\beta(2/\pi)(\text{sign}(\omega)\ln|\omega|)])} & \text{if } \alpha_Z = 1 \end{cases} \tag{3.33}$$

where G is the stable distribution function corresponding to the stable density function of Z.

The key idea of Zolotarev's fundamental Theorem is that α_Z and β determine the shape of the stable distribution, while c is a scale and d is a shift parameter. It shows that the standardized stable distribution has only two parameters: (1) an *index of stability, or stability (shape) exponent* $\alpha_Z \in (0,2]$ *and* (2) *a skewness parameter* $\beta \in [-1,1]$. *For the* $\alpha_Z = 1$ *case,* $0 . \ln 0$ *is always interpreted as* 0.

Remark 109 *The non-standardized stable distribution of the random variable* $X \sim S(\alpha_Z, \beta, \gamma, \delta; 0)$ *(e.g., in Mittnik et al., 1998 and in Rachev and Mittnik, 2000) has the characteristic function*

$$E\{e^{j\omega x}\} = \int_{-\infty}^{+\infty} e^{j\omega x} dH(x)$$

$$= \begin{cases} e^{(-\gamma^{\alpha_Z}|\omega|^{\alpha_Z}[1+j\beta \tan(\pi\alpha_Z/2)\,\mathrm{sign}(\omega)(\gamma|\omega|^{1-\alpha_Z}-1)]+j\delta\omega)} & if\, \alpha_Z \neq 1 \\ e^{(-\gamma|\omega|[1+j\beta(2/\pi)(\mathrm{sign}(\omega)(\ln|\omega|+\ln\gamma]+j\delta\omega)} & if\, \alpha_Z = 1 \end{cases}$$

$$\tag{3.34}$$

where H *is the stable distribution function corresponding to the stable density function of* X. *As we already discussed in Chapter 1, this non-standardized stable distribution has four parameters* (1) *a stability exponent* $\alpha_Z \in (0,2]$, (2) *a skewness parameter* $\beta \in [-1,+1]$, (3) *a scale parameter* $\gamma > 0$, *and* (4) *a location parameter* $\delta \in \mathbb{R}$.

Remark 110 *The computation of all stable densities is approximate in the sense that the density function* $S(\alpha_Z, \beta, \gamma, \delta; k), k = 0, 1$ *is approximated by Fast Fourier Transformation (FFT in Chapter 5) of these stable characteristic functions.*

3.5.2 General properties of stable distributions

Although explicit formulas exist for stable characteristic functions, in general no explicit formulas exist for the corresponding stable distribution densities. However, the theoretical properties of such distribution densities are well known. The basic property of stable distribution densities is given by the following so-called idealization theorem.

Theorem 111 *All (non-degenerate) stable distributions are continuous distributions with an infinitely differentiable density.*

The probability density function (p.d.f.) of a standardized $Z(\alpha_Z, \beta)$ stable distribution will be denoted by $f(z \mid \alpha_Z, \beta)$ and the cumulative distribution function (c.d.f.) will be denoted by $F(z \mid \alpha_Z, \beta)$. All stable densities are *unimodal*, i.e., they have each one "peak."[4] The mode $m(\alpha_Z, \beta)$ of a $Z(\alpha_Z, \beta)$ distribution can be *numerically* computed, even though no explicit algebraic formula for it exists. By the symmetry property, the densities have modes such that:

$$m(\alpha_Z, -\beta) = -m(\alpha_Z, \beta) \tag{3.35}$$

Furthermore, stable densities are positive on the whole real line, unless $\alpha_Z < 1$ and ($\beta = +1$ or $\beta = -1$), in which case the support is half a line. In more precise terms

Lemma 112   *The support of a stable $X(\alpha_Z, \beta, \gamma, \delta)$ distribution is*

support $f(z \mid \alpha_Z, \beta)$

$$= \begin{cases} [\delta - \tan(\pi\alpha_Z/2), \infty) & \text{if } \alpha_Z < 1 \text{ and } \beta = 1 \text{ (positively skewed)} \\ (-\infty, \delta + \gamma \tan(\pi\alpha_Z/2)] & \text{if } \alpha_Z < 1 \text{ and } \beta = -1 \text{ (negatively skewed)} \\ (-\infty, +\infty) & \text{otherwise} \end{cases}$$

(3.36)

Remark 113   *Notice that the constant $\tan(\pi\alpha_Z/2)$ is an important ingredient of stable distributions. It shows an essential discontinuity at $\alpha_Z = 1$, since as $\alpha_Z \uparrow 1$, $\tan(\pi\alpha_Z/2) \uparrow +\infty$ and $\alpha_Z \downarrow 1$, $\tan(\pi\alpha_Z/2) \downarrow -\infty$, while $\tan(\pi\alpha_Z/2)$ is undefined at $\alpha_Z = 1$.*

Another basic property of stable distributions is their symmetry.

Proposition 114   (Symmetry Property) *For any α_Z and β,*

$$Z(\alpha_Z, -\beta) \stackrel{d}{=} Z(\alpha_Z, \beta)$$

(3.37)

Therefore, the density and distribution function of a $Z(\alpha_Z, \beta)$ random variable satisfy $f(z \mid \alpha_Z, \beta) = f(-z \mid \alpha_Z, -\beta)$ and $F(z \mid \alpha_Z, \beta) = 1 - F(-z \mid \alpha_Z, \beta)$.

It is important to consider a few special cases:

(1) When $\beta = 0$, the symmetry property says $f(z \mid \alpha_Z, \beta) = f(-z \mid \alpha_Z, \beta)$, so the p.d.f. and c.d.f. are symmetric around 0.
(2) When $\beta > 0$, the distribution is skewed to the right with the right tail of the distribution heavier than the left tail: $P(Z > z) > P(Z < -z)$ for large $z > 0$. When $\beta = 1$, the stable distribution is *totally skewed to the right*.
(3) By the symmetry property, the behavior of the $\beta < 0$ cases is reflecting the behavior of the $\beta > 0$ cases, with a heavier left tail. Thus, when $\beta < 0$, the distribution is skewed to the left with the left tail of the distribution heavier than the right tail: $P(Z > z) > P(Z < -z)$ for large $z > 0$. When $\beta = -1$, the distribution is *totally skewed to the left*.
(4) The stability exponent $\alpha_Z \in (0, 2]$ determines the kurtosis of the distribution: the peakedness at δ and the fatness of the tails. As the stability exponent α_Z decreases, three things occur to the distribution density: its peak gets higher, the region flanking the peak gets lower, and the tails get heavier, or, in summary: the kurtosis of the distribution increases. Of course, when the stability exponent α_Z increases, the kurtosis of the distribution decreases. For example, when $\alpha_Z = 2$, the distribution is normal with its variance equal to

$\sigma^2 = 2\gamma^2$. In that case

$$\tan\left(\frac{\pi \alpha_Z}{2}\right) = \tan(\pi) = 0 \qquad (3.38)$$

so the characteristic function is real and hence the distribution is always symmetric, no matter what the value of β.

(5) When the stability exponent $\alpha_Z < 2$, the second moment, or variance, becomes infinite, or undefined. When $1 < \alpha_Z < 2$, the first moment exists, but when $\alpha_Z \leq 1$, the theoretical (population) average also becomes infinite or undefined (Samorodnitsky and Taqqu, 1994). Thus, there is only a very limited range of the stability exponent α_Z for which both the first and second moments exist. By *existence of moments* we mean that they have a well-defined value that can be determined within a prespecified error range, no matter how small.

Of course, we can always compute a (sample) average or a variance of a finite data set. Non-existent or undefined theoretical (population) averages and variances mean that there is no convergence to well-defined values, even when we substantially enlarge the data set. The computed mean and variance of that data set will never converge to a specific mean and variance, but will continue to "wander." It will never settle on a specific value. This is not a theoretical abstraction, as one can observe from the empirical data Exercises at the end of this chapter, based on the rates of return of the S&P500 Index. These stock market rates have defined, convergent finite mean, but no defined, convergent variance. Peters 1994 (pp. 200–205) provides many additional theoretical and empirical examples. These cases are seldom mentioned in the classical statistical literature, thereby creating the erroneous impression that these cases are pathological and special. But they are regularly occurring empirical cases in the financial markets!

3.5.3 Different Zolotarev parametrizations

Historically, several different Zolotarev parametrizations have been used for stable distributions, for which, in general, no closed form parametrization exists (because of the discontinuity at $\alpha_Z = 1$). We give the three most often used parametrizations. Here is the first one.

Definition 115 *A random variable X is the* parametrized stable distribution $S(\alpha_Z, \beta, \gamma, \delta; 0)$ *if*

$$X \overset{d}{=} \gamma Z + \delta \qquad (3.39)$$

where $Z = Z(\alpha_Z, \beta)$ *is implicitly given by its characteristic function in Theorem 1.*

This is the parametrization used for current numerical work on stable distributions. It has the simplest form for the characteristic function that is continuous in all parameters.

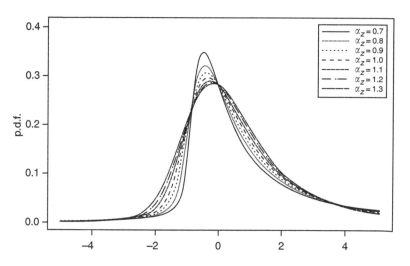

Figure 3.2 Stable density in the Zolotarev $S(\alpha_Z, \beta, \gamma, \delta; 0) = S(\alpha_Z, 0.8, 1, 0; 0)$ parametrization.

Remark 116 *Notice that γ is the scale parameter and δ the location parameter, in a rather natural fashion. For the standardized version $\gamma = 1$ and $\delta = 0$, so that $S(\alpha_Z, \beta, \gamma, \delta; 0) = S(\alpha_Z, \beta; 0)$.*

Let's show some numerical examples of stable distributions to demonstrate their properties mentioned in the preceding section. Figure 3.2 provides a graphical representation of stable densities in the $S(\alpha_Z, \beta, \gamma, \delta; 0) = S(\alpha_Z, 0.8, 1, 0; 0)$ parametrization, with the stability exponent α_Z (alpha) as indicated.

Here is the second parametrization:

Definition 117 *A random variable X is characterized by the parametrized stable distribution $S(\alpha_Z, \beta, \gamma, \delta; 1)$ if*

$$
X \overset{d}{=} \begin{cases} \gamma Z + (\delta + \beta \gamma \tan \dfrac{\pi \alpha_Z}{2}), & \text{if } \alpha_Z \neq 1 \\[2mm] \gamma Z + (\delta + \beta \dfrac{2}{\pi} \gamma \ln \gamma), & \text{if } \alpha_Z = 1 \end{cases}
\tag{3.40}
$$

where $Z = Z(\alpha_Z, \beta)$ is implicitly given by its characteristic function in Zolotarev's 1986 Theorem.

This $S(\alpha_Z, \beta, \gamma, \delta; 1)$ parametrization is the most common one currently in theoretical use, since it produces the simplest characteristic function, which is jointly continuous in all four parameters, and has therefore preferable algebraic properties. But it's practical disadvantage is that the location of the mode is unbounded in any neighborhood of $\alpha_Z = 1$.

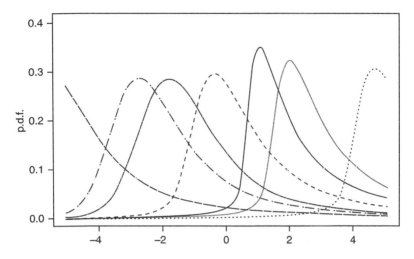

Figure 3.3 Stable density in the Zolotarev $\mathbf{S}(\alpha_Z, \beta, \gamma, \delta; 1) = \mathbf{S}(\alpha_Z, 0.8, 1, 0; 1)$ parametrization.

Figure 3.3 provides a graphical representation of stable densities in the $\mathbf{S}(\alpha_Z, \beta, \gamma, \delta; 1) = \mathbf{S}(\alpha_Z, 0.8, 1, 0; 1)$ parametrization, with the stability exponent α_Z being varied similarly as in Figure 3.2. Notice in Figure 3.3 that the mode is near 0 for α_Z near 0 or 2, or $\alpha_Z = 1$, but diverges to $+\infty$ as $\alpha_Z \uparrow 1$ and diverges to $-\infty$ as $\alpha_Z \downarrow 1$. When $\beta = 0$, both these parametrizations are identical.

Remark 118 *As $\alpha_Z \uparrow 2$ both parametrized distributions converge in distribution to a distribution with standard deviation $\sqrt{2}\gamma$ and not γ, as maybe would have been expected! In fact, when $\alpha_Z < 2$, no standard deviation exists. Thus, for comparison purposes, one should multiply γ by $\sqrt{2}$ to make the scale parameter of the stable distribution comparable with that of the standard Gaussian distribution, i.e., the deviation $\sigma = \sqrt{2}\gamma$, or, equivalently, $\gamma = \frac{1}{\sqrt{2}}\sigma$.*

The third parametrization focuses on the mode as a location parameter, since, as we saw, every stable distribution has a mode.

Definition 119 *A random variable X is characterized by the parametrized stable distribution $\mathbf{S}(\alpha_Z, \beta, \gamma, \delta; 2)$ if*

$$X \stackrel{d}{=} \alpha_Z^{-1/\alpha_Z} \gamma (Z - m(\alpha_Z, \beta)) + \delta \tag{3.41}$$

where $Z = Z(\alpha_Z, \beta)$ is implicitly given by its characteristic function in Theorem 1 and $m(\alpha_Z, \beta)$ is the mode of Z.

3.5.4 *Tail properties and stable Paretian laws*

When the stability exponent $\alpha_Z = 2$, the resulting Gaussian distribution has well understood asymptotic tail properties. For the purpose of comparison, we'll briefly discuss in this section the crucial tail properties of non-Gaussian ($\alpha_Z < 2$) stable distributions. In financial risk theory, it is the tails of such stable distributions, representing the less likely, outlying and sometimes catastrophic events, that are most important for financial analysts, hedgers and insurers.

Theorem 120 (Tail Approximation) *Let* $X \sim S(\alpha_Z, \beta; 0)$ *with* $0 < \alpha_Z < 2$, $-1 < \beta \leq 1$. *Then, as* $x \to \infty$,

$$P(X > x) \sim c_{\alpha_Z}(1 + \beta)x^{-\alpha_Z} \tag{3.42}$$

$$f(x \mid \alpha_Z, \beta; 0) \sim \alpha_Z c_{\alpha_Z}(1 + \beta)x^{-(\alpha_Z+1)} \tag{3.43}$$

where $c_{\alpha_Z} = \Gamma(\alpha_Z)(\sin \pi \alpha_Z/2)/\pi$.

Remark 121 *Notice the gamma function* Γ, *which is such that* $\Gamma(\alpha_Z + 1) = \alpha_Z\Gamma(\alpha_Z) = \alpha_Z!$, *with* $\Gamma(1) = 1$. *We'll discuss and use this important gamma function in much greater detail in Chapter 4.*

Remark 122 *Using the symmetry property, the lower tail properties are similar. For all* $\alpha_Z < 2$ *and* $-1 < \beta$, *the upper tail probabilities and densities are asymptotic power laws (i.e. scaling distributions).*

Having developed this arsenal of concepts and definitions of stable distributions, we can now define more specific non-Gaussian distributions, in particular the Pareto and heavy tailed distributions, which currently figure prominently in the recent financial research literature (Müller *et al.*, 1990; Janicki and Weron, 1994; Mantegna and Stanley, 1995; Samorodnitsky and Taqqu, 1994) .

Definition 123 Pareto distributions *are probability laws with upper tail probabilities given exactly by the right-hand side of the Tail Approximation Theorem.*

Remark 124 *The term* stable Paretian laws *is used to distinguish between the fast decay of the Gaussian distributions and the Pareto-like tail behavior in the* $\alpha_Z < 2$ *case.*

Definition 125 *A distribution is said to be* heavy tailed *if it's tails are heavier than exponential.*

Remark 126 *For* $\alpha_Z < 2$, *stable distributions have one tail (when* $\alpha_Z < 1$ *and* $\beta = \pm 1$), *or both tails (in all other cases) that are asymptotically power laws.*

One important consequence of heavy tails is that not all moments exist, or, when they exist, they may be fractional. In other words, the literature on frequency distributions has considerably expanded our arsenal of moments discussed in Chapter 1: from integer moments to fractional moments!

Definition 127 Fractional absolute moments:

$$E\{|X|^p\} = \int_{-\infty}^{\infty} |x|^p f(x)dx \tag{3.44}$$

where p is any-integer or fractional-real number.

The Tail Approximation Theorem implies that for $0 < \alpha_Z < 2$, the moments $E\{|X|^p\}$ are finite for $0 < p < \alpha_Z$, and that $E\{|X|^p\} = +\infty$ for all $p \geq \alpha_Z$. Thus, when $\alpha_Z < 2$, $E\{|X|^2\} = E\{X^2\} = +\infty$ and stable distributions do not have finite second moments or variances. This is the worrisome theoretical case to which Mandelbrot (1963, 1966) referred in the 1960s and which was then dismissed by most mathematicians as pathological. But empirical observations since then have demonstrated that this case is more prevalent in financial markets than was presumed by the theoreticians.

In fact, this is an important case for anybody studying financial risk, since it implies that particular investment return series may have measurable stable distributions, but still exhibit infinite risk! The empirical scientific question is, do such strange financial distributions exist in empirical reality? The unfortunate answer is: yes, since these are the distributions of variables moving in the range of the so-called persistent or pink noise, i.e., noise that lies in the range between white and red noise.[5]

Example 128 *The logarithmic plot of Figure 3.4 (borrowed from Mantegna and Stanley, 2000, p. 69) shows that the high-frequency p.d.f. for $\Delta t = 1$ minute price changes of the S&P500 index with an empirically measured $\alpha_Z = 1.67$ lies between the Gaussian p.d.f. with $\alpha_Z = 2.00$ and the p.d.f. of a Lévy stable distribution with $\alpha_Z = 1.40$ and a scaling factor of $\gamma = 0.00375$.*

Example 129 *Figure 3.5 shows that the daily observations on the rates of return of the S&P500 stock market index in 1998 (available in Appendix B) exhibit considerable persistence unlike Gaussian rates of return. The variance or volatility of these daily rates of return, computed over longer and longer horizons dissipates. But this dissipation of the S&P500's volatility is not gradual and smooth. It shows sudden and completely unpredictable discontinuities and the volatility never converges to one defined value. Peters (1994, pp. 141–146) observed similar phenomena and found that this volatility dissipation process is antipersistent, a term that we'll explain in Chapter 4.*

Let's analyze the specific case of the first moment, or mean, of stable distributions in somewhat greater detail.

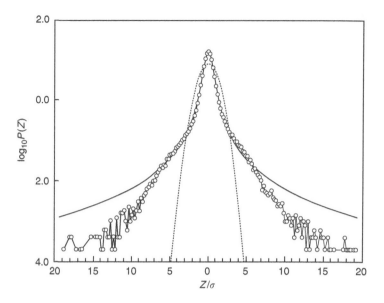

Figure 3.4 Comparison of the $\Delta t = 1$ minute p.d.f. for high-frequency S&P500 price changes (white circles) with the Gaussian p.d.f. (dotted line, smallest p.d.f. in middle) with $\alpha_Z = 2.00$ and with a Lévy stable p.d.f. (solid line, largest p.d.f.) of $\alpha_Z = 1.40$ and scale factor $\gamma = 0.00375$ (same as that of the S&P500).

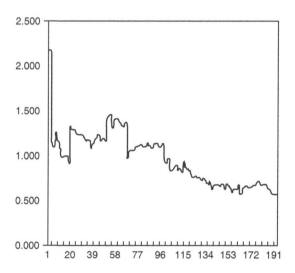

Figure 3.5 Non-convergent moving variance of 253 daily rates of return (in 100 percent) of the S&P500 stock market index in 1998, computed with a moving window of $\tau = 50$ observations. Notice that none of the window variances is the same and that they wander aimlessly.

Proposition 130   *When* $1 < \alpha_Z \leq 2$, $E\{|X|\} < \infty$ *and the mean of* $X \sim$ $S(\alpha_Z, \beta, \gamma_k, \delta_k; k)$ *exists, for* $k = 0, 1, 2$, *respectively, the mean is*

$$
\mu = \begin{cases} E\{X\} = \delta_1 \\ \delta_0 - \beta\gamma_0 \tan \dfrac{\pi\alpha_Z}{2} \\ \delta_2 - \alpha_Z^{-1/\alpha}\gamma_2\left(\beta \tan \dfrac{\pi\alpha_Z}{2} + m(\alpha_Z, \beta)\right) \end{cases} \tag{3.45}
$$

In other words, there is a clear relationship between the various location parameters, δ_1, δ_2 and δ_2 of these three parametrizations. On the other hand, when $\alpha_Z \leq 1$, the first absolute moment $E\{|X|\} = +\infty$, and these means are undefined. What happens geometrically with a stable distribution when its absolute mean does not exist?

Consider what happens to the mean of $X \sim S(\alpha_Z, \beta; 0)$ as $\alpha_Z \downarrow 1$. Even though the mode of the distribution stays close to 0, it has a mean $\mu = \beta \tan(\pi\alpha_Z/2)$. When $\beta = 0$, the distribution is symmetric and the mean is always 0. When $\beta > 0$, the mean $\mu \uparrow +\infty$, because both tails are getting heavier, but the right tail is heavier than the left. By symmetry, the $\beta < 0$ case has the mean $\mu \downarrow -\infty$. Finally, when α_Z reaches 1, the tails are too heavy for the integral

$$
E\{X\} = \int_{-\infty}^{\infty} xf(x)dx \tag{3.46}
$$

to converge and the mean becomes undefined or infinite: $E\{X\} \to \infty$.

However, this geometric description depends on the particular Zolotarev parametrization chosen. For example, the second parametrization, a $S(\alpha_Z, \beta; 1)$ distribution keeps the mean at 0 by shifting the whole distribution by an increasing amount as $\alpha_Z \downarrow 1$. For the third parametrization, a $S(\alpha_Z, \beta; 2)$ distribution keeps the mode exactly at 0, and the mean behaves like the mean of a $S(\alpha_Z, \beta; 0)$ distribution. Thus, a stable empirical distribution with a non-existent mean can best be parametrized by the first parametrization, when such a parametrization is required.

3.5.5   *Generalized Central Limit Theorem (GCLT)*

The classical Central Limit Theorem states that the normalized sums of i.i.d. variables with finite variance converges to a Gaussian distribution (Gnedenko and Kolmogorov, 1954). But the GCLT shows that if the finite variance (= finite risk) assumption is dropped, the only possible resulting limits are stable distributions.

Theorem 131   (GCLT) *Let* $X_1, X_2, \ldots, X_n$ *be an i.i.d. sequence of random variables. There exist constants* $c_n > 0$, $d_n \in \mathbb{R}$ *and a non-degenerate random variable* Z *with*

$$
c_n(X_1 + \cdots + X_n) - d_n \xrightarrow{d} Z \tag{3.47}
$$

if and only if Z *is stable, in which case* $c_n = n^{-1/\alpha_Z}$ *for some* $0 < \alpha_Z \leq 2$.

Remark 132   *Recall from Chapter 1 that for the normalized i.i.d. Random Walk volatility we have the stability exponent $\alpha_Z = 2$ and thus the normalizing constant $c_n = n^{-0.5}$.*

This GCLT implies that the only possible distributions with a *domain of attraction* (DOA) are stable distributions!

Definition 133   *A random variable X is in the DOA of Z if and only if there exist constants $c_n > 0, d_n \in \mathbb{R}$ with*

$$c_n(X_1 + \cdots + X_n) - d_n \overset{d}{\to} Z \tag{3.48}$$

where $X_1, X_2, \ldots$ are i.i.d. distributed copies of X.

By $DOA(Z)$ we will indicate the set of all random variables that are in the domain of attraction of Z. As Mittnik *et al.* (1998) and Rachev and Mittnik (2000) properly emphasize, a DOA is an important and, perhaps, even desirable property. Loosely speaking, any distribution in the DOA of a specified stable distribution has properties which are close to the properties of the stable distribution. These authors reason that, therefore, decisions will, in principle, not be affected by adopting an "idealized" stable distribution instead of using the true empirical distribution. Furthermore, they claim that it is possible to check whether or not a distribution is in the DOA of a stable distribution by examining only the tails of the distribution, since only these parts specify the DOA properties of the distribution. The stability, or continuity, of the adopted distribution is valid for any distribution with the appropriate tail.

3.6   Examples of closed form stable distributions

Although there are closed forms for the characteristic functions of all stable distributions, there are no closed formulas for the distribution densities and distribution functions for all but a few stable distributions, like for the Gaussian, Cauchy and Lévy distributions we encountered in Chapter 1. Here are their special closed form densities.

Definition 134   Gaussian distributions: $X \sim N(\mu, \sigma^2)$ *if it has density*

$$f(x) = \frac{1}{\sqrt{2\pi\sigma^2}} e^{-(x-\mu)^2/2\sigma^2}, \quad -\infty < x < +\infty \tag{3.49}$$

The normal distribution has an *infinite support* (infinite domain) on the whole real line from $-\infty$ to $+\infty$. In terms of Zolotarev's formula, $Z(2, \beta) \overset{d}{=} Z(2, 0) \sim N(0, 2)$.

Definition 135   Cauchy distributions: $X \sim Cauchy(\gamma, \delta)$ *if it has density*

$$f(x) = \frac{1}{\pi} \frac{\gamma}{\gamma^2 + (x - \delta)^2}, \quad -\infty < x < +\infty \tag{3.50}$$

The Cauchy distribution has also an *infinite support* on the whole real line from $-\infty$ to $+\infty$. In terms of Zolotarev's formula, $Z(1,0) \sim Cauchy(1,0)$.

Remark 136 *It can easily be shown that a Cauchy variable X, which has a stable distribution and is almost certainly finite, has an infinite variance and an infinite mean! (We return to this important issue in Chapter 12, when we discuss the particular consequences of their properties for portfolio management.)*

Definition 137 Lévy distributions: $X \sim L\acute{e}vy(\gamma, \delta)$ *if it has density*

$$f(x) = \sqrt{\frac{\gamma}{2\pi}} \frac{1}{(x-\delta)^{3/2}} e^{-\gamma/2(x-\delta)}, \quad \delta < x < \infty \tag{3.51}$$

The Lévy distribution has only *support in the positive domain* on the half line from δ to ∞. In terms of Zolotarev's formula, $Z(0.5,0) \sim L\acute{e}vy(1,0)$.

Both Gaussian and Cauchy distributions are symmetric, bell-shaped curves, but the Cauchy distribution has much heavier tails than the Gaussian distribution, i.e., the events further away from the mean are more likely to occur than under a Gaussian distribution. This is the reason why stable distributions other than the Gaussian are called *heavy tailed*. In contrast to both the Gaussian and Cauchy distributions, the Lévy distribution is highly skewed, with all the probability concentrated on $x > 0$, and it has an even heavier tail than the Cauchy distribution. General stable distributions allow for varying degrees of tail heaviness and varying degrees of skewness.

Table 3.1 demonstrates clearly the heavier tail probabilities of the Cauchy and Lévy distributions, compared to the tail probabilities of the Gaussian distribution.

Other than the Gaussian distribution, the Cauchy distribution, the Lévy distribution and the reflection of the Lévy distribution, there are no known closed form expressions for general stable densities and it is even unlikely that any other stable distributions, than the ones mentioned, have closed forms for their densities. Although there is no closed formula for the normal distribution function, there are numerical tables and accurate numerical computer algorithms for the standard distribution function (e.g., Mantegna, 1994). Financial analysts use such computed numerical values in normal models, e.g., for the

Table 3.1 Comparison of tail $P(X > c)$ probabilities

c	*Normal*	*Cauchy*	*Lévy*
0	0.5000	0.5000	1.0000
1	0.1587	0.2500	0.6827
2	0.0228	0.1476	0.5205
3	0.001347	0.1024	0.4363
4	0.00003167	0.0780	0.3829
5	0.0000002866	0.0628	0.3453

valuation of Black–Scholes options. Similarly, we have now also computer programs (like Nolan's STABLE.EXE software, available from his web site: http://www.cas.american.edu/~jpnolan/stable.html) to compute quantities of interest for stable distributions, so it is possible to use them in empirical problems, like the valuation of the risk in various assets and derivatives. Precise tabulations of the skewed stable distributions can be found in McCulloch and Panton (1997, 1998).

3.7　Stable parameter estimation and diagnostics

Nolan (1999b) discusses in detail the methods for estimating stable parameters from empirical data and the methods for model verification, i.e., how to assess whether the estimated stable parameters actually do a good job describing the empirical data.

3.7.1　Parameter computation

There are basically four methods of parameter computation:

(1) The computation of α_Z, β, γ and δ is usually performed by minimizing a distance function, (Mittnik *et al.*, 1998), like the Kolmogorov distance.

Definition 138　*Kolmogorov distance (KD):*

$$\rho = \sup_{x \in \mathbb{R}} |F(x) - \hat{F}_{\mathbf{S}}(x)| \tag{3.52}$$

where $F(x)$ is the empirical distribution and $\hat{F}_{\mathbf{S}}(x)$ the estimated distribution function for a particular parametrization **S**.

This method is used mostly when one is concerned about kurtosis.

(2) Alternatively, one maximizes numerically the so-called likelihood function of stable distributions.

Definition 139　Likelihood function (ML):

$$L(\alpha_Z, \beta, \gamma, \delta) = \prod_{t-1}^{T} \mathbf{S}(\alpha_Z, \beta; 0) \left(\frac{x - \delta}{\gamma} \right) \frac{1}{\gamma} \tag{3.53}$$

which is maximized with respect to the four parameters $\alpha_Z, \beta, \gamma, \delta$.

Under the i.i.d. assumptions the resulting estimates are consistent and asymptotically normal with the asymptotic covariance matrix given by the inverse of the usual Fisher information matrix, i.e., the matrix of second derivatives of the likelihood function evaluated at the ML point values (Mittnik *et al.*, 1996).

(3) The oldest method is the *quantile/fractile method* of Fama and Roll (1971) for the symmetric case and of McCulloch (1986) for the general

case. This method tries to match certain data quantiles with those of stable distributions.

(4) But the scientifically most convincing method is to compute the moments directly from the *empirical characteristic function*, as recommended by Nolan (1999a,b).

Nolan (1999b) provides many valuable applications of simulated data, exchange rate data, CRSP stock prices, Abbey National share prices, radar noise ocean wave energy, and simulated unstable data. Here, we reproduce Nolan's example of fitting stable distributions to exchange rate data.

Example 140 *Daily exchange rate data for 15 different currencies were recorded (in UK Pounds) over a 16-year period (January 2, 1980 to May 21, 1996). The data was logarithmically transformed by*

$$y(t) = \Delta \ln X(t + 1)$$
$$= \ln X(t + 1 - \ln X(t)) \tag{3.54}$$

giving $T = 4,274$ transformed data observations. The transformed data were fit with a stable distribution, using the maximum likelihood function method. The results, with 95 percent confidence intervals, are given in Figure 3.6. These empirical data are clearly not Gaussian: the heavy tails in the data cause the sample variance to be large, and the Gaussian fit poorly describes both the center and the tails of the distribution. Although the stable distribution fit does a reasonable job of describing the FX rate data, it never captures the extreme "peakedness" of FX rate data. With the stability or tail exponent $1 < \alpha_Z < 2$, we must conclude that although the mean of these daily FX returns exists, the variance is undefined and

Country	α	β	γ	δ
Australia	1.479 ± 0.047	0.033 ± 0.080	0.00413 ± 0.00013	-0.00015 ± 0.00022
Austria	1.559 ± 0.047	-0.119 ± 0.092	0.00285 ± 0.00009	0.00014 ± 0.00015
Belgium	1.473 ± 0.047	-0.061 ± 0.080	0.00306 ± 0.00010	0.00009 ± 0.00016
Canada	1.574 ± 0.047	-0.051 ± 0.093	0.00379 ± 0.00012	0.00004 ± 0.00020
Denmark	1.545 ± 0.047	-0.119 ± 0.090	0.00272 ± 0.00008	0.00022 ± 0.00014
France	1.438 ± 0.047	-0.146 ± 0.078	0.00245 ± 0.00008	0.00028 ± 0.00013
Germany	1.495 ± 0.047	-0.182 ± 0.085	0.00244 ± 0.00008	0.00019 ± 0.00013
Italy	1.441 ± 0.046	-0.043 ± 0.076	0.00266 ± 0.00009	0.00017 ± 0.00014
Japan	1.511 ± 0.047	-0.148 ± 0.086	0.00368 ± 0.00012	0.00013 ± 0.00019
The Netherlands	1.467 ± 0.047	-0.167 ± 0.081	0.00244 ± 0.00008	0.00016 ± 0.00013
Norway	1.533 ± 0.047	-0.070 ± 0.088	0.00253 ± 0.00008	0.00005 ± 0.00013
Spain	1.512 ± 0.047	-0.007 ± 0.083	0.00268 ± 0.00008	0.00012 ± 0.00014
Sweden	1.517 ± 0.047	-0.081 ± 0.085	0.00256 ± 0.00008	0.00006 ± 0.00013
Switzerland	1.599 ± 0.047	-0.179 ± 0.100	0.00295 ± 0.00009	0.00014 ± 0.00016
United States	1.530 ± 0.047	-0.088 ± 0.088	0.00376 ± 0.00012	0.00009 ± 0.00020

Figure 3.6 Estimates of four parameters of the Zolotarev parametrization of FX distributions.

thus also the fourth moment. In other words, the values of the variance and of the kurtosis of each of the FX series do not converge, but they "wander" aimlessly when more data are aggregated.[6] *In other words, the volatilities of these FX data are undefined and, therefore, cannot be priced or hedged by the usual pricing or hedging formulas! The currency with the heaviest tails ($\alpha = \alpha_Z = 1.441$) and thus most extreme outlying values was the Italian Lire, while the one with the lightest tails ($\alpha = \alpha_Z = 1.530$) was the Swiss Franc. Notice also that the Australian distribution was the only one in this period with a slight positive skewness ($\beta > 0$), indicating the depreciation of the Australian Dollar versus the UK Pound. All other currencies showed negative skewness ($\beta < 0$) and thus appreciated versus the UK Pound over the length of this 16-year period. For a similar, but earlier, set of daily foreign exchange data and their statistical properties, see Hsieh (1988).*

3.7.2   Diagnostics

In principle, it should be no surprise that one can fit the empirical data better with the four parameter stable distribution model than with the two parameter Gaussian model, since there are two more degrees of freedom available. But the relevant scientific question is whether or not the fitted stable distribution actually describes the empirical data well. In models of financial data, like rates of investment, stock prices or foreign exchange rates, we're interested in the whole distribution, and not only in the tails, even though risk sensitive financial managers may want to focus on the extreme values in these tails (Hols and DeVries, 1991), as we'll discuss in Chapter 12.

An important caveat is that non-Gaussian stable distributions are heavy-tailed distributions, but most heavy-tailed distributions are not stable, as we'll see in Chapters 4 and 5. In fact, *it is not possible to directly prove that a given empirical data set is or is not stable!* (Pincus and Kalman, 1997) Therefore, the elegance of the stable distributions may turn out to be irrelevant for empirical financial research, Gaussian or not, because of changes in the financial and economic situations over time that produce nonstationary, unstable time series, for which no definite stable distributions exist.

Even testing for normality or "Gaussianity" is still an active field of research and not as "cut and dried" as standard statistics and, in particular, econometrics textbooks (even in specialized textbooks such as Gourieroux and Jasiak, 2001) make it out to be! The best we can do at this point is to determine whether the data are consistent with the hypothesis of stability. But all these tests will fail if the departure from stability is small or occurs in an unobserved part of the range of observations. For example, it is found that because of the curvature (reflecting the degree of kurtosis) in the distribution functions, it is very difficult to compare the fitted and the empirical density functions visually, especially with respect to the (important) tails, where observations are, per definition, scarce.

3.8   Software

For more detailed information on stable distributions, papers and software, see John Nolan's expert web site at the American University:

http://academic2.american.edu/~jpnolan/stable/stable.html where you can find STABLE.EXE (900 KB) which calculates stable densities, cumulative distribution functions and quantiles, as well as Nolan's User Guide for STABLE Version 2.11. It also includes stable random number generation and maximum likelihood estimation of stable parameters using a fast three-dimensional cubic spline interpolation of stable densities. STABLE.TXT (16 KB) provides the description of the STABLE.EXE program.

Huston McCulloch of Ohio State University provides a stable distribution random number generator in the form of MATLAB® M - Files: STABRND.M: http://www.econ.ohio-state.edu/jhm/jhm.html.

3.9   Exercises

Exercise 141   *What does a power (scaling) law of price changes, or of cash rates of return on investments, mean in financial terms?*

Exercise 142   *With the four standard integer moments computed in the Exercises of Chapter 1, use Nolan's software program STABLE.EXE to numerically compute the marginal p.d.fs for each of the four data series. Try the two standardized parametrizations:* $S(\alpha_Z, \beta, \gamma, \delta; 0) = S(\alpha_Z, \beta; 0) = S0$ *and* $S(\alpha_Z, \beta, \gamma, \delta; 1) = S(\alpha_Z, \beta; 1) = S1$. *What's the difference between these two Zolotarev parametrizations?*

Exercise 143   *Are any of the four data series of the Exercises in Chapter 1 Gaussian? If not, what distributions do you suggest they represent and why?*

Exercise 144   *Looking at the plots produced in the second Exercise of Chapter 2, do all first four moments of these series exist? If, or if not, what does that imply?*

Exercise 145   *Use Nolan's software STABLE.EXE to generate, by the Chambers, Mallows and Stuck algorithm (corrected by Nolan), 1,000 stable random variates following the example in Nolan's User's Guide (initial random seed for the random number generator* $= -1$, $\alpha = \alpha_Z = 1.4$, $\beta = 0$, $\gamma = 1, \delta = 0$). *The output goes to a file STABLE.OUT, where it can be edited for other use (e.g., parameter estimation).*

Exercise 146   *Use STABLE.EXE to fit the S&P500 data series of* $X(t)$, $x(t) = \Delta \ln X(t)$ *and* $\Delta x(t)$ *of the Exercises of Chapter 1 with parameters using Maximum Likelihood estimation with the default ranges. A simple text file, e.g., 255.txt, works well as input file for this DOS-based program. You can check if your input file works by comparing the "Summary statistics for sample" of STABLE.EXE with the mean, standard deviation, coefficient of skewness and coefficient of kurtosis you've computed earlier in the Exercises of Chapter 1 (The EXCEL functions deliver slightly different values, because of their degrees of freedom corrections). Do exploratory analysis by making PP and QQ plots with confidence* *bounds, and by comparing the smoothed data distribution densities versus the fitted densities.*

Notes

1 An early user of such operator algebra was the famous Polish economist Oskar Lange, 1904–1965 (Lange, 1970). As a graduate student of Columbia University, I used such operator algebra in 1978 to solve the complex nonlinear growth system of Michael Kalecki (1945), to the delight of my economics lecturer Duncan Foley of Barnard College. Kalecki's dynamic mathematical system was more realistic, because it could model more complex nonstationary behavior, than Samuelson's more familiar, but much simpler accelerator-multiplier economic growth system, which can only model stationary behavior (i.e., trends, infinite sinusoidal waves, etc.) (Samuelson, 1947).

2 Vilfredo Pareto (1848–1923) was an Italian sociologist and professor of political economy at the University of Lausanne, Switzerland. In his book *Mind and Society* (1916; English translation, 1935), Pareto states that individuals act irrationally, but that mass action becomes more logical, the greater the number of individuals involved, because their desires and illusions cancel out. He thought that society, like physics, is a system of forces in equilibrium. Mathematics can therefore be applied to explain why the equilibrium holds, making a science of society possible. Unfortunately, Pareto's theory did not recognize that irrational behavior can also occur on a mass scale, e.g., like bubbles and catastrophes in the financial markets, and therefore his theory cannot account for crowd behavior. In 1897 he found that the distribution of incomes for individuals was approximately lognormally distributed for 97 percent of the population. But for the last 3 percent of the population incomes increased more sharply. We now know from finance theory why that is, because the more wealth one has, the more one can risk. The wealthy can *leverage* their wealth in ways the average, middle-income, individual cannot.

3 Other parametrizations are possible, but currently not as popular (cf. Rachev and Mittnik, 2000). In this book, which emphasizes concepts, definitions and empirical measurements of financial risk, all theorems, lemmas and propositions will be given without proof. Such mathematical proofs can be found in the references.

4 This unimodality, or "one-peakedness" of stable distributions is a potential shortcoming for research into empirical financial distributions, since some of them have been observed to be multi-modal. Multi-modality occurs, for example, in chaotic distributions.

5 These terms – white, pink and red noise – will be defined and discussed in greater detail in Chapter 4.

6 Interestingly, Nolan's (1999b) and Mittnik *et al.*'s (1999) measurements using the ML method and the implied conclusion regarding the nonconvergence of the variance of FX returns appears to conflict with the measurements by Müller *et al.* (1998). The Nolan–Mittnik measurements of α_Z are between 1.44 and 1.78. Müller *et al.* use the so-called bootstrap and jackknife methods and find values for the tail exponent α_Z between 3 and 5 for various US dollar exchange rates for various time intervals, suggesting that the second moment does converge. This inconsistency of the respective empirical measurements is not easily resolved. But my own α_Z measurements are compatible with the Nolan–Mittnik measurements (cf. chapter 8, section 8.42). Moreover the nonconvergence of the variance has been observed by myself and several other researchers. Perhaps, Müller *et al.* inverted the exponent and actually measured the homogeneous Lipschitz $\alpha_L = H$ (which will be discussed in Chapter 8). In that case their measured tail exponent is $1/3 = 1.33 \leq \alpha_Z \leq 2.00 = 1/5$ and, thus, much more in agreement with the (somewhat tighter) Nolan–Mittnik measurements of $1.44 \leq \alpha_Z \leq 1.78$. Both the physics and the

financial literature is full of confusion between the Lipschitz α_L and Zolotarev's tail or stability exponent α_Z, since most authors don't bother to index the α!

Bibliography

Adler, Robert J., Raisa E. Feldman and Colin Gallagher (1998) "Analyzing Stable Time Series," in Adler, Robert J., Raisa E. Feldman and Murad S. Taqqu (Eds) *A Practical Guide to Heavy Tails: Statistical Techniques and Applications*, Birkhäuser, Boston, MA, pp. 133–158.

Batten, Jonathan, Craig Ellis and Robert Mellor (1999) "Scaling Laws and Variance as a Measure of Long-Term Dependence," *International Review of Financial Analysis*, **8**(2), 123–139.

Boothe, P., and D. Glasserman (1987) "The Statistical Distribution of Exchange Rates, Empirical Evidence and Economic Implications," *Journal of International Economics*, **22**(3/4), 297–319.

Caldéron-Rossel, J. R., and M. Ben-Horim (1982) "The Behavior of Foreign Exchange Rates, Empirical Evidence and Economic Implications," *Journal of International Business Studies*, **13**(2), Fall 99–111.

Chobanov, G., P. Mateev, S. Mittnik and S. T. Rachev (1996) "Modeling the Distribution of Highly Volatile Exchange–Rate Time Series," in Robinson, P. *et al.* (Eds), *Time Series*, Springer Verlag, New York, NY, 1996, pp. 130–144.

Cont, R., M. Potters and J.-P. Bouchaud (1997) "Scaling in Stock Market Data: Stable Laws and Beyond, " in Dubrulle, B., F. Graner and D. Sornette (Eds) *Scale Invariance and Beyond*, Springer Verlag, Berlin, Germany.

Fama, Eugene F. (1963) "Mandelbrot and the Stable Paretian Hypothesis," *The Journal of Business*, **36**(4), 420–429.

Fama, Eugene F. (1965a) "The Behavior of Stock Market Prices," *Journal of Business*, **38**(1), 34–105.

Fama, Eugene F. (1965b) "Portfolio Analysis in a Stable Paretian Market," *Management Science*, **11**(A, 3), 404–419.

Fama, Eugene F., and R. Roll (1971) "Parameter Estimates for Symmetric Stable Distributions," *Journal of the American Statistical Association*, **66**(334), 331–338.

Friend, I., and R. Westerfield (1980) "Co-Skewedness and Capital Asset Pricing, " *Journal of Finance*, **35**(4), 897–913.

Gnedenko, B. V., and A. N. Kolmogorov (1954) *Limit Distributions for Sums of Independent Random Variables*, Addison-Wesley, Cambridge, MA.

Gopikrishnan, P., M. Meyer, L. A. N. Amaral and H. E. Stanley (1998) "Inverse Cubic Law for the Distribution of Stock Price Variations," *European Physics Journal*, B, **3**, 139–140.

Gourieroux, Christian, and Joann Jasiak (2001) *Financial Econometrics: Problems, Models and Methods*, Princeton University Press, Princeton, NJ.

Hols, M. C., and C. C. DeVries (1991) "The Limiting Distribution of Extremal Exchange Rate Returns," *Journal of Applied Econometrics*, **6**(3), 287–302.

Hsieh, D. A. (1988) "The Statistical Properties of Daily Foreign Exchange Rates: 1974–83," *Journal of International Economics*, **35**(1/2), 129–145.

Hsu, D., R. Miller and D. Wichern (1974) "On the Stable Paretian Character of Stock Market Prices," *Journal of the American Statistical Association*, **69**(345), 108–113.

Janicki, A., and A. Weron (1994) *Simulation and Chaotic Behavior of a Stable Stochastic Processes*, Marcel Dekker, New York, NY.

Jackwerth, J. C., and M. Rubinstein (1996) "Recovering Probability Distributions from Options Prices," *Journal of Finance*, **51**(5), 1611–1631.

Kalecki, Michael (1945) *Kapitalizm, Koniunktura i Zatrudnienie (Capitalism, Business Cycles and Full Employment*, edited by Osiatynsky, Jerzy, and translated by Kisiel, Chester Adam), Oxford University Press, New York, NY, 1990.

Kraus, A., and R. H. Litzenberger (1976) "Skewness Preference and the Valuation of Risk Assets," *Journal of Finance*, **31**(4), 1085–1100.

Lange, Oskar (1970) *Introduction to Economic Cybernetics*, edited by Banasiński, Antoni, and translated by Stadler, Józef, Pergamon Press, Oxford, UK.

Lévy, Paul (1925) *Calcul des Probabilités*, Gathier-Villars, Paris, France.

Los, Cornelis A. (1999) "Nonparametric Testing of the High-Frequency Efficiency of the 1997 Asian Foreign Exchange Markets," *Journal of Multinational Financial Management*, **9**(3–4), 265–289.

Los, Cornelis A. (2000) "Nonparametric Efficiency Testing of Asian Foreign Exchange Markets," in Abu-Mostafa, Yaser S., Blake LeBaron, Andrew W. Lo and Andreas S. Weigend (Eds) *Computational Finance 1999*, MIT Press, Cambridge, MA, 2000, pp. 229–245.

Los, Cornelis A. (2001) *Computational Finance: A Scientific Perspective*, World Scientific Publishing Co., Singapore.

Mandelbrot, Benoit B. (1962) "Sur Certain Prix Spéculatifs: Faits Empiriques et Modèle Basé sur les Processes Stables Additifs de Paul Lévy," ("About Some Speculative Prices: Empirical Facts and Model Based on the Stable Additive Processes of Paul Lévy"), *Comptes Rendus*, **254**, 3968–3970.

Mandelbrot, Benoit B. (1963a) "New Methods in Statistical Economics," *Journal of Political Economy*, **71**, 421–440.

Mandelbrot, Benoit B. (1963b) "The Variation of Certain Speculative Prices," *The Journal of Business*, **36**, 394–419, and **45**, 1972, 542–543. Reprinted as chapter E14, with annotations and corrections, in *Fractals and Scaling in Finance: Discontinuity, Concentration, Risk*, Springer Verlag, New York, 1997, pp. 371–418.

Mandelbrot, Benoit B. (1963c) "The Stable Paretian Income Distribution, when the Apparent Exponent is Near Zero," *International Economic Review*, **4**, 111–115.

Mandelbrot, Benoit B. (1966) "Forecasts of Future Prices, Unbiased Markets and Martingale Models," *The Journal of Business*, **39**(1), January (Special Supplement), 242–255.

Mantegna, Rosario N., (1994) "Fast, Accurate Algorithm for Numerical Simulation of Lévy Stable Stochastic Processes," *Physics Review*, E, **49**, 4677–4683.

Mantegna, Rosario N., and H. Eugene Stanley (1995) "Scaling Behavior in the Dynamics of an Economic Index," *Nature*, **376**, 46–49.

Mantegna, Rosario N., and H. Eugene Stanley (2000) *An Introduction to Econophysics: Correlations and Complexity in Finance*, Cambridge University Press, Cambridge, UK.

Markowitz, Harry M. (1952) "Portfolio Selection," *Journal of Finance*, **7**(1), 77–91.

Markowitz, Harry M. (1991; original 1959) "Portfolio Selection": Efficient Diversification of Investments, 2nd edn, Basil Blackwell, Cambridge, MA.

McCulloch, J. H. (1986) "Simple Consistent Estimators of Stable Distribution Parameters," *Communications in Statistics – Computation and Simulation*, **15**(4), 1109–1136.

McCulloch, J. H. (1996) "Financial Applications of Stable Distributions," in Maddala, G. S., and C. R. Rao (Eds) *Handbook of Statistics, Statistical Methods in Finance*, **14**, pp. 393–425, Elsevier Science B. V., Amsterdam, The Netherlands.

McCulloch, J. Huston, and Don B. Panton (1997) "Precise Tabulation of the Maximally-Skewed Stable Distributions and Densities," *Computational Statistics and Data Analysis*, **23**, 307–320.

McCulloch, J. Huston, and Don B. Panton (1998) "Table of the Maximally-Skewed Stable Distributions," in Robert Adler, Raya Feldman and Murad Taqqu (Eds) *A Practical*

Guide to Heavy Tails: Statistical Techniques for Analyzing Heavy Tailed Distributions, Birkhäuser, 1998, pp. 501–507.

McFarland, J. W., R. R. Petit and S. K. Sung (1982) "The Distribution of Foreign Exchange Price Changes: Trading Day Effects and Risk Measurement," *The Journal of Finance*, **37**(3), 693–715.

Melick, W. R., and C. P. Thomas (1997) "Recovering an Asset's Implied Probability Density Function from Options Prices: An Application to Crude Oil During the Gulf Crisis," *Journal of Financial and Quantitative Analysis*, **32**(1), 91–115.

Mittnik, Stefan, and Svetlozar T. Rachev (1993a) "Modeling Asset Returns with Alternative Stable Distributions," *Econometric Reviews*, **12**(3), 261–330.

Mittnik, Stefan, and Svetlozar T. Rachev (1993b) "Reply to Comments on 'Modeling Asset Returns with Alternative Stable Distributions' and Some Extensions," *Econometric Reviews*, **12**(3), 347–389.

Mittnik, Stefan, Svetlozar T. Rachev, T. Doganoglu and D. Chenyao (1996) "Maximum Likelihood Estimation of Stable Paretian Models," Working Paper, Institute of Statistics and Econometrics, Christian Albrechts University, Kiel, Germany.

Mittnik, Stefan, Svetlozar T. Rachev and Marc S. Paolella (1998) "Stable Paretian Modeling in Finance," in Adler, Robert J., Raisa E. Feldman and Murad S. Taqqu (Eds) *A Practical Guide to Heavy Tails: Statistical Techniques and Applications*, Birkhäuser, Boston, MA, pp. 79–110.

Müller, Ulrich A., Michel A. Dacorogna and Olivier V. Pictet (1998) "Heavy Tails in High-Frequency Financial Data," in Adler, Robert J., Raisa E. Feldman and Murad S. Taqqu (Eds) *A Practical Guide to Heavy Tails: Statistical Techniques and Applications*, Birkhäuser, Boston, MA, pp. 55–77.

Müller, Ulrich A., Michel A. Dacorogna, R. B. Olsen, Olivier V. Pictet, M. Schwarz and C. Morgenegg (1990) "Statistical Study of Foreign Exchange Rates, Empirical Evidence of a Price Change Scaling Law and Intraday Analysis," *Journal of Banking and Finance*, **14**(6), 1189–1208.

Nolan, John (1999a) "Basic Properties of Univariate Stable Distributions," chapter 1 in *Stable Distributions*, American University, 30 pages.

Nolan, John (1999b) "Fitting Data and Assessing Goodness-of-Fit with Stable Distributions," Working Paper, American University, 52 pages.

Pareto, Vilfredo (1897) *Cours d' Économie Politique*, Lausanne, CH and Paris, France.

Pareto, Vilfredo (1916; English translation 1935) *The Mind and Society*, Harcourt, New York, NY.

Peters, Edgar E. (1994) *Fractal Market Analysis*, John Wiley and Sons, New York, NY.

Pincus, Steve, and Rudolf E. Kalman (1997) "Not All (Possibly) 'Random' Sequences Are Created Equal," *Proceedings of the National Academy of Sciences USA*, **94**(8), 3513–3518.

Rachev, Svetlozar, and Stefan Mittnik (2000) *Stable Paretian Models in Finance*, John Wiley and Sons, New York, NY.

Samorodnitsky, G., and M. Taqqu (1994) *Stable Non-Gaussian Random Processes: Stochastic Models with Infinite Variance*, Chapman and Hall, New York, NY.

Samuelson, Paul (1947) *Foundations of Economic Analysis*, Harvard University Press, Cambridge, MA.

Sharpe, William F. (1966) "Mutual Fund Performance," *Journal of Business*, **39**(1), Supplement, 119–139.

Zolotarev, V. (1986) *One-Dimensional Stable Distributions*, American Mathematical Society, Providence, RI.

4 Persistence of financial risk

4.1 Introduction

In this chapter we focus on the issue of serial and global, or short-term and long-term, *temporal dependence* among asset returns, irrespective of the stable marginal frequency distributions discussed in Chapter 3.

For example, speculative market returns (and other financial and economic time series) tend to be characterized by the presence of aperiodic cycles of all conceivable "periods" of uncertain length – short, medium and long – where "long" means comparable up the length of the total available data set, and where the distinction between "long cycles" and "trends" is very fuzzy (Mandelbrot, 1972). Consider, for example, the business cycles in the United States which used to have, more or less defined, "periods" of somewhere between 3.5 and 10 years (Moore, 1980). In fact, the most recent business "cycle" in the United States had an expansion phase of about 12 years, from 1989–2001 and is one of the longest on record!

Although cyclical behavior of time series produced by economic models has been extensively studied, efforts to characterize the structure of actual empirical financial-economic time series has been minimal. The exceptions were the elegant and heroic efforts by Granger and Morgenstern (1963) and Granger (1966), who tried to characterize stationary time series of stock market prices by spectral analysis and who attempted to determine the "typical spectral shape of economic variables."[1] Similar spectral analysis of stationary and of nonstationary series will be presented in Chapter 5, when we discuss Fourier Transforms and Windowed Fourier Transforms, respectively. We'll have to understand these classical techniques to analyze stationary and semi-stationary financial time series first, before we can advance to the current technology of wavelet multiresolution analysis, also called multi-scale decomposition, to analyze nonstationary and unstable financial time series, which are not even convergent in their lower-order moments, and to analyze series of singularities.

4.2 Serial dependence

4.2.1 Mixing random processes

One way to describe serial, "weak," or short-term time dependence is that of *strong-mixing* processes. Informally, *mixing processes* are processes that gradually "mix" with new information, i.e., that gradually "forget" their initial conditions over time. In particular, a process is strong-mixing if the maximal dependence between any two events at two different dates becomes trivially small as the time span between these two dates increases. By controlling the rate at which this dependence between past and future events declines, it is possible to extend the usual laws of large numbers and the central limit theorems from sequences of independent random variables to sequences of dependent random variables. A formal definition of a strong-mixing random process is as follows.

Definition 147 (Strong-mixing process) *Let the random process* $\{X(t)\}$ *be defined on the probability space* $(\Omega, \mathcal{G}, P)$ *and define the distance measure:*

$$\gamma(\mathcal{A}, \mathcal{B}) \equiv \sup_{A \in \mathcal{A}, B \in \mathcal{B}} (|P(A \cap B - P(A)P(B)|), \mathcal{A} \subset \mathcal{G}, \mathcal{B} \subset \mathcal{G} \tag{4.1}$$

The quantity $\gamma(\mathcal{A}, \mathcal{B})$ *is a measure of the dependence between the two* σ-*algebras* $\mathcal{A}$ *and* $\mathcal{B}$ *in the measurable set* $\mathcal{G}$. *Denote by* $\mathcal{B}_s^t$ *the* σ-*algebra generated by the sequence* $\{X_s(\omega), \ldots, X_t(\omega)\}$, *i.e.,* $\mathcal{B}_s^t \equiv \sigma(X_s(\omega), \ldots, X_t(\omega)) \subset \mathcal{G}$. *Define the quantities*

$$\gamma(\tau) \equiv \sup \gamma(\mathcal{B}_{-\infty}^t, \mathcal{B}_{t+\tau}^\infty) \tag{4.2}$$

The random process $\{X(t)\}$ *is said to be* strong-mixing *if*

$$\lim_{\tau \to \infty} \gamma(\tau) = 0 \tag{4.3}$$

Such strong-mixing conditions are satisfied by all finite-order stationary auto-regressive moving average (ARMA) models. These ARMA models can all be transformed into stable Markov processes, as we will now demonstrate.

4.2.2 *Markov and finite-order ARMA processes*

The first efforts to characterize oscillatory behavior with exact periodicity was by postulating second- and higher-order affine Markov processes and their directly related cousins, the Box-Jenkins type ARMA models (Box and Jenkins, 1970; Anderson, 1994). Markov models provide only for short-term, or serial, time dependence. These models are identified by using autocovariance function analysis, or by using its cousin, spectral analysis, both to be discussed in detail in Chapter 5.

Definition 148 *The* first-order Markov process *is defined by*

$$X(t) = a_1 X(t-1) + \varepsilon(t)$$
$$= a_1 L X(t) + \varepsilon(t), \quad with\ \varepsilon(t) \sim i.i.d.(0, \sigma_\varepsilon^2) \tag{4.4}$$

which can also be written with the lag operator L *(cf. Chapter 3) as*

$$(1 - a_1 L)X(t) = \varepsilon(t), \quad with\ \varepsilon(t) \sim i.i.d.(0, \sigma_\varepsilon^2) \tag{4.5}$$

This first-order Markov process is stable when $0 < a_1 < 1$. The Random Walk is a first-order Markov process, which is marginally unstable (and has in the limit an infinite variance), since $a_1 = 1$. An unstable and geometrically exploding first-order Markov process has $1 < a_1$. This is easy to confirm, since this first-order autoregressive AR(1) Markov process $X(t)$ can also be viewed as an infinite-order moving average (MA) process with an infinite memory:

$$X(t) = \frac{1}{(1 - a_1 L)} \varepsilon(t)$$

$$= (1 + a_1 L + a_1^2 L^2 + a_1^3 L^3 + \cdots) \varepsilon(t)$$

$$= \left(1 + \sum_j a_1^j L^j\right) \varepsilon(t), \quad \text{with } \varepsilon(t) \sim \text{i.i.d.}(0, \sigma_\varepsilon^2) \tag{4.6}$$

When $0 < a_1 < 1$, the $\lim_{j \to \infty} \sum_j a_1^j L^j = q$ exists, where $0 < q < \infty$ is a real constant. Thus, in the limit, $\sigma_X^2 = (1 + q)^2 \sigma_\varepsilon^2$ is a finite (equilibrium) variance and over time the financial market risk remains bounded and is stable. When $1 \leq a_1$, the limit diverges, $\lim_{j \to \infty} \sum a_1^j L^j \to \infty$, and, in the limit, the variance of $X(t)$ is unbounded, $\lim \sigma_X^2 \to \infty$. The financial market risk diverges: in the limit the financial risk of $X(t)$ becomes unbounded and infinite.

But first-order Markov processes are too simple processes to describe financial pricing processes. Financial pricing processes are characterized by uncertain "periodicity," i.e., by oscillatory behavior of some sort, although without fixed periods. For such uncertain "periodicity" one needs at least second- to fourth-order Markov processes, or more likely, nonlinear processes.[2]

Definition 149   *The second-order Markov process is defined by*

$$(1 - a_1 L - a_2 L^2) X(t) = \varepsilon(t), \quad \text{with } \varepsilon(t) \sim \text{i.i.d.}(0, \sigma_\varepsilon^2) \tag{4.7}$$

Remark 150   *From straightforward solution analysis of quadratic equations we know that this second-order Markov process is stable when* $(a_1^2 - 4a_2) > 0$; *it is oscillatory* (= *showing strict periodic behavior*), *when* $(a_1^2 - 4a_2) < 0$; *and is unstable when* $(a_1^2 - 4a_2) = 0$.

Such higher-order Markov processes are easier to represent in a generic fashion in vector-matrix notation, as follows.

Definition 151   *The n-order Markov process is defined by*

$$\mathbf{x}(t) = \mathbf{A}\mathbf{x}(t-1) + \varepsilon(t), \quad \text{with } \varepsilon(t) = \begin{bmatrix} \varepsilon_1(t) \\ 0 \end{bmatrix} \quad \text{and} \quad \varepsilon_1(t) \sim \text{i.i.d.}(0, \sigma_\varepsilon^2) \tag{4.8}$$

where $\mathbf{x}(t)$ *is a* $(n \times 1)$ *vector and* $\mathbf{A}$ *a* $(n \times n)$ *matrix, which can also be written with the lag operator as*

$$(\mathbf{I} - \mathbf{A}L)\mathbf{x}(t) = \varepsilon(t) \quad \text{with } \varepsilon(t) = \begin{bmatrix} \varepsilon_1(t) \\ \mathbf{0} \end{bmatrix} \quad \text{and} \quad \varepsilon_1(t) \sim i.i.d.(0, \sigma_\varepsilon^2)$$

(4.9)

Example 152 *For* $n = 3$, *a third-order autoregressive* $AR(p, q) = AR(3, 0)$ *process can be written in such vector matrix notation as*

$$\mathbf{x}(t) = \begin{bmatrix} x(t) \\ x(t-1) \\ x(t-2) \end{bmatrix}$$

$$= \mathbf{A}\mathbf{x}(t-1) + \varepsilon(t)$$

$$= \begin{bmatrix} a_1 & a_2 & a_3 \\ 1 & 0 & 0 \\ 0 & 1 & 0 \end{bmatrix} \begin{bmatrix} x(t-1) \\ x(t-2) \\ x(t-3) \end{bmatrix} + \begin{bmatrix} \varepsilon_1(t) \\ 0 \\ 0 \end{bmatrix}$$

$$= a_1 x(t-1) + a_2 x(t-2) + a_3 x(t-3) + \varepsilon_1(t) \qquad (4.10)$$

with $\varepsilon_1(t) \sim i.i.d.(0, \sigma_\varepsilon^2)$.

Again, the behavior of this random process depends on the spectral analysis of the actual values of the $\mathbf{A}$-matrix, in particular, the parameters a_1, a_2 and a_3, which are to be determined from the A.cf. If the determinant

$$|\mathbf{A}| = \prod_{i=1}^{n} \lambda_i < 1 \qquad (4.11)$$

then the process is stable or *implosive*; if $|\mathbf{A}| = 1$, it is *marginally stable*; and if $|\mathbf{A}| > 1$, the process is unstable or *explosive*.

Remark 153 *Even more general Markov processes can be described by this type of model when the innovations are covarying, e.g.,* $\varepsilon(t) \sim i.i.d.(0, \Sigma)$, *with* $\Sigma > \mathbf{0}$, *a positive definite* $(n \times n)$ *matrix. Such general Markov processes form the basic random system structure for the Kalman filter, which tracks nonstationary processes* $\mathbf{x}(t)$ *(including unstable ones!) with time-varying covariance risk matrices symptomatic for the conditional heteroskedasticity of G(ARCH) processes to be discussed in Section 4.4.*[3]

4.3 Global dependence

However, financial and economic time series do not exhibit exact periodicity, or even uncertain periodicity; they exhibit distinct *aperiodic cyclicity*. In the frequency domain such time series are said to have risk (= power) at low frequencies.

Financial time series, in particular, exhibit such aperiodic cyclicity, or periods of relative stability, followed by periods of great turbulence. Such diverse behavior with periods of great intensity of uncertain movement followed by periods of low intensity of movement, where the periods are not well defined, is called *intermittency*. Intermittency is a property of nonlinear dynamic processes which are close to complete chaos, as discussed in Chapter 9.

While the occurrence of sharp discontinuities in the otherwise trend-wise financial and economic time series is called the "Noah effect" by Mandelbrot (1965), an appropriate reference to the Old Testamental catastrophic Flood, long-term aperiodic cyclicity is called the "Joseph Effect " by Mandelbrot and Wallis (1969). This is an appropriate biblical reference to the Old Testament prophet, who foretold of the seven years of plenty followed by the seven years of famine that Egypt was to experience. This cyclical phenomenon was explained by the long-term aperiodic, but somehow cyclical behavior of the water flows of the river Nile, which brought some time intervals of fertile sediment and thus rich harvests, followed by intervals of drought, no sediments and consequently poor harvests in Egypt. This aperiodic cyclic behavior of the Nile's floodwaters has been carefully analyzed by Harold Edwin Hurst, the British hydrologist in the 1950s.[4]

Hurst, who is known in Egypt as the "Father of the Nile," studied the behavior of the Nile's water level to determine the height and mass of the Aswan dam to be built by the Russians. In the process, he designed a new and powerful statistical measure, the "range-over-standard deviation," or R/S measure, to quantify such aperiodic cyclical persistence of floodwater levels. We will define this R/S measure and relate it to various exponents measuring the irregularity (= "randomness") of financial-economic time series.

4.3.1   Long-term persistence of speculative prices

Optimal consumption, savings, portfolio and hedging decisions may become extremely sensitive to investment horizons τ_i, when the investment returns are long-term time dependent, i.e., when they show long memory properties. Problems may also arise in the pricing of derivative securities (such as options and futures) with Fama's martingale methods, since the theoretical continuous-time random processes most commonly employed, e.g., Geometric Brownian Motions (GBMs), are inconsistent with such empirical long-term memory effects.

In such circumstances, traditional tests of the Capital Asset Pricing Model (CAPM) and Arbitrage Pricing Theory (APT) are no longer valid, since the usual forms of statistical inference do not apply to time series exhibiting long-term persistence (Lo and MacKinlay, 1988, 1999). Mandelbrot (1971) was the first to consider the implications of such persistent statistical dependence in asset returns in terms of the limitations of Fama's martingale model. This particular line of research has acquired a greater urgency in the 1990s, when the frequency of occurrence of financial crises appeared to increase and financial analysts and traders became more aware of such aperiodic cyclicity and intermittency.

The question arises: are such cycles of *condensation* and *rarefaction*, i.e., of financial crises, which interrupt periods of relative tranquility, predictable, or are such cycles essentially unpredictable? We'll defer a response to that crucial, but difficult question to Chapters 9–11.

4.3.2   *Fractionally differenced (ARFIMA) time series*

We will now introduce a theoretical model, which can represent such long-term time dependence and aperiodic cyclicity. Fractional Brownian Motion (FBM) is a nonstationary process with infinite time span of temporal dependence. *Fractional difference processes* were originally proposed by Mandelbrot and Van Ness (1968). But Hosking (1981) extended the range of these models in the form of *Autoregressive Fractionally Integrated Moving Average* or ARFIMA(p, d, q) models, with fractional $d \in \mathbb{R}$, where short-term, or serial, frequency effects are superimposed on the long-term, global, or long memory processes.[5] These fractionally differenced, respectively integrated, random processes are not strong-mixing. They are nonstationary, but have a risk spectrum with a *power law decay*. The autocorrelation functions (ACFs) of long memory or globally dependent processes decay at much slower rates than the better known and more intensely studied ACFs of serially dependent processes.[6]

Definition 154   *A fractionally differenced process is defined by*

$$(1 - L)^d X(t) = \varepsilon(t), \quad \text{with } \varepsilon(t) \sim i.i.d.(0, \sigma_\varepsilon^2) \tag{4.12}$$

where L is the lag operator and $0 < d < 1$ is a fraction $\in \mathbb{R}$ and $\varepsilon(t)$ is some sort of shock or innovation.

Remark 155   *When the $d < 0$ is a fraction $\in \mathbb{R}$, we have a* fractionally integrated *process of order d.*

Since the expression $(1 - L)^d$ can be expanded via the binomial theorem for fractional d powers, we have the general AR process (Lo and MacKinley, 1999):

$$(1 - L)^d X(t) = \left[\sum_{\tau=0}^{\infty} (-1)^\tau \binom{d}{\tau} L^\tau \right] X(t)$$

$$= \sum_{\tau=0}^{\infty} a(\tau) X(t - \tau)$$

$$= \varepsilon(t), \quad \text{with } \varepsilon(t) \sim i.i.d.(0, \sigma_\varepsilon^2) \tag{4.13}$$

where the AR coefficients

$$a(\tau) = (-1)^\tau \binom{d}{\tau} \tag{4.14}$$

are often re-expressed in terms of the gamma function $\Gamma(u)$ as follows.

Definition 156   *The gamma function $\Gamma(u)$ is defined by*

$$\Gamma(u) = \int_0^\infty x^{u-1} e^{-x} dx \qquad (4.15)$$

Integration by parts and iterated substitution gives the following important result

$$
\begin{aligned}
\Gamma(u+1) &= u\Gamma(u) \\
&= u(u-1)\Gamma(u-1) \\
&= u(u-1)(u-2)\Gamma(u-2) \\
&= u(u-1)(u-2)\cdots\Gamma(1) \\
&= u! \text{ for } u \text{ a positive integer} \qquad (4.16)
\end{aligned}
$$

since $\Gamma(1) = 1$.

Thus, we have for the AR coefficients:

$$
\begin{aligned}
a(\tau) &= (-1)^\tau \binom{d}{\tau} \\
&= (-1)^\tau \frac{d!}{\tau!(d-\tau)!} \\
&= (-1)^\tau \frac{d(d-1)\cdots(d-\tau+1)}{\tau!} \\
&= \frac{(\tau-d-1)\cdots(1-d)(-d)}{\tau!} \\
&= \frac{(\tau-d-1)!}{(-d-1)!\tau!} \\
&= \frac{\Gamma(\tau-d)}{\Gamma(-d)\Gamma(\tau+1)} \qquad (4.17)
\end{aligned}
$$

As the time horizon increases, $\tau \to \infty$, proportionally,

$$a(\tau) \sim \frac{\tau^{-d-1}}{(-d-1)!} \qquad (4.18)$$

Following Box and Jenkins (1970) and Anderson (1994), we can also view the AR process as an infinite-order MA process, since

$$
\begin{aligned}
X(t) &= (1-L)^{-d}\varepsilon(t) \\
&= \sum_{\tau=0}^\infty b(\tau)\varepsilon(t-\tau), \quad \text{with } \varepsilon(t) \sim \text{i.i.d.}(0, \sigma_\varepsilon^2) \qquad (4.19)
\end{aligned}
$$

where the MA coefficients $b(\tau)$ can also be expressed in terms of the gamma function

$$
\begin{aligned}
b(\tau) &= (-1)^\tau \begin{pmatrix} -d \\ \tau \end{pmatrix} \\
&= \frac{(\tau + d - 1)!}{(d-1)!\tau!} \\
&= \frac{\Gamma(\tau + d)}{\Gamma(d)\Gamma(\tau + 1)}
\end{aligned}
\tag{4.20}
$$

as can be checked by following the preceding steps with $-d$ substituted for d.

As the time horizon increases, $\tau \to \infty$, proportionally,

$$
b(\tau) \sim \frac{\tau^{d-1}}{(d-1)!}
\tag{4.21}
$$

Viewed this MA way, any time series $X(t)$, even a fractionally integrated one, can thus be represented as a summation (integration) of white noise $\varepsilon(t)$.

We can characterize such AR and MA processes by their *ACF*.

Definition 157 *The* (non-normalized) ACF *of* $x(t)$ *is defined by the integral*

$$
\begin{aligned}
\gamma(\tau) &= \int_{-\infty}^{\infty} x(t)x(t - \tau)dt \\
&= \int_{-\infty}^{\infty} x(t)L^\tau x(t)dt
\end{aligned}
\tag{4.22}
$$

ACFs and their Fourier Transforms (= risk spectra) will be discussed in greater detail in Chapter 5.[7] The ACFs of these long-term dependent random processes decay so slowly that for the case of *persistence*, when $d < 0$, the sum of the AR coefficients $a(\tau)$ diverges to infinity (= the financial market risk of investment returns increases) and for the case of *antipersistence*, when $d > 0$, their sum collapses to zero (= the financial market risk of investment returns vanishes). Of course, for the MA $b(\tau)$ coefficients the reverse is true. The main empirical research question is: how fast does financial risk divergence to infinity or financial risk convergence to zero occur?

In the next section, we'll discuss this persistence and antipersistence of random (investment return) processes in terms of a variety of (Lipschitz) exponents. First, we need the definitions of regularly and slowly varying functions to be able to define the important concept of long-term time dependence, which we have used thus far in a rather loose fashion, but which now needs to be rigorously defined.

Definition 158   *A function $f(x)$ is said to be* regularly varying at infinity *with index λ if*

$$\lim_{\tau \to \infty} \frac{f(\tau x)}{f(x)} = x^\lambda \quad \text{for all } x > 0 \tag{4.23}$$

i.e., if it behaves asymptotically as a power function. When $\lambda = 0$, the function $f(x)$ is said to be slowly varying at infinity, *since it behaves like a "constant" for a large horizon τ.*

We have finally arrived at the central definition of the first part of this book: the definition of a long-term time dependent random process. This random process figures now prominently in the financial literature concerned with the measurement of the efficiency and the microstructure of financial markets (cf. Lo and MacKinlay, 1999).

Definition 159   *A* long-term dependent *random process is a process with an ACF $\gamma(\tau)$, such that*

$$\gamma(\tau) = \begin{cases} \tau^\lambda H(\tau) & \text{for } \lambda \in [-1, 0), \text{ or} \\ -\tau^\lambda H(\tau) & \text{for } \lambda \in (-2, -1] \end{cases} \tag{4.24}$$

as the time interval lengthens, $\tau \to \infty$, where $H(\tau)$ is any slowly varying function at infinity.

As we will see in the next chapter, the ACF of the aforementioned fractionally differenced time series, when $\varepsilon(t) \sim$ i.i.d.$(0, \sigma_\varepsilon^2)$ is given by:

$$\gamma(\tau) = \frac{(-1)^\tau (-2d)!}{\tau!(-2d - \tau)!}$$
$$\sim \sigma_\varepsilon^2 \tau^{2d-1} \quad \text{as } \tau \to \infty \tag{4.25}$$

where $d \in (-\frac{1}{2}, \frac{1}{2})$. Thus, asymptotically, this ACF is *slowly decaying*.

We have now three important cases of noise processing in the financial markets:

(1) When $d \downarrow -\frac{1}{2}$, the market fractionally differentiates white noise $\varepsilon(t)$ and its ACF converges to $\gamma(\tau) \sim \sigma_\varepsilon^2 \tau^{-2}$, twice as fast as a hyperbolic decay. The market representing FBM produces an *antipersistent* financial time series.

(2) When $d = 0$, the market processes just white noise $\varepsilon(t)$, and its ACF converges to $\gamma(\tau) \sim \sigma_\varepsilon^2 \tau^{-1}$, a simple hyperbolic decay. The market representing FBM integrates the white noise once and produces thereby a neutrally persistent or *brown noise* financial time series.

(3) When $d \uparrow \frac{1}{2}$, the market fractionally integrates white noise $\varepsilon(t)$ and its ACF converges to $\gamma(\tau) \sim \sigma_\varepsilon^2$, a constant. The market representing FBM produces a *persistent* financial time series.

Remark 160 *One can measure these exponents by taking logarithms at both sides of the proportionality sign $\sim$:*

$$\ln \gamma(\tau) = (2d - 1) \ln \tau + \ln \sigma_\varepsilon^2 + \ln C \tag{4.26}$$

for any constant C. The empirically measured slope $(2d - 1)$ in this double-logarithmic picture provides us with the value of the differentiation exponent d.

ACFs, Fourier Transforms and spectral densities will be discussed in detail in Chapter 5, but, for the purpose of comparison, we already present here the spectral density of the fractionally-differenced time series at frequencies close to zero. The spectral density is the Fourier Transform of its ACF:

$$
\begin{aligned}
P(\omega) &\cong \sigma_\varepsilon^2 (1 - e^{-j\omega})^{-d} (1 - e^{j\omega})^{-d} \\
&\sim \sigma_\varepsilon^2 \omega^{-2d} \\
&= \sigma_\varepsilon^2 \omega^{-\upsilon} \quad \text{as } \omega \to 0
\end{aligned}
\tag{4.27}
$$

The spectral density $P(\omega)$ will be either infinite, as the frequencies approach zero, $\omega \to 0$, when $d > 0$: we differentiate the time series $X(t)$, c.q., we integrate white noise $\varepsilon(t)$. Or, the opposite is true and the spectral density is zero, as the frequencies approach zero, $\omega \to 0$, when $d < 0$: we integrate the time series $X(t)$, c.q., differentiate the white noise $\varepsilon(t)$. The exponent $\upsilon = 2d$ is called the *spectral exponent*.

Before we continue with our favorite model, the FBM model, we'll discuss now first some strong, and popular, contenders of the FBM: the (G)ARCH processes. We will demonstrate that the FBM dominates the GARCH model in representing long-term time dependence.

4.4 (G)ARCH processes

As we discussed in Chapters 1 and 2, there is strong empirical and theoretical evidence that the second moment, or variance, of the rates of return on financial assets are time-dependent random processes (cf. Nelson, 1991). The ARCH (= Auto-Regressive Conditional Heteroskedastic) processes, introduced by Engle (1982) are the only plausible alternative to fractal distributions and fractionally differenced time-series. ARCH processes appear to fit the empirical data of stock returns, interest rates, inflation rates and foreign exchange rates, since they can have sharp modes and fat tails, i.e., they can exhibit different degrees of leptokurtis for the same variances. Bollerslev (1986) generalizes the ARCH model further to GARCH (= Generalized ARCH) and IGARCH (= Integrated GARCH) models. Although ARCH models cannot explain correctly the measured long-term time dependence phenomena, the IGARCH models do a better, although still not perfect, job of explaining them, because of the incorporation of a unit root, i.e., a marginally stable process. For a promotional overview of ARCH models in finance, cf. Bollerslev *et al.* (1994), the collection of articles by Engle (1995) and Bollerslev *et al.* (1998).

4.4.1   Statistical properties of ARCH processes

ARCH models describe random processes, which are *locally nonstationary*, but *asymptotically stationary*. This implies that the parameters of its conditional p.d.f. are time-varying. Still the random process has a well-defined asymptotic p.d.f. ARCH processes are models for which the financial risk σ_t is conditioned on a finite series of past values of the square value of the process x_t itself, as follows.

Definition 161   *An ARCH(p), or ARCH random process x_t of order p is a random process defined by:*

$$\sigma_t^2 = a_0 + a_1 x_{t-1}^2 + \cdots + a_p x_{t-p}^2$$

with $a_0, a_1, \ldots, a_\tau > 0$, $E\{x_t\} = 0$ *and* $E\{x_t^2 \,|\, \mathcal{A}_{t-1}^{t-p}\} = \sigma_t^2$ (4.28)

where $E\{x_t^2 \,|\, \mathcal{A}_{t-1}^{t-p}\}$ *is the expectation of a conditional p.d.f., conditioned on the information of a finite memory of x_t of a lagged horizon of p time periods from $t-1$ through $t-p$.*

Remark 162   *An ARCH(p) process is completely determined when the horizon p and the shape of the p.d.f. are defined and parametrized by the coefficients $a_0, a_1, \ldots, a_p$. The conditional p.d.f. may be Gaussian or non-Gaussian.*

Example 163   *The, among currency traders popular, ARCH(1) process*

$$\sigma_t^2 = a_0 + a_1 x_{t-1}^2$$ (4.29)

with a Gaussian conditional p.d.f., is characterized by the finite asymptotic or limit ("unconditional") variance (= the variance observed over an infinite horizon)

$$\sigma^2 = \lim_{t \to \infty} \sigma_t^2$$

$$= \frac{a_0}{1 - a_1} \tag{4.30}$$

provided

$$1 - a_1 \neq 0, \quad 0 \leq a_1 < 1 \tag{4.31}$$

The limiting normalized kurtosis (cf. Chapter 1) of this ARCH(1) process is

$$\kappa = \lim_{t \to \infty} \frac{E\{x_t^4\}}{E\{x_t^2\}^2}$$

$$= \frac{m_4}{m_2^2} \tag{4.32}$$

$$= \frac{c_4}{m_2^2} + 3$$

$$= \frac{c_4}{\sigma^4} + 3$$

$$= \frac{6a_1^2}{1 - 3a_1^2} + 3 \tag{4.33}$$

which is finite if

$$0 \leq a_1 < \frac{1}{\sqrt{3}} \tag{4.34}$$

Notice the potential excess kurtosis of this ARCH(1) process, since $6a_1^2/(1 - 3a_1^2) + 3 \geq 3 =$ the kurtosis of a Gaussian distribution. By varying a_0 and a_1, one can obtain random processes with the same limit variance σ^2, but with different values of limiting kurtosis. An example for an ARCH(1) process is given in Table 4.1. Successive increments of simulations of these three ARCH(1) processes are shown in Figure 4.1 and their respective p.d.fs in Figure 4.2. Both figures are borrowed, with small modifications, from Mantegna and Stanley (2000, pp. 79–80).

4.4.2 Statistical properties of GARCH processes

Bollerslev (1986, 1987) proposed a generalized ARCH random process, called GARCH(p, q) process, which can represent a greater degree of inertia in its conditional volatility or risk, as follows.

Table 4.1 ARCH(1) limit kurtosis

For parameter	Limit kurtosis
$a_0 = 1, a_1 = 0$	3 (= Gaussian process)
$a_0 = a_1 = 0.5$	9
$a_0 = 0.45, a_1 = 0.55$	23

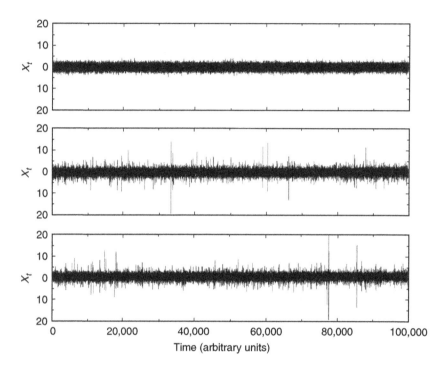

Figure 4.1 Successive increments of ARCH(1) simulations with the same unconditional variance ($\sigma^2 = 1$). Events outside three standard deviations are almost absent when $\kappa = 3$ (top: $\alpha_0 = 1, \alpha_1 = 0$). They are present when $\kappa = 9$ (middle: $\alpha_0 = \alpha_1 = 0.5$), and are more intense when $\kappa = 12$ (bottom: $\alpha_0 = 0.45$, $\alpha_1 = 0.55$).

Definition 164   *A GARCH(p, q), or GARCH random process x_t of orders (p, q) is a random process defined by:*

$$\sigma_t^2 = a_0 + a_1 x_{t-1}^2 + \cdots + a_p x_{t-p}^2 + b_1 \sigma_{t-1}^2 + \cdots + b_q \sigma_{t-q}^2$$

$$\text{with } a_0, a_1, \ldots, a_p, b_1, \ldots, b_q > 0, \quad E\{x_t\} = 0 \text{ and } E\{x_t^2 | \mathcal{A}_{t-1}^{t-p,t-q}\} = \sigma_t^2$$

$$(4.35)$$

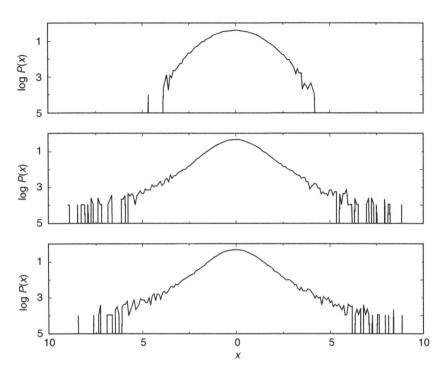

Figure 4.2 Logarithmic probability density function of the successive increments shown in Figure 4.1. The p.d.f. is Gaussian when $\kappa = 3$ (top) and is leptokurtic when $\kappa = 9$ or $\kappa = 23$ (middle and bottom).

where $E\{x_t^2 | \mathcal{A}_{t-1}^{t-p,t-q}\}$ is an expectation of a conditional p.d.f., conditioned on the information of a finite memory of x_t of p or q time periods, whichever is longest.

Example 165 *Baillie and Bollerslev (1992) show that the simplest GARCH(1, 1) process, with a Gaussian p.d.f. has as the finite asymptotic or limit ("unconditional") variance*

$$\sigma^2 = \frac{a_0}{1 - a_1 - b_1} \tag{4.36}$$

The limit normalized kurtosis of this GARCH(1, 1) process is given by

$$\kappa = \lim_{t \to \infty} \frac{E\{x_t^4\}}{E\{x_t^2\}} = \frac{m_4}{m_2^2}$$

$$= \frac{6a_1^2}{1 - 3a_1^2 - 2a_1 b_1 - b_1^2} + 3 \tag{4.37}$$

*which allows again excess kurtosis, depending on various configurations of the
values of the parameters a_1 and b_1. When $a_1 = 0$, the process is Gaussian. When
$b_1 > 0$ the variance feedback process of σ_t increases the kurtosis of the x_t process.*

4.4.3   (G)ARCH processes: uncorroborated time scaling

(G)ARCH processes are empirically deficient models since they don't exhibit
the correct empirical long-term dependence, in particular, proper scaling properties. For example, the empirical evidence shows that the variance of financial
market returns is characterized by power law correlations. Since the correlation
of the squared x_t of a GARCH(1, 1) process is exponential, a GARCH(1, 1)
process cannot be used to properly describe this empirical phenomenon. In other
words, (G)ARCH model processes can't represent the empirically observed long
memories. They are investment-horizon τ-specific and can represent only finite
memories. They measure conditional variances for specific finite horizons of maximally $\tau = p$ or q length and not of infinite length. In contrast, fractionally
differenced processes indiscriminately represent p.d.fs for all possible investment
horizons, finite and infinite and produce thus the proper scaling properties for the
unconditional p.d.fs.

Example 166 *Mantegna and Stanley (2000) compare empirical investigations
of the S&P500 high-frequency data with simulations of a GARCH(1, 1) process,
characterized by the same limiting variance and kurtosis. Such equality is ensured
by calibrating the three control parameters of the GARCH(1, 1) process, a_0, a_1
and b_1 subjectively and thus, non-scientifically. For example, Akgiray (1989)
arbitrarily chooses $b_1 = 0.9$. From the empirical analysis of the S&P500 minute-
by-minute data for the period January 1984–December 1989 (493, 545 minutes),
Mantegna and Stanley find that the limit variance $\sigma^2 = 0.00257$ and the limit
kurtosis $(m_4/m_2^2) \approx 43$. Using the preceding equations, with $b_1 = 0.9$, the
parameter values $a_0 = 2.30 \times 10^{-5}$ and $a_1 = 0.09105$ are obtained. The resulting simulated p.d.f. fits the $\Delta t = 1$ minute p.d.f. data well. But, as Mantegna
and Stanley (2000, p. 87) correctly conclude: "The fact that the GARCH(1, 1)
process describes well the $\Delta t = 1$ minute p.d.f. does not ensure that the same
process describes well the stochastic dynamics of the empirical data for any
time horizon Δt." To describe the dynamics of the price changes in a complete way, in addition to the p.d.f. of the price changes at a given time horizon,
the scaling properties of price change p.d.fs must be also considered. Although
there is no theoretical model for the scaling properties of the GARCH(1, 1) process, one can perform numerical simulations of the GARCH(1, 1) process, as
reported in the double-logarithmic Figure 4.3 (borrowed, with a correction, from
Mantegna and Stanley, 2000, p. 86). From Figure 4.3 it is clear that although
the GARCH(1, 1) process can accurately describe the $\Delta t = 10^0 = 1$ minute
empirical leptokurtic p.d.f. of price changes, it fails to describe the scaling properties of the empirical p.d.fs of the high-frequency S&P500 data for all higher
time horizons, using the same control parameters. The absolute value of the*

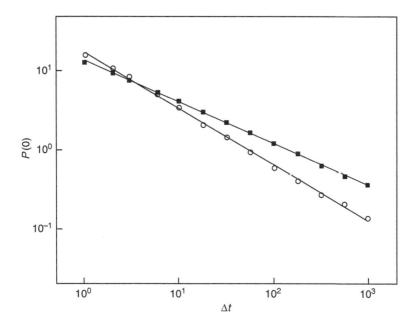

Figure 4.3 Comparison of the scaling properties of the unconditional p.d.f. of a GARCH(1, 1) stochastic process (black squares) with the ML estimated parameter values $a_0 = 2.30 \times 10^{-5}$, $a_1 = 0.09105$ and $b_1 = 0.9$ with the scaling properties of the p.d.f. of the S&P500 high-frequency data (white circles). The scaling of the GARCH(1, 1) process fails to describe the empirical behavior in the S&P500 high-frequency data.

empirical slope of the GARCH (1, 1) simulated price change data (black squares) is a Gaussian Hurst exponent $H = 1/\alpha_Z = (\ln 10^{1.5})/(\ln 10^3) = 0.5$, while the slope of the high-frequency S&P500 data (white circles) has a Hurst exponent $H = 1/\alpha_Z = (\ln 10^2)/(\ln 10^3) = 0.67$.[8]

The *Integrated variance GARCH*, or IGARCH models of Bollerslev (1986), a further generalization of his GARCH model, are characterized by infinite unconditional variance, because they contain a unit root. In those models, current information remains important for the forecasts of conditional variance for all investment horizons. It is still an open research question if these models produce the proper dynamic scaling properties (cf. Alexander, 1998). Numerical simulations are easy to execute, but the derivation of the theoretical scaling properties of these models is quite a difficult matter and the possible topic for a doctoral dissertation.

4.5 Fractional Brownian Motion

Thus, we have finally arrived at one of the most useful generic research models for a random process currently in existence in the financial markets literature, the *FBM*. This random process model encompasses virtually all of the observed empirical phenomena in the time series of financial markets. A recent theoretical paper by Elliott and van den Hoek (2000) discusses the theoretical niceties of the FBM and shows how easy it is to replace the GBM by the FBM in all the familiar dynamic valuation and hedging models in the finance literature, to present models that are much closer to empirical observations in their scaling properties. In this chapter, we'll focus on the empirical measurement analysis of the FBM and the wide range of empirical phenomena it is able to represent.

Definition 167   FBM *is defined by the fractionally differenced time series*

$$(1 - L)^d x(t) = \varepsilon(t), \ d \in \left(-\tfrac{1}{2}, \tfrac{1}{2}\right), \quad with \ \varepsilon(t) \sim i.i.d.(0, \sigma_\varepsilon^2) \tag{4.38}$$

where the gross rates of return $x(t) = \ln X(t) - \ln X(t-1) = (1 - L) \ln X(t)$.

A completely equivalent definition is that FBM $x(t)$ is fractionally integrated white noise, since

$$x(t) = (1 - L)^{-d} \varepsilon(t), \ d \in \left(-\tfrac{1}{2}, \tfrac{1}{2}\right), \quad with \ \varepsilon(t) \sim i.i.d.(0, \sigma_\varepsilon^2) \tag{4.39}$$

Remark 168   *The FBM can also be presented in terms of the original market price series* $X(t)$ *as*

$$(1 - L)^d (1 - L) \ln X(t)$$
$$= (1 - L)^{d+1} \ln X(t)$$
$$= \varepsilon(t), \quad with \ \varepsilon(t) \sim i.i.d.(0, \sigma_\varepsilon^2) \tag{4.40}$$

Table 4.2 provides a comparison of the ACFs of two simulated fractionally differenced time series, $(1 - L)^d x(t) = \varepsilon(t)$ for $d = -\tfrac{1}{3}$ and $\tfrac{1}{3}$, with long-term memory, with the ACF of a simulated AR(1) time series, $x(t) = \rho x(t-1) + \varepsilon(t)$

Table 4.2 ACFs of long- and short-memory series

Lag τ	$d = -1/3$	$d = 1/3$	AR(1), $a_1 = 0.5$
	$\gamma(\tau)$	$\gamma(\tau)$	$\gamma(\tau)$
1	−0.250	0.500	0.500
2	−0.071	0.400	0.250
3	−0.036	0.350	0.125
4	−0.022	0.318	0.063
5	−0.015	0.295	0.031
10	−0.005	0.235	0.001
25	−0.001	0.173	2.98×10^{-8}
50	-3.24×10^{-4}	0.137	8.88×10^{-16}
100	-1.02×10^{-4}	0.109	7.89×10^{-31}

with $\rho = 0.5$ and short-term memory. The variance σ_ε^2 of the i.i.d. noise was chosen to yield a unit variance for $x(t)$ in all three cases. Notice the very gradual decline and infinite continuation of the ACF when $d = \frac{1}{3}$ or when $d = -\frac{1}{3}$ and the initial steep decline and virtual non-existence of the ACF of the AR(1) after only 10 lags.

The standard GBM is the special case of a fractionally differenced time series, when $d = 1$, so that

$$\Delta x(t) = (1 - L)x(t) = \varepsilon(t) \tag{4.41}$$

or

$$x(t) = (1 - L)^{-1}\varepsilon(t), \quad \text{with } \varepsilon(t) \sim \text{i.i.d.}(0, \sigma_\varepsilon^2) \tag{4.42}$$

with its ACF decaying hyperbolically:

$$\gamma(\tau) \sim \sigma_\varepsilon^2 \tau^{-1} \tag{4.43}$$

which is proportional to the variance of the i.i.d. innovations $\varepsilon(t)$: σ_ε^2. Thus, obviously, the GBM is *self-similarly scaling*. Brownian Motion is once integrated white noise, since its innovations are white noise, i.e., they exhibit a flat, constant spectral density: $P_\varepsilon(\omega) = \sigma_\varepsilon^2$.

Example 169 *Figure 4.4 provides the standardized empirical ACFs (autocorrelograms) of equally-weighted CRSP daily and monthly stock returns indexes. The observation period for the daily index is July 1962–December 1987 and January 1926–December 1987 for the monthly index. Notice that these empirical ACFs are not as smooth and continuous as presented by the theoretical FBMs of Table 4.2, thus emphasizing the problem of identification of the proper difference exponent d from empirical ACFs. In Chapters 6 and 7 we'll discuss more advanced and better identification methodologies than the classical ACFs. What these empirical*

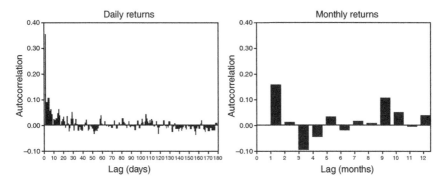

Figure 4.4 Autocorrelograms of equally-weighted CRSP daily (July 1962–December 1987) and monthly (January 1926–December 1987) stock return indices.

ACFs show is that the processes of daily and monthly returns have long memory, or long-term dependence, since they don't vanish quickly.

We'll now turn to Range/Scale Analysis, which is the basis for most of the recent efforts to measure homogeneous Hurst exponents to determine the degree of scaling in financial time series or in rates of return or in implied volatility.

4.6   Range/Scale analysis

To detect global, "strong,"or long-term time dependence, Mandelbrot (1965) suggested the use of Hurst's "rescaled range," or R/S statistic, which Hurst (1951) had developed in his study of the Nile river discharges. As we will see, the Hurst statistic leads to the Hurst or *H*-exponent. Although, recently, the *H*-exponent has become quite popular in finance (cf. Peters, 1992), there are reasons to consider this exponent as too limited to measure all forms of aperiodic cyclicities, in particular, with financial turbulence and chaos (cf. Chapter 9). There are already better defined exponents supported over larger domains, which cover more extreme cases, as we will see in this chapter.

4.6.1   *Hurst's original Range/Scale statistic*

Definition 170   (Hurst's R/S statistic) *Consider a sequence of investment returns* $\{x(t)\}$ *and its empirical mean* ($=$ *first cumulant* $=$ *first moment*).

$$c_1 = m_1 = \frac{1}{T} \sum_{t=1}^{T} x(t) \tag{4.44}$$

and its empirical variance ($=$ *second cumulant*)

$$c_2 = m_2 - m_1^2$$

$$= \frac{1}{T} \sum_{t=1}^{T} [x(t) - m_1]^2 \tag{4.45}$$

then Hurst's R/S statistic is defined by

$$RS_H(T) \equiv \frac{1}{c_2^{0.5}} \left[Max_{1 \leq t \leq T} \sum_{t=1}^{\tau} [x(t) - m_1] - Min_{1 \leq t \leq T} \sum_{t=1}^{\tau} [x(t) - m_1] \right] \geq 0 \tag{4.46}$$

The first term in brackets is the maximum (over interval τ) of the partial sums of the first τ deviations of $x(t)$ from the mean. Since the sum of all τ deviations of $x(t)$ from their mean is zero, this maximum is always nonnegative. The second term is the minimum (over interval τ) of this same sequence of partial sums; hence it is always nonpositive. The difference of these two quantities, called the "range" is thus always nonnegative. This range is then scaled by the empirical standard deviation for the whole data set $c_2^{0.5}$.

4.6.2 Lo and MacKinlay's (1999) "Modification"

Lo and MacKinlay (1999) modify the rescaled range measure of Hurst, so that it becomes robust to short-term dependence, and derives its limiting distribution under both short-term and long-term dependence. In contrast to many other authors in the current literature, including Mandelbrot (1965, 1972), Mandelbrot and Taqqu (1979), Mandelbrot and Wallis (1969), Lo and MacKinlay also claim that, when they apply their modified R/S statistic to daily and monthly stock return indices over different periods and sub-periods, there is no evidence of long-term dependence, once the effects of short-term dependence are accounted for. Therefore, they suggest that the time series behavior of stock returns may be adequately captured by the more conventional (Markov) models of short-term dependence. For now, the accumulated empirical evidence by Peters (1994) tends to shift the balance of proof in the direction earlier indicated by Mandelbrot c.s. But considering the conflicting evidence, this remains an open, very interesting and challenging, empirical and theoretical research question, which we'll reconsider in Chapters 7 and 8.

4.6.3 Homogeneous Hurst exponent

The Hurst statistic provides us with a means to analyze the dependence characteristics of time series and to determine if they are serially, or globally dependent, since it delivers the Hurst exponent as a fractal dimension, Hölder or Lipschitz irregularity coefficient (Mandelbrot, 1972).[9]

Definition 171 *The* Hurst exponent H *is defined as*

$$0 < H = \lim_{\tau \to \infty} \frac{\ln RS_H(\tau)}{\ln \tau} < 1 \tag{4.47}$$

For serially, or short-term, dependent time series, such as strong-mixing processes, $H \to 0.5$ when $\tau \to \infty$, but for globally dependent time series $H \to 0.5 + d$. In fact, the fractionally-differenced random processes satisfy the equality $H = 0.5 + d$. Thus, Mandelbrot (1965) suggests to plot $\ln RS(\tau)$ against $\ln \tau$ to compute H from the slope of the resulting plot. He calls any time series $x(t)$ which shows the R/S statistic time-scaling, $RS_H(\tau) \propto \tau^H$: *"Hurst noise."*

Example 172 *As Hurst (1951) showed, based on the water-level minima recorded in the period 622–1469, the annual water flow of the Nile river in Egypt shows a strong long-term persistence with $H = 0.91$, that requires unusually high barriers, such as the Aswan High Dam, to contain damage and rein in the floods. (We'll discuss such extreme risk value phenomena in Chapter 12.) As Mandelbrot and Wallis (1969) showed, for the rivers Saint Lawrence in Canada, Colorado in the USA and the Loire in France, the persistence is considerably lower with $0.5 < H < 0.9$. The river Rhine (at the Swiss-French-German triple point near Basel) is exceptional with a long-term exponent of $H = 0.5$, indicating that its* *water flow changes like white noise (Whitcher et al., 2002). In other words, the Rhine river tends to produce no major catastrophic floods.*

The ACF of the fractionally-differenced time series can now be written in terms of the H-exponent, since we can now substitute $d = H - 0.5$ into the previously defined ACF to get:

$$\gamma(\tau) = \frac{\sigma_\varepsilon^2 \Gamma(2 - 2H)\Gamma(\tau + H - 0.5)}{\Gamma(H - 0.5)\Gamma(1.5 - H)\Gamma(\tau + 1.5 - H)}$$

$$\sim \sigma_\varepsilon^2 \tau^{2H-2} \quad \text{as } \tau \to \infty \tag{4.48}$$

where $H \in (0, 1)$.

4.7   Critical color categorization of randomness

4.7.1   *Blue, white, pink, red, brown and black noise*

Following Schroeder (1991, pp. 121–137) we can now present a color categorization of randomness, or irregularity, by collecting the various descriptive exponents and relating them to each other. This comparison of exponents will facilitate the reading of a great variety of interdisciplinary research articles on phenomena of time dependence. In Chapter 8, we'll explain the intimate relationship between our concept of "randomness," as discussed in Chapter 1, and the concept of "irregularity" as defined by the mathematician Lipschitz.

Definition 173   *(1) When the Hurst exponent $0 < H < 0.5$, i.e., $-0.5 < d < 0$, the time series of increments is called* antipersistent. *(2) When $H = 0.5$, i.e., $d = 0$, the increments are independent or "white," and the time dependence of the series is* neutral *(or neutrally persistent). Examples are the increments of Random Walks or Arithmetic Brownian Motions (for speculative prices) and of GBM (for investment returns). The Brownian Motion series is once-integrated "white noise" and is called "brown" noise. Its ACF decays hyperbolically:*

$$\gamma(\tau) = \frac{\sigma_\varepsilon^2 \Gamma(\tau)}{\Gamma(\tau + 1)}$$

$$= \frac{\sigma_\varepsilon^2 (\tau - 1)!}{\tau!}$$

$$= \sigma_\varepsilon^2 \tau^{-1} \tag{4.49}$$

(3) When $0.5 < H < 1$, i.e., $0 < d < 0.5$, the time series of increments is called persistent.

In the case of extreme antipersistence, $H \downarrow 0$, so that the ACF of the time series decays faster than hyperbolically in a quadratic fashion:

$$\gamma(\tau) = \frac{\sigma_\varepsilon^2 \Gamma(\tau - 0.5)}{\Gamma(\tau + 1.5)}$$

$$= \frac{\sigma_\varepsilon^2 (\tau - 1.5)!}{(\tau + 0.5)!}$$

$$= \frac{\sigma_\varepsilon^2}{(\tau + 0.5)(\tau - 0.5)}$$

$$= \frac{\sigma_\varepsilon^2}{(\tau^2 - 0.25)}$$

$$\approx \sigma_\varepsilon^2 \tau^{-2} \quad \text{as } \tau \to \infty \tag{4.50}$$

At the other extreme of Hurst's limited *randomness spectrum* $H \uparrow 1$, so that the ACF of the time series remains a flat constant and it never vanishes:

$$\gamma(\tau) = \frac{\sigma_\varepsilon^2 \Gamma(\tau + 0.5)}{\Gamma(\tau + 0.5)}$$

$$= \sigma_\varepsilon^2 \text{ a constant, as } \quad \tau \to \infty \tag{4.51}$$

4.7.2 Irregularity exponents

We can make a connection with the stable distributions discussed earlier in Chapter 3, once we realize that, for globally (long-term) dependent time series, for which the autocovariance function has the form

$$\gamma(\tau) = \begin{cases} \tau^\lambda H(\tau) & \text{for } \lambda \in [-1, 0), \text{ or} \\ -\tau^\lambda H(\tau) & \text{for } \lambda \in (-2, -1] \end{cases} \tag{4.52}$$

as the time-interval lengthens, $\tau \to \infty$, and $H(\tau)$ is any slowly varying function at infinity, the *dependence exponent* λ equals

$$\lambda = 2d - 1$$

$$= \upsilon - 1$$

$$= 2H - 2$$

$$= \frac{2}{\alpha_Z} - 2$$

$$= 2\alpha_L - 2 \tag{4.53}$$

where d is the *difference (order) exponent*, υ is the *spectral exponent* (to be discussed in detail in Chapter 5), H is the aforementioned *Hurst exponent*, α_Z is the *stability exponent* of the Zolotarev parametrization of the stable distributions

Table 4.3 Equivalence of various critical irregularity exponents

Exponents: Color:	Dependence λ	Difference d	Spectral υ	Hurst H	Stability α_Z
Blue noise	$\lambda \downarrow -2$	$d = -0.5$	$\upsilon = -1$	$H \downarrow 0$	NA
Antipersistence	$-2 < \lambda < -1$	$-0.5 < d < 0$	$-1 < \upsilon < 0$	$0 < H < 0.5$	NA
White noise	$\lambda = -1$	$d = 0$	$\upsilon = 0$	$H = 0.5$	$\alpha_Z = 2$
Persistence (pink)	$0 < \lambda < -1$	$0 < d < 0.5$	$0 < \upsilon < 1$	$0.5 < H < 1$	$1 < \alpha_Z < 2$
Red noise	$\lambda \uparrow 0$	$d = 0.5$	$\upsilon = 1$	$H \uparrow 1$	$\alpha_Z = 1$
Brown noise	NA	$d = 1$	$\upsilon = 2$	NA	$\alpha_Z = 2/3$
Black noise	NA	$1 \leq d \leq 2$	$2 < \upsilon \leq 4$	NA	$2/5 \leq \alpha_Z < 2/3$

Note
NA = not applicable.

of Chapter 3, and α_L is the Lipschitz *regularity exponent* (to be discussed in Chapter 8).[10] Thus, the randomness, or irregularity, categorization can be expressed in terms of each of these *critical exponents*. For completeness of definition: $\lambda/2$ is the so-called *time-scaling exponent*.

The complete spectrum of randomness, or irregularity, in terms of the five critical exponents equivalent to the Lipschitz regularity exponent is given in Table 4.3, which provides the essential relationships between the exponents of the first difference of FBM (cf. also Keshner, 1982; Flandrin, 1989).

For example, for the Brownian Motion increments $\varepsilon(t)$, which are white noise:

$$\lambda = -1, \quad d = 0, \quad \upsilon = 0, \quad H = 0.5, \quad \alpha_Z = 2 \tag{4.54}$$

Thus, the time series of Brownian Motion increments is modelled by white noise:

$$x(t) = (1 - L)^0 \varepsilon(t)$$
$$= \varepsilon(t) \tag{4.55}$$

Fractional integration of such white noise, when $d = 0.5$ and $H \uparrow 1$, results in a red noise series (Gilman *et al.*, 1963):

$$x(t) = (1 - L)^{-0.5} \varepsilon(t) \tag{4.56}$$

One complete integer integration of the white noise, when $d = 1$, results in a brown noise series (= Brownian Motion)

$$x(t) = (1 - L)^{-1} \varepsilon(t) \tag{4.57}$$

Visual samples of time series of such white, red and brown noise are given by Figure 4.5.

In the case of $0.5 < H < 1$, the vital property of the FBM is that the persistence of its increments extends forever: *it never dies out* and gives rise to the empirically observed *catastrophes*. The strength of such persistence is measured by the critical H-exponent.

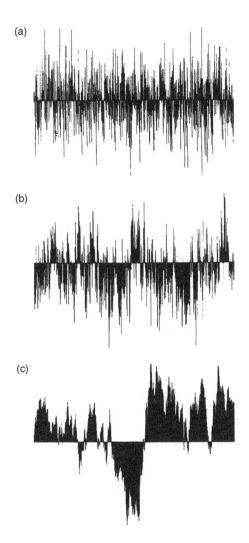

(a)

(b)

(c)

Figure 4.5 Sample of (a) white noise with $P(\omega) = \omega^{-0}$ power spectrum; (b) pink noise with $P(\omega) = \omega^{-1}$ power spectrum; and (c) brown noise with $P(\omega) = \omega^{-2}$ power spectrum.

Example 174 *The rates of return $x(t)$ of the S&P500 stock market index show mild persistence with $H = 0.67$. Indeed, their graph is less irregular than that of ordinary GBM increments. Its fractional dimension D is thus between the dimension of a line, $D = 1$, and the dimension of a plane, $D = 2$:*

$$1 < D = 2 - H = 1.33 < 2 \tag{4.58}$$

In Chapter 8 we'll discuss the fractional dimensions of financial time series in more detail. Curiously, the Dow Jones Industrials stock index shows neutral persistence, according to Li (1991), with $H = 0.5$.

Example 175   *The fractional dimension of GBM increments, with $H = 0.5$, is*

$$D = 2 - H = 1.5 = \frac{3}{2} \tag{4.59}$$

The case where $0.5 < d < 1.5$, or, equivalently, $1 < \upsilon < 3$, which cannot be measured directly by the *H*-exponent, but only after one differentiation, has been called the *infrared catastrophe* (Wornell and Oppenheim, 1992). It can be measured by the wavelet multiresolution analysis discussed in Chapter 8. More fractional integration, for example $d = 2$, results in heavily persistent, or pure *black noise*

$$x(t) = (1 - L)^{-2} \varepsilon(t) \tag{4.60}$$

As Schroeder (1991, p. 122) comments:

> Black-noise phenomena govern natural and unnatural catastrophes, like floods, droughts, bear markets, and various outrageous outages, such as those of electrical energy. Because of their black spectra, such disasters often come in clusters.

In contrast, the FBM increments with $0 < H < 0.5$ are antipersistent noise, hence they diffuse more quickly than the Brownian increments. Such FBM increments continuously return to the point they came from.

Remark 176   *Notably this means that the theoretical Random Walk innovations $\varepsilon(t)$ are rather exceptional. They exhibit the same stability, $\alpha_Z = 2$, and (in-)dependence, $H = 0.5$, as Gaussian random variables, but do not necessarily have to be Gaussian! Furthermore, their ACF drops off geometrically with $\lambda = -1$. By measuring the financial-economic, e.g., stock price innovations to be close to Gaussian, Granger and Morgenstern (1963) and Granger (1966) inferred that such innovations had a typical spectral shape. However, we'll learn in Chapters 6 and 7 that their inference was erroneous, and that there was nothing typical about that inferred shape, because it was biased by thinking exclusively in term of Gaussian innovations $\varepsilon(t) \sim N(0, \sigma_\varepsilon^2)$. For example, the covariance function of modern foreign exchange rates, like the Japanese Yen or the German Deutschemark, shows antipersistence, i.e., a slower drop-off of the ACF than the "typical" spectral shape based on this assumption of Gaussian i.i.d. innovations.*

4.7.3   Stability spectra

It is very important to understand that the Hurst exponent H is a rather limited measure of randomness and distributional stability with a very limited

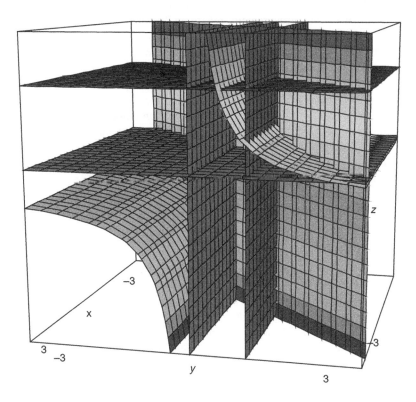

Figure 4.6 Relations between and constraints on d, H and α_Z. The axes measure $x = d$, $y = H$, $z = \alpha_Z$.

measurement domain, and that the α_Z-stability exponent, and the υ-spectral exponent have much more extensive measurement domains. This becomes clear, when we geometrically visualize the mathematical relationships, the constraints, and the respective domains of the various critical irregularity exponents in Figure 4.6.

The implied equality $\alpha_Z = 1/H$ does not hold for all values of α_Z, since the Hurst exponent, per definition, $0 < H < 1$, implies that $1 < \alpha_Z < \infty$, while the parametrized stable distributions of Chapter 3 are defined for the limited domain $0 < \alpha_Z \leq 2$. Apparently there exist empirical *ultra-stable* distributions (not yet parametrized!) in the domain $2 \leq \alpha_Z < \infty$, since we find *in extremo* $\alpha_Z \uparrow \infty$ when $H \downarrow 0$ (and $d \uparrow 0.5$), which is *complete stability*. These distributions are the distributions of *singularities*, or *singularity spectra*, which can be characterized and measured by the stability exponent α_Z. Considering that we have already empirically measured antipersistence in the FX markets, we will discuss such theoretical singularity spectra in Chapter 8.

As we recall from Chapter 3, and as is clearly visible in Figure 4.6, when the Hurst exponent vanishes, $H \downarrow 0$, the Zolotarev stability exponent becomes infinite,

$\alpha_Z \uparrow \infty$. In other words, for very small values of the Hurst exponent, $H \downarrow 0$, we acquire very uncertain measurements regarding Zolotarev's stability exponent α_Z.

In addition, there are now theoretically defined, parametrized stable distributions where $0 < \alpha_Z < 1$, which can also not be measured by the Hurst H-exponent directly, but can be measured by α_Z, if we can compute α_Z in some other fashion. These are the *ultra-unstable* distributions. However, empirically, there appears to be a physical turbulence barrier at $\alpha_Z = 2/5$. In other words, there appears not to exist any empirical α_Z such that $0 < \alpha_Z < 2/5$, even though there are theoretical Zolotarev-parametrized distributions defined for such α_Z values. Again, this is an area open for further theoretical and empirical research.

In conclusion, the best domain for using the H-exponent to compute the stability α_Z-exponent is in the Gaussian neighborhood of $H = 0.5$, where $\alpha_Z = 2$. Still, it is important to recognize that there exists a *stability spectrum* of randomness, or irregularity, completely specified by the stability exponent α_Z.

Remark 177 *Of course, one can still use the H-exponent for measuring infrared and black catastrophes, by measuring the H-exponent after proper integer-differentiation. For example, we hypothesize that $x(t)$ is pure black noise and has a spectral exponent $\upsilon = 4$, then differentiation of two full times $(d = 2)$ should theoretically result in white noise series with a flat spectrum, $\upsilon = 0$, so that $H = 0.5$. However, when we empirically measure, for example, $H = 0.2 \rightarrow \upsilon = -0.6$, then the original series must have a spectral coefficient of $\upsilon = -0.6 + 4 = 3.4$ and not 4.*

4.8 Software

Benoit 1.3: Fractal System Analysis (for Windows), Trusoft International Inc., 204, 37th Ave. N #133, St. Petersburg, FL 33704 Tel: (813) 925-8131; Fax: (813) 925-8141; sales@trusoft-international.com. See http://www.trusoft-international.com for details. This Benoit software enables you to measure the fractal dimension and/or Hölder–Hurst exponent of your data sets using your choice of method(s) for analysis of self-affine traces of speculative prices.

In the following Exercises you should use the Benoit software, Version 1.3. Once you've accessed Benoit, enlarge the working screen by the maximizing $ button in the upper-right corner of Benoit's initial screen, otherwise you will not see the crucial *OK* button. Always read the Benoit Help descriptions of the methods you use and relate them to the text of this chapter. To feed the empirical data as inputs into the Benoit program using EXCEL, read Benoit's Help instructions on Data Files (Data Formats).

4.9 Exercises

Exercise 178 *Compare the ACFs of the four data series of the Exercises of Chapter 1 against the theoretical benchmarks of Table 4.2. Are the series* *antipersistent, white noise, persistent (= pink) noise, red noise, brown noise or black noise, respectively? How can you tell?*

Exercise 179 *Following Kasdin (1995), simulate three types of FBMs with Hurst exponents H = 0.2, H = 0.5 and H = 0.8, respectively, by using Benoit's self-affine trace generator. Compare your results with the one in this chapter. Generate no more than 250 points for each case. Use a vertical range of 0–25. Generate both the traces and their first differences. The Benoit program provides three methods for generating synthetic self-affine traces (the successive random addition method, the Fourier Transform method and the wavelet method). Try all three methods and describe in your own words how the results differ from each other. In total you should generate 2 × 3 × 3 = 18 pictures. Save the traces and their first differences and display them either in an EXCEL spreadsheet or in Microsoft Power Point. These respective simulations will provide you with some "benchmark" pictures for the following Exercises.*

Exercise 180 *Compute the Hurst exponent and the fractal dimension of our S&P500 data of the Exercises of Chapter 1 using Hurst's Rescaled-Range (R/S) analysis for (1) the original share prices, (2) their total rates of return and (3) for first differences of the rates of total return. (Use the double logarithmic plot window.)*

Exercise 181 *Repeat the preceding Exercise, using the Irregularity (or Roughness)–Length method, which relates the standard deviation of windows of various length to the Hurst exponent, in the fashion described in this chapter. It plots the logarithm of the standard deviation (or Root-Mean-Squared (RMS) error) against the logarithm of the length of the window τ.*

Exercise 182 *Repeat the preceding Exercise, using the Variogram method, which is directly related to the autocovariance function.*

Notes

1 The current unorthodox efforts to characterize nonstationary financial-economic time series using more advanced signal processing technology are comparable with these early out-of-the-mainstream technical efforts by Granger and Morgenstern. For example, econometrician J. B. Ramsey of New York University performed the first wavelet multiresolution analysis (MRA) of macroeconomic data series (Ramsey, 1997).

2 Los (1999, 2000) provides some empirical examples of such "periodicity" for Asian FX markets, using non-parametric methods, based on high frequency data for 1997.

3 Cf. Los (1984) for theoretical discussions and Monte Carlo experiments with empirically estimated Kalman filters for econometric time-varying parameter models, including unstable ones.

4 We'll discuss in Chapter 12 possible insurance against such extreme catastrophic events, in the context of some dramatic hydrological and financial developments in mainland China.

5 Mandelbrot has questioned if Hosking's ARFIMA models were an improvement over his simpler fractionally differenced models, since such models with fractional exponents can trivially represent the integer exponent ARIMA models. But Hosking wanted to show the fractional and integer exponents separately within one modified framework, because they represent different phenomena: non-periodic and periodic cyclicity, respectively.

6 Cf. Meerschaert (1999) for the continuous time form of these long memory dynamic processes.

7 Such classical ACFs support the econometric measurements of Vector Auto-Regression (VARs) models. Classical VARs can represent higher order periodicities, but not the long-term time dependent phenomenon of non-periodic cyclicities, because they are expressed in terms of integer Markov processes. Of course, one can also, unconventionally, model fractional VARs to properly represent globally dependent or long memory processes.

8 And not the incorrect value of $H = 0.53$ provided by Mantegna and Stanley (2000, p. 86), who are proven wrong by their own figure 10.7, which we borrowed as our Figure 4.3.

9 Hölder (1859–1937) was a German mathematician, who devised treatment of divergent series of arithmetic summations, which led to a regularity exponent now recognized to be similar to Hurst's. However, Hölder was thinking about microscopic (physics) phenomena, in contrast to Hurst, who thought about macroscopic (hydrological) phenomena. The Hölder–Hurst exponents are also called critical Lipschitz irregularity exponents.

10 Somewhat confusingly presented in the literature, the Zolotarev stability $\alpha_Z = 1/\alpha_L$, where α_L is the Lipschitz regularity exponent. In the literature, one often finds just α and it is not always clear if the author(s) mean(s) the Zolotarev stability exponent α_Z or the Lipschitz α_L. We hope that this comparison of the various critical exponents and the presentation of their relationships will lift the dense fog between the various scientific disciplines, in particular in finance, physics and engineering, which deal with essentially the same signal processing phenomena.

Bibliography

Akgiray, V. (1989) "Conditional Heteroskedasticity in Time Series of Stock Returns: Evidence and Forecasts," *Journal of Business*, **61**(1), 55–80.

Alexander, Carol (1998) "Volatility and Correlation: Measurement, Models and Applications," chapter 4 in Alexander, Carol (Ed.) (1999), *Risk Management and Analysis, Volume 1: Measuring and Modelling Financial Risk*, John Wiley and Sons, New York, NY, pp. 125–171.

Anderson, T. W. (1994) *The Statistical Analysis of Time Series*, John Wiley and Sons, New York, NY.

Baillie, R. T., and T. Bollerslev (1992) "Conditional Forecast Densities From Dynamic Models with GARCH Innovations," *Journal of Econometrics*, **52**(112), 91–113.

Bollerslev, Tim (1986) "Generalized Autoregressive Conditional Heteroskedasticity," *Journal of Econometrics*, **31**(3), 307–327.

Bollerslev, Tim (1987) "A Conditionally Heteroskedastic Time Series Model for Speculative Prices and Rates of Return," *Review of Economics and Statistics*, **9**(3), 542–547.

Bollerslev, Tim, Ray Y. Chou and Kenneth F. Kroner (1992) "ARCH Modeling in Finance: A Review of the Theory and Empirical Evidence," *Journal of Econometrics*, **52**(112), 5–59.

Bollerslev, Tim, Robert F. Engle and Daniel B. Nelson (1994) "ARCH Models," chapter 49 in Engle, Robert F., and Dan L. McFadden (Eds) (1994), *Handbook of Econometrics*, Vol. 4, Elsevier-North Holland, Amsterdam.

Box, G. E. P., and G. M. Jenkins (1970) *Time Series Analysis: Forecasting and Control*, 2nd edn, Holden-Day, San Francisco, CA.

Elliott, Robert J., and John van den Hoek (2000) "A General Fractional White Noise Theory and Applications in Finance," *Quantitative Methods in Finance and Bernoulli Society 2000 Conference (Program, Abstracts and Papers)*, 5–8 December 2000, University of Technology, Sydney, pp. 327–345.

Engle, Robert F. (1982) "Autoregressive Conditional Heteroskedasticity with Estimates of the Variance of U.K. Inflation," *Econometrica*, **50**(4), 987–1002.

Engle, Robert F. (Ed.) (1995) *ARCH: Selected Readings*, Advanced Texts in Econometrics, Oxford University Press, Oxford, UK.

Flandrin, Patrick (1989) "On the Spectrum of Fractional Brownian Motion," *IEEE Transactions on Information Theory*, **35**(1), 197–199.

Gilman, D. L., F. J. Fuglister and J. M. Mitchell, Jr (1963) "On the Power Spectrum of 'Red Noise'," *Journal of Atmospheric Science*, **20**(2), 182–184.

Granger, C. W. J. (1966) "The Typical Spectral Shape of an Economic Variable," *Econometrica*, **34**(1), 150–161.

Granger, C. W. J., and O. Morgenstern (1963) "Spectral Analysis of New York Stock Exchange Prices," *Kyklos*, **16**, 1–27. Reprinted as chapter 8 in Cootner, Paul H. (Ed.) (1964), *The Random Character of Stock Market Prices*, The MIT Press, Cambridge, MA, pp. 162–188.

Hosking, J. R. M. (1981) "Fractional Differencing," *Biometrika*, **68**(1), 165–176.

Hurst, H. E. (1951) "Long-term Storage Capacity of Reservoirs," *Transactions of the American Society of Civil Engineers*, **116**, 770–799.

Kasdin, N. Jeremy (1995) "Discrete Simulation of Colored Noise and Stochastic Processes and $1/f^\alpha$ Power Law Noise Generation," *Proceedings of the IEEE*, **83**(5), 802–827.

Keshner, M. S. (1982) "1/f Noise," *Proceedings of the IEEE*, **70**, 212–218.

Li, W. (1991) "Absence of $1/f$ Spectra in Dow Jones Daily Average," *International Journal of Bifurcations and Chaos*, **1**, 583–597.

Lo, Andrew W., and A. Craig Mackinlay (1988) "Stock Market Prices Do Not Follow Random Walks: Evidence from a Simple Specification Tests," *The Review of Financial Studies*, **1**(1), 41–66.

Lo, Andrew W., and A. Craig MacKinlay (1999) "Long-Term Memory in Stock Market Prices," chapter 6 in *A Non-Random Walk Down Wall Street*, Princeton University Press, Princeton, NJ, pp. 147–184.

Los, Cornelis A. (1984) *Econometrics of Models with Evolutionary Parameter Structures*, PhD dissertation, Columbia University, University Microfilms International, Ann Arbor, MI, January.

Los, Cornelis A. (1999) "Nonparametric Testing of the High-Frequency Efficiency of the 1997 Asian Foreign Exchange Markets," *Journal of Multinational Financial Management*, **9**, 3 and 4 October, 265–289.

Los, Cornelis A. (2000) "Nonparametric Efficiency Testing of Asian Stock Markets, Using Weekly Data," in Fomby, Thomas B. and R. Carter Hill (Eds), *Advances in Econometrics: Applying Kernel and Nonparametric Estimation to Economic Topics*, Vol. 14, JAI Press, pp. 329–363.

Mandelbrot, Benoit B. (1965) "Une Classe de Processus Stochastiques Homothétique à Soi; Application à la Loi Climatologique de H. E. Hurst" ("A Class of Self-Similar Stochastic

Processes; Application to the Climatological Law of H. E. Hurst"), *Comptes Rendus (Paris)*, **260**, 3274–3277.

Mandelbrot, Benoit B. (1971) "Limitations of Efficiency and of Martingale Models," *The Review of Economics and Statistics*, **53**(3), 225–236.

Mandelbrot, Benoit B. (1972) "Statistical Methodology for Nonperiodic Cycles: From the Covariance to the R/S Analysis," *Annals of Economic and Social Measurement*, **1**(3), 259–290.

Mandelbrot, Benoit B., and John W. Van Ness (1968) "Fractional Brownian Motions, Fractional Noises and Applications," *SIAM Review*, **10**(4), 422–437.

Mandelbrot, Benoit B., and J. R. Wallis (1969) "Some Long-Run Properties of Geophysical Records," *Water Resources Research*, **5**(2), 321–340.

Mandelbrot, Benoit B., and M. Taqqu (1979) "Robust R/S Analysis of Long Run Serial Correlation," *Bulletin of the International Statistical Institute*, **48**(2), 59–104.

Mantegna, Rosario, N., and H. Eugene Stanley (2000) *An Introduction to Econophysics: Correlations and Complexity in Finance*, Cambridge University Press, Cambridge, UK.

Meerchaert, Mark (1999) "Fractional Diffusion," in *Proceedings of Applications of Heavy Tailed Distributions in Economics, Engineering and Statistics*, American University, Washington DC, 3–5 June 1999.

Moore, Geoffrey H. (1980) *Business Cycles, Inflation, and Forecasting*, published for the National Bureau of Economic Research, Ballinger Publishing Co., Cambridge, MA.

Nelson, Daniel B. (1991) "Conditional Heteroskedasticity in Asset Returns: A New Approach," *Econometrica*, **59**(2), 347–370.

Peters, Edgar E. (1992) "R/S Analysis Using Logarithmic Returns: A Technical Note," *Financial Analysts Journal*, **48**(6), 81–82.

Peters, Edgar E. (1994) *Fractal Market Analysis*, John Wiley and Sons, New York, NY.

Ramsey, J. B. (1997) "The Decomposition of Economic Relationships by Time Scale Using Wavelets: Expenditure and Income," *Studies in Nonlinear Dynamics and Econometrics*, **3**(1), 23–42.

Schroeder, Manfred (1991) "Noises: White, Pink, Brown, and Black," in *Fractals, Chaos, Power Laws*, W. H. Freeman and Co., New York, NY, pp. 121–137.

Whitcher, B., S. D. Byers, P. Gultrop and D. B. Percival (2002) "Testing the Homogeneity of Variance in Time Series: Long Memory, Wavelets and the Nile River," *Water Resources Research*, **38**(5), 1029–1039.

Wornell, G. W., and A. V. Oppenheim (1992) "Estimation of Fractal Signals from Noisy Measurements Using Wavelets," *IEEE Transactions of Signal Processing*, **40**(3), 611–623.

Part II
Financial risk measurement

5   Frequency analysis of financial risk

5.1   Introduction

In Chapter 3 we analyzed the marginal distribution and in Chapter 4 the temporal dependence of investment returns identified as Fractional Brownian Motion (FBM). We'll now prepare to look at these two aspects of the research problem to characterize the long-term temporal risks of such returns simultaneously in their frequency and time domains. As we discussed in the preceding four chapters, Geometric Brownian Motion (GBM) increments are, per definition, independent and stationary (i.i.d.). Their stationarity allows for Fourier analysis, i.e., linear analysis in the frequency domain, since their (co-) variances and therefore their (co-) frequencies are constant. These increment series can be expanded in series of scaling frequencies, the so-called *frequency spectra*. In the next chapter, when we discuss windowed Fourier analysis, we'll determine how the FBM scaling frequency spectra depend on, and vary through, time.

In particular, in this chapter we'll discuss first covariance or correlation functions, which measure the degree of linear dependence, time and frequency convolution, and Fourier (= frequency or spectral) analysis. This chapter will prepare us for the next chapter, where we will visualize nonlinear dependence measurements in the time-frequency domain using Gábor's spectrograms based on the Windowed Fourier Transform.

Our original financial-economic inspiration originated with the work by Granger and Morgenstern (1963), Granger (1966) and Priestley (1981).[1] For the following mathematical details of measuring the time-dependence of varying frequencies we are indebted to Bloomfield (1976), Hsu (1984), Champeney (1990), Nikias and Petropulu (1993) and Körner (1990). Additional and more recent examples of applied Fourier analysis can be found in Folland (1992).

5.2   Visualization of long-term financial risks

5.2.1   *Plot of absolute ACF against time horizons*

Because of time-reversals and reversals-to-the-mean in time series, it is difficult to detect long-term dependence and geometric scaling laws by just plotting the Autocorrelation Function (ACF) $\gamma(\tau)$, of first differences of the returns on investments

$$\Delta x(t) = \Delta[\ln X(t) - \ln X(t-1)] \tag{5.1}$$

or of first differences of foreign exchange (FX) rates

$$\Delta X(t) = X(t) - X(t-1) \tag{5.2}$$

The reason is that it is difficult to visually distinguish between the decays of the various ACFs corresponding to various fractional difference constants d, as was originally suggested by Box and Jenkins (1970). An only mildly better identifying picture of these slow geometric declines in dependence, which are indicative for long-term dependence, are plots of the absolute values of the ACFs, $|\gamma(\tau)|$, or of their squared values, $|\gamma(\tau)|^2$, against the time horizons τ, as in Figure 4.4 of Chapter 4.

5.2.2   *Time-frequency and time-scale visualizations*

In addition, there is a more fundamental problem with this particular identification methodology. The ACF, $\gamma(\tau)$, provides only second-order evidence for linear dependence, i.e., evidence for *weak* linear dependence (cf. Chapters 1 and 3). Following up on our conjecture at the end of Chapter 2, that financial risk involves more than just the second-order moments of variance and covariance of financial variables, we prefer to visualize the shape of their complete distributions, in particular, by way of their third- and fourth-order moments – their skewness and kurtosis. This is similar to what we did for the stable distributions discussed in Chapter 3. Moreover, we would like to visualize complete distributional evidence for all relative frequencies of occurrence for a time series for any form of time dependence, and not only for its correlation, i.e., for its linear dependence.

Thus, our preferred methodology should be to simultaneously visualize the marginal distributional evidence *and* the time-localized dependence evidence of these nonstationary time series, so that we can also better distinguish between serial (short term) time-dependence and global (long term) time-dependence. Such visualization and identification methodology exists already for more than half a century and it is very familiar to signal processing engineers.

In short, we need to analyze time-frequency pictures, or *spectrograms*, of financial time series, as discussed in Chapter 6, and time-scale pictures, or *scalograms*, as discussed in Chapter 7 to enable the required, and proper, identification of financial market risk.

5.3   Correlation and time convolution

In this section, we'll define the ACF of classical time series analysis (Jenkins and Watts, 1968; Box and Jenkins, 1970; Anderson, 1994) and establish its close relationship with the convolution of signal processing. It's important to recognize that all correlation functions, convolutions and Fourier Transforms discussed in this chapter are scalar products, based on simple integrations.

Definition 183   *The scalar product, or inner product, on the space of $L^2[a, b]$ of square integrable functions is defined by*

$$\langle x, y \rangle = \int_a^b x(t) y(t) \, dt \tag{5.3}$$

A scalar product of two vectors and a simple integral are essentially the same thing. The two operations exactly coincide in the following situation (Burke-Hubbard, 1998, pp. 159–160). The step functions $f(t)$ are defined for $0 \leq t \leq T$ and are constant, except possibly at the integers. For example, imagine a step function $\bar{Y}(t)$ representing an average quantity of a commodity in time period t and another step function $\bar{X}(t)$ representing the average price of that commodity in time period t. Then, the integral

$$\int_a^b \bar{X}(t) \bar{Y}(t) \, dt \tag{5.4}$$

gives the total revenue of the sale of this commodity over the period $(b - a)$. But the same information is given by the scalar product

$$\langle \bar{X}, \bar{Y} \rangle = \left\langle \begin{bmatrix} \bar{X}_a \\ \vdots \\ \bar{X}_b \end{bmatrix}, \begin{bmatrix} \bar{Y}_a \\ \vdots \\ \bar{Y}_b \end{bmatrix} \right\rangle$$

$$= \bar{X}_a \bar{Y}_a + \cdots + \bar{X}_b \bar{Y}_b$$

$$= \sum_{t=a}^b \bar{X}(t) \bar{Y}(t) \tag{5.5}$$

In a 2-Dimensional (2D) price–quantity diagram, the scalar product $\langle \bar{X}, \bar{Y} \rangle$ would represent the space under the average price curve.

5.3.1   Covariance functions

Let's now use this scalar product to specify the covariance and correlation functions.

Definition 184   *The* cross-covariance function *of two (random) variables* $x_1(t)$
and $x_2(t)$ *is*

$$R_{12}(\tau) = E\{x_1(t)x_2(t-\tau)\}$$

$$= \int_{-\infty}^{+\infty} x_1(t)x_2(t-\tau)\,dt$$

$$= \int_{-\infty}^{+\infty} x_1(t)L^\tau x_2(t)\,dt \qquad (5.6)$$

Of course, we also have

$$R_{21}(\tau) = E\{x_2(t)x_1(t-\tau)\}$$

$$= \int_{-\infty}^{+\infty} x_2(t)x_1(t-\tau)\,dt$$

$$= \int_{-\infty}^{+\infty} x_2(t)L^\tau x_1(t)\,dt \qquad (5.7)$$

where L is the familiar linear lag operator.

The cross-covariance function $R_{12}(\tau)$, or $R_{21}(\tau)$, provides a measure of linear similarity, or linear dependence, between the variables $x_1(t)$ and $x_2(t)$ as a function of the parameter τ, the time shift of one variable with respect to the other. If the cross-covariance function is zero for all time shifts τ, then the two variables are said to be uncorrelated.

Definition 185   *If the (random) variables* $x_1(t)$ *and* $x_2(t)$ *are identical, the covariance function*

$$R_{11}(\tau) = \int_{-\infty}^{+\infty} x_1(t)x_1(t-\tau)\,dt$$

$$= \int_{-\infty}^{+\infty} x_1(t)L^\tau x_1(t)\,dt \qquad (5.8)$$

is called the autocovariance function *of* $x_1(t)$.

Definition 186   *The normalized quantity* $\gamma(t)$ *defined by*

$$\gamma(\tau) = \frac{\int_{-\infty}^{+\infty} x_1(t)x_1(t-\tau)\,dt}{\int_{-\infty}^{+\infty} [x_1(t)]^2\,dt}$$

$$= \frac{\int_{-\infty}^{+\infty} x_1(t)L^\tau x_1(t)\,dt}{\int_{-\infty}^{+\infty} [x_1(t)]^2\,dt} \qquad (5.9)$$

is called the autocorrelation function (ACF) *of* $x_1(t)$, *and*

$$\gamma(0) = 1 \qquad (5.10)$$

The ACF of the FBM, which we interpreted in Chapter 4 as a fractional summation of white noise processes,

$$x(t) = (1 - L)^{-d}\varepsilon(t) \tag{5.11}$$

with $\varepsilon(t) \sim i.i.d.(0, \sigma_\varepsilon^2)$, is given by

$$
\begin{aligned}
\gamma(\tau) &= E\{x(t)x(t-\tau)\} \\
&= \int_{-\infty}^{+\infty} x(t)L^\tau x(t)\, dt \\
&= \int_{-\infty}^{+\infty} (1-L)^{-d}\varepsilon(t)L^\tau (1-L)^{-d}\varepsilon(t)\, dt \\
&= \int_{-\infty}^{+\infty} (1-L)^{-2d} L^\tau \varepsilon^2(t)\, dt \\
&= \int_{-\infty}^{+\infty} \left[\sum_{\tau=0}^{\infty} (-1)^\tau \binom{-2d}{\tau} L^\tau \right] L^\tau \varepsilon^2(t)\, dt \\
&= \left[\sum_{\tau=0}^{\infty} (-1)^\tau \binom{-2d}{\tau} \right] L^{2\tau} \int_{-\infty}^{+\infty} \varepsilon^2(t)\, dt \\
&= \sigma_\varepsilon^2 \sum_{\tau=0}^{\infty} c(\tau) \tag{5.12}
\end{aligned}
$$

using the results of Chapter 4. The coefficients $c(\tau)$ can again be expressed in terms of the gamma function

$$
\begin{aligned}
c(\tau) &= (-1)^\tau \binom{-2d}{\tau} \\
&= \frac{(-1)^\tau (-2d)!}{\tau!(-2d-\tau)!} \\
&= \frac{(-1)^\tau (-2d)(-2d-1)\cdots(-2d-\tau+1)}{\tau!} \\
&= \frac{(2d+\tau-1)\cdots(2d+1)(2d)}{\tau!} \\
&= \frac{(2d+\tau-1)!}{(2d-1)!\tau!} \\
&= \frac{\Gamma(\tau+2d)}{\Gamma(2d)\Gamma(\tau+1)!} \tag{5.13}
\end{aligned}
$$

As the time horizon increases, $\tau \to \infty$,

$$c(\tau) \sim \frac{\tau^{2d-1}}{(2d-1)!} \tag{5.14}$$

There are three cases: when $d \downarrow -\frac{1}{2}$,

$$c(\tau) \sim \tau^{-2} \tag{5.15}$$

When $d = 0$, the Gaussian case occurs

$$c(\tau) \sim \tau^{-1} \tag{5.16}$$

When $d \uparrow \frac{1}{2}$,

$$c(\tau) \sim 1 \tag{5.17}$$

Thus, the ACF of the FBM is proportional to

$$\gamma(\tau) \sim \sigma_\varepsilon^2 \tau^{2d-1}$$
$$= \sigma_\varepsilon^2 \tau^{2H-2} \tag{5.18}$$

This clearly shows that the ACF of the FBM is time-dependent, since it scales according to the time horizon τ. How fast it decreases in scale depends on the scaling exponent $2d - 1 = \lambda = 2H - 2$ or $2d + 1 = \lambda + 2 = 2H$, respectively (Table 4.2 in Chapter 4).

5.3.2   Symmetry properties of covariance functions

It is easy to show that, because of symmetry,

$$R_{12}(\tau) = R_{21}(-\tau) \tag{5.19}$$

and

$$R_{11}(\tau) = R_{11}(-\tau) \tag{5.20}$$

5.3.3   Time convolution

Signal engineers prefer to use the concept of time convolution, in contrast to time series statisticians, who prefer to use the concept of a covariance function. Shortly, we'll show that time convolution and the covariance function are equivalent.

Definition 187   *The convolution of two variables $x_1(t)$ and $x_2(t)$ is*

$$f(t) = \int_{-\infty}^{+\infty} x_1(u) x_1(t - u) \, du \tag{5.21}$$

which is often symbolically expressed by a "star" symbol $\star$ as

$$f(t) = x_1(t) \star x_2(t) \tag{5.22}$$

5.3.4 Properties of time convolution

Time convolution has three important algebraic properties, which are often used in theoretical Fourier analysis (Hsu, 1984):

(1) Convolution is *commutative*

$$x_1(t) \star x_2(t) = x_2(t) \star x_1(t) \tag{5.23}$$

(2) Convolution is *associative*

$$[x_1(t) \star x_2(t)] \star x_3(t) = x_1(t) \star [x_2(t) \star x_3(t)] \tag{5.24}$$

(3) Convolution is *distributive*

$$x_1(t) \star [x_2(t) + x_3(t)] = x_1(t) \star x_2(t) + x_1(t) \star x_3(t) \tag{5.25}$$

5.3.5 Covariance as time convolution

The cross-covariances of $x_1(t)$ and $x_2(t)$ are related to the convolutions of $x_1(t)$ and $x_2(-t)$, as follows. Let, by the definition of time convolution,

$$
\begin{aligned}
G_{12}(t) &= x_1(t) \star x_2(-t) \\
&= \int_{-\infty}^{+\infty} x_1(u) x_2[-(t-u)] \, du \\
&= \int_{-\infty}^{+\infty} x_1(u) x_2(u-t) \, du
\end{aligned}
\tag{5.26}
$$

Changing the variable t to τ and the dummy variable u to t, we have

$$
\begin{aligned}
G_{12}(\tau) &= \int_{-\infty}^{+\infty} x_1(t) x_2(t-\tau) \, d\tau \\
&= R_{12}(\tau)
\end{aligned}
\tag{5.27}
$$

Hence, a cross-covariance equals the following time convolution

$$R_{12}(\tau) = G_{12}(\tau) = x_1(t) \star x_2(-t)|_{t=\tau} \tag{5.28}$$

5.4 Fourier analysis of stationary price innovations

We will now first discuss the Fourier analysis of stationary periodic variables, e.g., of Random Walk price innovations, and, next, the Fourier analysis of stationary aperiodic variables.[2] Fourier analysis is a mathematical technique for transforming the view of a time series from a time-based one to a frequency-based one (Körner, 1990). It analyzes the "frequency content" of a time series.

This particular property is also the drawback of Fourier analysis, since in this transformation from the time domain to the frequency domain, the *timing* of information is lost, because a Fourier Transform (FT) is a global representation of a time series over the whole time domain $(-\infty, +\infty)$. But if a time series does not change much over time – i.e., if it is stationary – this drawback isn't very important. In fact, it's properties make it a very suitable tool for studying linear time-invariant operators (cf. Chapter 3), such as differentiation or integration with integer orders. Such classical research was the basis for the very first forays into empirical periodic analysis of financial price formation (Osborne, 1962).

However, if a given frequency is present in a time series $x(t)$ over only a limited time interval, the FT is unable to accurately detect this frequency and to give any information about its *lifetime* or *coherence* and about the moments of its appearance and of its disappearance.

The following analysis will culminate in the definition of the (constant) risk or power spectral density (PSD) for stationary aperiodic variables. This PSD can be visualized by a *spectrogram*. A spectrogram is a powerful visualization for empirical analysis of stationary random variables. The important Wiener–Khinchin Theorem will show that the risk spectrum is the FT of the auto-covariance function. Thus, we can analyze stationary aperiodic variables $x(t)$ by computing their covariance functions, or equivalently, their PSDs. This Fourier analysis of stationary series will be followed by the even more useful windowed Fourier analysis of slowly changing nonstationary variables in Chapter 6, since we have already observed that most financial market time series are nonstationary.

Definition 188   *A periodic* variable *is any variable for which*

$$x(t) = x(t - \tau) \quad \text{for all } t \tag{5.29}$$

The smallest constant τ that satisfies this equation is called the period τ *of this variable.*

Remark 189   *By iteration, we have for periodic variables the following relationship*

$$x(t) = x(t - n\tau) \quad \text{for } n = 0, \pm 1, \pm 2, \dots \tag{5.30}$$

5.4.1   *Fourier series for periodic variables*

Definition 190   *A periodic variable can be represented equivalently by two trigonometric forms and one complex exponential form of the* Fourier series, *as follows*

$$x(t) = \frac{a_0}{2} + \sum_{n=1}^{+\infty}(a_n \cos n\omega_0 t + b_n \sin n\omega_0 t) \tag{5.31}$$

$$= C_0 + \sum_{n=1}^{+\infty} C_n \cos(n\omega_0 t - \theta_n) \tag{5.32}$$

$$= \sum_{n=-\infty}^{+\infty} c_n e^{jn\omega_0 t} \tag{5.33}$$

where $\omega_0 = 2\pi/T$ and the imaginary number $j = \sqrt{-1}$.

The *Cartesian coefficients* a_n and b_n, respectively the *polar coefficients* C_n, as well as the *exponential coefficients* c_n are collectively called: the *Fourier resonance coefficients*. The second equivalent trigonometric Fourier series is called the *harmonics form*.

Notice that the Fourier series expansion of a periodic time variable describes a periodic variable as a sum of sinusoidal components having different frequencies. The sinusoidal component of *frequency* $\omega_n = n\omega_0$ is called the nth *harmonic* of the periodic variable and n is called the *wave number*. Here $\omega_0 = 2\pi f_0 = 2\pi/T$ is the *fundamental angular frequency* and $f_0 = 1/T$ is the *fundamental frequency* and the first harmonic $C_1 \cos(\omega_0 t - \theta_1)$ is called the *fundamental component* (because it has the same period as the variable $x(t)$). An increase in frequency decreases the wavelength.

The coefficients C_n and the angles θ_n are the *harmonic amplitudes*, i.e., they *scale* the amplitude of the sinusoidal waves, and *phase angles, respectively*, i.e., they *shift* the position of the sinusoidal waves, respectively. Thus, Fourier analysis scales and shifts the sinusoidal *bases* $e^{jn\omega_0 t}$ to achieve a complete analysis of the time series.

Example 191   *Fourier series can be used to approximate target time series $x(t)$, in this example, a step function, or square wave, as in Figure 5.1. We start with a mean $f_0 = C_0 = 1$ and, successively add the large wave $f_1 = \cos \omega_0$, subtract three times smaller and three times more frequent wave $f_2 = \frac{1}{3}\cos 3\omega_0$ to create the general "hat" shape. Next we add a five times smaller and faster wave $f_3 = \frac{1}{5}\cos 5\omega_0$. In the left column of Figure 5.1 are the target and terms f_1 through f_3. In the right column are f_0 and the succeeding sums, as each term is added to f_0. Notice that the approximation improves (i.e. each successive sum approximates the square wave more precisely) as the number of Fourier terms in the series increases. In the last graph, terms f_5 and f_6 are added (but not shown separately) to show further improvement in the approximation. Notice the Gibbs phenomenon, consisting of spurious $sinc(t)$ oscillations over the whole time domain. In older sound systems, which use Fourier approximation expansions for communication and transfer of information, this approximation error phenomenon causes a slight*

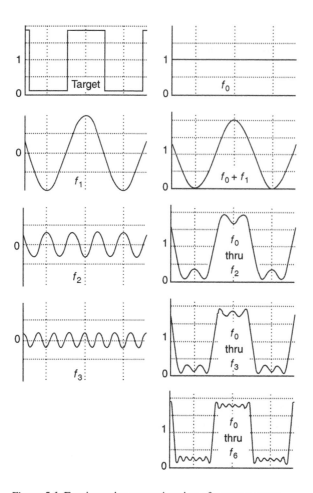

Figure 5.1 Fourier series approximation of a square wave.

"hiss." *The Gibbs phenomenon will be discussed in greater detail in Chapter 11, when we are looking at the various finite element numerical solution methods for nonlinear diffusion equations. We'll find that interpolating wavelet expansions more precisely locate the Gibbs phenomenon than the Fourier trigonometric expansions thereby eliminating most of the Gibbs phenomenon.*

Remark 192   *It is easy to proof (by checking) the following conversion formulas of the Fourier resonance coefficients.*
   For $n \neq 0$

$$C_n = \sqrt{a_n^2 + b_n^2} = 2|c_n| \quad and \quad \theta_n = \tan^{-1}\left(\frac{b_n}{a_n}\right) \tag{5.34}$$

and

$$c_n = |c_n|e^{j\phi_n} \quad \text{where} \quad |c_n| = \tfrac{1}{2}\sqrt{a_n^2 + b_n^2} \quad and \quad \phi_n = \tan^{-1}\left(-\frac{b_n}{a_n}\right) = -\theta_n$$

(5.35)

or

$$c_n = \tfrac{1}{2}(a_n - jb_n) \quad and \quad c_{-n} = \tfrac{1}{2}(a_n + jb_n) = c_n^*$$

(5.36)

*where the asterisk * indicates the* complex conjugate, *so that*

$$a_n = 2\,\mathrm{Re}[c_n] \quad and \quad b_n = -2\,\mathrm{Im}[c_n]$$

(5.37)

For n = 0

$$\frac{a_0}{2} = C_0 = c_0$$

(5.38)

Example 193 *The sophisticated heat analysis, conducted by J. B. J. Fourier himself during Napoleon's campaign in Egypt, allows for time-varying Fourier resonance coefficients, which are better analyzed in Chapter 6, when we analyze nonstationary time series. It illustrates how Fourier analysis can be used to solve problems that are difficult to analyze in the time domain, but easier to solve in the frequency domain, as can be seen in Figure 5.2. (adapted from Burke-Hubbard, 1998, p. 13). To determine the temperature at time t of a metal bar (in the case of J. B. J. Fourier, the barrel of a cannon in Napoleon's Grand Army) that is cooling, one starts by measuring the bar's initial temperature (at t = 0), representing it as a temperature function x(s, t) that depends on space s (= distance along the bar) and time t. Next one moves from physical space to the frequency domain, computing its time-dependent FT $\mathcal{F}(\omega, t)$, which tells us the coefficient c_n for each frequency $\omega_n = n\omega_0$, or heat wave number n, making up the heat function x(s, t) at time t = 0. The Fourier resonance coefficients at time t = 0, are given by the formula*

$$c_n(0) = n^{-0.5}$$

(5.39)

The Fourier resonance coefficients at time t are computed with the formula

$$c_n(t) = c_n(0)e^{(-n^2 t/100)}$$
$$= n^{-0.5}e^{(-n^2 t/100)}$$

(5.40)

It's clear that these time-dependent Fourier resonance coefficients decay over time: the heat waves vanish over time. Consider here just the coefficients for times t = 1, 5, 10 and 50. For each such time, the coefficients are the same for the entire bar (Fourier resonance coefficients are global coefficients) and the information on space x seems to have disappeared. But this space information reappears when

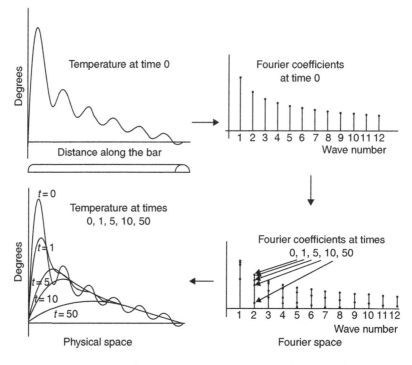

Figure 5.2 Heat diffusion analysis: by following the arrows we find a FT from the measured temperature in physical space to the heat wave frequency domain, and then analyze and return to physical space by the inverse FT.

we return from the frequency domain to the space domain: we invert the resolved FT $\mathcal{F}(\omega, t)$ to obtain the function $x(s, t)$, which provides the exact temperature for each point s of the bar at any time t.

5.4.2   Computation of the Fourier resonance coefficients

The constant Fourier resonance coefficients can be computed directly from the data, once we take account of the fundamental orthogonality of the sinusoidal bases.

5.4.2.1   Orthogonality of sinus and cosinus

Definition 194   *A set of functions* $\{\phi_k(t)\}$ *is* orthogonal *on an interval* $a < t < b$, *if, for any two functions* $\phi_m(t)$ *and* $\phi_n(t)$ *in the set* $\{\phi_k(t)\}$, *the following relationship holds*

$$\int_a^b \phi_m(t)\phi_n(t)dt = \begin{cases} 0 & \text{for } m \neq n \\ r_n & \text{for } m = n \end{cases} \tag{5.41}$$

Definition 195   *The set of functions* $\{\phi_k(t)\}$ *is orthonormal, when it is orthogonal and* $r_n = 1$ *for* $m = n$.

Using elementary calculus, one can easily show that sines and cosines form an orthogonal set of functions on the interval $-T/2 < t < T/2$, since

$$\int_{-T/2}^{T/2} \cos(m\omega_0 t) = 0 \quad \text{for } m \neq 0 \tag{5.42}$$

$$\int_{-T/2}^{T/2} \sin(m\omega_0 t) = 0 \quad \text{for all } m \tag{5.43}$$

$$\int_{-T/2}^{T/2} \cos(m\omega_0 t) \cos(n\omega_0 t)\, dt = \begin{cases} 0 & \text{for } m \neq n \\ T/2 & \text{for } m = n \neq 0 \end{cases} \tag{5.44}$$

$$\int_{-T/2}^{T/2} \sin(m\omega_0 t) \sin(n\omega_0 t)\, dt = \begin{cases} 0 & \text{for } m \neq n \\ T/2 & \text{for } m = n \neq 0 \end{cases} \tag{5.45}$$

$$\int_{-T/2}^{T/2} \sin(m\omega_0 t) \cos(n\omega_0 t)\, dt = 0 \quad \text{for all } m \text{ and } n \tag{5.46}$$

where $\omega_0 = 2\pi/T$.

Such a well-defined set of orthogonal analytic functions is called a *frame of reference*. When a frame of reference is *complete*, it forms a *basis* for analysis. Such a basis may contain functions that are not necessarily orthogonal (or orthonormal), but its analytic results, i.e., the computed correlation coefficients, are easier to understand when they are. Fortunately, each frame of reference can be orthogonalized. When we discuss wavelets in Chapter 7, we'll discuss more details of these important analytic frames of reference and bases.

5.4.2.2   *Valuation of the trigonometric Fourier resonance coefficients*

Using these orthogonality relations of the sines and cosines, we can now compute the Cartesian Fourier resonance coefficients a_n and b_n of the Fourier series $x(t)$ and, by using the conversion relations, also the polar Fourier resonance coefficients C_n and θ_n, and the exponential Fourier resonance coefficients of c_n and ϕ_n, as follows:

$$a_n = \frac{2}{T} \int_{-T/2}^{T/2} x(t) \cos(n\omega_0 t)\, dt \quad \text{for } n = 0, 1, 2, \ldots \tag{5.47}$$

$$b_n = \frac{2}{T} \int_{-T/2}^{T/2} x(t) \sin(n\omega_0 t)\, dt \quad \text{for } n = 0, 1, 2, \ldots \tag{5.48}$$

and

$$a_0 = \frac{2}{T} \int_{-T/2}^{T/2} x(t)\, dt \tag{5.49}$$

5.4.2.3   Valuation of complex Fourier resonance coefficients

First, we have the simple mean

$$c_0 = \frac{a_0}{2} = \frac{1}{T} \int_{-T/2}^{T/2} x(t)\, dt \tag{5.50}$$

Then, with the use of the identity

$$e^{-j\theta} = \cos\theta - j\sin\theta \tag{5.51}$$

we find

$$c_n = \tfrac{1}{2}(a_n - jb_n)$$
$$= \frac{1}{T}\left[\int_{-T/2}^{T/2} x(t)\cos(n\omega_0 t)\, dt - j\int_{-T/2}^{T/2} x(t)\sin(n\omega_0 t)\, dt \right]$$
$$= \frac{1}{T}\left[\int_{-T/2}^{T/2} x(t)[\cos(n\omega_0 t)\, dt - j\sin(n\omega_0 t)]\, dt \right]$$
$$= \frac{1}{T} \int_{-T/2}^{T/2} x(t)e^{-jn\omega_0 t}\, dt \tag{5.52}$$

Similarly,

$$c_{-n} = \tfrac{1}{2}(a_n + jb_n)$$
$$= \frac{1}{T} \int_{-T/2}^{T/2} x(t)e^{jn\omega_0 t}\, dt \tag{5.53}$$

These two formulas for c_n and c_{-n}, respectively, can be combined into a single exponential formula

$$c_n = \frac{1}{T} \int_{-T/2}^{T/2} x(t)e^{-jn\omega_0 t}\, dt \quad \text{for } n = 0, \pm1, \pm2, \ldots \tag{5.54}$$

These results have led to the powerful analytical identity of Parseval, which provides us with an exact accounting of the total amount of *risk = volatility = energy = power* contained in the financial time series $x(t)$, when decomposed into an infinite series of wave functions.

Proposition 196 (*Parseval's identity*) *If a_0, a_n and b_n are the coefficients in the Fourier expansion of a periodic function $x(t)$ with period T, then*

$$\frac{1}{T}\int_{-T/2}^{T/2} [x(t)]^2\, dt = \frac{a_0^2}{4} + \frac{1}{2}\sum_{n=1}^{+\infty}(a_n^2 + b_n^2) \tag{5.55}$$

$$= c_0^2 + 2\sum_{n=1}^{+\infty}|c_n|^2 \tag{5.56}$$

$$= \sum_{n=-\infty}^{+\infty}|c_n|^2 \tag{5.57}$$

This mean-square value is called the *risk content* of the periodic function $x(t)$. Thus, the finite estimate of the second moment of the periodic $x(t)$ equals this infinite sum of the squared Fourier resonance coefficients!

5.4.2.4 *Orthogonality of complex exponential functions*

The complex form of the Fourier series is the most useful. It is the initial platform for our discussion of wavelets in Chapter 7. Consider a set of *complex exponential functions* $\{e^{jn\omega_0 t}\}$ where the fundamental frequency is $\omega_0 = 2\pi/T$. Using elementary calculus, one can show that the mean

$$\frac{1}{T}\int_{-T/2}^{T/2} e^{jn\omega_0 t}\, dt = 0 \quad \text{for } n \neq 0 \tag{5.58}$$

and the (complex) variance

$$\frac{1}{T}\int_{-T/2}^{T/2} e^{jm\omega_0 t}(e^{jn\omega_0 t})^*\, dt = \begin{cases} 0 & \text{for } n \neq m \\ 1 & \text{for } n = m \end{cases} \tag{5.59}$$

The complex exponential functions $\{e^{jn\omega_0 t}\}$, $n = 0, \pm 1, \pm 2, \ldots$, form a set of orthogonal basis functions over the interval $-T/2 < t < T/2$. They form a complete frame of reference and, thus, a basis for analysis.

5.4.3 *Frequency spectra*

Definition 197 *A plot of the magnitude $|c_n|$ of the complex Fourier resonance coefficients c_n versus the angular frequency ω is called the* amplitude spectrum *of the periodic variable $x(t)$. A plot of the phase angle ϕ_n of c_n versus ω is called the* phase spectrum *of $x(t)$.*

Since for periodic series the index n assumes only integers, these two spectra are not continuous curves, but appear only at discrete frequencies $n\omega_0$. They are *discrete frequency spectra* or *line spectra*.

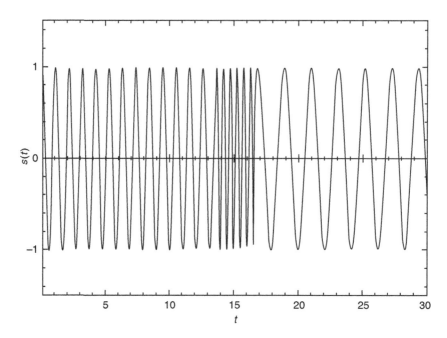

Figure 5.3 A sample signal constructed from sine functions representing three pulsations: $\omega_1 = 6, \omega_2 = 12, \omega_3 = 3$ with the same amplitude. The time coherence of ω_1 and ω_3 is identical. Discontinuities are present at the time of change of frequencies.

Example 198 *Figure 5.3 presents a sampled continuous time signal function $s(t)$ constructed from three successive sine functions with the same coherence or lifetime T_1 for frequency ω_1 and $\omega_3 < \omega_1$, and shorter coherence T_2 for frequency $\omega_2 > \omega_1$ (Bendjoya and Slezak, 1993, pp. 233–234). The signal $s(t)$ shows discontinuities at the time of change of frequencies. Figure 5.4 displays the modulus of the Fourier resonance coefficients $|c_n|$, i.e., its* line spectrum. *Notice the rather good detection of the three frequencies present in $s(t)$ and how the high frequency ω_2 is less precisely detected because of its shorter coherence. The spurious fluctuations all over this spectrum are due to the discontinuities. No information can be obtained from the line spectrum about the sequence of the changes in frequencies, the time at which the different frequencies appear and disappear in $s(t)$, or about their coherence. Only a "timeless" frequency analysis is performed, which can be distorted by discontinuities.*

Example 199 *Figure 5.5 shows examples of the magnitude spectra of several musical variables, which are, clearly, periodic, sinusoidal waves (Kemp, 1991, p. 12). The clarinet, the violin and the highland bagpipe playing the same note (B flat above middle C, 466 Hz). The* interferograms *(= correlograms)*

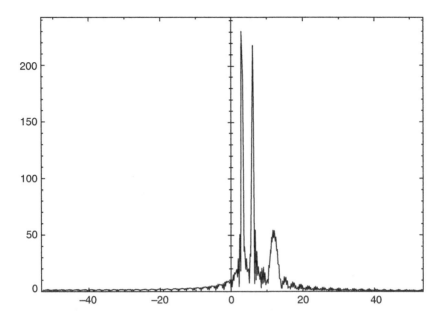

Figure 5.4 The FT of the sampled signal $s(t)$. The three frequencies $\omega_3 < \omega_1 < \omega_2$ are detected, but the frequency ω_2 with he shortest time coherence has the smallest resonance coefficient. The spurious fluctuations all over this spectrum are due to the discontinuities in the signal.

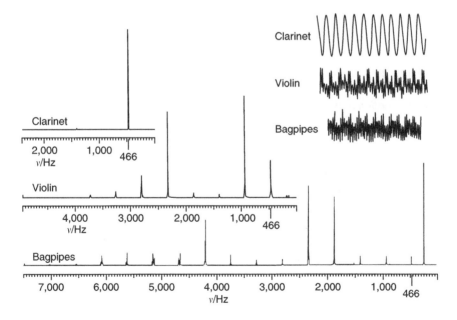

Figure 5.5 Fourier series analysis of pure musical harmonics: dominant frequencies of the clarinet, violin and bagpipe.

at the upper right-hand side were Fourier transformed to show the resonance coefficients of their individual frequencies, or resonances emitted, as shown at the lower left side. Notice that the clarinet is almost pure, with one dominant frequency at 466 Hz. The violin shows several dominating higher frequency overtones in addition to the 466 Hz. And the bagpipe shows both a dominant lower harmonic (from the bas drone) and several dominant higher frequency harmonics.

5.5   Software

The computations of the following Exercises can be executed by using the MATLAB® Signal Processing Toolbox and by the MATLAB® Higher-Order Spectral Analysis (HOSA) Toolbox (Swami *et al.*, 1998). Both Toolboxes are available from The MathWorks, Inc., 24 Prime Park Way Natick, MA 01760-1500, USA. Tel (508) 647-7000; Fax (508) 647-7001;

http://www.mathworks.com/products/wavelettbx.shtml.

The HOSA Toolbox (2.0.3) is a collection of MATLAB® M-files containing specialized tools for signal processing with higher order spectra. It was created by Jerry M. Mendel, Chrysostomos L. (Max) Nikias and Ananthram Swami of United Signals and Systems, Inc. The toolbox is a collection of MATLAB® routines whose primary features are functions for: higher order spectrum estimation either by conventional or parametric approaches; magnitude and phase retrieval; adaptive linear prediction; harmonic retrieval and quadratic phase coupling; time-delay estimation and array signal processing.

5.6   Exercises

Run MATLAB® Help, Examples and Demos, Toolboxes, Signal Processing:

Exercise 200   *Filtering a sinusoidal signal: look carefully at the creation of a sinusoidal signal with different frequencies by superposition, the creation and implementation of the IIR (= Infinite Impulse Response filter), the way the various series are plotted, the magnitude versus frequency diagram of the Fast Fourier Transform (FFT) (cf. Brigham, 1988).*

Exercise 201   *Spectral Analysis of the DTMF signal (with sound): study the spectrum diagram*

Exercise 202   *Discrete Fourier Transform (DFT) (try different windows): study the effects on the DFT by changing frequency and amplitude of the signal. Notice that there doesn't exist a DFT for an infinite signal. (It's somewhat confusing that the command for the DFT in MATLAB® is fft. For the inverse DFT it is ifft.)*

Exercise 203   *Continuous FT: study the effects of different modulation frequencies on the FT of the modulated Gaussian pulse. Notice the symmetry of the FT.*

Notes

1 Chapter 6 contains a visual example of the original spectral analysis of the Standard and Poor stock market series by Granger and Morgenstern (1963).
2 Jean Baptiste Joseph Fourier (1768–1830) was a French mathematician, who became famous for his mathematical treatise on the *Theorie Analytique de la Chaleur (Analytical Theory of Heat)*, 1822. He established the partial differential equation governing the heat diffusion in the barrels of the canons of Napoleon's Grand Army to determine how quickly these cannons could be safely reloaded. He solved it by using an infinite series of trigonometric functions. His diffusion (= partial differentiation) equation was used in 1973 to derive the Black–Scholes European option pricing model. This heat diffusion equation is also used in the theory of turbulence, as we will see in Chapter 11.

Bibliography

Anderson, T. W. (1994) *The Statistical Analysis of Time Series*, John Wiley and Sons, New York, NY.

Bendjoya, Ph., and E. Slézak (1993) "Wavelet Analysis and Applications to Some Dynamical Systems," *Celestial Mechanics and Dynamical Astronomy*, **56**, 231–262.

Bloomfield, P. (1976) *Fourier Analysis of Time Series: An Introduction*, John Wiley and Sons, New York, NY.

Box, G. E. P., and G. M. Jenkins (1970) *Time Series Analysis: Forecasting and Control*, 2nd edn, Holden-Day, San Francisco, CA.

Brigham, E. O. (1988) *The Fast Fourier Transform and Its Applications*, Prentice-Hall: Englewood Cliffs, NJ.

Burke-Hubbard, Barbara (1998) *The World According to Wavelets: The Story of a Mathematical Technique in the Making*, 2nd edn, A K Peters, Wellesley, MA.

Champeney, D. C. (1990) *A Handbook of Fourier Theorems*, Cambridge University Press, Cambridge, UK.

Folland, G. (1992) *Fourier Analysis and its Applications*, Wadsworth and Brooks/Cole, Belmont, CA.

Granger, C. W. J. (1966) "The Typical Spectral Shape of an Economic Variable," *Econometrica*, **34**(1), 150–161.

Granger, C. W. J., and O. Morgenstern (1963) "Spectral Analysis of New York Stock Exchange Prices," *Kyklos*, **16**, 1–27. Reprinted as chapter 8 in Cootner, Paul H. (Ed.) (1964) *The Random Character of Stock Market Prices*, The MIT Press, Cambridge, MA, pp. 162–188.

Hsu, Hwei P. (1984) *Applied Fourier Analysis*, Harcourt Brace College Publishers, San Diego, 1984, chapter 6.

Jenkins, G. M., and D. G. Watts (1968) *Spectral Analysis and its Applications*, Holden-Day, San Francisco, CA.

Körner, T. W. (1990) *Fourier Analysis*, Cambridge University Press, Cambridge, UK.

Kemp, William (1991) *Organic Spectroscopy*, 3rd edn, W. H. Freeman and Co., New York.

Osborne, M. F. M. (1962) "Periodic Structure in the Brownian Motion of Stock Prices," *Operational Research*, **10**, May–June, 345–379. Reprinted as chapter 13 in Cootner, Paul H. (Ed.) (1964), *The Random Character of Stock Market Prices*, The MIT Press, Cambridge, MA, pp. 262–296.

Nikias, Chrysostomos L., and Athina P. Petropulu (1993) *Higher-Order Spectral Analysis: A Nonlinear Signal Processing Framework*, PTR Prentice Hall, Englewood Cliffs, NJ.

Priestley, M. B. (1981) *Spectral Analysis and Time Series*, Academic Press, New York, NY.

Swami, Ananthram, Jerry M. Mendel and Chrysostomos L. (Max) Nikias (1998) *Higher-Order Spectral Analysis Toolbox User's Guide*, Version 2, January, The MathWorks, Inc., Natick, MA.

6 Fourier time–frequency analysis of risk

6.1 Introduction

As we discussed in Chapter 5, Fourier series are powerful tools for analyzing periodic variables, such as musical tones of instruments, or for determining the spectral lines of inorganic and organic chemical components. But very few practical problems of financial-economic analysis do involve such rigidly periodic variables. We need a form of Fourier analysis that can deal with aperiodic, but still "cyclical" variables and that can identify Mandelbrot's aperiodic cyclicity prevalent in the long memory financial return series. Therefore, we'll discuss a frequency representation of aperiodic variables by means of the Fourier Transform (FT), which analyzes the frequency contents of *any* time series, periodic or aperiodic, as the case may be.

The many properties of the FT make it particularly suitable for representation in terms of linear time-invariant system operators, such as integer differentiation or integration, discussed in Chapter 4. Its immediate shortcoming is the same as that of the Fourier series: the FT is a global, and not a local, representation of a time series, since it takes an integral, or average, of the available set of time series observations.

In the second half of this chapter we'll discuss the Windowed FT, which is suitable to analyze *transient* phenomena localized in time, although, perhaps, only suboptimally, since the support of the Fourier wave bases remains infinite. This Windowed FT was discovered by Gábor (1946) and produces the colorful spectrograms of instantaneous frequency distributions familiar from speech analysis and other, rather entertaining internet media, such as RealPlayer™, which lists real-time spectrograms among its audio statistics. Considering that financial time series of investment returns or foreign valuta prices are as nonstationary as speech, Windowed FT forms a powerful, and still heavily under-utilized, research tool for the time–frequency analysis of financial risk (Priestley, 1988; Cohen, 1989).

A very recent, optimal and complete way of analyzing such localized phenomena, which does not suffer from the "infinite support syndrome" of the FT, but which relies instead on finite support, will be discussed in the next chapter, when we focus on time series analysis by finite wavelet bases.

6.2 FT for aperiodic variables

The continuous FT for aperiodic time series is analogously defined to the discrete Fourier series for periodic time series of Chapter 5, as follows (Hsu, 1984; Champeney, 1990).

Definition 204 *The FT of time series $x(t)$ (symbolized by $\mathcal{F}$) in the square-integrable L^2 space is defined by the inner product (or correlation):*

$$F(\omega) = \mathcal{F}[x(t)]$$

$$= \int_{-\infty}^{+\infty} x(t)e^{-j\omega t}dt \tag{6.1}$$

Definition 205 *The inverse FT of $F(\omega)$ (symbolized by $\mathcal{F}^{-1}$) represents the time series $x(t)$ as an infinite integral ("sum") of sinusoids:*

$$x(t) = \mathcal{F}^{-1}[F(\omega)]$$

$$= \frac{1}{2\pi} \int_{-\infty}^{+\infty} F(\omega)e^{j\omega t}d\omega \tag{6.2}$$

Remark 206 *These two equations are often called the FT pair, symbolically denoted by*

$$F(\omega) \leftrightarrow x(t) \tag{6.3}$$

The condition for the existence of the FT $F(\omega)$ is given by

$$\int_{-\infty}^{+\infty} |x(t)|\,dt < \infty \tag{6.4}$$

In other words, the variable $x(t)$ must be *absolutely integrable*. This is the same restrictive condition as exists for martingales (cf. Chapter 2) and, again, it excludes discontinuities and jumps, but also periodic functions, because, for example, for any periodic function:

$$\int_{-\infty}^{+\infty} |x(t)|\,dt = \infty \tag{6.5}$$

Thus, strictly defined, the FT (which is NOT the Fourier series) cannot properly deal with discontinuities or singularities (catastrophes) and periodic functions. However, the Windowed FT can detect other transient phenomena. So let's see how we can understand this form of windowed analysis.

Since any periodic variable $x(t)$ is a function of slow growth, its FT exists in the sense of a generalized function, as follows.

Definition 207 A function $x(t)$ of slow growth *is defined if there exist real numbers C and R such that*

$$x(t) \leq Ct^n \quad where \ |t| > R > 0 \tag{6.6}$$

Immediately related to this concept of slow growth is the concept of a restricting device, such as a *taper*, which "tapers" the influence of the individual observations.

Definition 208 *A continuous function* $\phi(t)$ *is a* testing function of rapid decay, *or* taper, *if*

$$\lim_{t \to \pm\infty} |t^n \phi^{(r)}(t)| = 0 \quad for \ some \ n, r \geq 0 \tag{6.7}$$

where the rth derivative

$$\phi^{(r)}(t) = \frac{d^r \phi(t)}{dt^r} \tag{6.8}$$

In the Exercises, you'll find an application of such a taper for FT analysis. Such a taper can be used to define even more generalized functions, as follows.

Definition 209 *A generalized function of slow growth* $g(t)$ *is defined as a symbolic function, such that to each testing function of rapid decay* $\phi(t)$ *there is assigned a finite number to the inner product:*

$$\langle g, \phi \rangle = \int_{-\infty}^{+\infty} g(t)\phi(t)dt < \infty \tag{6.9}$$

with the linear properties of additivity and homogeneity. Thus

$$\langle g, a_1\phi_1 + a_2\phi_2 \rangle = a_1\langle g, \phi_1 \rangle + a_2\langle g, \phi_2 \rangle \tag{6.10}$$

Remark 210 *If* $\phi(t)$ *is a taper, then we can use advanced calculus to show that* $\phi(t)$ *is absolutely integrable:*

$$\int_{-\infty}^{+\infty} |\phi(t)| \, dt < \infty \tag{6.11}$$

Hence, the FT of this taper, $\Phi(\omega)$*, exists.*

In the next chapter we'll discuss the relaxation of this particular restraining condition of either $\int_{-\infty}^{\infty} |x(t)| \, dt < \infty$ or $\int_{-\infty}^{\infty} |\phi(t)| \, dt < \infty$ for the Wavelet Transform. The Wavelet Transform $\psi(t)$ of $x(t)$ exists, even when $x(t)$ includes discontinuities, jumps, periodicities and cyclicities – in other words, when $x(t)$ includes all the phenomena we observe in empirical financial time series! Because the Wavelet Transform has finite and not infinite support.

But let's now first define the generalized FT.

Definition 211   *The generalized FT $F(\omega)$ of a function of slow growth $x(t)$ is defined by the commuting integrals*

$$\int_{-\infty}^{+\infty} F(u)\phi(u)du = \int_{-\infty}^{+\infty} x(u)\Phi(u)du \tag{6.12}$$

Remark 212   *It can be shown that all the properties of ordinary FTs also hold for the generalized FTs of functions of slow growth (Hsu, 1984; Körner, 1990).*

6.2.1   Algebraic properties of FTs

FTs have some very useful properties, which makes it easy to *exactly* compute an enormous variety of FTs, which are discussed in a historically very interesting and enjoyable presentation by Körner (1990). Let $F(\omega) \leftrightarrow x(t)$ denote the FT pair. Then it's easy to prove the following nine properties (cf. Hsu, 1984, for the particulars of these proofs). In particular, translation = time shifting and scaling = frequency shifting, will be very useful, when we study empirical financial series that exhibit long time-dependence, such as the Fractional Brownian Motion (FBM) defined in Chapter 4. Here follow the nine fundamental properties of FT pairs often used in theoretical signal processing analysis, and now also in theoretical dynamic asset valuation:

(1) *Convolution* in the time domain = multiplication in the frequency domain:

$$x_1(t) \star x_2(t) = F_1(\omega)F_2(\omega) \tag{6.13}$$

(2) *Multiplication* in the time domain = convolution in the frequency domain:

$$x_1(t)x_2(t) = \frac{1}{2\pi} F_1(\omega) \star F_2(\omega) \tag{6.14}$$

(3) *Linearity* in the time domain = linearity in the frequency domain:

$$a_1 x_1(t) + a_2 x_2(t) \leftrightarrow a_1 F_1(\omega) + a_2 F_2(\omega) \tag{6.15}$$

(4) *Translation* (= time shifting) = complex exponential decay in the (imaginary) frequency domain:

$$x(t - t_0) \leftrightarrow F(\omega)e^{-j\omega t_0} \tag{6.16}$$

(5) *Modulation* (= frequency shifting) = complex exponential increase in the (imaginary) time-domain:

$$x(t)e^{j\omega_0 t} \leftrightarrow F(\omega - \omega_0) \tag{6.17}$$

(6) *Scaling up* in the time domain = scaling down in the frequency domain, and *vice versa*:

$$x(ct) \leftrightarrow \frac{1}{|c|} F\left(\frac{\omega}{c}\right) \tag{6.18}$$

(7) *Time-reversal* in the time domain = frequency-reversal in the frequency domain:

$$x(-t) \leftrightarrow F(-\omega) \tag{6.19}$$

(8) *Symmetry* of functions in time and frequency domain:

$$F(t) \leftrightarrow 2\pi x(-\omega) \tag{6.20}$$

(9) *Differentiation* in the time domain = frequency exponential in the frequency domain and *vice versa*:

$$x^{(p)}(t) \leftrightarrow (j\omega)^p F(\omega) \quad \text{and} \tag{6.21}$$

$$(-jt)^p x(t) \leftrightarrow F^{(p)}(\omega) \tag{6.22}$$

Using the fundamental linearity and time shifting properties, we can now find the FT of the Geometric Brownian Motion (GBM) as follows:

$$
\begin{aligned}
F(\omega) &= \mathcal{F}[x(t)] \\
&= \mathcal{F}[x(t-1) + \varepsilon(t)] \\
&= F(\omega)e^{-j\omega} + \mathcal{F}[\varepsilon(t)]
\end{aligned} \tag{6.23}
$$

Notice the frequency translation of the time shift! This implies that we can concisely represent the GBM in the frequency domain as follows:

$$F_{\text{GBM}}(\omega) = (1 - e^{-j\omega})^{-1} \mathcal{F}[\varepsilon(t)] \tag{6.24}$$

Similarly, the FT of the FBM is modeled in the frequency domain as follows:

$$F_{\text{FBM}}(\omega) = (1 - e^{-j\omega})^{-d} \mathcal{F}[\varepsilon(t)] \tag{6.25}$$

We'll need these spectral representations later in this chapter, when we focus on the spectral density of the stationary increments of the FBM.

6.2.2   *Some exact FTs*

Here are some additional important FTs of exact time functions, which can be easily checked (Hsu, 1984):

(1) The FT of a constant is an *impulse function* $\delta(\cdot)$, which is the first derivative of the unit step function $u(\cdot)$:

$$1 \leftrightarrow 2\pi\delta(\omega) = 2\pi \frac{du(\omega)}{d\omega} \tag{6.26}$$

(2) The FT of a complex exponential function results in an impulse with a shifted frequency:

$$e^{j\omega_0 t} \leftrightarrow 2\pi\delta(\omega - \omega_0) \tag{6.27}$$

(3) The FT of a cosine function consists of the sum of two frequency shifted impulse functions:

$$\cos \omega_0 t \leftrightarrow \pi \delta(\omega - \omega_0) + \pi \delta(\omega + \omega_0) \tag{6.28}$$

(4) The FT of a periodic function with period T, which, as we have seen, can always be expressed as a Fourier series of exponential functions, consists of a sequence of equidistant impulses located precisely at the harmonic frequencies of the function (cf. Chapter 5):

$$x(t) = \sum_{n=-\infty}^{+\infty} c_n e^{jn\omega_0 t}, \quad \text{with } \omega_0 = \frac{2\pi}{T}, \tag{6.29}$$

$$\leftrightarrow F(\omega) = 2\pi \sum_{n=-\infty}^{+\infty} c_n \delta(\omega - n\omega_0) \tag{6.30}$$

Remark 213   *To speed up the calculations by reducing the number of computing operations, often we implement the so-called* Fast Fourier Transform (FFT), *which separates its odd and even harmonics. The vector-matrix implementation of this FFT, discovered by Cooley and Tukey (1965), provides an interesting advanced topic in numerical analysis.*

6.2.3   Fourier spectra

The operational *raison d'être* for FTs is to enable the computation of frequency spectra of any continuous or discrete time series.

Definition 214   *The Fourier spectrum $F(\omega) = \mathcal{F}[x(t)]$ is, in general, complex, and thus represented by the sum of real and imaginary parts:*

$$F(\omega) = R(\omega) + jX(\omega)$$
$$= |F(\omega)| e^{j\phi(\omega)} \tag{6.31}$$

where $|F(\omega)|$ is called the magnitude (amplitude) spectrum *of $x(t)$ and $\phi(\omega)$ its* phase spectrum.

When $x(t)$ is a real-valued time series (and, empirically, it always is!), then, using the familiar goniometric identity for a complex exponential,

$$e^{-j\omega t} = \cos \omega t - j \sin \omega t \tag{6.32}$$

its FT can be rewritten as

$$F(\omega) = \int_{-\infty}^{+\infty} x(t)e^{-j\omega t}\,dt$$

$$= \int_{-\infty}^{+\infty} x(t)\cos(\omega t)\,dt - j\int_{-\infty}^{\infty} x(t)\sin(\omega t)\,dt$$

$$= R(\omega) + jX(\omega) \qquad (6.33)$$

so that, equating the real and imaginary parts of the complex $F(\omega)$, we have the real terms

$$R(\omega) = \int_{-\infty}^{+\infty} x(t)\cos(\omega t)\,dt \qquad (6.34)$$

$$X(\omega) = -\int_{-\infty}^{+\infty} x(t)\sin(\omega t)\,dt \qquad (6.35)$$

which are both easy to compute.

6.2.4 Convolution Theorems

The (general) FT can now be related to the earlier sections of Chapter 5, where we discussed correlation and convolution, by way of two powerful Theorems. These Theorems allow convolutions to be replaced by simple products (cf. Hsu, 1984; Champeney, 1990; Körner, 1990, for the respective proofs). The first Theorem shows that convolution in the time domain can be replaced by a product in the frequency domain. The second Theorem shows that convolution in the frequency domain can be replaced by a product in the time domain.

Theorem 215 (Time Convolution) *If* $\mathcal{F}[x_1(t)] = F_1(\omega)$ *and* $\mathcal{F}[x_2(t)] = F_2(\omega)$ *then*

$$\mathcal{F}[x_1(t) * x_2(t)] = F_1(\omega)F_2(\omega) \qquad (6.36)$$

Theorem 216 (Frequency Convolution) *If* $\mathcal{F}^{-1}[F_1(\omega)] = x_1(t)$ *and* $\mathcal{F}^{-1}[F_2(\omega)] = x_2(t)$ *then*

$$\mathcal{F}^{-1}[F_1(\omega) \star F_2(\omega)] = 2\pi x_1(t)x_2(t) \qquad (6.37)$$

or, equivalently,

$$\mathcal{F}[x_1(t)x_2(t)] = \int_{-\infty}^{+\infty} [x_1(t)x_2(t)]\,e^{-j\omega t}\,dt$$

$$= \frac{1}{2\pi}F_1(\omega) \star F_2(\omega)$$

$$= \frac{1}{2\pi}\int_{-\infty}^{+\infty} F_1(y)F_2(\omega - y)\,dy \qquad (6.38)$$

Using the second Theorem and setting the frequency $\omega = 0$, we obtain

$$\int_{-\infty}^{+\infty} [x_1(t)x_2(t)]dt = \frac{1}{2\pi} \int_{-\infty}^{+\infty} F_1(y)F_2(-y)dy$$

$$= \frac{1}{2\pi} \int_{-\infty}^{+\infty} F_1(\omega)F_2(-\omega)d\omega \qquad (6.39)$$

by changing the dummy variable of integration. If $x(t)$ is real valued, then

$$F(-\omega) = F^*(\omega) \qquad (6.40)$$

where $F^*(\omega)$ is the complex conjugate of $F(\omega)$. By substitution in the preceding equation we derive the following financial version of the well-known ergodic Theorem of Parseval, which provides a crucial link between the risk content of a financial time series, as measured in the time domain and in the frequency domain, respectively.

Theorem 217   (Parseval) *If the FT $\mathcal{F}[x(t)] = F(\omega)$, then the risk content (= second moment) of the aperiodic stationary financial time series $x(t)$ is*

$$E[x(t)^2] = \int_{-\infty}^{+\infty} [x(t)]^2 dt$$

$$= \frac{1}{2\pi} \int_{-\infty}^{+\infty} |F(\omega)|^2 d\omega$$

$$= \int_{-\infty}^{+\infty} |F(2\pi v)|^2 d\omega \qquad (6.41)$$

where the angular frequency is $\omega = 2\pi v$ and the frequency v is expressed in Hertz.

The quantity $|F(\omega)|^2$ is called the *risk* or *power spectrum*, or *power spectral density* (PSD) of $x(t)$. It is the frequency domain equivalent of risk in the time domain.

6.2.5   *Wiener–Khintchin Theorem*

Using the foregoing results, we can now present the FTs of the various covariance functions.

Corollary 218   *If $\mathcal{F}[x_1(t)] = F_1(\omega)$ and $\mathcal{F}[x_2(t)] = F_2(\omega)$, then*

$$S_{12}(\omega) = \mathcal{F}[R_{12}(\tau)] = F_1(\omega)F_2(-\omega) \qquad (6.42)$$

$$S_{21}(\omega) = \mathcal{F}[R_{21}(\tau)] = F_1(-\omega)F_2(\omega) \qquad (6.43)$$

$$S_{11}(\omega) = \mathcal{F}[R_{11}(\tau)] = F_1(\omega)F_1(-\omega) \qquad (6.44)$$

The measures $S_{12}(\omega)$ and $S_{21}(\omega)$ are referred to as cross-risk *or* cross-spectral densities (CSD), *and $S_{11}(\omega)$ is, as we saw, the risk spectrum or PSD of $x_1(t)$.*

If $x_1(t)$ is real valued, then

$$S_{11}(\omega) = \mathcal{F}[R_{11}(\tau)]$$

$$= F_1(\omega)F_1(-\omega)$$

$$= F_1(\omega)F_1^*(\omega)$$

$$= |F(\omega)|^2 \tag{6.45}$$

Thus, we have arrived at the famous Wiener–Khinchin Theorem relating the autocovariance function of a financial time series to its risk spectrum, and *vice versa*.[1] Thereby, the time dependence of a time series is translated into its frequency dependence, and *vice versa*.[2]

Theorem 219   (Wiener–Khinchin) *The autocovariance function $R_{11}(\tau)$ and the risk spectral density $|F(\omega)|^2$ constitute a FT pair:*

$$|F(\omega)|^2 = \mathcal{F}[R_{11}(\tau)]$$

$$= \int_{-\infty}^{+\infty} R_{11}(\tau)e^{-j\omega\tau}\,d\tau \tag{6.46}$$

and

$$R_{11}(\tau) = \mathcal{F}^{-1}\big[|F(\omega)|^2\big]$$

$$= \frac{1}{2\pi}\int_{-\infty}^{+\infty}|F(\omega)|^2 e^{j\omega\tau}\,d\omega \tag{6.47}$$

Since for *periodic* or *random* variables that exist over the entire time interval $(-\infty, \infty)$, the risk contents are infinite,

$$E[x(t)^2] = \int_{-\infty}^{+\infty}[x(t)]^2 dt \to \infty \tag{6.48}$$

the covariance functions, as defined earlier, do not exist as finite numbers, nor do their FTs. Therefore, pragmatically we must work with truncated, approximating average covariance functions, based on the assumed ergodicity of the time series, i.e., the assumed equivalence of the represented time series volatility in the time and frequency domains.

Definition 220   *The* average autocovariance function *of $x_1(t)$ is the limit*

$$\bar{R}_{11}(\tau) = \lim_{T\to\infty}\frac{1}{T}\int_{-T/2}^{T/2} x_1(t)x_1(t-\tau)\,dt \tag{6.49}$$

Definition 221   *Similarly, the* average cross-covariance function *of $x_1(t)$ and $x_2(t)$ is the limit*

$$\bar{R}_{12}(\tau) = \lim_{T\to\infty}\frac{1}{T}\int_{-T/2}^{T/2} x_1(t)x_2(t-\tau)\,dt \tag{6.50}$$

These definitions assist us to precisely define what we mean by *uncorrelatedness* of two time series, which is defined as their *linear independence*.

Definition 222   *Two variables $x_1(t)$ and $x_2(t)$ are uncorrelated, if we can decompose their cross-correlation into a product of two independent time averages:*

$$\bar{R}_{12}(\tau) = \lim_{T\to\infty} \frac{1}{T} \int_{-T/2}^{T/2} x_1(t)x_2(t-\tau)dt$$

$$= \left[\lim_{T\to\infty} \frac{1}{T} \int_{-T/2}^{T/2} x_1(t)dt\right]\left[\lim_{T\to\infty} \frac{1}{T} \int_{-T/2}^{T/2} x_2(t-\tau)dt\right] \qquad (6.51)$$

Then, if one time series, say $x_1(t)$, has also a zero average value (e.g. because it is measured as deviations from the mean)

$$\lim_{T\to\infty} \frac{1}{T} \int_{-T/2}^{T/2} x_1(t)dt = 0 \qquad (6.52)$$

then their cross-correlation equals zero:

$$\bar{R}_{12}(\tau) = 0 \quad \text{for all } \tau \qquad (6.53)$$

Thus, uncorrelatedness of two financial time series is empirically easy to verify: compute the deviations from their means and cross-correlate to see if the result equals zero. However, this procedure only measures uncorrelatedness = linear independence, and does not demonstrate anything about nonlinear independence or global independence, i.e., the kind of independence that financial risk analysts are currently most concerned about. Global dependence has major consequences for the way we conduct financial risk measurement, analysis and management if it does not exist, as we will see in Chapter 12.

Definition 223   *For time series with infinite risk content, the average risk of time series $x(t)$ is defined as the approximation*

$$\lim_{T\to\infty} \frac{1}{T} \int_{-T/2}^{T/2} [x(t)]^2 dt \qquad (6.54)$$

Definition 224   *The risk spectrum or PSD of the financial time series $x_1(t)$ is the FT of the average autocovariance function of $x_1(t)$, which does exist, since the* *average autocovariance function is finite. Thus*

$$P(\omega) = \mathcal{F}[\bar{R}_{11}(\tau)]$$

$$= \int_{-\infty}^{+\infty} \bar{R}_{11}(\tau)e^{-j\omega\tau}\,d\tau \tag{6.55}$$

Then, of course, the average autocovariance function *is the inverse FT of the risk spectrum or PSD:*

$$\bar{R}_{11}(\tau) = \mathcal{F}^{-1}[P(\omega)]$$

$$= \frac{1}{2\pi}\int_{\infty}^{+\infty} P(\omega)e^{j\omega\tau}\,d\omega \tag{6.56}$$

These are pragmatic, practical definitions for situations which are likely to occur. However, these pragmatic definitions can lead to distortions, in particular when the risk is infinite, as is the case when time series contain discontinuities, or other singularities. These formulas define only approximations to the information content of a financial time series and do not provide a complete analysis.

Corollary 225 *The average risk (or mean-square value) of a financial time series $x_1(t)$ is given by the integration of the PSD $P(\omega)$ over the entire frequency range, since*

$$\bar{R}_{11}(0) = \lim_{T\to\infty} \frac{1}{T}\int_{-T/2}^{T/2} [x_1(t)]^2\,dt$$

$$= \frac{1}{2\pi}\int_{-\infty}^{+\infty} P(\omega)\,d\omega \tag{6.57}$$

In the case of a stationary financial time series, it does not matter if we investigate its risk content in the time domain or in the frequency domain, since they are equivalent representations. But it does very much matter in which domain we investigate the risk content when the time series is nonstationary, since then the risk contents in the time and the frequency domains, respectively, are not equivalent. They cannot be transformed into each other and have to be looked at simultaneously to achieve a complete analysis.

Example 226 *Figure 6.1 shows the truncated financial risk spectrum of the Standard and Poor series computed by Granger and Morgenstern in 1963, after an important trend in the mean is removed, by using moving averages of lengths 80 and 36. In other words, the original time series was nonstationary! The spectrum was computed at 240 frequency bands, but only the first 100 are shown. A small resonance peak at 40 months can be observed, but is not statistically significant. Even after the trend removal, this peak only accounts for slightly less than 10 percent of the total remaining variance. Thus, the component corresponding with*

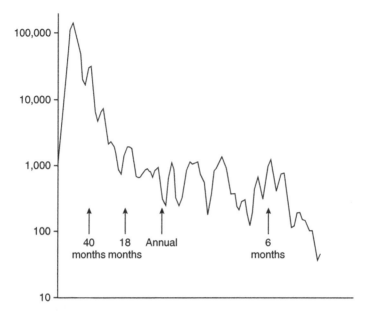

Figure 6.1 Granger and Morgenstern's global risk spectrum of Standard and Poor series, based on annual data, 1875–1952.

the American business cycle of approximately 40 months, although noticeable, is not of particular importance and is much less pronounced than the components with resonance periods of five years or more (Granger and Morgenstern, 1963).

Finally, we can now also properly define white noise in spectral terms.

Definition 227 White noise *is defined as any random variable whose risk spectrum or PSD is a constant flat line (= independent of frequency):*

$$P(\omega) = \sigma_\varepsilon^2 \tag{6.58}$$

when measured in the 2-dimensional (2D) spectrum-frequency $\{P, \omega\}$, *space.*

Thus, white noise is a very specific kind of noise with a particular characteristic: the *flatness* of its risk spectrum. Therefore, it cannot be considered "general noise," as is often, but erroneously, suggested by statisticians, econometricians, financial analysts, etc. Later on we will find how "general noise" is visualized and measured in both the time and frequency domains.

6.2.6   *Average financial risk spectrum of FBM*

From Chapter 4, we recall that the FBM provides a useful model for long-term dependent financial time series, whose empirical spectra obey self-similar power laws of a fractional order $d \in (-0.5, 0.5)$. However, due to the non-stationarity of these financial pricing processes, it is not clear how to measure their time-varying spectra, since the classical measurement by Fourier spectra requires the use of time-averaged measurements based on stationarity. An apparent contradiction exists between the stationarity assumption upon which the usual Fourier spectra are based and the fact that time-varying spectra cannot be associated with stationary processes.

The usual way to approach this difficult measurement issue is as follows. Although the FBM itself is nonstationary, its increments (and hence its derivatives) are stationary. This allows one to associate well-defined average spectral representations with the increments of FBMs.

The *financial risk spectrum or PSD, of the FBM* at frequency zero is the FT of its ACF, which, according to the Wiener–Khinchin Theorem, is the product of the two conjugate FTs of the FBM process, as follows. Recall that the FT of the FBM is modeled by:

$$F_{FBM}(\omega) = (1 - e^{-j\omega})^{-d} \mathcal{F}[\varepsilon(t)] \tag{6.59}$$

Next, apply the two exponential series expansions for $e^{j\omega}$ and $e^{-j\omega}$, with $j = \sqrt{-1}$, the imaginary number and ω is the angular frequency, and take the limit for $\omega \to 0$. Then we obtain the FT of the ACF of the FBM as follows:

$$
\begin{aligned}
P(\omega) &= \mathcal{F}[\gamma(\tau)] \\
&= F(\omega)F(-\omega) \\
&= (1 - e^{-j\omega})^{-d}(1 - e^{j\omega})^{-d}\mathcal{F}[\varepsilon^2(t)] \\
&= \sigma_\varepsilon^2 (1 - e^{j\omega})^{-d}(1 - e^{-j\omega})^{-d} \\
&= \sigma_\varepsilon^2 \left[1 - \left(1 + j\omega + \frac{(j\omega)^2}{2!} + \cdots\right)\right]^{-d} \\
&\quad \times \left[1 - \left(1 - j\omega + \frac{(-j\omega)^2}{2!} - \cdots\right)\right]^{-d} \\
&= \sigma_\varepsilon^2 \left[-j\omega + \frac{\omega^2}{2!} + \cdots\right]^{-d} \left[j\omega + \frac{\omega^2}{2!} + \cdots\right]^{-d} \\
&\sim \sigma_\varepsilon^2 [-j\omega]^{-d}[j\omega]^{-d} \quad \text{as } \omega \to 0 \\
&= \sigma_\varepsilon^2 \omega^{-2d} \tag{6.60}
\end{aligned}
$$

Again, for $d = 0$

$$P(\omega) = \sigma_\varepsilon^2 \tag{6.61}$$

the spectral density of white noise. Thus, the spectral density of the anti-persistent FBM increments, or fractionally differenced white noise time series with $d < 0$

Table 6.1 Risk spectrum of FBM increments

Noise characteristic	Difference	Spectrum $P(\omega)$
Fractionally differenced white noise	$d < 0$	$\sigma_\varepsilon^2 \omega^{-2d} \to 0, \omega \to 0$
White noise	$d = 0$	$\sigma_\varepsilon^2 \omega^{-2d} = \sigma_\varepsilon^2$
Fractionally integrated white noise	$d > 0$	$\sigma_\varepsilon^2 \omega^{-2d} \to \infty, \omega \to 0$

will be zero, when the frequency approaches zero $\omega \to 0$. *Vice versa*, the spectral density of persistent FBM increments, or fractionally integrated white noise with $d > 0$ will be infinite when the frequency approaches zero $\omega \to 0$, as summarized in Table 6.1.

Therefore, neither extreme can be observed in a risk spectrum $P(\omega)$. But, as we've observed in Chapter 4, there are different degrees of fractional integration of white noise in between these two extremes. For fractional differentiation of white noise by $d = 0.5$, the result is blue noise. For fractional integration of the white noise by $d = -0.5$, the result is red noise; for integrating white noise once, $d = 1$, the result is brown noise (= Brownian Motion), and for integrating it once more, $d = 2$, the result is black noise.

Since the financial risk spectrum of the fractional increments of the FBM is scaling and proportional to

$$\omega^{-2d} = \omega^{1-2H} \quad \text{as } \omega \to 0 \tag{6.62}$$

this suggests that the FBM self, which consists of once integrated FBM increments, has a scaling spectral density proportional to

$$\omega^{-2(d+1)} = \omega^{-2(H+0.5)}$$

$$= \omega^{-(2H+1)} \quad \text{as } \omega \to 0 \tag{6.63}$$

since the Hurst exponent $H = d + 0.5$ (cf. Chapter 4).

Remark 228 *Notice that these average financial risk spectra do not depend on time t. In other words, the average FBM spectra are not time-varying. This fundamental fact results from the stationarity of the FBM increments combined with the linearity of the integration!*

It is also clear that the financial risk spectrum of a scaled FBM, $x(ct)$, is *frequency-scaling* (= characterized by a power law of a fractional order d), which is in accordance to the fact that its second-order moments, represented by the ACF

$\gamma(\tau)$ are *time-scaling*:

$$\gamma(\tau) \sim \sigma_\varepsilon^2 \tau^{2d-1} \tag{6.64}$$

Recall that, according to the scaling property of FTs, there is the transform pair

$$x(ct) \leftrightarrow \frac{1}{|c|} F\left(\frac{\omega}{c}\right) \tag{6.65}$$

Thus, the financial risk spectrum of the scaled FBM is

$$
\begin{aligned}
\mathcal{F}[\gamma(\tau)] &= \frac{1}{|c|} F\left(\frac{\omega}{c}\right) \frac{1}{|c|} F\left(\frac{-\omega}{c}\right) \\
&= \frac{1}{|c|^2} P\left(\frac{\omega}{c}\right) \\
&= \begin{cases} \dfrac{\sigma_\varepsilon^2}{|c|^2} \left(\dfrac{\omega}{c}\right)^{-2d} = c^{2d-2}\sigma_\varepsilon^2 \omega^{-2d} = c^{2H-3}\sigma_\varepsilon^2 \omega^{-(2H-1)} \\[4pt] \qquad\qquad\qquad\qquad\text{for the FBM increments, and} \\[8pt] \dfrac{\sigma_\varepsilon^2}{|c|^2} \left(\dfrac{\omega}{c}\right)^{-2(d+1)} = c^{2d}\sigma_\varepsilon^2 \omega^{-2(d+1)} = c^{2H-1}\sigma_\varepsilon^2 \omega^{-(2H+1)} \\[4pt] \qquad\qquad\qquad\qquad\text{for the FBM self} \end{cases}
\end{aligned}
\tag{6.66}
$$

McCulloch *et al.* (2001) provide an alternative approach to spectral measures of the stable distributions of Chapter 3.

6.3   Hurst exponent identification from risk spectrum

It is this frequency scaling property of the FBM, which allows us to compute its financial risk spectrum to determine the Hurst exponent. How? Plot the logarithm of the financial risk spectrum $P(\omega)$ of the FBM against the logarithm of frequency ω:

$$
\begin{aligned}
\ln \mathcal{F}[\gamma(\tau)] &= \ln\left[\frac{1}{|c|^2} P\left(\frac{\omega}{c}\right)\right] \\
&= -(2H+1)\ln\omega + [(2H-1)\ln[c] + \ln\sigma_\varepsilon^2] \\
&= -b\ln\omega + C
\end{aligned}
\tag{6.67}
$$

The slope coefficient of the resulting negative line is

$$b = (2H+1) \tag{6.68}$$

so that

$$H = \frac{b-1}{2} \tag{6.69}$$

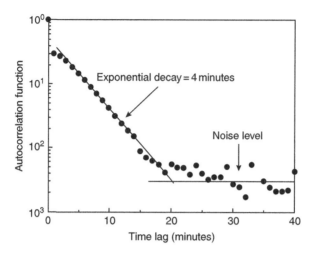

and the intercept is

$$C = (2H - 1)\ln[c] + \ln\sigma_\varepsilon^2 \qquad (6.70)$$

With H so computed and the intercept C and the scaling constant c known, we can even find the value of the noise variance σ_ε^2. This could not be done with Mandelbrot's logarithmic plot in Chapter 4. Let's now look at some empirical examples.

Example 229   *Figure 6.2, displayed also in Mantegna and Stanley (2000, p. 55; courtesy of Gopikrishnan et al., 1998), provides the semi-logarithmic plot of the autocorrelation function for the S&P500 index, sampled at the $\Delta t = 1$ minute time scale. The straight line corresponds to exponential decay with a characteristic decay time of $\tau = 4$ minutes. It is apparent that after about 20 minutes the correlations are at the level of pure noise.*

Example 230   *Figure 6.3, displayed in Mantegna and Stanley (2000, p. 56; adapted from Mantegna and Stanley, 1996), shows the spectral density of the S&P500 index, of which high-frequency minute-by-minute data were recorded during the four-year period from January 1984 to December 1987. The empirical behavior of the index is clearly described by the linear slope coefficient $\lambda/2 = (H-1) \approx -0.5$ in the time window from approximately 30 trading minutes to 100 trading days, corresponding with the independent increment case, $H = 0.5$. Such a linear slope coefficient is characteristic for the particular financial market investigated. Mantegna and Stanley (2000, p. 56) mention comparable studies*

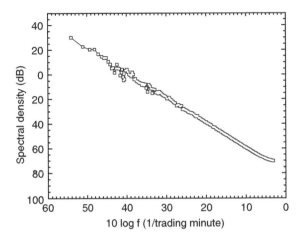

Figure 6.3 Spectral density of high-frequency data from the S&P500 index.

analyzing daily data on stock indices of New York (the New York Composite index), Frankfurt (the DAX index), and Milan (the MIB index) exchanges, with the empirical results of $\lambda = -1.04, -1.06$ *and* -1.14, *or, equivalently,* $H = 0.48, 0.47$ *and* 0.43, *respectively (Mantegna, 1991). These values show the presence of weak long-term dependence, in particular, of anti-persistence, since the empirical values of* H *are always slightly lower than* 0.5. *Based on our own empirical research, we concur with their conclusion that the strength of such long-term dependence is dependent on the particular financial market and that it "seems to be larger for less efficient markets." Using high-frequency data for the S&P500 index, one finds that the market's volatility, which is a measure of the market's risk, has two regimes: for very short trading horizons (*$\tau < 30$ *trading minutes), superdiffusive* $(-\lambda/2 < -0.5)$, *or anti-persistent (*$H < 0.5$*) behavior is observed. In the longer term (*$30 < \tau < 10^4$ *minutes* $= 167$ *hours* $= 7$ *days) the behavior is closer to diffusive or neutrally persistent (*$\lambda/2 = -0.5$ *or* $H = 0.5$*). In the very short-term* $\lambda/2 = -0.8$ *or* $H = 0.2$ *with strong superdiffusive or ultra-anti-persistent behavior, which borders on chaos. This anti-persistent behavior is most likely due to the fact that in the very short-term the time series has a memory of only a few minutes, as shown in the preceding example. For another example of spectral analysis of heavy-tailed data, cf. Mikosch (1998).*

6.4   Heisenberg Uncertainty Principle

The fundamental Uncertainty Principle of Heisenberg states that there exists no time series with finite risk which is *compactly supported* both in the time and frequency domains.[3] Since this principle has important consequences for our financial market risk analysis (Los, 2000), we will provide a very simple proof using the concepts of *equivalent time duration* and *spectral bandwidth*.

Definition 231   *The equivalent time duration T_D of $x(t)$ is defined by*

$$T_D = \frac{1}{x(0)} \int_{-\infty}^{+\infty} |x(t)| \, dt \tag{6.71}$$

where $x(0) \neq 0$.

Definition 232   *The equivalent spectral bandwidth W_B of $x(t)$ is defined by*

$$W_B = \frac{1}{F(0)} \int_{-\infty}^{+\infty} |F(\omega)| \, d\omega \tag{6.72}$$

where $F(0) \neq 0$.

Proposition 233   (Uncertainty Principle of Heisenberg): *The product of the equivalent spectral bandwidth and time duration of a time series $x(t)$ cannot be less than a certain minimum value.*

$$W_B T_D \geq 2\pi \tag{6.73}$$

Proof   By definition of T_D, we have

$$
\begin{aligned}
x(0)T_D &= \int_{-\infty}^{+\infty} |x(t)| \, dt \\
&\geq \int_{-\infty}^{+\infty} x(t) \, dt \\
&= \left[\int_{-\infty}^{\infty} x(t)e^{-j\omega t} \, dt \right]_{\omega=0} \\
&= F(0)
\end{aligned}
\tag{6.74}
$$

Similarly, by definition of W_B, we have

$$
\begin{aligned}
F(0)W_B &= \int_{-\infty}^{+\infty} |F(\omega)| \, d\omega \\
&\geq \int_{-\infty}^{+\infty} F(\omega) \, d\omega \\
&= \left[\int_{-\infty}^{+\infty} F(\omega)e^{j\omega t} \, d\omega \right]_{t=0} \\
&= 2\pi x(0)
\end{aligned}
\tag{6.75}
$$

Thus, we obtain

$$x(0)T_D \geq F(0) \geq \frac{2\pi x(0)}{W_B} \tag{6.76}$$

from which we conclude that

$$W_B T_D \geq 2\pi \tag{6.77}$$

∎

6.5 Windowed FT for transient price innovations

Classical time series analysis devotes most of its efforts to the design of time-invariant and frequency-invariant operators, that modify essentially stationary time series properties. The FT dominates linear time-invariant time series analysis, because the sinusoidal waves $e^{j\omega t}$ are the constant eigenvectors of linear time-invariant difference operators (cf. Chapter 3 for the relevant properties of linear time-invariant operators). As we discussed earlier, this makes it possible to compute the Hurst exponent and thus to establish some indication about the irregularity and the time and frequency scaling of financial time series.

Let's be a bit more precise about this particular aspect of the use of the FT, by defining the characteristic function of the linear time-invariant operator in terms of its eigenvalues, i.e., the solutions of its characteristic function (Mallat, 1999).

Definition 234 *A function satisfying the equation*

$$\Lambda\{x(t)\} = \lambda x(t) \tag{6.78}$$

is called an eigenfunction *(or* characteristic function*) of the operator Λ, and the corresponding value of λ is called an* eigenvalue *(or* characteristic value*) of Λ.*

Definition 235 *A linear time-invariant (convolution) operator L is entirely specified by the eigenvalue $H(\omega)$, which is the FT of the linear function h at the frequency ω:*

$$
\begin{aligned}
Le^{j\omega t} &= \int_{-\infty}^{+\infty} h(u)e^{j\omega(t-u)}\,du \\
&= e^{j\omega t} \int_{-\infty}^{+\infty} h(u)e^{-j\omega u}\,du \\
&= e^{j\omega t} H(\omega)
\end{aligned} \tag{6.79}
$$

The exponential basis $e^{j\omega t}$, which represents a sinusoidal wave, is the eigenvector of the linear convolution operator L.

Consequently, the eigenfunction of a linear time-invariant system is an exponential function, because we have the FT pair

$$x(t) = \frac{1}{2\pi} \int_{-\infty}^{+\infty} F(\omega)e^{j\omega t} d\omega \tag{6.80}$$

and

$$F(\omega) = \int_{-\infty}^{+\infty} x(t)e^{-j\omega t} dt \tag{6.81}$$

i.e., the Fourier coefficient obtained by correlating $x(t)$ and $e^{-j\omega t}$, and thus

$$Lx(t) = \frac{1}{2\pi} \int_{-\infty}^{+\infty} F(\omega)H(\omega)e^{j\omega t} d\omega \tag{6.82}$$

This construction explains the global character of the FT. The linear operator L amplifies, or attenuates, the sinusoidal component $e^{j\omega t}$ of $x(t)$ by the *transfer function $H(\omega)$*, which is the *frequency filter* of $x(t)$. Since the support of the sinusoidal wave $e^{j\omega t}$ covers the whole real line $(-\infty, +\infty)$, the Fourier coefficient $F(\omega)$ depends on the values $x(t)$ for all times $t \in \mathbb{R}$.

It is precisely this global "mix" of information spread over all the times considered by the set of observations why the FT $F(\omega)$ can excellently analyze the *global* frequency contents of the irregularity, or true risk, of $x(t)$, but not its *local* frequency contents of its irregularity. Thus, we can determine the overall risk level of the financial investment return series $x(t)$, but Fourier analysis cannot assist us with the determination of its local risk content, i.e., the market risk level of this financial series at a particular time t. But this is precisely the kind of risk information that fund managers require for proper market risk management by continuous *dynamic hedging*!

On the other hand, when each of the stacked frequencies can be precisely identified, we can produce a frequency or risk analysis that is localized in frequency as well as in time. Such an approach will require the understanding of the *time–frequency localization* of the systematic part of a time series, as already in 1946 had been achieved by Gábor's or Windowed Fourier Analysis (Cohen, 1989; Delprat *et al.*, 1992). In fact, there exist now two time–frequency localization transforms:

(1) the Gábor Transform.
(2) the Wavelet Transform (to be discussed in Chapter 7).

Gábor's Transform or Windowed Fourier Transform (WFT) replaces the FT's infinitely supported sinusoidal wave by the product of a sinusoid and a compact *taper*, which is localized in time (Allen, 1977).

6.5.1 Gábor's WFT

As we noted in the preceding section, the Uncertainty Principle states that there is no finite risk time series $x(t)$ which is compactly supported in both the time and frequency domains. In other words, the risk spread of a variable and its FT cannot be simultaneously arbitrarily small. Motivated by quantum mechanics, the Hungarian physicist Gábor (1946) defined elementary time–frequency "atoms" or "kernels" as wave forms that have minimal spread in the time–frequency plane. He demonstrated the importance of localized time–frequency time series analysis, when he implemented his invention in the form of the first *holograph*.[4] It took until the 1980s before his vision came to complete fruition in Wavelet Transforms and (multidimensional) wavelet multiresolution analysis, discussed in Chapter 7 and as now used in 3-dimensional (3D) image compacting and transmission over the internet.

Definition 236 Gábor atoms (*or* kernels) *are constructed by* time translation *(by period τ) and* frequency modulation *(by frequency ξ) of the original* time window $g(t)$:

$$g_{\tau,\xi}(t) = g(t - \tau)e^{j\xi t} \tag{6.83}$$

such that $\int_{-\infty}^{+\infty} g^2(t - \tau)dtd\tau = 2\pi$.

Notice that a Gábor atom is the product of a sinusoidal wave $e^{j\xi t}$ with a finite risk symmetric window g. Thus, the risk of $g_{\tau,\xi}(t)$ is symmetrically concentrated in the time neighborhood of τ over an interval of size σ_t, measured by the standard deviation of $|g|^2$, and it has a frequency center ξ. The atom $g_{\tau,\xi}(t)$ can be viewed as changing analyzing filters which adapt according to the frequency change in the time series $x(t)$ associated with the frequency ξ in the neighborhood of time horizon τ. The time and frequency spreads of these atoms are constant. The whole family of Gábor atoms is generated by time and frequency translations of one specific atom $g(t)$.

Example 237 *Figure 6.4 shows the Gábor atom $g_{0,\xi}$ for three frequencies: a: high frequency ξ_1, b: middle frequency ξ_2 and c: low frequency ξ_3, (Bendjoya and Slézak, 1993, p. 235).*

Definition 238 *The FT of the Gábor atom is a frequency translation by ξ:*

$$G_{\tau,\xi}(\omega) = \mathcal{F}[g_{\tau,\xi}(t)]$$

$$= \int_{-\infty}^{+\infty} g_{\tau,\xi}(t)e^{-j\omega t} dt$$

$$= \int_{-\infty}^{+\infty} g(t - \tau)e^{-j(\omega-\xi)t} dt$$

$$= G(\omega - \xi)e^{-j(\omega-\xi)\tau} \tag{6.84}$$

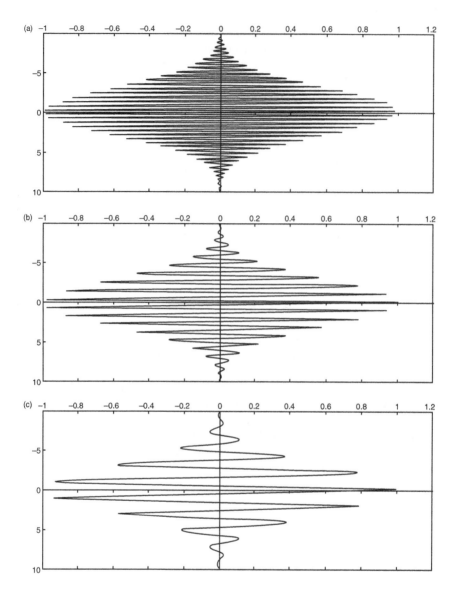

Figure 6.4 Gábor's atom g_{0,ξ_i} as a function of time for three frequencies: (a) high ξ_1, (b) middle ξ_2 and (c) low ξ_3.

Thus, the risk of $G_{\tau,\xi}(\omega)$ is localized near the frequency ξ, over an interval of size σ_ω, which measures the domain where the Gábor resonance coefficient $G(\omega)$ is non-negligible.

The original FT represents a time series as the sum of sinusoidal waves in which the resonance coefficients are correlation coefficients. As we discussed

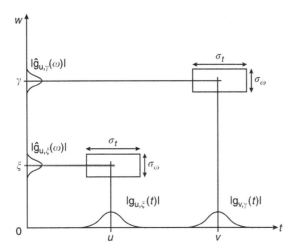

Figure 6.5 Heisenberg boxes of two windowed Fourier atoms $g_{u,\xi}$ and $g_{v,\gamma}$.

earlier, these *sinusoids* are very well localized in frequency, but not in time, since their support has infinite length $(-\infty, +\infty)$. This is a consequence of their exact periodicity. To represent the frequency behavior of a financial time series locally in time, the time series should be analyzed by functions that are localized both in time and frequency, i.e., that are compactly supported in both the time *and* frequency domains, like Gábor's atoms.

In a *time-frequency plane* (t, ω), the risk spread of the atom $g_{u,\xi}$ is measured in the mean squares sense and can symbolically be represented by the *Heisenberg box* illustrated in Figure 6.5. Gábor's Heisenberg box is centered at (u, ξ) and has a time dispersion σ_t and a frequency dispersion σ_ω. Although the shape of this time–frequency box may vary depending on the time width of the window g, the Uncertainty Principle proves that its area satisfies the following inequality

$$\sigma_t \sigma_\omega \geq \frac{1}{2} \tag{6.85}$$

where σ_t is the standard time deviation and σ_ω the standard frequency deviation of a time series $x(t) \in L^2$.

Remark 239 *The area of the Heisenberg box is minimal and this inequality is an equality if and only if the window, kernel or density function, g is Gaussian, in which case the atoms $g_{\tau,\xi}$ are called* Gábor chirps. *In other words, g is a Gábor chirp, if there are constants $(\tau, \xi, c, b) \in \mathbb{R}^2 \times \mathbb{C}^2$ such that*

$$g_{\tau,\xi}(t) = ce^{-b(t-\tau)^2} e^{j\xi t} \tag{6.86}$$

If the time series $x(t)$ is non-zero with a compact support, then its FT in the frequency domain cannot be zero on a whole frequency interval. Similarly, if its

FT is compactly supported, then the time series $x(t)$ cannot be zero on a whole time interval. Hence, even if the Heisenberg constraint is satisfied, it is impossible to have a function in L^2 space, which is compactly supported both in time and frequency domain. This means that there cannot exist an instantaneous frequency analysis for finite risk time series. Thus, time–frequency localization is achievable only in the mean squares sense as visualized by the Heisenberg box.

We can also represent Gábor's Transform as a scalar function, with two arguments, time horizon τ and frequency ξ, as follows.

Definition 240   Gábor's Transform *or* WFT *correlates (= computes the inner product of) the time series* $x(t)$ *with each Gábor atom* $g_{\tau,\xi}(t)$ *to produce the following* resonance coefficients:

$$G(\tau, \xi) = \langle x(t), g_{\tau,\xi}(t) \rangle$$

$$= \int_{-\infty}^{+\infty} x(t)g_{\tau,\xi}^*(t)dt$$

$$= \int_{-\infty}^{+\infty} x(t)g(t - \tau)e^{-j\xi t}dt$$

$$= \frac{1}{2\pi} \int_{-\infty}^{+\infty} F(\omega)G_{\tau,\xi}^*(\omega)d\omega \tag{6.87}$$

The last equation follows from Parseval's (ergodic) Formula, since we have (without proof):

Theorem 241   (Parseval's Formula)

$$\int_{-\infty}^{+\infty} x(t)h^*(t)dt = \frac{1}{2\pi} \int_{-\infty}^{+\infty} F(\omega)H^*(\omega)d\omega \tag{6.88}$$

Remark 242   *For* $h = x$ *it follows from Parseval's Formula that*

$$\int_{-\infty}^{+\infty} |x(t)|^2dt = \frac{1}{2\pi} \int_{-\infty}^{+\infty} |F(\omega)|^2d\omega \tag{6.89}$$

i.e., Parseval's Theorem.

The original time series $x(t)$ can be reconstructed from Gábor's resonance coefficients by the following double integral:

$$x(t) = \frac{1}{2\pi} \int_{-\infty}^{+\infty} \int_{-\infty}^{+\infty} G(\tau, \xi)g(t - \tau)e^{j\xi t}d\xi d\tau$$

$$= \frac{1}{2\pi} \int_{-\infty}^{+\infty} \int_{-\infty}^{+\infty} \int_{-\infty}^{+\infty} x(t)g(t - \tau)e^{j\xi t}g(t - \tau)e^{-j\xi t}dtd\xi d\tau$$

$$= \frac{1}{2\pi} \int_{-\infty}^{+\infty} \int_{-\infty}^{+\infty} x(t)g^2(t - \tau)dtd\tau \tag{6.90}$$

The time series $x(t)$ can thus be viewed as a sum of localized waves weighted by the profile of the chosen taper or window g. Gábor's Transform has a *constant time–frequency resolution*. This resolution can be changed by rescaling the window g. It is a complete, stable and redundant representation of the systematic part of the time series. Hence, it is invertible and easy to model.

6.5.2   Spectrograms: varying spectral densities

Gábor's WFT can be written both as a time integral and as a frequency integral. Measuring time-varying harmonics is the most important application of WFTs. For example, when listening to the human voice, we perceive sounds with frequencies that vary in time. They are clearly nonstationary: they are modulated over time.

A spectral line of $x(t)$ creates high amplitude windowed Fourier resonance coefficients $S(\tau, \xi)$ at frequencies $\xi(\tau)$ that depend on the time τ. The time evolution of such spectral components is therefore analyzed by following the location of such large amplitude coefficients. These color or grey level coded visualizations of the amplitude resonance coefficients are called spectrograms.

Definition 243   *A spectrogram is the squared modulus of the WFT, i.e., the time varying spectral density*

$$P_S(\tau, \xi) = |S(\tau, \xi)|^2$$

$$= \left| \int_{-\infty}^{+\infty} x(t)g(t - \tau)e^{-j\xi t}dt \right|^2 \tag{6.91}$$

A spectrogram measures the risk of financial time series $x(t)$ in the time–frequency neighborhood of (τ, ξ) specified by the Heisenberg box of $g_{\tau,\xi}(t)$. This means that we can now measure and visualize the *localized risk* of a financial time series, instead of the average risk.

6.5.3   Examples of spectrograms and sonograms

We will now show a few nonfinancial and financial examples, using these new technologies of signal processing, like the creation of histograms and spectrograms of the increments of financial rate of return series or the increments of foreign exchange rate series.[5] We will conclude that such financial increment series consist of series of singularities or jumps, with random arrival times and with modulated amplitudes, i.e., non-stationarities, like the sonogram of human laughter.

Example 244   *Figure 6.6 presents Gábor's time–frequency analysis using a grey level coding, of the time series presented in Chapter 5. (Adapted from Bendjoya and Slezak, 1993, p. 236.) The highest value of the Gábor resonance coefficients are coded in black and the lowest value in white. The Gábor Transform can detect the frequencies present in the time series $x(t)$ and also their temporal location.*

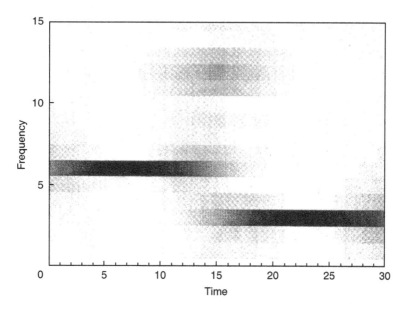

Figure 6.6 Time–frequency analysis by the Gábor Transform with σ adapted to the time coherence of frequencies ω_1 and ω_3. The Gábor resonance coefficients are coded in grey level, with the highest values in black and the lowest values in white. The abscissa represents time and the ordinate the frequency. The highest frequency with the shortest time coherence is worse detected than the other, lower frequencies for which the window size is well suited.

However, it's also clear from this spectrogram that the Gábor Transform has difficulty with detecting frequencies with a coherence shorter than the size of the window. In this spectrogram, the lower coefficients are associated with the highest frequency ω_2 present in the time series with a very short coherence T_2. Such high frequency could be interpreted as "noise" instead of a bona fide systematic signal. The contribution of the short coherence frequency is very easily underestimated. In short, Gábor's WFT is well suited only for financial time series with a coherence at least equal to and preferably larger than the temporal size of the window.

Example 245 *Daubechies (1992, p. 5) shows three spectrograms $P_S(\tau, \xi)$ of the same periodic time series $f(t)$, with only two discontinuities or unit steps $u(t)$ where the arrows are, as in Figure 6.7. The spectrograms show that the basic time series consists of the sum of two sinusoidal time series each with a different frequencies of 500 Hz and 1,000 Hz, respectively. The two discontinuities are clearly detected and show up as impulses $\delta(t)$ in the spectrograms, cutting through all frequencies. Notice the demonstration of Heisenberg's Uncertainty Principle occasioned by three widths of windows g: in the first spectrogram of panel (b): the emphasis is on precise determination of the basic frequencies of*

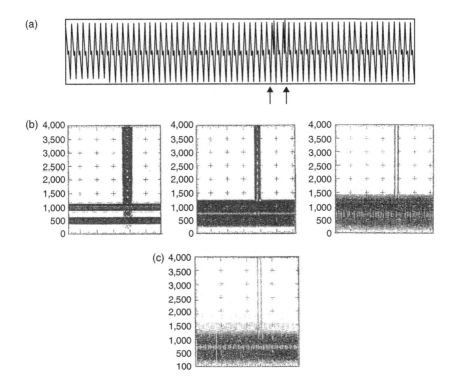

Figure 6.7 Signal, spectrograms and scalogram (a) the signal $f(t)$. (b) Three spectrograms or WFTs $P_S(\tau, \xi)$ of $f(t)$ with three different window widths. Actually
$\ln|S(\tau, \xi)|$ is plotted, using grey levels, high values = black, zero = white,
intermediate grey levels are assigned proportional to $\ln|S(\tau, \xi)|$ in the time t
(abscissa), frequency ω (ordinate) plane. (c) Wavelet Transform $P_W(\tau, a)$ of
$f(t)$. To make the comparison with (b) the $|W(\tau, a)|$ is plotted with the same
grey level coloration and a linear frequency axis (i.e., the ordinate corresponds
to a^{-1}).

*the sinusoids, but this blurs the precise localization of the impulses. Going to the
right, the precision of the localization of the impulses is increased, but this blurs
the precise determination of the basic frequencies. In panel (c): we've an example
of a wavelet-based scalogram, which will be discussed in Chapter 7. A scalogram
is an excellent devise for time localization of transient events, but is less useful for
the precise determination of basic frequencies. Thus spectrograms and scalograms
should be used in tandem for a complete time–frequency analysis of financial time
series.*

Example 246 *Figure 6.8 demonstrates that the spectrogram $P_S(\tau, \xi)$ is a great
device to visualize non-stationarity, in particular of time-varying frequencies, or*

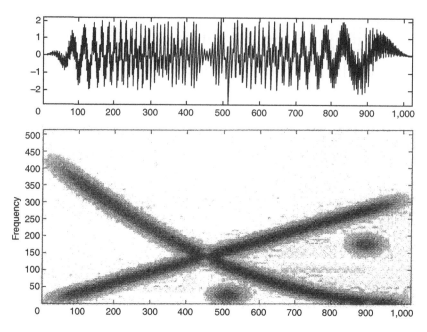

Figure 6.8 Spectrogram $P_S(\tau, \xi)$ of time series with two superimposed time-varying frequencies. Dark areas indicate large amplitude resonance coefficients $|S(\tau, \xi)|^2$.

so-called "chirps." The time series of $T = 1,000$ observations at the top is analyzed in the spectrogram below it. The time series includes a linear chirp, whose frequency increases linearly over time, a quadratic chirp, whose frequency decreases quadratically over time, and two modulated Gaussian noise functions located at $t = 512$ and $t = 896$ (Mallat, 1999, p. 72).

Example 247 *Human speech time series are very high frequency series, highly nonstationary and they are known to exhibit frequency- and phase-coupling phenomena, i.e., cross-correlation phenomena over time. The following analysis was performed on a data set of $T = 1,400$ observations by some of the Higher-Order Spectral Analysis (HOSA) Toolbox MATLAB® -files to illustrate such non-stationarity features (Swami et al., 1998, pp. 1–122/125). Time is measured in milliseconds. Figure 6.9 shows the sonogram of the laughter data in the first panel. The corresponding binned histogram in the second panel shows that its univariate frequency distribution is asymmetrical. The mean, standard deviation, skewness and kurtosis (cf. Chapter 1) are computed as 0.5621, 536.69, 0.1681 and 1.3277, respectively, indicting that these data are non-Gaussian, and that the univariate probability density function (p.d.f.) is not symmetrically distributed. Figure 6.10 shows the spectrogram $P_S(\tau, \xi)$ of the laughter chirp. An FFT length of 512 observation is used, so that the (Hanning) taper g has length $512/2 = 256$, with an*

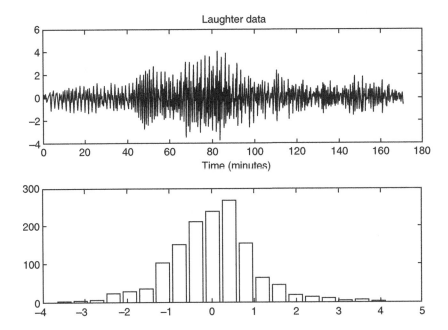

Figure 6.9 Laughter data and their global histogram.

overlap of 240 *observations. The spectrogram shows three dominant frequency tracks, approximately around* 550, 1,100 *and* 1,550 *Hz. The last frequency track or formant begins around* 30 *milliseconds. Additional fragments are visible around* 1,800 *Hz and* 2,100 *Hz. The spectrogram indicates that human laughter is essentially harmonic and that its frequencies appear to be approximately harmonically related. However, not all its fundamental frequencies occur at the same time!*

Example 248 *Figure 6.11 shows that data for the changes in the three-month Treasury Yield contains numerous one-day spikes, which strongly suggests that such series are not continuous, but that they are highly discontinuous (Chapman and Pearson, 2001, p. 86). They can be characterized as series of singularities with modulated amplitudes, i.e., a nonstationary jump process, with random arrival times of these jumps. These financial time series of changes in short-term cash rates of Figure 6.11 look very much like the sonogram of the high frequency nonstationary laughter data in Figure 6.9. However, the series of yield increments are unevenly distributed series of modulated singularities, while the laughter data is a sonogram with a continuous sound wave, consisting of superimposed sound waves of a few fundamental frequencies. This small, but crucial difference is not observable from the binned frequency distributions, which look very much alike. Under close inspection it is somewhat visible in the time domain. But it would be most*

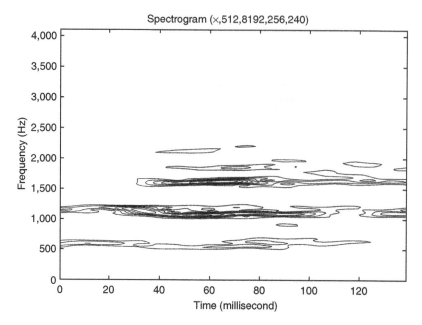

Figure 6.10 Spectrogram of laughter data with three dominant harmonics, approximately around 550 Hz, 1,100 Hz and 1,550 Hz. The last coherent harmonics begins around 30 milliseconds. Additional harmonic fragments are visible around 1,800 Hz and 2,100 Hz. Notice how much more (local) information a spectrogram displays than the statistician's global histogram in Figure 6.9.

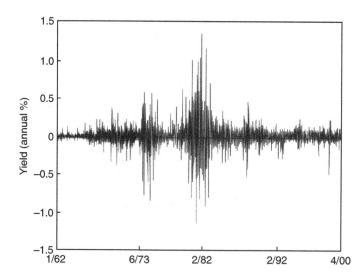

Figure 6.11 Changes in the daily level of the three-month Treasury yield, daily data, January 1962 to April 2000.

clearly visible in the time–frequency spectrogram. We've not been able to obtain this particular yield data set and to produce a spectrogram of it. But in the following example of foreign exchange rate (FX) increments we were able to analyze a very similar data set. It will show that FX increments are not like laughter, since there are no natural harmonics identifiable in the data. The FX increments consist of series of singularities (for which we can compute and visualize a singularity spectrum). It is a clear example of the situation where the frequency distributions of the FX increments and of laughter are similar, but where their respective time distributions are completely different.

Example 249 *Figure 6.12 shows the comparison between the modulated spectrogram* $P_S(\tau, \xi) = |S(\tau, \xi)|^2$ *of minute-by-minute FX data compared with the flat spectrogram of white noise. We compare* 10,800 *increments of the empirical German Deutschemark DEM/US Dollar (USD) rate in the first week of June 1997 in the left panel with the same number of observations on simulated white noise in the right panel with the same constant variance as the FX increments. The frequencies are standardized between* 0 *and* 1 *and are measured by the vertical axis, while the time intervals are measured by the horizontal axis. The lowest frequencies are at the bottom and the highest frequencies at the top. Notice, first, that the German FX increments have low financial risk (light grey and white) in the low frequencies and high financial risk (dark grey and black) in the high frequencies: the risk spectrum is modulated over time. The series is nonstationary. In contrast, the white noise has a constant financial risk over all frequencies and is evenly distributed over time: it is clearly stationary and has a flat spectrum. The financial risk of the German FX increments is intermittently distributed over time. The financial risk*

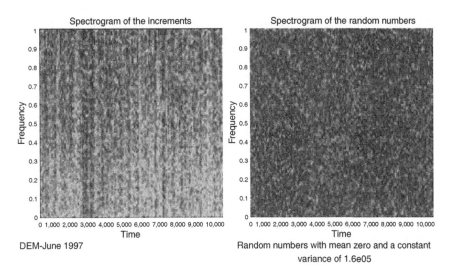

Figure 6.12 Comparison of the modulated spectrogram of empirical DEM/USD increments with the flat spectrogram of white noise.

of the white noise is evenly distributed over time. Thus, to emphasize, this time–frequency visualization shows that the German FX increments in Figure 6.12 are nonstationary, or modulated: their frequency distribution varies over time. Moreover, the German FX increments are unevenly distributed over time. In contrast: white noise is stationary, or unmodulated, and evenly distributed over time. This empirical analysis clearly calls into question the use of the GBM for the modeling of FX prices. In Chapter 8 we will see that scalograms improve the time location of the spectrograms and that such scalograms contain information about these singular FX increments, which can be extracted from the scalogram/spectrogram by modeling the FX process as an FBM.

6.6   Software

The computations of the following Exercises can be executed by using Benoit 1.3: Fractal System Analysis for Windows, Trusoft International Inc., 204 37th Ave. N #133, St Petersburg, FL 33704 Tel (813) 925-8131; Fax (813) 925-8141; sales@trusoft-international.com. See http://www.trusoft-international.com for details.

They can also be executed by using the MATLAB® Signal Processing Toolbox and the MATLAB® HOSA Toolbox (Swami *et al.*, 1998). Both Toolboxes are available from The MathWorks, Inc., 24 Prime Park Way Natick, MA 01760-1500, USA. Tel (508) 647-7000; Fax (508) 647-7001; http://www.mathworks.com/products/wavelettbx.shtml.

The HOSA Toolbox (2.0.3) of Nikias and Petropulu (1993) is a collection of MATLAB® M-files containing specialized tools for signal processing with higher order spectra. It was created by Jerry M. Mendel, Chrysostomos L. (Max) Nikias and Ananthram Swami of by United Signals and Systems, Inc. The toolbox is a collection of MATLAB® routines whose primary features are functions for: higher-order spectrum estimation either by conventional or parametric approaches; magnitude and phase retrieval; adaptive linear prediction; harmonic retrieval and quadratic phase coupling; time-delay estimation and array signal processing.

6.7   Exercises

Exercise 250   *Using the Benoit 1.3 software, compute the Financial Risk Spectrum for (1) the original share prices of Chapter 1, (2) their total rates of return, and (3) the first differences of the rates of total return. Use initially simple averaging of the spectrum. Then try tapering with a rapid-decay function to avoid Gibbsian edge effects and to minimize spectral leaking. Spectral leaking is the phenomenon that financial risk is added to the estimate at some wave number from neighboring wave numbers. In that case, there is no sharp discrimination between the risk levels at different frequencies. Spectral leaking is a particular concern if the spectrum is very red, i.e., if the long-wavelength components have greater risk than the short-wavelength components. This is always the case for self-affine traces, like the globally dependent financial time series, like we discuss in this book.*

Exercise 251 *Run MATLAB® Help, Help Desk (HTML), Online Manuals (in PDF). In the Signal Processing Toolbox User's Guide, study and implement the examples in MATLAB® for the DFT (pp. 1/43–1/45), Spectral Analysis (pp. 3/5–3/11), and FFT-based Time –Frequency Analysis (pp. 4 and 26). Find out what is a risk spectrum or PSD (= power spectral density)? What is a CSD (= cross-spectral density)? What is a periodogram? What is the Nyquist rate? What is a spectrogram?*

Run the following MATLAB® Help, Examples and Demos, Toolboxes, HOSA, Case Studies:

Exercise 252 *The classical sunspot data series (annual, 1700–1987): notice the two representations of the data, as time series and as histogram. Why is differencing helpful? Interpret the summary statistics of the histogram: mean, variance, skewness and kurtosis. How and why do we compute a singular value plot? Interpret the various representations of the risk spectrum and the harmonic analysis. Are the sunspot data periodic or cyclic? If periodic, what is their period? If cyclic, why? What's the difference between periodicity and cyclicity? Is the business cycle of GDP returns periodic or cyclic?*

Exercise 253 *Canadian lynx data (annual, 1821–1934): do the same as for the sunspot data.*

Exercise 254 *Speech data (laughter): this is an example of high-frequency (HF) data. What is a spectrogram? How do you interpret it? How can you determine if a series is stationary and why is that important? How do you determine if data is harmonic? How do you determine if data is Gaussian? What is linearity and how do you determine it (cf. Chapter 3)? What is a bi-spectrum and why it is useful? What is a cumulative spectrum? What is quadratic frequency coupling? What is self-coupling? What other terms don't you know and do you need to define?*

Exercise 255 *Run MATLAB® Fourier analysis on a data set of one day of High Frequency Foreign Exchange (HFFX tick-by-tick and minute-by-minute) data for some Asian currencies, available from the author, or from an international commercial, currency-trading bank like ABN-AMRO. Compute histograms and their summary statistics, risk (power) spectra and cumulative spectra. Conduct harmonic analysis on all series and determine the Fourier "signature,"or "fingerprint,"of each of the nine series, using MATLAB®'s programming facilities (You must also figure out how the EXCEL Link works to feed the raw input data in). Compute a spectrogram. Determine if the series are stationary, harmonic and Gaussian or not. Compute a bi-spectrum and determine if the HFFX series are linear.*

Notes

1 The American mathematician Norbert Wiener (1894–1964), is best known for his development of an interdisciplinary approach to the study of communication and control

processes in living organisms and machines, for which he coined the word *cybernetics*. He was doing work on automated control systems for anti-aircraft guns during the Second World War, when he wrote his famous "yellow peril" report on the optimal tracking solution in the frequency domain. Wiener also contributed to the theory of stochastic processes and the theory of Brownian motion, by constructing a rigorous mathematical description of physical processes that are subject to random change. He helped build the mathematics department at the Massachusetts Institute of Technology (MIT) into an outstanding research facility and taught there from 1919 to 1960.

2 Before Aleksandr Yakovlevich Khinchin graduated in 1916 he had already written his first paper on a generalization of the Denjoy integral. This paper began a series of publications by Khinchin on the properties of functions retained after deleting a set of density zero (probability zero) at a given point. He summarized these results in *Fundamental Mathematica* in 1927. In that same year he became a professor at Moscow University and published his *Basic Laws of Probability Theory*. Between 1932 and 1934 he laid the foundations for the theory of stationary random processes, culminating in a major paper in *Mathematische Annalen* in 1934. At Moscow University, Khinchin build the influential school of probability theory, together with Kolmogorov and Gnedenko. From the 1940s on he was interested in the theory of statistical mechanics and he helped to develop Shannon's ideas on information theory. Khinchin published his famous *Mathematical Principles of Statistical Mechanics* in 1943 and in 1951 he extended it into his *Mathematical Foundations of Quantum Statistics*. It included his fundamental treatment of *local* limit theorems for sums of identically distributed random variables.

3 German theoretical physicist Werner Karl Heisenberg (1901–1976) was one of the leading scientists of the twentieth century. The physical principles underlying the mathematics of quantum mechanics remained mysterious until 1927, when Heisenberg – following conversations with Bohr and Albert Einstein – discovered the uncertainty principle. An important book of Heisenberg published in 1928, *The Physical Principles of Quantum Theory*, described his ideas. The previous year he had become a professor at the University of Leipzig, and in 1932 he was awarded the Nobel Prize for physics. He remained in Germany during the Nazi period and became director of the Kaiser Wilhelm Institute, also heading the unsuccessful German nuclear weapons project. In 1958, Heisenberg became director of the Max Planck Institute for Physics and Astrophysics. He spent his later years working toward a general theory of subatomic particles.

4 The British scientist and inventor Dennis Gábor was born in Budapest, Hungary (1900–1979) and won the Nobel prize for physics (1971) for his invention (in 1947) and later development of holography, a means of numerically producing 3D photographic images without using a lens. Gábor began his career as an industrial research engineer in Germany but went to England with the rise of the Nazis in 1933. He began teaching in 1949 at the Imperial College of Science and Technology in London and became professor of applied electronic physics in 1958. In 1968, he was appointed staff scientist at CBS Laboratories in Stamford, Connecticut and stayed in the United States.

5 A recent interesting example of the application of the WFT in options markets is Benhamou (2002) of Goldman Sachs International, Fixed Income Strategy, Swaps, Division in London, who is impressed by the non-lognormal densities of discrete Asian options and examines the effects of fat-tailed distributions on price as well as on the delta. Using this technology he finds that fat tails lead to larger jumps in the (hedging) delta.

Bibliography

Allen, J. B. (1977) "Short-Time Spectral Analysis, Synthesis and Modification by Discrete Fourier Transform," *IEEE Transactions ASSP*, **25**(3), 235–238.

Bendjoya, Ph., and E. Slézak (1993) "Wavelet Analysis and Applications to Some Dynamical Systems," *Celestial Mechanics and Dynamical Astronomy*, **56**, 231–262.

Benhamou, Eric (2002) "Fast Fourier Transform for Discrete Asian Options," *The Journal of Computational Finance*, **6**(1), 49–68.

Champeney, D. C. (1990) *A Handbook of Fourier Theorems*, Cambridge University Press, Cambridge, UK.

Chapman, David A., and Neil D. Pearson (2001) "Recent Advances in Estimating Term-Structure Models," *Financial Analysts Journal*, **57**(4), 77–95.

Cohen, L. (1989) "Time – Frequency Distributions: A Review," *Proceedings of IEEE*, July, 941–981.

Cooley, J. W., and J. W. Tukey (1965) "An Algorithm for the Machine Calculation of Complex Fourier Series," *Mathematics of Computation*, **19**(90), 297–301.

Daubechies, Ingrid (1992) *Ten Lectures on Wavelets*, SIAM, Philadelphia, PA. (Notes from the 1990 CBMS-NSF Conference on Wavelets and Applications, at Lowell, MA.)

Delprat, N., B. Escudić, P. Guillemain, R. Kronland-Martinet, P. Tchamitchian and B. Torrésani (1992) "Asymptotic Wavelet and Gábor Analysis: Extraction of Instantaneous Frequencies," *IEEE Transactions in Information Theory*, **38**, 644–664.

Duhamel, P., and M. Vetterli (1990) "Fast Fourier Transform: A Tutorial Review and a State of the Art," *Signal Processing*, **19**(4), 259–299.

Gábor, D. (1946) "Theory of Communications," *Journal of the Institute of Electrical Engineering, London III*, **93**, 429–457.

Granger, C. W. J., and O. Morgenstern (1963) "Spectral Analysis of New York Stock Exchange Prices," *Kyklos*, **16**, 1–27. Reprinted as chapter 8 in Cootner, Paul H. (Ed.) (1964) *The Random Character of Stock Market Prices*, The MIT Press, Cambridge, MA, pp. 162–188.

Hsu, Hwei P. (1984) *Applied Fourier Analysis*, Harcourt Brace College Publishers, San Diego, CA.

Gopikrishnan, P., M. Meyer, L. A. N. Amaral and H. E. Stanley (1998) "Inverse Cubic Law for the Distribution of Stock Price Variations," *European Physics Journal*, B, **3**, 139–140.

Körner, T. W. (1990) *Fourier Analysis*, Cambridge University Press, Cambridge, UK.

Los, Cornelis A. (2000) "Frequency and Time Dependence of Financial Risk," *The Journal of Performance Measurement*, **5**(1), 72–73.

Mallat, Stéphane (1999) *A Wavelet Tour of Signal Processing*, 2nd edn, Academic Press, Boston, MA.

Mantegna, R. N. (1991) "Lévy Walks and Enhanced Diffusion in Milan Stock Exchange," *Physica*, A, **179**, 232–242.

Mantegna, Rosario, N., and H. Eugene Stanley (1996) "Turbulence and Financial Markets," *Nature*, **383**, 587–588.

Mantegna, Rosario, N., and H. Eugene Stanley (2000) *An Introduction to Econophysics: Correlation and Complexity in Finance*, Cambridge University Press, Cambridge, UK.

McCulloch, J. Huston, John P. Nolan and Anna K. Panorska (2001) "Estimation of Stable Spectral Measures," *Mathematical and Computer Modelling*, **34**, 1113–1122.

Mikosch, T. (1998) "Periodogram Estimates from Heavy-Tailed Data," in Adler, Robert J., Raisa E. Feldman and Murad S. Taqqu (Eds) (1998) *A Practical Guide to Heavy Tails: Statistical Techniques and Applications*, Birkhäuser, Boston, MA, pp. 241–257.

Nikias, Chrysostomos L., and Athina P. Petropulu (1993) *Higher-Order Spectra Analysis: A Nonlinear Signal Processing Framework*, PTR Prentice Hall, Englewood Cliffs, NJ.

Priestley, M. (1988) *Non-Linear and Non-Stationary Time Series Analysis*, Academic Press, San Diego, CA.

Swami, Anathram, Jerry M. Mendel and Chrysostomos L. (Max) Nikias (1998) *Higher-Order Spectral Analysis Toolbox User's Guide*, Version 2, January, The MathWorks, Inc., Natick, MA.

7 Wavelet time–scale analysis of risk

7.1 Introduction

In this chapter we continue to simultaneously analyze the marginal distributions and the temporal dependence of investment returns, as in Chapter 6, but we do it in a time–scale frame of reference, instead of in a time–frequency frame of reference. *Scale* is proportional to the inverse of frequency: $a \sim 1/\omega$.

Our basic model of analysis for the investment returns and foreign exchange rates is again the Fractional Brownian Motion (FBM) presented earlier in Chapter 4. In that chapter we discussed the analysis of stationary and of slowly varying nonstationary financial time series. In this chapter we discuss the analysis of financial time series that contain numerous transient, nonstationary characteristics, such as drifts, trends, discontinuities in higher derivatives of the series, the beginnings and ends of particular events, as well as the self-similarity and scaling exhibited by the FBM.

As we discussed in Chapter 5, classical Fourier analysis is *periodic* wave analysis. It expands signals or functions (of time) in terms of sinusoidal basis functions, or, equivalently, in terms of complex exponentials. Therefore, it is especially suited for the harmonic analysis of periodic, time-invariant, or stationary phenomena. Next, in Chapter 6, we approached the analysis of nonstationary phenomena in a time–frequency frame of reference by breaking the data set up into a sequence of finite horizon "windows," and implemented Fourier analysis to each consecutively overlapping window, in a moving average fashion. The problem with the windowed approach is that the Gábor–Fourier Transforms (FTs) are still not strictly localized. This non-localization leads to approximation, "time-smearing," and thus some time ambiguity of the analytic results.

In contrast, the wavelets discussed in this chapter comprise a complete set of finite basis functions, precisely localized in both time and frequency (or scale), which, in linear resonance combinations, can provide an extremely flexible, efficient and complete representation of a time series.

These wavelet basis functions have their risk concentrated in time. When correlated with a time series, the magnitudes of the resulting wavelet resonance or correlation coefficients provide a tool for the analysis of nonstationary, transient, rapidly or sharply developing dynamic processes (Wang, 1995; Ogden and Parzen, 1996). Such nonlinear dynamic phenomena often incorporate scaling behavior.

Wavelets are very good tools for detecting, quantifying and modeling scaling behavior at various resolutions. Thus, wavelet Multiresolution Analysis (MRA) is an improvement over Gábor's Windowed Fourier Analysis. By using non-overlapping, scaling and shifting windows wavelet MRA localizes the significant resonance correlations accurately, both in time and in frequency.

This chapter is heavily indebted to signal processing engineers and mathematicians like Mallat (1989a,b,c; 1999), Bruce *et al.* (1996), Burrus *et al.* (1998), Burke-Hubbard (1994, 1998), Flandrin (1989, 1992), Jawerth and Sweldens (1994), Kaplan and Kuo (1993), Rioul and Vetterli (1991), and Strang (1994). Holschneider (1995) of the Centre National de la Recherche Scientifique (CNRS = National Center for Scientific Research) in Marseille, France, and Cohen and Kovacevic (1996) provide excellent and detailed mathematical overviews of wavelet analysis, as do Benedetto and Frazier (1994). The Wavelet Transform (WT) was first introduced by Morlet *et al.* (1982) to obtain time–frequency information from seismic time series. The two (already) classic texts in wavelet theory are written by two mathematical founders of the subject: Yves Meyer (1990) and Ingrid Daubechies (1992). Meyer's book requires a research-level background in mathematics, but Daubechies' text is acessible to a somewhat wider audience. Simpler introductions to wavelets, using only linear algebra, can be found in Chui (1992a) and in Frazier (1999).

In the meantime, wavelet analysis and its applications have become a truly inter-disciplinary research methodology. Excellent first introductions to bridge the still existent chasm between signal processing and statistical analysis using wavelets can be found in Chui (1992b) and in Ogden (1997). In finance, this ingenious wavelet analysis has already provided us with the tools to identify and, perhaps even forecast, the pricing and trading processes that characterize our financial markets. The first instances of this new empirical analysis are only now slowly emerging in the financial literature, although much confusion remains regarding what the best ways are to use these powerful analytic signal processing tools in finance (Jensen, 1997). This situation is not unlike when the first instances of econometrics appeared in economics 60 years earlier.

But there is no doubt that wavelet MRA is extremely powerful and will lead to many new discoveries in both finance and economics (cf. Ramsey *et al.*, 1995; Ramsey and Zhang, 1996; Ramsey and Zhang, 1997; Aussem *et al.*, 1998; Ramsey and Lampart, 1998a,b; Gençay *et al.*, 2001), as it already has in medical and biomedical, seismic and oceanographic signal and image processing, in quantum mechanics and asteroid family identification from cluster analysis, meteorology and turbulence research (Ruskai *et al.*, 1992; Meyers *et al.*, 1993; Lau and Weng, 1995).

Wavelets have been used to solve serious electronic communications problems and, combined with fractals, they have been applied to time series that are chaotic, as we will discuss in Chapter 8. Since wavelets are self-similar and scaling, there is a natural affinity between wavelet MRA and fractal models, in particular in the research of the self-similar cascading risk levels of the vortices in turbulence research (Massopust, 1994; Wornell, 1995), as we will see in

Chapter 11. Moreover, the use of wavelets as basis functions for the discretization and numerical solution of nonlinear diffusion equations (e.g. used in the valuation and dynamic hedging of American and exotic options) have already achieved excellent success (Bendjoya and Slezak, 1993; Meyer, 1993).

7.2   Wavelet analysis of transient pricing

Wavelet analysis has a diverse historical background. In reflection seismology in the 1970s and 1980s, Morlet *et al.* (1982) found that modulated pulses sent underground have a time duration that is too long at high frequencies to separate the reflections of fine, closely spaced layers of rock, because of the Heisenberg Uncertainty Principle (cf. Chapter 6). Instead of emitting pulses of equal time and frequency duration, he then thought of sending shorter waveforms at high frequencies. Such waveforms are obtained by scaling a single basis function, called a (Morlet) wavelet.[1]

Alex Grossman of the Marseille Theoretical Physics Center recognized in Morlet's approach some ideas that were close to his own analysis of coherent (= correlating) quantum states (Grossman and Morlet, 1984). Thus, nearly forty years after Gábor *et al.*, reactivated a collaboration between theoretical physics and signal processing, this ultimately led to the formalization of the Continuous Wavelet Transform (CWT).

The basic ideas of wavelet time–scale analysis were already familiar to mathematicians and engineers working with the harmonic Fourier analysis discussed in Chapters 5 and 6. Thus, the acceptance of wavelets was rather rapid within the community of signal processing engineers. Wavelet analysis is now invading other applied fields in cognitology, biology and medicine, like computer vision, machine sensors, neurology, e.g., the study of electroencephalographs (EEGs) to find extreme brain waves, and in cardiology, e.g., the study of electrocardiograms (ECGs) to identify cardiac arrhythmias (Aldroubi and Unser, 1996).[2]

Wavelet analysis has now also reached the financial markets, to determine the periodicities, aperiodic cyclicities, intermittencies and arrhythmias of the financial time series produced in great abundance by these markets. It's our expectation that a study of the spectrograms and scalograms of the financial markets can assist us with their financial and economic diagnosis to prevent financial crises and other market inefficiencies (Jensen, 1997).[3]

The specific mathematical methods of wavelet analysis have been developed mainly by the French mathematician Yves Meyer (1985, 1993) and his colleagues. Complete wavelet MRA was discovered by Stéphane Mallat in 1988 (Mallat, 1989a,b). Since then, research on wavelets has become truly international. It is particularly active in the United States, where it is led by the work of mathematicians and scientists such as Ingrid Daubechies at Rutgers University and AT&T Bell laboratories, and Ronald Coifman and Victor Wickerhauser at Yale University (Coifman and Wickerhauser, 1992; Wickerhauser, 1994; Buckheit and Donoho, 1995).

After a lapse of more than thirty years, the thread of analyzing the fractality or self-affinity of financial-economic time series was picked up by Ramsey and Zhang (1996, 1997) at the Courant Institute of New York University by implementing wavelet analysis. It is currently a wide open field of research, ripe for a more complete exploration by students in finance and economics (Gençay *et al.*, 2001).

7.2.1 Wavelet Transform

Let's see how wavelet analysis works. Similar to the windowed Fourier Transform (WFT), the WT decomposes a 1-dimensional (1D) time series into 2-dimensional (2D) time–scale ($\sim$ frequency^{-1}) space. In particular, while Fourier analysis breaks down a time series of investment returns into constituent orthogonal sinusoids of different frequencies (= constant periodicities), wavelet analysis breaks down such a time series into constituent orthogonal wavelets of different scales.

Similar to the Gábor Transform, the WT replaces the basic sinusoidal waves of the FT by a family of basic wavelets generated by translations and dilations of one particular wavelet atom. Figure 7.1 compares an infinite sine wave basis for Fourier analysis with a finite Daubechies(20) wavelet basis.

Definition 256 *A continuous wavelet atom $\psi_{\tau,a}(t)$ is a wave function of zero average, centered around amplitude zero, with finite risk:*

$$E\{\psi_{\tau,a}(t)\} = \int_{-\infty}^{+\infty} \psi_{\tau,a}(t)dt = 0 \tag{7.1}$$

which is translated *by a limited time interval τ and* scaled, *or dilated, by a scale parameter a as follows:*

$$\psi_{\tau,a}(t) = \frac{1}{\sqrt{a}}\psi\left(\frac{t-\tau}{a}\right) \tag{7.2}$$

This scaled and translated wavelet is time centered around τ, like the Gábor atom. If the frequency center of ψ is η, then the frequency center of the dilated

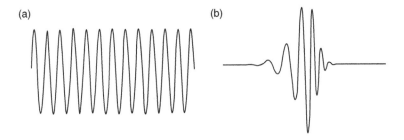

(a)   (b)

Figure 7.1 (a) A sine wave and (b) a Daubechies' wavelet ψ_{D20}.

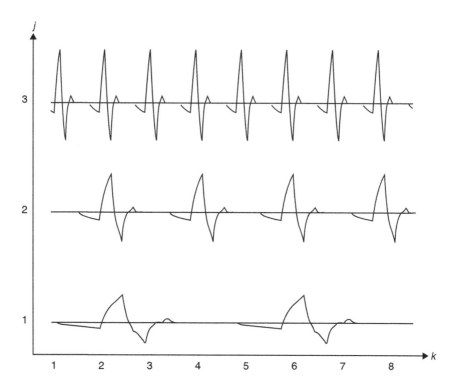

Figure 7.2 Self-similarity of wavelets: translation (every fourth k) and scaling of a wavelet ψ.

wavelet is $\xi = \eta/a$ (thus the scale $a \propto 1/\xi$). Figure 7.2 shows the translation and scaling of a Daubechies(4) wavelet, which we'll define later in this chapter. A continuous wavelet is simply a finite risk function with a zero mean. Besides its scaling and dilating Heisenberg box, the most important feature of a wavelet is the number of its vanishing moments:

$$\int_{-\infty}^{+\infty} t^r \psi(t) dt = 0 \quad \text{for } 0 \le r < n \tag{7.3}$$

This vanishing moments property of wavelets makes it possible to analyze the local regularity of a time series $x(t)$. A theorem characterizes fast decaying wavelets with r vanishing moments as the rth derivatives of a fast decaying function (cf. Chapter 6 for such testing functions of rapid decay, or *tapers*). We will meet these fast decaying wavelets again in Chapter 8, when we discuss the crucial Lipschitz irregularity analysis.

Usually wavelet analysis is done by orthonormal wavelets, to effectuate the completeness, or exhaustiveness of the analysis.

Definition 257 *An* orthogonal wavelet $\psi_{\tau,a}(t)$ *is a wavelet with the orthogonality property*

$$\int_{-\infty}^{+\infty} \psi_{\tau,a}(t)\psi_{v,b}(t)dt = 0 \quad \text{for } \tau \neq v \text{ or } a \neq b \tag{7.4}$$

Definition 258 *An* orthonormal wavelet $\psi_{\tau,a}(t)$ *is an orthogonal wavelet with the normalization*

$$\int_{-\infty}^{+\infty} \psi_{\tau,a}(t)\psi_{\tau,a}^*(t)dt = \int_{-\infty}^{+\infty} |\psi_{\tau,a}(t)|^2 dt = 1 \tag{7.5}$$

These few introductory definitions enable us now to define the CWT, which forms the basis for wavelet MRA.

Definition 259 *The CWT of $x(t)$ at position τ and scale a is an inner product computed by correlating (or convoluting) the time series $x(t)$ with a wavelet atom*

$$\begin{aligned} W(\tau, a) &= \int_{-\infty}^{+\infty} x(t)\psi_{\tau,a}^*(t)dt \\ &= \int_{-\infty}^{+\infty} x(t)\frac{1}{\sqrt{a}}\psi^*\left(\frac{t-\tau}{a}\right)dt \\ &= x(t) \star \psi_{\tau,a}(-t) \end{aligned} \tag{7.6}$$

Thus, the CWT resonance coefficient is the correlation (convolution) between the time series and the appropriate wavelets, as in Figure 7.3. In a (Morlet) Wavelet Transform, a wavelet is correlated with different sections of a financial time series $x(t)$. The inner product of a section and the wavelet is a new function. The volume of the area delimited by that function and computed by the integral is the wavelet resonance (or correlation) coefficient. Sections of the time series $x(t)$ that look like the wavelet give large resonance coefficients, as seen in Figure 7.3(c) and (d). (The (scalar) product of two negative functions is positive.) Slowly changing sections of $x(t)$ produce small resonance coefficients, as seen in (e) and (f). Accordingly, the time series $x(t)$ is analyzed at different scales, using wavelets of different widths.

Thus, the dilating and translating wavelet atoms can be used as the orthonormal basis for a unique, complete observation system, which allows continuously varying levels of resolution, like a microscope. Similar to Gábor's WFT, a WT can measure the time–frequency variation of spectral components, but it has a sharper, more localized time–frequency resolution than the WFT. One of the reasons is that wavelets tend to be irregular, fractal and asymmetric, while sinusoids are smooth, periodic and symmetric (Bruce *et al.*, 1996).

The CWT can operate at any scale, from that of the original financial time series up to some maximum scale, which is determined by trading off the need for

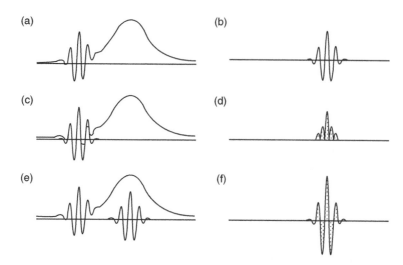

Figure 7.3 Wavelet coefficients are "correlation" or "resonance" coefficients. Here a wavelet is correlated with an irregular signal. Different sections of the signal produce different resonance coefficients.

detailed analysis with available computational power. The CWT is not only continuous in terms of scaling, it is also continuous in terms of shifting (translation): during computation, the analyzing wavelet $\psi_{\tau,a}(t)$ is shifted smoothly over the full domain of the analyzed series $x(t)$. When done, one has computed the wavelet resonance coefficients produced by different sections of the signal, translated by τ, and at different scales a.

The CWT $W(\tau, a)$ has four very useful mathematical properties:

(1) It's linear: $W(\tau, a)\{\gamma_1 x_1(t) + \gamma_2 x_2(t)\} = \gamma_1 W(\tau, a)\{x_1(t)\}$
$$+\gamma_2 W(\tau, a)\{x_2(t)\};$$
(2) It's invariant under translation $W(\tau, a) = W(\tau - \tau_0, a)$;
(3) It's invariant under dilation $W(\tau, a) = (1/k)W(k\tau, ka)$, using $k = 1/\sqrt{a}$;
(4) It's localized in time and frequency.

How to make analytic sense of the resulting multitude of wavelet resonance coefficients? How can we interpret them? Usually one makes a *visualization plot* in which the abscissa represents the position $t - \tau$ along the time axis, the ordinate represents the scale a, and the grey scale or color at each (τ, a) point represents the magnitude of the wavelet coefficient $|W(\tau, a)|$ as in Figure 7.4 (This is a grey scale example of a *scalogram*, defined in Section 7.2.3). These plots of wavelet coefficient resemble an irregular surface viewed from above. You can also represent the same coefficients in a 3-dimensional (3D) plot as in Figure 7.5. Notice the slope of the ridges from the small-scale to the large-scale coefficients. The maxima of these ridges are the maxima lines. The speed of their decay from the large to the

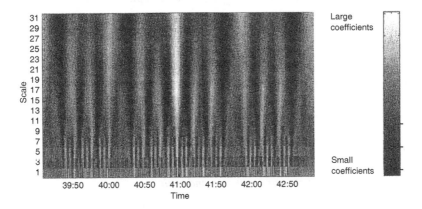

Figure 7.4 A scalogram: a plot of the magnitude of wavelet coefficients.

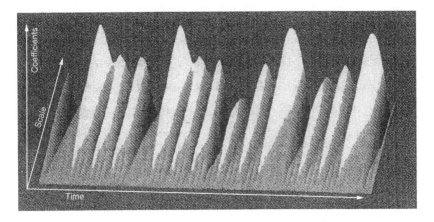

Figure 7.5 A 3D scalogram: a plot of the magnitude of the wavelet coefficients in three dimensions.

small scales can be used for very sophisticated irregularity analysis of singularities and to compute singularity spectra, as we will see in Chapter 8.

By applying Parseval's Formula (cf. Chapter 6), the CWT resonance coefficient, which is a time integral, can also be written as a frequency integral (Walker, 1997):

$$W(\tau, a) = \int_{-\infty}^{\infty} x(t)\psi_{\tau,a}^*(t)dt$$

$$= \frac{1}{2\pi} \int_{-\infty}^{\infty} F(\omega)\Psi_{\tau,a}^*(\omega)d\omega \qquad (7.7)$$

where $F(\omega)$ is the FT of $x(t)$ and $\Psi^*_{\tau,a}(\omega)$ is (the complex conjugate of) the FT of the wavelet atom $\psi_{\tau,a}(t)$:

$$\Psi_{\tau,a}(\omega) = \sqrt{a}\Psi(a\omega)e^{j\omega\tau} \tag{7.8}$$

In the time integral, the financial time series (e.g. of investment returns) $x(t)$ is correlated with the wavelet $\psi_{\tau,a}(t)$. Its risk is concentrated in a positive time interval centered at τ. In the equivalent frequency integral, the FT of the time series $F(\omega)$ is correlated with the FT of the wavelet $\Psi_{\tau,a}(\omega)$. This means that $\Psi(\omega) = 0$ for $\omega < 0$. The risk of $\Psi_{\tau,a}(\omega)$ is concentrated over a positive frequency interval centered at τ/a, whose size is scaled by a^{-1}.

7.2.2 Relationship between frequency and scale

In the time–frequency plane, a wavelet atom $\psi_{\tau,a}$ is again symbolically represented by a Heisenberg box centered at $(\tau, \eta/a)$, as in Figure 7.6. The time and frequency spread are proportional to a and a^{-1}, respectively. When the scale a varies, the height and width of the Heisenberg rectangle change, but *its area or volume remains constant*. When a decreases, i.e., when the time resolution decreases, the frequency support of the wavelet is shifted to the higher frequencies, and *vice versa*, in accordance with Heisenberg's Uncertainty Principle, discussed in Chapter 6.

As Figure 7.6 shows, the higher scales a correspond to the most dilated ("stretched") wavelets. The more dilated the wavelet $\psi_{\tau,a}(t)$, the longer the portion of the time series $x(t)$ with which it is being compared, and thus the coarser the

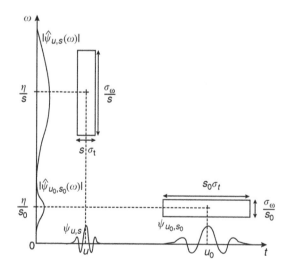

Figure 7.6 Heisenberg boxes of two wavelets. Smaller scales decrease the time dispersion, but increase the frequency support, which is shifted towards higher frequencies.

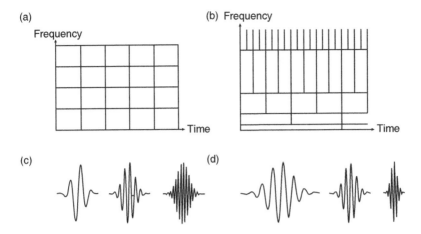

Figure 7.7 Time–frequency resolution and basis functions of the Windowed FT and the Wavelet Transform: (a) tiling of the time–frequency plane for the WFT, (b) for the WT, (c) corresponding basis functions for the WFT and (d) for the WT.

time series features being measured by the wavelet resonance coefficients $W(\tau, a)$. Therefore, there is an inverse correspondence between the scale parameter a and the radian frequency ω:

Low scale $a \Leftrightarrow$ compressed wavelet $\Leftrightarrow$ rapidly changing time series details $\Leftrightarrow$ high frequency ω.

High scale $a \Leftrightarrow$ dilated wavelet $\Leftrightarrow$ slowly changing, coarser time series features $\Leftrightarrow$ low frequency ω.

Remark 260 *Gábor's Windowed or Short-Term Fourier Transform (STFT) obtains frequency information with limited precision, and that precision is determined by the size of the window of the particular Gábor atom, which remains the same for all frequencies. In contrast, the WT uses wavelet windows that vary according to their scale (= "inverted frequency"). This can be clearly seen in Figure 7.7, which compares the basis functions and time–frequency resolution of Gábor's WFT and the WT in tiling diagrams. The tiles in these diagrams represent the essential concentration in the time–frequency plane of a given basis function (Herley et al., 1993; Strang, 1993). Notice in (d) that the shape of the wavelet basis functions is invariant under the changes in frequency. This is what produces the precise and unambiguous interpretation of a time–frequency analysis by a WT.*

7.2.3 Scalograms: varying scaled and localized densities

Thus, the wavelet coefficient $W(\tau, a)$ depends on the values of $x(t)$ and its FT $F(\omega)$ in the time–frequency region, where the risk of the wavelet atom $\psi_{\tau,a}$ and its FT $\Psi_{\tau,a}(\omega)$ is concentrated. Measuring time-varying frequencies is again the most important application of WTs. Sharp transitions in the time series $x(t)$ create large amplitude wavelet resonance coefficients $W(\tau, a)$ at scales a localized at time τ. The time evolution of such spectral or scale components is analyzed by following the location of such large amplitude coefficients. As we saw earlier, these visualizations are called scalograms (Figures 7.4 and 7.5). They are already used on an experimental basis in economics (Ariño and Vidakovic, 1995), and in finance (Jensen, 1997).

Definition 261   *A* scalogram, *or* local wavelet spectrum, *is the localized and scaled wavelet density (= modulus squared of the WT)*

$$P_W(\tau, a) = |W(\tau, a)|^2$$

$$= \left| \int_{-\infty}^{\infty} x(t)\psi^*_{\tau,a}(t)dt \right|^2 \tag{7.9}$$

Thus, a scalogram measures the *localized risk* of a financial time series $x(t)$ in the time–scale neighborhood of (τ, a) specified by the Heisenberg box of $\psi_{\tau,a}(t)$. If η denotes the frequency center of the base wavelet, then the frequency of a dilated wavelet is $\xi = \eta/a$.[4]

Definition 262   *The normalized scalogram is*

$$\frac{\xi}{\eta} P_W(\tau, a) \tag{7.10}$$

Example 263   *Figure 7.8 displays the scalogram of a wavelet analysis of our example of the Gábor Windowed Fourier Analysis in Chapters 5 and 6, using a Morlet wavelet for 25 different scale levels:*

$$\psi_{\tau,a}(t) = e^{-t^2/2}e^{j\omega_m t} + e^{-\omega_m^2/2} \tag{7.11}$$

for $\omega_m = 6$, where the term in ω_m^2 ensures admissibility (it is negligible for $\omega > 5$) and $j = \sqrt{-1}$ (adapted from Bendjoya and Slezak, 1993, p. 240). Scale a and frequency ω are related by $a = \omega_m/\omega$. Again, the abscissa measures time t and the ordinate the scale a. A grey coding is used with the largest resonance coefficients in black and the smallest in white. Notice the differences compared with the Gábor analysis. First, all three monochromatic frequencies present in the signal $x(t)$ with the same amplitude are detected in the same fashion. The three detected coherent frequencies have the same weight. Moreover, the discontinuities are detected by the two cones pointing towards the locations of these singularities at the small scales. The width of these cones contains information about the type of singularity, as will be discussed in Chapter 8.

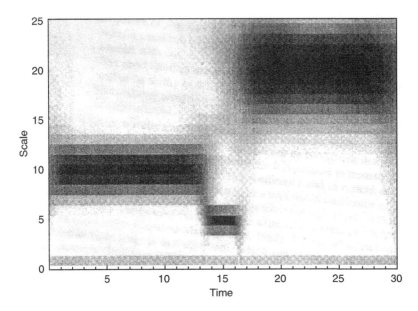

Figure 7.8 A scalogram with modulus $|W(\tau, a)|$ using a Morlet (6) wavelet for 25 different scales along the ordinate and time along the abscissa, with grey level coding. The three detected coherent frequencies $\omega_3 < \omega_1 < \omega_2$ in the signal $x(t)$ have the same weight. Discontinuities are visible at all scales through the cones pointing toward the location of their singularities at the smallest scale. The grey strip at the smallest scale is a finite sampling effect.

Example 264 *Figure 7.9 demonstrates that the normalized scalogram $(\xi/\eta) P_W(\tau, a)$ is also a device to visualize nonstationarity, in particular of time-varying frequencies, or "chirps." The time series of the one but last example in Chapter 6 of $T = 1,000$ observations is analyzed in the following scalogram. As we noted, the time series includes a linear chirp, whose frequency increases linearly over time, a quadratic chirp, whose frequency decreases quadratically over time, and two modulated Gaussian noise functions located at $t = 512$ and $t = 896$. Compare this scalogram with the spectrogram in Chapter 6. Despite the appearance to the contrary, the scalogram represents the data analysis more truthfully than the spectrogram, since the scalogram visualizes also the relative epistemic uncertainty of the computed frequencies, in particular, of the higher frequencies, as required by the Heisenberg Principle and the Heisenberg boxes.*

The reason for the varying relative epistemic (knowledge) uncertainty in scalograms is perfectly clear from the dyadic time–scale tiling diagram in Figure 7.10, which shows how a smooth sinusoidal function and an isolated singularity are represented in a scalogram. In contrast, the spectrograms in Chapter 6 represent

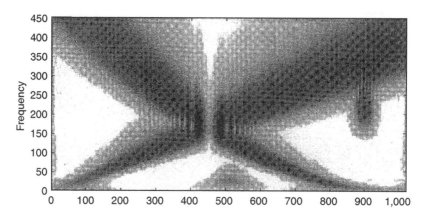

Figure 7.9 Normalized scalogram $(\xi/\eta)P_W(\tau, a)$ computed from the "chirped" time series of Figure 6.8. Dark points indicate large amplitude wavelet coefficients.

illusory analytic precision, where there can't be any, because it is tiled by scale-invariant, equally sized Heisenberg boxes.

Example 265   *Figure 7.11 provides an empirical example of a 3D normalized scalogram measuring a sharp discontinuity or break in a financial time series. This scalogram is computed from 44,640 minute-by-minute increments of the Thai baht quotations of July 1997. The large discontinuity at the beginning of the time axis (from front towards the right) is caused by the financial crisis of July 2, 1997 and is represented by very large wavelet resonance coefficients (measured along the vertical axis from 0 to 100 percent) over the various scales a along the scale axis (from the front, where $a = 1$ minute, towards the left, where $a = 60$ minutes = 1 hour). Notice that most of the risk of the discontinuity is concentrated on the smallest scale = highest frequency of Foreign Exchange (FX) trading: the discontinuity generated a short-lived vortex.*

Related to the scalogram is the scalegram or wavelet spectrum, which is the wavelet analog of the average risk spectrum.

Definition 266   *A scalegram, or* global (average) wavelet spectrum *is the scaled wavelet density (= average modulus squared of the WT):*

$$P_W(a) = \int_{-\infty}^{\infty} |W(\tau, a)|^2 d\tau$$

$$= \int_{-\infty}^{\infty} \left| \int_{-\infty}^{\infty} x(t)\psi_{\tau,a}^*(t)dt \right|^2 d\tau \qquad (7.12)$$

The wavelet spectrum is the scalogram projected (integrated) onto the scale or (inverted) frequency axis. It provides the wavelet equivalent of the classical

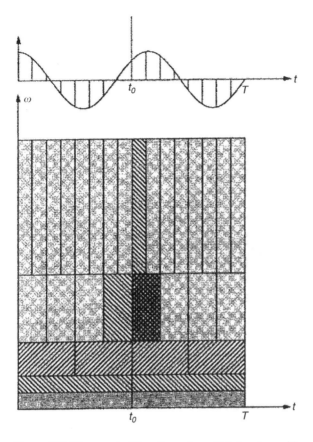

Figure 7.10 Time–scale tiling for a sinusoidal function with an isolated singularity represented by a "cone" in the scaleogram at t_0. The abscissa represents time. The ordinate represents either increasing frequency or decreasing scale $(1/a)$.

marginal frequency distribution (cf. Chapter 2) and Fourier risk spectrum (cf. Chapters 5 and 6).[5] Like the average risk spectrum, it is used to look at the components of a signal as a function of scale (or frequency), with disregard to location. The wavelet spectrum based on the WT contains much the same information as the risk spectrum based on the FT. The wavelet spectrum can be used to identify the homogeneous H-exponent(s) from scaling financial time series, as we will see in the next chapter. This, in turn, is used to identify special models of nonlinear deterministic behavior called *transient chaos* or *intermittency* (Scargle, 1997).

Remark 267 *When the noise model is based on counting photons, as in Chapter 1, this noise simply adds a constant (independent of scale) to the true average wavelet spectrum. That constant is the mean counting rate of the photon*

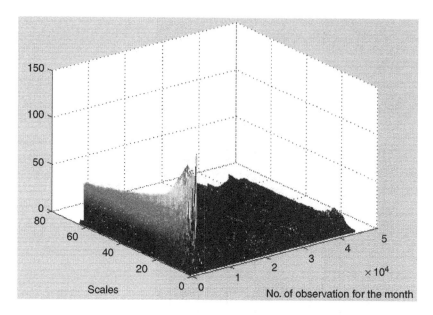

Figure 7.11 Empirical 3D scalogram of Thai baht increments in July 1997.

count. *In practice, it is quite easy to identify the true scalegram, although the identification remains uncertain when the signal-to-noise ratio is low.*

7.2.4 *Frame theory and wavelet bases*

Subsampling of Gábor's WFT, or of the CWT, defines a *complete* representation of the financial time series, if any such time series can be reconstructed from linear combinations of discrete families of windowed Fourier atoms $\{g_{\tau_n, \xi_k}\}_{(n,k) \in \mathbb{Z}^2}$, or, respectively, of wavelet atoms $\{\psi_{\tau_n, a_j}(n,j) \in \mathbb{Z}^2\}$. *Frame theory* discusses what conditions the families of wavelets must satisfy if they are to provide *stable and complete representations* of time series. Completely eliminating redundancy is equivalent to building an orthogonal basis of the time series space. The following discussion is meant to generalize for WTs what we already have learned from the FTs.

Definition 268 *A frame is a family of vectors $\phi_k(t)$, which can represent any financial time series with finite risk by the sequence of its inner products with the vectors of the family. More precisely, a family $\{\phi_k(t)\}_{k \in \mathbb{Z}}$ of vectors in the real square-integrable, or Hilbert space $L^2(\mathbb{R})$, is a frame of this L^2 space, if there are two constants $A > 0$ and $B > 0$ such that, for any $x(t)$ in the space $L^2(\mathbb{R})$,*

$$A\|x(t)\|^2 \leq \sum_{k \in \mathbb{Z}} |\langle x(t), \phi_k(t) \rangle|^2 \leq B\|x(t)\|^2 \tag{7.13}$$

where

$$\|x(t)\|^2 = \int_{-\infty}^{+\infty} |x(t)|^2 dt \tag{7.14}$$

is the risk content of x(t), aka the norm *of financial time series x(t).*

Definition 269   *If A = B, the frame is said to be* tight.

In general a frame is a stable, redundant and not necessarily linear representation of a financial time series. It is a generalization of the more familiar fundamental concept of the *basis* of a linear space, which we've encountered earlier. For example, an orthogonal basis is a complete, tight frame. The frame vectors $\{\phi_k(t)\}_{k\in\mathbb{Z}}$ are supposed to be of *unit norm*, that is

$$\|\phi_k(t)\|^2 = \int_{-\infty}^{+\infty} |\phi_k(t)|^2 dt = 1 \tag{7.15}$$

When is a frame not tight but redundant (Lawton, 1990)?

Definition 270   *A frame is* redundant, *if* $1 < A$.

There exist some specific bases for the wavelet decomposition space. For example,

Definition 271   *A* Riesz basis *is a frame of linearly independent vectors* $\{\phi_k(t)\}_{k\in\mathbb{Z}}$.

If the frame vectors $\{\phi_k(t)\}_{k\in\mathbb{Z}}$ form a Riesz basis, then $A \le 1 \le B$.

Definition 272   *An* orthonormal basis *is a tight (= complete = unique) Riesz basis.*

Thus, a frame is an orthonormal basis if and only if $A = B = 1$.

A financial time series $x(t)$ can always be expanded into a series of terms, as follows.

Definition 273   *An* expansion *is the linear decomposition*

$$x(t) = \sum_{k=-\infty}^{+\infty} a_k \phi_k(t) \tag{7.16}$$

where k is an integer index for the finite or infinite sum, a_k are the real-valued expansion coefficients, and $\phi_k(t)$ are a set of real-valued functions of t, called the expansion set.

We can always expand, decompose or analyze a financial time series into a series of terms, but the question is: when is such an analytic decomposition complete and thus unique? That depends on the set of terms $\{\phi_k(t)\}$. If this set is complete and thus unique, the expansion is.

Definition 274 *If an expansion (= linear decomposition) is unique, the set of frame vectors $\{\phi_k(t)\}$ is called a* basis *for the class of financial time series $x(t)$ that can be so decomposed.*

Remark 275 *For example, the set of exponential eigenvectors $\{e^{j\omega t}\}$ form the expansion set for the FT. Since it is a unique expansion, this particular expansion set forms a basis.*

One of the crucial consequences of dealing with an orthogonal basis is that the expansion coefficients a_k can always be computed by the inner product (or correlation):

$$
\begin{aligned}
a_k &= \langle x(t), \phi_k(t) \rangle \\
&= \int_{-\infty}^{+\infty} x(t)\phi_k(t)dt
\end{aligned}
\tag{7.17}
$$

As we discussed in Chapter 5, this was, indeed, the case with the computation of the FT resonance coefficients, and, we will see, it is also the case with a properly defined wavelet basis! We need also to define the extend or span of the basis set and what is maximally included in such a span.

Definition 276 *The* span *of a basis set, span $\{\phi_k(t)\}$, is the set of all financial time series $x(t)$ that can be decomposed in terms of this set of bases:*

$$
x(t) = \sum_{k=-\infty}^{+\infty} a_k \phi_k(t)
\tag{7.18}
$$

Definition 277 *The* closure *of the space spanned by the basis set, $\overline{\text{span}\{\phi_k(t)\}}$, contains not only all variables that can be expressed by a linear combination of the basis functions $\phi_k(t)$, but also the variables which are the limit of these infinite expansions.*

The closure is usually denoted by an over-bar, as we will see in Definition 291, when we discuss wavelet MRA, which is a particular form of unique expansion. To do so, we need the definition of a wavelet expansion.

Definition 278 *A* wavelet expansion *is the two-parameter (or 2D) expansion, such that*

$$x(t) = \sum_{j=0}^{+\infty} \sum_{n=-\infty}^{+\infty} a_{j,n} \psi_{j,n}(t) \tag{7.19}$$

where the integer indices $j, n \in \mathbb{Z}^2$ *and the* $\psi_{j,n}(t)$ *are the wavelet expansion functions that (usually) form an orthogonal basis.*

Similar to the preceding general frame definitions, we have for the wavelet bases the following specific definitions.

Definition 279 *An* orthogonal wavelet basis *is a complete set of orthogonal wavelets:*

$$\{\psi_{j,n}\}_{(j,n) \in \mathbb{Z}^2} \tag{7.20}$$

Definition 280 *An* orthonormal wavelet basis *(or tight wavelet frame) is a complete set of orthonormal wavelets.*

The term complete in these articular definitions means that there are no redundant wavelets in these set and that the set is unique.

Definition 281 *The set of expansion coefficients* $a_{j,n}$ *are called the* Discrete Wavelet Transform (DWT) *of* $x(t)$ *and the wavelet expansion is the* inverse DWT.

The following is a most remarkable and powerful theorem. It is clearly the foundation for the success and current popularity of wavelet MRA. For its proof we refer to the aforementioned mathematical wavelet literature, in particular to Mallat (1989a).

Theorem 282 (Wavelet expansion) *Any financial time series* $x(t)$ *with finite risk can be decomposed over a orthogonal wavelet basis*

$$x(t) = \sum_{j=0}^{+\infty} \sum_{n=-\infty}^{+\infty} \langle x(t), \psi_{j,n} \rangle \psi_{j,n} \tag{7.21}$$

This theorem is remarkable and powerful, because it states that *any* financial time series can be so *completely* analyzed. There is no approximation involved!

In summary:

(1) A wavelet basis is a set of *building blocks* to represent a function or time series $x(t)$. It is a 2D expansion set (usually a basis) for some class of 1- (or higher) dimensional functions.

(2) The wavelet expansion gives a *time–scale (frequency) localization* of $x(t)$. Most of the risk of the financial time series $x(t)$ is well represented by a few expansion coefficients $a_{j,n}$.

(3) The computation of these expansion coefficients from $x(t)$ can be done *efficiently* in discrete time.

7.2.5   DWT Systems

We will now present some specific examples of first-generation wavelet sets of
DWTs, which are all generated from a single scaling function, or a wavelet, by
simple time translation and frequency scaling.

Almost all useful wavelet sets also satisfy the so-called *multiresolution conditions*. This means that if a set of data series can be represented by a weighted sum
of laterally shifted wavelets $\psi(t-k)$, then a larger set (including the original) can
be represented by the weighted sum of $\psi(2t-k)$. The lower resolution coefficients can be computed from the higher resolution coefficients by a tree-structure
algorithm, called a *filter bank*. Mallat (1989a) provided the mathematical basis for
such an MRA, as we will discuss in detail in Section 7.3.

We will now first define some families of wavelets, which can be quite diverse.

7.2.5.1   Haar wavelet

The first recorded mention of the term "wavelet" was in 1909, in the PhD thesis of
Alfréd Haar (1910).[6] Haar realized that one can construct a very simple piecewise
constant function whose dilations and translations generate a complete *dyadic
orthonormal* basis in Hilbert space, i.e., in real quadratic linear space $L^2(\mathbb{R})$, as
follows.[7]

Definition 283   *A dyadic orthonormal wavelet basis in Hilbert space $L^2(\mathbb{R})$ is
defined by the set of dyadically scaling orthonormal wavelets:*

$$\psi_{j,n}(t) = \frac{1}{\sqrt{2^j}}\psi\left(\frac{t - 2^j n}{2^j}\right)$$
$$= 2^{-j/2}\psi(2^{-j}t - n) \tag{7.22}$$

The discrete *dyadic scale* parameter $a_j = 2^j$, while the translation interval is
$\tau_n = 2^j n$. The factor $2^{-j/2}$ maintains a constant norm independent of scale j.
Thus, we have the definition of the Haar wavelet.

Definition 284   *The discrete Haar wavelet is defined by:*

$$\psi^H(t) = \begin{cases} +1 & if\ 0 \le t < 0.5 \\ -1 & if\ 0.5 \le t < 1 \\ 0 & otherwise \end{cases} \tag{7.23}$$

The Haar wavelet is the (basic) wavelet that appears most useful for the analysis of financial time series, in particular of the increments or rates of return of
pricing series, since they are produced by independently shifting demand and
supply (curves), often in the form of discretely recorded tick data from trading
transactions, and contain many singularities.

7.2.5.2   Other families of wavelets

Of course, there exists a whole family of considerably more sophisticated wavelets other than the simple Haar wavelet. For example, other rather simple wavelets are the discrete time triangle wavelet and the continuous time Gábor wavelet.

Definition 285   *The discrete* Triangle Wavelet *is*

$$
\psi^T(t) = \begin{cases} +t & \text{if } 0 \leq t < 0.25 \\ 0.5 - t & \text{if } 0.25 \leq t < 0.75 \\ -1.0 + t & \text{if } 0.75 \leq t < 1 \\ 0 & \text{otherwise} \end{cases} \tag{7.24}
$$

Definition 286   *The continuous* Gábor wavelet *is a particular Gábor chirp* (cf. *Chapter 6*)

$$
\psi^G(t) = e^{j\eta t} g(t) \tag{7.25}
$$

with a Gaussian window

$$
g(t) = \frac{1}{\sigma^2 \pi^{0.25}} e^{-t^2/2\sigma^2} \tag{7.26}
$$

for $\sigma^2 \eta^2 \gg 1$.

The *Gábor wavelet* wavelet family, which has a Gaussian flavor, is often used in theoretical *continuous time* MRA, where it provides elegant solutions for difficult problems, as we will see in Chapter 8.

The family of wavelets is growing rapidly, since customized sets of wavelets can be carefully created to satisfy selected situations by applying particular zero-moment conditions, as Daubechies (1988) first demonstrated. There now exists already a remarkable *Daubechies(N) wavelet* family, where N = order of zero-moments of the Daubechies wavelets. But there are no explicit closed form Daubechies wavelets, except the Daubechies(1) wavelet, which is the same as the Haar wavelet. The $N > 1$ order Daubechies wavelets are all defined numerically by sets of recursive equations which define the filter coefficients of these wavelets. This is a similar situation as the no-closed form of most stable frequency distributions in Chapter 3.

7.3   Mallat's MRA

An efficient way to implement the DWT in the form of an MRA was invented in 1986 and developed in 1988 by Mallat (1989a–c). The operational Mallat algorithm is in fact a classical scheme known to signal processing engineers as a *two-channel subband coder*, or tree analysis. This very practical filtering algorithm yields a Fast Wavelet Transform, similar to the Fast Fourier Transform (FFT).

For many financial time series, the low-frequency content of a time series $x(t)$ is the most important part, since it gives the series its recognizable identity. Its high-frequency content, on the other hand, imparts its flavor or nuance. Mallat showed that one can completely decompose a time series $x(t)$ in terms of *approximations* (A), provided by so-called scaling functions, and *details* (D), provided by the wavelets. The approximations are the high-scale, low-frequency components of the time series. The details are the low-scale, high-frequency components.

This decomposition process can be iterated, with successive approximations being decomposed in turn, so that one time series $x(t)$ is broken down in many lower-resolution components. This is called the *wavelet decomposition tree*. Since the decomposition process is iterative, in theory it can be continued indefinitely. In reality, the decomposition can proceed only until the individual details consist of a single observation. For example, when one observes minute-by-minute data, the one-minute data point provides the smallest detail of resolution. The choice of the *wavelet filters* determines the shape of the wavelet we use to perform the analysis.

The following discussion of Mallat's MRA is adapted from Burrus *et al.* (1998) and from Hubbard (1998).

7.3.1 Low- and high-pass filters

Mathematically, for the MRA of the financial time series $x(t)$, one needs two closely related basic functions. In addition to the wavelet $\psi(t)$, which provides the details, one needs a second basis function, called the *scaling function*, which provides the low frequency approximation, e.g., like an average or mean. This scaling function and the wavelets are conjugated, as we will see. One cannot exist without the other. Mallat (1989a) proves that, using a combination of these scaling functions and wavelets, a very large class of time series can be represented by the following decomposition equation of scaling functions and wavelets:

$$x(t) = A + D$$

$$= \sum_{n=-\infty}^{+\infty} c_n \varphi_n(t) + \sum_{j=0}^{+\infty} \sum_{n=-\infty}^{+\infty} d_{j,n} \psi_{j,n}(t) \tag{7.27}$$

where the approximation (A) is provided by the 1D linear combination of the scaling functions, which form the so-called *low-pass filters*:

$$A = \sum_{n=-\infty}^{+\infty} c_n \varphi_n(t)$$

$$= \sum_{n=-\infty}^{+\infty} c_n \varphi(t - n) \tag{7.28}$$

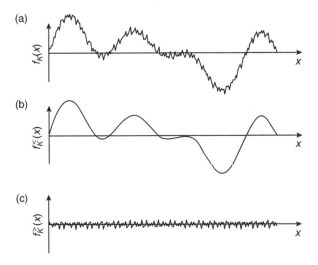

Figure 7.12 Time signal observations on $f(x)$ in panel (a) are subject to low-pass filtering in panel (b) and subject to high-pass filtering in panel (c).

and the details (D) by the 2D linear combination of the dyadic wavelets, which form the so-called *high-pass filters*:

$$D = \sum_{j=0}^{+\infty} \sum_{n=-\infty}^{+\infty} d_{j,n} \psi_{j,n}(t)$$

$$= \sum_{j=0}^{+\infty} \sum_{n=-\infty}^{+\infty} d_{j,n} \psi(2^{-j}t - n) \tag{7.29}$$

Example 287 *Figure 7.12 shows a primitive form of MRA or decomposition: 1D time series $f_K(x)$ (a) subject to low-pass filtering, (b) as indicated by the $<$ sign, and high-pass filtering, (c) as indicated by the $>$ sign. This kind of analysis is discussed in finance by, for example, Fama and French (1988). Obviously,*

$$f_K(x) = f_K^<(x) + f_K^>(x) \tag{7.30}$$

where $1/K$ is the scale of this filtering. This is a time series which possesses structures on only two very different scales: a small scale (of the order of a few millimeters) and a large scale (of the order of a few centimeters). The filter scale $1/K$ is chosen to be intermediate, say, c.1 cm. The passage from $f_K^<(x)$ to $f_K^>(x)$ may be generalized to filters of arbitrary shape, such as the WTs.

The coefficients of this MRA expansion, or DWT, are again computed as inner products, or basis correlations, as follows.

Definition 288   *The discrete (approximation)* scaling coefficients *are computed by the inner product*

$$c_n = \langle x(t)\phi_n(t)\rangle$$

$$= \int_{-\infty}^{+\infty} x(t)\phi_n(t)dt, \quad \text{with } n \in \mathbb{Z} \tag{7.31}$$

Definition 289   *The discrete (detail)* wavelet resonance coefficients *are computed by the inner product*

$$d_{j,n} = \langle x(t)\psi_{j,n}(t)\rangle$$

$$= \int_{-\infty}^{+\infty} x(t)\psi_{j,n}(t)dt, \quad \text{with } j, n \in \mathbb{Z} \tag{7.32}$$

Let's look now at some more clarifying definitions and see why this decomposition into approximating scaling functions $\phi_n(t)$ and detailing wavelets $\psi_{j,n}(t)$ leads to a *complete* MRA of the time series $x(t)$, due to the conjugation between these two functions.

Definition 290   *A set of (time)* scaling functions *is defined in terms of integer translates of the real square integrable basic scaling function by*

$$\varphi(t) = \varphi(t - n), \quad n \in \mathbb{Z}, \quad \varphi \in L^2(\mathbb{R}) \tag{7.33}$$

Thus, a scaling function is a strictly *periodic* function, as defined in Chapter 3. It exactly repeats itself with a lag n. Therefore, most of the concepts of the periodic wave theory of FTs can be applied to scaling functions.

Definition 291   *The square-integrable real (Hilbert) subspace of* $L^2(\mathbb{R})$ spanned *by these scaling functions is defined as*

$$\mathbf{V}_0 = \overline{\text{span}\{\varphi_n(t)\}} \tag{7.34}$$

for all integers k from $-\infty$ *to* $+\infty$*. The over-bar denotes* closure. *This means that*

$$x(t) = \sum_{n=-\infty}^{+\infty} a_n\varphi_n(t) \quad \text{for any } x(t) \in \mathbf{V}_0 \tag{7.35}$$

One can increase the size of the subspace spanned by changing the time scale of the time scaling functions. A 2D set of functions is generated from the basic scaling function by translation and scaling, as follows

$$\varphi_{j,n}(t) = 2^{-j/2}\varphi(2^{-j}t - n) \tag{7.36}$$

whose span over n is

$$\mathbf{V}_j = \overline{\text{span}_n\{\varphi_n(2^{-j}t)\}}$$
$$= \overline{\text{span}_n\{\varphi_{j,n}(t)\}} \quad \text{for all integers } n \in \mathbb{Z} \tag{7.37}$$

This means that any time series $x(t)$ can be linearly expanded strictly in terms of scaling functions as follows:

$$x(t) = \sum_{n=-\infty}^{+\infty} a_n\varphi_{j,n}(t)$$
$$= \sum_{n=-\infty}^{+\infty} a_n\varphi_n(2^{-j}t - n) \quad \text{for any } x(t) \in \mathbf{V}_j \tag{7.38}$$

For $j < 0$, the span can be larger, since the $\varphi_{j,n}(t)$ is narrower and is translated in smaller steps. Therefore, it can represent finer detail. For $j > 0$, $\varphi_{j,n}(t)$ is wider and is translated in wider steps. The wider scaling functions can represent only coarse information, and the space they span is smaller. Thus, the change in scale provides a change in resolution. The scale j indicates the *resolving power* of the analysis, similar to the resolving power of lenses in optics and photography.

7.3.2 MRA equation

Mallat formulated these intuitive ideas of scale and resolution into mathematical requirements for a *complete* MRA, by requiring a nesting of the spanned spaces $\mathbf{V}_j$ as follows

$$\mathbf{V}_{j+1} \subset \mathbf{V}_j \quad \text{for all } j \in \mathbb{Z} \tag{7.39}$$

with

$$\mathbf{V}_\infty = \{0\} \quad \text{and} \quad \mathbf{V}_{-\infty} = L^2(\mathbb{R}) \tag{7.40}$$

Thus, the linear space that contains low resolution will also contain the linear spaces of high resolution. This means that at the zero resolution, the only finite risk time series is 0, while at the infinite resolution all finite risk time series are perfectly reproduced. In other words, because of the definition of the spanned spaces $\mathbf{V}_j$, the spaces must satisfy the natural dyadic scaling condition

$$\varphi(t) \in \mathbf{V}_j \quad \Leftrightarrow \quad \varphi(2t) \in \mathbf{V}_{j+1} \tag{7.41}$$

which ensures that elements in a space are simply scaled versions of the elements in the next space. Thus, $\mathbf{V}_{j+1}$ is obtained from $\mathbf{V}_j$ by factor 2 rescaling.

This *dyadic nesting* of the spans of $\varphi(2^{-j}t - n)$, denoted by $\mathbf{V}_j$, is achieved by requiring that $\varphi(t) \in \mathbf{V}_1$, which means that if $\varphi(t) \in \mathbf{V}_0$, it is also $\varphi(t) \in \mathbf{V}_1$, the space spanned by $\varphi(2t)$. The resolution of V_j is generated by a basis which is obtained by 2^{-j} translations of a $2^{=j}$ rescaled φ. The φ is such a function that integer translations or lateral time shifts of φ creates a Riesz basis of $\mathbf{V}_\infty$. As we discussed earlier, a Riesz basis is a frame of linearly independent vectors.

Thus, we have now arrived at Mallat's formal definition of an MRA.

Definition 292   (Mallat's MRA) *A sequence $\{\mathbf{V}_j\}_{j \in \mathbb{Z}}$ of closed subspaces of $L^2(\mathbb{R})$ is an MRA, if and only if the following six properties are satisfied:*

(1) For all $(j, n) \in \mathbb{Z}^2$, $x(t) \in \mathbf{V}_j \Leftrightarrow x(2^{-j}t - n) \in \mathbf{V}_{j+1}$ ($\mathbf{V}_j$ is 2^{-j} dyadic translation invariant)
(2) For all $j \in \mathbb{Z}$, $\mathbf{V}_{j+1} \subset \mathbf{V}_j$ (nesting of resolutions)
(3) For all $j \in \mathbb{Z}$, $x(t) \in \mathbf{V}_j \Leftrightarrow x(2^{-1}t) \in \mathbf{V}_{j+1}$ (dyadic scaling of resolutions)
(4) $\lim_{j \to \infty} \mathbf{V}_j = \cap_{j=-\infty}^{+\infty} \mathbf{V}_j = \{0\}$ (at zero resolution, finite risk is 0)
(5) $\lim_{j \to -\infty} \mathbf{V}_j = Closure(\cup_{j=-\infty}^{+\infty} \mathbf{V}_j) = L^2(\mathbb{R})$ (at infinite resolution, perfect reproduction of finite risk)
(6) There exist a function φ, such that $\{\varphi(t - n)\}_{n \in \mathbb{Z}}$ is a Riesz basis of $\mathbf{V}_0$.

Remark 293   *When the Riesz basis is an orthogonal basis, the MRA is orthogonal, and its base atom is called a* scaling function. *It is always possible to orthogonalize any MRA. This implies that scaling functions always exist. However, orthogonalities impose constraints, such as that a compactly supported orthogonal scaling function cannot be symmetric and continuous, as Daubechies (1988, 1992) proved.*

The definition of an MRA implies that the scaling function $\varphi(t)$ can be expressed in terms of an expansion, i.e., a weighted sum of shifted $\varphi(2t)$ as follows (Strang, 1989).

Definition 294   *The MRA (dilation or scaling) equation is*

$$\varphi(t) = \sum_{n=-\infty}^{+\infty} h(n)\sqrt{2}\varphi(2t - n), \quad \text{for any } n \in \mathbb{Z} \tag{7.42}$$

where the coefficients $h(n)$ are real or complex numbers called the scaling (function) coefficients (= *the* scaling filter *or* scaling vector) *and the scaling factor $1/\sqrt{2}$ maintains the norm of the scaling function.*

An equivalent way to present the MRA equation is

$$\frac{1}{\sqrt{2}}\varphi\left(\frac{t}{2}\right) = \sum_{n=-\infty}^{+\infty} h(n)\varphi(t - n), \quad \text{for any } n \in \mathbb{Z} \tag{7.43}$$

Its FT is

$$\Phi(\omega) = \frac{1}{\sqrt{2}} \mathbf{H}\left(\frac{\omega}{2}\right) \Phi\left(\frac{\omega}{2}\right) \tag{7.44}$$

where $\mathbf{H}(\omega)$ is the transfer function, i.e., the FT of $h(n)$.

This recursive equation is fundamental to MRA and is analogous to a differential equation with coefficients $h(n)$ and a closed form solution $\varphi(t)$, that may or may not exist, or be unique or nonunique. For example, only for the Daubechies(1) wavelet (= Haar wavelet) exists an explicit expression, which is the Haar scaling function. For all higher order Daubechies wavelets only *numerical* solutions exist in the form of computed $h(n)$ coefficients, although the square modulus of the transfer function, $|\mathbf{H}(\omega)|^2$, is explicit and often fairly simple.

The coefficients $h(n)$ form a so-called *conjugate mirror filter*, which entirely determines the scaling function and most of its properties. In particular, the scaling function is compactly supported, if and only if $h(n)$ has a finite number of zero coefficients. In fact, we have the following crucial MRA design Theorem of Mallat and Meyer, which we present again without its proof, since it can be found in Mallat (1989a–c).

Theorem 295 (Mallat and Meyer MRA design) *Let $\varphi \in L^2(\mathbb{R})$ be any integrable scaling function. The Fourier series of the MRA coefficients $h(n)$, which are computed by the inner product*

$$h(n) = \left\langle \frac{1}{\sqrt{2}} \varphi\left(\frac{t}{2}\right), \varphi(t-n) \right\rangle \tag{7.45}$$

satisfies the two dyadic equations

$$\text{for all } \omega \in \mathbb{R}, \quad |\mathbf{H}(\omega)|^2 + |\mathbf{H}(\omega + \pi)|^2 = 2 \tag{7.46}$$

and

$$\mathbf{H}(0) = \sqrt{2} \tag{7.47}$$

Conversely, if $\mathbf{H}(\omega)$ is 2π periodic and continuously differentiable in a neighborhood of $\omega = 0$, if it satisfies the two dyadic equations, and if

$$\min_{\omega \in \left[-\frac{\pi}{2}, \frac{\pi}{2}\right]} |\mathbf{H}(\omega)| > 0 \tag{7.48}$$

then

$$\Phi(\omega) = \prod_{p=1}^{+\infty} \frac{\mathbf{H}(2^{-p}\omega)}{\sqrt{2}} \tag{7.49}$$

is the FT of a scaling function $\varphi \in L^2(\mathbb{R})$.

Remark 296   *This important FT of the scaling function is currently used for designs of new MRAs, which show up in the image compression filters, like the JPEG and MPEG filters of digital cameras and in the storage of digital movies on the Internet, and which are used for the digital restoration and coloration of old classic black and white movies in Hollywood (Mulcahy, 1996, 1997).*

7.3.2.1   Examples of MRA scaling filters

The following are examples of the scaling function and the corresponding MRA equation for some of the wavelet families we've introduced earlier in this chapter:

(1)   The *Haar (= Daubechies(1)) scaling function* is

$$\varphi(t) = \begin{cases} 1 & \text{if } 0 \leq t < 1 \\ 0 & \text{otherwise} \end{cases} \tag{7.50}$$

and its corresponding *Haar MRA equation* is

$$\varphi(t) = \varphi(2t) + \varphi(2t - 1) \tag{7.51}$$

i.e., the MRA equation with two scaling coefficients

$$h(0) = h(1)$$
$$= \frac{1}{\sqrt{2}} = 0.70711 \tag{7.52}$$

(rounded to five digits).

Figure 7.13 (left) shows how the Haar MRA equation corresponds with the graph of its scaling function.

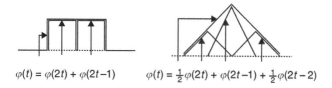

$$\varphi(t) = \varphi(2t) + \varphi(2t-1) \qquad \varphi(t) = \tfrac{1}{2}\varphi(2t) + \varphi(2t-1) + \tfrac{1}{2}\varphi(2t-2)$$

Figure 7.13 Haar (left) and triangle (right) scaling functions and their respective MRA equations.

(2) The *triangle scaling function* is

$$\varphi(t) = \begin{cases} t & \text{if } 0 \le t < 0.5 \\ 1 - t & \text{if } 0.5 \le t < 1 \\ 0 & \text{otherwise} \end{cases} \tag{7.53}$$

and the corresponding *triangle MRA equation* is

$$\varphi(t) = \frac{1}{2}\varphi(2t) + \varphi(2t - 1) + \frac{1}{2}\varphi(2t - 2) \tag{7.54}$$

i.e., the MRA equation is with three scaling coefficients

$$h(0) = \frac{1}{2\sqrt{2}} = 0.35355 \tag{7.55}$$

and

$$h(1) = h(2)$$

$$= \frac{1}{\sqrt{2}} = 0.70711 \tag{7.56}$$

Figure 7.13 (right) shows how the triangle MRA equation corresponds with the graph of its scaling function.

(3) The *Daubechies(4) scaling function* is the MRA equation with four scaling function coefficients

$$h(0) = 0.48296 \tag{7.57}$$
$$h(1) = 0.83652 \tag{7.58}$$
$$h(2) = 0.22414 \tag{7.59}$$

and

$$h(3) = -0.12941. \tag{7.60}$$

These scaling function coefficients are crucial for the "regularity" or "zero-moment" properties of the scaling filter. They summarize the density of information in the time series $x(t)$.

7.3.3 Relationship between wavelets and scaling functions

But what is the general relationship between wavelets and scaling functions? The wavelets are used to build a basis on which to represent the details of a time series that are gained between a particular resolution represented by a scaling function, and the next finer resolution, as is seen from the following set of definitions.

Definition 297   Sets of wavelets $\{\psi_{j,n}(t)\}$ *are sets of functions that span the differences between the spaces spanned by the various scales of a scaling function.*

Remark 298   *Usually it is required that the scaling functions and their corresponding wavelets are orthogonal, because orthogonal functions allow simple computation of expansion coefficients by inner (correlation) products and, consequently, as we will see at the end of this chapter, have a Parseval's Theorem that allows the* complete *partitioning of the financial time series' risk in the WT's time–scale domain.*

Definition 299   *The* orthogonal complement *(or* disjoint difference*) of* $\mathbf{V}_j$ *in* $\mathbf{V}_{j+1}$ *is* $\mathbf{W}_j$*. This means that all elements of* $\mathbf{V}_j$ *are orthogonal to all elements of* $\mathbf{W}_j$*, or the inner products of all scaling functions and wavelets equal zero*

$$\langle\varphi_{j,n}(t)\psi_{j,l}(t)\rangle = \int_{-\infty}^{\infty} \varphi_{j,n}(t)\psi_{j,l}(t)dt = 0 \tag{7.61}$$

for all appropriate $j, l, n \in \mathbb{Z}$.

This relationship between the orthogonal spaces is indicated as follows

$$\mathbf{V}_{j+1} = \mathbf{V}_j \oplus \mathbf{W}_j \tag{7.62}$$

where the symbol $\oplus$ indicates that the space $\mathbf{V}_{j+1}$ consist of the subspace $\mathbf{V}_j$ and its orthogonal complement $\mathbf{W}_0$. But then

$$\begin{aligned}\mathbf{V}_2 &= \mathbf{V}_1 \oplus \mathbf{W}_1 \\ &= \mathbf{V}_0 \oplus \mathbf{W}_0 \oplus \mathbf{W}_1\end{aligned} \tag{7.63}$$

and, in general, the whole real square-integrable (Hilbert) space is completely divided up as follows

$$L^2(\mathbb{R}) = \mathbf{V}_0 \oplus \mathbf{W}_0 \oplus \mathbf{W}_1 \oplus \mathbf{W}_2 \oplus \cdots \tag{7.64}$$

where $\mathbf{V}_0$ is the initial space spanned by the scaling function $\varphi(t - n)$.

The scale of the initial space $\mathbf{V}_0$ is arbitrary and can be chosen at any available resolution. Thus also

$$\mathbf{W}_{-\infty} \oplus \cdots \oplus \mathbf{W}_{-1} = \mathbf{V}_0 \tag{7.65}$$

which again shows the arbitrariness of the scale of the scaling space. In practice, the scale of the scaling space is chosen to represent the coarsest detail, or largest observation window, of interest in the time series $x(t)$. This will become clearer when we exhibit some of the empirical MRA examples.

The MRA equation for scaling functions is complemented by the MRA equation for wavelets.

Definition 300 *The* MRA *equation for wavelets is the weighted sum of shifted scaling functions*

$$\psi(t) = \sum_{n=-\infty}^{+\infty} h_1(n)\sqrt{2}\phi(2t-n), \quad n \in \mathbb{Z} \tag{7.66}$$

for some set of wavelet (generation) coefficients $h_1(n)$, since the wavelets reside in the space spanned by the next narrower scaling function, $\mathbf{W}_0 \subset \mathbf{V}_1$.

This MRA equation for wavelets can equivalently be presented as

$$\frac{1}{\sqrt{2}}\psi\left(\frac{t}{2}\right) = \sum_{n=-\infty}^{+\infty} h_1(n)\phi(t-n), \quad n \in \mathbb{Z} \tag{7.67}$$

Its FT is

$$\Psi(\omega) = \frac{1}{\sqrt{2}}\mathbf{H}_1\left(\frac{\omega}{2}\right)\Phi\left(\frac{\omega}{2}\right) \tag{7.68}$$

It can be easily proved, that, because of the MRA requirements and because of the orthogonality of the translates of the scaling function, these wavelet generation coefficients $h_1(n)$ (modulo translates by integer multiples of two) are required by orthogonality to be related to the scaling function coefficients by the following equation

$$h_1(n) = (-1)^n h(1-n) \tag{7.69}$$

The MRA equation for the wavelet $\psi(t)$ gives the prototype or *mother wavelet* for a class of expansion functions of the form

$$\psi_{j,n}(t) = 2^{j/2}\psi(2^j t - n) \tag{7.70}$$

7.3.3.1 Examples of MRA wavelet filters

The following are again examples of the wavelet resonance coefficients $h_1(n)$ that satisfy the wavelet coefficient equation, and show how easy it is to generate wavelets from sets of particular scaling functions:

(1) For the *Haar wavelet*, the MRA equation for wavelets is

$$\psi(t) = \phi(2t) - \phi(2t-1) \tag{7.71}$$

and the two wavelet generation coefficients are

$$h_1(0) = -h_1(1)$$

$$= \frac{1}{\sqrt{2}} = 0.70711 \tag{7.72}$$

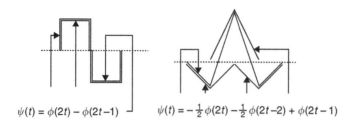

$\psi(t) = \phi(2t) - \phi(2t-1)$ $\psi(t) = -\tfrac{1}{2}\phi(2t) - \tfrac{1}{2}\phi(2t-2) + \phi(2t-1)$

Figure 7.14 Haar (left) and triangle (right) wavelets and their respective MRA equations.

Figure 7.14 (left) shows how the Haar MRA equation for wavelets corresponds with the graph of its wavelet.

(2) For the *triangle wavelet*, the MRA equation for wavelets is

$$\psi(t) = -\frac{1}{2}\phi(2t) + \phi(2t-1) - \frac{1}{2}\phi(2t-2) \tag{7.73}$$

and the three wavelet generation coefficients are

$$h_1(0) = -\frac{1}{\sqrt{2}} = -0.70711 \tag{7.74}$$

$$h_1(1) = -0.35355 \tag{7.75}$$

and

$$h_1(2) = 0.35355 \tag{7.76}$$

Figure 7.14 (right) shows how the triangle MRA equation for wavelets corresponds with the graph of its wavelet.

(3) For the *Daubechies (4) wavelet* (*cf.* Figure 7.2), the four wavelet generation coefficients are

$$h_1(0) = 0.12941 \tag{7.77}$$
$$h_1(1) = 0.22414 \tag{7.78}$$
$$h_1(2) = -0.83651 \tag{7.79}$$

and

$$h_1(3) = 0.48296 \tag{7.80}$$

The wavelet resonance coefficients summarize the detailed transient information in time series $x(t)$.

7.3.4 Design properties of MRA systems

Nowadays the optimal design of MRA systems consists of the choosing of the scaling coefficients $h(n)$ according to particular signal processing design criteria to improve the resolution of a single time series $x(t)$, or of a 2D time series, *c.q.*, digital pictures and movies, like the JPEG and MPEG criteria (Donoho, 1993a,b; Strichartz, 1993; Daubechies, 1996).[8] Let's have a look at some of the specific MRA design properties, such as the order of the vanishing moments, support, regularity and symmetry of the wavelet and scaling functions.[9]

7.3.4.1 Vanishing moments

Criterion 301 *A wavelet $\psi(t)$ has p vanishing moments*

$$\int_{-\infty}^{+\infty} t^k \psi(t) dt = 0 \quad \text{for } 0 \leq k < p \tag{7.81}$$

if and only if its scaling function can generate polynomials of degree smaller than or equal to p.[10]

When the wavelet's p moments are equal to zero, all the polynomial time series

$$x(t) = \sum_{0 \leq k < p} a_k t^k \tag{7.82}$$

have zero wavelet resonance coefficients and their details are also zero. This property ensures the suppression of time series that are polynomials, since the systematic polynomials are *exactly* captured by the scaling functions, just like cosine and sine waves are exactly captured by Fourier series.

Remark 302 *While this property of vanishing moments is described by the approximating power of scaling functions, for wavelets it has also the possibility to characterize the order of isolated singularities. The order of vanishing moments of a wavelet is entirely determined by the coefficients $h(n)$ of the filter h featured in the scaling function.*

If the FT of the wavelet is p times continuously differentiable, then the three following conditions are exactly equivalent:

(1) The wavelet ψ has p vanishing moments.
(2) The scaling function φ can generate polynomials if degree smaller than or equal to p.
(3) The FT of the filter h and its first $p - 1$ first derivatives vanish at $\omega = \pi$.

All these conditions can rather easily be checked.

Remark 303 *Daubechies (1988) proved that, to generate an orthogonal wavelet with p vanishing moments, a filter of minimum length $2p$ has to be used. Daubechies filters, which generate Daubechies wavelets, have a length of $2p$.*

7.3.4.2   Compact support

The following property of compact support has to do with the speed of convergence to zero at infinity of the scaling and wavelet functions, when either time or frequency goes to infinity.

Criterion 304   *If the support of the scaling function is $[N_1, N_2]$, then the wavelet support is $[(N_1 - N_2 - 1)/2, (N_2 - N_1 + 1)/2]$. The scaling function is* compactly supported *if and only if the filter h has finite support, and the support boundaries of h are not the same $N_1 \neq N_2$, i.e., the support is asymmetric.*

Remark 305   *Daubechies (1988, 1992) also showed that it is possible for the scaling function and the wavelets to have both compact support (i.e., to be nonzero only over a finite region) and to be orthonormal. This made possible the desired exhaustive and complete time–scale analysis. Thus, all risk of a financial time series can be completely presented by a* dyadic tiling *of its whole time–scale domain.*

7.3.4.3   Irregularity

We have discussed irregularity of time series somewhat in Chapter 4, and we will discuss it in more detail in Chapter 8. Wavelet regularity is less important than their vanishing moments. Wavelets can be very irregular. Consequently, the following two wavelet properties are crucial:

Criterion 306   *There is* no *compactly supported orthogonal wavelet which is indefinitely differentiable.*

Criterion 307   *For Daubechies wavelets with a large number of vanishing moments p, the scaling function and wavelet are α-Lipschitz, where α is of the order of $0.2p$. For large classes of orthogonal wavelets, more regularity implies more vanishing moments.*[11]

To represent $x(t)$ with K derivatives, one can choose a wavelet $\psi(t)$ that is K (or more) times continuously differentiable. The penalty for imposing greater *smoothness* in this sense is that the supports of the basis functions, the filter lengths and, hence, the computational complexity all increase. The most remarkable property is that smooth bases are also the "best" bases for representing time series with arbitrarily many singularities. This is a property that may become essential for the ongoing research of singularity spectra, as discussed in Chapter 8 (Donoho, 1993a).

7.3.4.4   Symmetry

Symmetric scaling functions and wavelets are important, because they are used to build bases of regular wavelets over any interval, rather than over only the real axis. Daubechies (1988, 1993) proved that, for a wavelet to be symmetric or anti-symmetric, its filter must have a linear complex phase and the following property.

Criterion 308   *There is no symmetric compactly supported orthogonal wavelet other than the Haar wavelet, which corresponds to a discontinuous wavelet with one vanishing moment. Thus, all compactly supported orthogonal wavelets other than the Haar wavelet are asymmetric.*

7.3.5   Usefulness of wavelets

Burrus *et al.* (1998, p. 216) summarize why wavelets are so useful for (financial) time series analysis:

(1) Wavelets, even very irregular ones, can represent *smooth* time series, in particular, those series which exhibit some form of scaling behavior, since wavelets themselves are self-similar.
(2) Wavelets can also represent series of *singularities* of various kinds.
(3) Wavelets are *local*. This makes most coefficient-based algorithms naturally adaptive to the heterogeneities in the time series.
(4) Wavelets have the *unconditional basis* property for a great variety of time series, implying that if one knows very little about a time series, as is often the case in the financial markets, the wavelet basis is usually a reasonable choice for measurement and analysis.

7.4   Wavelet Parseval Risk Decomposition Theorem

If the scaling functions and wavelets form an orthonormal basis (= a tight frame), there is a Parseval's (tiling) Theorem that relates the risk of the financial time series $x(t)$ exactly to the risk in each of the components and their wavelet resonance coefficients (Herley *et al.*, 1993).

Theorem 309   (Parseval's tiling) *For the general wavelet expansion the risk or variance of the financial time series can be expanded (or analyzed) as*

$$\int_{-\infty}^{+\infty} |x(t)|^2 dt = \sum_{n=-\infty}^{+\infty} |c_n|^2 + \sum_{j=0}^{+\infty} \sum_{n=-\infty}^{+\infty} |d_{j,n}|^2 \qquad (7.83)$$

with the risk in the expansion completely partitioned in time by n and in scale by j.

Parseval's Theorem for wavelets allows us to completely and uniquely decompose the overall risk of a financial market time series into subcomponent, i.e., into financial risk at any scale (frequency) and at any moment in time. Thus, we have achieved one of the major objectives of this book: to find a rigorous method to decompose the risk of a financial rate of return series into any time-localized scale or frequency of our choice.

Using Parseval's tiling one can check if volatility scales in foreign exchange markets, as Batten and Ellis (1999) claim, or if the volatility of credit spreads scales, as Batten *et al.* (1999) claim. In Chapter 8, we'll discuss how to use the wavelet MRA to identify the homogeneous Hurst exponent of the parametric scaling of the FBM.

7.5   Software

The computations of the following Exercises can be executed by using the MATLAB® Wavelet Toolbox, available from The MathWorks, Inc., 24 Prime Park Way Natick, MA 01760-1500, USA. Tel.: (508) 647-7000; Fax: (508) 647-7001; http://www.mathworks.com/products/wavelettbx.shtml.

A complete wavelet analysis toolkit called *Wavelab 802* can be obtained at no cost from Stanford University: http://playfair.stanford.EDU:80/~wavelab/.

This *Wavelab* is a very complete set of MATLAB® scripts that implement both the basic wavelet and related transforms and more advanced techniques. There is full documentation, a set of tutorials, and section of "Toons," short for *cartoons*. These Toon scripts reproduce from scratch the figures in many papers of Stanford's wavelet research group consisting of Dave Donoho, Ian Johnstone *et al.*, describing the theoretical research underlying the algorithms in *Wavelab*. By studying these scripts and by experimenting with the data, the reader can learn all the details of the process that led to each figure. This forms part of the new discipline of *Reproducible Research*, i.e., the idea to provide the reader full access to all details (data, equations, code, etc.) needed to completely reproduce all the results normally presented only in summary form in scientific publications. For example, there are MATLAB® scripts to generate and exactly reproduce all the figures in the book by Mallat (1998). The pioneer of such *Reproducible Research* is Jon Claerbout of Stanford University's Geophysics Department (Claerbout, 1994; Buckheit and Donoho, 1995).

In addition, one can use Benoit 1.3: Fractal System Analysis (for Windows 95/98 or Windows NT), Trusoft International Inc., 204 37th Ave. N #133, St Petersburg, FL 33704. Tel.: (813) 925-8131; Fax: (813) 925-8141; sales@trusoft-international.com. See http://www.trusoft-international.com for details. This Benoit software enables you to measure the fractal dimension and/or Hölder-Hurst exponent of your data sets using your choice of method(s) for analysis of self-affine traces of speculative prices. However, astonishingly, the wavelet routine in Benoit 1.3 is incorrect, although the other routines to compute the Hurst exponent are correct.

7.6   Exercises

Exercise 310   *Study and execute MATLAB® Exercises – Chapter 1, Wavelet Display, in Strang and Nguyen (1997), p. 454. This assignment is designed to familiarize the reader with the MATLAB® Wavelet Toolbox and its GUI (= Graphical User Interface). The assignment includes Wavelet Display, Continuous Wavelet Transform, 1D and 2D DWT. It is assumed that the Wavelet Toolbox is installed. At the MATLAB® prompt, type* **wavemenu**. *A window should pop up with choices* *ranging from* **Wavelet 1D** *to* **Wavelet Packet 2D** *to* **Continuous Wavelet 1D.** *Closely follow Strang and Nguyen's instructions.*

Exercise 311   *Study and execute MATLAB® Exercises – Chapter 1, CWT in Strang and Nguyen (1997), pp. 454–455. Under File menu option, select* **Load Signal.** *Choose the MATLAB® file MATLAB® on in* /toolbox/ wavelet/wavedemo/freqbrk.mat.

Exercise 312   *and follow Strang and Nguyen's instructions. Notice the scalogram. What does the scalogram show us (in detail)? Use the File menu option to load another signal file of MATLAB® on 'Nbs1'* (F:)/toolbox/wavelet/ wavedemo/qdchirp.mat, *and again follow Strang and Nguyen's instructions.*

Exercise 313   *Study and execute MATLAB® Exercises – Chapter 1, 1D DWT, Strang and Nguyen (1997), p. 455. Under File menu option, select* **Load Signal.** *Choose the MATLAB® file in* /toolbox/wavelet/wavedemo/noisdopp.mat.

Exercise 314   *and follow Strang and Nguyen's instructions. Study the various Decomposition and Statistics, Histogram, Compress and Denoise capabilities (Note: the MATLAB® GUI follows Daubechies' convention of giving the scaling function and the lowest frequency wavelet the highest scaling number. Strang and Nguyen gives them the lowest scaling number, i.e., the zero). Study in particular the automatic denoising and compression. Notice how few wavelet resonance coefficients are required for an acceptable synthesis and reconstruction of the original data series (= "signal").*

Exercise 315   *Study and execute MATLAB® Exercises – Chapter 6, Multiresolution Analysis in 1D, Strang and Nguyen (1997), p. 466.*

Exercise 316   *Study and execute MATLAB® Exercises – Chapter 6, Wavelet Packet in 1D, Strang and Nguyen (1997), p. 466.*

Notes

1 In Chapter 8, we'll provide an empirical analysis of Latin American financial markets using Morlet (6) wavelets.
2 An *electroencephalogram* (EEG) is a recording of the electrical activity of the brain, and an *electroencephalograph* is the instrument used for making the recording. The technique, called electroencephalography, was first reported in 1929 by Hans Berger, a German psychiatrist. The complexity of the brain and the inability of the electrical recording apparatus to distinguish the direction of nerve impulses within the brain, because it identifies correlations and not causalities, make it very difficult to interpret the EEG. The frequency of these impulses also varies in different parts of the brain. But certain distinctive, abnormal patterns are clearly associated with such situations as epilepsy, stroke and brain tumors. Thus, the study of a patient's EEG can aid in medical diagnosis.

3 Indeed, Brian Yuhnke Jr, one of the new media software programmers with whom I work at Kent State University, interprets my current research as trying to find a real-time "doppler radar for financial markets." No doubt, his comment is inspired by the doppler radar used for the weather report of Channel 3, the t.v. station in Cleveland, Ohio, close to our university, and also used for tornado warnings.

4 Thus, a scalogram shows the localized conventional "R-squareds" between the time series and each of the wavelets in the tiling diagram.

5 The scalegram corresponds with the *average* "R-squareds."

6 Alfréd Haar (1885–1933) was born in Budapest, Hungary. In 1904, Haar travelled to Germany to study at Göttingen under Hilbert's supervision, obtaining his doctorate in 1909 with a dissertation entitled *Zur Theorie der Orthogonalen Funktionensysteme* ("The Theory of Systems of Orthogonal Functions"). Haar then taught at Göttingen until 1912, when he returned to Hungary and held chairs at the university in Kolozsvár (which is now Cluj in Romania), Budapest University and Szeged University. Haar, together with Riesz, rapidly made the new Szeged University a major mathematical center. Later he went on to study partial differential equations. In 1932, he introduced a measure on groups, now called the Haar measure, which allows an analogue of Lebesgue integrals to be defined on locally compact topological groups. Thus, he generalized classical measure theory! The Haar measure was used by both von Neumann and Pontryagin in 1934 and by Weil in 1940 to set up an abstract theory of commutative harmonic analysis. Only now, after Mallat created its tree-algorithm in 1988 and combined it with the current advanced state of computing power, find these powerful abstract ideas feasible applications in advanced time series analysis and in the analysis of financial market risk.

7 *Dyadic* = based on a geometric sequence of ratio 2.

8 There exist now already better standards for the design of the multiresolution of signals than MPEG, e.g., the design criteria for the archives of the digitized FBI fingerprints and the design criteria for recent compact digital cameras, of which the filter allows hundreds of pictures to be compressed and stored in a relatively small physical memory.

9 This section is for specialists and can be skipped in a first reading. It was Daubechies who mathematically developed and researched these four important design criteria for WTs.

10 For example, the Gaussian distribution kernel, which can be presented as a wavelet, has vanishing moments at $p = 3$ and for all $p > 4$.

11 Since the Gaussian has vanishing moments at $p = 3$ and for all $p > 4$, the Gábor wavelet, which has a Gaussian atom, is very regular. We'll discuss the concept of α-Lipschitz irregularity in Chapter 8.

Bibliography

Aldroubi, Akram, and Michael Unser (Eds) (1996) *Wavelets in Medicine and Biology*, CRC Press, Boca Raton, FL.

Antoniadis, A., and G. Oppenheimer (Eds) (1995) *Wavelets and Statistics*, Springer Verlag, New York, NY.

Ariño, M. A., and B. Vidakovic (1995) "On Wavelet Scalograms and Their Applications in Economic Time Series," Discussion Paper 95(21), ISDS, Duke University, Durham, NC.

Aussem, Alex, Jonathan Campbell and Fionn Murtagh (1998) "Wavelet-Based Feature Extraction and Decomposition Strategies for Financial Forecasting," *Journal of Computational Intelligence in Finance*, **6**(2), 5–12.

Batten, Jonathan, and Craig Ellis (1999) "Volatility Scaling in Foreign Exchange Markets," CREFS Working Papers #99-04, Nanyang Technological University, Singapore, April, 23 pages.

Batten, Jonathan, Craig Ellis and Warren Hogan (1999) "Scaling the Volatility of Credit Spreads: Evidence from Australian Dollar Eurobonds," CREFS Working Papers #99-03, Nanyang Technological University, Singapore, April, 23 pages.

Bendjoya, Ph., and E. Slézak (1993) "Wavelet Analysis and Applications to Some Dynamical Systems," *Celestial Mechanics and Dynamical Astronomy*, **56**, 231–262.

Benedetto, J. J., and M. W. Frazier (Eds) (1994) *Wavelets: Mathematics and Applications*, CRC Press, Boca Raton, FL.

Bruce, A., David Donoho and H. Y. Gao (1996) "Wavelet Analysis," *IEEE Spectrum*, **33**(10), 26–35.

Buckheit, J. B., and D. L. Donoho (1995) "Wavelab and Reproducible Research," in Antoniadis, A., and G. Oppenheim (Eds) *Wavelets and Statistics*, Springer Verlag, Berlin, pp. 53–81.

Burke-Hubbard, Barbara (1994) "The Mathematical Microscope: Waves, Wavelets, and Beyond," in M. Bartusiak *et al.* (Ed.) *A Positron Named Priscilla, Scientific Discovery at the Frontier*, National Academy Press, Washington, DC, pp. 196–235.

Burke-Hubbard, Barbara (1998) *The World According to Wavelets: The Story of a Mathematical Technique in the Making*, 2nd edn, A K Peters, Wellesley, MA.

Burrus, Sidney, Ramesh A. Gopinath and Haitao Guo (1998) *Introduction to Wavelets and Wavelet Transforms: A Primer*, Prentice Hall, Upper Saddle River, NJ.

Chui, Charles K. (1992a) *An Introduction to Wavelets*, Academic Press, San Diego, CA.

Chui, Charles K. (Ed.) (1992b) *Wavelets: A Tutorial in Theory and Applications*, Academic Press, New York, NY.

Claerbout, J. (1994) "Reproducible Electronic Documents," http://sepwww.stanford.edu/research/redoc.

Coifman, R. R., and M. V. Wickerhauser (1992) "Entropy-based Algorithms for Best Basis Selection," *IEEE Transactions of Information Theory*, **38**(2), 713–718.

Cohen, Albert, and Jelena Kovacevic (1996) "Wavelets: The Mathematical Background," *Proceedings of the IEEE*, **84**(4), 514–522.

Daubechies, Ingrid (1988) "Orthonormal Bases of Compactly Supported Wavelets," *Communications on Pure and Applied Mathematics*, **41**(7), 909–996.

Daubechies, Ingrid (1992) *Ten Lectures on Wavelets*, SIAM, Philadelphia, PA (Notes from the 1990 CBMS-NSF Conference on Wavelets and Applications, at Lowell, MA).

Daubechies, Ingrid (1993) Orthonormal Bases of Compactly Supported Wavelets II. Variations on a Theme, *SIAM Journal on Mathematical Analysis*, **24**(2), 499–519.

Daubechies, Ingrid (1996) "Where Do Wavelets Come From? – A Personal Point of View," *Proceedings of the IEEE*, **84**(4), 510–513.

Donoho, David L. (1993a) "Unconditional Bases are Optimal Bases for Data Compression and for Statistical Estimation," *Applied and Computational Harmonic Analysis*, **1**(1), 100–115.

Donoho, David L. (1993b) "Nonlinear Wavelet Methods for Recovery of Signals, Densities, and Spectra from Indirect and Noisy Data," *Proceedings of Symposia in Applied Mathematics*, **47**, 173–205.

Fama, Eugene F., and Kenneth R. French (1988) "Permanent and Transitory Components of Stock Prices," *Journal of Political Economy*, **96**(2), 24–73.

Flandrin, Patrick (1989) "On the Spectrum of Fractional Brownian Motion," *IEEE Transactions on Information Theory*, **35**(1), January, 197–199.

Flandrin, Patrick (1992) "Wavelet Analysis and Synthesis of Fractional Brownian Motion," *IEEE Transactions on Information Theory*, **38**(2), March, 910–917.

Frazier, Michael W. (1999) *An Introduction to Wavelets Through Linear Algebra*, Springer Verlag, New York, NY.

Gençay, Ramazan, Faruk Selçuk and Brandon Whitcher (2001) *An Introduction to Wavelets and Other Filtering Methods in Finance and Economics*, Academic Press, San Diego, CA.

Grossman, A., and J. Morlet (1984) "Decomposition of Hardy Functions Into Square Integrable Wavelets of Constant Shape," *SIAM Journal of Mathematical Analysis*, **15**(4), 723–736.

Haar, Alfréd (1910) "Zur Theorie der Orthogonalen Funktionensysteme ('A Theory of Systems of Orthogonal Functions')," *Mathematical Analysis*, **69**(1), 331–371.

Herley, C., J. Kovacevic, K. Ramachandran and M. Vetterli (1993) "Tilings of the Time–Frequency Plane," *IEEE Transactions in Signal Processing*, **41**(12), 3341–3359.

Holschneider, M. (1995) *Wavelet: An Analysis Tool*, Clarendon Press, Oxford, UK.

Jawerth, Björn, and Wim Sweldens (1994) "An Overview of Wavelet Based Multiresolution Analysis," *SIAM Reviews*, **36**(3), 377–412.

Jensen, Mark J. (1997) "Making Wavelets in Finance," *Financial Engineering News*, **1**(1), 1 and 9–10.

Kaplan, Lance M., and C.-C. Jay Kuo (1993) "Fractal Estimation From Noisy Data, Via Discrete Fractional Gaussian Noise (DFGN) and the Haar Basis," *IEEE Transactions in Signal Processing*, **41**(12), 3554–3562.

Lau, K.-M., and H.-Y. Weng (1995) "Climate Signal Detection Using Wavelet Transform: How to Make a Time Series Sing," *Bulletin of the American Meteorological Society*, **76**, 2391–2402.

Lawton, W. (1990) "Tight Frames of Compactly Supported Wavelets," *Journal of Mathematical Physics*, **31**, 1898–1901.

Mallat, Stéphane G. (1989a) "A Theory for Multiresolution Signal Decomposition: The Wavelet Representation," *IEEE Transactions on Pattern Analysis and Machine Intelligence*, **11**(7), 674–693.

Mallat, Stéphane G. (1989b) "Multiresolution Approximation and Wavelet Orthonormal Bases of L^2," *Transactions of the American Mathematical Society*, **315**(1), 1989, 69–87.

Mallat, Stéphane G. (1989c) "Multifrequency Channel Decomposition of Images and Wavelet Models," *IEEE Transactions on Acoustics, Speech and Signal Processing*, **37**(12), 2091–2110.

Mallat, Stéphane (1999) *A Wavelet Tour of Signal Processing*, 2nd edn, Academic Press, Boston, MA.

Massopust, P. (1994) *Fractal Fluctuations, Fractal Surfaces and Wavelets*, Academic Press, San Diego, CA.

Meyer, Yves (1985) "Principe d'Incertitude, Bases Hilbertienne et Algèbres d'Opérateurs" ("Uncertainty Principle, Hilbert Bases and Operator Algebra"), in *Séminaire Bourbaki*, **145–146**, 209–223, Astérisque, Paris.

Meyer, Yves (1990) *Wavelets and Operators*, Cambridge University Press, Cambridge, UK.

Meyer, Yves (1993) *Wavelets: Algorithms and Applications* (translated and revised by Robert D. Ryan), Society for Industrial and Applied Mathematics (SIAM), Philadelphia, PA.

Meyers, S. D., B. G. Kelly and J. J. O'Brien (1993) "An Introduction to Wavelet Analysis in Oceanography and Meteorology: With Application to the Dispersion of Yanai Waves," *Monthly Weather Review*, **121**(10), 2858–2866.

Morlet, J., G. Arens, I. Fourgeau and D. Giard (1982) "Wave Propagation and Sampling Theory," *Geophysics*, **47**(2), 203–236.

Mulcahy, Colm (1996) "Plotting and Scheming with Wavelets," *Mathematics Magazine*, **69**(5), 323–343.

Mulcahy, Colm (1997) "Image Compression Using the Haar Wavelet Transform," *Spelman Science and Mathematics Journal*, **1**(1), 22–31.

Ogden, R. T. (1997) *Essential Wavelets for Statistical Applications and Data Analysis*, Birkhäuser, Boston, MA.

Ogden, R. T., and E. Parzen (1996) "Change-Point Approach to Data Analytic Wavelet Thresholding," *Statistics and Computing*, **6**, 93–99.

Ramsey, James B., and Zhifeng Zhang (1996) "The Application of Waveform Dictionaries to Stock Market Index Data," in Kravtsov, Yurii A., and James B. Kadtke (Eds) *Predictability of Complex Dynamical Systems*, Springer Verlag, New York, NY, 1996, pp. 189–205.

Ramsey, James B., and Zhifeng Zhang (1997) "The Analysis of Foreign Exchange Data Using Waveform Dictionaries," *Journal of Empirical Finance*, **4**, 341–372.

Ramsey, James B., and Camille Lampart (1998a) "Decomposition of Economic Relationships by Time Scale Using Wavelets: Money and Income," *Macroeconomic Dynamics*, **2**(1), 49–71.

Ramsey, James B., and Camille Lampart (1998b) "Decomposition of Economic Relationships by Time Scale Using Wavelets: Expenditure and Income," *Studies in Nonlinear Dynamics and Econometrics*, **3**(1), 23–42.

Ramsey, James B., Daniel Usikov and George M. Zaslavsky (1995) "An Analysis of U.S. Stock Price Behavior Using Wavelets," *Fractals*, **3**(2), 377–389.

Rioul, O., and M. Vetterli (1991) "Wavelets and Signal Processing," *IEEE Signal Processing Magazine*, October, 14–38.

Ruskai, M. B., Gregory Beylkin, Ronald Coifman, Ingrid Daubechies, Stéphane Mallat, Yves Meyer and Louis Raphael (Eds) (1992) *Wavelets and Their Applications*, Jones and Bartlett Publishers, Boston, MA.

Scargle, Jeffrey D. (1997) "Wavelets, Scaling, and Chaos," in Buchler, J. Robert, and Henry Kandrup (Eds) *Nonlinear Signal and Image Analysis*, Annals of the New York Academy of Sciences, **808**, January 30, 125–138.

Strang, Gilbert (1989) "Wavelets and Dilation Equations: A Brief Introduction," *SIAM Reviews*, **31**(4), 614–627.

Strang, Gilbert (1993) "Wavelet Transforms vs. Fourier Transforms," *Bulletin of the American Mathematical Society*, **28**(2), 288–305.

Strang, Gilbert (1994) "Wavelets," *American Scientist*, **82**, 250–255.

Strang, Gilbert, and Truong Nguyen (1997) *Wavelets and Filter Banks*, Wellesley-Cambridge Press, Wellesley, MA.

Strichartz, R. (1993) "How to Make Wavelets," *American Mathematical Monthly*, **100**(6), 539–556.

Vetterli, Martin (1986) "Filter Banks Allowing Perfect Reconstruction," *Signal Processing*, **10**(3), 219–244.

Walker, James S. (1997) "Fourier Analysis and Wavelet Analysis," *Notices of the American Mathematical Society*, **44**(6), 658–670.

Wang, Y. (1995) "Jump and Sharp Cusp Detection by Wavelets," *Biometrika*, **82**, 385–397.

Wickerhäuser, M. V. (1994) *Adapted Wavelet Analysis: From Theory to Software*, A K Peters, Boston, MA.

Wornell, G. W. (1995) *Signal Processing with Fractals: A Wavelet-Based Approach*, Prentice-Hall, New York, NY.

8 Multiresolution analysis of local risk

"Natura Saltus Facit"

(= "Nature Jumps")[1]

8.1 Introduction

For the first time in history, huge quantities of high-frequency financial data are currently being recorded and stored. Both financial price and volume data have been recorded (Gopikrishnan *et al.*, 1998):

- on a daily basis since the nineteenth century;
- with a sampling rate of one minute or less since 1984; and
- on a transaction-by-transaction (tick-by-tick) basis since 1993.

The first to collect and archive high-frequency, intraday foreign exchange (FX) data from Reuters composite FXFX page were the researchers of the institute of Olsen and Associates in Zürich, Switzerland (Müller *et al.*, 1990; Dacorogna *et al.*, 2001). This was quickly followed by the massive data archiving project under the directorship of Dr Würtz at the Eidgenössische Technische Hochschule (ETH: Federal Technical University) in Zürich, who collected high-frequency data from Reuters data selection feeds, mainly from RIC data records. His research group collected the series of quoted prices of 355 major financial instruments, including FX spot rates, forward rates, deposit rates, currency and deposit fixings, treasury market yields and FX cross rates at a rate of 60 megabytes per month. Financial futures, options and financial news subsequently followed.

Most of the series collected by both the Olsen and Associates and the ETH groups contain unequally spaced prices in the time domain. Such unequal spacing, or *time warping* of prices, produces a new research challenge in finance. Wavelet multiresolution analysis (MRA) can very effectively deal with such time warping. This ability of the wavelet MRA is one of the many reasons why this book advocates its use as a major research tool in finance.

The currencies involved in the instruments of the ETH project include those of the G10 countries, Switzerland, the European Community, Hong Kong and Australia. In Asia's financial *annus horibilis* 1997, when the Asian Financial Crisis erupted, I serendipitously collected, archived and analyzed a complete year of seven minute-by-minute Asian FX data series from Reuters FXFX pages with the assistance of three undergraduate students at the Nanyang Technological University in Singapore. Our Asian high-frequency FX series had the advantage of being equally spaced in time, like conventional time series. But we've already noticed the advantage of wavelet MRA in dealing with equally and unequally spaced, smooth and irregular data, in particular, with both discontinuous and turbulent pricing series.[2]

High-frequency records of financial prices, or of rates of return, in competitive markets exhibit three striking characteristics:

(1) They are conspicuously *discontinuous*, i.e., they are singular at almost every point, because the financial supply and demand curves move in unequal discrete steps, in instantaneous response to discrete news events. For example, Figure 8.1 shows on a time scale of 20 minutes the US Dollar/Deutsche Mark (USD/DEM) exchange rates as mid-prices and as associated logarithmic differences or rates of return (Schnidrig and Würtz, 1995, p. 2, figures 1 and 2). In the right panel the quiet sections represent the two days of the weekends, while there are daily fluctuations in the volatility of the log returns for the five-day trading week.

(2) They are *strictly non-stationary*. However, they adhere to stable scaling or power laws and they are stationary at particular scales. For example, Figure 8.2 shows the scaling law behavior for the USD/DEM exchange rate in a double-logarithmic plot. This scaling law is independent from the source of data (in the period 1993–1994) and holds over several orders of magnitude. The scaling exponent $H = 0.58$ is significantly different from the Gaussian process $H = 0.5$ (Schnidrig and Würtz, 1995, p. 4, figure 3).

(3) They show *aperiodic cyclicity*, i.e., they show intermittent periods of condensation, succeeded by periods of rarefaction. Figures 8.3 and 8.4 demonstrate the impact of the intraday cycles of average trading activity on the intensity of the price changes in the global FX market (Dacorogna *et al.*, 1993). Although the FX market is active 24 hours per day, the social organization of business, combined with the circadian cycle, forces the market activity to experience temporal constraints in each financial region of the world. This impacts the price formation. Similar day and weekend effects can be observed in the stock market returns (French, 1980). Figure 8.3 (left and right panel) shows the average hourly trading transaction density in the global FX market as measured by the number of transactions per hour (Schnidrig and Würtz, 1995, p. 5, figure 6). Figure 8.4 (left and right panel) shows the mean absolute hourly log-price change $E\{|\Delta \ln P_t|\}$ for the USD/DEM rate as a measure for weekly averaged price risk or volatility per hour (Schnidrig and Würtz, 1995,

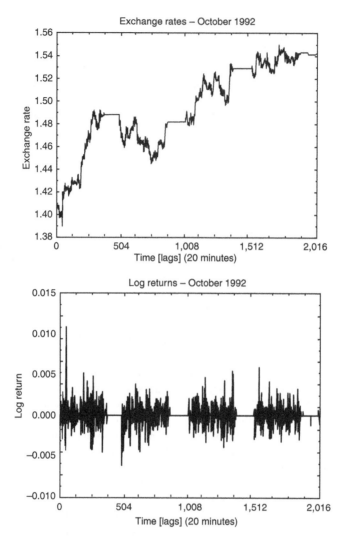

Figure 8.1 USD/DEM exchange rate, computed as a mid-price (upper) and as the
associated logarithmic difference (lower), on a time scale of $\Delta t = 20$
minutes, October 5–November 2, 1992.

Source: USD/DEM from Reuters FXFX pages 5.10.1992–2.11.1992.

p. 6, figure 8). The time on the abscissa of the weekly figures in Figure 8.3
(lower) and 8.4 (lower) is measured in $7 \times 24 = 168$ hours per week.
Time is measured in Greenwich Mean Time (GMT) and starts on Monday
0:00 GMT.

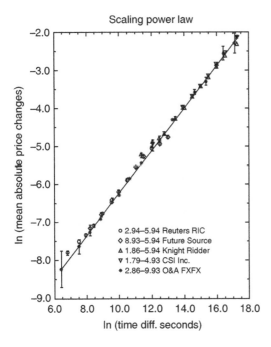

Figure 8.2 Scaling law behavior of the USD/DEM exchange rate in the period 1993–1994, for various subperiods: ln(mean absolute price changes) versus ln(time difference in seconds): $\ln E\{|\Delta P_t|\}/\ln \Delta t$.

Source: USD/DEM various vendors and time periods.

Notice that the three peaks in both Figures 8.3 (right) and 8.4 (right) relate to the maximum market activity in America (main peak), Asia (smallest peak), and Europe (small peak), respectively. There is very little trading during the weekends. The peaks in the trading activity in Figure 8.3 correspond with the peaks in price volatility or risk in Figure 8.4.

It is also observed that stock prices or foreign exchange rates are *singular at almost every point*, since their transaction records are essentially represented by step functions over time. The prices "jump" in small steps, because of small shifts in their respective supply and demand curves. The typical mechanism in price formation involves both knowledge of the present and expectations about the future. Even when the exogenous physical determinants of prices vary continuously, expectations can change drastically and instantaneously.

Such discontinuous price data are similar to particular physiological measurement data, such as heart records, electromagnetic fluctuations in galactic radiation noise, textures in images of natural terrain, variations of electric grid or traffic flows, etc. However, *not all singularities are alike!* Knowing the degree of irregularity

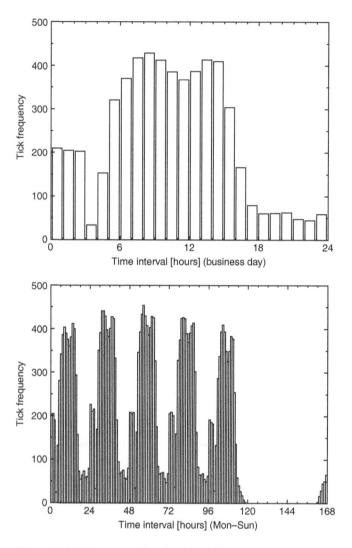

Figure 8.3 Trading transaction density: daily (upper) and weekly (lower) averaged
number of ticks per hour. The tick labels are in GMT and start on Monday
0:00 GMT (October 5, 1992–September 29, 1993).

Source: USD/DEM from Reuters FXFX page 5.10.1992–26.9.1993.

of such discontinuities, or singularities, is important in analyzing their properties.
In finance, knowing the distributions of the degrees of irregularity of financial
time series is necessary for a correct analysis and valuation of the non-stationary,
aperiodic, but cyclic financial risk.

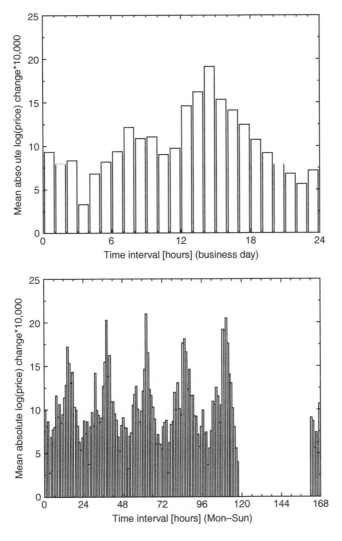

Figure 8.4 Daily (upper) and weekly (lower) averaged volatility per hour of the USD/DEM exchange rate. Tick labels are in GMT and start on Monday 0:00 GMT (October 5, 1992–September 26, 1993).

Source: USD/DEM from Reuters FXFX page 5.10.1992–26.9.1993

For this purpose, we return in this chapter to our original informal definition of irregularity or "randomness" of Chapter 1. This time we provide a proper formal definition of measurable irregularity, as measured by the Lipschitz (ir-) regularity exponent α_L.[3]

Pointwise measurements of Lipschitz regularity exponents, which measure the degree of irregularity of singularities, are not possible, because of finite numerical resolution of the empirical data. After discretization, each data set corresponds to a time interval where the time series has a very large (but finite) number of singularities. These singularities may show similarities, but they may also all be different. Such singularity distributions, or *singularity spectra* must therefore be computed from global measurements, which take advantage of *multifractal self-similarities* inherent in the financial data.

In the preceding chapters, we found that the Fractional Brownian Motion (FBM) provides a convenient uni-parametric model for such self-similar time series (cf. Chapter 4). FBMs are statistically self-similar i.i.d. processes, which exhibit long-term dependencies. Despite their non-stationarity, one can define a power spectrum, based on their stationary increments, that exhibits power decay. Thus, FBMs exhibit $1/\omega$-type spectral behavior over wide ranges of radian frequencies ω (cf. Chapter 4). Realizations of FBMs are almost everywhere singular, with the same *homogeneous* α_L-Lipschitz regularity at all points.

On the other hand, unlike FBMs, there exist fractal random processes that are not homogeneous α_L-Lipschitz irregular, although their power spectrum shows power decay. Empirical realizations of these processes may include increments of various types other than the familiar i.i.d. innovation processes of the classical Geometric Brownian Motion (GBM). Therefore, the computation of a complete singularity spectrum with a fractal dimension dependent on the Lipschitz regularity exponent α_L is important for such non-FBM cases, as we'll discuss at the end of this chapter.

To give a preview of the following topics: after discussing how to measure the irregularity or multifractal spectrum of time series $x(t)$, by implementing the wavelet MRA of Chapter 7, we'll discuss in the next chapter the phenomena of deterministic financial chaos. In Chapters 9 and 11 we'll present the current efforts to provide mathematical theories for financial turbulence. In Chapter 10 we'll give a simple example of a nonlinear dynamic interest rate term structure that demonstrates how financial intermittence and complete chaos can occur.

Financial turbulence theories are in debt to the original theory of physical turbulence of Kolmogorov of 1941, to his later amendment in 1962, and to the corrections by Mandelbrot in the 1970s and 1980s. Such theories are currently progressing far beyond Kolmogorov's fundamental insights, thanks to the analytic measurements provided by the wavelet MRA. One of the new insights by Frisch, Parisi and Farge is that turbulence is a heterogeneous multifractal phenomenon of which we can determine a multifractal spectrum of singularities from wavelet MRA. In addition, by using Galerkin's method of finite elements, wavelet MRA helps to numerically solve the dynamic Navier–Stokes nonlinear diffusion equations, which represent still the best dynamic model to explain turbulence, since it is based on fundamental mathematical and physical system laws.

8.2 Measurement of local financial market risk

8.2.1 Time-scale analysis of FBM

Due to the self-similarity, or scaling property of the FBM, Flandrin (1989, 1992) and Mallat (1989a) examined the FBM's behavior relative to different observational time scales, using self-similar wavelet MRA. A second-order moment analysis of the wavelet resonance coefficients of the FBM reveals a stationary structure at each scale and a power-law behavior of the wavelet coefficient's variance, from which the average Lipschitz exponent α_L of the FBM can be computed.

Reviewing the various aspects of the FBM that we discussed in Chapters 4 and 5, we first established that the autocovariance function of the FBM $x(t)$ is represented by:

$$
\begin{aligned}
\gamma(\tau) &= E\{x^2(\tau)\} \\
&= \sigma_\varepsilon^2 \tau^{2d-1} \\
&= \sigma_\varepsilon^2 \tau^{2H-2}
\end{aligned}
\tag{8.1}
$$

which shows it to be *non-stationary*, and *self-similar*, since the second moment is a scaling law of the time lag τ. Next, we established that the average power spectral density of the FBM is:

$$
\begin{aligned}
P(\omega) &= \sigma_\varepsilon^2 \omega^{-2(d+1)} \\
&= \sigma_\varepsilon^2 \omega^{-(2H+1)}
\end{aligned}
\tag{8.2}
$$

which is also a scaling law, this time of the frequency ω, or scale $a \sim 1/\omega$. Furthermore, the FBM is *statistically self-similar* in the sense that for any constant $c > 0$, and with the convention that $x(0) = 0$, we find the distributional scaling

$$
\begin{aligned}
x(c\tau) &\overset{d}{=} c^{d+0.5} x(\tau) \\
&= c^H x(\tau)
\end{aligned}
\tag{8.3}
$$

where $\overset{d}{=}$ means equality in distribution, as discussed in Chapter 3. This means in frequency terms that the power spectrum of the FBM is represented by

$$
\begin{aligned}
\mathcal{F}[\gamma(c\tau)] &= \frac{1}{|c|^2} P\left(\frac{\omega}{c}\right) \\
&= \frac{\sigma_\varepsilon^2}{|c|^2} \left(\frac{\omega}{c}\right)^{-2(d+1)} \\
&= c^{2H-1} \sigma_\varepsilon^2 \omega^{-(2H+1)}
\end{aligned}
\tag{8.4}
$$

Thus, any portion of a given FBM can be viewed as a scaled version of a larger part of the same process, both in the time domain and in the frequency domain.

Consequently, an individual realization of the FBM is a fractal time series and has a unique *fractal dimension D*, which is related to the Hurst H-exponent, as follows

$$D = 2 - H \tag{8.5}$$

In summary, the FBM has two important features:

(1) *non-stationarity*, which requires time-dependency analysis; and, more specifically,
(2) *self-similarity*, which requires time-scale power law analysis.

Since Mallat's wavelet MRA provides such a localized time-scale analysis, it is the natural tool to examine empirical FBMs.

8.2.2   Lipschitz analysis of local financial risk

The Fourier Transform analyzes the global regularity of a financial time series $x(t)$. The Wavelet Transform analyzes the pointwise irregularity of a financial time series $x(t)$. FBM traces are locally very irregular: they are continuous time series, but their first derivatives exist almost nowhere, i.e., their increments consist of singularities almost everywhere.

Definition 317   *A time series is called* regular *if it can be locally approximated by a polynomial, i.e., a particular mathematical system. If not, it is called* completely irregular.

Therefore, we must now introduce the formal definition of irregularity or "randomness."[4] It appears that there are degrees of local irregularity, from highly regular to highly irregular (Pincus and Singer, 1996). These degrees of irregularity are measured by the Lipschitz regularity exponent α_L.[5] If $x(t)$ has a singularity at time τ, which means that it is not differentiable at τ, the Lipschitz regularity exponent α_L characterizes this singular behavior at time τ. When we measure the Lipschitz α_L of a singularity, we assess how irregular or random such a singularity is. Consequently, we no longer have to assume the *degree of randomness* of a time series. We can measure the degree of its randomness by determining its Lipschitz α_L! In this section, we'll develop an apparatus to measure Lipschitz α_L, using Mallat's MRA from the preceding chapter.

The Lipschitz regularity exponent α_L is based on the approximation error of the Taylor expansion formula, which relates the differentiability of the continuous time series $x(t)$ to a local polynomial approximation.

Definition 318   *Suppose that $x(t)$ is d times differentiable in the bounded interval $[\tau - \epsilon, \tau + \epsilon]$ for a small ϵ. Then we can expand $x(t)$ in a Taylor expansion* *as follows*

$$x(t) = x(\tau) + x^{(1)}(\tau)(t - \tau) + \frac{x^{(2)}(\tau)}{2!}(t - \tau)^2 + \cdots$$

$$+ \frac{x^{(d-1)}(\tau)}{(d-1)!}(t - \tau)^{d-1} + \epsilon_\tau(t)$$

$$= \left[\sum_{k=0}^{d-1} \frac{x^{(k)}(\tau)}{k!}(t - \tau)^k\right] + \epsilon_\tau(t)$$

$$= \hat{x}_\tau(t) + \epsilon_\tau(t) \tag{8.6}$$

where $x^{(k)}(t)$ is the kth derivative of $x(t)$. The $\hat{x}_\tau(t) = [\cdots]$ part is the exact polynomial Taylor expansion *of $x(t)$ at time τ, or systematic component, and the* $\epsilon_\tau(t) = x(t) - \hat{x}_\tau(t)$ *is the approximation error, or unsystematic component, of this Taylor expansion.*

Remark 319 *Statisticians often call the approximation error $\epsilon_\tau(t)$: the residual. It is clear that the character of this residual depends on the number of differentiation terms included in the linear Taylor expansion. Therefore, one cannot ascribe inherent characteristics like "Gaussian distribution" to this residual, since such characteristics are* not sui generis. *Still, this is what statisticians conventionally (conveniently, but unfortunately) do!*

The Taylor expansion proves that the approximation error

$$\epsilon_\tau(t) = x(t) - \hat{x}_\tau(t) \tag{8.7}$$

satisfies

for all $t \in [\tau - \epsilon, \tau + \epsilon]$,

$$|\epsilon_\tau(t)| \leq \sup_{u \in [\tau - \epsilon, \tau + \epsilon]} \left| x^{(d)}(u) \right| \frac{|u - \tau|^d}{d!} \tag{8.8}$$

The dth-order differentiability of $x(t)$ in the neighborhood of τ yields an upper bound on the approximation error $\epsilon_\tau(t)$ when t tends to τ, i.e., when the time interval becomes smaller. The following Lipschitz regularity refines this upper bound with the fractional Hölder exponent d, introduced in Chapter 4.

Definition 320 (Lipschitz) *A time series $x(t)$ is pointwise α_L-Lipschitz regular, with regularity exponent $\alpha_L \geq 0$ at point τ, if there exists a $K > 0$, and a polynomial $\hat{x}_\tau$ of degree $\lfloor \alpha_L \rfloor$ such that for all real time $t \in \mathbb{R}$, the absolute value* *of the error is bounded by:*

$$|\epsilon_\tau(t)| = |x(t) - \hat{x}_\tau(t)|$$

$$\leq K|t - \tau|^d$$

$$= K|t - \tau|^{\alpha_L} \tag{8.9}$$

or, equivalently:

$$|\epsilon_\tau(t)|^{1/\alpha_L} = |x(t) - \hat{x}_\tau(t)|^{1/\alpha_L} \leq K'|t - \tau| \tag{8.10}$$

where $K' = K^{1/\alpha_L}$.

Definition 321

- *A time series* $x(t)$ *is* uniformly α_L-Lipschitz regular *over the interval* $[a, b]$ *if it is pointwise Lipschitz* α_L *for all* $\tau \in [a, b]$, *with a constant K that is independent of* τ.
- *The Lipschitz regularity exponent of* $x(t)$ *at point* τ *or over the interval* $[a, b]$ *is the* supremum *of* α_L *such that* $x(t)$ *is* α_L-Lipschitz *regular (pointwise or uniformly).*

This is a (very) technical definition of irregularity and a new definition of local (financial) risk, which requires some additional explication. At each time point τ, the polynomial $\hat{x}_\tau(t)$ is uniquely defined. If $x(t)$ is $d = \lfloor \alpha_L \rfloor$ times continuously differentiable in the neighborhood of τ, then $\hat{x}_\tau(t)$ equals the linear Taylor expansion of $x(t)$ at τ. Thus, when α_L is an integer, the regularity at point τ is defined as usual, with α_L indicating the order of differentiability of $x(t)$.

When α_L is not an integer, but a fraction, let d be an integer such that $d < \alpha_L < d + 1$, then $x(t)$ has an α_L- Lipschitz regularity at τ, if its derivative $x(t)^{(d)}$ of order d resembles $|t - \tau|^{\alpha_L - d}$ locally around point τ. Furthermore, the degree of regularity of $x(t)$ in a time domain is that of its least regular point. The greater α_L, the more regular is the time series $x(t)$. The smaller α_L, the more irregular, or "risky," is the time series $x(t)$.

Remark 322   *There exist* multifractal *time series* $x(t)$ *with non-isolated singularities, where* $x(t)$ *has a different Lipschitz* α_L *at each point* τ. *In contrast, uniform Lipschitz* α_L *exponents provide a more global measurement of regularity, which applies to a whole interval. If a time series* $x(t)$ *is uniformly Lipschitz* $\alpha_L > d$, *or monofractal, where d is an integer, then one can verify that* $x(t)$ *is d times continuously differentiable in that neighborhood.*

What values of the Lipschitz α_L exponent should one expect for the various kinds of singularities? If $0 \leq \alpha_L < 1$, then $\hat{x}_\tau(t) = x(\tau)$ and the Lipschitz condition becomes:

$$\text{for all } t \in \mathbb{R}, \quad |x(t) - x(\tau)| \leq K|t - \tau|^{\alpha_L} \tag{8.11}$$

A time series $x(t)$ that is bounded, but discontinuous at time τ is Lipschitz $\alpha_L = 0$ at the time of the discontinuity τ. If the Lipschitz regularity is $0 < \alpha_L < 1$ at

τ, then $x(t)$ is continuous, but not differentiable at τ and the α_L characterizes the degree, or type, of irregularity. If $\alpha_L = -1$, the discontinuity "flip-flops" (cf. Figure 8.7).

What is the Lipschitz regularity condition for the Fourier Transform and for the Wavelet Transform, respectively?

8.2.2.1 Fourier regularity condition

The precise definition of the Lipschitz-α_L regularity in the frequency domain, in addition to the one we already have in the time domain, is provided by the following theorem.[6]

Theorem 323 *A function $x(t)$ with Fourier Transform $F(\omega)$ is bounded and uniformly Lipschitz-α_L over the domain of real numbers $\mathbb{R}$, if*

$$\int_{-\infty}^{+\infty} |F(\omega)|(1 + |\omega|^{\alpha_L})d\omega < +\infty \tag{8.12}$$

Remark 324 *This uniform regularity condition is obviously a global regularity condition, since it holds true over the whole $(-\infty, +\infty)$ frequency domain.*

Next, we will discuss the required regularity condition of wavelets.

8.2.2.2 Wavelet regularity condition

The basic wavelet regularity condition is that it is a *fast decaying* wavelet with p vanishing moments.[7] In fact, if a function is continuous, has vanishing moments, decays quickly towards 0 when $t \to \infty$, or equals 0 outside a particular interval, it is already a likely candidate for a wavelet!

Theorem 325 *A wavelet $\psi(t)$ with a fast decay has p vanishing moments, if and only if there exists a function $\theta(t)$ with a fast decay such that*

$$\psi(t) = (-1)^p \theta^{(p)}(t)$$

$$= (-1)^p \frac{d^p \theta(t)}{dt^p} \tag{8.13}$$

As a consequence, the CWT or resonance coefficient is equivalent to the following *multiscale differential operator*

$$W(\tau, a) = \int_{-\infty}^{\infty} x(t)\psi_{\tau,a}^*(t)dt$$

$$= a^p \frac{d^p}{d\tau^p}\{[x(t) \star \theta_a(t)](\tau)\} \tag{8.14}$$

with the scaled wavelet

$$\theta_a(t) = \frac{1}{\sqrt{a}}\theta\left(\frac{t}{a}\right) \tag{8.15}$$

Table 8.1 Degree of Lipschitz irregularity of Daubechies wavelets

ψ	DB1($=$ *Haar*)	DB2	DB3	DB4	DB5	DB7	DB10
α_L	0		0.5	0.91	1.27	1.69	2.15	2.90

where the $\star$ sign indicates again the convolution operator (cf. Chapter 5). This provides a test whether the wavelet ψ has more than p vanishing moments. Compute

$$\int_{-\infty}^{+\infty} t^p \psi(t)\, dt = (i)^p \hat{\psi}^{(p)}(0) = (-i)^p p! \hat{\theta}(0) \tag{8.16}$$

Clearly, the wavelet $\psi(t)$ has no more than p vanishing moments if and only if:

$$\hat{\theta}(0) = \int_{-\infty}^{+\infty} \theta(t)\, dt \neq 0 \tag{8.17}$$

Remark 326   *An example of such a fast decaying wavelet is the Gábor's Gaussian wavelet, or chirp, discussed in Chapter 6.*

The degree of irregularity of certain wavelets is known. Table 8.1 gives some indications of the Lipschitz-α_L irregularity of Daubechies wavelets indexed by DBN.

Selecting an irregularity and a wavelet to measure this irregularity is useful for estimations of the local properties, like the *intrinsic* or *local risk*, of a financial time series. From a practical point of view, these questions arise in finance in dealing with financial markets for fine microstructure studies of high-frequency ($=$ very fast) trading transactions. Let's now see, how we can approach the measurement of the irregularity or intrinsic risk of such high-frequency financial transactions.

If $x(t)$ is a financial time series which is a little bit more than p times differentiable at point τ, then it can be approximated by a polynomial of degree p, as we've already seen in Chapter 4. For example, it can be approximated by a Markov process of order p, which can represent trends and regular periodic oscillations. As we noticed earlier, the Wavelet Transforms of such exact polynomials are zero. But around point τ, its order is that of the *error* between the polynomial and the time series $|x(t) - \hat{x}_\tau(t)|$. If this error can be uniformly estimated on an interval $[a, b]$, this insight yields a tool for irregularity or local risk analysis on that interval and we can estimate the *fractal order d* of the financial time series $x(t)$.

8.2.3   Asymptotically decaying wavelet amplitudes

The decay of the Wavelet Transform amplitude across all scales is related to the uniform and pointwise Lipschitz regularity of the financial time series $x(t)$. Measuring this asymptotic decay is equivalent to zooming into the time series structure with a scale that goes to zero. The following theorems relate the uniform and pointwise Lipschitz regularity of $x(t)$ on an interval to the amplitude of its Wavelet Transform at the very fine scales. If we then measure the amplitude of the measured decaying wavelet resonance coefficients, we can find out what the Lipschitz α_L regularity of $x(t)$ is and thus its fractal difference order d.

Theorem 327   (Mallat) *If $x(t) \in L^2(\mathbb{R})$, an element of the Hilbert space, and is uniformly Lipschitz $\alpha_L \leq p$ over the interval $[a, b]$ then there exists a constant A such that*

for all $(\tau, a) \in [a, b] \times \mathbb{R}^+$,

$$|W(\tau, a)| \leq A a^{\alpha_L + 0.5}$$
$$= A a^{d+0.5} \tag{8.18}$$

Conversely, if $|W(\tau, a)|$ satisfies this last inequality and if α_L is not an integer, but a fraction $\alpha_L < p$, then the time series $x(t)$ is uniformly α_L-Lipschitz on the interval $[a + \epsilon, b - \epsilon]$, for any $\epsilon > 0$.

Remark 328   *The inequality is really a condition on the asymptotic decay of the absolute value of the wavelet resonance coefficient $|W(\tau, a)|$, when its scale a goes to zero. At larger scales it does not introduce any constraints since the Cauchy–Schwarz inequality guarantees that the Wavelet Transform is always bounded:*

$$|W(\tau, a)| = |\langle x(t), \psi_{\tau,a}(t)\rangle|$$
$$\leq \|x(t)\| \|\psi_{\tau,a}(t)\| \tag{8.19}$$

where the norms (= risk contents) $\|x(t)\| < \infty$ and $\|\psi_{\tau,a}(t)\| < \infty$.

Jaffard (1991) generalized Mallat's Theorem to pointwise Lipschitz regularity, while Mallat's Theorem can be viewed as a corollary of Jaffard's Theorem (Jaffard, 1989; Farge, *et al.*, 1993). Jaffard's Theorem provides a necessary and a sufficient condition on the modulus of the Wavelet Transform for computing the Lipschitz regularity of $x(t)$ at point τ.

Theorem 329 (Jaffard) *If $x(t) \in L^2(\mathbb{R})$ is Lipschitz $\alpha_L \leq p$ at point υ in time, then there exists a constant A such that*

for all $(\tau, a) \in \mathbb{R} \times \mathbb{R}^+$,

$$|W(\tau, a)| \leq A a^{\alpha_L + 0.5} \left(1 + \left| \frac{\tau - \upsilon}{a} \right|^{\alpha_L} \right) \tag{8.20}$$

Conversely, if $\alpha_L < p$ is not an integer and there exist A and $\alpha_L^j < \alpha_L$ such that

for all $(\tau, a) \in \mathbb{R} \times \mathbb{R}^+$,

$$|W(\tau, a)| \leq A a^{\alpha_L + 0.5} \left(1 + \left| \frac{\tau - \upsilon}{a} \right|^{\alpha_L} \right) \tag{8.21}$$

then $x(t)$ is Lipschitz α_L at υ.

To interpret more easily the necessary and sufficient conditions of Jaffard's Theorem, suppose that the wavelet $\psi_{u,a}(t)$ has a compact support equal to $[-C, C]$. Then we can formulate the following definition of the *cone of influence* of a particular point υ on the time line.

Definition 330 *The* cone of influence *of υ in the scale-time plane is the set of points (τ, a) such that υ is included in the support of the CWT wavelet*

$$\psi_{\tau,a}(t) = \frac{1}{\sqrt{a}} \psi \left(\frac{t - \tau}{a} \right) \tag{8.22}$$

Since the support of this wavelet is equal to $[\tau - Ca, \tau + Ca]$, the cone of influence of υ is defined by

$$|\tau - \upsilon| \leq Ca \tag{8.23}$$

or, equivalently,

$$\frac{|\tau - \upsilon|}{a} \leq C \tag{8.24}$$

For example, Figure 8.5 shows the cone of influence for a time abscissa at $t = \upsilon$ in a scalogram.

Example 331 *Figure 8.6 shows the* regions of influence *in scalograms (a and c) for the CWT and spectrograms (b and d) for Gábor's Short-Term or Windowed Fourier Transform (STFT) for the singularity of a Dirac pulse $\delta(\omega)$ at time $t = t_0$, as well as three sinusoids of frequencies $\omega_0 = \omega_0$, $\omega_1 = 2\omega_0$, $\omega_3 = 4\omega_0$,*

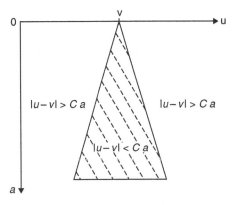

Figure 8.5 The cone of influence of an abscissa singularity v consists of the time-scale points (u, a) for which the support of the wavelet $\psi_{u,a}$ intersects the time point $t = v$.

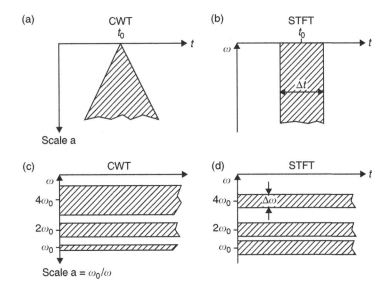

Figure 8.6 Singularity cones of influence of a Dirac pulse at $t = t_0$ for (a) the CWT and for (b) the STFT; versus monochromatic bands of influence of three sinusoids for (c) the CWT and for (d) the STFT.

respectively (cf. Chapter 6). The scale is $a = \omega_0/\omega$. Notice that for the CWT in (a) the width of the cone of influence of the Dirac pulse is scale-frequency dependent, while for the STFT in (b) it remains constant and is scale-frequency independent. Furthermore, for the CWT in (c) the monochromatic resonance bands differ in *width according to the scale-frequency, while for the STFT in (d) the width of the monochromatic resonance bands are scale-frequency independent.*

Using a reformulation of the cone of influence, Jaffard's necessary and sufficient conditions can be considerably simplified, as follows:

$$
\begin{aligned}
|W(\tau, a)| &\leq A a^{\alpha_L + 0.5} \left(1 + \left| \frac{\tau - \upsilon}{a} \right|^{\alpha_L} \right) \\
&\leq A a^{\alpha_L + 0.5} (1 + C^{\alpha_L}) \\
&= A' a^{\alpha_L + 0.5}
\end{aligned}
\tag{8.25}
$$

which is identical to the uniform Lipschitz condition of Mallat's Theorem!

Jaffard's Theorem relates the pointwise irregularity, e.g., the singularities, of a time series to the decay of the *modulus maximum* of its Wavelet Transform $|W(\tau, a)|$. This will assist us with the measurement of the degree of local financial risk.

8.2.4   Measuring various price singularities

We will now discuss the innovative concepts of modulus maxima and the maxima line to detect and measure the various kinds of singularities (Hwang and Mallat, 1994).

Definition 332   *The* modulus maximum *of a Wavelet Transform is any point* (τ_0, a_0) *such that* $|W(\tau, a)|$ *is locally maximum at* $\tau = \tau_0$. *This implies*

$$
\frac{\partial |W(\tau_0, a_0)|}{\partial \tau} = 0
\tag{8.26}
$$

Definition 333   *The* maxima line *is any connected curve* $a(\tau)$ *along the scale ordinate in the time-scale plane* (τ, a) *along which all points are modulus maxima.*

Singularities can thus be detected by finding the abscissa where the wavelet modulus maxima converge at the very fine scales of, say, high-frequency financial data. The following Theorem by Hwang and Mallat proves that if the Wavelet Transform $W(\tau, a)$ has no modulus maxima at fine scales, then the time series $x(t)$ is locally regular. Otherwise stated, there cannot be a singularity without a local maximum of the Wavelet Transform at the very fine scales.

Theorem 334   (Hwang, Mallat) *Suppose that the wavelet* $\psi(t)$ *is* C^p *($=$ continuous of order p) with a fast decay, has p vanishing moments with* *compact, finite support, and*

$$\psi(t) = (-1)^p \theta^{(p)}(t) \tag{8.27}$$

with the Gaussian wavelet $\theta(t)$ such that

$$\int_{-\infty}^{+\infty} \theta(t)dt \neq 0 \tag{8.28}$$

Let $x(t) \in L^1[c, d]$. If there exists $a_0 > 0$ such that $|W(\tau, a)|$ has no local maximum for $\tau \in [c, d]$ and $a < a_0$, then $x(t)$ is uniformly Lipschitz p on $[c + \epsilon, d - \epsilon]$ for any $\epsilon > 0$.

This important and insightful theorem implies that $x(t)$ can be singular (= not Lipschitz-1) at a point υ only if there is a sequence of wavelet maxima points that converges towards the time point υ at very fine scales:

$$\lim_{n \to +\infty} \tau_n = \upsilon \quad \text{and} \quad \lim_{n \to +\infty} a_n = 0 \tag{8.29}$$

This sequence of wavelet maxima indicates the presence of a maximum modulus of the Wavelet Transform at the very fine scales where a singularity occurs.

In the general case, a sequence of modulus maxima, or maxima line, may be detected, which converges to the particular singularity. When the wavelet is the pth derivative of a Gaussian wavelet $\theta(t)$ (= Gábor wavelet), these maxima lines are connected and go through all of the finer scales. The decay rate of the maxima along the maxima ridges indicates the order of the isolated singularities. This can be easily shown, since from the Jaffard Theorem for $\tau = \upsilon$, we have for the log–log inequality:

$$\log_2 |W(\tau, a)| \leq (\alpha_L + 0.5) \log_2 a + \log_2 A' \tag{8.30}$$

Thus, one should display the modulus maxima of the Wavelet Transform as a function of scale a in a log–log plot, and its computed slope will be $b = \alpha_L + 0.5$, from which we then can immediately identify the Lipschitz α_L. For example, when this slope is $b = \alpha_L + 0.5 = 0.5$, the time series is Lipschitz $\alpha_L = 0$ and, thus, exhibits a discontinuity. But when the slope $b = \alpha_L + 0.5 = 1$, the time series is Lipschitz $\alpha_L = 0.5$. In other words, the degree of irregularity (= "randomness") of each singularity can be separately assessed. No longer have we to assume that some price singularity is random. We can now precisely locally measure its degree of irregularity, randomness or riskiness, as the following examples demonstrate!

Example 335 *Figure 8.7 provides the first example of this kind of financial risk analysis. In the top panel (a) we see a time series or signal $S_1 = x(t)$, which*

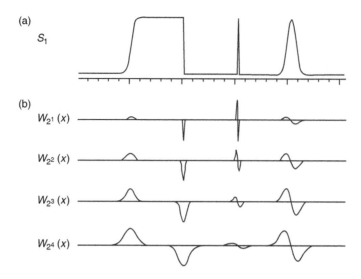

(a) S_1

(b) $W_{2^1}(x)$

$W_{2^2}(x)$

$W_{2^3}(x)$

$W_{2^4}(x)$

Figure 8.7 Wavelet decomposition of a time series with singularities. In the top panel
(a) we see a time series or signal $S_1 = x(t)$, which contains four singularities, characterized, respectively by the Lipschitz α_L and the smoothing
scale s: $(\alpha_L = 0, s = 0)$, $(\alpha_L = 0, s = 3)$, $(\alpha_L = -1, s = 0)$ and
$(\alpha_L = -1, s = 4)$. In the lower panel (b) we see four scales of wavelet
decomposition.

contains four singularities, characterized, respectively by the Lipschitz α_L and
the smoothing scale s: $(\alpha_L = 0, s = 0)$, $(\alpha_L = 0, s = 3)$, $(\alpha_L = -1, s = 0)$,
and $(\alpha_L = -1, s = 4)$. In the lower panel (b) we see four scales of wavelet
decomposition (Mallat and Zhong, 1992, p. 86). It is clear that the behavior of
the local maxima across the wavelet scales depend on the Lipschitz α_L and the
smoothing scale s. Notice that the "sharpest" singularity, $(\alpha_L = 0, s = 3)$, and
$(\alpha_L = -1, s = 0)$ are best detected at scale level $a = 1$, while the "softest"
singularity, $(\alpha_L = 0, s = 0)$ and $(\alpha_L = -1, s = 4)$ are best detected at scale
level $a = 4$. But each scale level provides its own piece of information about each
of the different singularities.

Example 336 *Figure 8.8 provides a more complex financial risk analysis. At
the top we have 256 observations of the irregular time series $x(t)$, which shows
different kinds of singularities: from step functions at the left, to a sharp peak
in the middle, followed by a discontinuity and a very "random" looking series.
The question is how we can characterize these singularities of $x(t)$ using the
scalogram based on the CWT $W(\tau, a)$. Panel (a) shows the scalogram $P_W(\tau, a)$.
The horizontal and vertical axes measure t and $\log_2 a$, where a is the dyadic scale.
Panel (b) shows the modulus maxima of the $W(\tau, a)$. Notice that the "random"
looking series part is represented by a series of modulus maxima. The continuous*

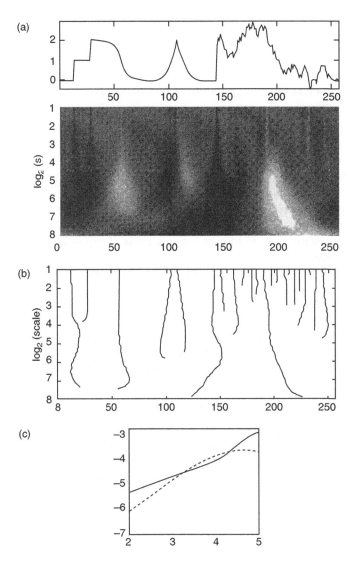

Figure 8.8 How to measure the degree of irregularity of local risk of a series of price singularities $x(t)$: (a) the scalogram $P_W(\tau, a)$, (b) the modulus maximae of the $W(\tau, a)$, (c) continuous line: the decay of $\log_2 |W(\tau, a)|$ as a function of $\log_2 a$ along the most left maxima line that converges on the abscissa point $t = 14$. Dashed line: the decay of $\log_2 |W(\tau, a)|$ along the maxima line that converges to time point $t = 108$.

line in panel (c) gives the decay of $\log_2 |W(\tau, a)|$ *as a function of* $\log_2 a$ *along the most left maxima line that converges to the abscissa* $t = 14$. *The dashed line in panel (c) gives the decay of* $\log_2 |W(\tau, a)|$ *along the maxima line that converges to* $t = 108$ *(Mallat, 1998, p. 180).*

8.3   Homogeneous Hurst exponents of monofractal price series

Now, let's discuss how this mathematical apparatus of wavelet regularity conditions can be used: first, to compute the *uniform* Lipschitz regularity exponent α_L, or, equivalently, the *homogeneous* Hurst H-exponent for our main model for financial risk, the FBM. This is followed by computation of the pointwise Lipschitz α_L to characterize the *singularity* or *local risk spectrum* of multifractal non-FBM processes. We begin with simple computations of homogeneous H-exponents for the FBM, using the wavelet detail coefficients $d_{j,n}$ from Mallat's MRA. Next, we will compute a multifractal spectrum of *heterogeneous* H-exponents or α_L's for non-FBM processes.

The heterogeneous or multifractal local risk spectrum characterizes the scaling and singularity structures of time series and has already proved to be a useful tool for numerous applications, from (electric) network traffic analysis to the analysis of turbulence in high-frequency financial time series. The computation of the complete local multifractal risk spectrum from a finite data record has long escaped the capability of the turbulence researcher, but the preceding general irregularity analysis shows that this kind of local risk analysis is now completely possible.

8.3.1   *Logarithmic scalegram based on discrete wavelet MRA*

Let's begin with the computation of the homogeneous Hurst exponent of global financial risk. When we discussed the MRA in Chapter 7, we stated that the *Discrete wavelet Transform (DWT) coefficient* of the FBM $x(t)$ is computed as the inner product of $x(t)$ and the basic discrete, dyadic, orthonormal wavelet ψ, e.g., the Haar wavelet, by the usual approach, as follows

$$d_{j,n} = 2^{-j/2} \int_{-\infty}^{+\infty} x(t)\psi(2^{-j}t - n)dt, \quad \text{with} j, n \in \mathbb{Z} \tag{8.31}$$

The tiling of the time-scale space by the resulting wavelet Heisenberg boxes is shown in Figure 8.9. For example, the $d_{0,0}$ coefficient represents the mean of $x(t)$. These wavelet resonance coefficients $d_{j,n}$ of an FBM have the following four properties, as proved by Flandrin (1992) and by Flandrin and Gonçalvès (1996):

(1) The wavelet resonance coefficients are *stationary in distribution*, i.e., they are *stably distributed*:

$$d_{j,n} \overset{d}{=} d_{j,0} \quad \text{for all } n \tag{8.32}$$

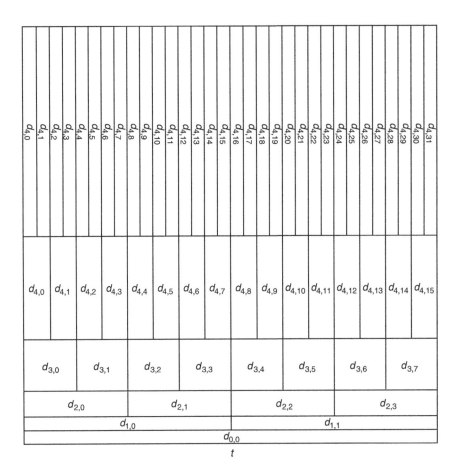

Figure 8.9 Complete wavelet tiling: the relation of the DWT coefficients $d_{j,n}$ to the time-scale tiles. This demonstrates the completeness of a financial risk analysis by wavelet MRA.

(2) The wavelet resonance coefficients are *Gaussian distributed:*

$$d_{j,n} \sim N(0, \text{Var}(d_{j,n})) \tag{8.33}$$

Remark 337 *Consequently, the squared resonance coefficients, or local wavelet risk, are Chi-squared distributed:*

$$|d_{j,n}|^2 \sim \chi^2 \tag{8.34}$$

This statistical property allows for significance testing of the wavelet coefficients.

Remark 338   *If one wants to verify that the statistical distribution for the local wavelet risk is, indeed, Chi-squared distributed, one can apply the following Monte Carlo method: (1) create a large number, say 100,000 random time series, each with as many points as the financial time series $x(t), t = 1, \dots, T$ to be analyzed; (2) then take the Wavelet Transform for each of the random time series and compute all the local wavelet risks $|d_{j,n}|^2$; next, (3) take a time slice from the middle (time $n = T/2$); (4) at each scale j, sort all selected 100,000 local wavelet risks into increasing order; (5) then make a plot of the local wavelet risk versus the sorted index number; (6) look at what the local wavelet risk is for number 95,000 out of 100,000, then 95 percent of the local wavelet risk is below that value, and only 5 percent is above; (7) this 95 percent level is the staistician's conventional 95 percent confidence level (or 5 percent significance level). This Monte Carlo method can be generalized to any process where the statistical distribution is unknown, yet one wants to determine statistical confidence, or significance levels.*

Flandrin (1989, 1992) and Kaplan and Kuo (1993) also proved that the variance of these wavelet resonance coefficients $d_{j,n}$ of the FBM is represented by the following scaling law, which is the integration of the Chi-squared distribution of the squared resonance coefficients:

$$\text{Var}\{d_{j,n}\} = E\{|d_{j,n}|^2\}$$

$$= \frac{\sigma_\varepsilon^2}{2} V_\psi(H)(2^j)^{-(2H+1)} \tag{8.35}$$

where the constant $V_\psi(H)$ depends on both the ACF $\gamma_\psi(\tau)$ of the chosen wavelet $\psi(t)$ and the H-exponent, as follows:

$$V_\psi(H) = -\int_{-\infty}^{+\infty} \gamma_\psi(\tau)|\tau|^{2H} d\tau \tag{8.36}$$

with

$$\gamma_\psi(\tau) = \int_{=\infty}^{+\infty} \psi(t)\psi(t-\tau)dt \tag{8.37}$$

Thus, by taking the dyadic logarithm of $\text{Var}\{d_{j,n}\}$, we find the linear relationship from which we can compute H

$$\log_2[\text{Var}\{d_{j,n}\}] = -(2H+1)j + \log_2\left[\frac{\sigma_\varepsilon^2}{2} V_\psi(H)\right] \tag{8.38}$$

Since the second (intercept) term is a constant, we plot $\log_2[\mathrm{Var}\{d_{j,n}\}]$ against the scale coefficient j to find the slope value $(2H + 1)$ and thus H (Wornell and Oppenheim, 1992; Wornell, 1993). This average or global wavelet (log) scalegram delivers the same analytic irregularity measurement result of the homogeneous Hurst exponent H as the (log) Fourier power spectrum.

The other two properties of importance for this MRA analysis:

(3) The wavelet resonance coefficients are *almost uncorrelated*:

$$E\{d_{i,n}d_{j,m}\} \simeq |2^{-i}n - 2^{-j}m|^{2(H-R)} \text{ and} \tag{8.39}$$

(4) The wavelet resonance coefficients *scale:*

$$d_{j,n} \overset{d}{=} 2^{jH}d_{0,n} \tag{8.40}$$

Remark 339 *Because of property (2) and (3) it is often asserted that the FBM wavelet resonance coefficients are exactly uncorrelated and hence independent (Gonçalvès et al., 1998). But this is, strictly speaking, not true since they scale. They are stably distributed (cf. Chapter 4).*

8.3.2 Scalegrams of heart arrhythmias and stock prices

We will now discuss two applications of the preceding analysis to compute homogeneous Hurst exponents from the dyadic logarithmic plot of wavelet resonance coefficients: a wavelet MRA of the heartbeat of a healthy human and of the Dow Jones Industrial Average Index (DJIA). The heartbeat inter-arrival times resemble those of foreign exchange quotations. Both these exemplary analyses are from Flandrin (1992). The persistence of the DJIA has also been studied by Lo and Mackinlay (1999) by non-wavelet, econometric time series methods. They produced similar results. In addition, we include some interesting scalograms and scalegrams based on wavelet MRA of Latin American financial markets around the times of major trading regime changes.

8.3.2.1 Scalegram of heart beats

Figure 8.10 shows the computation of the global or homogeneous Hurst exponent for heartbeat inter-arrival times $X(t)$ in seconds for a healthy human patient, of which 65,536 heartbeats are shown in the top panel. It is clear that this heart is not strictly periodic and that it shows arrhythmias: it is aperiodic cyclical. Fractal analysis is thus warranted. The time series is again analyzed using a Daubechies(5) wavelet basis and MRA tiling. In panel (a) the $\log_2[\mathrm{Var}\{d_{j,n}\}]$ is plotted versus the scale $j = m$. The scale in this panel (a) is such that a low scale j means low frequency while a high scale means low frequency. The approximate slope of the

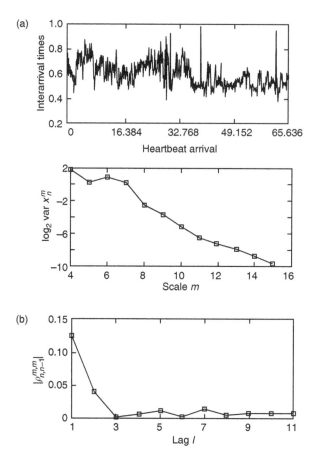

Figure 8.10 Wavelet-based persistence analysis of heartbeat interarrival times for a
healthy patient with a Daubechies(5) wavelet. Top panel: data; (a) scale-
to-scale wavelet coefficient variance progression; (b) average magnitude
of normalized along-scale correlation between wavelet coefficients.

line that is not completely straight is:

$$b = (2H + 1)$$
$$= \frac{2 - (-10)}{15 - 4}$$
$$= 1.0909 \tag{8.41}$$

from which we derive the Hurst exponent $H = 0.04545$. This implies that the
heartbeat inter-arrival times are almost blue noise, i.e., highly antipersistent. Differently stated, the human heart self-reverses or corrects itself (almost) immediately.

It is an extremely efficient pump. Notice, however, that the slope of the dyadic plot line is not strictly straight and thus the Hurst exponent is not strictly homogeneous, in particular around scales $a = 2^6 = 64$ seconds, or close to one minute, and $a = 2^7 = 128$ seconds, or close to two minutes. Panel (b) shows again the average magnitude of the normalized along-scale empirical correlation

$$\rho_{n,n-l}^{m,m} = \sqrt{E\{d_{i,n}d_{j,m}\}} \tag{8.42}$$

$$= \begin{cases} =0.125 & \text{for } l = 1 \\ =0.04 & \text{for } l = 2 \quad \text{and} \\ <0.01 & \text{for } l > 2 \end{cases} \tag{8.43}$$

This shows that there is virtually no serial correlation between the wavelet resonance coefficients although they clearly scale.

8.3.2.2   Scalegram of Dow Jones Industrial Average

Figure 8.11 shows the computation of the homogeneous Hurst exponent for 4,096 weekly DJIA data as follows. The time series $X(t)$ in the top panel is analyzed using a Daubechies(5) wavelet basis and MRA tiling. In panel (a) the $\log_2[\text{Var}\{d_{j,n}\}]$ is plotted versus the scale $j = m$. Consequently, the value of the slope of this (almost straight) line is:

$$b = (2H + 1)$$
$$= \frac{24 - 10}{11 - 4}$$
$$= 2 \tag{8.44}$$

from which we derive the Hurst exponent $H = 0.5$. This implies that the difference operator exponent $d = H - 0.5 = 0$ for the price increments $\Delta X(t) = \varepsilon(t)$ (cf. Chapter 4). Thus, the weekly DJIA series $X(t)$ follows a pure Random Walk (cf. Chapter 2). Panel (b) shows the average magnitude of the normalized along-scale empirical correlation between the wavelet resonance coefficients:

$$\rho_{n,n-l}^{m,m} = \sqrt{E\{d_{i,n}d_{j,m}\}} \tag{8.45}$$

$$= \begin{cases} =0.08 & \text{for } l = 1 \\ =0.03 & \text{for } l = 2 \quad \text{and} \\ <0.03 & \text{for } l > 2 \end{cases} \tag{8.46}$$

This shows again that there is virtually no serial correlation between the wavelet resonance coefficients.

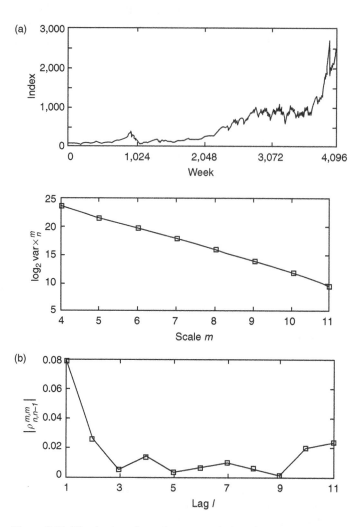

Figure 8.11 Wavelet-based persistence analysis of weekly Dow Jones Industrial
Index data with Daubechies(5) wavelet. Top panel: data; (a) scale-to-
scale wavelet coefficient variance progression; (b) average magnitude of
normalized along-scale correlation between wavelet coefficients.

8.3.3   *Persistence analysis of Latin American financial markets*

The following persistence analysis of Latin American financial stock and foreign
exchange markets, using wavelet scalograms and scalegrams, was performed by
Kyaw *et al.* (2002), and uses daily data.[8]

8.3.3.1 Mexico's Peso/Dollar rate

In panel (a) of Figure 8.12, we look at the time series of 3,253 daily observations on Mexico's Peso/Dollar exchange rate for the period January 4, 1993 – November 30, 2001. At the top right-hand side is portrayed the analyzing Morlet (6) wavelet. A mother Morlet wavelet $\psi_0^M(t)$ is a sine wave $\pi^{-1/2}e^{j\omega_0 t}$ multiplied by a Gaussian "envelope" $\pi^{-1/2}e^{(-t^2/2)}$, as follows:

$$\psi_0(t) = \pi^{(-1/4)}e^{j\omega_0 t}e^{(-t^2/2)} \tag{8.47}$$

where $\psi_0^M(t)$ is the wavelet value at non-dimensional time t and ω_0 is the wave number. The scaled Morlet wavelet is:

$$\psi\left[\frac{(n'-n)\delta t}{a}\right] = \left(\frac{\delta t}{a}\right)^{0.5}\psi_0\left[\frac{(n'-n)\delta t}{a}\right] \tag{8.48}$$

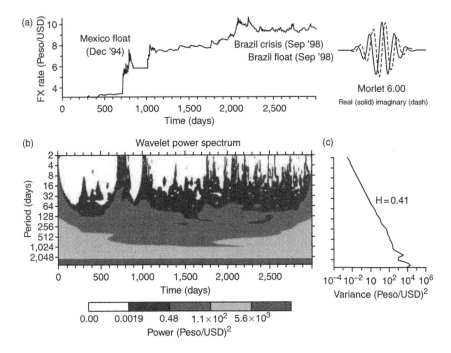

Figure 8.12 Wavelet MRA by Morlet(6) wavelet of the various exchange rate regimes of the Mexican Peso/USD in the 1990s and the various Brazilian financial market crises. Notice the impact of the Mexican float in December 1994, the Brazilian stock market crisis in September 1998 and the Brazilian float in January 1999. Globally, the Mexican Peso is antipersistent with a homogeneous $H = 0.41$. (a) Foreign exchange rate – Mexican Peso/USD; (b) wavelet power spectrum; (c) global wavelet.

where a is the *dilation* parameter used to change the scale and n is the *translation* parameter used to slide in time. The factor of $a^{-0.5}$ is a normalization to keep the total risk of the scaled wavelet constant and δt is the marginal time step. The Morlet wavelet is very popular, because (1) it's simple and (2) it looks like a wave. But there are a very large number of other mother wavelets that could be chosen. We choose the wave number of this Morlet wavelet to be $\omega_0 = 6$, so that the errors due to the non-zero mean are smaller than the typical computer round-off errors and the precision of the local risk measurement is enhanced.[9]

The CWT or wavelet resonance coefficient, $W(n', a) = d_{j,n}$, is just the inner product (or convolution) of the wavelet function with our original time series $x(t)$:

$$W(n', a) = \sum_{n'=0}^{N-1} x(n'\delta t)\psi^* \left[\frac{(n' - n)\delta t}{a} \right] \tag{8.49}$$

where the asterisk ($*$) denotes the complex conjugate. The above "integration" can be evaluated for various values of the scale a (usually taken to be multiples of the lowest possible frequency), as well as all values of n between the start and end dates. Panel (b) shows the localizing wavelet scalogram, MRA, or *local risk or power spectrum:*

$$P_W(n', a) = |W(n', a)|^2$$
$$= |d_{j,n}|^2 \tag{8.50}$$

It presents the relative risk at a certain scale and a certain time. The abscissa measures the wavelet location in time. The ordinate measures the wavelet period in days. In panel (b) the localized power $|d_{j,n}|^2$ is colorized into five levels, from white = no power to dark grey = highest power.

Panel (c) shows the global wavelet scalegram, or *global (risk) power spectrum:*

$$P_W(a) = E\{|W(\tau, a)|^2\}$$
$$= E\{|d_{j,n}|^2\}$$
$$= \text{Var}\{d_{j,n}\} \tag{8.51}$$

The dark grey monochromatic resonance band at the largest scale is again a sampling effect. On the vertical axes of both panel (b) and (c) the frequency is indicated by the number of days included in the time horizon $\tau = n'\delta t$. At the top of both panels are the high frequencies and at the bottom the low frequencies measured in days. The horizontal axis of panel (c) indicates the global risk or power of the wavelet resonance coefficients, $\text{Var}\{d_{j,n}\}$, on a decimal logarithmic (decibel) scale.

The slope of the scalegram in panel (c) shows that the negative slope, computed from logarithmic base 2, is:

$$b = (2H + 1)$$

$$= \frac{\log_2 10^4 - \log_2 10^{-2}}{\log_2 2^{12} - \log_2 2}$$

$$= 1.8120 \tag{8.52}$$

Thus the global, or homogeneous Hurst exponent for the whole period that has been portrayed is $H = 0.41$. Overall, the Mexican Peso is now an antipersistent currency.

But it is clear that there are at least five discernible subperiods, each having its own "local" Hurst exponent, as indicated in Table 8.2.

In other words, there is marked evidence for the existence of heterogeneous Hurst exponents, each applicable for the frequency scaling in a subperiod, i.e., there is evidence for so-called *multifractality*.

Of course, there exists no computable Hurst exponent for a fixed exchange rate regime, since there is no power or variation in the observed time series of the fixed exchange rate. Notice that when the Mexican Peso/Dollar rate was pegged in the period February 24, 1994 to December 19, 1994, the exchange rate showed a Hurst exponent of $H = 0.57$ and was persistent (pink). It showed Hurst exponents below 0.5 and was thus antipersistent in all other periods. Notice also that after the Brazilian crises, the Mexican Peso became slightly more antipersistent than in the period after the second float announcement.

More remarkable even is to observe that in the violent vortex of the first float in the period December 20, 1994 to May 3, 1994, the computed Hurst exponent dipped to $H = 0.20$, the light blue noise or highly antipersistent area of turbulence. The adjustment vortex, immediately after the announcement of the first float on December 20, 1994, shows a dark cone of influence with power at all analyzing frequencies between two days and about one year, as is shown in the companion Figure 8.13, where the first (log) differences of the daily rates are analyzed in the same fashion as in Figure 8.12. Recall that for this Morlet (6) Wavelet Transform

Table 8.2 Heterogeneous Hurst exponents of subsequent exchange rate regimes in Mexico in the 1990s

Subperiods	Mexico's FX regime	Hurst exponents
01/04/93–02/23/94	Loose peg	0.33
02/24/94–12/19/94	Pegged	0.57
12/20/94–05/03/95	First float	0.20
05/04/95–10/15/95	Fixed	N/A
10/16/95–09/09/98	Second float	0.37
09/10/98–11/30/01	Float after Brazilian crisis	0.29

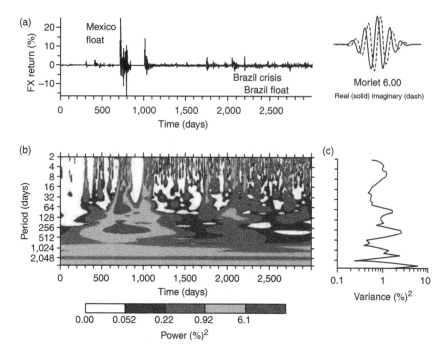

Figure 8.13 Wavelet MRA of the various exchange rate regimes of the first (log) differences
of the Mexican Peso/USD in the 1990s, based on daily data. Taking first
differences sharpens the MRA analysis. Notice (a) the two powerful adjustment
vortices occurring after the two float announcements, in particular, the one
immediately after the Mexican float announcement in December 1994. The
remaining innovations show clearly identifiable periodicities in the scalegram
in the lower right. (a) Foreign exchange returns–Mexican Peso/US Dollar;
(b) wavelet power spectrum; (c) global wavelet.

CWT the width of the cone of influence is scale-frequency dependent. The second
float, announced on October 16, 1995 caused a much smaller adjustment vortex,
with power at frequencies between two days and about two weeks.

Again, the monochromatic resonance band at the largest scale is a sampling
effect. Recall that for the CWT such monochromatic resonance bands differ in
width according to the scale-frequency.

The scalegram or global risk or power spectrum in panel (c) of Figure 8.13
shows that the differencing does not result in white noise, i.e., in a flat spectrum.
First, the slope of that risk spectrum is $2H - 1 = 0.8120 - 1 = -0.188$ so that
$H = 0.41$, consistent with Figure 8.12. Second, the spectrum shows clearly identifiable reporting periodicities with spectral peaks at the 5- trading day or "weekly"
frequency, and, in particular, the 63- trading day or "quarterly" frequency and the
252- trading day or "annual" frequency. In the scalegram, the increased power of

the high-frequency trading after the Brazilian crises is also clearly observable. The Brazilian crises are indicated by some red color in the original colorized scalograms, but it is clear that these external events emerging from outside Mexico had much less impact on the Mexican Peso, than the two domestic float announcements.

8.3.3.2 Comparison of degrees of persistence of Latin American stock and FX markets

Figure 8.14 shows an MRA of the volatile Chilean stock index return rates. Notice the severe turbulence vortices caused by the Brazilian stock market crisis of September 1998 and the Brazilian float of January 15, 1999. Another sharp singularity occurred, when a tender offer of Enerquinta shares failed, because accounting information became available that had been secret before: the Chilean stock market collapsed by ca. 30 percent! The global risk again shows reporting periodicities at the weekly, bi-weekly and quarterly frequencies, but also at the

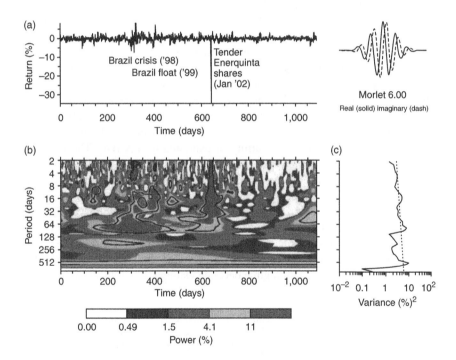

Figure 8.14 Wavelet MRA, based on daily data, of Chilean stock index rate of returns in the 1990s. Notice the two powerful adjustment vortices occurring immediately after the Brazilian stock market crisis of September 1998 and the Brazilian float of January 15, 1999. A sharp singularity occurred when the tender of Enerquinta shares in January 2002 failed and the Chilean stock market was drawn down by more than 30%. The scalegram shows that the residual noise is not white, but shows periodicities. (a) Chilean Stock returns; (b) wavelet power spectrum; (c) global wavelet.

biennial frequency. The dotted line is the spectrum for white noise. It is clear that stock rates of return are not white noise: the global risk spectrum is too much differentiated and shows periodicity peaks. The colorized scalogram makes that also abundantly clear on a localized basis.[10]

It is important to note that we not only observe adjustment vortices immediately after domestic trading regime changes in the foreign exchange markets, like the changes from a pegged to a floating exchange rate regime in Mexico. But we observe also adjustment vortices occurring in well-working financial markets caused by disturbances in neighboring interconnected markets, like the impact of the stock market crisis in Brazil on the stock market pricing process in Chile. This particular interconnection between various financial markets in different countries is of current concern because of the threat of contagion (Forbes and Rigobon, 2002) and we will research it in greater detail at Kent State University, because of its importance for financial market regulatory advice for, *i.a.*, the IMF.

In Table 8.3 all measured homogeneous Hurst exponents are collected for both the stock and foreign exchange markets of several Latin American counters.[11] This shows that most of these markets have homogeneous Hurst exponents above 0.5, i.e., they are globally persistent, with the exception of the Colombian stock market and the Mexican Peso market, which have measured Hurst exponents of below 0.5. These two markets are globally antipersistent. While the Brazilian and Mexican stock market indices follow a GBM and are brown noise, the Argentinean, Chilean and Venezuelan stock indices are persistent, pink noise and show major stretches of continuity interspersed by sharp discontinuities. The Argentinian Peso was dollarized, i.e., kept at a fixed exchange rate by its Currency Board. Since the Argentinian Peso has thus no volatility, it exhibited no FX risk. The Brazilian Real and Chilean, Colombian and Venezuelan Pesos were all persistent. That is an indication of administered or controlled foreign exchange rate trading and not of completely floating exchange rate regimes!

Strictly speaking, the Brazilian Real was first pegged until January 15, 1999, when it became floating. Since its exchange rate trading process clearly breaks into two very different trading regimes, it is somewhat misleading to represent the Brazilian exchange rate process by one homogeneous Hurst exponent. For Brazil's pegged exchange rate regime between October 22, 1995 and January 14,

Table 8.3 Measured homogeneous Hurst exponents of Latin American stock and foreign exchange markets. Only the Columbian stock market and the Mexican Peso/USD market are antipersistent

	Stock indices	*Foreign exchange rates*
Argentina	0.79	N/A
Brazil	0.50	0.66
Chile	0.79	0.66
Colombia	0.42	0.61
Mexico	0.50	0.41
Venezuela	0.79	0.66

1999, the Hurst exponent was $H = 0.67$, indicating considerable persistence. For Brazil's floating exchange rate regime between January 15, 1999 and December 18, 2001, the Hurst exponent was $H = 0.46$, indicating mild, but hardly significant, anti-persistence.

As we have already noted, the Mexican Pesos is antipersistent with a global Hurst exponent of $H = 0.41$, just like the Japanese Yen and the German Deutschmark (and now the Euro), as we will see in the next section.

8.3.4 Persistence analysis of Asia's foreign exchange markets

The persistence of FX rates had earlier attracted the attention of financial analysts, but their conventional correlation methodology did not allow them to reach precise or correct conclusions (Huizinga, 1987; De Long *et al.*, 1990; Dacorogna *et al.*, 1993). After all, an uncorrelated series can still be dependent, scaling and show long-term memory. For a technically correct analysis of the volatility scaling of FX rates, cf. Gençay *et al.*, 2001a,b). In Chapter 7 we presented the 3D scalogram for the July 1997 minute-by-minute data of the Thai baht (THB), which clearly shows the sharp discontinuity in that FX market on July 2nd, 1997, when the Asian Financial Crisis erupted, not surprisingly, only one day after the handover of Hong Kong by the former British colonial empire to Communist mainland China.

The first four moments of the distributions of the minute-by-minute FX rates for nine currencies (eight Asian currencies, plus the DEM and the Yen) for the four months in 1997 are collected in Figure 8.15.

Next, let's look at a uniform or homogeneous persistence analysis by Karuppiah and Los (2000) of foreign exchange rates in Asia, around the time of the onset of the Asian Financial Crisis in the summer of 1997.

Using the dyadic logarithmic scalegram, we compute the homogeneous H-components, fractal dimensions $D = 2 - H$, and Zolotarev stability exponent $\alpha_Z = 1/H$, for ten currencies (eight Asian currencies, plus the DEM and the Yen) for the four months in 1997 surrounding the onset of the Asian Financial Crisis on July 2nd, 1997. The results of this analysis are collected in Table 8.4.[12]

Notice the uniform antipersistence of these currency rates, but, since we compute the H-exponents for each month, notice also that the H- exponents are not entirely homogeneous. Still, the DEM and the Japanese Yen (JPY) are clearly antipersistent with $0.24 \leq H \leq 0.36$ for all four months. This implies that the FX markets for these two currencies were very liquid and *self-correcting* or *mean-reverting* (Poterba and Summers, 1988). They are trading so fast, that they possibly exhibit financial turbulence, an efficiency-enhancing phenomenon, as we will discuss in Chapters 10 and 11.

In contrast, the Hong Kong Dollar (HKD), the Malaysian Ringgit (MYR), and the Singapore Dollar (SGD) were only mildly antipersistent with $0.42 \leq H \leq 0.48$. They exhibited price formations close to the GBM. The Philippine Pesos (PHP) showed about GBM with $0.43 \leq H \leq 0.52$. The Taiwanese Dollar (TWD) was mostly persistent with $0.49 \leq H \leq 0.67$. The Thai Baht (THB) was more strongly antipersistent in May and June, i.e., in the pre-currency break period, with $0.36 \leq H \leq 0.39$, than in July and August, i.e., in the post-currency break period,

Distributional statistics for the countries from May 97–August 97

DEM	May	June	July	August
Mean	1.7031	1.7262	1.7909	1.8405
Std	0.0140	0.0077	0.0345	0.0258
Kurtosis	−0.5491	0.4164	−1.4497	−0.9763
Skew	0.5804	−0.3969	0.1340	−0.1470
No. of trans	1,18,398	1,20,770	1,24,037	1,14,134

PHP	May	June	July	August
Mean	26.3718	26.3764	28.2078	29.5979
Std	0.0044	0.0065	1.4209	0.6881
Kurtosis	−0.3712	0.5364	−1.1713	−1.2000
Skew	−0.6215	0.0941	−0.0549	−0.6468
No. of trans	115	106	131	97

JPY	May	June	July	August
Mean	118.99	114.25	115.19	117.90
Std	4.4264	1.3381	1.7569	1.1365
Kurtosis	−1.0165	−0.3634	−0.8565	0.0376
Skew	0.7130	−0.1944	0.2107	−0.7009
No. of trans	83,557	1,02,676	85,524	62,774

SGD	May	June	July	August
Mean	1.4359	1.4279	1.4508	1.4967
Std	0.0064	0.0030	0.0151	0.0182
Kurtosis	−1.0674	0.9688	−1.5323	−1.1382
Skew	0.7064	−0.9178	0.0792	−0.3221
No. of trans	5,009	4,086	7,375	6,204

HKD	May	June	July	August
Mean	7.7422	7.7439	7.7450	7.7437
Std	0.0038	0.0024	0.0029	0.0025
Kurtosis	−1.3658	−0.6572	−1.1694	0.0765
Skew	0.0107	0.4250	−0.0161	0.7313
No. of trans	1,534	1,347	1,862	1,979

THB	May	June	July	August
Mean	25.8336	24.5466	30.0950	32.2345
Std	0.2761	0.6592	1.4849	1.0602
Kurtosis	0.9915	0.3408	3.2011	−1.0948
Skew	−1.1526	−0.2749	−1.2732	0.4413
No. of trans	1,828	1,433	1,807	1,884

IDR	May	June	July	August
Mean	2436.08	2429.54	2516.46	2750.28
Std	6.421	1.543	77.958	136.647
Kurtosis	−1.3170	−1.0468	−1.7310	−1.0332
Skew	−0.3258	−0.0011	0.1473	0.5100
No. of trans	1,842	1,827	3,417	3,643

TWD	May	June	July	August
Mean	27.7755	27.8808	28.0055	28.7137
Std	0.0685	0.0336	0.2038	0.0645
Kurtosis	−0.8579	−0.4860	3.2741	3.4474
Skew	0.1035	−0.5162	2.1013	1.2671
No. of trans	1,627	1,293	1,629	1,036

MYR	May	June	July	August
Mean	2.5071	2.5162	2.5710	2.7523
Std	0.0079	0.0042	0.0553	0.0826
Kurtosis	0.9704	−0.2647	−1.6296	−0.3709
Skew	−0.6024	0.1373	0.0548	−0.0271
No. of trans	1,637	1,346	1,568	1,525

Figure 8.15 The first four monthly moments of the distributions of the minute-by-minute quotations of nine currency rates in May–August 1997 (USD is the numéraire).

with $0.43 \leq H \leq 0.47$. Finally, the Indonesian rupiah consisted only of a few singularities with $H = 0.06$ in May, but showed almost GBM in the following three months with $0.46 \leq H \leq 0.48$.

This suggests that, although the FBM model is an improvement over the GBM model, even the FBM may not be the best model for FX pricing, since the FBM is a model with a homogeneous H-exponent (or uniform Lipschitz-α_{L0}), while the empirical results in Table 8.1 suggest that the H-exponent changes, almost imperceptibly, over time. The increases in kurtosis (= condensation periods), as measured by the monthly $1/H_{it}$ kurtosis exponent, are followed by decreases in

Table 8.4 Values of homogeneous Hurst and Zolotarev exponents for nine currencies (eight Asian currencies and one European) in May–August 1997

Month:	May			Jun			Jul			Aug		
FX/USD:	H	D	α_Z	H	D	α_Z	H	D	α_Z	H	D	α_Z
DEM	0.28	1.72	3.52	0.27	1.73	3.72	0.27	1.73	3.71	0.36	1.64	2.78
JPY	0.34	1.66	2.96	0.25	1.75	4.03	0.24	1.76	4.23	0.30	1.70	3.37
HKD	0.45	1.55	2.21	0.46	1.54	2.19	0.47	1.53	2.11	0.46	1.54	2.16
IDR	0.06	1.94	16.25	0.48	1.52	2.10	0.46	1.54	2.17	0.47	1.53	2.15
MYR	0.45	1.55	2.20	0.42	1.58	2.38	0.46	1.54	2.19	0.48	1.52	2.07
PHP	0.52	1.48	1.93	0.43	1.57	2.32	0.51	1.49	1.97	0.49	1.51	2.03
SGD	0.44	1.56	2.30	0.46	1.54	2.17	0.45	1.55	2.21	0.42	1.58	2.37
THB	0.36	1.64	2.77	0.39	1.61	2.56	0.47	1.53	2.13	0.43	1.57	2.34
TWD	0.55	1.45	1.81	0.55	1.45	1.82	0.67	1.33	1.49	0.49	1.51	2.06

kurtosis (= rarefaction periods). It appears that most of the condensation occurred in the months of June and July 1997, i.e., in the pre-currency break period. But the Indonesian rupiah experienced very high kurtosis in May, followed by a sharp drop in the subsequent months.

In conclusion, FX rates are almost homogeneous, multifractal random processes, of which the density distributions change kurtosis usually almost imperceptibly over time, but, occasionally, rather drastically. Therefore, a complete, non-uniform, time-dependent, local financial risk or singularity spectra should be computed.

8.4 Multiresolution analysis of multifractal price series

8.4.1 *Local risk analysis of financial pricing processes*

As we discussed earlier, singularities of any kind can be detected by following the decay of the maximum local Wavelet Transform amplitudes in a scalogram across all scales.[13] The data-microscopic zooming capability of the Wavelet Transform not only locates isolated events, but also characterizes more complex multifractal time series, having non-isolated singularities (Mallat and Hwang, 1992; Gonnet and Torrésani, 1994). Therefore, it is ideal, not only for the detection of unique discontinuities, but also for the analysis of the very antipersistent behavior of step functions, such as the speculative market prices driven by tick-by-tick innovations of FX markets, scaling of individual or bank loan credit risk, and other financial market scaling phenomena. In recent years, Mandelbrot has been leading a broad search for multifractals, showing that they occur in almost every corner of nature and science, e.g., in signal processing, hydrology, climatology and high-frequency financial pricing processes (Mandelbrot, 1997, 1999, 2002).

In Chapter 4, we discussed the natural occurrence of the scaling phenomena of fractionally differenced time series of investment rates of return. Scaling one part of a multifractal process produces a series that is statistically similar to the whole.

This self-similarity appears already in the Wavelet Transform, which modifies the analyzing scale a. Thus we can use the Wavelet Transform to take advantage of the multifractal self-similarities to compute the distribution of the very large number of singularities. This singularity spectrum of the high-frequency financial time series is then used to analyze the local risk properties of these multifractal pricing processes. One does no longer have to assume a homogeneous, monofractal FBM model for speculative market prices. From the global Wavelet Transform decay visualized in the scalogram, one can now measure the singularity spectrum of multifractal financial rates of return series.[14]

8.4.2   *Fractal (capacity) dimensions*

We will now introduce the concept of *fractal dimension*, which is a simplification of the well-known *Hausdorff dimension*, so that it is easier to compute, as follows.[15]

Definition 340   *Let S be a bounded set of points in n-dimensional real space $\mathbb{R}^n$. We count the minimum number $N(a)$ of balls of radius a to cover the set S. If S is a set of dimensions D with a finite length $(D = 1)$, surface $(D = 2)$, or volume $(D = 3)$, then it is easy to see that*

$$N(a) \approx \frac{S}{a^D}$$

$$\sim a^{-D} \tag{8.53}$$

so that

$$\log N(a) \sim -D \log a \tag{8.54}$$

Then the Hausdorff dimension *is*

$$D = -\lim_{a \to 0} \frac{\log N(a)}{\log a}$$

$$= \lim_{a \to 0} \frac{\log N(a)}{\log a^{-1}} \tag{8.55}$$

Remark 341   *When $D =$ integer, this Hausdorff dimension is the classical Euclidean dimension. But D may be a fraction.*

The Hausdorff dimension D is the exponent that keeps the product $N(a)a^D$ finite and nonzero as the radius or scale $a \to 0$. If D is altered even by an infinitesimal amount, this product will diverge either to 0 or to ∞. For a continuous curve $D = 1$ and the number N of covering line segments is proportional to a^{-1}. For a continuous surface $D = 2$ and the number N of covering disks is proportional to

a^{-2}. For a continuous volume $D = 3$ and the number N of balls is proportional to a^{-3}.

Definition 342 *The fractal (or capacity) Hausdorff dimension D of S generalizes this definition and is defined by*

$$D(\alpha_L) = -\lim_{a \to 0} \inf \frac{\log N_{\alpha_L}(a)}{\log a}$$

$$= \lim_{a \to 0} \inf \frac{\log N_{\alpha_L}(a)}{\log a^{-1}} \tag{8.56}$$

Or, equivalently, by

$$N_{\alpha_L}(a) \sim a^{-D(\alpha_L)} \tag{8.57}$$

Example 343 *For the nth generation in the construction of the famous fractal Koch snowflake, produced by Helge von Koch in 1904, choosing the measurement length $a = a_0/3^n$, the number of pieces $N \sim 4^n$ (Figure 8.16). Thus the fractal Hausdorff dimension of the Koch snowflake is $D = \log 4/\log 3 = 1.2619$. This is between $D = 1$ and $D = 2$, because an infinitely long curve is, in some metric sense, more than just a 1-dimensional object, but less than a 2-dimensional area, and the curve does not cover a region in a plane.*

The concept of one fractal can now be expanded to a set of fractals, of which we can measure the fractal dimension.

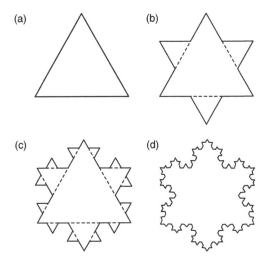

Figure 8.16 Development of Koch's snowflake with Hausdorff dimension $D = 1.2619$.

Definition 344   *Let S_{α_L} be the set of all (time) points $t \in \mathbb{R}$ where the pointwise Lipschitz regularity of the time series $x(t)$ is equal to α_L. The* multifractal *(or singularity) spectrum $D(\alpha_L)$ of $x(t)$ is the fractal dimension of this set S_{α_L}. The* support *of $D(\alpha_L)$ is the set of α_L such that S_{α_L} is not empty.*

Remark 345   *The multifractal spectrum was originally introduced by Parisi and Frisch (1985) to analyze the homogeneity of multifractal measures that model the energy dissipation of turbulent fluids (cf. Chapters 9, 10 and 11). It was then extended by Arnéodo et al. (1989) to multifractal time series, in particular to a set of FBMs. They were also the first to call Mallat's (1989) MRA a "mathematical microscope" in Bacry et al. (1993).*

The fractal dimension is therefore now no longer one number, but consists of a whole spectrum of dimensions of all the fractals in the set. In fact, this multifractal spectrum provides the frequency distribution of α_L-Lipschitz singularities that appear at any scale a. We will use the multifractal spectrum to measure all the dimensions of the set of cash flows in a financial market in Chapter 9. All cash flows in a financial market have different cyclicities: they originate at different moments and are discontinued at different maturities or investment horizons τ.

The multifractal or risk spectrum provides us with a tool to analyze the set of fractal rates of return in a financial market, each separately modeled by FBMs, and *to determine the resulting degree of persistence of such a market!* This will enable us to achieve our goals set out in Chapters 1 and 2: how to measure time and frequency localized financial market risk. We now have to define homogeneous, or monofractal, time series and heterogeneous, or multifractal, time series.

Definition 346   *The fractal time series $x(t)$ is said to be* homogeneous, *or* monofractal, *if all its singularities have the same Lipschitz exponent α_{L0}. This means that the support of the singularity spectrum $D(\alpha_L)$ is restricted to one point $\{\alpha_{L0}\}$, which is measured by the homogeneous Hurst exponent: $H = \alpha_{L0}$.*

Definition 347   *The fractal time series $x(t)$ is said to be* heterogeneous, *or* multi- *fractal if not all its singularities have the same Lipschitz exponent α_L. This means that the support of the singularity spectrum $D(\alpha_L)$ consists of more than one point, which is identified by more than one Lipschitz α_L exponent.*

FBMs are examples of homogeneous multifractal processes. We demonstrated that the fractal FX series are probably heterogeneous fractals, *ergo* they must be multifractals and that therefore the FBM is not likely to be the empirically correct model, even though it is a considerably more general model than the classical GBM. For example, a term structure of interest rates consists of a system of related FBMs. One cannot compute the pointwise Lipschitz regularity of a multifractal, because its singularities are not isolated: the finite numerical resolution is not sufficient to discriminate between them (Hwang and Mallat, 1994). Only very recently the differentiation between homogeneous and heterogeneous scaling risk has become a topic of research in hydrology (Whitcher *et al.*, 2002). One can, however, measure the singularity spectrum of multifractals from the local maxima of Wavelet Transforms, using a global wavelet partition function of Bacry *et al.* (1993), as shown in the next section.

8.4.3 Measuring the local financial risk spectrum

The procedure of Mallat (1998, pp. 199–216) and Gonçalvès *et al.* (1998) is to compute the complete singularity spectrum of multifractals or local risk spectrum from the local modulus maxima of the Wavelet Transform discussed earlier, implementing the prescriptions of the theorems in the preceding section, in the following five cookbook style steps. This research cookbook recipe will be empirically supported by the case of the $3D$ turbulent flow in Chapter 11.

Step (1) compute the Wavelet Transform $W(\tau, a)$ for all translations τ and all dilations a. In other words, compute the scalogram $P_W(\tau, a)$.

Remark 348 *In the MRA it is necessary to use a wavelet with enough vanishing moments to measure all Lipschitz exponents up to $\alpha_{L\max}$.*

Step (2) Find the *modulus maxima* of $W(\tau, a)$ for each time scale a:

$$\sup_a |W(\tau, a)| \sim a^{(\alpha_L + 0.5)} \tag{8.58}$$

and chain the wavelet maxima across scales into *maxima lines*.

Remark 349 *The largest dyadic scale $a = 2^j$ depends on the number of available sample points and the distances between the singularities.*

As we will see, the FBM generates a very large number of close range singularities and maxima lines. A parabolic interpolation is usually performed between three successive scales to better localize the maxima lines. Let $\{\tau_n(a)\}_{n\in\mathbb{Z}}$ be the position of all local maxima of $|W(\tau, a)|$ at a fixed scale a.

Step (3) Following the example of Frisch and Parisi (1985), compute Gibbs' (thermodynamic) partition function in wavelet terms, as proposed by Bacry *et al.* (1993).[16]

Definition 350 *The partition function is the sum of the modulus maximae raised to the power of $q \in \mathbb{R}$:*

$$Z(q, a) = \sum_\tau \sup_a |W(\tau, a)|^q$$

$$\sim a^{(\alpha_L + 0.5)q} \tag{8.59}$$

The partition function $Z(q, a)$ measures the sum at the power q of all these wavelet modulus maxima. It measures the scaling of the higher-order moments and higher-order dependencies of the wavelet resonance coefficients and the singularity structure of the time series, all in one. This partition function is as always concave, since moment generating functions are log-convex (cf. Chapter 1).

Definition 351   *For each real power exponent $q \in \mathbb{R}$, the* scaling exponent $\tau(q)$ *measures the asymptotic decay of the partition function $Z(q, a)$ at fine scales a, using dyadic logarithms, as follows:*

$$\tau(q) = \lim_{a \to 0} \inf \frac{\log_2 Z(q, a)}{\log_2 a} \tag{8.60}$$

This typically means that the partition function is scale-dependent:

$$Z(q, a) \sim a^{\tau(q)} \tag{8.61}$$

Step (4) Compute the decay scaling exponent $\tau(q)$ as the slope in the following double-logarithmic plot:

$$\log_2 Z(q, a) \approx \tau(q) \log_2 a + C(q) \tag{8.62}$$

The following important theorem proves that the scaling exponent $\tau(q)$ is the so-called Legendre Transform of the multifractal spectrum $D(\alpha_L)$ for self-similar time series and relates the fractal dimension $D(\alpha_L)$ to the order q of the partition function $Z(q, a)$.

Theorem 352   (Arnéodo, Bacry, Jaffard, Muzy) *Let $\Lambda = [\alpha_{L \min}, \alpha_{L \max}]$ be the support of the multifractal spectrum $D(\alpha_L)$. Let ψ be a wavelet with p vanishing moments, $p > \alpha_{L \max}$. If $x(t)$ is a self-similar time series, then we have the Legendre Transform:*

$$\tau(q) = \inf_{\alpha_L \in \Lambda} [(\alpha_L + 0.5)q - D(\alpha_L)] \tag{8.63}$$

Suppose such an α_L exists, then for a given fractal dimension $D(\alpha_L)$

$$(\alpha_L + 0.5) = \frac{\partial \tau(q)}{\partial q} \tag{8.64}$$

which is the slope of the plot of the scaling exponent $\tau(q)$ versus the order q. Now we need to invert this Legendre Transform to recover the singularity spectrum $D(\alpha_L)$ for self-similar time series $x(t)$ by the tenets of following important proposition.

Proposition 353

- *The scaling exponent $\tau(q)$ is a convex and increasing function of q.*
- *The Legendre Transform is invertible if and only if the multifractal singularity spectrum $D(\alpha_L)$ is convex, in which case*

$$D(\alpha_L) = \min_{q \in \mathbb{R}}[(\alpha_L + 0.5)q - \tau(q)] \tag{8.65}$$

- *The spectrum $D(\alpha_L)$ of a self-similar time series $x(t)$ is convex.*

Step (5) Compute this (Legendre) multifractal spectrum $D(\alpha_L)$ by plotting all $D(\alpha_L) > 0$ versus α_L for all $0 \le \alpha_L < 1$ and for all q.

The Legendre Transform transforms the relationship between the order q and the decay scaling exponent $\tau(q)$ into the relationship between the Lipschitz α_L and the multifractal spectrum $D(\alpha_L)$. It proves that the maximum of the multifractal spectrum is reached at order $q = 0$:

$$D(\alpha_{L0}) = \max_{\alpha_L \in \Lambda} D(\alpha_L) = -\tau(0) \tag{8.66}$$

$$D(\alpha_{L\,min}) = 0 \quad \text{for } q \to +\infty \quad \text{and} \tag{8.67}$$

$$D(\alpha_{L\,max}) = 0 \quad \text{for } q \to -\infty \tag{8.68}$$

This becomes clear in Figure 8.17: the mode of the multifractal spectrum $D(\alpha_{L0})$ is the fractal dimension of the Lipschitz exponent α_{L0} most frequently encountered in the financial time series $x(t)$. It is the same as the homogeneous Hurst exponent.

Since all other Lipschitz α_L singularities appear over sets of lower dimension, if $0 < \alpha_{L0} < 1$, then $D(\alpha_L)$ is also the fractal dimension of the singularity support of

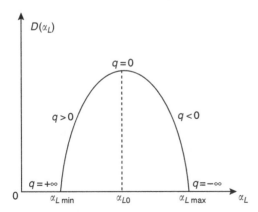

Figure 8.17 Schematic convex multifractal singularity spectrum $D(\alpha_L)$, with various Gibbs exponent regimes.

$x(t)$. For $\alpha_L < \alpha_{L0}$ the spectrum $D(\alpha_L)$ depends on the scaling exponent $\tau(q)$ for $q > 0$. For $\alpha_L > \alpha_{L0}$ it depends on $\tau(q)$ for $q < 0$. The value $\alpha_{L \min}$ represents the least frequently occurring part of the multifractal and $\alpha_{L \max}$ the most frequently occurring.

Remark 354   *When $q = 2$, to compute the second-order moments of the wavelet resonance coefficients of the homogenous FBMs – as in the MRA based on the DWT of FBMs by Flandrin (1989, 1992) and Kaplan and Kuo (1993) discussed earlier – the partition function is, indeed, proportional to the variance of the wavelet resonance coefficients:*

$$Z(2, a) = \sum_\tau \sup_a |W(\tau, a)|^2 \sim E\{d_{j,n}^2\} \tag{8.69}$$

for the dyadic scale $a = 2^j$ and

$$\log_2 Z(2, a) \approx \tau(2) \log_2 a + C(2) \tag{8.70}$$

Several types of dimensions have been defined in the physics literature using Gibbs' thermodynamic partition function, like the *information dimension* and the *correlation dimension*, depending on the moment order q.

Definition 355   *The* information *(or first moment) dimension*

$$D_{\text{information}} = \lim_{a \to 0} \inf \frac{\log_2 Z(1, a)}{\log_2 a} \tag{8.71}$$

The information dimension plays an important role in the analysis of nonlinear dynamic systems, like the parabolic logistic equation, to be discussed in Chapter 9, which can produce intermittency and chaotic behavior. This dimension is particularly used for measuring the loss of information as a chaotic system evolves over time.

Definition 356   *The* correlation *(or second moment) dimension*

$$D_{\text{correlation}} = \lim_{a \to 0} \inf \frac{\log_2 Z(2, a)}{\log_2 a} \tag{8.72}$$

The correlation dimension indicates how likely it is to find, within the distance a of a given member of the particular fractal set S_{α_L}, another member (Theiler, 1987). Thus, measuring this likelihood comes down to a simple counting process. This overcomes some of the problems of computing this correlation dimension from chaotic time series (Ding *et al.*, 1993; Fraedrich and Wang, 1993). Osborne and Provenzale (1989) present the correlation dimension of the kind of random dynamic systems with a power-law spectra we discussed in Chapter 6. We propose now a further extension of the series of definitions of moment dimensions.

Definition 357 *The* skewness *(or third moment)* dimension

$$D_{\text{skewness}} = \lim_{a \to 0} \inf \frac{\log_2 Z(3, a)}{\log_2 a} \tag{8.73}$$

The skewness dimension indicates the distortion, bias or skewness of a particular fractal set S_{α_L}. In all fairness, the multifractal spectra measured thus far appear to all be symmetric, but precise measurements of this skewness dimension have not yet been executed. It is easily imaginable that turbulence is an asymmetric fractal process.

Definition 358 *The* kurtosis *(or fourth moment)* dimension

$$D_{\text{kurtosis}} = \lim_{a \to 0} \inf \frac{\log_2 Z(4, a)}{\log_2 a} \tag{8.74}$$

The kurtosis dimension indicates the curvature of a particular fractal set S_{α_L} and thus the relative concentration or density of particular singularities. Infinitely many more moment dimensions immediately follow (cf. Chapter 1).

8.4.4 Computing local risk spectra: a few examples

We'll now provide three examples of the computations of singularity or local risk spectra for homogeneous or monofractal, and for heterogeneous or multifractal *singular* time series. The first theoretical example computes a singularity spectrum for the abstract Devil's staircase. This is followed by the computation of the spectrum of a simulated FBM. We conclude with an even more complicated example with a *time-warped* GBM, using the increments of one realization of a binomial cascade with a time warp. A time-warped GBM is a potential model for high frequency tick-by-tick financial data, which have notoriously heterogeneous time differences (Dacorogna *et al.*, 2001).

Example 359 *Figure 8.18 shows in panel (a) a Devil's staircase with $p_1 = 0.4$ and $p_2 = 1 - p_1 = 0.6$, which provides us with 4,000 data points $x(t)$. The devil's staircase is an example of an* intermittent *function: long periods of no change are interrupted by short periods of steep ascent. Panel (b) shows the partition function $\log_2 Z(q, a)$ for several values of order q, from which we derive the scaling exponent $\tau(q) = \lim_{a \to 0}(\log_2 Z(q, a)/\log_2 a)$ plotted against q in panel (c) by measuring the slope of a line of $\log_2 Z(q, a)$ versus $\log_2 a$ for each order q. For example, for $q = 10.00$ we find $\tau(q) = [-20 - (-60)]/(10 - 2) = 5.0$. In panel (d) the theoretical singularity spectrum $D(\alpha_L)$ is shown with a solid line. The $+$ signs are the spectrum values computed numerically with the Legendre Transform of $\tau(q)$. The singularity spectrum reaches its maximum $\max D(\alpha_L) = 0.62$ at $\alpha_L = 0.65$ for $q = 0$. The spectrum measures the dimensions of the fractal sets of various Lipschitz α_L that measure the degree of irregularity, randomness,*

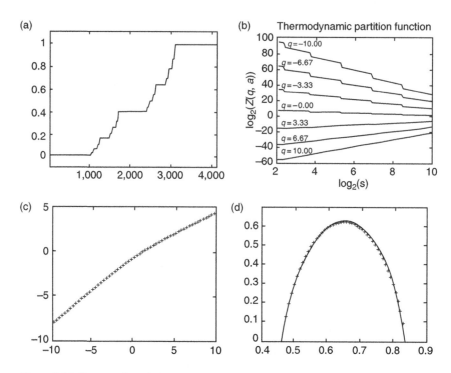

Figure 8.18 Computation of singularity spectrum of (a) the devil's staircase with $p_1 = 0.4$ and $p_2 = 0.6$; (b) partition function $Z(q, a)$ for various values of q; (c) scaling exponent $\tau(q)$; (d) theoretical spectrum $D(\alpha_L)$ represented by a solid line. The $+$ signs form the empirical spectrum values computed with the Legendre transform of $\tau(q)$.

or local risk of the set of many fractals constituting the Devil's staircase (Source: Mallat, 1998, p. 210).

Example 360 *Figure 8.19 displays in panel (a) one realization of 8,100 data points of a FBM $x(t)$ with a homogeneous Hurst exponent $H = 0.7$. Panel (b) provides the scalogram $W(\tau, a)$ based on the CWT with Gábor's Gaussian wavelet ψ basis. Panel (c) shows the corresponding local modulus maxima $|W(\tau, a)|$ from which the partition function $Z(q, a) \sim a^{\tau(q)}$ is computed. Panel (d) gives the scaling exponent $\tau(q)$. The maximum of the multifractal spectrum is reached at $q = 0$, when*

$$D(\alpha_{L0}) = \max_{\alpha_L \in \Lambda} D(\alpha_L)$$

$$= -\tau(0)$$

$$= 1 \tag{8.75}$$

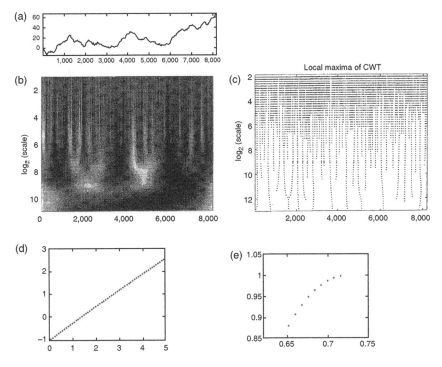

Figure 8.19 Wavelet MRA of Fractional Brownian Motion: (a) One realization of a theoretical FBM with a Hurst exponent $H = 0.7$. (b) Scalogram with CWT; (c) Modulus Maxima of the CWT. (d) Scaling exponent $\tau(q)$ versus order q; (e) Resulting singularity spectrum $D(\alpha_L)$ over its support $[\alpha_{L\,min}, \alpha_{L\,max}]$.

Recall that FBM are fractals (= self-similar time series) with uniform Lipschitz or Hurst exponents $\alpha_{L0} = H$. The theoretical singularity spectrum $D(\alpha_L)$ has thus a support consisting of one point $\alpha_{L0} = d\tau(q)/dq = \{0.7\}$ with $D(0.7) = 1$. Using the Theorem of Arnéodo, Bacry, Jaffard and Muzy, the empirical singularity spectrum in panel (e) is computed with the Legendre Transform of the $\tau(q)$ in panel (d). We find that its empirical support is $\Lambda = [0.65, 0.72]$. i.e., it is not a single point, as we theoretically expect from the FBM model, but it is a very narrow finite range. According to Mallat (1998, p. 213) the probable cause of this finite estimation error is that the computations are performed on a time series $x(t)$ of finite length. Thus, we find a frequency distribution of Lipschitz α_L, because of the finiteness of the data set ("sampling"), and not because of a non-unique theoretical reality. A lengthening of the data set would narrow the frequency distribution of the α_L. This statistical conclusion was also reached by Kalman (1994) using non-technical mathematical arguments.

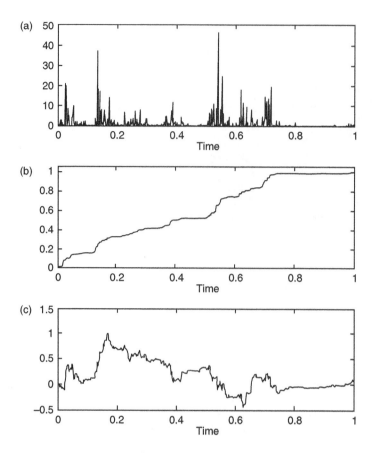

Figure 8.20 Time-warped Geometric Brownian Motion: (a) increments of one real-
    ization of a binomial cascade $\Delta z(2^j t, 2^j (t + 1))$, $t = 0, \ldots, 2^{-j} - 1$;
    realization of a binomial cascade $z(2^j t)$; one realization of GBM warped
    with the realization of (b), $x(2^j k) = x_{1/2}(z(2^j t))$.

Example 361   *Figure 8.20 shows in panel (a) the increments of one realization
of the binomial cascade*

$$z(a(t + 1)) - z(at) = z(2^j (t + 1)) - z(2^j t)$$
$$= \Delta z([2^j t, 2^j (t + 1)]) \qquad (8.76)$$

with $t = 0, \ldots, 2^{-j} - 1$. Panel (b) shows the realization of the binomial cascade

$$z(at) = z(2^j t) \qquad (8.77)$$

*with $t = 0, \ldots, 2^{-j} - 1$. This binomial cascade produces the warped time, i.e.,
the irregularly spaced time intervals for the GBM. Panel (c) shows one realization*

of a GBM time-warped with the realization of (b),

$$x(at) = x(2^j t)$$
$$= x_{1/2}(z(2^j t)) \tag{8.78}$$

with $t = 0, \ldots, 2^{-j} - 1$ *(Argoul et al., 1989; Gonçalvès et al., 1998).*

Example 362   *Figure 8.21 provides the multifractal analysis of the time-warped GBM displayed in Figure 8.20. The dot – dashed line is the theoretical multifractal spectrum of the warp time z displayed in Figure 8.20(b). The dashed line is the theoretical multifractal process of the time-warped GBM itself, which is displayed in Figure 8.20(c). The solid line is the wavelet-based computation of the multifractal spectrum of the simulated time-warped GBM x(t). The singularity spectra of warp time z and the warped process x are related by*

$$D_x(\alpha_L) = D_z\left(\frac{\alpha_L}{H}\right) \tag{8.79}$$

where H is the Hurst exponent. Notice that the mode α_{L0} *of this singularity spectrum of time-warped GBM,* $\alpha_{L0} > 0.5$, *i.e., above the Lipschitz measure for a pure GBM. Thus, a time-warped GBM is a potential candidate for empirical stock market returns which exhibit a homogeneous Lipschitz* $\alpha_{L0} \approx 0.62$, *although*

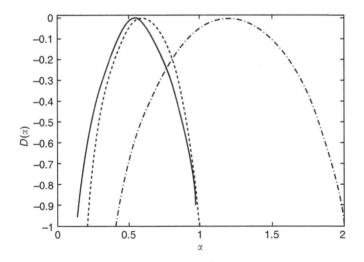

Figure 8.21 Multifractal spectrum analysis of time-warped GBM: -·-: theoretical multifractal spectrum of warp time z; - - -: theoretical multifractal spectrum of GBM; —: wavelet-based estimate of multifractal spectrum of a time-warped GBM.

most measured homogeneous Hurst exponents of stock markets are slightly larger,
$H \approx 0.67$. *Again, this is a current field of research, where the differences between
the empirical measurement results are not yet settled.*

As this example demonstrates, *time-warping* is an important modeling concept
for financial time series, since most financial time series are tick-by-tick data with
random arrival times (= random time intervals), similar to the random arrival
times of the heartbeat of a healthy human patient analyzed earlier in Section 3.1.
In other words, one should be able to analyze the arrhythmias of the financial
markets for diagnostic purposes to determine how efficiently a market actually
operates! Finally, we can identify the degree of persistence and thus the *degree of
efficiency* of a financial market by objective measurement and analysis. Financial
market efficiency is no longer a matter of black noise (no efficiency) or white noise
(efficiency). There are different colors of market noise, or degrees of efficiency.

8.4.5 Multifractals in financial turbulence modeling

Multifractals, or non-homogeneous series of singularities, are currently used in
describing a wide range of natural phenomena, from the distributions of people or
minerals on earth to energy dissipation in fluid turbulence, or to fractal computer
networks (Schroeder, 1991, pp. 187–210). If we divide the world into regions,
each characterized by a different level of oil resources, it happens that each of
these regions is nearly a fractal set. So the pattern of global oil distribution is not
itself a fractal set, but a novel combination of a multitude of fractal sets. It's called
a *multifractal distribution*, or *multifractal measure*. Figure 8.22 provides a typical
multifractal time series, similar to what we observed in Figure 8.20(a). This trace
is modeling the turbulence in a laboratory experiment using a multifractal model.
It shows the variability of risk (energy) dissipation in a turbulent fluid. But it brings
to mind the graphs representing the variability of the variance of price increments,

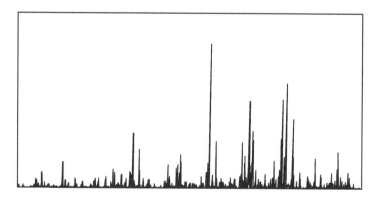

Figure 8.22 Mandelbrot's early multifractal turbulence trace modeling in a laboratory
experiment.

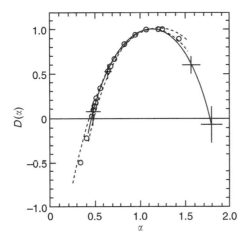

Figure 8.23 Multifractal spectrum of physical (windtunnel generated) turbulence, i.e.,
energy dissipation in the time domain measured at the atmospheric surface
layer at high Reynolds number.

thus revealing a deep link between the uses of the fractal modeling in the study
of physical turbulence and of pricing in the financial markets (Mandelbrot, 1972,
1997). This link we'll discuss in greater detail in Part III of this book.

Figure 8.23 shows the empirically measured multifractal spectrum for the
energy dissipation in fully developed physical turbulence along a 1-dimensional
straight-line path (= *Gagne signal*) through such turbulent flow (Meneveau and
Sreenivasan, 1987a,b, 1991). The turbulent regions form the *support*

$$\Lambda = [\alpha_{L\,min}, \alpha_{L\,max}]$$
$$= [0.51, 1.74] \tag{8.80}$$

of the multifractal, which has perfectly deterministic fractal subsets. The experimental points $\square, \circ$ and $+$ of the spectrum $D(\alpha_L)$ are from different physical
realizations of turbulence (such as atmospheric turbulence, boundary-layer turbulence, and turbulence in the wake behind a circular cylinder or wire grid). Note
that these empirical measurements are well matched by a single $D(\alpha_L)$ curve. The
fact that the spectrum $D(\alpha_L)$ achieves a maximum around unity, near α_L, is indica-
tive that there is a nonsingular ($\alpha_L = 1$) background of space-filling ($D(\alpha_L) = 1$)
dissipation, which confirms Kolmogorov's 1941 turbulence theory, to be discussed
in Chapter 11. It appears that financial turbulence may be well modeled by such
multifractal processes.

Many strange attractors of nonlinear dynamic systems are also clearly multifractals, as we will see in Chapter 9. As we will argue in Chapter 11, the term
structure of rates of return on investment cash flows of various maturities has

a similar multifractal distribution as the global geographic distribution of oil, or as physical turbulence in nonlaminar fluids. Recall from our earlier study of the antipersistence of foreign exchange rates in Section 3.2, that some currency markets, e.g., of the DEM/USD rate and the Yen/US dollar rate, measure levels of antipersistence that physicists have shown to harbor potential turbulence.

For a comparison with the stock markets and futures markets, review the following example.

Example 363 *It appears that the correlation between the S&P500 spot and futures markets in Figure 8.24 shows intermittency which is similar to that of turbulence in Figure 8.22 and of the increments of one realization of the binomial cascade in Figure 8.20(a). The thin line in Figure 8.24 shows the empirical correlation between the S&P500 spot market in New York and the S&P500 futures market in Chicago. The bold line shows the moving average correlation. Although most of the time the bivariate correlation ρ_{sf} between these two markets has values $0.9 < \rho_{sf} < 1.0$, it clearly is not perfect correlation. In fact, quite frequently during these nine years the correlation has had much lower values $0.8 < \rho_{sf} < 0.7$. Figure 8.24 shows that in the period 1982–1991 there were at least eleven instances when $\rho_{sf} < 0.7$, when the coefficient of determination $\rho_{sf}^2 < 0.5$. The almost complete breakdown of the trading link between the spot and futures markets on Black Monday, October 19, 1987 – an instance of financial crisis – when the correlation was $\rho_{sf} < 0.3$, is easily detected (Los, 2001, p. 225).*

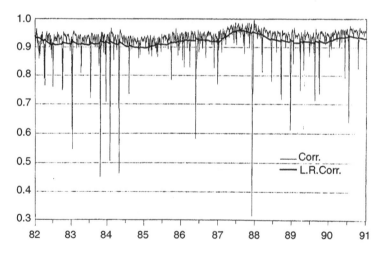

Figure 8.24 Turbulent correlation between the S&P500 spot and futures market, 1982–1991. The correlation between these two financial markets often breaks down, despite the fact that they are interlinked by arbitrage. Notice the complete lack of correlation on Black Monday, November 19, 1987.

8.5   Software

The computations of the following Exercises can be executed by using the MATLAB® Wavelet Toolbox, available from The MathWorks, Inc., 24 Prime Park Way Natick, MA 01760-1500, USA. Tel (508) 647-7000; Fax (508) 647-7001; http://www.mathworks.com/products/wavelettbx.shtml.

A complete wavelet analysis toolkit called *Wavelab* can be obtained at no cost from: http://playfair.stanford.EDU:80/~wavelab/.

This *Wavelab* is a very complete set of MATLAB® scripts that implement both the basic wavelet and related transforms and more advanced techniques. There is full documentation, a set of tutorials, and a section of "Toons," short for *cartoons*. These Toon scripts reproduce from scratch the figures in many papers of Stanford's wavelet research group consisting of Dave Donoho, Ian Johnstone *et al.*, describing the theoretical research underlying the algorithms in *Wavelab*. By studying these scripts and by experimenting with the data, the reader can learn all the details of the process that led to each figure in these papers. This forms part of the new discipline of *Reproducible Research*, i.e., the idea to provide the reader full access to all details (data, equations, code, etc.) needed to completely reproduce all the results normally presented only in advertising summary form in scientific publications. The pioneer of *Reproducible Research* is Jon Claerbout of Stanford University's Geophysics Department (Claerbout, 1994; Buckheit and Donoho, 1995).

In addition, one can use Benoit 1.3: Fractal System Analysis (for Windows 95/98 or Windows NT), Trusoft International Inc., 204 37th Ave. N #133, St Petersburg, FL 33704. Tel.: (813) 925-8131; Fax: (813) 925-8141; sales@trusoft-international.com. See http://www.trusoft-international.com for details. This Benoit software enables you to measure the fractal dimension and/or Hölder–Hurst exponent of your data sets using your choice of method(s) for analysis of self–affine traces of speculative prices. However, astonishingly, the wavelet routine in Benoit 1.3 is incorrect, although the other routines to compute the Hurst exponent are correct.

8.6   Exercises

Exercise 364   *Compute the Hurst exponent and the fractal dimension of the S&P500 data of Appendix B introduced in the Exercises of Chapter 1, using the Power Spectrum analysis of Chapter 6.*

Exercise 365   *Repeat the Exercise of question 1, using the Wavelet MRA analysis with Haar wavelets of Chapter 7 or with Morlet wavelets of Chapter 8. Follow the Flandrin (1992) and Kaplan and Kuo (1993) procedure. Notice that the Benoit software uses the detail wavelet resonance coefficients $d_{j,n}$ differently than the Flandrin (1992) and Kaplan and Kuo (1993) approach presented in this chapter. The Benoit software takes an average over the n translations of the successive ratios of the standard deviations of the wavelet detail coefficients $d_{j,n}$, as the description of Benoit's wavelet method indicates. This Benoit approach is incorrect, in comparison to the one explained in this chapter for computing homogeneous Hurst exponents, for which we used the MATLAB® Wavelet Toolboxes! You may want to* *use the quick and easy internet based interactive computation facility provided by Torrence and Compo (1998): http://ion.researchsystems.com/IONScript/wavelet/*

Exercise 366   *Study and execute MATLAB® Exercises – Chapter 11, Denoising in 1D, Strang and Nguyen (1997), p. 474.*

Exercise 367   *Study and execute MATLAB® Exercises – Chapter 11, Discontinuity Detection, Strang and Nguyen (1997), p. 474.*

Exercise 368   *In this chapter we've also discussed the third, and even more accurate, approach of Mallat and Jaffard, which uses the continuous Gábor chirp wavelets of Chapter 7, and which is based on tracing the slopes of the maxima lines of the $d_{j,n}$ coefficients in continuous scalograms (Mallat, 1998, pp. 199–216). Mallat and Jaffard exploit the local self-affinity of these $d_{j,n}$ coefficients. This new approach can compute non-homogeneous, multifractal Hurst exponents, as explained at the end of this chapter. If you want to apply this approach to, say, the detection and, perhaps, even prediction of sharp financial markets drawdowns or catastrophes, using a set of high-frequency stock market, foreign exchange or derivatives data, read the article by Zbigniew Struzik (2001) for some excellent suggestions. Struzik computes the instantaneous Hölder–Hurst exponent or Lipschitz-α_L, for all times, in a similar fashion as we have done that for various values of the chaos controlling parameter κ of the parabolic logistic equation in Chapter 9. He also computes a complete multifractal spectrum for a stock market. For this procedure you may want to use Scilab 6.0 for Windows, produced by I.N.R.I.A in France (Email: scilab@inria.fr).*

Notes

1 I propose this Latin phrase as a contemporary alternative – natural market pricing processes are essentially discontinuous – for the phrase written by the Victorian – Edwardian British economist Alfred Marshall (1842–1924) in his book *Principles of Economics* (1890), which integrated the modern and classical economic theory of his time: "Natura Saltus Non Facit" (= "Nature Does Not Jump"). By this phrase, Marshall erroneously asserted that market pricing processes are continuously differentiable, although they empirically consist of many singularities and are not continuously differentiable.

2 Financial turbulence must be sharply distinguished from financial catastrophes or discontinuities. Financial turbulence occurs in *antipersistent* financial markets, when the Hurst exponent $H \approx 0.3$. In contrast, financial catastrophes occur mostly in *persistent* financial markets, when $0.6 \leq H \leq 1.0$.

3 We've already met the stability or characteristic exponent α_Z in Chapters 3 and 4, based on the Zolotarev parametrization of stable distributions $S(\alpha_Z, \beta, \gamma, \delta; k)$. However, the Lipschitz regularity exponent α_L of the current chapter is exactly the inverse of Zolotarev's stability α_Z of Chapters 3 and 4: $\alpha_L = 1/\alpha_Z$. We have distinguished both by a proper subscript, in contrast to the literature, where such identifying subscripts are lacking, thereby causing confusion between α_Z and α_L.

4 The mathematical definition of irregularity corresponds with the informal definition of irregularity or "randomness" discussed in Chapter 1, since the irregularity is the difference between the empirical data and the regular approximating polynomial. Cf. also Chapter 7, where we looked at low- and high-pass filters.

5 Rudolf Lipschitz (1832–1903) studied at the universities of Königsberg and Berlin, where he received his doctorate in 1853. In 1862 he became an extraordinary professor

at Breslau, and in 1864 Lipschitz was nominated for an ordinary professorship at the University of Bonn in 1864, where he spent the rest of his very fruitful career. He investigated the number theory, Bessel functions, Fourier series, ordinary and partial differential equations, analytical mechanics, potential theory and quadratic differential forms (which can lead to chaos). Lipschitz's work on the Hamilton – Jacobi method for integrating the equations of motion of a general dynamic system led to important applications in celestial mechanics. He is most remembered for the "Lipschitz condition," an inequality that guarantees a unique solution to the differential equation $\partial y / \partial t = f(x, y)$.

6 Mallat (1998) provides the proofs for this theorem and for the following theorems.

7 In Chapter 4, we encountered slowly decaying functions, i.e., the opposite of fast decaying functions. In Chapter 7 we discussed the vanishing moments condition of properly behaving wavelets.

8 Wavelet software for these computations was provided by Christopher Torrence and Gilbert P. Compo of the Program in Atmospheric and Oceanic Sciences, University of Colorado, Boulder, Colorado (Torrence and Compo, 1998) and is available on the internet at the URL: http://ion.researchsystems.com/IONScript/wavelet/

9 Due to the extended tails of the Gaussian envelop, it is not possible to construct a truly orthogonal set or MRA for the Morlet wavelet. There remains some redundancy or inefficiency in the analysis. However, for other wavelets, such as the Daubechies wavelets, it is possible to construct an exactly orthogonal set and thus en efficient, i.e., non-redundant or efficient MRA.

10 The *monochromatic* light green strip at the 512-day scale is the same artificial sampling effect as before.

11 For all foreign exchange rates the US dollar is the numéraire.

12 The US dollar is again the numéraire. The fractal dimension $D = 2 - H$; Zolotarev's stability exponent $\alpha_Z = 1/\alpha_L$, the inverse of the Lipschitz irregularity exponent α_L, as measured by the homogeneous Hurst exponent.

13 Financial discontinuities, or catastrophes, are a particular kind of singularities and they can be properly identified by measuring their unique pointwise Lipschitz-α_L (Struzik, 2001).

14 Why would such multifractality exist? We speculate at this moment that it is because the yield curves in the various countries are segmented: each maturity spectrum has its own characteristic trading process that differs from the trading processes in neighboring maturity segments.

15 Felix Hausdorff (1868–1942) graduated from Leipzig in 1891 where he taught until 1910 when he went to Bonn. There he worked until 1935 when, because he was a Jew, he was forced to retire by the Nazi regime. In 1942, when he was at the point of being sent to a concentration camp, together with his wife and his wife's sister, he committed suicide. Hausdorff introduced the concept of a partially ordered set. He proved results on the cardinality of Borel sets in 1916. Building on work by Fréchet and others, he created a theory of topological and metric spaces (a term he invented) with *Grundzüge der Mengenlehre (Foundations of Set Theory)*, 1914. In 1919 he introduced the notion of the Hausdorff dimension, which is a real number lying between the topological dimensions of Euclidean objects. He also introduced the Hausdorff measure.

16 The original *partition function* was an analytical tool invented by the theoretical physicist and engineer J. Willard Gibbs (1839–1903), who was an American mathematician best-known for the distorting *Gibbs effect* seen in the Fourier Analysis of a discontinuous function (cf. Chapter 5, Figure 5.1). In 1854, he entered Yale College, winning prizes for excellence in Latin and Mathematics. At Yale, Gibbs did geometrical research in engineering, for which in 1863 he was awarded the first doctorate of engineering to be conferred in the United States. After a three-year-study sojourn in Europe, in 1871, he was appointed professor of mathematical physics at Yale, surprisingly, without any publications, based only on his lectures. It was not until 1873 that he published his first works *Graphical Methods in the Thermodynamics of Fluids* and *A Method of Geometrical Representation of the Thermodynamic Properties of Substances by Means of Surfaces*.

In 1876 Gibbs published his most famous work *On the Equilibrium of Heterogeneous Substances*. Using the vector methods of Grassmann, Gibbs produced an analytical system much more easily applied to physics than the non-vector system of Hamilton.

Bibliography

Argoul, F., A. Arnéodo, G. Grasseau, Y. Gagne, E. F. Hopfinger and U. Frisch (1989) "Wavelet Analysis of Turbulence Reveals the Multifractal Nature of the Richardson Cascade," *Nature*, **338**, 51–53.

Arnéodo, A., G. Grasseau and M. Holschneider (1989) "Wavelet Transform of Multifractals," *Physical Review Letters*, **61**(20), 2281–2284.

Bacry, E., J. F. Muzy and A. Arnéodo (1993) "Singularity Spectrum of Fractal Signals: Exact Results," *Journal of Statistical Physics*, **70**(3/4), 635–674.

Buckheit, J. B., and D. L. Donoho (1995) "Wavelab and Reproducible Research," in Antoniadis, A. and G. Oppenheim (Eds) *Wavelets and Statistics*, Springer Verlag, Berlin, pp. 53–81.

Claerbout, J. (1994) "Reproducible Electronic Documents," http://sepwww.stanford.edu/research/redoc

Dacorogna, M. M., U. A. Müller, R. J. Nagler, R. B. Olsen and O. V. Pictet (1993) "A Geographical Model for the Daily and Weekly Seasonal Volatility in the Foreign Exchange Market," *Journal of International Money and Finance*, **12**(4), 413–438.

Dacorogna, Michel M., Ramazan Gençay, Ulrich Müller, Richard Olsen and Olivier V. Pictet (2001) *An Introduction to High-Frequency Finance*, Academic Press, San Diego, CA.

De Long, J. Bradford, Andrei Shleifer, Lawrence H. Summers and Robert J. Waldmann (1990) "Noise Trader Risk in Financial Markets," *Journal of Political Economy*, **98**(4), 703–738.

Ding, M., C. Grebogi, E. Ott, T. Sauer and J. York (1993) "Estimating Correlation Dimension from a Chaotic Time Series: When Does Plateau Onset Occur," *Physica*, D, **69**, 404–424.

Farge, M., J. C. R. Hunt and J. C. Vassilicos (Eds) (1993) *Wavelets, Fractals and Fourier Transforms*, Clarendon Press, Oxford, UK.

Feinstone, L. J. (1987) "Minute by Minute: Efficiency, Normality, and Randomness in Intra-Daily Asset Prices," *Journal of Applied Econometrics*, **2**(3), 193–214.

Flandrin, Patrick (1989) "On the Spectrum of Fractional Brownian Motion," *IEEE Transactions on Information Theory*, **35**(1), 197–199.

Flandrin, Patrick (1992) "Wavelet Analysis and Synthesis of Fractional Brownian Motion," *IEEE Transactions on Information Theory*, **38**(2), 910–917.

Flandrin, Patrick, and Paulo Gonçalvès (1996) "Geometry of Affine Time – Frequency Distributions," *Applied and Computational Harmonic Analysis*, **3**(2), 10–39.

Forbes, Kristin J., and Roberto Rigobon (2002) "No Contagion, Only Interdependence: Measuring Stock Market Comovements," *The Journal of Finance*, **57**(5), 2223–2261.

Fraedrich, K., and R. Wang (1993) "Estimating the Correlation Dimension of an Attractor from Noisy and Small Data Sets Based on Re-embedding," *Physica*, D, **65**, 373–398.

French, Kenneth R. (1980) "Stock Returns and the Weekend Effect," *Journal of Financial Economics*, **8**(1), 55–69.

Frisch, U., and G. Parisi (1985) "Fully Developed Turbulence and Intermittency," in M. Ghil, R. Benzi and G. Parisi (Eds), *Turbulence and Predictability in Geophysical Fluid Dynamics*, North-Holland Publishing Co., Amsterdam, p. 84.

Gençay, Ramazan, Faruk Selçuk and Brandon Whitcher (2001a) "Scaling Properties of Foreign Exchange Volatility," *Physica A: Statistical Mechanics and Its Applications*, **289**(1/2), 249–266.

Gençay, Ramazan, Faruk Selçuk and Brandon Whitcher (2001b) "Differentiating Intraday Seasonalities Through Wavelet Multiscaling," *Physica A: Statistical Mechanics and Its Applications*, **289**(3/4), 543–556.

Gonçalvès, Paulo and Rudolf Riedi (1999) "Wavelet Analysis of Fractional Brownian Motion in Multifractal Time," *Proceedings of the 17th Colloquium GRETSI*, Vannes, France, September, 4 pages.

Gonçalvès, Paulo, Rudolf Riedi and Richard Baraniuk (1998) "A Simple Statistical Analysis of Wavelet-Based Multifractal Spectrum Estimation," *Asilomar 32nd Conference on "Signals, Systems and Computers,"* Monterey, CA, 5 pages.

Gonnet, C., and B. Torrésani (1994) "Local Frequency Analysis with the Two-Dimensional Wavelet Transform," *Signal Processing*, **37**, 389–404.

Gopikrishnan, P., M. Meyer, L. A. N. Amaral and H. E. Stanley (1998) "Inverse Cubic Law for the Distribution of Stock Price Variations," *European Physics Journal*, B, **3**, 139–140.

Huizinga, J. (1987) "An Empirical Investigation of the Long Run Behavior of Real Exchange Rates," *Carnegie – Rochester Conference Series on Public Policy*, **27**, 149–214.

Hwang, W. L., and S. Mallat (1994) "Characterization of Self-Similar Multifractals with Wavelet Maxima," *Journal of Applied and Computational Harmonic Analysis*, **1**(4), 316–328.

Jaffard, S. (1989) "Exponant de Hölder et Coefficients d' Ondelettes" ("Hölder Exponents and Wavelet Coefficients"), *C. R. Academie des Sciences*, **308**, 79–81.

Jaffard, S. (1991) "Pointwise Smoothness, Two-Microlocalization and Wavelet Coefficients," *Publicacions Matemátiques*, **35**, 155–168.

Kaplan, Lance M., and C.-C. Jay Kuo (1993) "Fractal Estimation From Noisy Data Via Discrete Fractional Gaussian Noise (DFGN) and the Haar Basis," *IEEE Transactions on Signal Processing*, **41**(12), 3554–3562.

Karuppiah, Jeyanthi, and Cornelis A. Los (2000) "Wavelet Multiresolution Analysis of High-Frequency FX Rates," *Quantitative Methods in Finance and Bernoulli Society 2000 Conference (Program, Abstracts and Papers)*, University of Technology, Sydney, Australia, 5–8 December, pp. 171–198.

Kyaw, Nyonyo, Cornelis A. Los and Sijing Zong (2002) "Persistence Characteristics of Latin American Financial Markets," Working Paper, Department of Finance, Graduate School of Management, Kent State University (Presented at the Financial Management Association International Meetings in San Antonio, TX, October 17–19).

Lo, Andrew W., and A. Craig MacKinlay (1999) "Long-Term Memory in Stock Market Prices," chapter 6 in *A Non-Random Walk Down Wall Street*, Princeton University Press, Princeton, NJ, pp. 147–184.

Los, Cornelis A. (2001) *Computational Finance: A Scientific Perspective*, World Scientific Publishing Co., Singapore.

Mallat, Stéphane (1998) "A Theory for Multiresolution Signal Decomposition: The Wavelet Representation," *IEEE Transactions on Pattern Analysis and Machine Intelligence*, **11**(7), July, 674–693.

Mallat, S., and W. L. Hwang (1992) "Singularity Detection and Processing with Wavelets," *IEEE Transactions on Information Theory*, **38**(2), 617–643.

Mallat, S., and S. Zhong (1992) "Characterization of Signals From Multiscale Edges," *IEEE Transactions on Pattern Recognition and Machine Intelligence*, **14**(7), 710–732.

Mandelbrot, Benoit B. (1972) "Possible Refinement of the Lognormal Hypothesis Concerning the Distribution of Eenergy Dissipation in Intermittent Turbulence," in Rosenblatt, M., and C. Van Atta (Eds) *Statistical Models and Turbulence*, Lecture Notes in Physics, 12, Springer Verlag, New York, NY, pp. 333–351.

Mandelbrot, Benoit B. (1997) *Fractals and Scaling in Finance: Discontinuity, Concentration, Risk*, Springer Verlag, New York, NY.

Mandelbrot, Benoit B. (1999) *Multifractals and 1/f Noise: Wild Self-Affinity in Physics (1963–1976)*, Springer Verlag, New York, NY.

Mandelbrot, Benoit, B. (2002) *Gaussian Self-Affinity and Fractals: Globality, The Earth, 1/f Noise, and R/S*, Springer Verlag, New York, NY.

Meneveau, C. M., and K. R. Sreenivasan (1987a) "Simple Multifractal Cascade Model for Fully Developed Turbulence," *Physical Review Letters*, **59**(13), 1424–1427.

Meneveau, C. M., and K. R. Sreenivasan (1987b) "The Multifractal Spectrum of the Dissipation Field in Turbulent Flows," *Nuclear Physics*, B, Proceedings Supplement, **2**, 49–76.

Meneveau, C. M., and K. R. Sreenivasan (1991) "The Multifractal Nature of Turbulent Energy Dissipation," *Journal of Fluid Mechanics*, **224**, 429–484.

Müller, U. A., M. M. Dacorogna, R. B. Olsen, O. V. Pictet, M. Schwarz and C. Morgenegg (1990) "Statistical Study of Foreign Exchange Rates, Empirical Evidence of a Price Scaling Law, and Intraday Analysis," *Journal of Banking and Finance*, **14**, 1189–1208.

Osborne, A., and A. Provenzale (1989) "Finite Correlation Dimension for Stochastic Systems with Power-Law Spectra," *Physica*, D, **35**, 357–382.

Parisi, G., and U. Frisch (1985) "On the Singularity Structure of Fully Developed Turbulence," in Ghil, M., R. Benzi and G. Parisi (Eds) *Turbulence and Predictability in Geophysical Fluid Dynamics, Proceedings of the International School of Physics*, E. Fermi, 1983, North-Holland Publishing Co., Amsterdam, pp. 84–87.

Pincus, S., and B. H. Singer (1996) "Randomness and Degrees of Irregularity," *Proceedings of the National Academy of Sciences (USA)*, **93**(5), 2083–2088.

Poterba, James M., and Lawrence H. Summers (1988) "Mean Reversion in Stock Prices: Evidence and Implications," *Journal of Financial Economics*, **22**(1), 27–60.

Schnidrig, Remo, and Diethelm Würtz (1995) "Investigation of the Volatility and Autocorrelation Function of the USDDEM Exchange Rate on Operational Time Scales," Interdisciplinary Project Center for Supercomputing (IPS) Research Report No. 95-04, Eidgenössische Technische Hochschule, Zürich.

Schroeder, Manfred (1991) "Multifractals: Intimately Intertwined Fractals," in *Fractals, Chaos, Power Laws: Minutes from an Infinite Paradise*, W. H. Freeman and Co., New York, NY, pp. 187–210.

Strang, Gilbert, and Truong Nguyen (1997) *Wavelets and Filter Banks*, Cambridge Press, Wellesley, MA.

Struzik, Zbigniew R. (2001) "Wavelet Methods in (Financial) Time-Series Processing," *Physica*, A, **296**, 307–319.

Theiler, J. (1987) "Efficient Algorithm for Estimating the Correlation Dimension from a Set of Discrete Points," *Physics Review*, A, **36**(9), 4456–4462.

Torrence, Christopher, and Gilbert P. Compo (1998) "A Practical Guide to Wavelet Analysis," *Bulletin of the American Meteorological Society*, **79**(1), 61–78.

Whitcher, B., S. D. Byers, P. Guttorp and D. B. Percival (2002) "Testing for Homogeneity of Variance in Time Series: Long Memory, Wavelets and the Nile River," *Water Resources Research*, **38**(5), 1029–1039.

Wornell, Gregory W. (1993) "Wavelet-Based Representations for the 1/f Family of Fractal Processes," *Proceedings of the IEEE*, **81**(10), 1428–1450.

Wornell, G. W., and A. V. Oppenheim (1992) "Estimation of Fractal Signals From Noisy Measurements Using Wavelets," *IEEE Transactions of Signal Processing*, **40**, 611–623.

Part III

Term structure dynamics

Part 12

9 Chaos – nonunique equilibria processes

9.1 Introduction

Chaos theory, a modern theory development in mathematics and science, provides a framework for understanding irregular, intermittent and turbulent fluctuations (Gleick, 1987; Lorenz, 2001). Chaotic systems are found in many fields of science and engineering (Hall, 1991; Prigogine, 1997). The study of their dynamics is an essential part of the burgeoning science of *complexity* (Nicolis and Prigogine, 1998). Complexity science researches the behavior of nonlinear dynamic processes and has now reached advanced financial time series analysis, but mostly in academic circles (Parker and Chua, 1987; Savit, 1988; Abarnel, 1994; Patterson and Ashley, 2000); and, in particular after the stock market crash of October 19, 1987, in the form of a search for chaos in the financial markets (Hsieh, 1991, 1993; Urbach, 2000). However, the initial assessment by these analysts was clearly misdirected, since the stock market crash of October 19, 1987 was a discontinuity occurring in a persistent financial market, i.e., a clear example of market failure or inefficiency. In contrast, turbulence is a phenomenon that can only occur in antipersistent financial markets, i.e., in hyper-efficient markets like the foreign exchange (FX) markets we discussed in Chapter 8, and which we will continue to discuss in Chapter 11, when we examine the quantitative modeling and simulation of turbulence in FX markets.

Historically, financial economics has been cast in terms of linearized Newtonian physics, i.e., in the form of simple linear price or volatility diffusion equations. However, many phenomena in financial economics are complex, nonlinear, self-organizing, adaptive, feedback processes. An example is financial turbulence, which we currently conjecture to be a process to minimize friction between cash flows with different degrees of liquidity, with different investment horizons, or with different trading speeds, resulting in different degrees of persistence (Peters, 1994, pp. 39–64). Moreover, if an investment portfolio contains options as well as stocks, not only is the sum of lognormally distributed stock prices not lognormal, but the option price distribution is also complicated and the portfolio's rates of return form a nonlinear process. Understanding these nonlinear pricing processes is of importance to portfolio management, dynamic asset valuation, derivative pricing, hedging and trading strategies, asset allocation, risk management and the development of market neutral strategies (cf. MacDonald, 2002, pp. 763–770).

Nonlinear dynamic processes are not new to financial economists. Mandelbrot (1963) found that speculative market prices followed a fractional differentiation process and introduced the Fractional Brownian Motion (FBM) to describe these processes, as we discussed in Chapter 4 (Mandelbrot and Van Ness, 1968). More than 35 years later and using an econometric misspecification approach, Lo and MacKinlay (1999) came to the same conclusion. Moreover, nonlinear market dynamics had already been detected in high frequency, intraday trading data by Müller *et al.* (1990). Their conclusion was recently confirmed with different data sets and the more sophisticated signal processing technique of wavelet Multiresolution Analysis (MRA) by Karuppiah and Los (2000), as we discussed in Chapter 8.

Why should the study of nonlinear dynamic systems be of interest to financial economics? The simple answer is that it offers a differentiated perspective on the *predictability* in the financial markets (Franses and van Dijk, 2000). This is clearly recognized, for example, by Richard Urbach (2000), who, with a PhD in Mathematical Statistics from Columbia University, co-manages a $110 million investment fund at Panther Capital Management. Urbach has been impressed by the work of physicists on turbulence, in particular by Pawelzik and Shuster (1991). Financial processes can be differentiated according to their degree of predictability, as discussed by Edgar Peters, the Chief Investment Officer and Co-Chair of the Investment Committee of PanAgora Asset management in Boston, which manages $13+ billion in assets for pension plans, endowments, foundations, unions and financial service providers around the world. Peters discerns four cases of predictability (Peters, 1999, p. 164), as in Table 9.1.

The current financial-economic models of speculative market pricing processes are often linear or linearized, but most such models cannot differentiate between the various degrees of short- and long-term predictability. Linear models have high predictability in the long term. In order to identify financial-economic models that differentiate between the short- and long-term predictability of pricing processes, one needs to introduce nonlinearity or complexity.

Deterministic linear dynamic systems show high predictability, in the long term, deterministic nonlinear dynamic systems show high predictability in the short term, but low predictability in the long term. Random nonlinear systems, in general, show low predictability, both in the short and the long term. In contrast, complex systems show low short-term, but high long-term predictability, which is attractive to long-term institutional investors.[1]

Table 9.1 Levels of short- and long-term predictability

Short term	Long term	
	Low	High
High	Nonlinear dynamic	Linear dynamic
Low	Nonlinear random dynamic	Complex dynamic

One particular research question motivating this book is the following. Since we find that financial market pricing processes contain feedback and are nonlinear, do they have high short-term and low long-term predictability, or are they complex, with low short-term, but high long-term predictability? For example, stock market pricing processes appear to have some kind of short-term predictability, or persistence, which is exploited by technical traders, but they are often unpredictable in the longer term, to the dismay of fundamental traders and investors (Savit, 1988). In addition, stock market return series show severe discontinuities, like the US stock market crises in 1929, 1987 and, possibly, in 2002, attesting to their persistence. The same is true for bond market returns, which show sometimes abrupt discontinuities, like the defaulting Russian bond market did in 1998, when it triggered, the debacle of the Long-Term Capital Management (LTCM) company, by severely distressing the German bond market. LTCM was heavily invested in German bonds, issued by German banks, which were heavily invested in Russian bonds.

On the other hand, FX pricing processes are unpredictable, or antipersistent, in the short term, but they tend to show some kind of global predictability in the longer term. For example, they appear to be rather resilient to exogenous shocks, like the European Monetary System (EMS) break in 1993, or the Thai baht break on July 2, 1997, or to any other drastic revaluation of a pegged or currency-board-controlled currency like the Argentinian Peso in the spring of 2002. FX processes do not often show sharp discontinuities. In fact, the Thai baht break in 1997 was exceptional. It was probably induced by malfunctioning fundamental asset markets, e.g., of commercial bank loans, in the Southeast Asian region, following the confidence reducing handover of Hong Kong on July 1, 1997 by a colonial capitalist United Kingdom to a communist mainland China. Perhaps, the best characterization of FX processes is that the innovations in FX rates show intermittency: periods of stability and persistence are interrupted by periods of instability and chaos.

Remark 369 *As the evidence in Chapter 1 shows, the rates of investment return: (1) are highly complex with structures at all frequency and time scales; (2) are mostly unpredictable in their detailed behavior; (3) have some properties, like their statistical distributions, that are quite reproducible and which can be captured in histograms and which can often be often summarized in a few moment statistics.*

In this chapter, we'll simulate and analyze the properties of a particular complex, nonlinear (parabolic) feedback process in an effort to understand these various predictability regimes. Parabolic (= quadratic) deterministic processes exhibit a whole range of behaviors, determined by the values of their main scaling parameter(s). We run simulation experiments with the so-called *logistic parabola*, since that is a simple discrete version of the celebrated Navier–Stokes partial differentiation equation, which can describe (physical) turbulence. In particular, we'll observe four types of behavioral regimes generated by this model, depending on the value of its scaling parameter: (1) regimes of unique dynamic equilibria;

(2) regimes of complex multiple dynamic equilibria; (3) regimes of intermittency, i.e., a mixture of multiple dynamic equilibria and chaos and (4) complete chaos.

Visualization of the distributions of intermittency and of complete chaos, i.e., of deterministically random behavior, and particularly the visualization of the chaotic attractor, produces several jarring surprises for conventional-probability and linearity-based statistics (Parker and Chua, 1987). Such experiments with the simple logistic parabola convincingly demonstrate that complex behavior does not necessitate the formulation of complex laws. Very simple nonlinear laws, like the Black–Scholes diffusion equation of a derivatives price, can produce very complex and unpredictable behavior based on a simple iterative feedback process.

One of the goals of empirical financial market research has been to identify the strange attractors present in chaotic time series and to measure their dimensions, which has not been an easy task. The most reliable identification of the chaotic dimension D had been when the inequality $D > 6$. For chaotic systems with $3 < D \leq 6$, it has been rather difficult to distinguish between chaotic time evolution and a purely random process, especially if the underlying deterministic dynamics are unknown. That is why even Mantegna and Stanley (2000, p. 5) despairingly state: "Hence, from an empirical point of view, it is quite unlikely that it will be possible to discriminate between chaotic and random hypotheses." That's also why in this chapter we mostly focus on *simulation* and not on the still not completely solved *identification* of the underlying real complex system, like we did in the preceding chapters. In this fashion we gain an intuitive understanding of the phenomena of turbulence and chaos.

However, we should not completely give up on the identification of complex systems, as Nicolis and Prigogine (1998) do and as we demonstrate through a very simple visualization technique of Mindlin and Gilmore (1992), also reported in Urbach (2000). This technique exploits the occasional aperiodic cyclicity of intermittency and turbulence to detect its attracting points and aperiodic orbits. The technique can be further improved by using wavelet MRA, as will be discussed in Chapter 10, so that it allows a sharp discrimination between a chaotic and random process, refuting Mantegna and Stanley's pessimism regarding the possibility of identifying the correct processes.

9.2   Logistic parabola regimes

Let's start with the simple definition of a logistic dynamic process, where $x(t)$ may be the relative increments of a market price of a security (a stock or a bond) or of an FX rate. The logistic parabola has been used to model nonlinearly restrained growth processes and has been applied in many fields, in particular in ecology and in socio-economics. In this chapter, we'll simulate, visualize and analyze its most salient features, in particular the self-similarities generated by its nonlinear iteration. We'll also compute Hurst exponents of its various stability regimes using wavelet MRA. This will demonstrate why it is difficult, if not impossible, to characterize the various stability regimes of the logistic process by the Hurst exponent, since it has a too limited range, and why we need to compute the multifractal spectrum of the heterogeneous Lipschitz-α_L.[2] We'll look at the stable and unstable regimes of the logistic parabolic process, the deterministic chaos it can produce, its bifurcation and phase shifting phenomena, its intermittency and the surprising shape of the frequency distribution of complete chaos.

Let's first formally define the logistic parabolic dynamic process.

Definition 370 *The* logistic parabola *is the following parabolic difference equation*

$$x(t) = f(x)$$
$$= \kappa x(t-1)[1 - x(t-1)]$$
$$= \kappa x(t-1) - \kappa[x(t-1)]^2$$
$$\text{with } 0 \leq x(t) < 1 \quad \text{and} \quad 0 \leq \kappa \leq 4 \tag{9.1}$$

where κ is a real number, for physical reasons. This equation can also be written as:

$$\Delta x(t) = -\kappa[x(t-1)]^2 + (\kappa - 1)x(t-1) \tag{9.2}$$

Remark 371 *This logistic parabola, or* quadratic map, *was introduced in 1845 by the Belgian sociologist and mathematician Pierre-Francois Verhulst (1804–1849) to model the growth of populations limited by finite resources (Verhulst, 1845). The designation* logistic, *however, did not come into general use until 1875. It is derived from the French* logistique, *referring to the* lodgment *of troops, given finite resources. Interesting details of this logistic process, particularly about its strange attractor set, can be found in Schroeder (1991). Notice that there is no harm in assuming that the variable x is suitably scaled so as to lie between zero and one.*

Remark 372 *The range of $x(t)$ represents a percentage between zero and one. When multiplied by a constant, it can represent the diffusion of a dynamic volatility of a financial market, or the price diffusion of a derivative.*

The logistic parabola is an extremely simple nonlinear difference equation, which consists of a linear element, $(\kappa - 1)x(t-1)$, representing the one-period (feedback) delay or "viscosity," and a nonlinear, quadratic or parabolic element, $-\kappa[x(t-1)]^2$, representing the quadratic or parabolic resource constraint. It exhibits stable, bifurcating, intermittent and completely chaotic process regimes for certain values of the scaling parameter κ, caused by its implied iterative, binomial "folding" process. The process can swing from stable behavior to intermittent behavior, and then back to chaotic behavior, by relatively small changes in the value of its single *scaling* or *stability parameter* κ (Feigenbaum, 1981).[3] This scaling parameter κ governs the transitions between the various stability regimes of this nonlinear dynamic feedback process.

Example 373   *Let's look at the standard theoretical Black–Scholes continuous time framework for derivatives pricing and see how it relates to the logistic equation. Suppose that the price of the underlying asset $X(t)$ is governed by the Geometric Brownian Motion (GBM), which is called in finance a* one-factor affine model, *because it is driven by one stochastic process $z(t)$:*

$$dX(t) = \mu X(t)dt + \sigma X(t)dz(t) \tag{9.3}$$

where $z(\tau)$ is a normalized Wiener process, $z(\tau) \sim N(0, \tau)$. Assume that there is a constant risk-free rate r. Finally, suppose that the price of the derivative of the underlying asset is some unknown time-dependent function $f[X(t), t]$. Then it can be shown, by implementing Itô's Lemma, that the price of the derivative follows the following forced parabolic diffusion process:

$$\frac{\partial f[X(t), t)]}{\partial t} = -rX(t)\frac{\partial f[X(t), t]}{\partial X(t)} - \frac{1}{2}\sigma^2 X(t)^2\frac{\partial^2 f[X(t), t]}{\partial X(t)^2}$$
$$+ rf[X(t), t] \tag{9.4}$$

which is the Black–Scholes equation (Luenberger, 1998, p. 439). Interestingly, this Black–Scholes derivatives pricing equation has three interpretations: (1) the no-arbitrage interpretation that a combination of two risky assets can reproduce a risk-free asset and its rate of return must be identical to the risk-free rate r; (2) the interpretation that this is a backward solution process of the risk-neutral pricing formula; and (3) the interpretation that this equation is a special case of the log-optimal pricing formula. The parabolic viscosity *term $-\frac{1}{2}\sigma^2 X(t)^2(\partial^2 f[X(t), t])/(\partial X(t)^2)$ governs the global behavior of this Black–Scholes equation, while the* convection *term $-rX(t)\partial f[X(t), t]/\partial X(t)$ is the feedback delay term. In particular, the viscosity term $-1/2\sigma^2\partial^2 f[X(t), t]/\partial X(t)^2$ corresponds with the scaling parameter κ in the logistic equation. The value of this term determines if and when the behavior of the diffusion is stable, intermittent or chaotic. Examples of such single factor price diffusion processes used for bond option pricing are the Vasicek (1977) and extended Vasicek* mean-reversion *models (Jamshidian, 1989). We'll encounter such one-factor models again in Chapter 10.*

Example 374   *Other authors have explicitly constructed mathematical financial models with the built-in capacity to produce chaotic behavior. For example, Tice and Webber (1997) devised a* three-factor *model to explain the term structure of interest rates, with two linear factors and one quadratic, which is a stochastic version of the original Lorenz system of differential equations (Lorenz, 2001). The three factors in their financial model are the short-term interest rate $r(t)$, the short rate reversion level $x(t)$ and a feedback parameter $p(t)$, with the following* *stochastic processes:*[4]

$$dr(t) = \alpha[x(t) - r(t)]dt + \sigma_r dz_r(t) \tag{9.5}$$

$$dx(t) = \beta\{p(t)r(t) + [1 - p(t)]\mu - x(t)\}dt + \sigma_x dz_x(t) \tag{9.6}$$

$$dp(t) = \gamma\{\delta - \phi[x(t) - \mu][r(t) - \mu] - p(t)\}dt + \sigma_p dz_p(t) \tag{9.7}$$

If $\phi = 0$, so that $p(t)$ has no cross-products in its drift, then this model reduces to a simple three-factor affine interest rate model. The quadratic cross-product term $[x(t) - \mu][r(t) - \mu]$ is sufficient to cause this dynamic system to become chaotic. The first two equations are a generalized Vasicek mean-reversion model where $r(t)$ reverts to $x(t)$ and $x(t)$ reverts to the weighted sum of $r(t)$ and a constant μ. This nonlinear model generalizes the drift functions of Hull and White (1993), and Bakshi and Chen (1997), whose models have $p(t) = 0$. It also generalizes a drift function used by Babbs and Webber (1994). Models of this sort have been extensively studied by Beaglehole and Tenney (1991). James and Webber (2001, pp. 284–290) provide an economic justification for this "IS–LM based" model and simulate it with what they call "reasonable" parameter values $(\alpha, \beta, \gamma, \delta, \mu, \phi) = (5, 0.5, \frac{5}{12}, 23, 0.1, 22{,}000)$, although they don't provide any justification why these calibration values are "reasonable." Their simulation produces an interesting cyclical and apparently intermittent time series behavior for the short-term rate $r(t)$.

Remark 375 *As we will see in Chapter 11, the dynamic Navier–Stokes equation describes the energy diffusion process of the physical flow of an incompressible fluid and it provides a theoretical model for laminar flow, intermittency and turbulence (Navier, 1823). It is the proto model for the Black–Scholes equation. The logistic parabola simulated and analyzed in this chapter has been called the "poor man's Navier–Stokes equation" (Frisch, 1995, p. 31). It can be rewritten in a way paralleling the continuous time (unforced) Navier–Stokes equation, because it has a nonlinear, parabolic term, representing the imposed nonlinear resource constraint, and a linear delay, or viscosity, term.*

9.2.1 Stability and dynamic persistence regimes

The various process regimes of the logistic parabola are summarized by the following *Feigenbaum diagram*, or "fig tree" plot in Figure 9.1, which shows the steady-state equilibrium values of $x(t)$ in the observation range $t = 101, \ldots, 200$ for various values of the scaling parameter κ, which is the sole control parameter of the logistic process.

Notice in Figure 9.1 at the far left the unique stationary, timeless, homogeneous states of equilibrium for $\kappa < 3$, and the apparent multiplicity of equilibrium states after the critical value of $\kappa = 3.0$. The first bifurcation occurs at $\kappa = 3.0$. Then there is a cascade of supercritical, period-doubling pitchfork bifurcations (to be explained in later sections of this chapter) and $180°$ phase shifting crossovers for

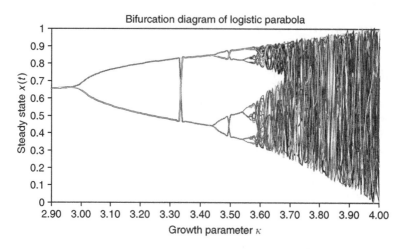

Figure 9.1 Nonunique dynamic equilibria of the logistic parabola. At the far left, the stable, so-called thermodynamic path splits into two paths when $\kappa = 3.00$. There is a clear $180°$ phase shift at $\kappa = 3.34$. The next bifurcations occur at $\kappa = 3.45$, with $180°$ phase shifts at close to $\kappa = 3.50$.

$3 < \kappa < 3.6$, followed by moderate chaos. The shading in Figure 9.1 clearly shows that there are $180°$ phase shifts in the process paths, signifying the occurrence of *bi-stability* along particular paths. The first crossover $180°$ phase shift occurs at $\kappa = 3.34$. This is followed by a set of bifurcations at $\kappa = 3.45$, followed by another phase shift at $\kappa = 3.50$, etc.

In the post $\kappa = 3.0$ regime in Figure 9.1, the steady-state equilibrium value of $x(t)$ is strictly unpredictable, because it depends on the initial state value and the precision of the computations or computation noise. However, it can be characterized by one or the other path. This simultaneous dependence of the system on different steady-state equilibrium paths according to past history is called *hysteresis*.[5]

Figure 9.2 provides the corresponding Hurst exponents, computed from only three resolution levels of wavelet resonance coefficients, indicating the relative persistence of the logistic process for various values of κ.[6] For $H = 0.5$ the process is white noise or non-persistent; for $0 < H < 0.5$ the process is antipersistent; for $0.5 < H < 1$ the process is persistent.

Notice in Figure 9.2, that sharp changes in the Hurst exponent do indicate the bifurcations. At $\kappa = 3.0$ the simple symmetry of the steady-state equilibrium is broken. Between $\kappa = 3.0$ and $\kappa = 3.45$ the Hurst exponent is homogeneous $H = 0.924$, indicating substantial persistence, because of the resulting bi-stability. At $\kappa = 3.45$ many more bifurcations appear and the Hurst exponent drops in value to the antipersistent level of $H = 1/3$. At $\kappa = 3.6$ chaos appears, in the sense that the Hurst exponent has no homogeneous value. The Hurst exponent

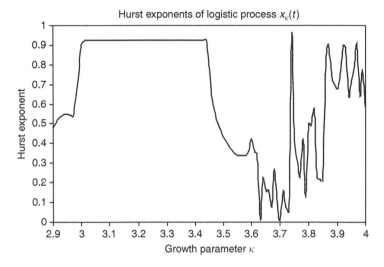

Figure 9.2 The Hurst exponent may not be the best measure of the global dependence of intermittent and chaotic processes, although a sharp change in the Hurst exponent tends to indicate a bifurcation. Unique or bi-modal equilibria result in homogeneous Hurst exponents indicating high persistence, while multi-equilibria result in Hurst exponents indicating antipersistence. Most surprising is that intermittency and complete chaos tends to result in homogeneous Hurst exponents indicating persistence of the degree observed in empirical stock markets.

drops sharply to below $H = 0.2$ and even reaches a few times its extreme value of $H = 0$ in both cases. Obviously, the Hurst exponent, which measures the relative persistence of a process, does not detect the phase shifts in the process at $\kappa = 3.34$ and $\kappa = 3.50$.

Chaos, which is unpredictable, nonunique deterministic evolutionary behavior, appears in the range $3.6 < \kappa < 4$. Here the sharp classical distinction between chance and necessity, between random and deterministic behavior is blurred and we witness the emergence of *complexity*. It appears that, in this particular range of κ, there exist *deterministic dynamic irregularity*. In this range the Hurst exponent is heterogeneous, indicating the emerging multi-fractality of the logistic process. Between $\kappa = 3.6$ and $\kappa = 3.74$, $0 < H < 0.3$ and the process becomes antipersistent. Then, at $\kappa = 3.74$ the process becomes suddenly very persistent, but immediately thereafter, between $\kappa = 3.74$ and $\kappa = 3.83$, $0.3 < H < 0.6$, the process is only moderately antipersistent. This situation of moderate antipersistence, with occasional moderate persistence is similar to the situation observed in the FX markets.

In particular, this moderate chaos regime is interleaved at certain values of κ with periodic "windows" of relative calm and persistence. The most prominent being the three-period window starting at $\kappa = 1 + 2\sqrt{2} = 3.83$. Once the period length three has been observed, all possible periods and frequencies appear and complete deterministic chaos results (Li and Yorke, 1975). Interestingly, after $\kappa = 3.83$, $0.6 < H < 0.9$: chaos has become, counter-intuitively, persistent, because of the emergence of "complex structure," and "self-organization" of the simplest inter-folding dynamic feedback processes. However, on very close detailed observation, within the three-period window period-doubling reappear, leading to stable orbits of period length $3 \times 2 = 6$, $3 \times 2^2 = 12$, $3 \times 2^3 = 24$, etc., and renewed chaos, in which another three-period window is embedded, and so on, *ad infinitum* into other *self-similar cascades of orbits* of period length 3×2^n. There we enter the final process regime of turbulence. We'll see that the cascades of dynamic orbits start to form 1-dimensional (1D) "vortices."[7]

Now, we'll first discuss each of the four regimes of evolutionary behavior of the logistic parabolic process in a cursory fashion at low values of t to see how quickly the dynamic process stabilizes. Notice the changes in the behavior of $x(t)$, by looking at its first 20 iterations, $t = 1, \ldots, 20$, for various values of the scaling parameter κ, starting at $x(0) = 0.1$ in Figure 9.3.[8]

When $\kappa = 1.5$, $x(t)$ reaches its steady state of $x^* = \frac{1}{3}$ at about $t = 8$. When $\kappa = 2.0$, $x(t)$ reaches its steady state of $x^* = \frac{1}{2}$ at about $t = 4$. In these regimes of unique uniform steady states (which are also asymptotically stable), the system ignores time. Once it has reached a steady state, it does not matter where we are in time: the value of the system remains one and the same for each t. These dynamic regimes are thus uniquely Newtonian and stationary.

But for $\kappa = 3.2$, the system produces oscillations between two steady states. First, it appears to settle in a periodic rhythm by about $t = 16$. Now the system is clearly time-dependent: it differs in value depending on the phase of the periodicity.

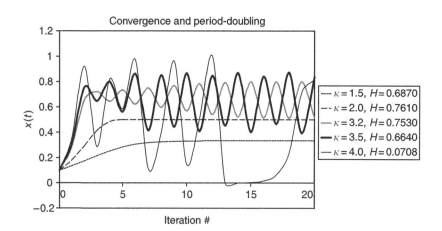

Figure 9.3 The various stability regimes of the logistic process are determined by the value of the scaling parameter κ: from stationarity ($\kappa = 1.5$ and 2.0), via oscillation ($\kappa = 3.2$), to overlapping oscillations ($\kappa = 3.5$), to aperiodic cyclicity ($\kappa = 4.0$).

For about $\kappa = 3.5$, there appear to be two different periodicities superimposed on each other and thus oscillations between four different steady states. For $\kappa = 4$, any specific periodicity has completely vanished, although there are still aperiodic cyclical oscillations.

The Hurst exponent, which ranges between 0 and 1, computed for these first 20 observations, is $H \geq 0.664 > 0.5$ for $\kappa = 1.5$, 2.0, 3.2 and 3.5, indicates that these particular logistic processes are persistent or pink, i.e., between white and red noise. But $H = 0.07 < 0.5$ for $\kappa = 4.0$, indicating that this chaotic process is initially antipersistent or light blue.

The completely chaotic process at $\kappa = 4.0$ is very unstable: the logistic process is extremely sensitive to the initial condition, i.e., to the starting point of the process $x(0)$. Small changes in the initial condition lead to large amplifications of the effects of these changes. In Figure 9.4, we show two paths for $x(t)$ for when $x(0) = 0.100000$ and when $x(0) = 0.100001$, with a small change in the sixth position after the decimal point.

Notice that until the two process traces split, they are exactly the same: their maxima and minima follow in exactly the same order at the same time. But at iteration 15, the temporal symmetry of the steady-state solutions is broken: the equilibrium has become time-dependent. Meteorological processes are often considered to exhibit regime changes, from stable to chaotic regimes. An even simpler example of such a regime change is visible in the smoke rising from a burning cigarette. When it arises from a cigarette, the smoke is first a smooth stable laminar flow, until it rather suddenly becomes a chaotic "whirl."

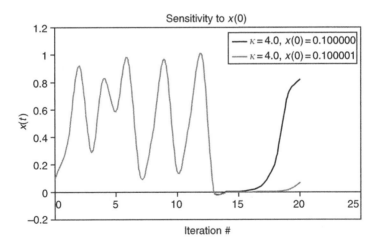

Figure 9.4 When a dynamic process is chaotic, its later values are directly dependent on the precision of its initial condition. Here a small change in the sixth digit after the decimal point of the initial condition only causes a change in the equilibrium part after 15 iterations.

We will now discuss the four major stability regimes of the logistic process in greater detail, visualize them, and then algebraically analyze when and why these various dynamic regimes occur.

9.2.2   Steady-state solutions

Since we observed that the logistic process stabilizes rather quickly to its steady states, in the following only its equilibria are analyzed. These equilibria are strictly dependent on the scaling parameter κ. For values of $0 < \kappa < 3.0$, the logistic process settles to a unique static equilibrium, as follows.

Definition 376   *The static equilibrium or steady-state solution is reached when*

$$x(t) = x(t-1) = x^*, \quad a\ constant \tag{9.8}$$

For the 1-orbit, from solving the not iterated logistic equation,

$$\kappa x^*(1 - x^*) = \kappa x^* - \kappa(x^*)^2$$
$$= x^* \tag{9.9}$$

for a nontrivial steady-state solution

$$x^* = \frac{\kappa - 1}{\kappa} \tag{9.10}$$

The slope of the logistic parabola is

$$\frac{\partial x(t)}{\partial x(t-1)} = \kappa[1 - 2x(t-1)] \tag{9.11}$$

which equals κ for $x(t-1) = 0$ and $2 - \kappa$ for the unique steady-state solution $x^* = (\kappa - 1)/\kappa$.[9]

This dynamic equilibrium is stable as long as the absolute value of the slope of the logistic parabola is smaller than unity:

$$\left| \frac{\partial x(t)}{\partial x(t-1)} \right| = |\kappa[1 - 2x(t-1)]| < 1 \tag{9.12}$$

Since this is a quadratic equation there must, in principle, be two steady-state solutions. The first trivial steady-state solution $x(t-1) = x^* = 0$ is stable for $0 \le \kappa < 1$, and marginally stable for $\kappa = 1$, but it is unstable for $1 < \kappa$.

The second nontrivial steady-state solution $x^* = (\kappa - 1)/\kappa$ is stable for $1 < \kappa < 3$, because then

$$\left| \frac{\partial x(t)}{\partial x(t-1)} \right| < 1 \tag{9.13}$$

For example when $\kappa = 1.5$, $x^* = \frac{1}{3}$ and $|\partial x(t)/\partial x(t-1)| = 0.5$. When $\kappa = 2.0$, $x^* = \frac{1}{2}$, and $|\partial x(t)/\partial x(t-1)| = 0$. The steady state $x^* = \frac{1}{2}$ is always *superstable* (with period length 1), and convergence to this particular state is always very rapid.

However, something happens when $\kappa = 3$. At $\kappa = 3$ the steady state is $x^* = \frac{2}{3}$, but the slope of the logistic parabola is $|\partial x(t)/\partial x(t-1)| = 1$ and the process no longer converges (= stably attracted) to the point x^*! This particular steady state is *marginally stable*: nearby values of $x(t)$ are no longer attracted to, nor repelled from the point $x^* = \frac{2}{3}$. The dynamic process has become indecisive or uncertain.

9.2.3 Mathematical self-organization: period-doubling

What happens is that at $\kappa = 3$ actually two possible steady-state solutions x^* appear, where one was a fixed attraction point. Initially these two steady-state solutions were very close together, but clearly separated, between which the process $x(t)$ alternates, as indicated by points x_0 and x_1 of the logistic parabola for $\kappa = 3.24$ in Figure 9.5. The result is a cobweb process that does not converge to one fixed point, but remains orbiting between the two attracting points. This cobweb pattern is essentially a *vortex*. The process remains very predictable, since the oscillation between the two stable states is periodic, as can be observed in the time series plot of $x(t)$ in Figure 9.6.[10] When $x(t)$ is shocked at the scaling parameter value immediately above $\kappa = 3$, it still quickly returns to this periodic oscillation

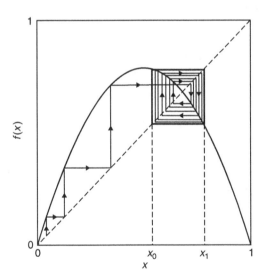

Figure 9.5 After a fixed attraction point turns unstable, an orbit of period length $p = 2$ emerges. The orbit of the logistic process is here depicted for scaling parameter $\kappa = 3.24$.

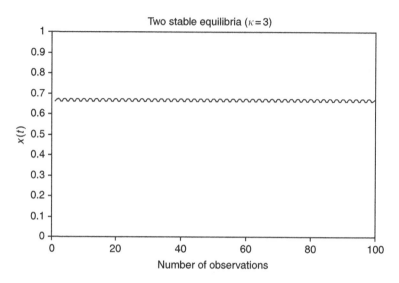

Figure 9.6 Period-doubling appears first at a scaling parameter value just above $\kappa = 3$ in the form of a tiny oscillation in the value of $x(t)$ over time, between two steady-state equilibrium states.

sequence, which therefore represents a dynamic steady-state equilibrium. This event, which emerges at scaling parameter value, $\kappa = 3$ is called a (*Myrberg*) *bifurcation* or *period-doubling* of the steady-state equilibrium (Auerbach *et al.*, 1987).

Let's first analyze this regime with two steady-state equilibria. A cyclical trajectory, or orbit, having a period length of $p = 2$, is called a 2-orbit. It is the steady-state solution x^*, which satisfies the $1\times$ iterated logistic equation:

$$f(f(x^*)) = \kappa\{\kappa x^*(1 - x^*)[1 - \kappa x^*(1 - x^*)]\} = x^* \qquad (9.14)$$

The relationship between the parabolic map for an orbit of period length $p = 2$ and the $1\times$ iterated logistic equation $f(f(x^*)) = f^{(2)}(x^*) = x^*$ is presented in Figure 9.7.

The value of κ for the superstable steady-state solutions $x^* = 0.5$ is obtained from solving this once iterated logistic equation

$$\kappa\{0.5\kappa(1 - 0.5)[1 - 0.5\kappa(1 - 0.5)]\} = 0.5 \qquad (9.15)$$

or

$$\kappa^3 - 4\kappa^2 + 8 = 0 \qquad (9.16)$$

which has three solutions for the scaling parameter: $\kappa = 2$. These solutions correspond, first, to $x^* = 0.5$, $\kappa = 1 + \sqrt{5} = 3.2361$, second, to $x^* = 0.8090$, and, third, to the inadmissible solution $\kappa = 1 - \sqrt{5} = -1.2361 < 0$.

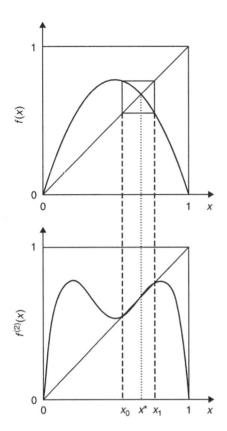

Figure 9.7 The relationship between the parabolic map $f(x)$ for an orbit of period
length $p = 2$ and the $1\times$ iterated map $f^{(2)}(x)$ with the two stable steady-
state equilibria points x_0 and x_1 and the former stable fixed point x_*, which
has become unstable because of the curving of the $1\times$ iterated map, when
the scaling parameter κ increases in value above $\kappa = 3$.

Remark 377 *Solve the once iterated equation* $(1 + \sqrt{5})\{(1 + \sqrt{5})x^*(1 - x^*)$
$[1 - (1 + \sqrt{5})x^*(1 - x^*)]\} = x^*$ *for* x^*. *The growth parameter* $\kappa = 1 + \sqrt{5} =$
$3.2361 = 2/\gamma$, *where* $\gamma = 0.618, \dots$, *i.e., the golden mean.*

Thus, for $\kappa = 2$ and $\kappa = 1 + \sqrt{5}$, respectively, there are two admissible stable
steady states or frequencies, i.e., two alternating, stable orbits of period length
$p = 2$. Accordingly, $x(t)$ consecutively takes on the values $x(0) = 0.5 \to x(1) =$
$0.8090 \to x(2) = x(0) = 0.5 \to x(3) = x(1) = 0.8090$, etc. as is clearly
observed in the time series plot of $x(t)$ in Figure 9.8.

When κ is increased further, then these two steady-state equilibria points of the
once iterated logistic parabola will further separate from each other and in turn

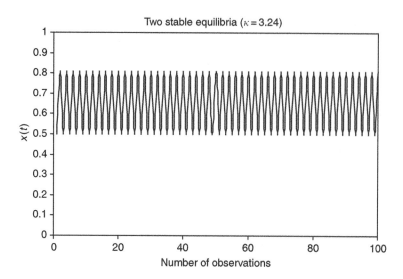

Figure 9.8 Oscillation of the logistic process between two steady-state equilibria at $x^* = 0.5$ and $x^* = 0.809$ for scaling parameter $\kappa = 1 + \sqrt{5} = 3.24$.

become unstable at precisely one and the same value of the scaling parameter κ, as shown by the $1\times$ iterated parabolic map $f^{(2)}(x)$ in Figure 9.9. It is not a coincidence that this happens at exactly the same value of κ, since, according to the chain rule of differentiation:

$$\frac{\partial}{\partial x}[f(f(x))]_{x=x(0)} = [f'(f(x))]_{x=x(0)} \cdot [f'(x)]_{x=x(0)}$$

$$= f'(x(1)) \cdot f'(x(0)) \tag{9.17}$$

When $x(0)$ becomes unstable, because

$$\left|\frac{\partial}{\partial x}[f(f(x))]_{x=x(0)}\right| > 1 \tag{9.18}$$

so does $x(1)$ at the same value of κ. Thus, both these steady-state solutions of the once iterated logistic equation $f(f(x))$ will bifurcate at the same value of the scaling parameter κ, leading to an orbit of period length $p = 2^n = 2^2 = 4$. In other words, the $3\times$ iterated logistic equation

$$f(f(f(f(x^*)))) = x^* \tag{9.19}$$

will have $n = 4$ consecutive steady-state equilibrium orbits or frequencies.

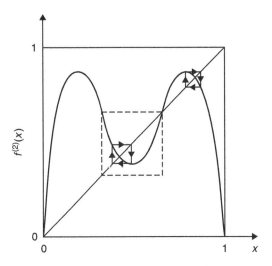

Figure 9.9 The 1× iterated map $f^{(2)}(x)$ for period length $p = 4$, with 2×2 stable steady-state equilibria and one unstable equilibrium. Notice the similarity between the contents of the (180° phase shifted) small dashed square and Figure 9.5. This self-similarity is characteristic for period-doubling and facilitates its analysis.

Again, the value of $\kappa = 3.4985$ for the superstable steady-state solutions x^* with a 4-orbit is obtained from solving the 3× iterated logistic equation

$$f(f(f(f(0.5)))) = 0.5 \tag{9.20}$$

Accordingly, $x(t)$ produces the superstable resonating orbit of period length $p = 4$ of $f(x)$: $x(0) = 0.5 \rightarrow x(1) = 0.875 \rightarrow x(2) = 0.383 \rightarrow x(3) = 0.827 \rightarrow x(4) = x(0) = 0.5$, etc. as observed in in the time series plot of $x(t)$ in Figure 9.10.

Again, because of the chain rule of differentiation, the four derivatives are the same at all four points of the orbit. Thus if, for a given value of κ, the magnitude of one of the derivatives exceeds 1, then the magnitude of each of the four derivatives will. Hence, all four iterated $x(t)$ will bifurcate at the same value of κ, leading to a cyclical trajectory, or orbit, of period length $p = 2^n = 2^3 = 8$, etc., as shown in Figure 9.11 for the 2× iterated parabolic map $f^{(3)}(x)$ for the scaling parameter $\kappa = 1 + \sqrt{2^3} + \varepsilon = 3.8284 + \varepsilon$, with very small $\varepsilon = 10^{-3}$.

In summary, the general method for finding the value of the scaling parameter κ for which a superstable orbit with period length p exists, is to solve the superstable solution equation

$$f^{(p)}(0.5) = 0.5 \tag{9.21}$$

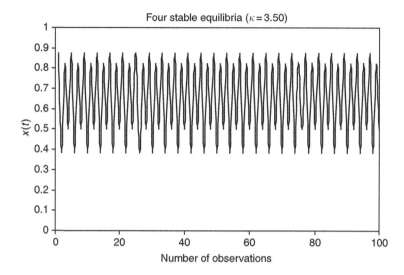

Figure 9.10 Oscillation of the logistic process between four steady-state equilibria at $x^* = 0.5$, 0.875, 0.383 and 0.827, respectively, for scaling parameter $\kappa = 3.4985$.

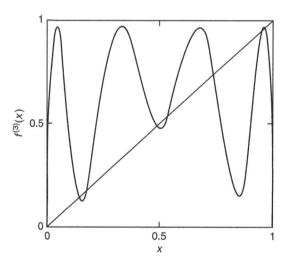

Figure 9.11 The 2× iterated parabolic map for the scaling parameter $\kappa = 1 + \sqrt{8} + 10^{-3}$. This iterated map has acquired six additional steady-state equilibria by "tangent bifurcation." Three of these equilibria are stable, i.e., with an absolute slope smaller than 1, and are members of the stable period-3 orbit visible in Figures 9.9 and 9.10.

exactly for scaling parameter κ, where p is the period length of the orbit and $f^{(p)}$ is the $(p-1)th$ iteration of the steady-state logistic parabola

$$f(x^*) = \kappa x^*(1 - x^*) \tag{9.22}$$

The other solutions then follow from all lower order orbits.

9.2.3.1 Self-similarity and scaling of the logistic parabolic process

The period-doubling transformation of the logistic parabola is asymptotically self-similar and therefore lends itself to both fractal and spectral analysis. Feigenbaum (1979) proved that this period-doubling process obeys a scaling law with the following scaling factor:

$$\alpha(n)_{n\to\infty} = \frac{x_{p/2}^{(n)} - x(0)}{x_{p/2}^{(n+1)} - x(0)} \to \alpha = -2.5029\ldots \tag{9.23}$$

where $x_{p/2}^{(n)}$ is the value of the iterate x at the half period $p/2$ for a superstable orbit of period length $p = 2^n$, with $n = log_2(p)$, starting with $x(0) = 0.5$. This scaling factor is related to Feigenbaum's *universal constant* δ, which appears in the following geometric law of the scaling parameter κ:[11]

$$\delta(n)_{n\to\infty} = \frac{\kappa^{(n)} - \kappa^{(n-1)}}{\kappa^{(n+1)} - \kappa^{(n)}} \to \delta = 4.6692016091029\ldots \tag{9.24}$$

Feigenbaum also discusses a simplified theory, which yields the following approximating relationship between the scaling factor α of the scaling parameter scaling law and the universal constant δ:

$$\delta \approx \alpha^2 + \alpha + 1 \approx 4.76 \tag{9.25}$$

9.2.3.2 Spectral analysis of periodic orbits

Since here we discuss periodic dynamic phenomena, with well-defined periodic orbits, Fourier series analysis can be applied to the resulting periodic time series. Let $c_k^{(n)}$ be the Fourier coefficient of the $x^{(n)}(t)$ for a period length $p = 2^n$. In going from an orbit of period length $p = 2^n$ by a period-doubling bifurcation to an orbit of period length $p = 2^{n+1}$, the new Fourier resonance coefficients with an even index $c_{2k}^{(n+1)}$, which describe the *harmonics* or periodicities of the regular orbits, are approximately equal to the old Fourier resonance coefficients:

$$c_{2k}^{(n+1)} \approx c_k^{(n)} \tag{9.26}$$

because periodicity causes the following equality to be approximately true:

$$x^{(n+p)}(t) \approx x^{(n)}(t) \tag{9.27}$$

The odd-indexed Fourier resonance coefficients $c_{2k+1}^{(n+1)}$, which describe the subharmonics appearing in the spectrum as a result of period-doubling, are determined by the difference

$$x^{(n+p)}(t) - x^{(n)}(t) \tag{9.28}$$

Feigenbaum (1979) showed that the squared magnitudes, or power ratios, of these odd-indexed Fourier resonance coefficients, $|c_{2k+1}^{(n+1)}|^2$, are roughly equal to an adjacent component from the previous orbit, scaled down by a factor of

$$\frac{8\alpha^4}{(1+\alpha^2)} = \frac{8(-2.5029)^4}{1+(-2.5029)^2}$$

$$= 43.217 \tag{9.29}$$

corresponding to

$$10\log_{10} 43.217 = 16.357\, dB$$

$$\approx 16\, dB \tag{9.30}$$

where dB = decibels.[12] When the scaling parameter κ is increased, more and more subharmonics appear until deterministic chaos or noise is reached, as we will discuss in the subsequent sections.

9.2.4   Intermittency and turbulence

The bifurcation scenario repeats itself as κ is increased, yielding orbits of period length $2^5 = 32$, $2^6 = 64$, etc., *ad infinitum*, until at about $\kappa = 3.6$, this dynamic process appears to become unstable. The process ends up in an undefined orbit of infinite period length, of which the time series plot as in Figure 9.12 gives only a sample "window" of 100 observations.

The cyclical trajectory or orbit is now *aperiodic*, comprising a strange point set of infinitely many values of $x(t)$ that never precisely repeat, although there is observable cyclicity. The approximate self-similarity of this point set shows Feigenbaum's self-similarity scaling factor of about $\alpha = -2.5029$. The fractal Hausdorff dimension $D = 0.538\ldots$ of this point set, which is a *Cantor set*, was derived analytically and numerically by Grassberger (1981).[13] A good approximation is:

$$D = \frac{\log \gamma}{\log \frac{1}{2.5}} \approx 0.525 \tag{9.31}$$

where the *golden mean* $\gamma = (\sqrt{5} - 1)/2 = 0.61803\ldots$. Thus this trajectory trace has a dimension almost half way in between the Euclidean dimension of a line

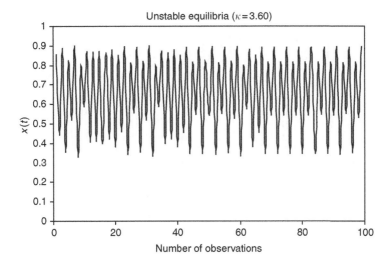

Figure 9.12 A sample window of 100 observations of an undefined orbit, or frequency, of infinite period length with scaling parameter $\kappa = 3.6$.

$(D = 1)$ and the Euclidean dimension of a set of points $(D = 0)$, with a slight balance in favor of the dimension of a line.

9.2.4.1 Intermittency

However, within the chaotic region, when $3.6 \leq \kappa < 4.0$, some "windows of stability" do occur in between periods of chaos. This alternation of stability and chaos when κ is increased is called *intermittency* (Frisch and Parisi, 1985). For example, for $\kappa = 3.82$ we have substantial intermittency or moderate chaos in the time series plot of $x(t)$ in Figure 9.13.

But then, stability reappears at the scaling parameter value of $\kappa = 1 + \sqrt{p} = 1 + \sqrt{2^3} = 3.83$. There occurs the so-called *tangent bifurcation* at the value of $\kappa = 3.83$. Figure 9.14 shows the time series plot of $x(t)$ for $\kappa = 3.83$. It looks as if for $\kappa = 3.83$ there are only two stable equilibria $x^* = 0.154$ and $x^* = 0.958$, but the process $x(t)$ passes straight through the nonattracting, now only marginally stable equilibrium $x^* = 0.5$.

Just above $\kappa = 3.83$, the now thrice iterated logistic parabola acquires six additional steady-state points x^*: three with an absolute slope $|(\partial f^{(3)}(x(t)))/(\partial x(t-1))| > 1$, which belong to the *unstable* orbit of period length 3, and three with a slope $|(\partial f^{(3)}(x(t)))/(\partial x(t-1))| < 1$, which are the three points belonging to the *stable* orbit with period length 3 and the apparent periodicity starts to break down again. Why this happens is clear from Figure 9.11, which shows the $3\times$ iterated logistic equation with the scaling parameter $\kappa = 1 + \sqrt{8} + 10^{-3}$, i.e., just above the value of $\kappa = 3.83$. Figure 9.15 shows the time series plot of $x(t)$

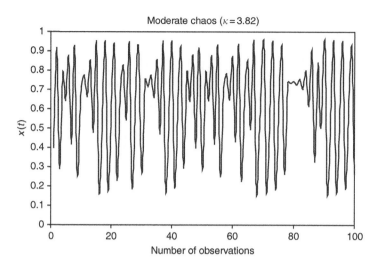

Figure 9.13 Intermittency in time series is characterized by periods of stability alternating with periods of chaos with scaling parameter $\kappa = 3.82$.

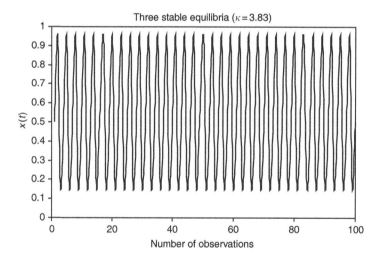

Figure 9.14 The reappearance of a period of apparent stability: periodicity with three steady-state equilibria, two stable and one unstable for $\kappa = 1 + \sqrt{8} = 3.83$.

of the three stable and the three unstable steady-state equilibria for $\kappa = 3.85$, which appears to be the same as in Figure 9.14. But then Figure 9.16 shows the same process for $\kappa = 3.86$. The renewed breakdown into intermittency, after the apparent stability at $\kappa = 3.85$, is now clearly visible.

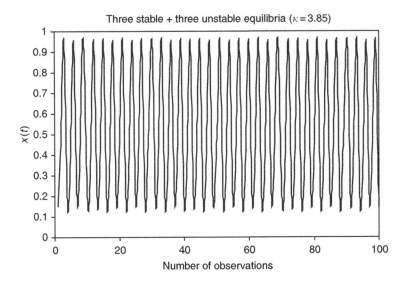

Figure 9.15 Another period of apparent stability with periodicity with six steady-state equilibria: three stable and three unstable ones for $\kappa = 3.85$. Notice that the unstable steady-state equilibria are not visible, since the time series $x(t)$ of the logistic process passes straight through these marginally stable points.

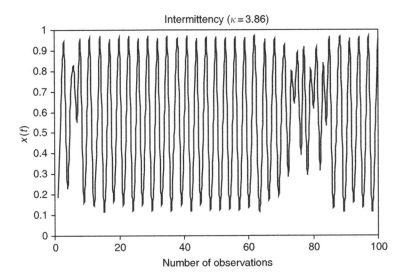

Figure 9.16 Another instance of intermittency in the time series of the logistic process, after the birth of period length 3, where the periods of apparent stability are interrupted by short periods of chaos for scaling parameter $\kappa = 3.86$.

The birth of period length 3 is one of the most intriguing research topics in the history of nonlinear dynamic theory, because it leads to the turbulence phenomena of intermittency and complete chaos (Bechhoefer, 1996; Gordon, 1996; Burm and Fishback, 2001).

Thus, we encounter the famous 3-orbit, an orbit with three distinct frequencies, which guarantees that all other orbits, or frequencies exist, albeit as unstable orbits, at the same parameter value.[14] In other words, the $2\times$ iterated process:

$$f(f(f(x^*))) = x^* \tag{9.32}$$

has a 3-orbit with three consecutive steady-state solutions x^*, which satisfies the twice iterated logistic parabola:

$$f(f(f(0.5))) = \kappa \left[\begin{array}{c} \kappa\{0.5\kappa(1-0.5)[1-0.5\kappa(1-0.5)]\} \\ \times(1-\kappa\{0.5\kappa(1-0.5)[1-0.5\kappa(1-0.5)]\}) \end{array} \right]$$

$$= \frac{\kappa^3}{4}\left(\frac{4-\kappa}{4}\right)\left(1 - \frac{\kappa^2}{4}\left(\frac{4-\kappa}{4}\right)\right) = 0.5 \tag{9.33}$$

or

$$\kappa^3(4-\kappa)(16-4\kappa^2+\kappa^3) - 128 = 0 \tag{9.34}$$

This polynomial in κ has seven exact solutions, three of which are real and four of which are conjugate complex. Numerically, these solutions are:[15]

- $\kappa = 2$, which corresponds with the superstable equilibrium $x^* = 0.5$.
- $\kappa = 3.832$, which corresponds with the equilibria $x^* = 0$ (marginally stable), $x^* = 0.154$ (stable), $x^* = 0.165$ (unstable), $x^* = 0.499$ (stable), $x^* = 0.529$ (unstable), $x^* = 0.739$ (stable), $x^* = 0.955$ (unstable), $x^* = 0.958$ (stable).
- $\kappa = -1.832$, which is inadmissible, because we must have $\kappa \geq 0$.
- $\kappa = 2.553 + 0.959i$ and $2.553 - 0.959i$, which are inadmissible, because κ must be real.
- $\kappa = -0.553 + 0.959i$ and $-0.553 - 0.959i$, which are inadmissible, because κ must be real.

The eight equilibria corresponding to $\kappa = 3.832$ are found from the equation:

$$3.832\left(\begin{array}{c} 3.832(3.832x^*(1-x^*)(1-3.832x^*(1-x^*))) \\ \times(1-3.832(3.832x^*(1-x^*)(1-3.832x^*(1-x^*)))) \end{array} \right) - x^* = 0 \tag{9.35}$$

After period length 3 has appeared at $\kappa = 3.83$, orbits of any period length are possible. As Li and Yorke (1975) state "period three implies chaos." Finally, at $\kappa = 4.0$ we encounter *complete chaos*, shown by the time series plot of $x(t)$ in Figure 9.17. *Complete chaos* is thus defined by the coexistence of an infinite number of unstable deterministic orbits.

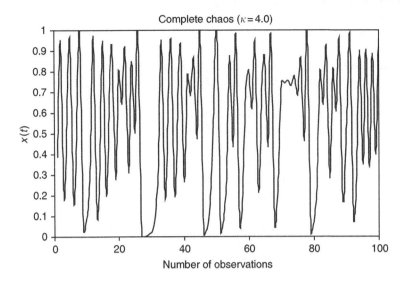

Figure 9.17 Complete chaos is defined by the coexistence of an infinite number of deterministic unstable equilibrium orbits, with the scaling parameter of the logistic process having the extreme value $\kappa = 4.0$.

9.2.4.2 *Universal order of period lengths*

The reason for the appearance of any period length, or frequency, after period length 3 is that the different period lengths or frequencies p of stable periodic orbits of unimodal maps, like the logistic parabola, *do not appear randomly*, as is often believed. In fact, these natural frequencies appear in a so-called *universal order*, as proved by Sharkovskii (1964).

Theorem 378 (Sharkovskii) *If κ_p is the value of the scaling parameter κ at which a stable period of length p first appears, as κ is increased, then $\kappa_p > \kappa_q$ if $p \succ q$ (read: period length p precedes period length q) in the following* Sharkovskii *order:*

$$3 \succ 5 \succ 7 \succ 9 \succ \cdots$$
$$2 \cdot 3 \succ 2 \cdot 5 \succ 2 \cdot 7 \succ \cdots$$
$$\cdots$$
$$2^n \cdot 3 \succ 2^n \cdot 5 \succ 2^n \cdot 7 \succ \cdots$$
$$\cdots$$
$$\cdots \succ 2^m \succ \cdots \succ 2^2 \succ 2 \succ 1$$

$$(9.36)$$

Example 379   *The minimal κ value for an orbit with period length or frequency $p = 10 = 2 \cdot 5$ is larger than the minimal κ value for $p = 12 = 2^2 \cdot 3$ because period length or frequency $10 \succ 12$.*

Remark 380   *(1) Thus, the existence of period length or frequency $p = 3$ guarantees the existence of any other period length or frequency q for some $\kappa_q < \kappa_p$. (2) If only a finite number of period lengths or frequencies occur, their frequencies must be powers of 2. (3) If a period length or frequency p exists that is not a power of 2, then there exist infinitely many different frequencies.*

Interestingly, the intervals of κ for the stable orbits are dense but not continuous. That implies that the values of the scaling parameter κ for which no stable periodic orbits exist form no closed intervals: they are fractal (Grebogi *et al.*, 1988). Nevertheless, they possess a positive Lebesgue measure. This means that a random choice of the scaling parameter κ has a *nonvanishing probability* of leading to an aperiodic cycle, orbit or frequency. These aperiodic orbits, cycles or frequencies are thus not "unlikely." They have a particular probability of occurrence, although that probability may be extremely small.

9.2.5   Complete chaos

With $\kappa = 4$, the process has become *completely chaotic*. In Figure 9.18 we look at the ultimate chaotic pattern of the logistic $x(t)$ for $\kappa = 4.0$ and $t = 101, \ldots, 1,100$. The Hurst exponent $H = 0.58$, indicating that this logistic chaos surprisingly exhibits some persistence and is not a white noise process. No pseudo-random number generator is used! The deterministic logistic parabola generates these 1,000 values of $x(t)$, after the first 100 values were discarded, starting from $x(0) = 0$. The process $x(t)$ has a bounded range: $0 \leq x(t) \leq 1$, but its mean is undefined, as is its variance, no matter how many observations generated. Ergo, the logistic chaos process is completely nonstationary or unstable. When more observations are generated, the mean and variance will continue to change.[16] There is no convergence to a unique steady-state equilibrium or to a few steady-state equilibria. There are infinitely many steady-state orbital equilibria!

Figure 9.19 is the same as Figure 9.18, but this time the dots representing the steady states are connected, to show the aperiodic oscillations with each oscillation having its own amplitude. There are as many amplitudes as there are oscillations. This chaotic noise appears to be a bit persistent, i.e., on average it moves a bit slower than white noise, because its measured homogeneous Hurst exponent $H = 0.58 > 0.5$. The fractal dimension of this continuous fractal (non-differentiable) space-filling line is: $D = 2 - H = 1.42$, which is almost halfway between the Euclidean dimension of a line ($D = 1$) and the Euclidean dimension of a flat space ($D = 2$).

Figure 9.20 shows the global frequency distribution of chaos formed by computing a histogram $H(0.10)$ with 10 percent equally spaced bins. A similar distribution of chaos was first presented by Taylor (1935, 1938; Ruelle, 1989). This frequency distribution of the 1,000 values of the constrained $x(t)$, $0 < x(t) < 1$, is not flat,

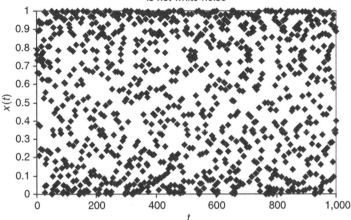

Figure 9.18 Complete logistic chaos consists of infinitely many coexisting steady-state dynamic equilibria and is not white noise. Here are 1,000 steady-state dynamic equilibrium points of the logistic process $x(t)$ for scaling parameter $\kappa = 4.0$, with a measured homogeneous Hurst exponent of $H = 0.58$.

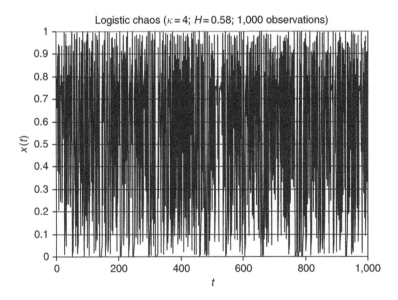

Figure 9.19 Complete chaos exhibits infinitely many aperiodic oscillations with each oscillation having its own amplitude. This graph connects the steady-state equilibrium points of Figure 9.18 and thereby shows the time series oscillations generated by the logistic process $x(t)$.

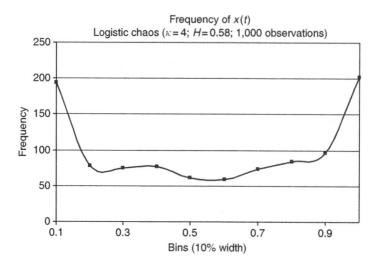

Figure 9.20 Complete chaos exhibits infinitely many aperiodic oscillations with each oscillation having its own amplitude. This graph connects the steady-state equilibrium points of Figure 9.19 and thereby shows the time series oscillations generated by the logistic process $x(t)$.

as would be the case with uniformly distributed white noise. It is highly *platykur-tic*, with a kurtosis $c_4 = -1.48$ (or a normalized kurtosis $= 3 - 1.48 = 1.52$), compared with that of the Gaussian distribution's kurtosis $c_4 = 0$ (or a normalized kurtosis $= 3$).

This surprising frequency distribution has an imploded mode and very fat tails against the "wall" constraints $x(t) = 0$ and $x(t) = 1$ that are considerably heavier than the mode. It is an example of a stable distribution with a (Zolotarev) stability exponent: $\alpha_Z = 1/H = \frac{1}{0.583} = 1.715$ and with a divergent second moment (Mandelbrot, 1974). This very heavy-tailed distribution jarringly contrasts with the conventional bell-shaped, unimodal, thin-tailed Gaussian distribution, with which most statisticians are familiar. Frequency distributions with imploded modes are not considered "normal," but may be more prevalent than is conventionally assumed.

In Figure 9.21 we present, for the very first time, a scalogram of the completely chaotic logistic parabola process with scaling parameter $\kappa = 4.0$.[17] Notice that most of the local risk appears to reside in the very small scales, although the scalegram in the lower right panel shows a "flat" spectrum with $H = 0.58$. There is a paucity of local risk at the $a = 2^5 = 32$ and $a = 2^8 = 256$ scales, respectively. Also, the scalegram does not show a constant flat spectrum and does not represent white noise: there is "periodicity" at various scale levels. The scalogram looks "choppy" with most local risk below the $a = 2^5 = 32$ scale. Our conjecture is that this scalegram is not constant when different size data sets of the complete

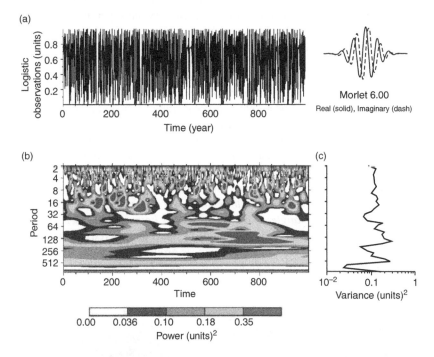

Figure 9.21 Wavelet scalogram and scalegram of the completely chaotic logistic parabola process with scaling parameter $\kappa = 4.0$. Most of the local risk appears to reside at the very small scales, but the scalegram does not show white noise. There is periodicity in chaotic noise. There is a paucity of local risk at the $a = 2^5 = 32$ and $a = 2^8 = 256$ scale levels. But there appear to be some finite dominant scale/frequency tracks at the $a = 2^6 = 64$ and $a = 2^9 = 512$ scale levels. (a) Chaotic logistic parabola data; (b) wavelet power spectrum and (c) global wavelet.

observations are analyzed, although it will remain "flat," with a homogenous Hurst exponent close to $H = 0.5$. But more study by wavelet MRA of the various dynamic regimes of the logistic parabola is required. Notice also the occurrence of finite dominant frequency tracks at the $a = 2^6 = 64$ and $a = 2^9 = 512$ scales, respectively, like in the laughter data of Figure 6.10 in Chapter 6. Compare this scalogram and scalegram also with the ones for the Mexican Pesos/USD exchange rate increments and the Chilean stock market increments, which show, perhaps, somewhat less local risk at the small-scale levels, *except where financial adjustment vortices occur.*

9.3   General nonlinear dynamic systems

Many of the properties of the logistic parabola are paradigmatic, not only for other unimodal maps, but for different nonlinear maps as well, such as the Navier–Stokes partial differential equation, which is either a model for a Black–Scholes type price diffusion equation for a derivative, or for a nonlinear volatility diffusion equation. These simple maps model a broad range of contemporary problems in which nonlinear constraints play an essential role (Lyubich, 2000).

Example 381 *Before 1900, the mathematical foundation of physics was anchored in simple* linear, *Newtonian, deterministic dynamic systems. We have now seen that simple* nonlinear *deterministic dynamic systems can generate very complex motion and even chaos. It may come as a surprise that the motion of a billiard ball – the archetypical Newtonian system – can become complex when subject to nonlinear environmental constraints. We can idealize the billiard ball as a point reflected* elastically, *i.e., without any loss of energy, from the boundary of the region in which it moves. Figure 9.22 shows what happens to the billiard ball when its motion is constrained to regions with different shapes. If the enclosure is a Euclidean rectangle or a circle, the ball bounces around in a* regular pattern. *But if the boundary is a* combination of linear and curved constraints, *like a "stadium" or like "Africa," the ball bounces around chaotically, in an* irregular pattern *(Berry, 1991, pp. 185). Recall that both the logistic parabola and the*

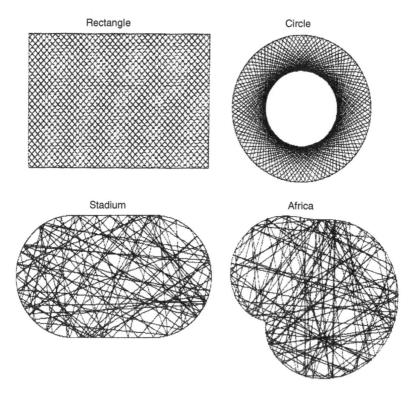

Figure 9.22 The trajectory of a billiard ball depends on the shape of the elastic boundary that constraints it. In the rectangular and circular areas, the orbits are regular, but in the "stadium" and in "Africa," they are chaotic (aperiodic cyclic).

Navier–Stokes equation have each such a combination of a linear and a nonlinear (quadratic) constraint built into their respective dynamic systems.

Therefore, we must first generalize our definition of a dynamic system to include such nonlinear dynamic systems, to better understand the concept of chaotic behavior of a financial dynamic system's evolutionary process.

Definition 382 *A dynamic system is described by its state at time t, which is a vector point $x(t)$ in a real Euclidean phase space $\mathbb{R}^D$, with (integer) dimension D, and its evolution between time t and time $t + \Delta t$ is determined by certain invariant rules. Each point in phase space can be taken as the initial state $x(0)$, and is followed by a trajectory $\mathbf{x}(t)$ for all $t > 0$.*

Let's now return to examine in detail the state space trajectory of the logistic parabola in its chaotic regime. Figure 9.23 shows the remarkable state space trajectory for the 2-state vector $[x(t), x(t-1)]$ of the chaotic logistic process, when the scaling parameter $\kappa = 4.0$.

None of these trajectory cycles, or aperiodic orbits, overlap (even under a microscope). Notice that there are two definite areas: the lighter area contains single orbits almost parallel to each other, and the darker areas with "crossed" orbits, which traces out a second parabola with a "mode" close to $x(t-1) = 0.4$. While the outer parabola represents the parabolic constraint directly, the inner parabola is a slightly shifted and deformed version of it. How was the graph of this deterministic dynamic process trajectory of 1,000 iterations, generated? Let's follow

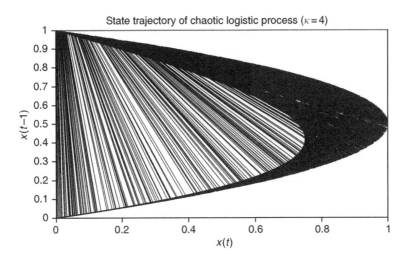

Figure 9.23 The state space trajectory of a chaotic system shows aperiodic cyclicity, so that none of the orbits overlap each other. The frequencies of the trajectory's orbits are all slightly different from each other. There are two areas: a lighter area with single orbits, and a dark area with "crossed" orbits, tracing out a second parabola.

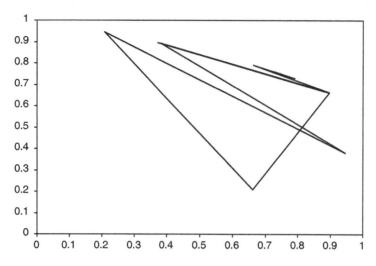

Figure 9.24 First 10 observations of the state space trajectory of the chaotic logistic process $x(t)$ for $\kappa = 4.0$.

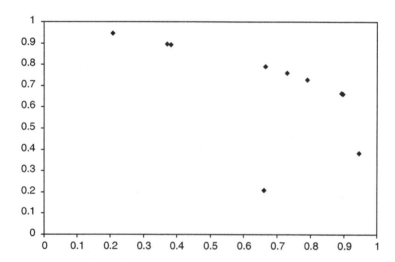

Figure 9.25 First 10 observations of the steady-state equilibrium points where the trajectory "touches" the parabolic constraint of the chaotic logistic process $x(t)$ for $\kappa = 4.0$.

the first 10 iterations in Figures 9.24 and 9.25. Figure 9.24 shows the actual state space trajectory of the first 10 orbits of the chaotic logistic process $x(t)$, while Figure 9.25 shows the steady-state equilibrium points where the trajectory "touches" the parabolic constraint of this logistic process, i.e., the attractor set of the trajectory's steady-state equilibria.

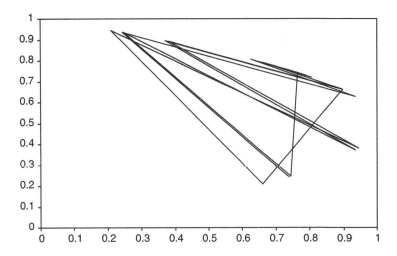

Figure 9.26 First 20 observations of the state space trajectory of the chaotic logistic process $x(t)$ for $\kappa = 4.0$.

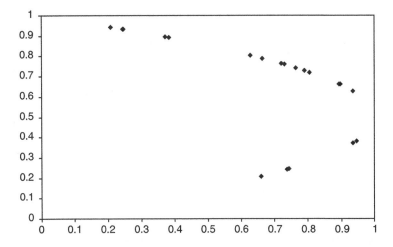

Figure 9.27 First 20 steady-state equilibria points on the attractor set of the chaotic logistic process $x(t)$ for $\kappa = 4.0$.

This is a clear example of Mandelbrot's aperiodic cyclicity (=having orbits of different length). Let's continue the state space trajectory and the process of passing through steady-state equilibrium points. Figures 9.26 and 9.27 show the trajectories and the attractor set of steady-state equilibria of the first 20 iterations. This is followed by the trajectories and attractor set of the steady-state equilibria of the first 50 iterations in Figures 9.28 and 9.29.

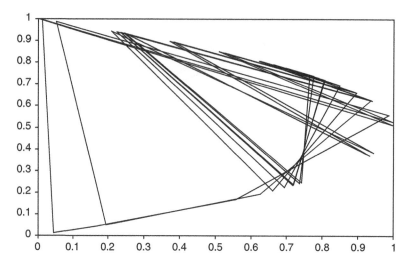

Figure 9.28 First 50 observations of the state space trajectory of the chaotic logistic process $x(t)$ for $\kappa = 4.0$.

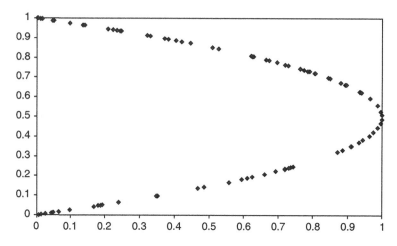

Figure 9.29 First 50 steady-state equilibria points on the attractor set of the chaotic logistic process $x(t)$ for $\kappa = 4.0$.

Figures 9.30 and 9.31 show the trajectories and attractor set of state equilibria of the first 90 iterations. Notice how these points in state space lie precisely on a well-defined object, the parabolic resource constraint, but the position of each of these state points is completely irregular or unpredictable and no point is ever visited twice. Their positions depend on the precision of numerical computation of the

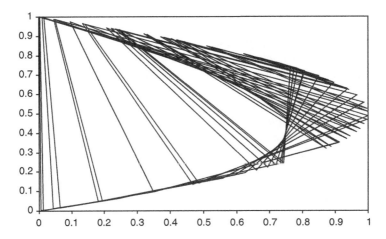

Figure 9.30 First 90 observations of the state space trajectory of the chaotic logistic process $x(t)$ for $\kappa = 4.0$.

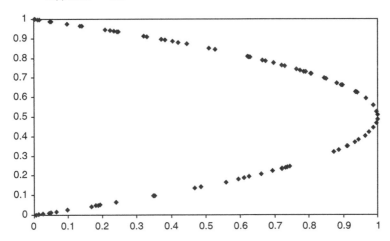

Figure 9.31 First 90 steady-state equilibria points on the attractor set of the chaotic logistic process $x(t)$ for $\kappa = 4.0$.

logistic evolutionary trajectory, which depends on the length of the digital registers of the computer. A computer with a different computing precision, delivers a different series of points, as can be easily demonstrated. This is an example of dynamic *deterministic, non-probabilistic irregularity*.

9.3.1 Fractal attractors

What is the defining character of the chaotic logistic parabola as a dynamic process? To discuss this properly we need a new concept that is particular to nonlinear dynamic systems and that we have already used earlier in this chapter: the attractor set.

Definition 383   *A dynamic process is said to have an* **attractor**, *if there exists a proper subset $\mathcal{A}$ of the Euclidean phase space $\mathbb{R}^D$, such that for almost all starting points* $\mathbf{x}(0)$, *and t large enough,* $\mathbf{x}(t)$ *is close to some point of* $\mathcal{A}$.

In other words, the attractor set $\mathcal{A}$ is the subset of the real Euclidean phase space with infinitely many *equilibrium* states $\mathbf{x}(t)$ of the system and their limiting points. The multifractal attractor characterizes the long-term behavior of the process. In fact, the shape and, in particular, the compactness of the multifractal attractor determines the degree of predictability of a system. The well-defined parabolic object in the state space $\{x(t), x(t-1)\}$ in Figure 9.32, which defines the aperiodic cycles, is the attractor of the logistic parabola.

Notice that a chaotic process, like the logistic process with a scaling parameter $\kappa = 4.0$, is not an *anarchic* process, since it clearly has a well-defined macroscopic structure determined by its (parabolic) resource constraint. It is complex in the sense that it combines the *global stability* of the logistic parabola with the *local uncertainty* of where the process at any time is on the parabolic attractor. Thus, the macroscopic or long-term trendwise predictability of a chaotic complex process depends on the shape of its resource constraints. The physical or institutional constraints of the chaotic process determine its long-term predictability. When the shape of these physical or institutional constraints are changed, the long-term shape

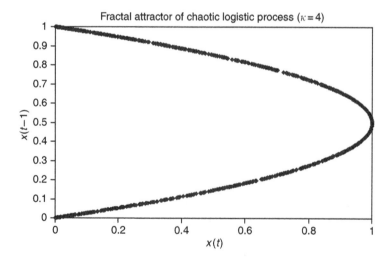

Figure 9.32   The physical or institutional resource constraint of the chaotic process determines its global, long-term predictability, i.e., the shape of the attractor set. But it remains completely uncertain when and where the chaotic process will hit this constraint, even though its steady-state trajectory is deterministic and well defined.

of the trend of the chaotic process changes accordingly. But it remains always uncertain when and where the chaotic process hits the physical or institutional resource constraint(s) and the chaotic complex process remains locally or short-term unpredictable.

This attractor set of steady-state equilibrium points is itself a Cantor-like set, with its Hausdorff dimension a fraction between the Euclidean values of zero (a set of points) and one (a line). The attractor is thus the set of all the deterministically random steady-state equilibria of $\mathbf{x}(t)$. The limited dimension D of an attractor $\mathcal{A}$ is almost always fractional and one speaks of *fractal attractors,* also called *strange* or *chaotic attractors* (Grassberger and Procaccia, 1983). As said, the Hausdorff dimension of the attractor of the logistic parabola is $D = 0.538\ldots$. Fractal attractors are aperiodic, but cyclic! Their state trajectories in phase space never intersect, although these trajectories wander about the whole attractor set in orbital fashion. Thus, fractal attractors are sets with infinitely many coexisting *dynamic steady-state equilibria.*[18]

Fractal attractors are called *strange*, because they differ from *familiar* attractors. Familiar attractors have one of three distinct forms, as we saw in Section 9.2. They consist either of:

(1) single points (fixed or steady-state points);
(2) finitely many points (periodic orbits); or
(3) continuous manifolds (polynomials) that give rise to periodic orbits.

However, strange attractors, which are aperiodic cyclic, do have the structure of the imposed nonlinear constraint and thus contain information, although this information is clearly incomplete. The global information that we often can extract from observing such chaotic process only pertains to the physical or institutional constraints. By continuously monitoring a chaotic process we can identify the complete abstract set of equilibrium points of its fractal attractor, i.e., the shape and structure of its global constraint, as we have demonstrated in the case of the parabolic constraint built into the logistic process.[19]

We cannot extract local information from a chaotic time series, unless we monitor all individual aperiodic cycles in real time. Then, we can only determine where the process is in the time–frequency plane, but we cannot predict its next local orbit. Often such processes are self-similar, or approximately so, and therefore they have fractal Hausdorff dimensions (Ruelle, 1989).

Remark 384 *Because of its property of self-similarity, the behavior of fractal attractors can be approximately described by wavelet functions, i.e., by linear expansions of wavelets over orthonormal wavelet bases, because they contain aperiodic, but cyclic behavior. This is currently a hot area of research: the modeling of (financial) turbulence by using wavelet multiresolution theory, in particular their identification and simulation using scalograms, and we'll return to that exciting topic in the next two chapters.*

9.3.2   *Chaotic processes*

Returning to the initial figures of this chapter, we can now define the chaotic behavior of a nonlinear dynamic process in terms of its globally defining fractal attractor set.

Definition 385   *A chaotic process is one of which the behavior shows sensitivity to initial conditions $x(0)$, so that no point of its attractor set $\mathcal{A}$ is visited twice in finite time.*

Thus, any uncertainty in the initial state of the given system, no matter how small, will lead to rapidly growing errors in any effort to predict the future behavior of $x(t)$. Although the attractor has a well-defined abstract shape (like a parabola), it is fractal: it consists of a set of singularities, which can only be characterized by a multi-fractal spectrum (cf. Chapter 8).

It is actually typical for multidimensional dissipative dynamic systems to have more than one attractor and each attractor has its own associated *basin of attraction*. The statistical properties of the dynamic solution depend on to which basin the initial conditions belong. Thus, not only may the detailed behavior of the orbits be unpredictable (because of the sensitivity to the initial conditions), but even their global, average statistical properties may be unidentifiable, insofar as it may be impossible to determine to which basin of attraction the initial conditions belong. Meteorologists face such problems with the prediction of the weather, which has many different basins of attraction.[20] Not only the weather, but also the climate may be unpredictable in the short run, but still be predictable in the long run, due to its natural resource constraints. For example, the El Niño effect is clearly an aperiodic cyclic global weather phenomena generated by the natural physical resource constraints of the Pacific Ocean. As we observed earlier, the plight of financial economists studying the global financial markets, in particular the FX markets, is very similar to that of global meteorologists (Los, 1991).

Indeed, the transition from stable, equilibrium, behavior to chaotic behavior when the scaling parameter κ is increased, as exhibited by the logistic parabola, has been observed in many physical systems, in fields as diverse as meteorology, seismology, ecology, epidemiology, medicine, economics and finance, to name just a few.[21] In particular, *intermittency of turbulence*, where some regions are marked by very high dissipation or chaos, while other regions seem by contrast to be stable and nearly free of dissipation, is symptomatic of the observed behavior of financial markets, both spatially and in time.

Example 386   *In the second half of 1997, the Southeast Asian financial markets saw a rapid succession of such periods of turbulence and temporary stability. At the same time, while the Southeast Asian FX markets exhibited this temporal intermittency in the second half of 1997, the Japanese Yen and Deutsche mark markets were completely unperturbed. This suggests that interacting financial markets can simultaneously exhibit a wide variety of dynamic pricing processes,* *some of which may be stable, intermittent or even completely chaotic (Karuppiah and Los, 2000).*

9.4   Detecting attracting points and aperiodic orbits

How can one empirically detect the location of attracting points and aperiodic cyclical orbits in an arbitrary financial time series, if there are any? Even without an estimate of the system's diffusion equation or phase space reconstruction, one can acquire a pretty good idea by the following simple procedure (adapted from Urbach, 2000, pp. 307–308).

If a system passes close to an aperiodic attracting equilibrium orbit of period τ, then it is likely to circulate near this attracting point for a while, and measurements $x(t)$ will reflect that *temporary periodicity* or cyclicity by nearly repeating after a horizon of τ time units – for a while at least. Thus, for a small positive value $\varepsilon > 0$ and some contiguous sequence of values of time t, the following inequality of absolute time differences will hold:

$$|x(t + \tau) - x(t)| < \varepsilon \tag{9.37}$$

To see the location and temporal periodicity of the attractor points is by plotting the truth value $\text{sign}\{|x(t + \tau) - x(t)| < \varepsilon\}$ as a function of both time t and horizon τ. Such a plot is called a *close return* or *recurrence plot*. Figure 9.33 provides an example for the Belousov–Zhabotinsky chemical reaction (Mindlin and Gilmore, 1992, p. 231; also in Nicolis and Prigogine, 1998, pp. 18–24).

Another visualization of such temporary periodicity is the *recurrence* or *close returns histogram*, defined by:

$$H(\tau) = \sum_t \Theta[\varepsilon - |x(t + \tau) - x(t)|] \tag{9.38}$$

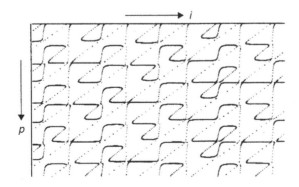

Figure 9.33 A close return or recurrence plot of the Belousov–Zhabotinsky chemical reaction. In this plot a pixel (i, p) is colored black if $|x(t + \tau) - x(t)| < \varepsilon$, and white if $|x(t + \tau) - x(t)| > \varepsilon$. The discriminating constant ε is about 2 percent of the diameter of the attractor.

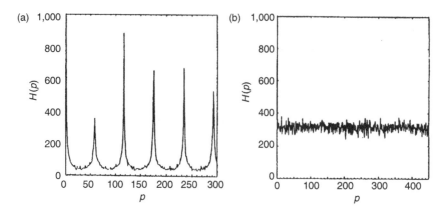

Figure 9.34 Close return histograms (a) of a chaotic time series with aperiodic cyclicity, and (b) of Geometric Brownian Motion increments.

where $\Theta[\cdots]$ is the Heaviside function:[22]

$$\Theta[z] = \begin{cases} 1 & \text{if } z > 0 \\ 0 & \text{otherwise} \end{cases} \tag{9.39}$$

Figure 9.34 provides examples of such recurrence histograms, that also clearly shows the distinction between an aperiodic cyclic chaotic time series and a truly random time series (Mindlin and Gilmore, 1992, p. 232). Notice the aperiodic cyclic singularities in the histogram of the chaotic time series and the very narrow and almost time-invariant bandwidth in the histogram of the random time series over all time horizons τ.

Since this simple nonstationary histogram method of Mindlin and Gilmore exploits the aperiodic cyclicity observable in the time-varying histograms or frequency distributions, it is a primitive form of windowed Fourier analysis. Thus, it is easy to see how the wavelet MRA in the form of a scalogram discussed in Chapter 7, can sharply improve the identification of simultaneous frequency and time cyclicity in high frequency financial time series, since such scalograms are superb instruments for simultaneous local and global system identification, as we will see in Chapter 11 (Farge, 1992; Buchler and Kandrup, 1997).

9.5   Summary of aperiodic cyclical steady-state equilibria

In this chapter, we've studied the behavior of a simple nonlinear dynamic system by simulation in preparation of a quantitative study of a wide variety of financial market processes. The logistic parabola is capable of producing widely different dynamic process regimes, depending on the value of its single scaling parameter κ. These regimes are summarized in Table 9.2.

For the lower values of $\kappa < 3$, the logistic process is like a classical, stable, linearized, Newtonian process with a single stable equilibrium. Thus, in this

Table 9.2 Steady-state equilibrium regimes of the logistic process

Scaling	Orbital steady-state equilibria	Stability regime
$0 \leq \kappa < 1$	$x^* = 0$	Stable
$\kappa = 1$	$x^* = 0$	Marginally stable
$1 < \kappa < 3$	$x^* = \dfrac{\kappa - 1}{\kappa}$	Superstable (1-period)
$\kappa = 3$	$x^* = \dfrac{2}{3} \to x^* = \dfrac{2}{3} + \varepsilon \ (\varepsilon \text{ very small}) \to x^*$ $= \dfrac{2}{3}, \text{ etc.}$	First bifurcation (2-period)
$3 < \kappa < 3.58$	$x^*(1) \to x^*(2) \to \cdots \to x^*(n+1) = x^*(1)$	Multiple stability (n-period)
$\kappa = 3.34$		First 180° phase shift
$\kappa = 3.45$	$x^*(1) \to x^*(2) \to x^*(3)$ $\to x^*(4) \to x^*(1), \text{ etc.}$	Second bifurcation (4-period)
$\kappa = 3.50$		Second 180° phase shift
$\kappa = 3.58$	$x^*(1) \to x^*(2) \to \cdots \to x^* \ (\text{large})$	Moderate chaos
$3.58 < \kappa < 4$		Complexity
$\kappa = 3.82$	$x^*(1) \to x^*(2) \to \cdots \to x^* \ (\text{large})$	Moderate chaos
$\kappa = 3.83$	$x^*(1) \to x^*(2) \to x^*(3) \to x^*(1), \text{ etc.}$	Apparent stability (3-period)
$\kappa = 3.86$	$x^*(1) \to \cdots \to x^*(3) \to x^*(1)$ and $x^*(1) \to \cdots \to x^* \ (\text{large})$	Intermittency
$\kappa = 4.0$	$x^*(1) \to x^*(2) \to \cdots \to x^*(\infty)$	Complete chaos

dynamic regime the process is completely predictable in the short- and the long-term, or both locally and globally. For $\kappa = 4.0$ the logistic process is completely chaotic, i.e., it is unstable in both the short- and the long-term, or unstable both locally and globally (Pawelzik and Shuster, 1991). A small change in the initial condition will cause it to move to a completely different magnitude at an unpredictable time.

The most interesting process regimes from the point of view of current research into financial market processes, are the logistic parabolic processes that lie in between these two extreme regimes. These processes are complex and highly structured, like the period-doubling bifurcation processes, when $3 < \kappa < 3.83$, which oscillate between even numbers of stable equilibria, i.e., a set of equilibria with different but even period lengths. They can become very complex when the number of stable equilibria in these sets increases and they can even exhibit moderate chaos, but with periods of intermittency. Thus, periods of stability are interlaced by periods of moderate chaos, or *vice versa*. Intermittency processes contain processes that are stable in the short term or locally, and unstable in the long term or globally, and processes that are unstable in the short term, or locally, and stability in the long term or globally.

Such complex processes are prevalent in nature because they tend to be better able to survive changing environmental constraints. They always operate in high states of uncertainty. This is the same with financial markets. This environmental uncertainty cannot be eliminated, because the reasons for the buying and selling actions of the individual market participants cannot be predicted. But lack of local or short-term predictability may give such free market pricing systems their global or long-term stability.

We saw that intermittency process regimes are very finely balanced. There are small ranges of the scaling parameter κ where the parabolic logistic process is in a period of calmness and stability, but when the parameter moves outside these windows of stability ranges, the process is plunged into moderate chaos. This should provide cause for extreme caution for tinkering with well-working financial markets, which show intermittency, i.e., fairly long periods of relative stability, interrupted by fairly short periods of chaos. Institutional policy changes, which change the shape of the institutional constraints, i.e., the scaling parameters, can cause a stable market mechanism to move into moderate chaos and regimes of intermittency. On the other hand, it can also be rescued from such chaos and periods of intermittency, by counteracting institutional policy changes, i.e., by correcting the shape of the institutional constraints. This does not mean that one should eliminate or arbitrarily constrain the uncertain market pricing processes. But it does mean that we must first understand the actual quantitative parametrization of the institutional and physical constraints of these complex market pricing processes, before we let politicians tinker with them!

It is clear that the current level of theoretical and engineering understanding of market pricing systems, which still relies on linearized models borrowed from Newtonian physics, is highly insufficient, because actual market pricing process are not both short- and long-term predictable, due to their nonlinear environmental constraints. They show heterogeneous levels of predictability. We suspect that most market pricing processes may be globally predictable, but short-term unpredictable. The logistic parabola is just a simple analogue simulation model, and a simple version of the parabolic Navier–Stokes diffusion equation, but it provides some clear guidelines. Considerable more empirical research is required for the identification of the proper nonlinear dynamic configuration and the scaling parametrization of actual financial market pricing processes.

9.6   Software

The computations of the first three Exercises can be executed in Microsoft EXCEL spreadsheets or by using the Statistics Toolbox available from The MathWorks, Inc., 24 Prime Park Way Natick, MA 01760-1500, USA. Tel. (508) 647-7000; Fax (508) 647-7001; http://www.mathworks.com/products/wavelettbx.shtml.

The last Exercise uses Benoit 1.3: Fractal System Analysis (for Windows 95/98 or Windows NT), Trusoft International Inc., 204 37th Ave. N #133, St Petersburg, FL 33704 Tel. (813) 925-8131; Fax (813) 925-8141; sales@trusoft-international.com.

See http://www.trusoft-international.com for details. This Benoit software enables you to measure the fractal dimension and/or Hölder–Hurst exponent of your data sets.

9.7   Exercises

Exercise 387   *Starting with an initial rate of return on investment $x(0) = 0.1$, compute and plot the next 20 iterates of the parabolic logistic equation for a Feigenbaum scaling parameter of $\kappa = 1.5$, $\kappa = 2$, $\kappa = 3.2$, $\kappa = 3.5$ and $\kappa = 4.0$. Your results should illustrate the convergence to equilibrium for $\kappa < 2$ and the period doubling route to chaos for $\kappa > 2$. How do these results illustrate that? Determine the H-exponent of each of the five series, using wavelet MRA. Which series are persistent and which antipersistent?*

Exercise 388   *Iterate the parabolic logistic equation with the Feigenbaum parameter $\kappa = 4.0$ twenty times using initial values of $x(0) = 0.1$ and $x(0) = 0.100001$ and plot the sequence of $x(t)$. Your results should illustrate the initial sensitivity of a chaotic system to initial conditions.*

Exercise 389   *Write a simple computer program to graph the values of $x(t)$ versus varying scaling parameters κ, $2 < \kappa < 4$, that result from repeated iteration of the logistic equation. Do not plot the first 100 iterates during which the solution approaches the strange attractor. Plot the next 10 iterates in a bifurcation diagram. Show also that the bifurcation diagram is independent of the initial value of $x(0)$.*

Exercise 390   *The strange or fractal attractor is the odd region plotted in the phase space, to which the "trajectory" of the nonlinear discrete dynamic system, represented by the logistic equation, is attracted. It represents all stable equilibrium points of the system's evolutionary process, and their limits. It is an attractor, because no matter where in the phase space the process is started, the $x(t)$ is quickly attracted to the plotted region. It is strange, because the attractor is neither a line nor a surface, but rather an object with a fractional dimension. A strange attractor is not a real physical entity, but an abstraction that exists in phase space, i.e., a Euclidean space with as many (integer) dimensions as are needed to describe the dynamic behavior of the process under investigation. For our process, this Euclidean space is the 2D $[x(t), x(t-1)]$ plane. One point in the phase space represents a single measurement of the state of the rate of return process as it evolves over time. When all such points are connected, they form a trajectory that lies on the surface of a strange attractor. Determine the shape of the strange attractor of the chaotic logistic equation (when $\kappa = 4.0$)? Why is the global shape of the attractor a parabola? Show the system's state trajectory for $t = 101, \ldots, 1{,}001$ and demonstrate its "deterministic irregularity."*

Exercise 391   *Using the Benoit software, can you determine the fractal dimension D of the strange attractor, which must be a fractional number $1 < D < 2$?*

Notes

1 Crack and Ledoit (1996) present an interesting example of the existence of an observable nonlinear robust structure in stock market pricing without any predictability of the stock market returns.

2 The simulations with the logistic parabola were executed in a Microsoft® Excel 97 spreadsheet, on a simple Compaq ARMADA1700 notebook with Intel Pentium II processor. The growth parameter κ was varied in steps of 0.1 for $t = 1, 2, \ldots, 1,100$. The Hurst exponents based on wavelet MRA of level 3 of the simulated data using the software Benoit, Version 1.2, of TruSoft Int'l Inc. 1997, 1999. This is not the best procedure, but it was the one available to us at this time. We prefer to compute the Hurst exponent using the Haar wavelet MRA of MATLAB®.

3 This scaling or stability parameter is, indeed, the first cousin of the Lipschitz $\alpha_L = 1/\alpha_Z$, where α_Z is Zolotarev's stability exponent.

4 Cf. James and Webber, 2001, p. 234 and their section 11.3 "An IS–LM Based Model," pp. 284–290, for more details on the behavior of this intriguing financial economic model.

5 The stability of differential maps which map the unit interval into itself is discussed in greater detail in Singer (1978).

6 We used the wavelet routine in TruSoft's Benoit, Version 1.3, to compute the Hurst exponent (cf. Section 9.6). However, there are some doubts about the reliability of the this wavelet procedure incorporated in the Benoit software and we are in the process of redoing the identification of the Hurst exponents for the various stability regimes.

7 For more images of critical points of nonlinear dynamic mappings, cf. Jensen and Myer (1985).

8 Notice that the Excel spreadsheet plotter has a problem with sharp discontinuities at the bottom of the chaotic, $\kappa = 4.0$ process. Excel's spline smoother curves the line below $x(t) = 0$, although the process $x(t) \geq 0$, always, by definition.

9 This is a familiar result for economists who have studied Solow's one-period delayed stable market pricing spiral, towards a unique price equilibrium, also called the dynamic *cobweb* pricing model.

10 Figure 9.6 and the following time plots portray $x(t)$ for $t = 901–1,000$, after the logistic process has completely stabilized. These oscillations are not transients, but cyclic fluctuations between two steady-state equilibria.

11 This so-called *Feigenbaum constant δ* was originally found by Grossman and Thomae (1977).

12 The number of decibels is, by definition, $10 \log_{10}$ of a squared magnitude ratio, such as the spectral power ratio (cf. Chapters 5 and 6).

13 George Ferdinand Ludwig Phillip Cantor (1845–1918) was a Russian-born German mathematician best known as the creator of set theory and for his discovery of the transfinite numbers. He also advanced the study of trigonometric series, was the first to prove the non-denumerability of the real numbers, and made significant contributions to dimension theory. Cantor received his doctorate in 1867 and accepted a position at the University of Halle in 1869, where he remained.

14 In 1971, a Belgian physicist, David Ruelle and a Dutch mathematician, Floris Takens, together predicted that the transition to chaotic turbulence in a moving fluid would take place at a well-defined critical value of the fluid's velocity. They predicted that this transition to turbulence would occur after the system had developed oscillations with at least three distinct frequencies. Experiments with rotating fluid flows conducted by American physicists Jerry Gollub and Harry Swinney in the mid-1970s supported these predictions. Another American physicist, Mitchell Feigenbaum, then predicted that at the critical point when an ordered system begins to break down into chaos, a consistent sequence of period-doubling transitions would be observed. This so-called "period-doubling route

to chaos" was thereafter observed experimentally by various investigators, including the French physicist Albert Liebhaber and his coworkers.

15 All solutions were obtained with Maple symbolic algebra software in TCI's Scientific Workplace, Version 4.0.

16 Cf. Chapter 3 for the comparison with stable processes with inexistent, i.e., nonconverging, means and variances.

17 Wavelet software for these computations was provided by Torrence and Compo, 1998 (cf. Chapter 8).

18 In classical financial-economics, equilibria are commonly static. Dynamic equilibria have just started to appear in the theoretical financial-economic literature in the form of state space and phase diagrams, although they were already familiar to mathematical economists in the 1970s. For example, Takayama (1974, pp. 321–330) illustrates the use of the *phase diagram technique* for a proof of global stability for the static three-commodity market case (with gross substitutability).

19 For an example of the identification of such a chaotic attractor, cf. Peters (1991).

20 Indeed, the modern study of chaotic dynamics began in 1963, when the American meteorologist Edward Lorenz demonstrated that a simple, deterministic model of thermal convection in the Earth's atmosphere showed sensitivity to initial conditions or, in current terms, that it was a chaotic process (Lorenz, 2001). Cf. also the picture of fractal atmospheric convection, i.e., the empirical breaking-wave patterns in clear-air turbulence, due to changes in the wind within and around the jet stream, in chapter 2.

21 The term *chaotic dynamics* refers to the evolution of a process in time. Chaotic processes, however, also often display spatial disorder – e.g., in complicated fluid flows. Incorporating spatial patterns into theories of chaotic dynamics is now a very active area of study. Researchers hope to extend theories of chaos to the realm of fully developed physical turbulence, where complete disorder exists in both space and time. This effort is widely viewed as among the greatest challenges of modern physics. The equivalence in financial economics would be to find a complete chaotic dynamic theory of multiple coexisting global market pricing processes, which can explain financial crises occurring in several interlinked regional pricing markets (cf. Dechert, 1996).

22 Oliver Heaviside, 1850–1925, was an English physicist, who made important advances in electromagnetism. He was the co-discoverer of the Kennelly–Heaviside Layer, a layer in the earth's atmosphere, occurring at 100–120 km above sea level, in which short-wave radio waves are reflected and temperature increases with increasing altitude.

Bibliography

Abarnel, H. (1994) "Analyzing and Utilizing Time Series Observations from Chaotic Systems," in Thompson, J., and S. Bishop (Eds) *Nonlinearity and Chaos in Engineering Dynamics*, John Wiley and Sons, New York, NY, pp. 379–392.

Auerbach, D., P. Critanovic, J. Eckmann, G. Gunaratne and I. Procaccia (1987) "Exploring Chaotic Motion Through Periodic Orbits," *Physical Review Letters*, **58**(3), 2287–2389.

Babbs, S. H., and N. J. Webber (1994) "A Theory of the Term Structure with an Official Short Rate," Working Paper, FORC 94/49, University of Warwick.

Bakshi, G. S., and Z. Chen (1997) "An Alternative Valuation Model for Contingent Claims," *Journal of Finanical Economics*, **44**, 123–165.

Beaglehole, D. R., and M. S. Tenney (1991) "General Solutions of Some Interest Rate – Contingent Claim Pricing Equations," *Journal of Fixed Income*, **1**, June, 69–83.

Bechhoefer, J. (1996) "The Birth of Period 3, Revisited," *Mathematics Magazine*, **69**, 115–118.

Berry, Michael (1991) "Quantum Physics on the Edge of Chaos," chapter 15 in Hall, Nina (Ed.) *Exploring Chaos: A Guide to the New Science of Disorder*, W.W. Norton & Co., New York, NY, pp. 184–195.

Buchler, J. Robert, and Henry Kandrup (Eds) (1997) *Nonlinear Signal and Image Analysis*, Annals of the New York Academy of Sciences, **808**, The New York Academy of Sciences, New York, NY.

Burm, Jacqueline, and Paul Fishback (2001) "Period–3 Orbits via Sylvester Theorem and Resultants," *Mathematics Magazine*, **74**(1), 47–51.

Crack, Timothy Falcon, and Olivier Ledoit (1996) "Robust Structure Without Predictability: The Compass Rose Pattern of the Stock Market," *The Journal of Finance*, **51**(2), 751–762.

Dechert, Davis (Ed.) (1996) *Chaos Theory in Economics: Methods, Models and Evidence* (International Library of Critical Writings in Economics, No. 66), Edward Elgar Publisher, London, UK.

Farge, Marie (1992) "Wavelet Transforms and Their Applications to Turbulence," *Annual Review of Fluid Mechanics*, **24**, 395–407.

Feigenbaum, M. J. (1979) "The Universal Metric Properties of Nonlinear Transformations," *Journal of Statistical Physics*, **21**, 669–706.

Feigenbaum, M. J. (1981) "Universal Behavior in Nonlinear Systems," *Los Alamos Science*, **1**(1), 4–27, and *Physica*, D7, **83**(1/3), 16–39.

Franses, Philip H., and Dick van Dijk (2000) *Non-Linear Time Series Models in Empirical Finance*, Cambridge University Press, Cambridge, UK.

Frisch, Uriel (1995) *Turbulence: The Legacy of A. N. Kolmogorov*, Cambridge University Press, Cambridge, UK.

Frisch, U., and G. Parisi (1985) "Fully Developed Turbulence and Intermittency," in M. Ghil, R. Benzi and G. Parisi (Eds), *Turbulence and Predictability in Geophysical Fluid Dynamics*, North-Holland Publishing Co., Amsterdam, p. 84.

Gleick, J. (1987) *Chaos: Making a New Science*, Viking Press, New York, NY.

Gordon, W. (1996) "Period Three Trajectories of the Logistic Map," *Mathematics Magazine*, **69**, 118–120.

Grassberger, P. (1981) "On the Hausdorff Dimension of Fractal Attractors," *Journal of Statistical Physics*, **26**(1), 173–179.

Grassberger, P., and I. Procaccia (1983) "Measuring the Strangeness of Strange Attractors," *Physica*, D, **9**, 189–208.

Grebogi, C., E. Off and J. A. Yorke (1988) "Unstable Periodic Orbits and the Dimension of Multifractal Chaotic Attractors," *Physics Review*, A, **37**(5), 1711–1724.

Grossman, S., and S. Thomae (1977) "Invariant Distributions and Stationary Correlations of One-Dimensional Discrete Processes," *Zeitschrift für Naturforschung*, **32**, A, 1353–1363.

Hall, N. (Ed.) (1991) *Exploring Chaos: A Guide to the New Science of Disorder*, W. W. Norton and Co., New York, NY.

Hsieh, David A. (1991) "Chaos and Nonlinear Dynamics: Application to Financial Markets," *The Journal of Finance*, **46**(5), 1839–1877.

Hsieh, David A. (1993) "Chaos and Order in Capital Markets: A New View of Cycles, Prices, and Market Volatility," *The Journal of Finance*, **48**(5), 2041–2044.

Hull, J. C., and A. D. White (1993) "One-Factor Interest-Rate Models and the Valuation of Interest-Rate Derivative Securities," *Journal of Financial and Quantitative Analysis*, **28**(2), June, 235–254.

James, Jessica, and Nick Webber (2001) *Interest Rate Modelling*, John Wiley and Sons, Chichester, NJ.

Jamshidian, F. (1989) "An Exact Bond Option Formula," *Journal of Finance*, **44**, 205–209.

Jensen, R. V., and C. R. Myer (1985) "Images of the Critical Points of Nonlinear Maps," *Physics Review*, A, **32**, 1222–1224.

Karuppiah, Jeyanthi, and Cornelis A. Los (2000) "Wavelet Multiresolution Analysis of High-Frequency FX Rates," *Quantitative Methods in Finance and Bernoulli Society 2000 Conference (Program, Abstracts and Papers)*, University of Technology, Sydney, Australia , 5–8 December, pp. 171–198.

Li, T.-Y., and J. A. Yorke (1975) "Period Three Implies Chaos," *American Mathematical Monthly*, **82**(10), 985–992.

Lo, Andrew W., and A. Craig MacKinlay (1999) "Long-Term Memory in Stock Market Prices," chapter 6 in *A Non-Random Walk Down Wall Street*, Princeton University Press, Princeton, NJ, pp. 147–184.

Lorenz, Edward N. (2001) *The Essence of Chaos*, University of Washington Press, Seattle, WA (original 1993).

Los, Cornelis A. (1991) "A Scientific View of Economic Data Analysis," *Eastern Economic Journal*, **17**, (1), 61–71.

Luenberger, David G. (1998) *Investment Science*, Oxford University Press, New York, NY.

Lyubich, Mikhail (2000) "The Quadratic Family as a Qualitatively Solvable Model of Chaos," *Notices of the American Mathematical Society*, **47**(9), 1042–1052.

McDonald, Robert (2002) *Derivatives Markets*, Addison-Wesley, New York, NY.

Mandelbrot, Benoit B. (1963) "The Variation of Certain Speculative Prices," *The Journal of Business*, **36**, 394–419 and (1972) **45**, 542–543. Reprinted as chapter E14, with annotations and corrections, in *Fractals and Scaling in Finance: Discontinuity, Concentration, Risk*, Springer Verlag, New York, 1997, 371–418.

Mandelbrot, Benoit B. (1974) "Intermittent Turbulence in Self-similar Cascades. Divergence of High Moments and Dimension of the Carrier," *Journal of Fluid Mechanics*, **62**, 331–358.

Mandelbrot, Benoit B., and John W. Van Ness (1968) "Fractional Brownian Motions, Fractional Noises and Applications," *SIAM Review*, **10**(4), 422–437.

Mantegna, Rosario, N., and H. Eugene Stanley (2000) *An Introduction to Econophysics: Correlations and Complexity in Finance*, Cambridge University Press, Cambridge, UK.

Mindlin, G., and R. Gilmore (1992) "Topological Analysis and Synthesis of Chaotic Time Series," *Physica*, D, **58**, 229–242.

Müller, U., M. Dacorogna, R. Olsen, O. Pictet, M. Schwarz and C. Morgenegg (1990) "Statistical Study of Foreign Exchange Rates, Empirical Evidence of a Price Change Scaling Law, and Intra-Day Analysis," *The Journal of Banking and Finance*, **14**, 1189–1208.

Navier, C. L. M. H. (1823) "Mémoire sur les Lois du Mouvement des Fluides," ("Report on the Dynamic Laws of Fluids") *Memoires d' Académie Royale des Sciences*, **6**, 389–440.

Nicolis, Gregoire, and Ilya Prigogine (1998) *Exploring Complexity: An Introduction*, W. H. Freeman and Co., New York (original 1989; 5th print).

Parker, T., and L. Chua (1987) "Chaos: A Tutorial for Engineers," *Proceedings of the IEEE*, **75**(8), 982–1008.

Patterson, D. M., and R. A. Ashley (2000) *A Nonlinear Time Series Workshop: A Toolkit for Detecting and Identifying Nonlinear Serial Dependence*, Kluwer Academic Publishers, Boston, MA.

Pawelzik, K., and H. Shuster (1991) "Unstable Periodic Orbits and Prediction," *Physics Review*, A, **43**(4), 1808–1812.

Peters, Edgar E. (1994) *Fractal Market Analysis: Applying Chaos Theory to Investment and Economics*, John Wiley and Sons, Inc., New York, NY.

Peters, Edgar E. (1999) *Patterns in the Dark: Understanding Risk and Financial Crisis with Complexity Theory*, John Wiley and Sons, Inc., New York, NY.

Prigogine, Ilya (1997) *The End of Certainty: Time, Chaos and the New Laws of Nature*, The Free Press, New York, NY.

Ruelle, D. (1989) *Chaotic Evolution and Strange Attractors*, Cambridge University Press, Cambridge, UK.

Saha, P., and S. Strogatz (1995) "The Birth of Period Three," *Mathematics Magazine*, **68**(1), 42–47.

Savit, Robert (1988) "When Random is Not Random: An Introduction to Chaos in Market Prices," *Journal of Future Markets*, **8**(3), 271.

Schroeder, Manfred (1991) *Fractals, Chaos, Power Laws: Minutes from an Infinite Paradise*, W. H. Freeman and Co., New York, NY.

Sharkovskii, A. N. (1964) "Coexistence of Cycles of a Continuous Map of a Line into Itself," *Ukrainische Mathematische Zeitschrift*, **16**, 61–71.

Singer, D. (1978) "Stable Orbits and Bifurcations of Maps of the Interval," *SIAM Journal of Applied Mathematics*, **35**, 260–267.

Takayama, Akira (1974) *Mathematical Economics*, The Dryden Press, Honsdale, IL.

Taylor, G. I. (1935) "Statistical Theory of Turbulence," *Proceedings of the Royal Society of London*, A, **151**, 421–478.

Taylor, G. I. (1938) "The Spectrum of Turbulence," *Proceedings of the Royal Society of London*, A, **164**, 476–490.

Tice, J., and N. J. Webber (1997) "A Non-Linear Model of the Term Structure of Interest Rates," *Mathematical Finance*, **7**(2), 177–209.

Torrence, Christopher, and Gilbert P. Compo (1998) "A Practical Guide to Wavelet Analysis," *Bulletin of the American Meteorological Society*, **79**(1), 61–78.

Urbach, Richard M. A. (2000) *Footprints of Chaos in the Markets: Analyzing Non-Linear Time Series in Financial Markets and Other Real Systems*, Prentice Hall, London, UK.

Vasicek, O. A. (1977) "An Equilibrium Characterization of the Term Structure," *Journal of Financial Economics*, **5**(2), 177–188.

Verhulst, Pierre-François (1845) "Récherches Mathématiques sur la Loi d'Accroissement de la Population" ("Mathematical Research into the Law of Population Growth"), *Nouvelles Mémoires de l'Académie Royale des Sciences et Belles-Lettres de Bruxelles*, **XVIII**(8), 1–38.

10 Measuring term structure dynamics

10.1 Introduction

Financial turbulence is a phenomenon occurring in antipersistent financial markets. In contrast, financial catastrophes occur in persistent financial markets. A relationship can be established between these two extreme phenomena of long-term market dependence and the older financial concept of illiquidity. The measurement of the degree of financial market persistence and the measurement of the degree of financial market illiquidity are related.

It has been suggested by Peters (1989, 1994) of PanAgora Management, that to understand financial turbulence, the dynamics of cash flows between the various market participants, within and between different asset markets, should be measured, identified and analyzed more carefully. Although there exists not yet a complete theory of physical turbulence, let alone of financial turbulence, many parallels between the two have been noted by Mandelbrot (1972, 1997, p. 43), as we observed earlier in Chapter 8 and as we'll discuss in greater detail in Chapter 11.

On the other hand, the accurate measurement of illiquidity and illiquidity risk has gained in importance, as the example of the $4 billion bail-out of the collapsed Long-Term Capital Management (LTCM) hedge fund in 1998 demonstrates. This hedge fund applied a trading strategy known as *convergence arbitrage* (Jorion, 1999; Dunbar, 2000). This strategy is based on the idea that if two securities have the same theoretical price, because they have the same return-risk profile, their market prices should eventually, in the long run, be the same. But this strategy only looks at the frequency distribution of the rates of return and ignores that risk is a long-term memory or time-dependent phenomenon. Indeed, in the summer of 1998, LTCM made a huge $4 billion loss, because Russia defaulted on its debt, which caused a flight to quality in the German bond market. There was a historical sequence of events which caused a fairly rapid dissipation of the market value of the German bond assets and thus of the equity of highly leveraged LTCM.

LTCM did not have a large direct exposure to illiquid and politically risky Russian debt, but it tended to be long in illiquid German (off-the-run) bonds and short in the corresponding liquid German (on-the-run) bonds. The spreads between the prices of the illiquid bonds and the corresponding liquid bonds widened sharply after the Russian default. Credit spreads also increased and LTCM was highly leveraged, with liabilities 30 times larger than its equity. Its financial leverage was about three times larger than the financial leverage of an average commercial bank. When it was unable to make its projected "risk-free" arbitrage profits, it experienced huge losses and there were margin calls on its positions that it was unable to meet.

LTCM's position in 1998 was made even more difficult by the fact that many other hedge funds followed similar convergence arbitrage strategies. When LTCM tried to liquidate part of its portfolio to meet its margin calls by selling its illiquid off-the-run bonds and by buying its liquid on-the-run bonds, other hedge funds were facing similar problems and tried to do similar trades. The price of the on-the-run bonds rose relative to the price of the off-the-run bonds. This caused illiquidity spreads to widen even further and to reinforce the flight to quality. Thus, the illiquidity problem was exacerbated and not alleviated. This is a clear example of long-term illiquidity risk-dependence that was not foreseen by the assumptions of the Geometric Brownian Motion (GBM) models used by LTCM's dynamic hedging managers and their illustrious Nobel Memorial Prize winning partners.

Despite its obvious importance, the proper measurement and analysis of credit and illiquidity risks is still in its infancy. For example, there is still no agreement on how market illiquidity should be measured. More precisely stated: there does not yet exist a measurement standard for the various *degrees of illiquidity*. Which levels of *hypo-liquidity* are prone to generate financial discontinuities or catastrophes, which neutral levels of liquidity are prone to generate normal trading activity, and which levels of *hyper-liquidity* are prone to generate financial turbulence?

Therefore, in this chapter we discuss the empirical measurement of the dynamics of market illiquidity, in particular the illiquidity of cash flows, which is directly related to the dynamics of the term structure of rates of return on cash investments and to the concept of (bond and equity) duration (Culbertson, 1957). For a recent survey on current theoretical work on term structure dynamics, cf. the article by Hong Yan (2001). For a thorough discussion about a few traditional approaches to the model identification of term structure dynamics, particularly by classical principal component analysis, cf. the companion article in the same issue of the *Financial Analysts Journal* by Chapman and Pearson (2001).

In Chapter 9, we discussed the phenomenon of chaos or nonunique deterministic steady-state dynamic equilibria, by way of simple simulations with the parabolic logistic equation, which is the "poor man's version" of the celebrated parabolic Navier–Stokes partial differential equation (PDE). The Navier–Stokes PDE is the standard dynamic physical flow or risk (energy) dissipation model, which inspires to replace the large set of affine multi-factor diffusion models by new nonlinear financial diffusion models. In Chapter 11, we discuss more details of the identification and dynamic simulation modeling of financial turbulence. We'll discuss also how wavelets can be used to solve a discrete version of the nonlinear Navier–Stokes PDE via the Galerkin finite elements solution method for such dynamic simulations.

To accomplish the two ambitious objectives of measurement and simulation of financial illiquidity, we reformulate and reinterpret the classical laws of fluid mechanics into cash flow mechanics, in particular, the law of conservation of investment capital (= "mass"), of the cash flow rate (= "momentum") and of the second moment of the rate of cash return (= financial market risk = 2× "energy"). Therefore, our newly proposed cash flow laws are modeled on the basic conservation laws of hydraulics and aerodynamics.[1]

For example, we'll study Richardson (1926)-type "scale-by-scale cash-flow rate of return budget equations," e.g., the *term structure* of default-free government zero-coupon bonds, which allows us to interpret the transfer of cash returns among the different maturities, scales or frequencies of investment cash flow. It is on the borders between fixed maturities that nonlinear mixing processes of cash flows occur and where long-term dependence phenomena are found. For more detailed background on the formulation of these laws in the mechanics of incompressible physical fluids, cf. Batchelor (1970), Landau and Lifshitz (1987) and Tritton (1988). Van Dyke's (1982) photographic album provides inspiring 2-dimensional (2D) visualizations of fluid dynamics and turbulence.

At first our new approach may appear somewhat contrived and artificial, but the final result of these reformulations and reinterpretations consist of a set of various useful quantifiable financial quantities, which will assist us with the measurement, analysis and characterization of the complex dynamic financial markets. They will do that in ways that cannot be achieved by most of the current concepts of finance and economics, which were developed for Marshallian comparative static pricing models and for Debreu and Arrow's static general equilibrium pricing models, and not for the current affine dynamic partial differentiation models. The comparative static and the general equilibrium pricing models provided us with many imaginative concepts and powerful qualitative insights, but they contributed little to robust explanations and predictions of the empirically observed financial market dynamics.

Despite the difficulties we encounter with such a "copy-cat" approach, the current underdeveloped status of the liquidity analysis of the financial markets commands us to break new grounds through interdisciplinary comparisons of analytical methodologies, so that we can make slow but steady progress in the difficult areas of measurement and analysis of the risks of dynamic cash flow markets.

The fundamental cash growth rate accounting framework for multi-asset and multi-country investment portfolios has already been developed by Karnosky and Singer (1994) and Singer and Karnosky (1995). Los (1998, 1999, 2002) established its empirical applicability and extended that accounting framework to a classical Markowitz' mean–variance portfolio optimization and risk attribution framework by using tensor algebra. In Chapter 12, we will extend this simple accounting-cum-optimization framework even further to beyond Markowitz' mean–variance analysis, so as to include stable and heavy-tailed, skewed and excess-kurtosis, rate of return distributions based on long-term dependence relationships.

In the current chapter we'll focus on the term structure of so-called *laminar* and *turbulent* investment cash flows. By way of several Examples and in the Exercises we'll demonstrate the empirical applicability of these new ways of measuring the dynamics of the cash flows of investments and the term structure. For example, we'll compute the coefficient of illiquidity (= "dynamic viscosity of cash flows") for a term structure based on the S&P500 stock market index.

For the discussion of financial turbulence in Chapter 11, starting with Kolmogorov's 1941 explanation for homogeneous fluid turbulence, we'll draw upon examples from meteorology and hydrology, because advanced dynamic financial modeling encounters similar problems as in dynamic meteorological and hydrological flow modeling, as originally suggested in Los (1991a,b). In Chapter 11, we'll describe the wavelet Galerkin finite elements method, based on the wavelet multiresolution analysis (MRA) of Chapter 7, to dynamically solve the nonlinear Navier–Stokes equations.

We expect that such identification and simulation of similar nonlinear diffusion models will become a leading example for the study of transient dynamics – in particular the occurrence of discontinuities, intermittency and turbulence – in the global financial markets, as originally envisioned by Benoit Mandelbrot in the 1960s. Currently, we have the high frequency data, the advanced dynamic physics modeling methodology, the signal and process engineering technology, and the (graphics) computer power to realize Mandelbrot's original vision.

One particular point we should emphasize right from the beginning: financial turbulence is not a "negative " or a "disastrous" phenomenon. Intermittency and turbulence may be unsettling for market participants, but they are *efficiency enhancing*, deterministic, dynamic phenomena, which we must understand better for a full appreciation of the ongoing proper functioning of the financial markets and the risks they contain. Financial intermittency and turbulence are limited phenomena that occur under particular nonlinear institutional constraints of well-functioning financial markets, such as the foreign exchange markets of the Deutschemark, the Euro or the Japanese Yen, when these markets are experiencing severe *differentials in liquidity persistence*, respectively.

In other words, financial *turbulence*, which occurs in antipersistent financial markets, must be sharply differentiated from the more fearsome financial *crises*, which are unpredictable discontinuities. Truly catastrophic crisis phenomena – like the 1929 and 1987 market crashes – occur when there is a large differential in persistence between the various interconnected financial markets. Such financial crises we either need to prevent by changing the institutional structure of the existing financial markets to make them all less persistent and more liquid, or against which we must hedge ourselves by trading financial catastrophe bonds or derivatives, to prevent their truly catastrophic consequences, as originally suggested by Chichilnisky and Heal (1993) and Chichilnisky (1996). Such completion of the finanical markets by enhanced arbitrage will make them more liquid and less prone to discontinuities.

10.2   Dynamic investment cash flow theory

We will now discuss *general cash flow streams*.[2] When cash is in motion, its properties are described at each point in time by the properties of its cash flow rate.

Definition 392 *A cash flow rate $\Delta X_\tau(t)$ at time t is the product of the cash invested (= cash position) $X_\tau(t)$ at the beginning of investment horizon τ and the spot, zero or cash rate of return (= cash velocity) $x_\tau(t)$ for investment horizon τ:*

$$\Delta X_\tau(t) = x_\tau(t) X_\tau(t) \tag{10.1}$$

since the invested value of an asset grows approximately as

$$\begin{aligned} X_\tau(t+1) &= X_\tau(t) + \Delta_\tau X(t) \\ &= [1 + x_\tau(t)] X_\tau(t) \\ &= X_\tau(t) \cdot e^{x_\tau(t)} \end{aligned} \tag{10.2}$$

The most important part of this definition is the term cash rate of return $x_\tau(t)$, which can be used in many different exact cash accounting frameworks (Karnosky and Singer, 1994; Singer and Karnosky, 1995; Los, 1998, 1999, 2001; Leow, 1999).

Remark 393 *The current price based on the investment with horizon τ is then the discounted price*

$$X_\tau(t) = X_\tau(t+1) e^{-x_\tau(t)} \tag{10.3}$$

Remark 394 *Continuous compounding gives*

$$X_\tau(t+\tau) = X_\tau(t) \cdot e^{x_\tau(t)\tau} \tag{10.4}$$

so that

$$x_\tau(t) = \frac{\ln X_\tau(t+\tau) - \ln X_\tau(t)}{\tau} \tag{10.5}$$

Example 395 *According to the exact cash rate of return accounting framework for multi-asset- multi-country portfolios, at time t an investor has three possible investment instruments: (1) investment in an asset k in country i with rate of return $r_{ik}(t)$, (2) a cash swap with rate of return $c_j(t) - c_i(t)$, with $c_j(t)$ being the risk free cash rate in country j into which the nominal is swapped, and $c_i(t)$ being the risk free cash rate in country i out of which the nominal is swapped, and (3) the foreign currency appreciation rate $f_j(t)$ of country j.[3] Thus, one particular bilateral investment strategy at time t is represented by the following strategic rate of return:*

$$x_{ijk}(t) = r_{ik}(t) + [c_j(t) - c_i(t)] + f_j(t) \tag{10.6}$$

with $i, j \in \mathbb{Z}_1^2$ being the indices for bilateral cash flows between the various countries and $k \in \mathbb{Z}_2$ being the index for the various assets (stocks, bonds, real estate, commodities, etc.). Notice that, according to the Capital Asset Pricing Model (CAPM), such an international investment strategy is, equivalent to $[r_{ik}(t) - c_i(t)]$, the sum of the asset risk premium in local market i, and $[c_j(t) + f_j(t)]$, the cash return on currency j (Los, 1998, 1999, 2002; Leow, 1999).

This leads to the following definitions of *continuous* and *steady* cash flows.

Definition 396   Continuous cash flow *occurs in a particular cash flow channel, when its cash flow rate* $\Delta X_\tau(t)$ *is constant*

$$\Delta X_\tau(t) = x_\tau(t) X_\tau(t)$$

$$= constant\ (= independent\ of\ time) \tag{10.7}$$

Remark 397   *This equation is also called the* cash flow continuity equation.

Continuous cash flow does not mean that the cash rate or return is constant, but that the first difference of the cash flow is constant. A constant cash rate of return defines a steady cash flow.

Definition 398   Steady cash flow *occurs in a particular investment channel, when its spot return rate*

$$x_\tau(t) = x_\tau$$

$$= constant\ (= independent\ of\ time) \tag{10.8}$$

It's obvious that, under conditions of continuous cash flows, the spot return rate x_τ is high when the cash flow channel is constricted, i.e., where the investment position X_τ is small, and the cash flow return rate x_τ is low where the channel is wide, i.e., where the investment position X_τ is large.

Remark 399   Day traders, *who have very short daily investment horizons, trade very quickly with small investment positions, in the order of a* $1,000 *and reap highly volatile returns* $x_\tau(t)$ *with very large amplitudes* $|x_\tau(t)|$. *In contrast, insti-tutional investors, such as pension funds, insurance funds or large mutual funds, who usually have very long-term investment horizons, trade much slower with very large investment positions in the order of* $100 *million and more, and who invest for steady rates of return* $x_\tau(t)$ *with moderate amplitudes* $|x_\tau(t)|$. *The trillion dollar research question is: can such different types of traders, with investment positions of different size and investment horizons of different lengths, coexist in the same global markets without financial intermittency and turbulence, or are these phenomena necessary and unavoidable consequences? Since day traders add liquidity and reduce the persistence of a financial market, it is likely that they reduce the possible occurrence of financial crises or catastrophes, which are phe-nomena occurring in illiquid, persistent financial markets, when suddenly large investment positions are set up, or, more likely, suddenly unwound in a panic atmosphere. However, since day traders trade very fast and institutional traders, such as the managers of pension funds and insurance funds usually trade very slow, it is likely that the confluence of these cash flows with different investment horizons and maturities and trading speeds causes vortices and turbulence, which is an efficiency-enhancing phenomena, since it reconciles the variety of velocities (= cash rates of return) of the confluent cash flows.*

10.2.1 *Perfectly efficient dynamic financial markets*

The motion of empirical cash flows in globally interconnected financial markets is very complex and still not fully understood, because the flows start and stop at various times and go back and forth between billions of bilateral positions.[4] Until very recently, financial economists have proceeded by making several heroic, simplifying assumptions for stationary, and often static, markets. Following the classical definitions of ideal, perfectly efficient physical flows, the following is my own suggestion for a new idealization definition of perfectly efficient dynamic financial markets, which can provide a new standard for the comparative measurement of dynamic cash flows in nonstationary markets. This effort, to define what empirical financial markets clearly are not, is intended to formulate benchmark quantities for the measurement for the highly nonstationary financial market dynamics.

Definition 400 Perfectly efficient dynamic financial markets *have cash flows, which are:*

(1) perfectly liquid *(or* nonviscous*): there is no internal (institutional) friction in the financial markets and all assets of different maturities in all markets can be instantaneously purchased and liquidated. This means that the financial markets instantaneously clear and that they are always in equilibrium.*
(2) steady: *the term rate of return* $x_\tau(t)$ *of each cash flow remains constant, i.e., it is not volatile.*
(3) incompressible*: the density of the cash transactions remains constant in time, i.e., the volume of the markets' buy and sell transactions remains uniform over time. There are no cyclicities, no intermittencies, no rarefaction and condensation periods, and no discontinuities ("gapping") in the market trading.*
(4) irrotational*: there is no angular momentum of the cash flows, i.e., all cash flows in a particular investment channel at a time t are in the same direction and are not reversed within the same channel and all flows in all channels are in the same direction. All decision makers with different time horizons for investment receive the same information at the same time and interpret that information correctly, simultaneously and in the same fashion (= the markets are rational and show a "herd instinct").*

Remark 401 *There is some contradiction between this idealization of irrotational cash flows and the financial-economic concept of a market of buyers and sellers, or of risk hedgers and speculators, since in a market one needs two parties with opposite views to conduct one arbitrage trade to establish a price. When everybody within a particular financial market has the same idea and invest in the same direction, that market's prices go ballistic, i.e., the phenomenon of a market bubble, of the kind we have experienced in the technology sector in the late 1990s and which has just gone bust in 2002. But, of course, this also implies that there are counterparts in coexistent financial markets, where prices become severely depressed.*

In the idealized situation of a perfectly efficient dynamic financial market, the cash flows in a particular investment channel are all streamlined in the same direction (there are no reversal trades within a channel or crossover trades between channels) and move at the same constant flow rates $x_\tau(t)$. There are no "bulls" (positive investors) and "bears" (negative investors) trading at the same maturity levels. This means, e.g., that the term structure of interest rates is horizontal can only move up and down parallel to itself, because of changing inflation expectations, and it does not rotate or curve. There is no time preference and there is no risk differentiation. This is, of course, an abstraction from empirical financial market reality, where slopes, rotations and curving of the term structures of interest rates are difficult to model empirical phenomena (cf. Chapman and Pearson, 2001; James and Webber, 2001).

10.2.2   *Financial pressure and cash flow risk*

Under such abstract, perfectly efficient dynamic financial market conditions, one can formulate a Bernoulli equation for cash flows which quantifies the concept of *financial pressure*.[5]

Definition 402   (Bernoulli equation for cash flows) *In perfectly efficient dynamic financial markets*

$$\mathrm{FP}(t) + \tfrac{1}{2}\rho x_\tau^2(t) = constant \tag{10.9}$$

where $\mathrm{FP}(t)$ *is the* financial pressure *at time t and* $\rho = 1/\$$ *is the* uniform cash density *in the investment channel with a particular horizon (maturity)* τ.

Remark 403   *The uniform cash density* $\rho = 1/\$$ *is, in financial terms, the* purchasing power *of one dollar.*

Remark 404   *The Bernoulli cash flow equation is also called the* cash risk equation. *It implicitly defines and measures the concept of financial pressure, since*

$$\mathrm{FP}_\tau(t) = constant - \tfrac{1}{2}\rho x_\tau^2(t) \tag{10.10}$$

This implies that financial pressure is relatively large where investment cash moves slowly and relatively low where it moves fast.

This Bernoulli equation for cash flows states that the sum of financial pressure $\mathrm{FP}_\tau(t)$ and the *local risk* of the cash flow per dollar invested, $\tfrac{1}{2}\rho x_\tau^2(t)$, is constant in a cash flow investment channel (or "streamline") of a particular term.

Remark 405   *The* local risk $\tfrac{1}{2}\rho x_\tau^2(t)$ *is not the same as the* average risk $\tfrac{1}{2}\rho E\{x_\tau^2(t)\}$ *familiar from classical finance. In Chapter 8, we learned to measure local volatility by wavelet MRA.*

This Bernoulli equation for cash flows describes a *Venturi cash flow channel* to measure the difference in financial pressure between two different places along an investment cash flow channel, as follows. The Bernoulli equation implies that

$$\text{FP}_{\tau_i}(t) + \tfrac{1}{2}\rho x_{\tau_i}^2(t) = \text{FP}_{\tau_j}(t) + \tfrac{1}{2}\rho x_{\tau_j}^2(t), \quad \text{where } (i, j) \in \mathbb{Z}^2 \qquad (10.11)$$

so that the *financial pressure differential* $\text{FP}_{\tau_i}(t) - \text{FP}_{\tau_j}(t)$, measured simultaneously at two different horizons τ_i and τ_j at time t, is the difference between the local volatilities or risks (= "dynamic energies") of the uniform cash flow at these two maturity points

$$\begin{aligned}
\Delta_{\tau_i \tau_j} \text{FP}(t) &= \text{FP}_{\tau_i}(t) - \text{FP}_{\tau_j}(t) \\
&= \tfrac{1}{2}\rho [x_{\tau_j}^2(t) - x_{\tau_i}^2(t)] \\
&= -\tfrac{1}{2}\rho \Delta_{\tau_i \tau_j} x^2(t) \qquad (10.12)
\end{aligned}$$

When the financial pressure at an "upstream" point, investment horizon, or maturity, τ_i is higher than at "downstream" point or horizon τ_j, the cash flow velocity $x_{\tau_j}(t)$ at maturity τ_j is higher than at maturity τ_i, and *vice versa*.

This point about the cash flow pressure differential $\Delta_{\tau_i \tau_j} \text{FP}(t)$ becomes clearer, when we take account of the size of the investment positions at the two investment horizons. When the cash flow between the two investment horizons is continuous, as thus far we have assumed, when

$$x_{\tau_i}(t) X_{\tau_i}(t) = x_{\tau_j}(t) X_{\tau_j}(t) = \text{constant} \qquad (10.13)$$

then

$$x_{\tau_j}(t) = \frac{X_{\tau_i}(t)}{X_{\tau_j}(t)} x_{\tau_i}(t) \qquad (10.14)$$

and

$$\begin{aligned}
\Delta_{\tau_i \tau_j} \text{FP}(t) &= -\tfrac{1}{2}\rho \Delta_{\tau_i \tau_j} x^2(t) \\
&= \tfrac{1}{2}\rho [x_{\tau_j}^2(t) - x_{\tau_i}^2(t)] \\
&= \frac{1}{2}\rho \left[\frac{X_{\tau_i}(t)}{X_{\tau_j}(t)} x_{\tau_i}(t) \right]^2 - x_{\tau_i}^2(t) \\
&= \frac{1}{2}\rho \left[\left(\frac{X_{\tau_i}(t)}{X_{\tau_j}(t)} \right)^2 - 1 \right] x_{\tau_i}^2(t) \\
&= \frac{1}{2}\rho \left[\frac{X_{\tau_i}^2(t) - X_{\tau_j}^2(t)}{X_{\tau_j}^2(t)} \right] x_{\tau_i}^2(t) \qquad (10.15)
\end{aligned}$$

Note that, under the condition of a continuous cash flow, $\Delta_{\tau_i \tau_j} \text{FP}(t) > 0$ if and only if $X_{\tau_i}^2(t) > X_{\tau_j}^2(t)$. This financial market cash flow system operates as follows. Consider a particular very crowded asset investment market at a particular investment horizon, with many market participants, where a lot of cash is squeezed together. As soon as an extra investment channel at another investment horizon opens up and cash begins to exit that particular asset market, the squeezing, or pressure FP, is least near this small exit, where the motion (= cash flow rate of return $x(t)$) is greatest. Thus, under the assumption of perfectly efficient dynamic financial markets, the lowest financial pressure occurs where the investment channel is smallest and the cash return rate or local risk is highest, e.g., in emerging financial markets, where the marginal productivity and the risk of capital investment is highest. In contrast, the highest financial pressure occurs where the investment channel is largest and the cash return rate or local risk is lowest, e.g., in developed financial markets, where the marginal productivity and the risk of capital investment is lowest.

Remark 406   *One should be on the alert for financial intermittency and turbulence when the difference in financial pressure between the upstream and downstream financial markets, $\Delta_{\tau_i \tau_j} \mathrm{FP}(t)$, is large. When the difference in the cash investments in each of the two connected markets, $X_{\tau_i}^2(t) - X_{\tau_j}^2(t)$, is very large, the local risk $x_{\tau_j}^2(t) = ((X_{\tau_i}(t))/(X_{\tau_j}(t))x_{\tau_i}(t))^2$ in the downstream market is very large. Under such circumstances, the uniform local risk term, $\frac{1}{2}\rho x_\tau^2(t)$, begins to figure prominently in the form of the* financial Reynolds number *(see below). A typical high financial Reynolds number empirically measures the onset of intermittency and financial turbulence.*

Multiplying the local risk of the uniform cash flow by its flow rate provides the rate at which the risk is transferred, i.e., it provides its financial *power*.

Definition 407   *The* Cash Flow Risk *(CFR) with investment horizon τ at time t is defined by*

$$\begin{aligned}
\mathrm{CFR}(t) &= \tfrac{1}{2}\rho x_\tau^2(t)\Delta X(t) \\
&= \tfrac{1}{2}\rho x_\tau^2(t)[x_\tau(t)X_\tau(t)] \\
&= \tfrac{1}{2}\rho x_\tau^3(t)X_\tau(t)
\end{aligned} \tag{10.16}$$

This leads to the definition of available cash flow risk per dollar invested.

Definition 408   *The* Available Cash Flow Risk (ACFR) per dollar invested *is given by*

$$\mathrm{ACFR}(t) = \frac{\mathrm{CFR}(t)}{X_\tau(t)} = \frac{1}{2}\rho x_\tau^3(t) \tag{10.17}$$

Remark 409   *The ACFR is the local skewness of the term rate $x_\tau(t)$.*

Definition 410 *The* Average Available Cash Flow Risk (AACFR) per dollar invested *is given by*

$$\text{AACFR}(t) = \tfrac{1}{2}\rho E\{x_\tau^3(t)\} \tag{10.18}$$

Remark 411 *The AACFR is similar to the third distribution moment or the global skewness of the term rate $x_\tau(t)$. It is a classical result that the skewness is a measure of vortex stretching (Frisch, 1995, p. 156), to be discussed in Chapter 11.*

This last definition involves the third moment (skewness) $m_3 = E\{x_\tau^3(t)\}$ of the distribution of the cash flow rate of return $x_\tau(t)$ in the term structure of spot rates $\{x_\tau(t)$ for all $\tau\}$. For (symmetric) Gaussian investment rates returns $m_3 = 0$ and thus the AACFR $= 0$. Gaussian distributions do not exhibit any AACFR phenomena. In contrast, asymmetric distributions of investment rates of return $m_3 \neq 0$, as we discussed in Chapters 1 and 3. Thus, the AACFR is nil, when the distribution of the rates of return is symmetric around zero, e.g., when it is as likely to make money as it is to lose it. The AACFR is positive when the distribution of the rate of return $x_\tau(t)$ is positively skewed, and negative when its distribution is negatively skewed. Interestingly, as we mentioned in Chapters 1, 2 and 3, most empirical financial distributions are skewed and thus exhibit AACFR $\neq 0$. Until recently, by systematically assuming most return distributions in finance to be Gaussian, financial economists avoided to discuss the dynamic CFR phenomena in which signal processing engineers and physicist are so interested! By *assuming* Gaussian distribution financial economists prohibited themselves from discovering why financial turbulence occurs.

10.3 Nonlinear relationships in finance

Now, we need first to make a digression to a few essential financial concepts and definitions and relationships to see that investment cash flows $X_\tau(t)$ are nonlinearly related to the yields $x_\tau(t)$, both in a static and a dynamic sense. The *static* nonlinear relationship is represented by the term structure of interest rates at a particular time t. The *dynamic* nonlinear relationship is represented by the nonlinear price diffusion equations and related curve-fitting functions of generalized dynamic term structure models of each of the spot interest rates on the term structure. To understand the importance of these relationships it is crucial to understand that in finance

asset (or liability) price = discounted cash flow related to investment horizon τ

Next, to motivate further our use of wavelet MRAs, we'll propose to use the Navier–Stokes *nonlinear* diffusion equation as a generalized version of the Black–Scholes pricing equation. Such a nonlinear diffusion equation can lead to stability, periodicity, cyclicity, turbulence and intermittency, as we discussed in Chapter 9, using the logistic equation as a simplified example of such a nonlinear diffusion equation. In Chapter 11, we'll then discuss how we can measure the essential parameter values of this generalized price diffusion equation using wavelet MRA. In Chapter 11, we'll also discuss how we can solve this nonlinear diffusion equation using wavelet–Galerkin method and use the solution to simulate each type of yield and thus price behavior of the various cash flows in the financial markets. We'll see that the results of such simulations crucially depend on the correct value of the parameter value of the nonlinear term in the diffusion equation.

After the motivational discussion of the generalized price diffusion equation, and, again, analogously to definitions in physical flow dynamics, we continue with the definition of a *coefficient of cash flow illiquidity*, which allows us to measure the degree of illiquidity in the financial markets using wavelet MRAs.

10.3.1 Linear combinations of assets and liabilities

To understand the centrality of a dynamic valuation of assets, which relates cash flows, prices and rates of return, we only have to look at the basis structure of finance: double-entry bookkeeping and the *law of one price* or, equivalently, *pricing by arbitrage*.

The double-entry bookkeeping model of accounting shows that the value of any concern can be represented as a linear portfolio of fundamental and derivative financial instruments (cf. Los, 2001, p. 24). The *Accounting Identity* of the *balance sheet* with current market values is

$$\text{Assets}(t) = \text{Liabilities}(t) + \text{Equity}(t)$$

$$\text{or } A(t) = L(t) + E(t)$$

$$\text{or, slightly rewritten, } E(t) = A(t) - L(t) \tag{10.19}$$

This Accounting Identity is the basic model for exact financial modeling, since financial instruments can be viewed as combinations of long and short positions of the fundamental securities. Changes in the net equity position $\Delta_\tau E(t)$ over the accounting period τ, which is usually one quarter of a year or a year, are produced by the corresponding changes in the assets and liabilities, as reflected in the *income statement*[6]

$$\Delta E_\tau(t) = \Delta A_\tau(t) - \Delta L_\tau(t)$$

$$\text{or } x_\tau^E(t) E_\tau(t) = x_\tau^A(t) A_\tau(t) - x_\tau^L(t) L_\tau(t)$$

$$\text{or Net Income}_\tau(t) = \text{Revenues}_\tau(t) - \text{Expenses}_\tau(t) \tag{10.20}$$

on a *market value basis*, where $x_\tau^A(t)$ is the market valued Rate of Return on Assets (ROA) over the period τ, $x_\tau^L(t)$ is the market valued rate of debt liability expense (= rate of interest on all debt) over the period τ, and $x_\tau^E(t)$ is the market valued Rate of Return on Equity (ROE) over the period τ. Thus, the Accounting Identity combines the bundles of discounted cash flows in a linear fashion and these discounted cash flows are nonlinearly related to the rates of return.

The rational law of pricing by arbitrage implies that all other financial instruments, like derivatives, can be derived from fundamental asset valuations by simple linear combinations. Call and put options can be synthesized from a linear portfolio of bonds and stocks (cf. Los, 2001, pp. 164–166). Forwards and futures can be represented as time-shifted bonds or stocks (cf. Los, 2001, pp. 225–227). Swaps can be represented by a combination of a long and a short bond, or, equivalently, by a series of zero coupon bonds, or a series of long and short forwards (cf. Los, 2001, pp. 239–243). But the resulting portfolios may not behave in a linear fashion. This can lead to quite complex situations in international cash flow analysis, as the following simple example shows.

Example 412 *One can form a square matrix of bilateral cash flow channels between all investment horizons within the same country, so that every cash flow investment channel associated with a particular term rate of return $x_{\tau_i}(t)$ is adjacent to every other cash flow investment channel, resulting in a net rate of return for both cash channels together*

$$\Delta_{\tau_i \tau_j} x(t) = x_{\tau_i}(t) - x_{\tau_j}(t)$$
$$= x_{ij}(t)$$

so that we form the bilateral cash rate of return matrix *or* strategic investment return matrix

$$\mathbf{x}(t) = \begin{bmatrix} x_{11}(t) & x_{12}(t) & \cdots & x_{1,T_2}(t) \\ x_{21}(t) & x_{22}(t) & \cdots & \cdots \\ \cdots & \cdots & \cdots & \cdots \\ x_{T_1,1}(t) & \cdots & \cdots & x_{T_1,T_2}(t) \end{bmatrix} \tag{10.21}$$

Each side of the matrix represents the term structure of assets in the same country. Alternatively, one can form a matrix of all the cash rates of one particular maturity of a whole set of countries. This means that the global term structure problem is at least a 3-dimensional (3D), or a cubic array problem. Such a cubic array can be reduced to a 2-dimensional (2D), or matrix problem by vectorization and the use of tensor algebra. Using tensor algebra, Los (2002) provides empirical examples of such bilateral cash rates of return matrices based on the short-term cash rates and stock market index return rates in 10 Asian countries (including Japan) plus Germany.

Thus, we need to look at the nonlinear structures of the fundamental assets and liabilities of various horizons in various countries, which can be combined in myriad ways into advanced financial instruments.

10.3.2 Nonlinear term structure of interest rates

The term structure relates the yields of the assets and liabilities to the cash flows invested, in a nonlinear, exponential relationship.

Definition 413 *The* term structure *or* spot rate curve *$\{x_\tau(t), \tau\}$ of any asset at time t is defined by the functional relationship between spot or zero rates $x_\tau(t)$*

and the investment horizons or maturities τ, written in continuous and discrete time forms as

$$x_\tau(t) = e^{x_\tau(t)} - 1$$

$$= \left[\frac{X_\tau(t+\tau)}{X_\tau(t)}\right]^{1/\tau} - 1 \tag{10.22}$$

The term structure measures the current, spot rates of return on investments with different maturities or investment horizons. A related definition is that of the *discount function*.

Definition 414   *The discount factors $\delta_\tau(t) = e^{-x_\tau(t)}$ form the* discount function *or* discount curve $\{\delta_\tau(t), \tau\}$.

Example 415   *The fundamental security of a simple (Treasury) bond at time t can be decomposed into a series of* zero coupon *bonds. A* zero coupon bond, *or* pure discount bond, *with maturity τ and principal payment $B_\tau(t)$, has zero coupons, so that its (discounted) present value is*

$$PB_0(t) = \begin{cases} B(t+\tau)e^{-x_\tau(t)\tau} & \text{in continuous time} \\ \dfrac{B(t+\tau)}{[1+x_\tau(t)]^\tau} & \text{in discrete time} \end{cases} \tag{10.23}$$

Thus, we have, ex post, *by approximation the nonlinear balance relationship between rates of return and cash flows*

$$[1+x_\tau(t)]^\tau = e^{x_\tau(t)\tau}$$

$$= \frac{B(t+\tau)}{PB_0(t)} \tag{10.24}$$

A τ-year spot interest rate at time t is the interest rate of a zero bond

$$x_\tau(t) = \left[\frac{B(t+\tau)}{PB_0(t)}\right]^{1/\tau} - 1 \tag{10.25}$$

This term structure of interest rates *is the nonlinear relationship between the spot interest rate $x_\tau(t)$ and the maturity τ for a particular grade of credit quality of obligations (e.g., bills, notes, bonds) (Barclay and Smith, 1995). The research question is either how do the spot rates $x_\tau(t)$ develop over time for each investment time horizon τ, or how does the term structure (or cash flow velocity field) $\{x_\tau(t), \tau\}$ develop over time?*

Example 416   *For the second fundamental security of a stock we have the following valuation. For (not necessarily constant) dividend payments $D_\tau(t)$ and a cost of capital $x_\tau(t)$ at time t, the dividend discount model (DDM) of stock valuation for an ongoing concern (= a firm with an infinite life time) computes the stock's* *present value at time t to be equivalent to an infinite series of "zero coupon bonds" with maturities* $\tau = 1, 2, \ldots, \infty$

$$
\begin{aligned}
\text{PS}_0(t) &= \sum_{\tau=1}^{\infty} \frac{D(t+\tau)}{[1+x_\tau(t)]^\tau} \\
&= \sum_{\tau=1}^{\infty} D(t+\tau)e^{-x_\tau(t)\tau}
\end{aligned}
\tag{10.26}
$$

Thus, for each of the dividend payments we have the cash flow relationship

$$
\begin{aligned}
[1+x_\tau(t)]^\tau &= e^{x_\tau(t)\tau} \\
&= \frac{D(t+\tau)}{\text{PS}_0(t)}
\end{aligned}
\tag{10.27}
$$

so that the τ-year spot dividend yield *is*

$$
x_\tau(t) = \left[\frac{D(t+\tau)}{\text{PS}_0(t)}\right]^{1/\tau} - 1
\tag{10.28}
$$

10.3.3   Parametrized term structure models

We can generalize this financial constellation further. For a $m \times 1$ vector $\mathbf{X}(t)$ of current asset spot prices within a particular currency and an $m \times n$ matrix $\mathbf{X}(t, \tau)$ of (certain or uncertain) cash flows between now and the investment horizon, or time to maturity τ, one wants to find an $n \times 1$ vector $\boldsymbol{\delta}_\tau(t)$ of discount factors at time t, so that

$$
\mathbf{X}(t) = \mathbf{X}(t, \tau)\boldsymbol{\delta}_\tau(t) + \boldsymbol{\varepsilon}(t)
\tag{10.29}
$$

where the $m \times 1$ vector of residual errors $\boldsymbol{\varepsilon}(t)$ are small.[7] The $n \times 1$ vector of discount factors $\boldsymbol{\delta}_\tau(t)$ is a function of investment horizons, or times to maturity, defined for all maturity times $\tau \in [0, \infty)$, so that $\boldsymbol{\delta}_\tau(t) = [\delta(\tau_1), \ldots, \delta(\tau_n)]'$, where $\{\tau_j\}_{j=1, \ldots, n}$ is a set of n cash flow times. The term structure can be easily found from this vector of discount factors since the $n \times 1$ vector of spot rates $\mathbf{x}_\tau(t) = [x_{\tau_j}(t) = -\ln \delta_{\tau j}(t)/\tau_j]'_{j=1, \ldots, n}$. If the vector $\boldsymbol{\delta}_\tau(t)$ depends on a small ($\ll n$) number of parameters, $\boldsymbol{\delta}_\tau(t) = \boldsymbol{\delta}_\tau(t|a, b, \ldots)$, then fitting the discount function or curve to the empirically observed discount factors involves choosing this small set of parameters via *error minimization* or a *calibration* search. The resulting calibrated vector of discount factors $\boldsymbol{\delta}_\tau(t)$ represents a coherent curve (as it should based on rational expectations, c.q. market arbitrage), instead of a set of independent discount factors $\{\delta(\tau_i)\}$.

There are two main types of curves commonly used in fitting this discount function: affine interest rate diffusion models and term structure fitting models.

10.3.3.1   *Affine interest rate diffusion models*

Term structures are currently directly derived from many different theoretical affine interest rate diffusion models, like the very popular one-factor term structure models with mean-reverting short rate dynamics of Vasicek (1977) and Cox *et al.* (1985), the two-factor extended Vasicek term structure models of Heath *et al.* (1990, 1992) and Hull and White (1990, 1993), the two-factor dynamic mean model of Sørensen (1994), the three-factor model of Balduzzi *et al.* (1996) and the stochastic volatility term structure models of Longstaff and Schwartz (1992). We'll discuss the one-factor affine diffusion model in some detail to provide a flavor of these parameterized affine term structure models.

The one-factor diffusion models of the term structure of interest rate are the simplest (Hong Yan, 2000). The dynamics of the short rate $x_0(t)$ are described by the stochastic differential equation

$$dx_0(t) = \mu[x_0(t)]\,dt + \sigma[x_0(t)]\,dz(t) \tag{10.30}$$

which means that the change in the short-term interest rate can be decomposed into a drift $\mu[x_0(t)]\,dt$ over the time period $(t, t+dt)$ and an increment of a GBM, $dz(t)$, with an *instantaneous volatility* or *risk* measure $\sigma[x_0(t)]$.

Remark 417   *Since empirical evidence shows that, in a principal component analysis of the covariance matrix of the term structure about 90 percent of the variation of the term structure is attributable to the first component, which is interpreted to be the level of the interest rate, any point on the term structure may be used as a proxy for it (Chapman and Pearson, 2001). This factor is generally taken to be the instantaneous short rate of interest (= the intercept of the term structure). The scientific problem with principal component analysis is, though, that the percentage of variation attributable to a particular component is dependent on the number of components that are retained from the covariance matrix. If all n components are retained, the question becomes: what is the size of the covariance matrix, since that determines the percentage of variation decomposition.*

The return on a zero coupon bond of maturity τ can then be expressed as

$$\frac{dX_\tau(t)}{X_\tau(t)} = \mu_{X_\tau}\,dt + \sigma_{X_\tau}\,dz(t) \tag{10.31}$$

where the expected return on the bond $\mu_{X_\tau}\,dt$ is directly related to the drift $\mu[x_0(t)]\,dt$ and volatility $\sigma[x_0(t)]$ of the short rate and the volatility of the bond return, σ_{X_τ}, is related to $\sigma[x_0(t)]$. The no-arbitrage condition applied to the whole set of zero coupon bond prices requires that the *market price of risk* is

$$\frac{\mu_{X_\tau} - x_0(t)}{\sigma_{X_\tau}} = \lambda[x_0(t)] \tag{10.32}$$

where $x_0(t)$ is the credit risk-free rate of return. The *market price of risk* $\lambda[x_0(t)]$ is the required compensation (or premium) in the form of excess return over the credit risk-free rate for bearing one unit of bond price risk as measured by the bond's volatility of return.

By applying Itô's Lemma, the bond price $X_\tau(t)$ satisfies a partial differential (diffusion) equation:

$$\frac{\partial X_\tau(t)}{\partial t} = -\frac{\partial\{\mu[x_0(t)] - \lambda[x_0(t)]\sigma[x_0(t)]\}X_\tau(t)}{\partial x_0(t)}$$

$$-\frac{1}{2}\frac{\partial^2 X_\tau(t)}{\partial x_0(t)^2}\sigma^2[x_0(t)] + x_0(t)X_\tau(t) \tag{10.33}$$

This simple diffusion model can be solved by symbolic integration. But for some diffusion models no closed form symbolic integration solution exists and they have to be solved by numerical integration.

Example 418 *In the very popular Vasicek (1977) one-factor mean-reversion model, the short rate follows an Ornstein–Uhlenbeck process as follows*

$$dx_0(t) = \kappa[\bar{x} - x_0(t)]\,dt + \sigma_x\,dz(t) \tag{10.34}$$

where κ measures the speed of mean reversion, $\bar{x}$ is the long-term mean to which the short rate is reverting, and σ_x is the instantaneous volatility of the short rate; all are assumed constant. In this model, the market price of risk is a constant

$$\lambda[x_0(t)] = \lambda_0 \tag{10.35}$$

After integration the resulting diffusion equation, the price of a zero bond is then shown to be of the form

$$X_\tau(t) = e^{[A(\tau) - B(\tau)x_0(t)]} \tag{10.36}$$

where τ is the remaining time horizon. Thus the zero bond price $X_\tau(t)$ is exponentially linear in the short rate $x_0(t)$

$$\ln X_\tau(t) = A(\tau) - B(\tau)x_0(t) \tag{10.37}$$

This implies that the spot rates of all maturities, $x_\tau(t)$, are linear in the short term rate $x_0(t)$. The horizon dependent deterministic functions $A(\tau)$ and $B(\tau)$ relate the spot rates of varying horizons (maturities) to the short rate $x_0(t)$, as follows

$$A(\tau) = [B(\tau) - \tau]\left[\bar{x} - \left(\frac{\lambda_0\sigma_x}{\kappa}\right) - \frac{1}{2}\left(\frac{\sigma_x}{\kappa}\right)^2\right] - \frac{[\sigma_x^2 B(\tau)^2]}{4\kappa} \tag{10.38}$$

$$B(\tau) = \frac{(1 - e^{-\kappa\tau})}{\kappa} \tag{10.39}$$

This one-factor Vasicek model produces thus term structure shapes that are either upward sloping, downward sloping or humped. Notice that when the parameter κ (which regulates the speed by which the short rate returns to its mean) is very *large, i.e., when we have an ultra-efficient or ultra-liquid instantaneously adjusting market*

$$\ln X_\tau(t) = A(\tau)$$

$$= -\tau \bar{x} \tag{10.40}$$

or the value of the zero coupon bond of maturity τ is

$$X_\tau(t) = e^{-\tau \bar{x}} \tag{10.41}$$

Because of the symmetric Gaussian distribution of $z(t)$ the model can generate negative interest rates $x_\tau(t)$. This is not a problem for real interest rates, but it is a problem for modeling nominal interest rates and the pricing of interest rate (fixed income) derivatives (Bakshi and Chen, 1996; Rogers, 1996).

Example 419   *To eliminate negative nominal interest rates, the Cox, Ingersöll and Ross (1985) (CIR) term structure propose a one-factor affine term structure (CIR) model with a square root process for the short rate:*

$$dx_0(t) = \kappa[\bar{x} - x_0(t)]\,dt + \sigma_x \sqrt{x_0(t)}\,dz(t) \tag{10.42}$$

This process has a reflecting boundary *at $x_0(t)$ if $2\kappa\bar{x} \geq \sigma_x^2$. Hence, it can exclude negative short rates of interest. The market price of risk is now depending on the short rate, since:*

$$\lambda[x_0(t)] = \frac{\lambda_0 \sqrt{x_0(t)}}{\sigma_x} \tag{10.43}$$

The resulting price of the zero bond still has the same form as in the Vasicek model, since it is still exponentially linear in the short rate:

$$X_\tau(t) = e^{[A(\tau) - B(\tau)x_0(t)]} \tag{10.44}$$

although now the horizon dependent deterministic functions $A(\tau)$ and $B(\tau)$ are as follows

$$A(\tau) = \frac{2\kappa\bar{x}}{\sigma_x} \ln\left[\frac{2\gamma e^{(\kappa+\lambda_0+\gamma)\tau/2}}{2\gamma + (\kappa+\lambda_0+\gamma)(e^{\gamma\tau}-1)}\right] \tag{10.45}$$

$$B(\tau) = \frac{2(e^{\gamma\tau}-1)}{2\gamma + (\kappa+\lambda_0+\gamma)(e^{\gamma\tau}-1)}, \tag{10.46}$$

where

$$\gamma = \sqrt{(\kappa+\lambda_0)^2 + 2\sigma_x^2} \tag{10.47}$$

The fact that the price of the zero bond is exponentially linear in the short rate and that the drift and variance terms are linear in the one or two factor(s) is characteristic of the general class of affine term structure models (Duffie and Kan,

1994; Dai and Singleton, 2000). This characteristic of linearity makes these affine models theoretically very tractable.

The ultimate kind of theoretical affine term structure modeling is found in the so-called "random field" or "stochastic string" models, developed initially by Kennedy (1994, 1997) and extended and characterized by Goldstein (2000), and Santa-Clara and Sornette (2001). These random field models describe the dynamics of the forward rate curve through an *infinite-dimensional* Gaussian (Wiener) shock vector $d\mathbf{z}(t)$, i.e., each point on the forward curve is driven by its own affine model. With a carefully defined correlation structure between the shocks $dz_i(t)$, $i = 1, 2, \ldots, \infty$ these infinite-dimensional models allow a flexible, consistent and complete description of the evolution of forward rates that matches the market prices at all times. Unfortunately, in reality we have only information about a finite number of shocks $dz_i(t)$ and these models are therefore scientifically uncorroborated.

For interesting discussions and generalizations of affine models, cf. Brown and Schaefer (1994a,b) and Duffie and Kan (1994, 1996), respectively. For example, affine term structure models may incorporate jump diffusion processes, like in Ahn and Thompson (1988), Das and Foresi (1996), Duffie and Kan (1996), who formally specified restrictions on the jump–diffusion processes to maintain the exponentially affine structure for bond prices, and Duffie *et al.* (2000), who provided a general treatment of a transform class readily applicable to valuing fixed-income securities. James and Webber (2001) present a complete classification of affine term structure models.

10.3.3.2 Nonlinear term structure models

Based on the discussion in Chapter 9, the quadratic term structure models, in which the term interest rates $x_\tau(t)$ are quadratic functions of the factors, should attract special attention for more detailed empirical research, because they harbor the potential for chaotic dynamic equilibrium regimes. Examples are Longstaff's (1989) nonlinear term structure model, its modification by Beaglehole and Tenney (1992) and Constantinides (1992) model for a nominal term structure. We already discussed the nonlinear, three-factor, Lorenz term structure model of Tice and Webber (1997) in Chapter 9.

10.3.3.3 Empirical identification of affine interest rate diffusion models

There is now a large proliferation of theoretical parametrized term structure models in the finance literature. For example, Luenberger (1998, pp. 406–408) lists no less than seven of the best-known one-factor affine models: the Rendleman and Bartter (1980) model, the Ho and Lee (1986) model, the Black, Derman and Toy (1990) model, the Vasicek (1977) model, the CIR (1985) model, the Hull and White (1990, 1993) model, and the Black and Karasinski (1991) model.

One-factor and two-factor affine term structure models assume that the dynamics of zero bond prices are driven by the same source or two sources of random shocks, respectively, and, therefore, that the term structure spot rates are locally perfectly correlated with each other. This assumption is empirically falsified (Hong, 2001). Empirical evidence suggests much more complex volatility or risk term structures than any of these simple affine term structure models allow for (Chapman and Pearson, 2001). Empirical studies show that (1) correlation between the various spot rates $x_\tau(t)$ are different from unity, and (2) these spot rates are highly correlated if they have the same horizon τ, but their correlations are significantly reduced for different time horizons or terms τ. In other words, the term structure and yield curves are highly segmented. Moreover, based on empirical evidence, the shorts rate covolatility structure is much more complex than these simple affine factor models can accommodate.

These observations are all quite important for the financial markets, because, e.g., the value of interest rate derivatives critically depends on the specification of the volatility term structure. But, once more than one factor is introduced to explain the shape of the term structure, confluence phenomena begin to occur and the diffusion processes become more complex, because of the mixing of the random processes. When these mixing diffusion processes are subject to nonlinear constraints, we have the model setting for possible chaotic phenomena.

It is now high time that rigorous and meticulous empirical identification and analysis weeds out the theoretical models that cannot be corroborated by empirical evidence. The reason that this has not yet happened is that the emphasis in the empirical corroboration process has traditionally been placed only on explaining the first two moments of the resulting theoretical frequency distributions. This procedure provides insufficient discriminating identification for proper empirical falsification. No attention has been paid by the empirical financial researchers to (1) the higher order moments of these frequency distributions and (2) the distribution and dependence relationships over time. If they had done so, most, if not all, of the proposed parametrized term structure models would already have been falsified.

10.3.3.4   Term structure fitting models

Term structure fitting models, like smoothing splines and Nelson and Siegel (1987) curves, do not derive from a particular interest rate model and do not explain the observed dynamics. They rely on the prevalence of stationary price developments. These curve-fitting families of curves also depend on a set of parameters. They are often used to *calibrate* interest rate models at a particular time, such as the extended Vasicek model. Since they rely on stationary market conditions, they promptly become very inaccurate in volatile times. These families of spot or forward rate curves may be linear or nonlinear.

Linear families of curves   A linear family forms a vector space with a set of a finite, preferably small number of basis functions – like sinuses or wavelets – so that every curve in the family can be represented as a linear combination of these basis functions – like in the Fourier and wavelet analyses. In a linear family the discount factor $\delta(\tau)$ can be represented as

$$\delta(\tau) = \sum_{k=1}^{K} \lambda_k \phi_k(\tau) \tag{10.48}$$

for some fixed set of finite basis functions $\phi_k(\tau)$, $k = 1, \ldots, K$, where $K \ll n$. Otherwise stated, the nonlinear discount factor can be expanded into a linear basis. The set $\{\phi_k(\tau)\}_{k=1,\ldots,K}$ is the small set of basis functions. The function $\delta(\tau)$ is determined by the vector of *resonance coefficients* $\lambda = [\lambda_1, \ldots, \lambda_K]$. Form the matrix $K \times n$ matrix $\Phi = [\phi_k(\tau_j)]_{k=1,\ldots,K, j=1,\ldots,n}$, so that the $n \times 1$ vector of discount factors $\delta(\tau) = \Phi' \lambda$, and define the $m \times K$ matrix $\mathbf{D}(t, \tau) - \mathbf{X}(t, \tau)\Phi'$, then we have to find the $K \times 1$ vector λ from:

$$\mathbf{X}(t) = \mathbf{D}(t, \tau)\lambda + \varepsilon(t) \tag{10.49}$$

so that the residual errors in the vector $\varepsilon(t)$ are very small. There are now only K resonance coefficients λ_i to find. Typically, in a term structure problem, $K = 6$ or 7, for a suitable set of basis functions.

Other linear curve fitting methods are splines. Splines are linear non-parametric interpolation methods, in particular smoothing, cubic, exponential and B-splines, as described by De Boor (1978) and Dierckx (1995) and implemented to term structures by Vasicek and Fong (1982) and Steeley (1991).

Nonlinear families of curves   These are mostly a family of static curves with relatively few parameters, often advocated by economists, to directly model either the spot rate curve or the forward rate curve. The resulting curves succeed fairly well in capturing the overall shape of the term structure or the forward rate curve at one particular time t_0, as long as it is not too complex, and as long a high accuracy is not required, and as long as the market conditions are stationary, which is, unfortunately, seldom the case. There are different versions of this family of curves.

Nelson and Siegel (1987) proposed the original family of such forward rate curves with a parsimonious four parameters $(\beta_0, \beta_1, \beta_2, k)$

$$f_\tau(t_0) = \beta_0 + (\beta_1 + \beta_2)e^{-k\tau} \tag{10.50}$$

If this represents a curve fitted to forward rates, then the term structure at time t_0 is

$$x_\tau(t_0) = \beta_0 + \left(\beta_1 + \frac{\beta_2}{k}\right)\frac{1 - e^{-k\tau}}{k\tau} - \frac{\beta_2}{k}e^{-k\tau} \tag{10.51}$$

The immediate short rate at time t_0 is $x_0(t_0) = \beta_0 + \beta_1$ and the corresponding long rate is $\lim_{\tau \to \infty} x_\tau(t_0) = \beta_0$ so that the parameters β_0 and β_1 have a direct intuition. β_2 and k control the height and the location of the hump in the

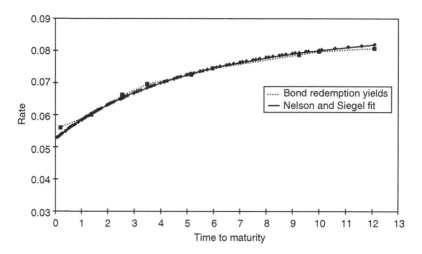

Figure 10.1 Nelson and Siegel curve fitted to UK government bond (gilt) rates derived from nine bonds for t_0 = September 4, 1996. Notice the slight overspricing of the short bond by five basis points.

term structure. Figure 10.1 shows a Nelson and Siegel (1987) curve fitted to UK government bond (gilt) rates derived from nine bonds for t_0 = September 4, 1996 (This is Figure 15.15 in James and Webber, 2000, p. 447). The fitted term structure is remarkably smooth. If anything, it is too smooth. It does not fit the empirical term structure well at the short end: it over-prices the short maturity bond rate by five basis points. James and Webber (2001, p. 444) unearthed many working papers with similar examples, with variations in the number of parameters to be fitted.

10.4   Liquidity and financial turbulence

In the imperfect empirical international financial markets, in which asset investors with different cash investment horizons – day traders, bank treasurers and pension fund managers – trade, friction can occur between the various investment cash flows, which show a great diversity of changing strategic cash flow rates of return $x_{ij}(t)$. Such friction can cause financial turbulence, or financial crises, depending on the degree of persistence of the financial markets. Now that we have defined continuous and steady cash flows, let's, initially rather informally, define turbulent cash flow. A more precise definition will be provided later in this chapter.

Definition 420   Turbulent cash flow *is irregular cash flow characterized by vortices, whirlpool-like regions, or "eddies"*

$$\Delta X_\tau(t) = x_\tau(t)X_\tau(t) = \textit{irregular, with possible vortices, or} \qquad (10.52)$$

$$\Delta^d X_\tau(t) = \varepsilon(t), \quad \textit{with } \varepsilon(t) \sim \textit{i.i.d.} \quad \textit{and} \quad -0.5 < d < 0.5 \qquad (10.53)$$

Remark 421 *This effectively means that the cash flow rates of return series $x_\tau(t)$ are irregular for some or all investment horizons τ. Recall that, in Chapter 8, we've already characterized and measured various degrees of irregularity by computing the fractal spectrum based on the Lipschitz α_L and the corresponding fractal dimensions.*

But what can we imagine a cash flow vortex to be? It clearly forms a cascade or term structure according to the time horizons τ_i. Therefore, we suggest the following definition.

Definition 422 *A cash flow vortex occurs, when the fractional differences $\Delta^d X_\tau(t)$ first rapidly increase in density (become quickly more rapid) and then rapidly decreases in density (become quickly less rapid). In other words, a cash vortex occurs, when the fractional differentiation (in particular the second-order differentiation, or convexity) of the cash flow $X_\tau(t)$ is heterogeneous and there exists a fractal spectrum of Lipschitz irregularity coefficients α_{L_i}, such that $d < \alpha_{L_i} < d + 1$.*

Thus, cash flow vortices are regions of heterogeneous fractional differentiation of the cash flows $X(t)$, which can lead to period-doubling and intermittent behavior. It shows up in the records of financial time series as *clustering* of the increments of the FBM.

Example 423 *Figure 10.2 shows the series of vertical ocean shear at various depths (in meters), collected by Mike Gregg of the Applied Physics Laboratory of the University of Washington. At the right side, around 1,000 m deep, there is a shear stress/strain vortex, where two ocean flows of different temperature and density flow above each other. Figure 10.3 shows a 6-scale wavelet coefficient*

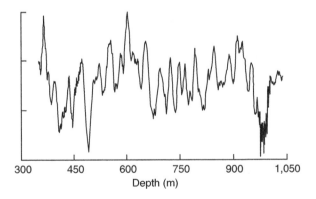

Figure 10.2 Vertical ocean shear at various depths. At the right side, around 1,000 m deep, there is a shear stress/strain vortex where two ocean flows of different temperature and density flow along each other.

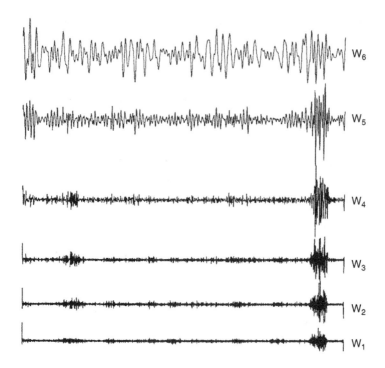

Figure 10.3 A 6-scale wavelet coeficient sequence decomposition of ocean shear
series in Figure 10.2. The high frequency wavelet resonance coefficients
are at the bottom, the low frequency resonance coefficients at the top.
The physical adjustment vortex at *c*. 1,000 m depth is noticeable at all
decomposition levels.

*sequence decomposition of this series. The high frequency wavelet coefficients are
at the bottom. The physical adjustment vortex is noticeable at all decomposition
levels. This means that it consists of a cascade of singularities. It is defined by first
showing volatility with increasing amplitude, immediately followed by volatility
with decreasing amplitude.*

Example 424   *In Figure 10.4 we have a financial time series plot of more than
9,300 minute-by-minute quotations on the Philippine pesos collected in real time
by my students on the trading floor of the Nanyang Business School of Nanyang
Technological University in Singapore for the month of July 1997. At the left side of
Figure 10.4, we notice the sharp discontinuity in the Philippine pesos immediately
after the Thai baht crisis break on July 2, 2001. The Philippine pesos had been
constant (= 100 percent persistent) until that instance. Immediately after the
break, there is adjustment turbulence, when the pesos adjusts to its new level, after
which it (relatively) stabilizes. Later in July, after a period of relative tranquility*

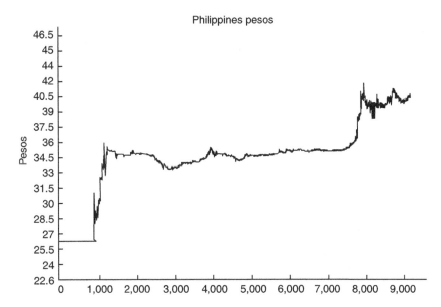

Figure 10.4 More than 9,300 minute-by-minute quotations on the Philippine pesos collected in real time for the month of July 1997. Immediately after the Thai baht
crisis break on July 2, 2001, there is adjustement turbulence in the pesos/USD
exchange rate, when it adjusts to its new, more stable, depreciated level. Later
in July, there is another sharp discontinuity, immediately followed by financial
adjustment turbulence, which includes a financial vortex.

(persistence), there is another, although somewhat less abrupt, discontinuity at the
right side in the plot, again immediately followed by adjustment turbulence, which
includes a vortex. In Figure 10.5 this dramatic sequence of the Philippine pesos is,
somewhat crudely, analyzed in a 3-scale wavelet resonance coefficient sequence
decomposition, using Benoit software, which shows that the dynamic phenomena
of vortices are identifiable at all three scale (∼ inverted frequency) levels. The low
scale (= high frequency) wavelet coefficients are in the top panel. Vortices show
an integrated cascade of frequencies. At this point we conjecture that the reason
for such adjustment turbulence to occur is the friction between the persistent cash
flow investments in pesos in the Philippines and the antipersistent cash flows of
the US dollar cash markets, when the cash flowed rapidly out of the now more
risky Philippine emerging market back to the safe haven of the United States.
Such an adjustment takes place apparently in several turbulent cash flow bursts,
interspersing periods of relatively calm laminar cash flows. Compare now the
preceding physical time series analysis of vertical ocean shear with this financial
time series analysis. Notice the striking similarity between the 6-scale wavelet
decomposition in Figure 10.3 and this 3-scale decomposition of the Philippine
pesos in Figure 10.5. It is clear that more in-depth study needs to be done of

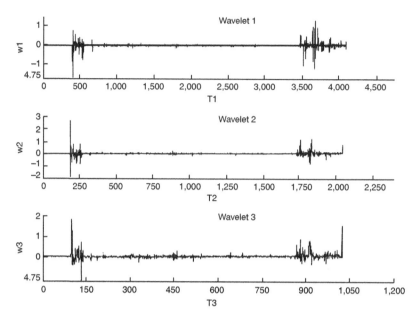

Figure 10.5 Three-scale wavelet resonance coefficient series of the minute-by-minute quotations on the Philippine pesos in Figure 10.4. The disturbances with the
subsequent financial adjustment vortices are clearly visible at all three scale
levels.

*1-dimensional (1D) cash flows in the global financial markets to identify the correct
model for this kind of intermittency that cannot be generated by GBMs.*

10.4.1   Illiquidity: cash flow viscosity

Why would such financial turbulence, consisting of a series of financial vortices,
occur? In Chapter 9, we learned that nonlinear constraints combined with a feedback process increases the number of coexistent steady-state equilibria via the
period-doubling process. In addition, the physical *theory of flow dynamics* provides us with some clues, or, at least, with some quantifiable entities, which can
measure when turbulence may occur, even though no completely acceptable model
or theory of financial turbulence exists. The term *viscosity* is used in flow dynamics
to characterize the degree of *internal friction*, *illiquidity*, or *persistence* in a fluid.
Equivalently, we can informally define in finance:

Definition 425

cash flow viscosity $= $ *cash flow illiquidity*

$\qquad\qquad\qquad = $ *degree of persistence of adjacent cash flows*   (10.54)

It's clear that differences in viscosity, illiquidity or persistence of the cash flows implies that they can't quickly mix and adjust to each other in an infinitely fast fashion.[8] This internal cash flow friction is associated with the resistance of two adjacent layers of cash flows to move relative to each other, due to *Newton's Second Law* for flows.

Proposition 426 (*Newton's Second Law*) *Any force applied to a flow results in an equal but opposite reaction, which in turn causes a rate of change of momentum in the flow.*

Because of the illiquidity or persistence of investment cash flows, part of their steady financial risk, represented by a finite, integrated amount of local risk

$$E\{x_\tau(t)\} = \int |x_\tau(t)|^2 \, dt < \infty \qquad (10.55)$$

is converted to random risk, represented by an infinite integrated amount of local risk

$$E\{x_\tau(t)\} = \int |x_\tau(t)|^2 \, dt \to \infty \qquad (10.56)$$

which can cause cash vortices on the edges of the adjacent investment cash flow channels.

In physics, *shear stresses* are the internal friction forces opposing flowing of one part of a substance past the adjacent parts. But how does cash flow stress and strain occur in finance and what do these phenomena mean in financial terms, in particular, in terms of the term structure of interest rates $f[x_\tau(t), \tau]$? In the financial markets, there are stresses of investment cash flows with different degrees of illiquidity adjacent in the complete term structure, flowing past each other within and between the various financial term markets and their maturity "buckets," indexed by the investment horizons τ_i, as follows.

Definition 427 *Financial cash flow stress is the change in the asset term structure relative to the original asset prices, $\Delta x_\tau(t)/X_\tau(t)$. It is the quantity that is proportional to the cash flow supply of earnings on an investment with a time horizon of τ periods, causing deformation of the term structure of the asset return rates.*

Definition 428 *Financial cash flow strain is the change in an asset price relative to its maturity $\Delta X_\tau(t)/\tau$. It is the quantity that is proportional to the cash flow demand in a particular maturity "bucket."*

When we express the cash strain per unit of time $\Delta t = 1$ we have the *cash rate of return gradient*, or *term structure gradient*.

Definition 429   *The financial term structure gradient (TSG) is given by*

$$TSG_\tau(t) = \frac{Cash\ flow\ strain\ (t)}{\Delta t}$$

$$= \frac{\Delta X_\tau(t)/\tau}{\Delta t}$$

$$= \frac{x_\tau(t)}{\tau} \tag{10.57}$$

This TSG is the cash flow rate of return of an asset with investment horizon or maturity τ relative to its term τ, as a measure of the degree of term structure deformation caused by cash flow *shearing*, i.e., caused by the differences between the cash flow rates of return with different investment horizons. The $TSG_\tau(t)$ measures the steepness of the term structure of interest rates from its origin at a particular moment in time t, as in Figure 10.6. This gradient is conceptually similar to the laminar velocity profile of the physical hydraulic flow in pipes.

The $TSG_\tau(t)$ is largest when the short-term rates $x_\tau(t)$ (for small τ) are large, e.g., because of an inverted term structure, or because of high inflation expectations. However, the size of the $TSG_\tau(t) > 0$ is less important than the speed by which the $TSG_\tau(t)$ changes for a given term τ. The $TSG_\tau(t)$ for a particular maturity

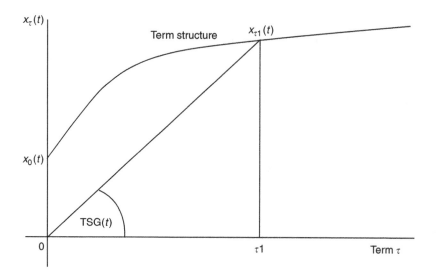

Figure 10.6 The term structure gradient, TSG(t), is the cash flow rate of return $x_\tau(t)$ of an asset with investment horizon or maturity τ relative to its term τ, as a measure of the degree of term structure deformation caused by cash flow shearing. The TSG(t) measures the steepness of the term structure of interest rates from its origin, at time t.

term τ changes most when the term rate $x_\tau(t)$ changes a lot, i.e., when $|\Delta x_\tau(t)|$ or $|\Delta x_\tau(t)\tau|$ is large. This leads us to the coefficient of dynamic cash flow illiquidity

For small cash flow stresses, financial stress is proportional to strain and we can define a coefficient of cash flow illiquidity, or dynamic cash viscosity, based on this simple linear financial stress–deformation relationship.

Definition 430 *The coefficient of dynamic cash flow illiquidity or viscosity at time t is*

$$
\eta_\tau(t) = \left| \frac{\text{cash flow stress}}{\text{cash flow strain}} \right|
$$

$$
= \left| \frac{\Delta x_\tau(t)/X_\tau(t)}{x_\tau(t)/\tau} \right|
$$

$$
= \left| \frac{\Delta x_\tau(t)\tau}{x_\tau(t)X_\tau(t)} \right|
$$

$$
= \left| \frac{\Delta x_\tau(t)\tau}{\Delta X_\tau(t)} \right| \tag{10.58}
$$

This relative illiquidity coefficient measures the (small) change in the term structure $\Delta x_\tau(t)$ multiplied by its term (maturity) τ relative to the cash flow rate $\Delta X_\tau(t) = x_\tau(t)X_\tau(t)$. When the investment cash flow is continuous, i.e., when the investment cash flow rate $\Delta X_\tau(t) = x_\tau(t)X_\tau(t)$ is constant, all illiquidity is measured by the empirical change in the term structure $\Delta x_\tau(t)$ for each term τ, i.e., by $\Delta x_\tau(t)\tau$.

Notice that for very short maturity terms τ, even a fairly large change in the short-term rate, $\Delta x_\tau(t) = $ small, does not indicate illiquidity, because the product $|\Delta x_\tau(t)\tau|$ remains small, for a continuous cash flow rate. On the other hand, for very long maturity terms even a small change in the long-term rate, $\Delta x_\tau(t) = $ large, can indicate illiquidity. Indeed, we observe most volatility or risk at the short-term end of the term structure and least volatility or risk at the long-term end, even for markets, like in the United States, which are considered most liquid in the world, for all maturity terms (Jamdee and Los, 2003).

Notice also that when the illiquidity measured by $\eta_\tau(t)$ is large for a given change in the term cash flow $\Delta X_\tau(t)$, the term structure gradient $\text{TSG}_\tau(t)$ is large, which occurs, as we noted earlier, when the short-term rates are very high, i.e., $x_\tau(t) = $ large for small τ. This situation occurred in the Eurodollar market around 1980, as can be observed in Figure 2.7 in Chapter 2.

When the $\Delta x_\tau(t)$ varies inversely with the term τ, the illiquidity coefficient is constant, $\eta_\tau(t) = \eta_\tau$ for continuous cash flow. Another way of expressing this, is to state

$$
\Delta x_\tau(t)\tau = \eta_\tau x_\tau(t)X_\tau(t) = \text{constant} \tag{10.59}
$$

Thus, for *laminar cash flow*, the "force of illiquidity" or "of viscosity resistance" is

$$
\Delta x_\tau(t)\tau \propto x_\tau(t)X_\tau(t) \tag{10.60}
$$

It is proportional to the cash flow rate, i.e., the rate of cash return $x_\tau(t)$ for maturity τ and the size of the original cash investment $X_\tau(t)$. The constant illiquidity coefficient η_τ is then the proportionality coefficient.

Still a different way of interpreting this relative illiquidity coefficient is to state that it measures the absolute relative change in the interest rates of a particular maturity $|\Delta x_\tau(t)/x_\tau(t)|$, relative to the size of the average cash flow $|X_\tau(t)/\tau|$ in a particular maturity market:

$$\eta_\tau(t) = \left| \frac{\Delta x_\tau(t)/x_\tau(t)}{X_\tau(t)/\tau} \right| \tag{10.61}$$

After these introductory definitions – which can and should all be calculated from empirical financial data – we are in the position to define the abstract perfect cash flow liquidity.

Definition 431   Perfect cash flow liquidity *exists when* $\eta_\tau(t) = 0$.

Thus, perfect cash flow liquidity exists either

(1) when $\Delta x_\tau(t) = 0$ for finite invested cash flows $X_\tau(t)$ and finite investment horizon terms τ, implying that the finite term structure remains unchanged under financial stress, and each cash rate of return $x_\tau(t)$ for investment horizon τ is constant; or
(2) when the term rates of return are infinite $x_\tau(t) = \infty$ for all finite cash flows $X_\tau(t)$ and finite terms τ; or
(3) when the cash flow for a finite term τ and a finite term structure rate $x_\tau(t)$ is infinitely large $X_\tau(t) = \infty$, i.e., the situation of deep liquid financial markets, like in the United States; or
(4) when the term equals zero, $\tau = 0$, for a finite investment cash flow $X_\tau(t)$ and a finite spot rate of return $x_\tau(t) = x_0(t)$ (= instantaneous cash).

Alternatives (2)–(4) are, in principle, unrealistic mathematical extremes, so that perfect cash flow liquidity only exists, when the term structure remains unchanged (= alternative (1))! But there are also situations where alternatives (2) and (3) combine, i.e., when the term rates $x_\tau(t)$ and the cash flows $X_\tau(t)$ are both very large for a finite term τ. In such situations $\eta_\tau(t) \downarrow 0$, and perfect liquidity is approached. Alternative (4) identifies the intercept of the term structure or (theoretically) instantaneous cash, e.g., the almost perfectly liquid Fed funds rate for overnight interbank lending.

Most real world cash flows are non-perfectly liquid with $\eta_\tau(t) > 0$, because most real world cash flows are term-dependent. There is not much instantaneous cash in comparison. Also, infinite term rates of return and invested cash flows empirically don't exist, nor do zero investment horizons. Thus, the only realistic outcome is that perfect cash flow liquidity exists when the cash rate of return for each investment horizon is constant and $\Delta x_\tau(t) = 0$ for finite invested cash flows $X_\tau(t)$ and finite investment horizon terms τ. That is the situation of small or no term structure volatility.

This particular expression for the illiquidity coefficient $\eta_\tau(t)$ is only valid when the term structure $x_\tau(t)$ varies linearly with the term τ, i.e., when the rate of cash return gradient $x_\tau(t)/\tau$ is uniformly constant for each term τ. That is when the term structure is constant. Then one may speak of *Newtonian cash flows*, in which stress, illiquidity and the rate of cash flow strain are linearly related. This is, of course, seldom the case with the *dynamic term structures* in the international financial markets, where nonlinear institutional constraints exist, as we already discussed in Chapter 9. Empirically, the term structures of the cash investment markets vary nonlinearly, in such a way that the short-term cash rates of return vary relatively more (= have larger amplitudes), and vary more frequently, than the long-term cash rates of return.[9]

Remark 432 Term structure modelers *have, somewhat inconsistently, attempted to capture this nonlinear dynamics of the term structure by, first, (linearly) correlating the various terms $x_\tau(t)$ with each other for a limited number of terms $1 < \tau < T$, and, then, by analyzing the resulting covariance matrix using a static principal component, or factor analysis (cf. the comprehensive survey of term structure models by Chapman and Pearson, 2001). The objective of such spectral analysis is to capture most of the variation of the term structure by retaining a small number, say three, principal component factor loadings, like Factor 1 = level, Factor 2 = slope and Factor 3 = curvature of the term structure. Such inexact (linear) identification schemes analyzing covariance matrices is inherently subjective, because which eigenvalues are to be considered significant and to be retained, when there are more than three term rates $x_\tau(t)$, and which should be considered representing noise? (For a detailed discussion of such "prejudices" of principal components analysis, cf. Los, 1989). One of the biggest current research challenges is to model the nonlinear diffusion dynamics of the interrelated terms of the stochastic term structure vector $\mathbf{x}_\tau(t) = [x_1(t), x_2(t), \ldots, x_T(t)]'$. The empirical evidence overwhelmingly shows that simple linear diffusion models of the Markov type cannot properly capture the complex dynamics of the empirical term structures of interest rates in the various countries in the world.*

When the rate of return gradient is not uniform, as is usually the case, we must express the illiquidity coefficient in the general marginal form:

$$\eta_\tau(t) = \left| \frac{\Delta x_\tau(t)/X_\tau(t)}{\partial x_\tau(t)/\partial \tau} \right|$$

$$= \left| \frac{\Delta x_\tau(t) \cdot \partial \tau}{\partial x_\tau(t) \cdot X_\tau(t)} \right| \tag{10.62}$$

Thus, we compare the empirical change in the required cash flow over an infinitesimal small change in the term or horizon, $\Delta x_\tau(t) \cdot \partial \tau$, with the infinitesimal change in the available cash flow rate $\partial x_\tau(t) \cdot X_\tau(t)$. That is, a measurable comparison is made between the marginal financial cash flow stress and the marginal financial cash flow strain.[10] This invariably means that we have to measure the changing illiquidity of each financial market continuously, and preferably, in real time.

10.4.2   *Laminar and turbulent financial cash flows*

We'll now define the important identifying concepts of laminar and turbulent cash flows. We are already familiar with the whole spectrum of dynamic steady-state cash flow regimes from the discussion in Chapter 9, from stable, via period-doubling and intermittent to completely chaotic equilibria. Here we look, still informally, at only two regimes: the completely stable, unique or laminar regime and the completely chaotic, nonunique or turbulent regimes.

Definition 433   *If the adjacent layers of illiquid term cash flow smoothly along-side each other in a financial market, and the term structure rates $x_\tau(t)$ are constant, and thus the whole term structure remains immobile, the stable stream-line flows of investment cash through the financial markets (of particular term and risk profiles) are called* laminar.

Definition 434   *If the streamlined term cash flows in a financial market, at suf-ficiently high term structure rates $x_\tau(t)$, become highly irregular cash flows with highly irregular cash flow (velocity) rates $x_\tau(t)$, so that part of the term structure or the whole term structure is very volatile, they are called* turbulent.

Both, laminar and turbulent cash flows are easily illustrated by hot cigar smoke, which initially, when it leaves the cigar is laminar, but then turns turbulent due to the nonlinear constraints imposed by the interactive heat exchange with the cooler environment. One can measure and visualize such changes in the whole term structure of interest rates by a properly formulated wavelet scalogram that displays a series of scalograms of all investment horizons or maturities τ.[11]

My current conjecture is that the nonlinear expectation constraints inherent in the logical term structure $x_\tau(t)$ can cause chaos in the short-term cash flows in finan-cial markets to emerge, when particular parametric thresholds in the interlocking term structures are surpassed. In other words, particular shapes of interlocking term structures, at sufficiently high-term rates, can cause irregularities to emerge particularly in the short term range.

Remark 435   *Small, perfectly liquid, laminar cash flow motions are called* acous-tic *cash flow motions and (linear) Fourier Transform (FT) analysis can be used to decompose such steady and continuous global cash flow motions in subcompo-nent flows. However, when any of these conditions do not apply, and we deal with large-scale, so-called* non-acoustical *cash flow motions, like cash flow turbulence, we need (nonlinear) wavelet MRA to analyze and decompose the volatility or risk of cash flow rates $x_\tau(t)$.*

10.4.3   *Financial Reynolds number*

Analogously to physical turbulence measurements, I also conjecture that the onset of cash flow turbulence can be identified by a dimensionless parameter, called the Reynolds number for uniform cash flow. In hydrodynamics and aerodynamics, the *Reynolds number* is a dimensionless ratio related to the velocity at which smooth flow shifts to turbulent flow.[12] There is no fundamental reason why we should not be able to measure a similar Reynolds numbers for financial cash flows. The end-of-chapter Exercises show how, using the S&P500 data in Appendix B.

Definition 436   *The financial Reynolds number* $Re_\tau(t)$ *for a uniform cash flow of maturity term* τ *is given by:*

$$
\begin{aligned}
Re_\tau(t) &= \left| \frac{a\rho x_\tau(t)}{\eta_\tau(t)} \right| \\[2mm]
&= \left| \frac{\rho x_\tau(t)\tau}{\Delta x_\tau(t)\tau/x_\tau(t)X_\tau(t)} \right| \\[2mm]
&= \left| \frac{\rho x_\tau^2(t)X_\tau(t)}{\Delta x_\tau(t)} \right|
\end{aligned}
\tag{10.63}
$$

where $a = \tau$ *is the length of the particular cash flow channel, and* $\rho = 1/\$$ *is again the uniform cash flow density, which renders the Reynolds number dimensionless.*

The beauty of the Reynolds number is that it is a dimensionless number that measures dynamic similarity (Reynolds, 1883). It characterizes the ratio of the nonlinear *advection* $\rho x_\tau^2(t)X_\tau(t)$ to the linear *dissipation* $\Delta x_\tau(t)$. Cash flows with the same Reynolds number look the same, whereas cash flows with different Reynolds numbers look quite different. It is a measure of the amount of cash flow volatility present at a particular time in a particular channel. When the financial Reynolds number is constant, $Re_\tau(t) = Re_\tau$, for turbulent cash flows with investment horizon τ, we have:

$$
\Delta x_\tau(t) = \frac{\rho x_\tau^2(t)X_\tau(t)}{Re_\tau}
\tag{10.64}
$$

This is the same very simple nonlinear diffusion equation of the type we encountered in Chapter 9, when we discussed the logistic parabola. Also, for turbulent cash flow, the "force of illiquidity resistance" contains clearly a quadratic cash rate of return $x_\tau^2(t)$. It is proportional to the square of the rate of cash return and the size of the cash flow:

$$
\Delta x_\tau(t)\tau \propto x_\tau^2(t)X_\tau(t)
\tag{10.65}
$$

This conforms to what we learned in Chapter 9 about the chaotic regimes of a dynamic growth system governed by quadratic constraints. This quadratic expression has a much higher value than the "force of illiquidity resistance" for laminar cash flow, which we know to be linearly proportional to both the rate of cash return and the size of the cash flow:

$$
\Delta x_\tau(t)\tau \propto x_\tau(t)X_\tau(t)
\tag{10.66}
$$

Remark 437   *The financial Reynolds number is proportional to the uniform local cash flow volatility per dollar squared $\frac{1}{2}\rho x_\tau^2(t)$ at the "downstream" measurement point. When the financial pressure "upstream" is high, this uniform local "downstream" volatility increases rapidly, producing a large financial Reynolds number. Turbulent cash flows have violent and erratic fluctuations in velocity and financial pressure, which are not associated with any corresponding fluctuations in the exogenous forces driving the flows, as the simulations in Chapter 9 clearly demonstrated. Thus, the classical financial-economic models where "shocks" are exogenous, i.e., impacting from outside the dynamic financial systems, are currently being replaced by dynamic models where the volatility is endogenous, i.e., self-generated.*

Financial turbulence should be considered a manifestation of the nonlinear nature of the underlying fundamental price diffusion equations. The "force of illiquidity resistance" is measured by a quadratic term. As we discussed in Chapter 9, this quadratic term is the essential nonlinear constraint "causing" deterministic chaos or turbulence to occur at particular values of the growth rate parameters of the underlying simple dynamic processes. Feedback loops of the simple dynamic investment cash flow processes quickly increases the complexity of the aggregated dynamic investment cash flow process of several interconnected financial markets.

Remark 438   *The physical flows in round pipes are laminar for $\mathrm{Re}_\tau(t) < 2,000$, but physical turbulence begins to occur for Reynolds numbers, $\mathrm{Re}_\tau(t) > 3,000$, when the nonlinear advection term begins to dominate the negligible linear dissipation. On the other hand, in physical turbulent flow over flat surfaces $\mathrm{Re}_\tau > 500,000$. We don't know yet what the critical values are for the financial Reynolds numbers. This is an important issue for the empirical research into the antipersistence regimes of financial markets.*

Since we have $a\rho = \tau/\$$, the Reynolds number for uniform cash flows can be interpreted as a term based *return/liquidity risk ratio* per dollar invested and sized for the horizon τ:

$$
\begin{aligned}
\mathrm{Re}_\tau(t) &= \left| \frac{a\rho x_\tau(t)}{\eta_\tau(t)} \right| \\
&= \left| \frac{x_\tau(t)}{\eta_\tau(t)} \right| \frac{\tau}{\$}
\end{aligned}
\tag{10.67}
$$

The higher the cash rate of return $x_\tau(t)$ on an investment asset with horizon τ, and the lower the cash illiquidity $\eta_\tau(t)$ (= the higher the cash liquidity) for that same horizon τ, and the longer the investment horizon, the larger the financial Reynolds number and, thus, the opportunity for financial turbulence.[13]

In other words, the financial Reynolds number measures the cash rate of return on a cash investment relative to its *illiquidity coefficient* $\eta_\tau(t)$, which is quite a different, and, perhaps, just as important financial measure as the usual market volatility risk $\sigma_\tau(t)$.

It's a matter of current empirical financial research to determine at which magnitudes of this financial Reynolds number financial turbulence begins to occur. This expression shows that the financial Reynolds number for finite term rates of return $x_\tau(t)$ becomes very large when the illiquidity risk approaches zero, *while the investment horizon τ is very long*! As we discussed earlier, under the conditions of perfect liquidity, $\eta_\tau(t) \downarrow 0$, and the financial Reynolds number becomes very large. Thus, financial turbulence is a phenomenon of very liquid, antipersistent financial markets and not of illiquid, very persistent markets. Efficiency-enhancing financial turbulence of liquid, antipersistent, ultra-efficient financial markets contrasts sharply with the high-risk discontinuity phenomena of very illiquid, persistent and inefficient markets, and the two should not be confused!

10.4.4 *Wavelet financial Reynolds numbers and intermittency*

How can we translate this financial Reynolds number in terms of the wavelet MRA of Chapters 7 and 8? Recall from Chapter 7 the definition of the scalogram of the cash rate of return $x_\tau(t)$. Then, analogously to Farge *et al.* (1996), we have the following definition:

Definition 439 *The local financial wavelet spectrum $S_W(\tau, a)$ of the term rate of return $x_\tau(t)$ is defined as its scale-standardized scalogram*

$$S_W(\tau, a) = \frac{P_W(\tau, a)}{a}$$

$$= \frac{|W(\tau, a)|^2}{a} \tag{10.68}$$

where the Wavelet Transform (WT) $W(\tau, a)$ of $x_\tau(t)$ is defined as in Chapter 7.

Remark 440 *The scale a refers both to the dyadic scale proportional to the inverse of the frequency of the financial time series and to the length of the horizon of the cash flow channel: $a \sim 1/\omega \sim \tau$.*

A characterization of the local "activity" of $x_\tau(t)$ is given by its *wavelet intermittency*, which measures local deviations from the mean spectrum of $x_\tau(t)$ at every horizon τ and dyadic scale *a*. It is a local measure of *financial risk*, i.e., a measure of risk localized in the scale (frequency)–time domain. We no longer need the idealized statistical concept of ergodicity of Chapter 1 to measure average financial risk. With a scalogram we can measure local or instantaneous financial risk. In addition, we can now measure financial intermittency by wavelet MRA as follows.

Definition 441 *The financial wavelet intermittency of the term cash rate of return $x_\tau(t)$ is defined as the relative wavelet spectrum:*

$$I_W(\tau, a) = \frac{|W(\tau, a)|^2}{\int_\mathbb{R} |W(\tau, a)|^2 d\tau} \tag{10.69}$$

Remark 442   *One advantage of this financial wavelet intermittency measure is again that it is dimension-free and expressed as a simple percentage between zero and one.*

Next, we implement the suggestion by Farge *et al.* (1996, p. 651) to express the financial Reynolds number in terms of wavelets, as follows.

Definition 443   *The* wavelet financial Reynolds number *is defined as*

$$
\begin{aligned}
\mathrm{Re}_W(\tau, a) &= \left| \frac{a\rho |W(\tau, a)|}{\eta_\tau(t)} \right| \\
&= \left| \frac{\tau |W(\tau, a)|}{\eta_\tau(t)\sigma_\psi} \right|
\end{aligned}
\tag{10.70}
$$

where $\rho = 1/\sigma_\psi$, *and the standard deviation*

$$
\sigma_\psi = \left| \int_{\mathbb{R}^2} |\psi_{\tau,a}(t)|^2 d\tau da \right|^{0.5}
\tag{10.71}
$$

is the standard deviation of the analyzing wavelet $\psi_{\tau,a}(t)$ *of the scalogram* $W(\tau, a)$ *over all time horizons* τ *and all scales a.*

Remark 444   *Our expectation is that at large scales* $a \sim \tau$, *i.e., at very long time horizons* τ, *the wavelet financial Reynolds number coincides with the usual large-scale Reynolds number* $\mathrm{Re}_\tau(t)$. *In the smallest scales, i.e., at very short time horizons, like time ticks, one expects this wavelet financial Reynolds number to be close to unity, when averaged over time.*

Analogously to Farge *et al.* (1996), the current empirical research questions regarding the analysis of financial market dynamics are the following. With such a wavelet financial Reynolds number defined for time horizons τ and scales a, are there time horizons τ where such a Reynolds number is much larger than at others? How do such time periods correlate with time periods of small-scale activity within the cash flow? If so, then $\mathrm{Re}_W(\tau, a)$ could give an unambiguous answer of the activity at very small scales (or at any desired scale a). Such time periods of high $\mathrm{Re}_W(\tau, a)$ can then be interpreted as periods of *strong nonlinearity*, i.e., periods of financial turbulence.

In other words, if this interpretation of Farge *et al.* (1996) is correct, we can just look at these scalograms of financial Reynolds numbers to detect periods of strong nonlinearities and thus of financial turbulence.

10.5   Software

The computations of the first four Exercises can be executed in Microsoft EXCEL spreadsheets, or by using the Statistics Toolbox available from The MathWorks,

Inc., 24 Prime Park Way Natick, MA 01760-1500, USA. Tel (508) 647-7000; Fax (508) 647-7001; http://www.mathworks.com/products/wavelettbx.shtml.

The computations of the following three Exercises can be executed by using the MATLAB® Wavelet Toolbox, available from The MathWorks, Inc., 24 Prime Park Way Natick, MA 01760-1500, USA. Tel (508) 647-7000; Fax (508) 647-7001; http://www.mathworks.com/products/wavelettbx.shtml.

A complete wavelet analysis toolkit called *Wavelab* can be obtained at no cost from: http://playfair.stanford.EDU:80/~wavelab/.

This *Wavelab* is a very complete set of MATLAB® scripts that implement both the basic wavelet and related transforms and more advanced techniques. There is full documentation, a set of tutorials, and section of "Toons," short for *cartoons*. These Toon scripts reproduce from scratch the figures in many papers of Stanford's wavelet research group consisting of Dave Donoho, Ian Johnstone *et al.*, describing the theoretical research underlying the algorithms in *Wavelab*. By studying these scripts and by experimenting with the data, the reader can learn all the details of the process that led to each figure. This forms part of the new discipline of *Reproducible Research*, i.e., the idea to provide the reader full access to all details (data, equations, code, etc.) needed to completely reproduce all the results normally presented only in an advertising summary form in scientific publications. The pioneer of *Reproducible Research* is Jon Claerbout of Stanford University's Geophysics Department (Claerbout, 1994; Buckheit and Donoho, 1995).

10.6 Exercises

Exercise 445 *Compute the daily changing term structure $x_\tau(t)$ of total rates of return for the S&P500 stock index (use the daily observations for 1988 of Sherry, 1992, pp. 29–32, available in Appendix B) for the terms $\tau = 1$ day, 21 days (= 1 month), 63 days (= 1 quarter), 126 days (= 1 half year) and 252 (= 1 year) investment terms (= investment horizons τ).*

Exercise 446 *Plot the average term structure of the total rates of return for the S&P500 stock index for overlapping observations (only).*

Exercise 447 *Compute for each term τ its coefficient of financial illiquidity $\eta_\tau(t)$, for each day, for the available data. (Eliminate DIV0! and VALUE! expressions by inserting asterisks *).*

Exercise 448 *Compute the daily and average financial Reynolds numbers for each cash investment channel for a standard unit cash flow, for the available data. Can you point to days of potential financial turbulence?*

Exercise 449 *Compute the term structure of volatility for the rates of return for the S&P500 stock index for non-overlapping windows.*

Exercise 450   *In the spirit of the risk dissipation model of Mandelbrot and Wallis (1969), compute the term structure of implied volatility for any high frequency FX option data available to you (cf. Xu and Taylor, 1994).*

Exercise 451   *Compute the local wavelet financial spectrum $S_W(\tau, a)$ of $x_\tau(t)$ for the available S&P500 data. Do the same for any high frequency FX data available to you.*

Exercise 452   *Compute the financial wavelet intermittencies $I_W(\tau, a)$ of $x_\tau(t)$ for the available S&P500 data. What is the advantage of the wavelet intermittency over the wavelet spectrum? Do the same for any high frequency FX data available to you.*

Exercise 453   *Compute the financial wavelet Reynolds numbers $\mathrm{Re}_W(\tau, a)$ of $x_\tau(t)$ for the available S&P500 data and compare them with the results from the previous Exercises. Is there financial turbulence in the available data? Do the same for any high frequency FX data available to you.*

Notes

1 A flow dynamics approach to the cash flows in financial markets is not new in economics. Compare, for example, the Keynesian circular income–expenditure flow dynamics modeling of an economy in the 1950s at the London School of Economics and Political Science (LSE) by engineer A. W. Phillips, familiar from the (expectations-augmented) Phillip's Curve in undergraduate textbooks on macroeconomics. Unfortunately, the financial-economic research of markets has focused on the static "equilibrium theory" of market pricing of Nobel Memorial prize winners Gerard Debreu and Kenneth Arrow, while the crucial dynamic "transport theory" has mostly been neglected. Consequently, the dynamics of cash flows has not been further developed since Phillips' heuristic macroeconomics research using hydraulic models in the basement of LSE. But fluid dynamics has a long mathematical history going back to Dutch mathematician and engineer Simon Stevin's (1586) work on the principles of "weighting" or pressure, in particular water pressure, Italian Evangelista Torricelli's law of efflux (1644), and French Blaise Pascal's uniform pressure law of hydrostatics (1653). Sir Isaac Newton devoted over one quarter of his famous *Principia Philosophae Naturalis* to the analysis of fluids (Book II, 1713) and added some original ideas, like his hypothesis of *viscosity*. This was followed by the mathematical explanations of the mechanics of ideal, frictionless fluid mechanics by Daniel and Jacques Bernouilli (1738) and Leonhard Euler (1755). In 1827, Claude Navier derived the equations of viscous flow, which were published by Sir George Gabriel Stokes in 1845, the celebrated Navier–Stokes equations. Work by Joseph Boussinesq (1877) and Osborne Reynolds (1883) on laminar (streamlined) flow and turbulent (erratic) flow extended these Navier–Stokes equations to turbulent flow, by including the Reynolds stresses and measurements, to be discussed in this chapter for cash flow dynamics.

2 This terminology is borrowed from "Part IV: General Cash Flow Streams" in Luenberger, 1998, pp. 417–474, and the title of the book of Van Horne, 1998). Cash and capital flows are abstractions, since there are no physical flows, but abstract investment flows over time. An electronic "transfer" is in physical reality a changing of a few digits on computer and communication lines. But the abstract images of "transfers" and "diffusions" are very helpful in explaining financial valuation and risk analysis.

3 In such cash accounting frameworks, one usually adopts the US dollar as the *base* currency, or numéraire.

4 Currently a very intense research effort is emerging to understand these complex inter-connecting cash and capital markets, as signified by the accelerating pace of publications by physicists and operation research analysts on studies of the financial markets (cf. Mantegna and Stanley, 2000; Urbach, 2000; Ilinski, 2001).

5 Daniel Bernoulli's most famous work, *Hydrodynamics* (1738) is both a theoretical and practical study of equilibrium, pressure and velocity of fluids. He demonstrated that as the velocity of fluid flow increases, its pressure decreases.

6 It is easy to view liabilities as "negative assets," when a balance sheet is viewed in terms of portfolio analysis, e.g., when immunizing a bank's balance sheet against term structure volatility.

7 The survey in this subsection is adapted and summarized from James and Webber (2001), pp. 425–453 an excellent source for recent term structure modeling. The error represents, e.g., unexpected default risk.

8 In Chapter 4, we introduced and discussed the definition of mixing random processes, in particular strong-mixing random processes.

9 Craig Holden, of the Kelley School of Business at Indiana University has made is a simple historical demonstration of this nonlinearly varying term structure: "Craig Holden's Excel-based Interactive 'Movie' of Term Structure Dynamics" (1996), which can be downloaded from his web page: http://www.bus.indiana.edu/cholden/
The spreadsheet movie demonstrates that historically the short-term interest rates are much more volatile than the long-term rates. It also demonstrates the great variety of shapes a term structure can exhibit over time.

10 We use the partial derivatives ∂ to indicate that we're interested in variation on the term structure $x_\tau(t)$ caused by a marginal change in the term τ at a fixed time t.

11 At Kent State University, we're developing a full color liquid crystal display of the scalogram of the real time term structure of US Treasury rates for the new derivatives trading floor affiliated with our new Master of Science in Financial Engineering program (http://business.kent.edu/msfe/).

12 Osborne Reynolds (1842–1912) was an English scientist whose papers on fluid dynamics and turbulence remain basic to turbine operation, lubrication, fluid flow and streamlining, cavitation, the effects of tides and temperature differentials of global oceanic flows.

13 The value of an asset is computed as the sum of the discounted (future) cash flows associated with that asset. Each asset has a particular maturity, even though it is sometimes assumed to have an infinite maturity, as in the case of, e.g., the assets of a firm, based on the accounting principle of an "ongoing concern." However, in reality, any firm has finite assets, i.e., projects with finite maturities.

Bibliography

Ahn, C. M., and H. E. Thompson (1988) "Jump–Diffusion Processes and Term Structure of Interest Rates," *Journal of Finance*, **43**(1), 155–174.

Bakshi, G., and Z. Chen (1996) "Inflation, Asset Prices, and the Term Structure of Interest Rates," *Review of Financial Studies*, **2**(1), 241–276.

Balduzzi, P., S. R. Das, S. Foresi and R. Sundaram (1996) "A Simple Approach to Three Factor Affine Term Structure Models," *Journal of Fixed Income*, **6**(3), 43–53.

Barclay, M., and C. Smith (1995) "The Maturity Structure of Corporate Debt," *Journal of Finance*, **50**(2), 609–632.

Batchelor, G. K. (1970) *Introduction to Fluid Dynamics*, Cambridge University Press, Cambridge, UK.

Beaglehole, D., and M. Tenney (1992) "Corrections and Additions to 'A Nonlinear Equilibrium Model of the Term Structure of Interest Rates'," *Journal of Financial Economics*, **32**(3), 345–353.

Bernoulli, Daniel (1738) *Hydrodynamica*, Johann Reingold, Strassburg.

Black, F., E. Derman and W. Toy (1990) "A One-Factor Model of Interest Rates and Its Application to Treasury Bond Options," *Financial Analysts Journal*, **46**(1), 33–39.

Black, F., and P. Karasinski (1991) "Bond and Option Pricing when Short Rates are Lognormal," *Financial Analysts Journal*, **47**(4), 52–59.

Brown, R. H., and S. M. Schaefer (1994a) "The Term Structure of Real Interest Rates and the Cox, Ingersöll and Ross Model," *Journal of Financial Economics*, **35**(1), 3–42.

Brown, R. H., and S. M. Schaefer (1994b) "Interest Rate Volatility and the Shape of the Term Structure," *Philosophical Transactions of the Royal Society of London*, A, **347**, 563–576.

Buckheit, J. B., and D. L. Donoho (1995) "Wavelab and Reproducible Research," in Antoniadis, A. and G. Oppenheim (Eds) *Wavelets and Statistics*, Springer-Verlag, Berlin, pp. 53–81.

Chapman, David A., and Neil D. Pearson (2000) "Is the Short Rate Drift Actually Nonlinear?," *Journal of Finance*, **55**(1), 355–388.

Chapman, David A., and Neil D. Pearson (2001) "Recent Advances in Estimating Term-Structure Models, " *Financial Analysts Journal*, **57**(4), 77–95.

Chichilnisky, G. (1996) "Markets with Endogenous Uncertainty: Theory and Policy," *Theory and Decision*, **41**(2), 99–131.

Chichilnisky, G., and G. M. Heal (1993) "Global Environmental Risks," *Journal of Economic Perspectives*, **7**(4), 65–86.

Claerbout, J. (1994) "Reproducible Electronic Documents," http://sepwww.stanford.edu/research/redoc.

Constantinides, G. (1992) "A Theory of Nominal Terms Structure of Interest Rates," *Review of Financial Studies*, **5**(4), 531–552.

Cox, J. C., J. E. Ingersöll and S. A. Ross (1985) "A Theory of the Term Structure of Interest Rate," *Econometrica*, **53**(2), 385–407.

Culbertson, J. M. (1957) "Term Structure of Interest Rates," *Quarterly Journal of Economics*, **71**(4), 485–517.

Dai, Q., and K. Singleton (2000) "Specification Analysis of Affine Term Structure Models," *Journal of Finance*, **55**(5), 385–407.

Das, S. R., and S. Foresi (1996) "Exact Solutions for Bond and Option Prices with Systematic Jump Risk," *Review of Derivatives Research*, **1**(1), 7–24.

De Boor, C. (1978) *A Practical Guide to Splines*, Springer-Verlag, New York, NY.

Dierckx, P. (1995) *Curve and Surface Fitting with Splines*, Oxford Science Publications, London, UK.

Duffie, D., and R. Kan (1994) "Multi-Factor Term Structure Models," *Philosophical Transactions of the Royal Society of London*, A, **347**, 577–586.

Duffie, D., and R. Kan (1996) "A Yield-Factor Model of Interest Rates," *Mathematical Finance*, **6**(4), 379–406.

Duffie, D., J. Pan and K. Singleton (2000) "Transform Analysis and Option Pricing for Affine Jump-Diffusions," *Econometrica*, **68**(6), 1343–1376.

Dunbar, N. (2000) *Inventing Money: The Story of Long-Term Capital Management and the Legends Behind It*, John Wiley and Sons, Chichester, UK.

Farge, Marie (1992) Wavelet Transforms and Their Applications to Turbulence. *Annals of Review of Fluid Mechanics*, **24**, 395–457.

Farge, Marie, Nicholas Kevlahan, Valérie Perrier and Éric Goirand (1996) "Wavelets and Turbulence," *Proceedings of IEEE*, **84**(4), 639–669.

Frisch, Uriel (1995) *Turbulence: The Legacy of A. N. Kolmogorov*, Cambridge University Press, Cambridge, UK.

Goldstein, R. (2000) "The Term Structure of Interest Rates as a Random Field," *Review of Financial Studies*, **13**(2), 365–384.

Heath, D., R. A. Jarrow and A. J. Morton (1990) "Bond Pricing and the Term Structure of Interest Rates: A Discrete Time Approximation," *Journal of Financial and Quantitative Analysis*, **25**, 419–440.

Heath, D., R. A. Jarrow and A. J. Morton (1992) "Bond Pricing and the Term Structure of Interest Rates: A New Methodology for Contingent Claims Valuation," *Econometrica*, **60**(1), 77–105.

Ho, T. S. Y., and S.-B. Lee (1986) "Term Structure Movements and Pricing Interest Rate Contingent Claims," *Journal of Finance*, **41**(5), 1011–1029.

Hong Yan (2001) "Dynamic Models of the Term Structure," *Financial Analysts Journal*, **57**(4), 60–76.

Hull, J. C., and A. D. White (1990) "Pricing Interest Rate Derivative Securities," *Review of Financial Studies*, **3**(4), 573–592.

Hull, J. C., and A. D. White (1993) "One-Factor Interest-Rate Models and the Valuation of Interest-Rate Derivative Securities," *Journal of Financial and Quantitative Analysis*, **28**(2), 235–254.

Ilinski, Kirill (2001) *Physics of Finance: Gauge Modelling in Non-Equilibrium Pricing*, John Wiley and Sons, Chichester, UK.

Jamdee, Sutthisit, and Cornelis A. Los (2003) "Dynamic Risk Profile of the U.S. Term Structure by Wavelet MRA," Working Paper, Department of Finance, Graduate School of Management, Kent State University, January 23 (to be presented at the Tenth Annual Conference of the Multinational Finance Society, Montrial, Quebec, June 28–July 4, 2003).

James, Jessica, and Nick Webber (2001) *Interest Rate Modelling*, John Wiley and Sons, Chichester, NJ.

Jorion, P. (1999) "How Long-Term Lost Its Capital," *RISK*, September.

Karnosky, D. S., and B. D. Singer (1994) *Global Asset Management and Performance Attribution*, The Research Foundation of the Institute of Chartered Financial Analysts, Charlottesville, VA.

Kennedy, D. P. (1994) "The Term Structure of Interest Rates as a Gaussian Random Field," *Mathematical Finance*, **4**(3), 247–258.

Kennedy, D. P. (1997) "Characterizing Gaussian Models of the Term Structure of Interest Rates," *Mathematical Finance*, **7**(2), 107–118.

Landau, L. D., and E. M. Lifshitz (1987) *Fluid Mechanics*, 2nd edn, Pergamon Press, Oxford, UK.

Leow Cheng Boon (1999) "Optimal Global Investment Strategy," MSc Thesis (under extramural supervision by Dr Los), University of Durham, Durham, UK.

Longstaff, F. A. (1989) "A Nonlinear General Equilibrium Model of the Term Structure of Interest Rates," *Journal of Financial Economics*, **23**(2), 195–224.

Longstaff, F. A., and E. S. Schwartz (1992) "Interest Rate Volatility and the Term Structure: A Two-Factor General Equilibrium Model," *Journal of Finance*, **47**(7), 1259–1282.

Los, Cornelis A. (1989) "The Prejudices of Least Squares, Principal Components and Common Factors," *Computers & Mathematics With Applications*, **17**(8/9), 1269–1283.

Los, Cornelis A. (1991a) "A Scientific View of Economic Data Analysis," *Eastern Economic Journal*, **17**(1), 61–71.

Los, Cornelis A. (1991b) "A Scientific View of Economic Data Analysis: Reply," *Eastern Economic Journal*, **17**(4), 526–532.

Los, Cornelis A. (1998) "Optimal Multi-Currency Investment Strategies With Exact Attribution in Three Asian Countries," *Journal of Multinational Financial Management*, **8**(2/3), 169–198.

Los, Cornelis A. (1999) Comment on "Combining Attribution Effects Over Time," *The Journal of Performance Measurement*, **4**(1), 5–6.

Los, Cornelis A. (2001) *Computational Finance: A Scientific Perspective*, World Scientific Publishing Co., Singapore.

Los, Cornelis A. (2002) "Optimal Asian Multi-Currency Strategy Portfolios With Exact Risk Attribution," in Batten, Jonathan, and Thomas Fetherstone (Eds) *Financial Risk and Financial Risk Management*, Research in International Business and Finance, **16**, Elsevier North-Holland, Amsterdam, pp. 215–260.

Luenberger, David G. (1998) *Investment Science*, Oxford University Press, New York, NY.

Mandelbrot, Benoit B. (1972) "Possible Refinement of the Lognormal Hypothesis Concerning the Distribution of Energy Dissipation in Intermittent Turbulence," in Rosenblatt, M., and C. Van Atta (Eds) *Statistical Models and Turbulence*, Lecture Notes in Physics, **12** Springer-Verlag, New York, NY, pp. 333–351.

Mandelbrot, Benoit B. (1997) *Fractals and Scaling in Finance: Discontinuity, Concentration, Risk*, Springer-Verlag, New York, NY.

Mandelbrot, B. B., and J. R. Wallis (1969) "Some Long-run Properties of Geophysical Records," *Water Resources Research*, **5**(2), 321–340.

Mantegna, Rosario N., and H. Eugene Stanley (2000) *An Introduction to Econophysics: Correlation and Complexity in Finance*, Cambridge University Press, Cambridge, UK.

Nelson, C. R., and A. F. Siegel (1987) "Parsimonious Modelling of Yield Curves," *Journal of Business*, **60**(4), 473–489.

Newton, Isaac (1713) *Philosophiae Naturalis Principia Mathematica, Cambridge, UK.*

Peters, Edgar E. (1989) "Fractal Structure in the Capital Markets," *Financial Analysts Journal*, **45**(4), 32–37.

Peters, Edgar E. (1994) *Fractal Market Analysis*, John Wiley and Sons, New York, NY.

Rendleman, R., and B. Barrter (1980) "The Pricing of Options on Debt Securities," *Journal of Financial and Quantitative Analysis*, **15**(1), 11–24.

Reynolds, O. (1883) "An Experimental Investigation of the Circumstances Which Determine Whether the Motion of Water Shall Be Direct or Sinuous, and the Law of Resistance in Parallel Channels," *Philosophical Transactions of the Royal Society of London*, **174**, 935–982.

Richardson, L. F. (1926) "Atmospheric Diffusion Shown on a Distance–Neighbour Graph," *Proceedings of the Royal Society of London*, A, **110**, 709–737.

Rogers, L. C. G. (1996) "Gaussian Errors," *Risk*, **9**(1), 42–45.

Santa-Clara, P., and D. Sornette (2001) "The Dynamics of the Forward Interest Rate Curve with Stochastic String Shocks," *Review of Financial Studies*, **14**(1), 149–185.

Sherry, Clifford J. (1992) *The Mathematics of Technical Analysis: Applying Statistics to Trading Stocks, Options and Futures*, Probus Publishing Co., Chicago, IL.

Singer, B. D., and D. S. Karnosky (1995) "The General Framework for Global Investment Management and Performance Attribution," *The Journal of Performance Measurement*, **21**(2), 84–92.

Sørensen, C. (1994) "Option Pricing in a Gaussian Two-Factor Model of the Term Structure of Interest Rates," Working Paper, WP-94-4, Copenhagen Business School, Copenhagen, Denmark.

Stanton, R. (1997) "A Nonparametric Model of Term Structure Dynamics and the Market Price of Interest Rate Risk," *Journal of Finance*, **52**(5), 1973–2002.

Steeley, J. M. (1991) "Estimating the Gilt-Edged Term Structure: Basis Splines and Confidence Intervals," *Journal of Business Finance and Accounting*, **18**, 513–530.

Stevin, Simon (1586) *De Beghinselen der Weeghconst, De Weeghdaet, De Beghinselen der Waterwichts (The Principles of Weighting, The Actual Weighting, The Principles of Water Pressure)*, Cristoffel Plantin, Antwerp.

Tice, J., and N. J. Webber (1997) "A Non-Linear Model of the Term Structure of Interest Rates," *Mathematical Finance*, **7**(2), 177–209.

Tritton, D. J. (1988) *Physical Fluid Dynamics*, 2nd edn, Clarendon, Oxford, UK.

Urbach, Richard M. A. (2000) *Footprints of Chaos in the Markets: Analyzing Non-Linear Time Series in Financial Markets and Other Real Systems*, Prentice Hall, London, UK.

Van Dyke, M. (1982) *An Album of Fluid Motion*, The Parabolic Press, Stanford, CA.

Van Horne, James C. (1998) *Financial Market Rates and Flows*, 5th edn, Prentice Hall, NJ.

Vasicek, O. A. (1977) "An Equilibrium Characterization of the Term Structure," *Journal of Financial Economics*, **5**(2), 177–188.

Vasicek, O., and G. Fong (1982) "Term Structure Modelling Using Exponential Splines," *Journal of Finance*, **37**(2), 339–348.

Xu, X., and S. J. Taylor (1994) "The Term Structure of Volatility Implied by Foreign Exchange Options," *Journal of Financial and Quantitative Analysis*, **29**(1), 57–74.

11 Simulation of financial turbulence

> Big whirls have little whirls,
> That feed on their velocity;
> And little whirls have lesser whirls,
> And so on to viscosity.
>
> > (Richardson, 1922)

11.1 Introduction

In this chapter, we will first address the few available basic laws of fully developed physical turbulence and interpret them in financial terms, in a similar fashion as we've interpreted the laws of fluid mechanics in terms of financial cash flows in Chapter 10. Physical turbulence is a phenomenon measured in a 4-dimensional (4D) space–time frame of reference in cubic meter seconds. Financial turbulence is, on the surface, a simpler phenomenon measured in a 2-dimensional (2D) magnitude–time reference frame of percentage seconds.

However, it is also clear from the examples we encountered in Chapters 8 and 10 that it is probably interaction between the cash flows of the various financial markets that causes vortices to arise. Very recently, the issue of how interdependent financial markets are and how they transmit financial contagion has become an important research question (Forbes and Rigobon, 2002).

In Chapter 8, not only did we observe adjustment vortices immediately after domestic trading regime changes in the foreign exchange markets, like the changes from pegged to floating exchange rate regimes, but we also observed adjustment vortices occurring in well-working financial markets caused by disturbances in neighboring interconnected markets, like the impact of a stock market crisis in Brazil on stock market pricing process in Chile.

Next, we'll spend some time on how we can obtain numerical solutions for the nonlinear diffusion equations that describe financial turbulence, like the finite difference method, the spectral method, and the Galerkin finite element method. In particular, we'll explain the considerable analytic power of the new wavelet Galerkin method in both its scalar and matrix forms.

11.2 Theories of physical and financial turbulence

How does the *critical phenomenon* of physical turbulence occur? Universally accepted exact or inexact mathematical models to completely explain physical turbulence do not yet exist. We are obliged to provide, first, an informal interpretation of the existing theory of physical turbulence, which is part of the theory of *vortex formation* or *vorticity dynamics*, before we can interpret these theories in financial terms.

The statistical theory of turbulence was introduced by Kolmogorov (1941a–c), Obukhov (1941a,b) and Taylor (1935, 1938). This involved applying the statistical tools used for stationary stochastic processes to understand the partition of risk at different scales or frequencies, using Parseval's Theorem (cf. Chapter 5), in the solutions of the Navier–Stokes diffusion equation, i.e., the nonlinear dynamic equations that can produce intermittency and chaos. Kolmogorov's statistical point of view, and assumption of ergodicity, was justified by the loss of the uniqueness of the dynamic solutions, i.e., the emergence of chaos, or *fully developed turbulence*, for very large Reynolds numbers and large values of time.

The intermediate scales of turbulence – the *inertial zone* – lie between the smallest scales, where through viscosity, the dynamic risk is dissipated in noise, and the largest scales, where exterior forces supply the risk.[1] The theory of Kolmogorov states that, in this inertial zone, risk is neither produced nor dissipated, but only transferred, without dissipation, from one scale to another and according to a constant rate σ_ε. In the financial markets and in financial terms, this inertial zone is represented by the fundamental term structure of interest rates. Major amounts of risk are supplied at the long-term end of the term structure, which are transferred along the term structure until they are completely dissipated in noise at the short-term end. Thus, the problem of term structure analysts of how to dynamically model the term structure of interest rates is the same problem of turbulence physicists and flow dynamics specialists. In both cases, no universally acceptable dynamic model exists for this inertial zone of risk.

The ergodicity assumption asserts that turbulence is *statistically homogeneous* (= translation invariant through time), *isotropic* (= invariant under rotation) and *self-similar* (scaling invariant). The velocity components $x_\tau(t)$ are then treated as random variables, in the probabilistic sense, and their statistical description is then derived from the corresponding auto- and cross-correlation functions (ACFs and CCFs) to measure their dynamic forms of stationarity.

The mathematical tool uniquely adapted to Kolmogorov's ergodic statistical theory of dynamic stationarity phenomena is the Fourier Transform (FT) of Chapter 6. By associating scale and frequency in the usual way, Kolmogorov arrived at the following expression for the average spectral distribution of risk

$$P(\omega) = \sigma_\varepsilon^{2/3}|\omega|^{-5/3} \tag{11.1}$$

where $P(\omega)$ is the FT of the (fractal) time series variable $x_\tau(t)$.

This ergodic statistical model of turbulence is self-similar, i.e., scale-invariant, and are determined by a specific scale exponent (cf. Chapters 3 and 4 for the theory of scaling invariance). The theoretical value $\frac{1}{3}$ of the scaling exponent of turbulence is obtained from physical principles in Kolmogorov's 1941 theoretical paper on turbulence (Kolmogorov, 1941c).

The main problem with this ergodic statistical approach is the assumption of statistical homogeneity. As the following example clearly demonstrates, two time series may exhibit exactly the same spectral distribution, but their distribution through time is not the same: while the first time series is homogeneous, the second time series is heterogeneous and contains a vortex spiral.

Example 454   *The top and bottom panels in Figure 11.1 show two fractal time series with exactly the same risk spectrum $P(\omega) \propto \omega^{-(5/3)}$. The ordinates measure the amplitudes, while the abscissas measure the respective time lines. While the top panel in Figure 11.1 shows a fractal time series of regularly distributed noise, the bottom panel shows a fractal time series with a vortex spiral. Notice the intermittency of the vortex spiral: there is a period of increasing frequency of variation or* condensation, *followed by a period of decreasing frequency of variation, or* rarefaction. *A comparison of these two time series clearly demonstrates that average statistical or frequency information alone is insufficient to completely*

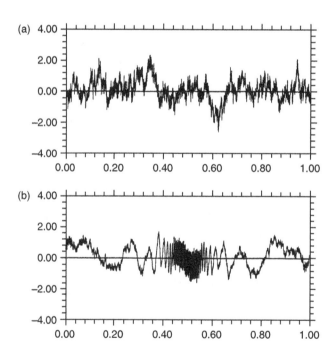

Figure 11.1 An indictment of global (average) statistical analysis: two very different fractal time series with the same global risk spectrum $P(\omega) \propto \omega^{-(5/3)}$ of turbulence. However, the fractal time series in the top panel (a) is homogeneous, while the time series in the bottom panel and (b) is heterogeneous and shows a vortex spiral.

identify and model a time series, that the ergodic assumption is not satisfied, and that time information must simultaneously be used in combination with frequency information to obtain an accurate picture of a risk diffusion process.

Various laboratory experiments, like in wind tunnels and in fluid basins, have shown that the risk associated with the small scales of turbulent flow is not distributed uniformly in space. This particular observation, that the systematic model of the transfer of risk is not homogeneous, but heterogeneous, or spatially intermittent, has led several authors to hypothesize that this dynamic model must be either monofractal (Mandelbrot, 1975), or multifractal (Frisch and Parisi, 1985). If so, the use of the stationarity-based FT cannot identify and elucidate the multifractal structure of fully developed turbulence. This observation has led to the important application of wavelet Multiresolution Analysis (MRA) by Marie Farge (1992a,b; cf. also Farge *et al.*, 1996).

As we discussed in Chapter 8, the Wavelet Transform (WT) is the ideal tool for analyzing multifractal structures, and Uriel Frisch (1995) has verified his conjecture by going into the heart of a turbulence, or Gagne signal and by traveling across the scales to compute the multifractal spectrum. His empirical observation results have already been reviewed in Chapter 8. After earlier theoretical speculations about the shape and dynamics of vortices, Frisch's empirical measurement results are currently used by Farge *et al.* (1996) to simulate physical turbulence by numerically solving the Navier–Stokes diffusion equation using the wavelet Galerkin method, to be discussed later in this chapter.

Example 455   *Although physical turbulence is spatially a* $3D$ *phenomenon, it's simulations are often presented in 2-dimensional* $(2D)$ *isocontour projections, where we look down on* $2D$ *snapshots of* $3D$ *vortices at different moments in time. In Figure 11.2, Farge et al. (1996) simulate the formation and dissipation of a* $2D$ *vortex, based on a pseudo-wavelet computation of* $2D$ *Navier–Stokes equations. The first three panels show the evolution of the* $2D$ *vortex spiral for* $t = 10, 20, 40$. *The final panel shows its the scalegram with the average risk spectrum of its diameter at* $t = 40$, *from which the slope* $-(2H + 1) = -\frac{5}{3}$ *is measured, so that the Hölder–Hurst exponent is identified as* $H = \frac{1}{3}$. *Notice the slight periodicities in the scalegram.*

11.2.1   Informal theory of physical turbulence

But what causes physical turbulence? A complete theory of turbulence has not yet been formulated, and the following remains therefore a strictly informal presentation of the physics involved. In physical terms, when the relative speed difference between adjacent flows increases, because of an increase in pressure difference, the friction between these adjacent flows increases too, according to the risk equation. Newton's Equation of State informs us that, for incompressible fluids with constant volumes (= *homogeneity* assumption), when the pressure of the adjacent

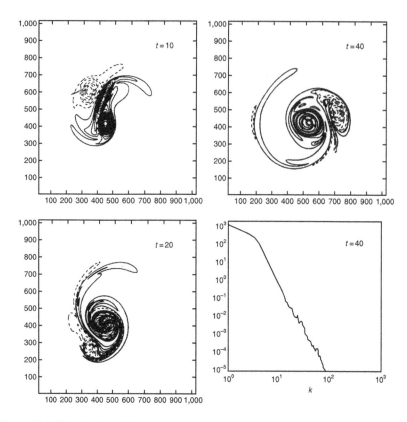

Figure 11.2 Simulated evolution, $t = 10, 20, 40$, of a 2D vortex spiral, based on a pseudo-wavelet computation of 2D Navier–Stokes equations, with its risk (energy) spectrum computed at $t = 40$. In the last panel, the ordinate measures the scale $\sim 1/\omega$, while the abscissa measures the spectrum $P(\omega)$.

flows increases marginally, the local temperature or risk of the *boundary layer* rises with it, as follows.

Proposition 456   (Newton's equation of state)

$$\frac{\text{pressure} \times \text{volume}}{\text{absolute temperature}} = \frac{\text{FP}_{mn} \times V}{\text{Temp}_{mn}} = \text{constant} \tag{11.2}$$

For constant volume V, this equation in marginal form equals:

$$\Delta \text{Temp}_{mn} = \Delta \text{FP}_{mn} \tag{11.3}$$

$$= -\tfrac{1}{2}\rho \Delta_{mn} x^2(t) \tag{11.4}$$

where the pressure difference $\Delta F P_{mn}$ is the same we encountered in Chapter 10, i.e., essentially a difference in local risk $\Delta_{mn} x^2(t)$.

Thus, the local risk difference results in a temperature or local risk change, which causes differences in risk dissipation and time dependency. The rising temperature or risk of the boundary layer leads to faster risk dissipation, and ultimately to irregularity, or randomness, of the microscopic flows on both sides of the boundary layer between the adjacent flows. This boundary layer of local risk, or *shock wave front*, defines the funnel shape of a vortex, which is, essentially, the shape of the term structure of interest rates.[2] We can thus look at the dynamic FT transform of the financial term structure to interpret the changing of its shape. The convexity deformation (or "stretching") of the shape of a vortex, and of the financial term structure, is responsible for risk transduction and subsequent risk dissipation. Thus, such convexity vortices effectively transduce the risk between high risk flows and low risk flows.

Indeed, these spiral vortices come into existence, when a flow gets stalled against its boundaries, or against another slower flow, or against a flow moving in the opposite direction. The stalled flow breaks into pieces that roll over themselves, like the waves on a sandy beach. Right at the boundary, the flow has zero velocity. But we don't know when a specific vortex will come into existence or will die away. Vortex formation appears to be a random occurrence, although it is actually deterministic: it is a set of non-unique equilibria, therefore, a chaotic development, i.e., clearly a nonlinear dynamic development. Because it is essentially chaotic, based on a period-doubling feedback process, we cannot describe the initial conditions with enough accuracy to be able to predict all the resulting consequences (cf. Chapter 8 why this is the case). Although we cannot yet predict precisely how such highly structured vortices form and interact, we can predict something about the average case of the formation of a vortex.

> For instance, the average eddy moves a distance about equal to its own diameter before it generates small eddies that move, more often than not, in the opposite direction. Those smaller eddies generate still smaller eddies and the process continues until all the energy dissipates as heat through molecular motion.
>
> (Stevens, 1974, p. 55)

If this "shock wave front" theory of vortex formation is correct, then we know from *acoustics* what the shape of the initial vortex is, since the *envelope of a wave front* forms a cone, whose apex half angle θ is given by the expression

$$\sin\theta = \frac{x_m(t)}{x_n(t)}, \quad \text{with } x_n(t) > x_m(t) \tag{11.5}$$

which is the inverse of the *Mach number* $= x_n(t)/x_m(t)$.[3]

Example 457 *The left panel of Figure 11.3 provides a graphical model of a (horizontal) vortex with its shock wave front produced when a source moves from position S_0 to S_n with a speed v_s, which is greater than the wave speed v in that particular medium (e.g., liquid or gas). The envelope of the wavefront forms a cone whose apex half-angle is given by $\sin\theta = v/v_s$, the inverse of the Mach number.*

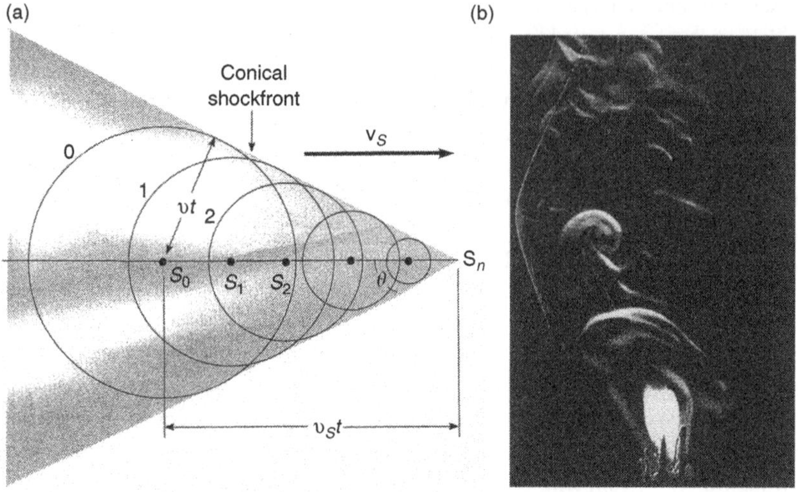

Figure 11.3 Theoretical and empirical representations of a shock wave. At the left (a) the
envelope of the wavefronts forms a cone whose apex half-angle is given by
$\sin \theta = v/v_s$. At the right (b) a stroboscopic photograph of a bullet moving
from right to left at supersonic speed through the hot air above the candle
forming a wave front.

*The right panel of Figure 11.3 shows an empirical strobographic photograph of
a bullet moving at supersonic speed through the hot air above a candle. Note the
thin hyperbola of the shock wave in front of the bullet fired from the right to the
left in this picture. (Source: Serway, 1992, pp. 467–468).*

The shock wave front carries thus a large amount of risk on the boundary layer,
which defines the cone of the vortex. The higher the "downstream" velocity x_n,
compared with the "upstream" velocity x_m, the narrower the angle of the cone of
the vortex. However, because the risk of the various flows dissipates at different
rates at different velocity levels, the shape of the developing vortex cone is not
constant, but actually a hyperbolic "funnel" shape, which stretches its shape over
time. The absolute apex of such a vortex is a singularity.[4]

In a sense, it is the much faster velocity by which the singularity of the vortex
is created relative to the velocity of the surrounding medium, why the vortex is
formed in the first place (Farge and Holschneider, 1990). Thus, *vortex dynamics*
(the rate at which vortices are created and then vanish) is intimately related to two
phenomena:

(1) the *relative velocity differences* between the velocity of a singularity (which
     is "infinite" by definition) and the finite velocity of the medium in which it is
     created, and

(2) the *relative rates of risk dissipation*, i.e., the stability of the singularity
     distribution (which we discussed in Chapter 8).

11.2.2 Informal theory of financial turbulence

My financial interpretation of this informal theory of physical turbulence for the critical phenomenon of financial turbulence and the formation of vortices in financial market pricing processes is now as follows. Financial cash flows dynamics is "spatially" 2D, because of the dynamic interaction between two rates of return of adjacent investment cash flow channels, e.g., within a domestic term structure of interest rates.

Suppose, there is an increase in financial pressure $\Delta FP_{mn}(t) > 0$, because of major differences in the rates of return $x_i(t), i \in \{m, n\}$ on cash investments at the beginning and the end of existing investment cash flow channels between segments of a steep domestic term structure, or between two term structures, e.g., in two different countries. These major differences may have been caused by the sudden announcement of a change in trading regime from a pegged exchange rate to a floating exchange rate, or by a sudden insight in the true valuation of corporate shares due to the due diligence auditing for an initial public offering (IPO) in a stock market. Similar examples, we've earlier discussed in Chapter 8.

This increased financial pressure requires rising of the local risk of the boundary layer or wave front between the two adjacent cash flows. This I interpret to mean an increase on the margin in the frequency of buy and sell transactions in the adjacent markets, i.e., a steep increase in the number of independent transactions per unit of time. The consequent increased transaction frequency of price singularities could lead to turbulent, i.e., rotational and random, rapidly mean-reverting flows: small cash flows that go rapidly back and forth between adjacent investment cash flow channels, caused by *noise traders* (= *small risk arbitragers*), of which we find more and more trading on the world-wide web.

Eventually we'll observe intermittency: periods of *condensation* = periods of increased velocity and efficiency of transactions, i.e., of antipersistence and stability, followed by periods of *rarefaction* = periods of reduced velocity and efficiency of transactions, i.e., of persistence and fundamental instability. These periods of temporarily increased scaling followed by periods of temporarily reduced scaling are observable in scalograms, as a variation in price singularity frequencies. Interpreted in statistical terms, such intermittency should be observable as a shift in the singularity spectrum from low Lipschitz irregularity α_L (= high Zolotarev stability α_Z = lepto-kurtosis of the distribution of the rate of cash return $x(t)$), to high Lipschitz irregularity α_L (= low Zolotarev stability α_Z = platy-kurtosis of the distribution of the rate of cash return $x(t)$).

Such intermittency of sequences of condensations and rarefactions of price singularities may thus cause the emergence of financial market vortices. When these cash vortices remain relatively small in amplitude and duration, because of high efficiency of trading (= fractal antipersistence = low Lipschitz α_L = high stability α_Z = lepto-kurtosis of distribution of the rates of cash return $x(t)$) in the financial markets, the financial markets will not experience major disruptions in their trading. But when this concentration, or increase in frequency of cash flow trading, cannot occur because of low efficiency (= fractal persistence = high Lipschitz α_L = low stability α_Z = platy-kurtosis of distribution of the rates of cash return $x(t)$) in the financial markets, the existing financial pressure may produce very large amplitude price singularities, i.e., financial crises, which will disrupt the cash flow rates, by disrupting the investment cash positions $X(t)$.

That's why I introduced in the preceding chapter the definition of a cash vortex, which I repeat here:

Definition 458   *A cash flow vortex occurs, when the fractal differences $\Delta^d X_\tau(t)$ first rapidly increase in density (become quickly more rapid) and then rapidly decreases in density (become quickly less rapid). In other words, a cash vortex occurs, when the fractional differentiation (in particular the second-order differentiation, or convexity) of the cash flow $X_\tau(t)$ is non-homogeneous and there exists a fractal spectrum of irregularities. Or, differently stated, when many values of $-0.5 < d < 0.5$ are co-existent.*

This is an observable phenomenon. As we demonstrated in Chapter 8, we can now measure the fractal spectrum of market rates of return series from which we can measure $H = d + 0.5$. In both the physical and financial sense, it is clear that the observable essence of turbulent flow motion is (1) spiral vortex or convexity dynamics, i.e., the interaction between the magnitude scales of rate of cash return $x_\tau(t)$ relative to the dependency structure of the risk dissipation and (2) periods of intermittency. This requires a simultaneous time–frequency analysis, preferably in real-time.

11.3   Measurement and simulation of turbulence

The phenomenon of turbulence was discovered physically. But the mathematical modelling of turbulence is still a major problem of modern science, which remains incomplete, despite an intense research effort since the first theory of Kolmogorov of 1941 and Kolmogorov's amendment of 1961. It is only very recently that we have drastically improved the measurement technology, thanks to wavelet MRA. No mathematical model exists yet to build a complete statistics–physics framework based on the Navier–Stokes equations for turbulence, that would enable us to truly understand the behavior of turbulent physical flows and, by analogy, of turbulent financial flows.

The physical experimentation that led to these and similar discoveries is quite peculiar. To a great extent, experimentation in flow dynamics is done while the underlying physical principles, like the Navier–Stokes equations, are in no doubt.[5] In fact, the quantities observed are completely determined by these known non-linear partial differential equations (PDEs).[6] So, the purpose of the recent and current experiments is not to verify the proposed theory but to replace a computation from an unquestioned theory by direct measurements. Wind tunnels were used as analogue computers to integrate these PDEs.

The main reason often given for this paucity of mathematical turbulence models is that the number of degrees of freedom needed to compute the spatially

3D Navier–Stokes is so large. At high Reynolds number, the solutions of these 3D PDEs scale as $\mathrm{Re}_\tau^{(3/2)^2} = \mathrm{Re}_\tau^{9/4}$, by direct numerical integration. Since the Reynolds number Re_τ runs into the thousands, this integration involves a very large number of measurements and real-time computations and produces extremely complex spatio-temporal behavior. Vector–matrix computation can now be done in an extremely fast fashion and in real time. Wavelet MRA is a vector–matrix based measurement and computation technique to visualize such complex nonlinear dynamic behavior.

Moreover, the argument that the computations become (too) complex and time-consuming is not valid for finance. In finance, the problem of the high number of degrees of freedom is considerably less. In finance, we only deal with 1D turbulence (vorticity) caused by the friction within the same market caused by adjustment problems over time, or with 2D turbulence between adjacent bilateral cash flows of two different markets, like, for example, the spot and futures markets. The solutions of the 1D Navier–Stokes equations scale as $\mathrm{Re}_\tau^{(1/2)^2} = \mathrm{Re}_\tau^{1/4}$ and the solutions of the 2D equations only scale linearly as $\mathrm{Re}_\tau^{(2/2)^2} = \mathrm{Re}_\tau$. That is quite a relief for financial vortex dynamics and makes such computations feasible using real time tick-by-tick data from the financial markets. Still, wavelet MRA computations can reduce the computational burden even more, since they are based on vector computations.

11.3.1 *Kolmogorov's homogeneous (isotropic) turbulence*

Let's now step back for a moment and review in greater detail what we have learned thus far about turbulence theory, measurement and analysis. In 1941, the Russian mathematician Kolmogorov formulated an analytic statistical theory of homogeneous, isotropic turbulence for viscous (= illiquid), incompressible (-constant density) fluids with high Reynolds numbers, based on the notion of self-similarity or scaling (Kolmogorov, 1941a–c).[7] He expanded on the earlier work by Richardson (1926), who introduced the notion of self-similarity in the form of a hierarchy of vortices linked by a *cascade*.[8] Such a cascade model we discussed by way of an example in Chapter 8. It is now tested by physicists in physical fluids (Meneveau and Sreenivasan 1987a,b, 1991), in foreign exchange markets (Ghasghaie *et al.*, 1996) and in stock markets (Mantegna and Stanley, 1996, 1997; Arnéodo *et al.*, 1998).

A crucial descriptor of such financial vortices is the velocity field.

Definition 459 *A velocity field is the nD density distribution of the nth-order velocity vector* $\mathbf{x}(t)$*. For turbulence and vortices* $n = 1, 2$ *or* 3.

In the following definitions this density distribution is described by only its second moment. When a Gaussian density distribution is assumed, this is sufficient to describe also its fourth moment or kurtosis (cf. Chapter 1). However, this is an insufficient description, when the velocity fields are actually stable non-Gaussian distributions (cf. Chapter 3), as is currently accepted by most scientists. Therefore, the kurtosis of these velocity fields should be determined for each dimension separately and conjunctively. It is usually assumed that there is no skewness, since risk dissipation is considered symmetric, because of the assumption of a uniform medium. But even this uniformity assumption is now being challenged, because of the *Doppler effect* (Farge *et al.*, 1996; Nolan, 1999a,b).[9]

But let's begin with Kolmogorov's original theoretical physical turbulence model.

Definition 460   *For Kolmogorov's homogeneous turbulence, the velocity field of* $\mathbf{x}(t)$ *is modeled by n orthogonal time series processes* $x_i(t)$, *whose increments have a variance proportional to the time lag* τ:

$$E\{|x_i(t) - x_i(t-\tau)|^2\} \sim (\sigma_\varepsilon \tau)^{2H} = (\sigma_\varepsilon \tau)^{2/3} \tag{11.6}$$

where σ_ε *is the (noise) risk dissipation coefficient, which is independent of spatial location.*

Kolmogorov's homogeneity assumption of the independence of location of the diffusion errors ε, and the constancy of the risk dissipation coefficient σ_ε, exclude intermittence, i.e., the convolution of the dissipation at various locations, since the dissipation rate $2H = \frac{2}{3}$ is assumed to be the same in all three orthogonal spatial dimensions (giving rise to the connotation "isotropic"). Thus, Kolmogorov (1941a–c) predicted that the velocity of a vortex is proportional to the cube root of its size. He predicted, e.g., a vortex moving twice as fast as another will usually be eight times as large; or that a vortex moving ten times as fast will be a thousand times as large.

Remark 461   *Notice that in Kolmogorov's model the nD risk density distribution of* $\mathbf{x}(t)$, *described by its second-order moment, dissipates over time at a constant rate. Thus, turbulence eventually ends in risk dissipation. Due to the viscosity of the adjacent flows, the risk of the macro-scale visible motions transforms via period-doubling processes into complete micro-scale chaos.*

Kolmogorov's model implies that each 1D time series process $x_i(t)$ is statistically homogeneous with Lipschitz regularity $\alpha_L = H = \frac{1}{3}$, so that its fractal Hausdorff dimension is zero (a point dimension), according to the inverted Legendre transformation of Chapter 8:

$$D(\alpha_L) = \inf_{q \in \mathbb{R}} [(\alpha_L + 0.5)q - \tau(q)]$$

$$= \inf_{q \in \mathbb{R}} \left[\left(\frac{1}{3} + 0.5 \right) 2 - \tau(2) \right]$$

$$= \inf_{q \in \mathbb{R}} \left[\frac{5}{3} - \tau(2) \right] = 0 \tag{11.7}$$

Thus, Kolmogorov's (1941) turbulence theory predicts that his 1D velocity trace $x_i(t)$ is a fractal random process with stationary increments, whose power spectrum decays with a scaling exponent $\tau(2) = 2H + 1 = \frac{5}{3}$ (cf. Chapter 8):

$$P(\omega) = \sigma_\varepsilon^2 |\omega|^{-(2H+1)}$$

$$= \sigma_\varepsilon^2 |\omega|^{-\frac{5}{3}} \qquad (11.8)$$

The success of Kolmogorov's average statistical theory comes from numerous empirical verifications of this power law of spectrum decay, initially from measurements of turbulence of shear flows, empirically, in the oceans and, experimentally, in wind tunnels (Grant *et al.*, 1962; Batchelor, 1969; Anselmet *et al.*, 1984), and more recently from measurements of turbulence in the atmosphere by Kida and Okhitani (1992), Gagne and Castaing (1991) and Schmitt *et al.* (1992). All empirical measurements show that the actual scaling exponent of turbulence is very close to Kolmogorov's predicted value of $\tau(2) = \frac{5}{3}$. Figure 11.4 shows the results of Gagne and Castaing (1991), as reproduced in Frisch (1995, p. 154).

As Mandelbrot (1982, p. 278) states:

This verification constitutes a striking triumph of abstract a priori thought over the messiness of raw data. It deserves (. . .) to be known outside the circle of specialists.

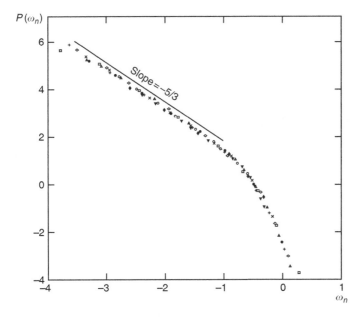

Figure 11.4 Data in the time domain from nine different turbulent flows with dissipation scales ranging from 130 to 13,000, plotted in a spectrogram with log–log coordinates. The abscissa measures the wavenumber ω_n and the ordinate the energy spectrum $P(\omega_n)$. Both axes have been standardized and the resulting curves have been shifted to give the best possible superposition for measurement of the common slope $-(2H+1) = -5/3$.

Physical antipersistent processes show approximately $H \approx \frac{1}{3} = 0.33$ and persistent processes $H \approx \frac{2}{3} = 0.66$. Similarly, in the financial markets, we find that the very antipersistent developed FX markets of the (former) German Deutsch mark (DEM) (now the Euro) and of the Japanese Yen (JPY) show a homogeneous $H \approx 0.32$. (Karuppiah and Los, 2000), while the rate of return in the slightly persistent S&P500 stock market shows a homogeneous $H \approx 0.60$ (Peters, 1994, p. 137).

The volatilities priced by option markets exhibit (scaling) power law phenomena with antipersistent $H \approx 0.44$ (Peters, 1994, p. 150), where the large-scale phenomena are the sum of many small-scale phenomena. Peters speculates that this is caused by the amplification process that underlies the long-memory process of computed implied volatilities. These striking analogous results again strongly suggest that there might be a relationship between financial cash turbulence and the persistence of investment cash flows.

As we discussed in Chapter 10, the financial equivalent of turbulence, caused by friction between adjacent illiquid (viscous) cash flows, would be the cash flow exchanges between short-term (small scale) investors, like day traders, and long-term (large scale) institutional investors, like pension and insurance funds, as Peters (1994, p. 177) conjectured:

> (1) In the stock, bond, and currency markets, volatility increased at a faster rate than the square root of time. This relationship of one investment horizon to another, amplifying the effects of smaller horizons, may be the dynamic reason that volatility has a power law scaling characteristic. At any time, the fractal structure of the markets (that is, many investors, who have different investment horizons, trading simultaneously), is a snapshot of the amplification process. This would be much like the snapshot taken of turbulent flow.
>
> (2) The stock and bond markets do have a maximum scale, showing that the memory effect dissipates as the energy in turbulent flow does. However, currencies do not have this property, and the energy amplification, or memory, continues forever. Volatility, which has a similar value of $\tau(q)$ to turbulent flow, should be modeled as such.

In contrast to Peters (1994), we find that the world's bond and stock markets are predominantly persistent, while the anchor currency markets are predominantly antipersistent. That's also why Mantegna and Stanley (1997, 2000) cannot find turbulence in the stock markets, since turbulence is essentially an antipersistence phenomenon.

11.3.2   Intermittent turbulence and chaos theory

Kolmogorov's (1941) average statistical turbulence theory does also not account for the *coherent structures* within turbulent flows, such as vortices and intermittent turbulence. Turbulence in fluid flows is characterized by *localized regions* or coherent structures of strong variations in the velocity and pressure of vorticity fields.

It is assumed, that these coherent structures control the dynamics and statistics of the turbulent flows.

These phenomena contradict Kolmogorov's hypothesis of homogeneity, which is at the root of his (1941) statistical theory of turbulence. The low-order flow structures follow Kolmogorov's law, but the higher order flow structures depart strongly from this law, since turbulent flows are actually highly intermittent.

Confronted with the empirical evidence of the 1940s and 1950s, Kolmogorov modified his homogeneity assumption in 1961, by introducing a time-varying risk dissipation rate to give an *ad hoc* explanation of the intermittency of turbulence (Kolmogorov, 1962). Although Kolmogorov's *ad hoc* modification is conceptually flawed, it opened the door, first, to the homogeneous monofractal turbulence models developed by Mandelbrot (1974, 1975) to explain risk exchanges between fine-scale time series structures and large-scale time series structures, and, second, to the current heterogeneous multifractal turbulence models. The computation of the singularity spectrum $D(\alpha_L)$, discussed in Chapter 8, plays thus an important role in the current testing the various proposed turbulence models to corroborate if the average statistical theory is true, or, currently already much more likely, if the localized non-statistical theory is true.

Let's now first examine Kolmogorov's (1962) amendment.

Definition 462 *For* monofractal (fractally homogeneous) turbulence, *the (cash) velocity field of* $\mathbf{x}(t)$ *is modeled by n orthogonal time series processes* $x_i(t)$, *whose increments have a variance proportional to the time lag* τ *as follows*

$$E\{|x_i(t) - x_i(t - \tau)|^2\} \sim (\sigma_\varepsilon \tau)^{2H} = (\sigma_\varepsilon \tau)^{(2/3)+B} \tag{11.9}$$

where $B = [3 - D]/3$.

In classical homogeneous physical turbulence the Hausdorff dimension $D = 3$, and the constant B vanishes, leaving the classic Kolmogorov exponent $2H = \frac{2}{3}$. However, Mandelbrot (1982) found that in nature $2 < D < 3$. Such a wide range is not helpful and more precise determination of the fractal dimension D was thus required, since a shape with a Hausdorff dimension $2 < D < 3$ may be either "sheet-like," "line-like,"or "dust-like." Nowadays, we find that there is a whole dimensional spectrum $D(\alpha_L)$ for a range of co-existent $\alpha_L s$.

The next phase of research is represented by the following much more sophisticated definition of the risk dissipation in vortices, which does allow for intermittency, and which is based on the work of *inter alia*, Frisch and Parisi (1985), Farge *et al.* (1996) and Mallat (1999).

Definition 463 *For* fractally heterogeneous *or* multifractal turbulence, *the velocity field of* $\mathbf{x}(t)$ *is modeled by n orthogonal time series processes* $x_i(t)$, *whose increments have a variance proportional to the time lag* τ *as follows*

$$E\{|x_i(t) - x_i(t - \tau)|^2\} \sim (\sigma_\varepsilon \tau)^{2\alpha_{L_i}} \tag{11.10}$$

so that $\alpha_{L,i} \neq \alpha_{L_j}$ *for* $i \neq j$.

Remark 464 *Notice that this most recent description of risk dissipation does allow for intermittency, i.e., covariance between the orthogonal dissipation processes, since the dissipation rates differ from each other for each n orthogonal direction. This implies that no longer Gaussian velocity fields are assumed, which have the same kurtosis (and skewness) in all dimensions, but stable non-Gaussian velocity fields, since the velocity field may have different kurtosis in each direction. The kurtosis of the velocity field in each dimension i is measured by $\alpha_{Z_i} = 1/\alpha_{L_i}$.*

To find the multifractal support for turbulence, Frisch and Parisi (1985) used the experimental wind tunnel time series (= the "Gagne" signal) supplied by Anselmet *et al.* (1984). As Meyer (1993, p. 120) relates, they evaluated the average power of the qth power of the change in the 3D velocity vector $x(t)$ in a turbulent flow, i.e., they computed Gibbs' *partition function* of the change (cf. end of Chapter 8):

$$Z(q, \Delta_\tau x_i) = E\{|\Delta_\tau x_i|^q\}$$
$$= E\{|x_i(t) - x_i(t - \tau)|^q\} \tag{11.11}$$

To their surprise, Frisch and Parisi (1985) found a power law in terms of

$$|\Delta_\tau x_i|^{\tau(q)} \tag{11.12}$$

where the exponent $\tau(q)$ does depend *nonlinearly* on the moment order q. They interpreted that to mean that turbulent flow develops multifractal singularities (by a period-doubling process), when the Reynolds number $\text{Re}_\tau(t)$ becomes very large.

What is the relationship between this multifractal structure and the nonlinear power law? When one discusses a multifractal "structure," one means that for each difference order $d > 0$, there is a set of singular points, with Hausdorff dimension $D(d)$, on which the increase in velocity, or the *acceleration*, acts like $|\Delta_\tau x_i|^d$. The contribution of each of these "singularities of difference (order) exponent d" to the average value $E\{|\Delta_\tau x_i|^q\}$ is of the order of magnitude of the product:

$$|\Delta_\tau x_i|^{dq}|\Delta_\tau x_i|^{3-D(d)} = |\Delta_\tau x_i|^{dq+3-D(d)} \tag{11.13}$$

whereby the second factor, $|\Delta_\tau x_i|^{3-D(d)}$, is the probability that a ball of radius $|\Delta_\tau x_i|$ intersects a fractal set with Hausdorff dimension $D(d)$.

When the radius of this ball approaches zero, $|\Delta_\tau x_i| \to 0$, the dominant term is the one with the smallest possible exponent, which implies that:

$$\tau(q) = \inf_{d>0, q\in\mathbb{R}} [dq + 3 - D(d)] \tag{11.14}$$

The exponent $\tau(q)$ is therefore given by the Legendre transform of the Hausdorff $\in$ dimension $D(d)$. The *nonlinear dependence* of the exponent $\tau(q)$ on the moment order q is caused by this Hausdorff dimension $D(d)$ of the singularity set, and thus indicates that the abrupt changes in velocity correspond to a multifractal structure.

As we discussed in Chapter 8, the wavelet MRA is the ideal research tool to analyze such multifractal structures. Nowadays, the measurements of turbulence in wind tunnels, ocean shear flows and, for the first time, in financial markets, are analyzed with wavelet MRA. Thanks to colorized visualization one can actually display the multifractal structure of turbulent flows in scalograms, as we've already done in Chapter 8.

Everson *et al.* (1990) criticized this *ad hoc* or phenomenological approach to study turbulence by showing that wavelet MRA of Brownian motion produces very similar 2D visualizations. In the past decade, their critique has moved turbulence research into a higher gear. It has moved from the qualitative to the quantitative and to extract the fractal exponents α_L and the corresponding Hausdorff dimensions $D(\alpha_L)$ from various turbulent time series $x(t)$, like financial market pricing series, as we also already learned in Chapter 8.

These theoretical and empirical measurement developments already induced Zabusky (1984), the discoverer of the *soliton*, to comment on Kolmogorov's FT-based spectral theory as follows:

> In the last decade we have experienced a conceptual shift in our view of turbulence. For flows with strong velocity shear . . . or other organizing characteristics, many now feel that the *spectral description has inhibited fundamental progress*. The next "El Dorado" lies in the *mathematical understanding of coherent structures in weakly dissipative fluids*: the formation, evolution and interaction of metastable vortex-like solutions of nonlinear partial differential equations . . .

In other words, the statistician's averaging spectral decomposition, which is based on the ergodic stationarity assumption (cf. Chapter 1), has inhibited and slowed down scientific progress. As Farge (1992a,b) points out, ignorance of the elementary physical, and for the purpose of this book, financial mechanisms at work in turbulent (cash) flows arises in part from the fact that, until very recently, we reasoned in Fourier modes (wave vectors), constructed from functions that are not well localized but have infinite support.

This particular ergodicity-based statistical viewpoint ignores the presence of clearly observable coherent structures that can be observed in physical time space and whose dynamics appear to be essential (Van Dyke, 1982). These coherent structures are observed in natural flows, experimental flows in laboratories and in numerical simulations (Basdevant *et al.*, 1981; McWilliams, 1984; Couder and Basdevant, 1986; Farge and Sadourney, 1989). But these coherents are not represented in the prevailing statistical theories based on the ergodic stationarity assumption (cf. Monin and Yaglom, 1975).

Farge (1988) and Farge and Sadourney (1989) conjectured, based on their visualization of the simulation results of dynamic 2D turbulent velocity fields, that the dynamics of such 2D turbulent flow is essentially dominated by the interactions between the coherent structures (vortices) that advect the residual flow situated between them, while the latter seems to play no dynamic role.

Indeed, in terms of the financial markets, the 1D and 2D financial vortices, generated in the rate of return and risk dissipation processes by the major announcements and political interventions, advect the residual cash flows of the noise traders, but the latter flows appear to play no dynamic role.

As Farge discovered, wavelet MRA, which decomposes the velocity fields on a set of functions with compact support, does provide well-localized time-scale analysis to delineate and interpret the coherent structures of such vortices, as we will see in the following simulation analyses.

We'll discuss first some simulation models of financial cash flow turbulence to see what actually happens when a laminar cash flow turns into a turbulent cash flow and dissipates into complete chaos.

11.4   Simulation of financial cash flow turbulence

11.4.1   *Intermittency of financial turbulence?*

Since we can characterize the degree of randomness, or irregularity, c.q., the instability of financial innovations in pricing series, is it possible to summarily measure turbulence in the financial markets, as we observed such financial turbulence, e.g., in 1994, following the Mexican Financial Crisis, or in 1997, following the Asian Financial Crisis, or in 1997 and 1998, following the Brazilian stock market and FX market crisis, respectively? And may such measurement of financial turbulence ultimately lead to a quantitative financial-economic theory of financial turbulence, which would be contrasted to the current financial-economic theory of stationary financial innovations underlying the normal valuation of risk by derivatives?

Peters (1994, pp. 167–183) produces a simple treatment of financial turbulence, while Farge *et al.* (1996) provide a more elaborate, but very similar treatment for physical turbulence. Schroeder (1991, p. 126) provides the same 1D model for a simple additive *relaxation process* as they use, which can exhibit long-term dependence, i.e., both antipersistent and persistent behavior:

$$x_\tau(t+1) = \rho x_\tau(t) + \sqrt{(1-\rho^2)}\varepsilon(t),$$

$$\text{with } 0 < \rho < 1, x_\tau(0) = 0, \text{ and } \varepsilon(t) \sim \text{uniform distribution} \tag{11.15}$$

Here ρ measures the correlation coefficient between adjacent data intervals. It is related to the *relaxation time* interval τ by the equation

$$\rho = e^{-1/\tau} \tag{11.16}$$

For a set of relaxation times that are scaled a factor of 10 (e.g. $\tau = 1, 10, 100, \ldots$), the correlation coefficients are obtained by taking decimal roots, e.g., $\rho = 0.37$, $0.90, 0.99, \ldots$

This equation has a complex interaction between its various parts. The first term

$$x_\tau(t+1) = \rho x_\tau(t)$$

$$= e^{-1/\tau}x(t) \tag{11.17}$$

is a simple AR(1) process, like we examined earlier in Chapter 4. Thus, this equation contains an infinite memory. Pure AR(1) processes are only serially persistent. But this turbulence equation can produce antipersistent time series. The secret lies in the second term, which is a random shock with a feedback twist. Its coefficient:

$$\sqrt{(1 - \rho^2)} = (1 - e^{-2/\tau})^{0.5} \tag{11.18}$$

is inversely related to the correlation coefficient ρ in the first term. The stronger the AR(1) process, i.e., the larger ρ, the less strong the random shock with its $\sqrt{(1 - \rho^2)}$ coefficient, and the weaker the AR(1) process, the stronger the random shocks. This shock becomes then part of the infinite memory process.

This inverse influence of the random shock feedback prevents the system from ever reaching equilibrium. If these random shocks were not included, each $x_\tau(t)$ series would reach its own unique equilibrium by its relaxation time τ. But the system continues to be perturbed. It continually reverses itself and therefore never settles down, since it creates coexistent nonunique equilibria. Although this model can produce both antipersistent and persistent behavior, it is still not the correct model, since it cannot produce intermittent behavior or vorticity.

Indeed, Peters (1994, pp. 177–180) proceeds to model the antipersistent volatility processes by the logistic equation we already discussed in Chapter 9, since that is the simplest method for simulating the self-similarity model of turbulence. It is characterized by a period-doubling route from orderly to chaotic behavior. Indeed, many financial economists have empirically observed the clustering phenomena in market pricing processes, e.g., large price changes are followed by more large price changes and small ones by more small ones, as well as the intermittent periods of complete unpredictability.

The current important research question is: what imposes the parabolic or higher-order constraints in the financial markets? Are the convexity constraints of the zero coupon bonds of the basic term structure providing sufficient nonlinearity on the cascade of the term structure to cause chaos to emerge when this convexity increases simultaneously with the speed of trading? Many financial economists have already proposed two- and multi-factor price diffusion models for the term structure (cf. Chapter 10).

11.4.2 Visualization of financial vorticity attractors

We have now two theoretical models of light blue (= antipersistent) random processes, which produce averaged behavior for which the homogeneous Hurst exponent is $0 < H < 0.5$: the additive relaxation model discussed in this chapter and, more importantly, the multiplicative logistic equation or "poor man's Navier–Stokes equation," which we studied in Chapter 9. Both are iterated feedback processes, i.e., processes that fractionally integrate over time. In the relaxation model, the power decay is due to correlation time and random events. In the logistic equation, power decay is due to a nonlinear transformation of the random process itself. The logistic equation can produce richer behavior than the relaxation model, since it can produce intermittent turbulence and 1D vortices.

But there is a significant empirical problem with both models, as models for empirical financial turbulence. Neither of these two time series processes generates the lepto-kurtic, high-peaked, heavy-tailed frequency distributions that we find to be characteristic of financial time series $x_\tau(t)$ with $0 < H < 0.5$, except when they are close to complete chaos! And none of the existent theoretical financial diffusion models shows the aperiodic cyclicity in their power spectra, that is emphirically observable!

Considering that kurtosis, measured by

$$c_4 = m_4 - 3m_2^2$$

$$= E\{x^4(t)\} - 3E\{x^2(t)\} \tag{11.19}$$

can be viewed as an alternative *measure of intermittency*, as Mandelbrot (1975) suggested, this lack of proper kurtosis produced by the various turbulence models is a very serious theoretical and empirical research issue. Therefore, it is necessary to carefully study the spectrum of the singularities found in the empirical rates of return (velocities) $x_\tau(t)$ to find an explanation for the non-Gaussian kurtosis of these rates. Next, we must numerically integrate the nonlinear Navier–Stokes equations in such a way that they exactly reproduce the vorticity observe in the financial market pricing series.

In Chapter 8, we have seen that the singularity analysis by wavelet MRA provides a powerful visualization and analysis tool for exactly this kind of research. Indeed, Mandelbrot already conjectured in 1976 the following statement regarding the multifractal nature of turbulence (Mandelbrot, 1982, p. 107):

> the turbulent solutions of the basic equations [of flow dynamics] involve singularities or "near singularities" of an entirely new kind. The singularities are locally scaling fractal sets, and the near singularities are approximations thereto.

11.5   Multiresolution analysis of financial turbulence

Since the early 1990s, the measurement analysis of turbulence has considerably improved by the use of wavelet MRA to compute multifractal spectra $D(\alpha_L)$. Computations with wavelet maxima on turbulent processes show that the multifractal spectrum $D(\alpha_L)$ is at a maximum at $\alpha_{L0} = \frac{1}{3}$, as predicted by the Kolmogorov (1941) theory of homogeneous, isotropic turbulence.[10] However, the computed singularity spectrum $D(\alpha_L)$ does not have its support reduced to a single point $\{\alpha_{L0}\} = \{\frac{1}{3}\}$, which verifies that turbulent processes are not homogenous, monofractal processes, but must be heterogeneous, multifractal processes (Muzy *et al.*, 1991).

Indeed, other dimensional estimates of α_L than Kolmogorov's (1941) homogeneous $H = \frac{1}{3}$ have already been conjectured and corroborated. In his work on homogeneous fractal turbulence, Mandelbrot (1975, 1976) conjectured that turbulence in real 3D-space is a risk dissipation phenomenon carried by a fractal set of dimension around $2.5 < D(\alpha_L) < 2.6$, but probably below 2.66, i.e., somewhere between a flat 2D-plane and truly 3D-space. Numerical work in support for his conjecture is provided by, e.g., Hentschel and Procaccia (1983), Chorin (1988) and Hentschel (1994). The boundary of such a turbulent area in space reveals a hierarchy of indentations, whose depth increases with the value of the classic measure of hydrodynamic scale, the Reynolds number $Re_\tau(t)$. These scaling indentations show up as aperiodic cyclicity in the power spectra of the rates of return $x_\tau(t)$

To put this within our scientific perspective of possible turbulence in 1D financial cash flows, charted in the Euclidean return time space $\{x(t), t\}$, financial turbulence would be characterized by a rate of return variance exponent of $2H = \frac{2}{3} + B$, where we should find according to Mandelbrot's (1976) corroborated conjecture that the value of the Kolmogorov's (1962) correction term is lying in the narrow range:

$$(3 - 2.6)/3 = 0.1333 < B < 0.1666 = \frac{(3 - 2.5)}{3} \tag{11.20}$$

so that the homogeneous Hurst exponent is

$$0.3999 < H < 0.4166 \tag{11.21}$$

and the Zolotarev stability exponent

$$2.4 < \alpha_Z \left(= \frac{1}{\alpha_L} \right) < 2.5 \tag{11.22}$$

which indicates that turbulence is antipersistent and considerably more stable noise than Gaussian noise. From the Legendre transformation for homogeneous fractals in Chapter 8, the equivalent time decay scaling exponent for turbulence $\tau(2) = 2H + 1$, so that

$$1.7999 < \tau(2) < 1.8332 \tag{11.23}$$

As we discussed in Chapter 8, we empirically find that the developed FX markets for the German DEM (now the Euro) and the JPY show an average $H \approx 0.32$, suggesting that these developed markets may contain truly antipersistent turbulent cash flows, since we also find that the equivalent Zolotarev $\alpha_Z = 3.125$ shows substantial distributional stability. In addition, the Mexican peso market shows a homogeneous $H = 0.41$, i.e., within the bound conjectured by Mandelbrot. Indeed, as we observed, the Mexican Peso/US Dollar (USD) rate shows several adjustment vortices in the observed period in the 1990s. Similar results we have already observed for several European financial markets. (Lipka and Los, 2002).

In contrast, most of the developing Asian FX markets in the period May–August 1997 had a Hurst exponent $0.42 \le H \le 0.67$, or $1.49 < \alpha_Z < 2.38$, with mostly $H \approx 0.48$, or $\alpha_Z = 2.083$, suggesting that they behaved more like Random Walks, even though some of these FX markets were unstable and others stable. Not all financial markets are alike: they exhibit different degrees of persistence.

These observations also suggest that the 1997 Asian Financial Crises was not due to imperfections in the Asian FX markets, since they behaved overall as Random Walks, which conventional financial economics considers sufficiently efficient. It is more appropriate to conclude that the outcome of this series of financial crises was initiated by a black-noise crisis in a imperfectly functioning commercial loan market, which spilled over in the turbulent Asian FX markets, i.e., more like the consequences of the subsequent Russian sovereign bond and German bund market crises in 1998, which brought down Long Term Capital Management, Inc., and the Brazilian stock market crisis in September 1998 and its FX market crisis in January 1999.

It is then possible that the subsequent contagion turbulence in the international FX markets is caused by the difference in cash flow rates of return between the developed JPY, DEM (now Euro) and USD anchor FX markets and the Asian FX markets. Cash flows in the developed FX markets show higher liquidity and less persistence than the cash flows in the developing FX markets. The friction between these laminar cash flows may have caused turbulence and "cash vortices," because of the differences in financial pressure, i.e., because of different rates of financial risk dissipation.

11.5.1   *Recent advanced research of financial turbulence*

Mandelbrot (1982, p. 98), the "Father of Fractal Geometry," said:

> Our knowledge of the geometry of turbulence remains primitive indeed, and part of fractal analysis of turbulence is the geometric counterpart of the analytic analysis of correlation and spectra.

Farge, who measures and simulates the Navier–Stokes equations using wavelet MRA, confronted this issue even more directly and bluntly stated:

> The main factor limiting our understanding of turbulent flows is that we have not yet identified the structures responsible for its chaotic and there-fore unpredictable behavior. Based on laboratory and numerical experiments, we think that vortices (or coherent structures) are these elementary objects, from which we may be able to construct a new statistical mechanics and define equations appropriate for computing fully developed turbulent flows.
>
> (Farge *et al.*, 1996, p. 664)

Farge proceed by introducing models based on the WT to explain the distribution of vortices in turbulent fluids (Farge *et al.*, 1996; Kevlahan and Farge, 1997). As we observed in Chapter 10, indeed, wavelet MRA of financial market time series detects regions of intermittent turbulence and financial vortices. Peters (1994) conjectures that these are caused by the cash flow exchanges between short-term horizon investors, like day-traders, and long-term (institutional) investors, but other explanations are likely to be found.

Much better mathematical modeling of the empirical observations is required to corroborate such far-reaching conjectures and to construct a reliable financial-economic theory of financial cash flow dynamics.

The current idea is to find simple models of financial cash flow turbulence that mimic the behavior of financial 2D Navier–Stokes nonlinear PDEs at high Reynolds numbers, but which would be easier to solve numerically and, perhaps, even analytically. These cascade, hierarchical and similar models can then be used to study some properties of turbulent cash flows, such as the risk cascade between small and large scales, the associated probability distribution functions, intermittency and all departures from Kolmogorov's ergodic homogeneity assumption.

All the simplifying 3D physical turbulence models are very recent. The first attempt was only made in the early 1970s by Desnyanski and Novikov (1974), who devised a so-called *shell* or *cascade model*, where the 3D Navier–Stokes equations are represented on a discrete set of wavenumbers in Fourier space, each Fourier shell corresponding to one octave. These models were popular, since with these models it is easy to obtain a very large inertial range, up to Reynolds numbers $Re_\tau = 10^{10}$, at limited computational cost. The reason is that the degrees of freedom of these models scale only as Re_τ, i.e., the same way as in 2D. However, these simple models are known to be unrealistic and are used mainly for simulation and training purposes.

Zimin (1981) proposed a *hierarchical model* that was defined in both space and scale. To solve this model, he projected the 3D Navier–Stokes equations onto a so-called Paley–Littlewood basis and then discretized by octaves, few in the large scales and more in the small scales, in accordance with the uncertainty principle. Next Zimin used semi-Lagrangian wavelets to compute the evolution of the flows. His work foreshadowed the current wavelet decomposition models of 2D *contour dynamics*, of which we showed an example by Farge *et al.* (1996) earlier in this chapter.[11]

As Farge emphatically stated in 1990 (quoted in Meyer, 1993, p. 122):

> The use of the wavelet transform for the study of turbulence owes absolutely nothing to chance or fashion, but comes from a necessity stemming from the current development of our ideas about turbulence. If, under the influence of the statistical approach, we had lost the need to study things in physical space, the advent of supercomputers and the associated means of visualization have revealed a zoology specific to turbulent flows, namely, the existence of coherent structures and their elementary interactions, none of which are accounted for by the statistical theory...

The time–scale wavelet MRA allows us to decouple the dynamics of the coherent structures of turbulence from the residual flow. The difficulty arises because the Navier–Stokes equations are nonlinear. Thus, the interactions between the coherent structures and the residual flow cannot be eliminated. The coherent structures differ from solitons in that they are not particular solutions of the Navier–Stokes equations. By using the WT one can extract these particular coherent turbulence structures from the residual flow and study them in much greater detail.

11.5.2   *Wavelet representation of turbulent financial flows*

The WT bases have two very useful properties, allowing us to construct adaptive wavelet MRA-based numerical schemes for solving the complex 3D Navier–Stokes PDEs:

(1) *Velocity field compression.* The use of wavelet bases allow a much larger nonlinear approximation compression of a velocity field, e.g., of the rates of cash flow returns $x(t)$, than Fourier bases. Less wavelet coefficients have to be computed for a nonlinear approximation of a vorticity field than Fourier coefficients to obtain the same explanatory power. Furthermore, as we saw in Chapter 8, the magnitude of the approximation error $\epsilon_\tau(t) = x(t) - \hat{x}_\tau(t)$ between $x(t)$ and its wavelet series expansion, as represented by the $d - 1$ largest coefficients ($=$ integer order of the Taylor approximation $\hat{x}_\tau(t)$), can be estimated in some Lebesgue space by a fractional power – the Lipschitz α_L. This fractional power exponent only depends on the irregularity of $x(t)$, since we saw in Chapter 8 that

$$|x(t) - \hat{x}_\tau(t)| \leq K|t - \tau|^{\alpha_L} \tag{11.24}$$

The nonlinear wavelet approximation of the dynamic cash flow return rate $x(t)$ is associated with a discrete time grid, which is refined where there are singularities of this function. Considering that a rate of return series $x(t)$ is almost always fractal ($=$ consist of a sequence of singularities), this implies that we need to focus on high frequency financial data with very small time scales and identify their singularity spectra to properly model financial turbulence.

(2) *Differential operator compression.* A second consequence of the double localization of wavelet bases (in time τ and scale a) of wavelet bases is that some pseudo-differential operators become almost diagonal when projected ($=$ decomposed as linear expansion) onto these bases. This means that they have very few significant coefficient and their discretization matrices are very sparse, so that fewer computations are needed, speeding up the computations and reducing computing time.

The first wavelet adaptive schemes for the Navier–Stokes equations were derived by Charton (1996), and Fröhlich and Schneider (1995). The most commonly used method for solving nonlinear PDEs is currently the Galerkin Finite Element method based on the discrete WT, which we'll discuss in the next section.

11.6   Wavelet solutions of financial diffusion equations

In the 1990s, wavelets have become a popular tool to solve nonlinear PDEs. One of the reasons is that simulations of nonlinear phenomena in, e.g., financial turbulence can produce solutions with discontinuities and singularities. This is particularly the case when one models the financial cash flow in the vicinity of a linear boundary condition, like for the early exercise decision of American options.

As we've observed in Chapter 8, discontinuities in velocity and density are also due to shock waves-like the announcement of the change from a pegged to a floating exchange rate regime, generating vortex and other small-scale fluctuations along the linear boundary, i.e., phenomena with different scale lengths (Perrier, 1989).[12]

Three kinds of methods are applied to solve the PDEs, which model this class of nonlinear phenomena: (1) the finite differences method, (2) the finite elements method of Galerkin and (3) the spectral method.

(1) The *finite difference method* replaces the differential operator by a difference operator by discretization of the space–time field.
(2) The *finite elements* or *Galerkin method* uses a set of test functions with small compact support. The equation is then integrated against these functions and the final solution appears as a combination of this finite set of functions (Thomee, 1984).
(3) The *spectral method* decomposes the solution onto a basis of global support consisting of sinusoidal functions and then truncates that solution into a finite number of terms.

The robustness of the first two methods in the representation of irregular functions and the accuracy of the spectral method in smooth regions have together led to a search for a mixed method that is numerically inexpensive and whose accuracy is independent from the solutions geometry. This search has led to the current focus on the Galerkin's finite elements method in combination with the spectral method and through them on the wavelet Galerkin method.

As we have seen in Chapter 7, discontinuous functions can be approximated using a wavelet basis without spurious fluctuations all over the spectral domain, since wavelets are localized functions. Perrier (1989) was the first to exploit this particular property to construct the new *wavelet method* for solving PDEs, but many others have improved this method further (Xu and Shann, 1992; Beylkin, 1993; Dahlke and Weinreich, 1993; Qian and Weiss, 1993; Amaratunga and Williams, 1994; Beylkin and Keiser, 1997).

Although the details of the numerical solution of nonlinear PDEs by wavelets are difficult, the overall approach is quite straightforward.

11.6.1 *Wavelet Galerkin solution of Burgers diffusion equation*

The following two sections are adapted from the excellent review of wavelet applications by Bendjoya and Slezak (1993). It will demonstrate how the localization properties of the WT incorporate the advantages of both the finite difference and spectral methods. In particular, how the WT localizes the distorting *Gibbs phenomenon* (cf. Chapter 5).

11.6.1.1   Solution of 1D diffusion equation and the Gibbs phenomenon

Consider first the following solution of a simple 1D diffusion equation as an example to show how the localization properties of the WT can direct us to the advantages of both finite difference and spectral solution methods:

$$\frac{\partial f}{\partial t}[x(t), t] = -u[x(t), t]\frac{\partial f}{\partial x}[x(t), t] \quad \text{with } t > 0 \text{ and } x(t) \in [0, 1]$$

(11.25)

where the unknown function is f and $u[x(t), t]$ stands for the *transport velocity* assumed to be 1-periodic in space. This function is now quite well-known among financial engineers (Wilmott *et al.*, 1998, pp. 58–70, etc.).

We can now choose an approximating expansion $\phi(x)$, using the basis set $\{\psi_k\}, k = 1, \ldots, N$:

$$\phi(x) = \sum_{k=1}^{N} c_k \psi_k(x)$$

(11.26)

such that at each *collocation point*, i.e., a point where $f(x)$ is known:

$$\phi(x_i) = f(x_i)$$

(11.27)

and also

$$\frac{\partial \phi}{\partial x}(x_i) = \sum_{k=1}^{N} c_k \frac{\partial \psi_k}{\partial x}(x_i)$$

(11.28)

is an approximation of $\partial f/\partial x(x_i)$. In other words, information can then be obtained from the approximating expansion $\phi(x)$ on the unknown function $f(x)$ and on its derivatives $\partial f/\partial x$ at the known collocation points x_i, and then between these collocation points by interpolating expansion.

For example, as we saw in Chapter 5, a sharp shock, modeled by a 1-periodic Heaviside function as in Figure 11.5 can be interpolated using a Fourier trigonometric basis (Perrier, 1989). The Fourier resonance coefficients c_k are easily computed by inner products, so that the Fourier expansion

$$\phi(x) = \sum_{k=-N/2}^{N/2} c_k e^{2j\pi kx}$$

(11.29)

approximates $f(x)$ with $\phi(x_i) = f(x_i)$ at each collocation point.

If, instead of the Fourier basis, one uses the orthonormal wavelet basis $\{\psi_k\}, k = 1, \ldots, N$, the wavelet resonance coefficients are again computed as inner products:

$$c_k = \int_0^1 f(x)\psi_k(x)dx$$

$$\simeq \frac{1}{N} \sum_{i=0}^{N-1} f(x_i)\psi_k(x_i) \tag{11.30}$$

Since the collocation condition $\phi(x_i) = f(x_i)$ is not automatically satisfied, the following Nth-order constraint linear system needs to be solved to get a numerically closely approximating result:

$$\phi(x) = \sum_{k=1}^{N} c_k \psi_k(x) \tag{11.31}$$

with

$$\phi(x_i) = f(x_i) \quad \text{for all } x_i \tag{11.32}$$

From careful analysis it appears that the amplitude of the remaining approximation error – the Gibbs phenomenon or spurious $sinc(t)$ oscillations – strongly correlates with the irregularity of the particular analyzing wavelet used, as can be seen in Figure 11.5. Notice in panel (d) of Figure 11.6 how the discontinuities are sharply localized, since the Gibbs phenomenon is localized due to the intrinsic localization property of the wavelet.

The fundamental difference between the use of a Fourier basis and the use of a wavelet basis is that the Gibbs phenomenon in the Fourier case extends to the whole domain, while in the wavelet case it is sharply localized. Therefore, it is possible to detect and compensate for the discontinuities using the wavelet

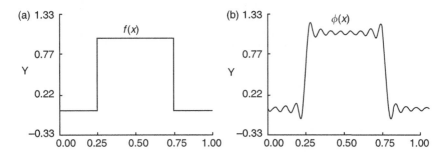

Figure 11.5 Gibbs phenomenon: panel (a) shows the 1-periodic Heaviside function $f(x)$, which represents a singular solution like a shock; panel (b) shows the interpolated expansion $\phi(x)$ using a Fourier trigonometric basis. The Gibbs phenomenon (= spurious $sinc(t)$ oscillations) extends over the whole domain. The number of collocation points is 32.

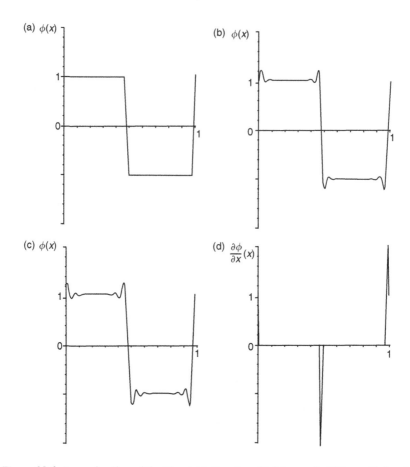

Figure 11.6 Approximation of the Heaviside function $f(x)$ in panel of Figure 11.5, using a wavelet basis. Panel (a) shows the Haar W^0 analyzing wavelet basis. Panel (b) the W^2 wavelt basis. Panel (c) the W^4 wavelet basis. Notice that the Gibbs phenomenon of spurious $sinc(t)$ oscillations is now localized near the discontinuities and that its amplitude is related to the irregularity of the analyzing wavelet. (Here W^n is the functional space of n times differentiable functions.) Panel (d) shows the derivative $\partial\phi/\partial x$ derived from the interpolated expansion $\phi(x)$ using the Haar W^0 wavelet basis.

basis of interpolation with finite support. This is impossible by using the Fourier trigonometric basis, since it has infinite support.

11.6.1.2   *Wavelet solution of the regularized Burgers equation*

Thus, wavelets can be used to solve partial differential equations because of their multiscale property, which helps to approximate functions, without losing their discontinuities. This enables the filtering of numerical volatility without smoothing out the empirical physical volatility. The wavelet (MRA) decomposition provides the best compromise between the accuracy, the efficiency and the adaptability of numerical solutions. The wavelet MRA is adaptable, as it automatically determines the smallest scale, and the corresponding sampling grid, that needs to be taken into consideration according to the local gradient. Consequently, it is currently accepted that the natural approach is to decompose the numerical solution into a wavelet basis $\{\psi_k(t)\}$ and not into a Fourier basis. The simplest 1D diffusion equation is the Burgers equation with periodic boundary conditions and which, in the case of small-scale diffusion (with variance $\sigma^2 = 10^{-3}$), has a close affinity with the Black–Scholes equation:[13]

$$\frac{\partial f[x(t), t)]}{\partial t} = -f[x(t), t]\frac{\partial f[x(t), t]}{\partial x(t)} + \sigma^2\frac{\partial^2 f[x(t), t]}{\partial x(t)^2}$$

with $t \geq 0$ and $x(t) \in [0, 1]$ (11.33)

where $f[0, t]$ is given and $f[0, t] = f[1, t]$.

This equation can be viewed as a 1D Navier–Stokes equation with a *convection* term $f[x(t), t](\partial f[x(t), t]/\partial x(t))$ and a *viscosity* term $\sigma^2(\partial^2 f[x(t), t]/\partial x(t)^2)$. As we observed from our simulation of the parabolic logistic equation in Chapter 9, the nonlinear viscosity term generates larger and larger gradients $(\partial f[x(t), t])/(\partial x(t))$ leading to the formation of local small-scale vortex structures via period-doubling and to singular discontinuities, when the solution $f[x(t), t]$ becomes singular. A competition takes place between the convection term and an increasing viscosity term. The gradients are damped and discontinuities do not occur after the critical time when the viscosity term has become largest: then the solution collapses to zero. Thus, the solution shows a clear *multiscale* or *cascade* behavior.

The Burgers equation can be rewritten in a discrete way as follows

$$f_{n+1} - f_n = -f_n\frac{\partial f_n}{\partial x}\delta t + \sigma^2\frac{\partial^2 f_{n+1}}{\partial x^2}$$ (11.34)

so that

$$\left[I - \sigma^2\frac{\partial^2}{\partial x^2}\right]f_{n+1} = f_n - f_n\frac{\partial f_n}{\partial x}\delta t$$ (11.35)

with the boundary condition

$$f_{n+1}(0) = f_{n+1}(1)$$ (11.36)

where δt is a constant time step, so that $t = n\delta t$, $f_n = f(x, n\delta t)$, and I is the identity operator. This gives us the parabolic difference equation:

$$f_{n+1} = \left[I - \sigma^2\frac{\partial^2}{\partial x^2}\right]^{-1}\left[f_n - f_n\frac{\partial f_n}{\partial x}\delta t\right]$$ (11.37)

Knowing now f_n and the discrete wavelet ψ_{jk}, the resonance coefficient of f_{n+1}
and the wavelet vector ψ_{jk} is computed by the inner product:

$$\langle f_{n+1}, \psi_{jk} \rangle = \left\langle \left[I - \sigma^2 \frac{\partial^2}{\partial x^2}\right]^{-1} \left[f_n - f_n \frac{\partial f_n}{\partial x} \delta t\right], \psi_{jk} \right\rangle$$

$$= \left\langle \left[I - \sigma^2 \frac{\partial^2}{\partial x^2}\right]^{-1} \left[f_n - f_n \frac{\partial f_n}{\partial x} \delta t\right], \left[I - \sigma^2 \frac{\partial^2}{\partial x^2}\right] \theta_{jk} \right\rangle$$

$$= \langle f_n, \theta_{jk} \rangle - \delta t \left\langle f_n \frac{\partial f_n}{\partial x}, \theta_{jk} \right\rangle$$

$$= \langle f_n, \theta_{jk} \rangle + \frac{1}{2} \delta t \left\langle f_n^2 \frac{\partial \theta_{jk}}{\partial x} \right\rangle \tag{11.38}$$

by application of the product differentiation rule. Here θ_{jk} is a precomputed family
of functions, such that for each wavelet ψ_{jk} we have

$$\psi_{jk} = \left[I - \sigma^2 \frac{\partial^2}{\partial x^2}\right] \theta_{jk} \tag{11.39}$$

Now, we can reconstitute the following expression for f_{n+1}:

$$f_{n+1} = \langle f_{n+1}, \psi_{jk} \rangle \psi_{jk} \tag{11.40}$$

The strong gradient regions are detected by the WT. Therefore, the required
lattice, or grid refinements occur only for sharp gradients and not for the moderate
extended gradients.

Thus far, the solution $f[x(t), t]$ of the Burgers equation has been computed
using (1) a Fourier spectral method, (2) a fixed non-adaptive wavelet decomposition method and (3) an adaptive wavelet decomposition method. As we saw,
the Fourier spectral method produces the Gibbs phenomenon, spreading all over
its time domain. The second method presents spurious numerical volatility in the
neighborhood of the discontinuities. Both these artifacts are caused by lack of resolution in these neighborhoods. The numerical solution has proven to behave only
satisfactorily with the WT method, since the strong gradient regions are then sampled at sufficiently fine scales. Compactly supported wavelets (such Daubechies
wavelets are localized in space, which means that the solution can be refined in
regions of high gradient, e.g., regions of stress concentrations, without having to
regenerate the scale–time grid for the entire problem.

11.6.2   Matrix wavelet Galerkin method

The solution method we just discussed is an application of the wavelet Galerkin
finite element method. Wavelet Galerkin methods employ appropriate wavelet
bases for the discretization of boundary integral operators. This yields quasi-sparse
system matrices which can be compressed to $O(NJ)$ relevant matrix entries without

compromising the accuracy of the underlying Galerkin method. Herein, $O(NJ)$ denotes the total number of unknowns.

The Galerkin method is now one of the most widely used methods for treating the spatial portion of time-dependent parabolic problems, like those common in models of cardiac wave propagation and in the parabolic diffusion models of the interest rate term structure (James and Webber, 2001, p. 333). A very general definition of the Galerkin method is the following.[14]

Definition 465   *The* Galerkin method *is a method of determining coefficients* c_k *in an expansion:*

$$x(t) = \sum_{k=1}^{n} c_k \phi_k(t) \tag{11.41}$$

of the linear (differential) equation $L[x(t)] = 0$, *so that the linear operator* $L[x(t)]$ *is orthogonal to every finite element* $\phi_k(t)$ *for* $k = 1, \ldots, n$.

Often the differential equations are time-dependent, $L[x(t), t] = 0$, and the Galerkin's finite element approximation is done in the form of a spatial variable $x(t)$, thereby reducing the PDE first to a system of ODEs in the frequency or scale domain and then to an eigenvalue or *spectral problem* in the time domain.

The general Galerkin method reduces to the simple solution of a linear system as follows. Suppose, we have a forced dynamic system of the form:

$$Lx(t) = q(t) \tag{11.42}$$

where L is a linear operator, like the difference or differential operator of Chapter 3, $q(t)$ is a given function, and $x(t)$ is the unknown process. We try to solve for $x(t)$ by selecting a set of basis functions $\psi_1, \psi_2, \ldots, \psi_n$ with the property that the $x(t)$ is expanded as follows:

$$x(t) = \sum_{k=1}^{n} c_k \psi_k(t) \tag{11.43}$$

The resonance coefficients c_k can be solved using the linearity of the operator L:

$$Lx(t) = \sum_{k=1}^{n} c_k L\psi_k(t) = q(t) \tag{11.44}$$

Since $q(t)$ doesn't lie in the space spanned by the transformed basis functions $L\phi_k$, we solve this linear equation by the approximation:

$$\phi_i \left(\sum_{k=1}^{n} c_k L\psi_k - q(t) \right) = 0, \quad \text{for all } i, \quad \text{where } 1 \leq i \leq n \tag{11.45}$$

where the function $\phi_i(\cdot)$ is the inner product $\phi_i(\upsilon) = \langle \phi_i, \upsilon \rangle$, so that

$$\phi_i\left(\sum_{k=1}^{n} c_k L\psi_k - q(t)\right) = \sum_{k=1}^{n} c_k \phi_i L\psi_k - \phi_i q(t) = 0 \qquad (11.46)$$

or

$$\sum_{k=1}^{n} c_k \phi_i L\psi_k = \phi_i q(t) \quad \text{for all } i, \text{ where } 1 \leq i \leq n \qquad (11.47)$$

Thus, an original PDE can always be reduced to a solvable linear system of ODEs of the matrix–vector form (Cooper, 2000, pp. 442–446):

$$\mathbf{Ac} = \mathbf{b} \qquad (11.48)$$

where the square $n \times n$ matrix

$$\mathbf{A} = [\phi_i L\psi_k] \qquad (11.49)$$

the $n \times 1$ vector

$$\mathbf{c} = [c_k] \qquad (11.50)$$

and the $n \times 1$ vector

$$\mathbf{b} = [\phi_i]q(t) \qquad (11.51)$$

This linear system can be solved for the vector of resonance coefficients $\mathbf{c} = [c_k]$, from which we can then reconstruct the unknown time series $x(t)$:

$$\mathbf{c} = \mathbf{A}^{-1}\mathbf{b} \qquad (11.52)$$

Often the linear dynamic system must be solved subject to initial and terminal constraints on $x(t)$, which imply constraints on the resonance coefficients $\mathbf{c} = [c_k]$.

The Galerkin approximation method provides thus an orthogonal projection of the true solution onto the given finite dimensional space of possible approximate wavelet solutions. The error between the solution in the infinite dimensional data space $\mathbf{V}$ and the finite N-dimensional wavelet space is orthogonal to all wavelets spanning the space of possible Galerkin solutions. Therefore, the orthogonal projection of the Galerkin approximation is always the best approximation in the risk space. Since the differential operator is positive definite, the matrix $\mathbf{A}$ is invertible and the approximate solution is unique.

11.6.3 Wavelet Galerkin solution of Navier–Stokes equations

Studies of turbulence are now increasingly making use of the wavelet Galerkin method (Argoul *et al.*, 1989; Farge and Holschneider, 1990; Farge, 1992a,b; Farge *et al.*, 1996). Let's discuss the *adaptive wavelet method* to solve the financial Navier–Stokes equations, based on the theory of acoustic spherical waves, in which the (Lagrangian) wavelets represent vorticity and behave as particles evolving over phase–space coordinates.

We look for an approximate *wave function*, $w(\tau, t)$ (= the solution of the Navier–Stokes equations), which is the *superposition* or linear expansion of wavelets evolving in phase–space, as follows:

$$w(\tau, t) = \sum_{k=1}^{d} c_k(t) \psi \left(\frac{\tau - b_k(t)}{a_k(t)} \right) \tag{11.53}$$

Here ψ is the base wavelet, and $a_k(t)$, $b_k(t)$ and $c_k(t)$ are the time-dependent *scale*, *translation* and *resonance* coefficients, respectively. For the PDEs in financial cash flow dynamics, there is the simplifications $b_k(t) = t$. The wave function $w(\tau, t)$ represents the *vorticity*.

In the financial markets this vorticity $w(\tau, t)$ is the convexity of the cash position at time t. In bond markets, e.g., this would be the *convexity* of the invested zero coupon bond value. The longer the maturity term, or horizon, τ, the higher the convexity $w(\tau, t)$, and *vice versa.*[15]

The continuous time Navier–Stokes parabolic diffusion equations in terms of the velocity field and vorticity are as follows:

$$\left. \begin{array}{l} \dfrac{\partial w(\tau, t)}{\partial t} + \mathbf{x}_\tau(t) \nabla w(\tau, t) = \dfrac{\eta_\tau(t)}{\rho} \nabla^2 w(\tau, t) + g(t) \\[2ex] w(\tau, t) = \nabla^2 X_\tau(t), \quad \text{and} \quad \mathbf{x}_\tau(t) = \left(\dfrac{\partial X_\tau(t)}{\partial \tau_i}, -\dfrac{\partial X_\tau(t)}{\partial \tau_j} \right) \end{array} \right\} \, \tau \in [0, 1], \; t > 0 \tag{11.54}$$

Here $w(\tau, t)$ = vorticity, $\mathbf{x}_\tau(t)$ = term structure of all rates of cash return (= velocity vector), $\eta_\tau(t)$ = dynamic cash viscosity (or illiquidity), which tends to zero in the limit of large Reynolds numbers Re_τ, i.e., for very turbulent flows, $g(t)$ = exogenous force in investment channel of term τ, $X_\tau(t)$ = investment cash flow of term τ; and there are usually some boundary conditions. Here $\nabla w(\tau, t) = \partial w(\tau, t)/\partial \tau$ is the first-order differential operator for all available terms τ, while $\nabla^2 w(\tau, t) = \partial^2 w(\tau, t)/\partial \tau_1 \partial \tau_2$ is the second-order differential operator for all available terms τ. Thus, we have the viscosity or convexity term

$$\begin{aligned} w(\tau, t) &= \nabla^2 X_\tau(t) \\[1ex] &= \frac{\partial^2 X_\tau(t)}{\partial \tau_1 \partial \tau_2} \end{aligned} \tag{11.55}$$

This system of dynamic equations has several recognizable parts:

(1) *Financial risk dissipation equation:*

$$\left[\frac{\partial w(\tau, t)}{\partial t} - \frac{\eta_\tau(t)}{\rho} \nabla^2 w(\tau, t) \right] = g(t) \tag{11.56}$$

where the left-hand side is the *risk kernel*, describing the financial risk dissipation process. This is the parabolic second-order partial differential equation that can cause chaos by period-doubling, as we noticed in Chapter 9.

(2) *Vorticity (Poisson) equation:*

$$w(\tau, t) = \nabla^2 X_\tau(t) \tag{11.57}$$

the solution of which can be obtained as the steady state solution $w^*(\tau, t)$ of the risk dissipation equation, which is usually reached within a few iterations.

(3) *Nonlinear interaction term:*

$$\mathbf{x}_\tau(t) \nabla w(\tau, t) \tag{11.58}$$

which can be computed by the wavelet Galerkin method. This term is then written as a convolution between the wavelet coefficients of $x(t)$ and the vorticity derivatives $\partial w(\tau, t)/\partial \tau$.

(4) *Boundary or collocation conditions.* These are in general included in the definition of the spaces $\mathbf{V}_J$, when constructing the multiresolution analysis (MRA) for the scale-discretization of the equations.

When $\eta_\tau(t) \to 0$ as $Re_\tau \to \infty$, the Navier–Stokes equation collapses to *Euler's equation:*

$$\frac{\partial w(\tau, t)}{\partial t} + \mathbf{x}_\tau(t) \nabla w(\tau, t) = g(t) \tag{11.59}$$

and the nonlinear advection term is no longer controlled by the linear dissipation term. Moreover, Euler's equation models how financial risk is conserved, whereas the Navier–Stokes equation models how it dissipates. *Risk conservation* is reversible in time, whereas *risk dissipation* is irreversible.

If one then considers a particular risk regime state, i.e., a state of cash flow such that the risk contribution from external forces is dissipated by the viscous friction, then the vorticity dynamics are described by:

$$\frac{\partial w(\tau, t)}{\partial t} - w(\tau, t) \nabla \frac{\partial X_\tau(t)}{\partial \tau_j} = 0 \tag{11.60}$$

or

$$\frac{\partial w(\tau, t)}{\partial t} = w(\tau, t) \nabla \frac{\partial X_\tau(t)}{\partial \tau_j} \tag{11.61}$$

Thus, the Lagrangian variation of vorticity, $\partial w(\tau, t)/\partial t$, is equal to the product of the vorticity $w(\tau, t)$ and the velocity gradients $\nabla(\partial X_\tau(t)/\partial \tau_j)$, which leads to *stretching of the term structure* $x_\tau(t)$ (velocity tube) at all terms τ_j by the rate of return (velocity) gradients $\nabla(\partial X_\tau(t)/\partial \tau_j) = \Delta x_{\tau_j}(t)$. This stretching or flattening of the term structure may then explain the transfer of financial market risk from the macro scales of the cash flows, e.g., long-term institutional capital flows, toward the smallest scales of the cash flows, e.g., the short-term money traders cash flows.

Remark 466 *Such* term structure stretching *by the rate of return gradients is mathematically only possible in* 3D. *In 2D, the vorticity is a Lagrangian invariant of the motion, because in the absence of risk dissipation, it is conserved throughout time along a cash flow trajectory, or:*

$$\frac{\partial w(\tau, t)}{\partial t} = 0 \tag{11.62}$$

Thus, financial term structure stretching in a particular country can only occur when cash flows of three separate domestic maturity terms are simultaneously considered, or the cash flows of a particular term from three different countries, or the cash flows with two foreign currency ratios, e.g., in the form of a cross-currency swap. For example, for three different maturity terms, $\tau_1 < \tau_2 < \tau_3$, *we can have that the rate of the moderate term* $x_{\tau_2}(t)$ *is too low, while the rates of the short term* $x_{\tau_1}(t)$ *and and the long term* $x_{\tau_3}(t)$ *are too high. Then the rates of the short and long term is usually lowered and the middle rate be raised by the market forces, i.e., the sale of the bonds of moderate terms and the buying of the short- and long-term bonds. In other words, by simple average return arbitrage along the term structure. This will stretch or flatten the term structure of the three zero rates. But more analogously to the risk (energy) redistribution by a vortex, one can consider a credit risk premium situation, where the risk premium of the short and long terms is partially transferred to the moderate term, for a more even distribution of the financial risk along the term structure. In other words, by simple risk (second moment) arbitrage along the term structure.*

For numerical solution of the Navier–Stokes diffusion equations, their discretization can be performed by introducing again a finite time step δt setting $w(\tau, t) \approx w(\tau, n\delta t)$ to be the approximate solution at time $t = n\delta t$. The discrete wavelet coefficient $w_J(\tau, n) \approx w(\tau, n)$ belongs to a finite dimensional subspace $\mathbf{V}_J$ obtained from an MRA $\{\mathbf{V}_j\}_{j\geq 0}$ of the Hilbert space $L^2[0, 1]$.

The wavelet Galerkin method is then implemented as follows. Suppose $\mathbf{V}_J = 2^J$ (dyadic space). Then, according to Chapter 8, $w_J(\tau, n)$ can be expanded onto a wavelet basis $\{\psi_{jk}\}$ of $\mathbf{V}_J$, so that we get the simple discrete MRA:

$$w_J(\tau, n) = c_{0,0}(n) + \sum_{j=0}^{J-1} \sum_{k=0}^{2^j-1} d_{j,k}(n)\psi_{j,k}(\tau) \tag{11.63}$$

Remark 467 *The Galerkin method uses only the few (non-negligible) wavelet detail coefficients* $d_{j,k}(n)$ *larger than a given threshold* $\{d_{j,k}(n) : |d_{j,k}(n)| > \varepsilon\}$, *further saving on computing time and memory.*

After discretization, the risk dissipation equation is:

$$\left(1 - \frac{\eta}{\rho}\delta t \nabla^2\right) w(\tau, n+1) = w(\tau, n) + \delta t f(n) \tag{11.64}$$

so that we obtain the parabolic difference equation:

$$w(\tau, n+1) = \left(1 - \frac{\eta}{\rho}\delta t \nabla^2\right)^{-1} [w(\tau, n) + \delta t f(n)] \tag{11.65}$$

An easy way to reduce this 2D system to several 1D systems is to use a tensor wavelet basis and to approximately diagonalize and split the 2D risk kernel into two 1D operators:

$$\left(1 - \frac{\eta}{\rho}\delta t \nabla^2\right)^{-1} \approx \left(1 - \frac{\eta}{\rho}\delta t \frac{\partial^2}{\partial \tau_1^2}\right)^{-1} \left(1 - \frac{\eta}{\rho}\delta t \frac{\partial^2}{\partial \tau_2^2}\right)^{-1} \tag{11.66}$$

Remark 468   *This adaptive wavelet Galerkin method works well for linear(-ized) equations, and was very recently applied to the study of the formation of galaxies (cf. Farge et al., 1996). A global simulation at resolution $1,024^2$ can be run on a simple workstation and doesn't need a supercomputer. But in the nonlinear case there are technical difficulties when two wavelets approach each other in phase–space. That is when the intended operator split can't work because of too much interconnectivity between the wavelets. This non-splitting effect is called an "atom's collision" (Teng and Uhlenbeck, 2000).*

11.7   Software

The computations of the following Exercises can be executed in Microsoft EXCEL spreadsheets, or by using the basic MATLAB® software available from The MathWorks, Inc., 24 Prime Park Way Natick, MA 01760-1500, USA. Tel.: (508) 647-7000; Fax: (508) 647-7001; http://www.mathworks.com/products/wavelettbx.shtml.

11.8   Exercises

Exercise 469   *Nowadays, financial markets have many different kinds of market participants, e.g., institutional investors with long investment horizons of several years and day traders with ultra short investment horizons of no more than a day. These participants trade parallel to each other in the same financial market. Peters (1994, p. 173) states that: "Under the Fractal Market Hypothesis, it is more likely that different investors, with different investment horizons, react to the information with multiple relaxation times; that is, the information affects different investors differently, depending on their investment horizon." Simulate the resulting fractal speculative market pricing process by implementing the EXCEL spreadsheet instructions of Peters (1994, p. 174), for four values of $t = 1, 21, 63$*

and 126 *days.* (*What correlation coefficients? Result?*) *What is the homogeneous H-exponent of the resulting summation process? Use the wavelet analysis of Chapter 8, to compute the homogeneous H-exponent for the simulated time series. Is the resultant financial market pricing process persistent, or antipersistent?*

Exercise 470 *Vary the time constant of the simulated process in the preceding question. What are the mean, variance, skewness and kurtosis of the resulting summation processes?*

Exercise 471 *What is financial turbulence? Is financial turbulence common in the S&P500 stock market? And in the FX markets? Would you be able to visualize it? What may cause it when it occurs? Is financial turbulence desirable or problematic in financial markets? Why, or why not?*

Exercise 472 *Construct a simple Navier–Stokes model for a derivative pricing risk diffusion process, identify its monofractal Hurst exponent. Identify its multifractal dimension, when it has one. Corroborate the results with high-frequency empirical data, if you can.*

Exercise 473 *Take a well-known Black–Scholes financial diffusion equation, resulting from an application of Itô's lemma and numerically solve it for different parameter values using the Galerkin wavelet method. Use MATLAB® software (cf. Cooper, 2000 for an introduction on how to numerically solve PDEs with MATLAB®) and high-frequency data for an empirically collocated or calibrated simulation.*

Notes

1 In financial terms, noise in the financial market time series would indeed be produced by *noise trading*, i.e., small, fast cash trade transactions, that are almost immediately reversed.

2 The funnel shape of an adjustment vortex we've already measured in the Thai baht, when we visualized this adjustment in a 3D scalogram in Chapter 8. We noticed it also in the scalograms of the vortices generated by the discontinuities of the Mexican and Brazilian Financial Crises.

3 When the Mach number >1, we speak of *supersonic* velocity. When the Mach number <1, we speak of *subsonic* velocity. When the Mach number $=1$, we speak of *sonic* velocity. Thus, the terms super- and subsonic are relative terms! They measure the velocity relative to the velocity of the surrounding medium.

4 The basic cone shape of a vortex has been corroborated by many natural phenomena. However, the measured geometric shape of the funnels of tornados and cyclones is much more elongated than this simple proportional relationship suggests, due to the change in viscosity, when risk or energy dissipation enters the equation, as we will see. The 1997 movie "Twister" shows the direct approach to the measurement and modeling of catastrophic tornado vortices by a team of courageous tornado chasers, which places a mass of tracers with built-in radio transmitters in the singularity of a tornado. By tracking all the tracers in the funnel of the tornado, the exact geometric shape of the tornado and the dynamics of the boundary layer can be established. Fortunately, in the financial

markets we do not have to make such dramatic and heroic empirical measurements, since the term structure is directly observable.

5 The French engineer Claude Louis Marie Henri Navier (1785–1836) was born in Dijon. His father, who was a member of the National Assembly in Paris during the time of the French Revolution, died in 1793. Thereafter, Navier was cared for by his uncle Emiland Gauthey, who was considered the leading civil engineer in France. During this first year at the École Polytechnique, Navier was taught analysis by Fourier, who became a lifelong friend of Navier as well as his teacher. Navier became soon recognized as a scholar of engineering science, by editing the works of his uncle Gauthey and by adding a somewhat analytical flavor. When Navier became a professor at the École des Ponts et Chaussées in 1830, he changed the syllabus to put much more emphasis on physics and on mathematical analysis and less on empirical principles. A specialist in road and bridge building, he was the first to develop a theory of suspension bridges, using variational calculus. But Navier is remembered today, not as the famous builder of bridges, for which he was known in his own day, but rather for the Navier–Stokes equations of fluid dynamics. He gave the well-known Navier–Stokes equations for an incompressible fluid in 1821, and the equations for viscous fluids in 1822. Navier derived his correct equations despite not understanding the physics of shear stress in a fluid, but rather he based his work on modifying Euler's equations based on (what is now considered) unacceptable reasoning.

6 Sir George Gabriel Stokes (1819–1903) was a British physicist and mathematician whose law of viscosity (1851), describing the movement of a small sphere through a viscous fluid, established the science of hydrodynamics. *Stokes Law* (1847) states that the frictional force on a particle $= 6\pi a \eta_\tau(t) x(t)$, where a = radius or scale of particle, $\eta_\tau(t)$ = coefficient of viscosity (illiquidity) and $x(t)$ = flow velocity, provided that the Reynold's number $R_\tau(t) = 2a\rho x(t)/\eta_\tau(t) < 1$.

7 Russian mathematician Andrei Nikolaevich Kolmogorov (1903–1987) made fundamental contributions to mathematical logic, the theory of functions, differential equations, topology and other branches of mathematics. However, as we noted in Chapter 1, Kolmogorov is most renowned for his work in the field of probability, for which he published his first paper in 1929. He then expanded it into a landmark book, published in German in 1933 and translated into English in 1950 as *The Foundations of the Theory of Probability*. The book presented the first full axiomatic treatment of the subject.

8 Lewis Fry Richardson (1881–1953) was a very interesting, original and industrious researcher, who broke new ground with his studies of turbulence, but who was often not understood by his contemporaries. He attended Cambridge University on a scholarship and earned his BA in physics, mathematics, chemistry, biology and zoology, since he could not make up his mind what career to follow. He started out as a meteorologist and wrote a path-breaking book on *Weather Prediction by Numerical Process* (1922), on which modern weather prediction is based. Eventually, at age 47, he obtained a PhD in mathematical psychology from London University, with a study of the psychology of armed conflict between states, founding what is now called *differential game theory*. Differential game theory led to the development of dynamic war games studied *inter alia* by polemologists of my Dutch Alma Mater, Groningen University in The Netherlands. He thereby made the Von Neuman and Morgenstern game theory dynamic. Richardson numerous posthumous articles include an investigation (in 1961) of the length of coastlines, which inspired Mandelbrot (1982) to develop his *Fractal Geometry*.

9 The Doppler effect is named after the Austrian Christian Johann Doppler (1803–1853). The *Doppler effect* occurs when there is relative motion between the vortex source (singularity) and an observer. The ratio of the observed frequency $f_n(t)$ relative to the source frequency $f_m(t)$ is $f_n(t)/f_m(t) = [x(t) \pm x_n(t)]/[x(t) \mp x_m(t)]$, where $x(t)$

is the common velocity of the inertial frame, $x_m(t)$ is the velocity of the source relative to the frame and $x_n(t)$ is the velocity of the observer relative to the frame. In this expression, the upper signs ($+x_n(t)$ and $-x_m(t)$) refer to motion *toward* each other, and the lower signs ($-x_n(t)$ and $+x_m(t)$) refer to motion *away* from each other. The word *toward* is associated with $f_n(t)/f_m(t) > 1$ and the word *away* with $f_n(t)/f_m(t) < 1$.

10 That is equivalent to a Zolotarev stability $\alpha_{Z0} = 1/\alpha_{L0} = 3$.

11 In Australia you can see daily examples of the current (almost real-time) computation of dynamic 2D barometric pressure contours on ABC t.v., where the popular weatherman ("Monty") presents the changing 2D airflow fields, between high and low pressure areas and points out where the airflow vortices develop. Weather derivatives, which hedge against the damage costs caused by these vortices, provide a direct bridge between the physical vortex risk valuation and the corresponding financial risk valuation (Banks, 2002). This suggests that derivatives can be used to hedge against financial vorticity and occasional crises risks in the financial markets.

12 However, it should be emphasized that it still is difficult to distinguish genuine intrinsic turbulent volatility from numerical solution volatility.

13 Frazier (1999, pp. 470–481) discusses the numerical wavelet solution for a class of Ordinary Differential Equations (ODEs), known as Sturm–Louisville equations.

14 Boris Grigorievich Galerkin, 1871–1949, entered in 1893 the Petersburg Technological Institute, where he studied mathematics and engineering. He became employed as a design engineer and, in 1909, he began teaching at the Petersburg Technological Institute and he published an article on longitudinal curvature, relevant to the construction of bridges and frames for buildings. Today Galerkin is best known for his finite element method of approximate integration of differential equations known as the Galerkin method, published in 1915. In 1920, Galerkin became Head of Structural Mechanics at the Petersburg Technological Institute and held chairs in elasticity at the Leningrad Institute of Communications Engineers and in structural mechanics at Leningrad University. From 1940 until his death, Galerkin was head of the Institute of Mechanics of the Soviet Academy of Sciences. Galerkin investigated stress in dams and breast walls with trapezoidal profile and was a consultant in the planning and building of many of the Soviet Union's largest hydrostations, like the Dnepr dam.

15 Coupon bonds show the largest convexity, while zero-coupon bonds have zero convexity. This suggests that when coupon bonds, or bank loans become non-performing, the convexity can suddenly change, thereby rapidly reshaping the term structure and, perhaps, causing financial turbulences.

Bibliography

Amaratunga, K., and J. Williams (1994) "Wavelet–Galerkin Solutions for One-Dimensional Partial Differential Equations," *International Journal of Numerical Methods in Engineering*, **37**(16), 2703–2716.

Anselmet, F., Y. Gagne, E. J. Hopfinger and R. A. Antonia (1984) "High-Order Velocity Structure Function in Turbulent Shear Flows," *Journal of Fluid Mechanics*, **140**, 63–89.

Argoul, F., A. Arnéodo, G. Grasseau, Y. Gagne, E. F. Hopfinger and U. Frisch (1989) "Wavelet Analysis of Turbulence Reveals the Multifractal Nature of the Richardson Cascade," *Nature*, **338**, 51–53.

Arnéodo, A., J. F. Muzy and D. Sornette (1998) "Direct' Causal Cascade in the Stock Market," *European Physics Journal*, B, **2**, 277–282.

Banks, Erik (Ed.) (2002) *Weather Risk Management: Markets, Products and Applications*, Palgrave, New York, NY.

Basdevant, C., B. Legras, R. Sadourny and I. Beland (1981) "A Study of Barotropic Model Flows: Intermittency, Waves and Predictability," *Journal of Atmospheric Sciences*, **38**, 2305–2326.

Batchelor, G. K. (1969) "Computation of the Energy Spectrum in Homogeneous Two-Dimensional Turbulence," *Physics of Fluids* (Supplement II), **12**, 233–239.

Bendjoya, Ph., and E. Slézak (1993) "Wavelet Analysis and Applications to Some Dynamical Systems," *Celestial Mechanics and Dynamical Astronomy*, **56**, 231–262.

Beylkin, G. (1993) "On Wavelet-Based Algorithms for Solving Differential Equations," in Benedetto, J. and M. Frazier (Eds) *Wavelets: Mathematics and Applications*, CRC Press, Boca Raton, FL, pp. 449–466.

Beylkin, G., and J. M. Keiser (1997) "On the Adaptive Numerical Solutions of Nonlinear Partial Differential Equations in Wavelet Bases," *Journal of Computational Physics*, **132**(2), 233–259.

Charton, P. (1996) "Produits de Matrices Rapides en Bases Ondelettes: Application à la Résolution Numérique d' Équations aux Dérivées Partielles" ("Products of Fast Matrices in Wavelet Bases: Application to the Numerical Solution of Partial Differential Equations"), PhD dissertation, Université Paris 13.

Chorin (1988) "Spectrum, Dimension, and Polymer Analogies in Fluid Turbulence," *Physical Review Letters*, **60**(19), 1947–1949.

Cooper, Jeffrey M. (2000) *Introduction to Partial Differential Equations with MATLAB®*, Birkhäuser, Boston, MA.

Couder, Y., and C. Basdevant (1986) "Experimental and Numerical Study of Vortex Couples in Two-Dimensional Flows," *Journal of Fluid Mechanics*, **173**, 225–251.

Dahlke, S., and I. Weinreich (1993) "Wavelet–Galerkin Methods: An Adapted Biorthogonal Wavelet Basis," *Constructive Approximation*, **9**(2), 237–262.

Desnyansky, V. N., and E. A. Novikov (1974) "The Evolution of Turbulence Spectra to the Similarity Regime," *Izvestia Akademii Nauk SSSR, Fizika Atmosfera i Okeana (News of Academy of Sciences, USSR, Physics of Atmosphere and Ocean)*, **10**(2), 127–136.

Everson, R., L. Sirovich and K. R. Sreenivasan (1990) "Wavelet Analysis on the Turbulent Jet," *Physics Letters*, A, **145**(6/7), 314–324.

Farge, Marie (1988) "Vortex Motion in a Rotating Barotropic Fluid Layer," *Fluid Dynamics Research*, **3**, 282–288.

Farge, Marie (1992a) "Wavelet Transforms and their Applications to Turbulence," *Annual Review of Fluid Mechanics*, **24**, 395–407.

Farge, Marie (1992b) "The Continuous Wavelet Transform of Two-Dimensional Turbulent Flows," in Ruskai, M. B., G. Beylkin, R. Coifman, I. Daubechies, S. Mallat, Y. Meyer and L. Raphael (Eds) *Wavelets and Their Applications*, Jones and Bartlett Publications, Boston, MA, pp. 275–302.

Farge, M., and M. Holschneider (1990) "Interpretation of Two-Dimensional Turbulence Spectrum in Terms of Singularity in the Vortex Cores," *Europhysics Letters*, **15**(7), 737–743.

Farge, Marie, Nicholas Kevlahan, Valérie Perrier and Éric Goirand (1996) "Wavelets and Turbulence," *Proceedings of IEEE*, **84**(4), 639–669.

Farge, M., and R. Sadourney (1989) "Wave–Vortex Dynamics in Rotating Shallow Water," *Journal of Fluid Mechanics*, **206**, 433–462.

Forbes, Kristin J., and Roberto Rigobon (2002) "No Contagion, Only Interdependence: Measuring Stock Market Comovements," *The Journal of Finance*, **57**(5), 2223–2261.

Frazier, Michael W. (1999) *An Introduction to Wavelets Through Linear Algebra*, Springer Verlag, New York, NY.

Frisch, Uriel (1995) *Turbulence: The Legacy of A. N. Kolmogorov*, Cambridge University Press, Cambridge, UK.

Frisch, U. and G. Parisi (1985) "Fully Developed Turbulence and Intermittency," in Ghil, M., R. Benzi and G. Parisi (Eds) *Turbulence and Predictability in Geophysical Fluid Dynamics and Climate Dynamics*, North-Holland Publishing Co., Amsterdam, pp. 71–88.

Fröhlich, J., and K. Schneider (1995) "An Adaptive Wavelet Galerkin Algorithm for One and Two-Dimensional Flame Computations," *European Journal of Mechanics*, B, **13**(4), 439–471.

Gagne, Y., and B. Castaing (1991) "A Universal Representation Without Global Scaling Invariantce of Energy Spectra in Developed Turbulence," *Cahiers de Recherche d'Academie des Science de Paris*, Serie II, **312**, 441–445.

Ghasghaie, S., W. Breymann, J. Peinke, P. Talkner and Y. Dodge (1996) "Turbulent Cascades in Foreign Exchange Markets," *Nature*, **381**, 767–770.

Grant, H. L., R. W. Stewart and A. Moiliett (1962) "Turbulent Spectra From A Tidal Channel," *Journal of Fluid Mechanics*, **12**, 241–268.

Hentschel, H. G. E., (1994) "Stochastic Multifractality and Universal Scaling Distributions," *Physics Review*, E, **50**, 243–261.

Hentschel, H. G. E., and I. Procaccia (1983) "The Infinite Number of Generalized Dimensions of Fractals and Strange Attractors," *Physica*, D, **8**, 435–444.

Itô, K. (Ed.) (1980) "Methods Other Than Difference Methods," in *Encyclopedic Dictionary of Mathematics*, 2nd edn, Vol. 2, MIT Press, Cambridge, MA, p. 1139.

James, Jessica, and Nick Webber (2001) *Interest Rate Modelling*, John Wiley and Sons, Chichester, NJ.

Karuppiah, Jeyanthi, and Cornelis A. Los (2000) "Wavelet Multiresolution Analysis of High-Frequency FX Rates," *Quantitative Methods in Finance & Bernoulli Society 2000 Conference (Program, Abstracts and Papers)*, University of Technology, Sydney, Australia , 5–8 December, pp. 171–198.

Kevlahan, N., and M. Farge (1997) "Vorticity Filaments in Two-Dimensional Turbulence: Creation, Stability and Effect," *Journal of Fluid Mechanics*, **346**, 49–76.

Kida, S., and K. Okhitani (1992) "Spatio–Temporal Intermittency and Instability of a Forced Turbulence," *Physics, Fluids* A, **4**, 1018–1027.

Kolmogorov, A. N. (1941a) "The Local Structure of Turbulence in Incompressible Viscous Fluid for Very Large Reynolds Number," *Doklady Akademii Nauk SSSR*, **30**, 299–303 (reprinted in *Proceedings of the Royal Society of London*, A, **434**, 1991, 9–13).

Kolmogorov, A. N. (1941b) "On Degeneration (Decay) of Isotropic Turbulence in an Incompressible Viscous Liquid," *Doklady Akademii Nauk SSSR*, **31**, 538–540.

Kolmogorov, A. N. (1941c) "Dissipation of Energy in Locally Isotropic Turbulence," *Doklady Akademii Nauk SSSR*, **32**, 299–303 (reprinted in *Proceedings of the Royal Society of London*, A, **434**, 1991, 15–17).

Kolmogorov, A. N. (1962) "A Refinement of Previous Hypotheses Concerning the Local Structure of Turbulence in a Viscous Incompressible Fluid at High Reynolds Number," *Journal of Fluid Mechanics*, **13**, 82–85.

Koster, F., K. Schneider, M. Griebel and M. Farge (2002) "Adaptive Wavelet Methods for the Navier–Stokes Equations," in E. H. Hirschel (Ed.) *Notes on Numerical Fluid Mechanics*, Vieweg Verlag, Braunschweig.

Lipka, Joanna M., and Cornelis A. Los (2002) "Persistence Characteristics of European Stock Indexes," Working Paper, Department of Finance, Graduate School of Management, Kent State University, January 2002 (Accepted at the Annual Meeting of the

National Business and Economics Society, March 5–8, 2003, St Thomas, U.S. Virgin Islands).

McWilliams, J. C. (1984) "The Emergence of Isolated Coherent Vortices in Turbulent Flow," *Journal of Fluid Mechanics*, **146**, 21–43.

Mallat, Stéphane (1999) *A Wavelet Tour of Signal Processing*, 2nd edn, Academic Press, Boston, MA.

Mandelbrot, Benoit B. (1975) "Intermittent Turbulence in Self-Similar Cascades. Divergence of High Moments and Dimension of the Carrier," *Journal of Fluid Mechanics*, **62**, 331–358.

Mandelbrot, Benoit B. (1976) "Intermittent Turbulence & Fractal Dimension: Kurtosis and the Spectral Exponent $5/3 + B$," in Teman, R. (Ed.) *Turbulence and Navier Stokes Equations*, Lecture Notes in Mathematics, Springer Verlag, New York, NY.

Mandelbrot, Benoit B. (1982) *The Fractal Geometry of Nature*, W. H. Freeman, New York, NY.

Mantegna, R. N. (1999) "Hierarchical Structure in Financial Markets," *European Physics Journal*, B, **11**, 193–197.

Mantegna, Rosario N., and H. Eugene Stanley (1996) "Turbulence and Financial Markets," *Nature*, **383**, 587–588.

Mantegna, Rosario N., and H. Eugene Stanley (1997) "Stock Market Dynamics and Turbulence: Parallel Analysis of Fluctuation Phenomena," *Physica*, A, **239**, 255–266.

Mantegna, Rosario, N., and H. Eugene Stanley (2000) *An Introduction to Econophysics: Correlations and Complexity in Finance*, Cambridge University Press, Cambridge, UK.

Meneveau, C. M., and K. R. Sreenivasan (1987a) "Simple Multifractal Cascade Model for Fully Developed Turbulence," *Physical Review Letters*, **59**(13), 1424–1427.

Meneveau, C. M., and K. R. Sreenivasan (1987b) "The Multifractal Spectrum of the Dissipation Field in Turbulent Flows," *Nuclear Physics*, B (Proceedings Supplement), **2**, 49–76.

Meneveau, C. M., and K. R. Sreenivasan (1991) "The Multifractal Nature of Turbulent Energy Dissipation," *Journal of Fluid Mechanics*, **224**, 429–484.

Meyer, Yves (1993) *Wavelets: Algorithms & Applications* (translated and revised by Robert D. Ryan), Society for Industrial and Applied Mathematics (SIAM), Philadelphia, PA.

Monin, A. S., and A. M. Yaglom (1975) *Statistical Fluid Mechanics*, The MIT Press, Boston, MA.

Muzy, J. F., E. Bacry and A. Arnéodo (1991) "Wavelets and Multifractal Formalism for Singular Signals: Application to Turbulent Data," *Physical Review Letters*, **67**(25), 3515–3518.

Navier, C. L. M. H. (1823) "Mémoire sur les Lois du Mouvement des Fluides," ("Report on the Dynamic Laws of Fluids"), *Memoires d'Académie Royale des Sciences*, **6**, 389–440.

Nolan, John (1999a) "Basic Properties of Univariate Stable Distributions," chapter 1 in *Stable Distributions*, American University, April 19, 30 pages.

Nolan, John (1999b) "Fitting Data and Assessing Goodness-of-Fit with Stable Distributions," Working Paper, American University, June, 52 pages.

Obukhov, A. N. (1941a) "On the Distribution of Energy in the Spectrum of Turbulent Flow," *Dokladi Akademii Nauk SSSR*, **32**(1), 22–24.

Obukhov, A. M. (1941b) "Spectral Energy Distribution in a Turbulent Flow," *Izwestia Akademii Nauk SSSR, Seri Geografii i Geofiziki*, **5**(4/5), 453–466.

Perrier, V. (1989) "Towards a Method for Solving Partial Differential Equations Using Wavelet Basis," in Combes, J. M., A. Grossman and Ph. Tchamitchian (Eds) *Wavelets, Time–Frequency Methods in Phase Space*, Springer Verlag, New York, NY, pp. 269–283.

Peters, Edgar E. (1994) *Fractal Market Analysis*, John Wiley & Sons, Inc., New York, NY.

Qian, S., and J. Weiss (1993) "Wavelets and the Numerical Solution of Partial Differential Equations," *Journal of Computational Physics*, **106**(1), 155–175.

Richardson, L. F. (1922) *Weather Prediction by Numerical Process*, Cambridge University Press, Cambridge, UK.

Richardson, L. F. (1926) "Atmospheric Diffusion Shown on a Distance–Neighbour Graph," *Proceedings of the Royal Society of London*, A, **110**, 709–737.

Schroeder, Manfred (1991) *Fractals, Chaos, Power Laws: Minutes from an Infinite Paradise*, W. H. Freeman and Co., New York, NY.

Schmitt, F., D. Lavallée, D. Schertzer and S. Lovejoy (1992) "Empirical Determination of Universal Multifractal Exponents in Turbulent Velocity Fields," *Physical Review Letters*, **68**(3), 305–308.

Serway, Raymond A. (1992) *Physics: For Scientists & Engineers with Modern Physics*, 3rd ed. (updated version), Harcourt Brace College Publisher, Philadelphia, PA.

Stevens, Peter S. (1974) *Patterns in Nature*, Atlantic Monthly Press–Little, Brown and Co., Boston, MA.

Taylor, G. I. (1935) "Statistical Theory of Turbulence," *Proceedings of the Royal Society of London*, A, **151**, 421–478.

Taylor, G. I. (1938) "The Spectrum of Turbulence," *Proceedings of the Royal Society of London*, A, **164**, 476–490.

Teng, Chuu-Lian, and Karen Uhlenbeck (2000) "Geometry of Solitons," *Notices of the American Mathematical Society*, **47**(1), 17–25.

Thomee, V. (1984) *Galerkin Finite Element Methods for Parabolic Problems*, Lecture Notes in Mathematics, Springer Verlag, New York, NY.

Van Dyke, M. (1982) *An Album of Fluid Motion*, The Parabolic Press, Stanford, CA.

Vergassola, M., and U. Frisch (1991) "Wavelet Transforms of Self-Similar Processes," *Physica*, D, **54**, 58–64.

Weng, H., and K.-M. Lau (1994) "Wavelets, Period Doubling, and Time–Frequency Localization with Application to Organization of Convection over the Tropical Western Pacific," *Journal of Atmospheric Science*, **51**, 2523–2541.

Wilmott, Paul, Sam Howison and Jeff Dewynne (1998) *The Mathematics of Financial Derivatives: A Student Introduction*, Cambridge University Press, Cambridge, UK.

Xu, J.-C., and W.-C. Shann (1992) "Galerkin–Wavelet Methods for Two-Point Boundary Value Problems," *Numerical Mathematics*, **63**(1), 123–142.

Zabusky, Norman (1984) "Computational Synergetics," *Physics Today*, July, 2–11.

Zimin, V. (1981) "Hierarchical Model of Turbulence," *Izvestia Akademii Nauk SSSR, Fizika Atmosfera i Okeana (News of Academy of Sciences, USSR, Physics of the Atmosphere and the Ocean)*, **17**, 941–949.

Part IV

Financial risk management

12 Managing VaR and extreme values

12.1 Introduction

In this chapter we will summarize some of the results and the consequences of the empirical results of non-Gaussianity, irregularity and nonstationarity of rates of return on cash investment, both for investment in individual assets and for investment in portfolios of assets. In particular, we will focus on the measurement and management of the Value-at-Risk (VaR) of an investment. The VaR measure summarizes the exposure of an investment to market risk as measured by the variance or standard deviation of rates of return. This makes it a popular tool for conveying the magnitude of the market risks of portfolios to senior fund management, directors, sponsors, shareholders and regulators (Hopper, 1996; Duffie and Pan, 1997; Hua and Wilmott, 1997; Jorion, 1997; Dowd, 1998).

However, we've learned in the preceding chapters (cf. Chapter 1) that such a simple risk measure based on only the second moment of a rates of return distribution is insufficient, since it ignores both the higher moments of the pricing distributions, like skewness and kurtosis, and all fractional moments, measuring the long-term or global dependencies of dynamic market pricing. The VaR methodology also devotes insufficient attention to the truly extreme financial events, i.e., those events that are *catastrophic* (Embrechts *et al.*, 1997; Bassi *et al.*, 1998). There exists considerable anecdotal literature on such catastrophic financial events (Kindleberger, 1996), but relatively little rigorous measurement, analysis or theory, the exceptions being the recent article and book by Sornette (1998, 2003).

12.2 Global dependence of financial returns

As we've observed in the preceding chapters, the pricing processes of financial markets show global dependencies, i.e., they are long-term memory processes, with slowly declining autocovariance functions and with scaling spectra. The reason for this phenomenon is the aggregation in the markets of investment flows of different time horizons and degrees of cash illiquidity. The pricing processes of stocks, bonds and currencies are nonlinear dynamic processes, which show short- and long-term aperiodic cyclicities, and intermittency, i.e., periods of laminar flows interspersed with periods of turbulent cash flows. Financial turbulence is characterized by successive velocity fluctuations and successive periods of condensation and rarefaction in the frequency of trading transactions. However, there are major differences among these various financial pricing processes:

(1) Foreign exchange (FX) is traded, but FX does not consist of securities. The FX appreciation rates are usually antipersistent with Hurst exponents of the order $0.2 < H < 0.5$. The cash flows in the FX markets are potentially turbulent and may show vortices, in particular when $H \approx 1/3$, as was the case with the DEM/USD, now replaced by the Euro/USD, and as is the case with the Yen/USD, when these cash flows are adjacent to much less liquid cash flows in, for example, Asian FX markets with $0.33 < H < 0.5$, as we discussed in Chapter 8.

Long term investment in FX rates is dangerous, since the volatility (= standard deviation) of their appreciation rates does not scale according to the square root of the investment time horizon $\tau^{0.5}$, as it does for a Geometric Brownian Motion (GBM). In the short term, FX rates are about as volatile as stock prices. But Figure 12.1 shows that when the investment horizon τ increases, the volatility of FX rates tends to increase *more slowly* than that of a GBM. In popular opinion, FX markets are considered more risky than stock markets in the long run, while the opposite is true. It depends on the investment horizon. FX rates are less risky in the long term than stock prices.

(2) Stock and bonds are traded securities. Their rates of return are persistent, with Hurst exponents $0.5 < H < 0.8$, e.g., the S&P500 and Dow Jones stock

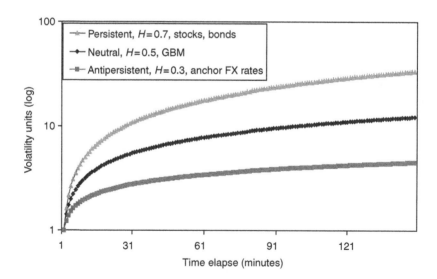

Figure 12.1 Typical time dependence of financial price volatility, $\log \sigma^2$. The volatility or second moment risk of the persistent stock prices increases faster with the time horizon τ than the volatility of the conventional GBM, while the volatility of FX rates increases more slowly.

indices have $H \approx 2/3$. Their rates of return behave closer to that of black noise, with occasional, and essentially unpredictable sharp discontinuities up or down, called *financial catastrophes*. These discontinuous catastrophes cause the frequency distributions of black noise processes to have fat tails (Sornette, 2003). It occurs because the originators of such events are amplified in the financial system. Stock and bond market prices are close to brown noise, and their first differences are persistent pink noise: $0.5 < H < 1$. Thus, their rates of return (= *velocity* of the stock and bond prices) which are first differences normalized on the lagged price, are also persistent pink noise.

Long-term investments in stocks and bonds are potentially very risky. When the investment horizon τ increases, bond and stock return volatility tends to increase faster than that of a GBM. Of course, the *level* of volatility of stock prices is much higher than that of bond prices (cf. Chapter 1).

(3) Real estate investments have equity and bond characteristics, but their liquidity is usually much lower than that of stocks or bonds. Consequently, their prices are extremely persistent and their rates of return truly black noise.[1] Financial catastrophes are a frequent occurrence in such consistently persistent and illiquid markets, as the real estate events of the past two decades testify.

Therefore, our advice regarding speculation in the FX, stock, bond and real estate markets runs counter to that of both professional and popular investment advice. It is based on the established relationship between financial market risk and investment horizon. One cannot judge the riskiness of an investment on the basis of a one-time picture of volatility, but needs to take account of long-term dependence.

Remark 474 *Considering the nature of the time dependencies in these three separate sets of markets, we suggest that the Asian Financial Crisis in 1997, which had the characteristics of a financial catastrophe and not that of financial turbulence, originated in the local real estate and, perhaps, the stock markets; then got amplified along the term structure of bank loans and bond markets; and only then spilled over into the FX markets, where it caused continuous financial turbulence, which then slowly dissipated its financial market risk in intermittent periods of frantic trading and periods of relative calm in the FX markets in 1997–1998.*

International cash investments of investors with different time horizons simultaneously flow in and out of all these international financial markets. Our understanding of these cash flow and pricing processes is still very limited, but, as we argued in Chapter 9, it is improving now that more high frequency data are accumulated and more research efforts are becoming directed towards the measurement and analysis of the various dependence phenomena of financial market risk.

12.3   VaR for stable distributions

12.3.1   *Subjectivity of VaR*

Informally, the VaR measure summarizes the expected maximum loss (or worst loss) over a limited investment horizon, within a given confidence interval (Wilson, 1998). Thus, measuring VaR involves the choice of two quantitative inputs: the length of the investment horizon τ, and the confidence level. Both are arbitrary, subjective choices. Therefore, by definition, VaR is not an objective, or scientific measure of the exposure to market risk, but a subjective, game type measure, according to some recent theoreticians (Shafer and Vovk, 2001).[2]

Example 475   *The internal bank risk model approach of the 1992 and 1996 (amended) Basle Committee Accords takes as investment horizon 10 working days and accepts a 99 percent confidence interval. The resulting VaR is then multiplied by a subjective safety factor of 3 to compute the minimum level of capital for regulatory purposes.*

Of course, portfolio investors can determine the length of their own investment horizon τ. Commercial banks in the United States currently report their trading VaR over a daily horizon or a horizon of 10 days (= two working weeks of 5 days each), because of the rapid turnover in their portfolios, in agreement with the amended Basle Accords. In contrast, pension funds tend to report their risk over one-month or one-quarter investment horizons. As Jorion (1997, p. 86) correctly states:

> As the holding period should correspond to the longest period needed for an orderly portfolio liquidation, the horizon should be related to the liquidity of the securities, defined in terms of the length of time needed for normal transaction volumes.

There is much less consensus about the subjective choice of the confidence level. There is a trade-off between the requirements set by the regulators to ensure a safe and sound financial system, and the adverse effects of the requirement for a minimum level of (expensive) capital on bank returns and thus on bank share prices. For example, Bankers Trust sets a 99 percent confidence level, Chemical and Chase use a 97.5 percent level, Citibank uses a 95.4 percent level, while Bank of America and JP Morgan use a 95 percent confidence level. These differences are allowed under the current Basle Accord guidelines, since the commercial banks are allowed to construct their own internal financial risk management models.

Higher confidence levels imply higher VaR figures, which in turn imply higher minimally required equity capital cushion for risk insurance. But higher confidence levels imply also longer testing periods. For example, suppose our investment horizon is 1 day and we accept a confidence level of 95 percent, we would expect a loss worse than the VaR in 1 day out of 20. If we choose a 99 percent confidence level, we would have to wait on an average 100 days, or more than 3 months, to confirm that our risk model conforms to reality! When our investment horizon is 1 month, then a 99 percent confidence level would force us to observe on average 100 months, or about eight years of data, before we can confirm our financial risk model.

The VaR measure can be derived either from actual empirical distributions or from an abstract formal distribution, like the Gaussian distribution, in which case it is based on its second moment only. The Basle Committee, which recommended VaR measures in 1988 and again in 1992 to summarize overall risk exposure, also recommended "back-testing" and "stress-testing" as means to verify the accuracy of VaR figures, as did the landmark *G-30* study (cf. chapter 2 of Jorion, 1997, pp. 23–39; Hanley, 1998; Grau, 1999).

12.3.2 *VaR as a quantile risk measure*

We will now first provide a formal definition of VaR, within the context of our cash flow model of investments of Chapter 9.

Definition 476 *For $X(t - \tau)$ as the initial investment and $x_\tau(t)$ its rate of return, the investment at the end of the investment horizon is*

$$X(t) = [1 + x_\tau(t)]X(t - \tau) \tag{12.1}$$

Assume that $x_\tau(t)$ is from a stable distribution. The lowest expected portfolio level at the end of the investment horizon τ at a given confidence level c is

$$X^*(t) = [1 + x_\tau^*(t)]X(t - \tau) \tag{12.2}$$

Then the VaR *relative to the mean at time t for investment horizon τ is*

$$
\begin{aligned}
\text{VaR}_{\text{mean}}(t, \tau) &= E\{X(t)\} - X^*(t)\} \\
&= E\{[1 + x_\tau(t)]X(t - \tau)\} - [1 + x_\tau^*(t)]X(t - \tau) \\
&= [\mu - x_\tau^*(t)]X(t - \tau) \tag{12.3}
\end{aligned}
$$

and the absolute VaR, *or* VaR *relative to zero at time t for investment horizon τ is*

$$
\begin{aligned}
\text{VaR}_{\text{zero}}(t, \tau) &= 0 - X^*(t) \\
&= -x_\tau^*(t)X(t - \tau) \tag{12.4}
\end{aligned}
$$

In both cases, finding the VaR is equivalent to determining the quantile cut-off rate of return $x_\tau^*(t)$ from its available empirical distribution of $x_\tau(t)$ and the confidence level $c(t)$, such that

$$c(t) = P[x_\tau(t) > x_\tau^*(t), t] = \int_{x_\tau^*(t)}^{+\infty} f[x_\tau(t)]dx \tag{12.5}$$

where $f[x_\tau(t)]$ is the empirical probability density function (p.d.f.). This assumes that the p.d.f. $f[x_\tau(t)]$ is continuously integrable, which may not be the case with (empirical) fractal distributions. Notice that, in general, the confidence level $c(t)$ can be time-varying, because the probability distribution $P[..]$ may be time-dependent.

This representation still allows for some kind of nonstationarity and long-term time dependence, i.e., the kind of nonstationarity associated with stable scaling distributions. But in the literature this distribution is usually assumed to be stationary in the strict sense, thus the confidence level c is assumed to be constant (= independent of time t):

$$c = P[x_\tau(t) > x_\tau^*(t)] = \int_{x_\tau^*}^{+\infty} f[x_\tau(t)]dx \tag{12.6}$$

For example, $c = 95$ percent for all t. Or, equivalently, we can express everything in terms of a constant *significance level*

$$1 - c = P[x_\tau(t) \le x_\tau^*(t)] = \int_{-\infty}^{x_\tau^*} f[x_\tau(t)]dx \tag{12.7}$$

For example, the significance level $1 - c = 5$ percent for all t.

It's important to emphasize that the quantile determination of the VaR is also *valid for any nonstationary stable distribution* of the rates of return on assets – discrete or continuous, skewed or symmetric, leptokurtic or platykurtic – as long as we know how the distribution scales over time! See, for example, the recent investigations by Hull and White (1998a,b) into the impact of non-Gaussian distributions on the VaR, or the VaR bounds for portfolios with assets with non-normal returns (Luciano and Marena, 2001).

Example 477   *The annual report of 1994 of JP Morgan provides an empirical example in the form of a histogram of its daily revenues $X(t)$ (Figure 12.2). From the graph, the average revenue $\mu = USD\,5.1m = USD\,5.1m$. There are $T = 254$ daily observations. We try to find $X(t)$, such that the number of observations to its left is $T \times (1 - c) = 254 \times 5$ percent $= 12.7$ days. Because of the coarseness of the histogram we need to interpolate. There are 11 daily observations to the left of $-USD\,10m$, and 15 observations to the left of $-USD\,9m$. Interpolation gives*

$$USD\left[-9 - \frac{12.7 - 15}{11 - 15}\right]m = -USD\,9.575m \tag{12.8}$$

Thus the VaR of daily revenues measured relative to the mean is

$$\begin{aligned} VaR_{mean}(t) &= E\{X(t)\} - X^*(t) \\ &= USD\,5.1m - (-USD\,9.575m) \\ &= USD\,14.57m \end{aligned} \tag{12.9}$$

and the VaR of daily revenues in absolute dollar loss is

$$\begin{aligned} VaR_{zero}(t) &= 0 - X^*(t) \\ &= USD\,9.575m \end{aligned} \tag{12.10}$$

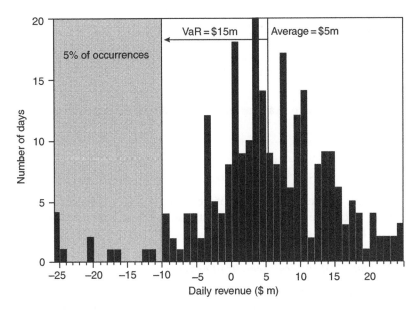

Figure 12.2 Empirical distribution of daily revenues of JP Morgan in 1994. Notice some extreme daily losses in the left tail, as indicated by the grey area, left of the $10m daily loss.

12.4 VaR for parametric distributions

12.4.1 Gaussian VaR

The VaR computation is simplified considerably when as theoretical parametric distribution the Gaussian distribution is assumed: $x_\tau(t) \sim N(\mu, \sigma^2 \tau)$. Then the VaR can be derived directly from the portfolio volatility $\sigma \tau^{0.5}$, using a multiplicative factor depending on the confidence level.

First, we transform the general stationary density function $f[x_\tau(t)]$ into a standardized normal distribution $g[z(t)]$, which has mean zero and a unitary standard deviation: $z(t) \sim N(0, 1)$, so that the standardized variable is defined by

$$z(t) = \frac{x_\tau(t) - \mu}{\sigma \sqrt{\tau}} \qquad (12.11)$$

and its cut-off rate by

$$z^* = \frac{x_\tau^* - \mu}{\sigma \sqrt{\tau}} \qquad (12.12)$$

so that the VaR can be expressed by

$$1 - c = P(x_\tau(t) \le x_\tau^*) = \int_{-\infty}^{x_\tau^*} f[x_\tau(t)]dx_\tau(t)$$

$$= \int_{-\infty}^{z^*} g[z(t)]dz(t) \tag{12.13}$$

Now we only have to examine the tables of the *cumulative standard normal distribution*

$$F_{z^*}[z(t)] = \int_{-\infty}^{z^*} g[z(t)]dz(t) \tag{12.14}$$

which provide the integrated area left of the value $z(t) = z^*$. We can always return to the original parametrized Gaussian distribution, since $x_\tau(t) = z(t)\sigma\sqrt{\tau} + \mu$ and $x_\tau^* = z^*\sigma\sqrt{\tau} + \mu$.

12.4.2   *Statistical problem: scarcity of extreme values*

The main problem facing the statistical VaR practitioners is that the VaR is an extreme quantile of a rate of return distribution (Bassi *et al.*, 1998). Therefore, we have relatively few historical observations with which to estimate it (Hendricks, 1996). This we had already observed in Figure 4.2. VaR estimates are usually imprecise, and become even more so, the more we move further out onto the tail of the distribution. Practitioners have responded by relying on assumptions to make up for the lack of data. The common, but decidedly unrealistic, assumption is that the empirical rates of return are from the parametric Gaussian distribution.

However, financial returns are usually fat-tailed and assuming Gaussianness can lead to serious under-estimates of VaR (Hull and White, 1998a; Ju and Pearson, 1999). This has led to the suggestion of adaptive updating of a time-varying volatility (Hull and White, 1998b). A more satisfactory assumption is that the returns follow a heavy-tailed stable distribution, as discussed in chapter 3 (Rachev and Mittnik, 2000). Even then we still face the problem that most observations are central ones. The estimated distribution fits the central observations best, and therefore remains ill-suited to the extreme observations with which financial risk analysts are mainly concerned. The estimation of low frequency events with finite data remains highly problematic and therefore *stress testing* is often recommended (Grau, 1999).

Market-makers are very much interested in large moves in the prices of stocks, bonds or other traded assets, since the largest price moves cause market-makers to lose money. Market-makers make money only for small price moves. The loss from large price moves result from the option's *gamma*. Market-makers are *delta-hedgers*. If prices move sufficiently, their delta-hedged positions become unhedged. For example, when a market-maker delta-hedges a stock position, he is short a call option and a large move generates a loss. As the stock price rises, the delta of the call option increases and it loses value faster than the stock gains value. *Vice versa*, as the stock price fall, the delta of the call option decreases and it gains value more slowly than the fixed stock position loses value. In effect, the market-maker becomes unhedged net long as the stock price falls and unhedged net short as the stock price rises.

It can be shown that the market-maker's profit depends on the squared change in the stock price, i.e., on the magnitude and not the direction of the stock price move. It can also be shown that a market-maker breaks even for a one standard deviation move in the stock price $\epsilon = \sigma \tau^H S$ (measured on an annual basis), makes money within that range and loses money outside that range. The market-maker's regular profit and occasional large loss can thus be explained by the preponderance of small price movements in the financial market and the occasional large moves. Differently stated, the leptokurtosis of the distribution of the financial market price increments explains the leptokurtosis of the distribution of the market-maker's profits. When the distributions are close to normal, a market-maker expects to make small profits about two-thirds of the time, and large losses about one-third of the time and on average to break even (McDonald, 2002, Chapter 13, pp. 401–430).[3]

Extreme value problems are not unique to financial risk management, but occur also in other scientific and engineering disciplines. They are particularly prominent in hydrology, where statisticians and engineers, like "Father-of-the-Nile" hydrologist Hurst in the 1950s, have long struggled with the problem of how high dams should be to contain flood probabilities within reasonable limits. These hydrologists have usually even less data than financial risk managers and often have to estimate quantiles well out the range of their historical data. Let's have a closer look at an interesting contemporary example of such extreme risk measurement and analysis, and what lessons it contains for the management of extreme financial risks.

12.4.3   A Gargantuan example of extreme risk

A Gargantuan example of the measurement, analysis and *dynamic management of extreme risks* is the determination of the required safety height of $x^* = 185$ m (607 feet) for the Three Gorges (Sanxia) Dam on the Yangtze, or Chiang Jiang (= Long River), near the village of Sandouping, Yichang, in the Hubei Province of the People's Republic of China (Figure 12.3).[4]

The water level will eventually rise to an average Normal Pool Level, of $\mu = 175$ m (574 feet), thus the excess security is $x^* - \mu = 10$ m. Since the flood control storage capacity of this dam is said to reduce the frequency of big downstream floods from every 10 to every 100 years, the extreme value percentage is $1 - c = 1.0$ percent (or $c = 99.0$ percent) for all time t. Assuming the distribution of the water level of the Yangtze to be approximately Gaussian sets the excess security equal to $x^* - \mu = 2.33 \times \sigma = 10$ m. This provides us with an estimated annual volatility of the water level of $\sigma = 4.3$ m for all time t.

However, it is well known that the Hurst exponent of such a long unregulated river is closer to $H = 0.9$ than to the Gaussian $H = 0.5$ (Mandelbrot and Wallis,

Figure 12.3 Potential large-scale catastrophic flow risk: the Yangtze River in Sandouping, Yichang, Hubei Province of the People's Republic of China.

1969; Whitcher *et al.*, 2002) In other words, the Yangtze has a very persistent water level distribution. Such a dependent volatile water level behaves more like brown or even black noise and, therefore, requires extra risk-reducing height for the dam.

Indeed, that's the reason why the engineers opted for *dynamic risk management* of the water storage level. The water level in the reservoir will be lowered during the dry winter season between January and May to the minimum flood control level of 145 m, creating an extreme risk hedge of 30 m $\approx 7 \times \sigma$ m, ready for the flood season from the end of May to the beginning of September. Notice that this is considerably larger than the $6 \times \sigma$, where the empirical distribution of outliers starts to deviate drastically from that of a Lévy stable distribution, as discussed in Chapter 3.

Why is the Yangtze River so persistent? The Yangtze flows from the 6,670 m (20,000 feet) high Tibetan Plateau to the East China Sea and is, with its length of 6,300 km (3,900 miles) the longest river in Asia and the third longest in the world (after the Nile and the Amazon). It is also the deepest river in the world. It is the third largest river in terms of annual runoff, after the Amazon and Congo rivers. Its drainage basin covers more than 1.8 million km^2 (705,400 miles^2), accounting for 18.8 percent of China's territory. The Three Gorges Dam reservoir will be 615 km. (370 mile) long (comparable to Lake Superior) and 175 m (525 feet) deep, storing 39.3 billion m^3 (51.4 billion cubic yards or 10.4 trillion gallons) of water (Figure 12.4).

Figure 12.4 In this drawing of the completed Three Gorges Dam, the spillway to release
water and control flooding is in the center, with electric generating plants on
either side. On the right is a shiplift for comparatively small vessels, and on
the far right is the five-step shiplock, which will allow ocean-going vessels to
travel up the Yangtze to the western reaches of Chongqing.

The Three Gorges Dam is China's largest infrastructure project since the building
of the 2,400 km (1,500 miles) long Great Wall in the third century BC and the
digging of its 1,600 km (1,000 miles) long Grand Canal in the sixth century AD. It
has a length of 2.3 km (1.4 miles) and is the largest hydroelectric dam in the world:
40 per cent larger than the Itaipu Dam on the border between Brazil and Paraguay,
which is 8 km, or 5 mile long, delivers 12.6 million kilowatt and was completed
in 1991 at a total cost of more than USD 20 billion. The Three Gorges Dam is
70 percent larger than the Aswan Dam in Egypt and will displace 1.2 million
people. The Aswan Dam was completed in 1970 for USD 1 billion, is 111 m (364
feet) high and 3.26 km (2.3 miles) long, has a capacity of 2.1 million kilowatt
(= 25 percent of Egypt's electricity needs) and displaced "only" 100,000 people.
The hydrologist Hurst determined the safety height for this Aswan High Dam in
the 1950s using his Hurst exponent to correct the standard deviation approach,
from $\epsilon_\tau = \sigma \tau^{0.5} S$ to $\epsilon_\tau = \sigma \tau^H S$ with $0.5 < H < 1$. Notice how crucial the τ^H
term is, when τ represents a very long time horizon, e.g., of hundred years or more.

The Three Gorges Dam project, modelled on the Tennessee Valley Authority
multiple-use dam project of 1933, is designed for *flood control*, *power generation*
and *improved navigation*.

During the 2,200 years from the beginning of the Han Dynasty in 202 BC to the end of the Qing Dynasty in 1911, there have been 214 floods, an average of one flood every 10 years. These floods have claimed 1 million lives in the past 100 years alone. In the twentieth century there have been five severe floods. In 1931 it drowned 145,000 people, in 1935 142,000 people and in 1954 30,000 people. Most recently, major floods caused by the Yangtze River in 1996 killed 2,700 people and in 1998 more than 3,000. The economic cost of Yangtze's flooding in August 1998 was $30 billion. The 1998 flood completely destroyed no less than 10 percent of China's grain supply.

The electricity generating capacity of the 26 generators in the Three Gorges Dam will be 18.2 million kilowatts, enough power for a city ten times the size of Los Angeles and equivalent to that generated by 18 nuclear power stations or by 36 coal-burning plants, satisfying 10 percent of the electricity needs of China. Per year it will generate 84.7 billion kilowatt hours, replacing the burning of 50 million tons of coal. The entire project started in 1994, after a final decision in 1992, and it is to be completed in 2009 (Figure 12.5). Thereby, after almost one century it will realize the vision formulated in 1919 by Sun Yat-Sen, the founding father of China's Republic.

We discuss the Three Gorges Dam project not only as an example of extreme risk management; it is also as a financially a very important project, since it is absorbing a very substantial amount of global capital every year, which is diverted from many alternative investment projects in the world. The original 1994 estimated cost

Figure 12.5 Emergence of large-scale dynamic catastrophic flow risk management: the Three Gorges Dam under construction.

of the dam was US$25 billion, more than any other single construction project in global history. However, unofficial estimates put its costs already closer to $75 billion. For that reason, the World Bank, the US Export–Import Bank and the Asian Development Bank have all three refused to finance this environmentally controversial project.

However, ignoring the warnings of the many critics, and rather ironically, in January 1997 and May 1999 the private American investment bank Morgan Stanley underwrote $830 million in bonds for the China Development Bank (CDB) and thereby became a 35 percent owner of China International Capital Corporation (CICC), the project corporation's advisor on overseas capital raising. Following Morgan Stanley's lead, in the year 2000, Salomon Smith Barney (a subsidiary of the Citigroup) and Merrill Lynch and Co., together with Credit Suisse First Boston, JP Morgan, Lehman Brothers, Goldman Sachs and Chase Manhattan Bank became lead managers of this private financing consortium. It is the largest privately underwritten capital investment project, with the longest maturity, in a (still officially) Communist society. Thus, it is a global project highly exposed to multi-dimensional, political, economic, financial and country risk, not unlike many other global investment projects subject to extreme risks. It focuses the attention of financial researchers in commercial banks and insurance companies on how to measure and analyze extreme financial risks (Embrechts *et al.*, 1997, 1998). Catastrophic reinsurance linked securities are already viewed as a new asset class (Litzenberger *et al.*, 1996).

12.5 Extreme value theory

A small group of theorists has recently discovered an extreme value (EV) theorem based on the (strong) assumption of i.i.d. returns, which tells us that the limiting distribution of extreme returns has always the same form, whatever the unknown i.i.d. distribution from which the data are drawn.[5]

Theorem 478 (Extreme value) *Subject to the i.i.d. condition, the density of extreme returns converges asymptotically to*

$$H(x; \mu, \sigma, \xi) = \begin{cases} e^{(-[1+\xi(x-\mu)/\sigma]^{-1/\xi})} & \text{if } \xi \neq 0 \\ e^{(-e^{-(x-\mu)/\sigma})} & \text{if } \xi = 0 \end{cases} \qquad (12.15)$$

The parameters μ and σ correspond to the mean and standard deviation, respectively, and the third parameter, the *tail index* ξ, indicates the heaviness of the tails. The bigger ξ, the heavier the tail (Longin, 1996; McNeil, 1996, 1998; Lauridsen, 2000). For some applications, cf. Koedijk *et al.*, 1990, and, most recently, Blum and Dacorogna, 2002. For a critique to use the ξ measure of the fatness of the tails of distributions to identify the stability exponent α_Z, cf. McCulloch (1997).

Remark 479 *Notice the similarity of the EV Theorem to the Zolotarev parametrization of stable distributions in Chapter 3. This EV Theorem is related* *to the classical CLT, but applies to the extremes of observations rather than their means (= the concentrations). It allows for estimation of the asymptotic distribution of extreme values, without making assumptions other than the i.i.d. assumption, about the unknown empirical distribution. The first step is to estimate these parameters. There is a choice between semi-parametric methods, like the Hill estimator, which focus on the estimation of the tail index ξ, and parametric methods, like the ML method, which estimate all three parameters μ, σ and ξ simultaneously. However, the estimation is complicated by nonlinearities and the properties of these estimators are still not well understood.*

EV theory faces, at least, two complications. First, the choice of the tail size of the distribution of our rate of return observations affects the VaR estimates through the effect on the estimate of the tail index ξ. Second, the EV theorem assumes that the rates of return are i.i.d. But we know from the empirical research reported in the preceding chapters that empirical financial rates of return show forms of clustering, with periods of alternating high and low volatility, due to global dependencies. These empirically observed global dependencies violate the key assumption of EV theory!

12.5.1   Increased inter-correlation of financial exceedences

A paper by Dacorogna *et al.* (2001), presented at the University of Konstanz, provides vivid evidence that the extreme values or so-called *exceedences* (i.e., the values exceeding certain confidence boundaries, like 95 percent of the distribution) of international rate of return distributions tend to cluster and to highly positively correlate at times of financial distress (cf. also Blum and Dacorogna, 2002)! Thus, in times of distress, portfolio diversification tends to be defeated by increased positive inter-correlations between the extreme rates of return of the various portfolio investments. This severely diminishes the value of the VaR approach to financial risk management, since it appears that portfolios behave very differently in times of distress compared with in times of normality. In other words, portfolio variances and covariances are time-varying and they are varying in such a way that they defeat conventional risk diversification rules. This a very important area of financial portfolio research to which our time-frequency signal processing approach expects to significantly contribute in the coming years.

12.5.2   Fractional Brownian Motion (FBM) and VaR

The VaR can be put in a dynamic context, with nonstationary distributions, as long as the risk is measurable by the second moment only. Thus, for the GBM, which has i.i.d. increments and a second-order risk measure dependent on the investment horizon τ, since

$$\sigma_\tau = \sigma_\varepsilon \tau^{0.5} \tag{12.16}$$

the VaR relative to the mean for investment horizon τ is

$$\text{VaR}_{\text{mean}}(t, \tau) = [\mu - x_\tau^*(t)]X(t - \tau)$$
$$= -z^*\sigma_\varepsilon\tau^{0.5}X(t - \tau) \tag{12.17}$$

since

$$[\mu - x_\tau^*(t)] = -z^*\sigma_\tau \tag{12.18}$$

and the corresponding absolute loss VaR is thus

$$\text{VaR}_{\text{zero}}(t, \tau) = -x_\tau^*(t)X(t - \tau)$$
$$= -(\mu\tau + z^*\sigma_\varepsilon\tau^{0.5})X(t - \tau) \tag{12.19}$$

This method generalizes to other cumulative distributions, as long as all the uncertainty can be measured by the volatility σ_τ. For example for the FBM (Elliott and van der Hoek, 2000), the VaR relative to the mean for investment horizon τ is easily generalized to

$$\text{VaR}_{\text{mean}}(t, \tau) = -z^*\sigma_\varepsilon\tau^H X(t - \tau) \tag{12.20}$$

and the corresponding absolute loss VaR to

$$\text{VaR}_{\text{zero}}(t, \tau) = -(\mu\tau^{2H} + z^*\sigma_\varepsilon\tau^H)X(t - \tau) \tag{12.21}$$

Remark 480 *The Black-Scholes option based on the FBM is as follows. The null option value is:*

$$C(t) = S(t)e^{-g\tau}N(d_1) - Ke^{-r\tau}N(d_2) \tag{12.22}$$

with

$$d_1 = \frac{ln(S(t)/K) + (r - g + 1/2\sigma^2)\tau^{2H}}{\sigma\tau^H} \tag{12.23}$$

$$d_2 = d_1 - \sigma\tau^H, \quad 0 < H < 1 \tag{12.24}$$

where $C(t)$ – call option value, $S(t)$ – underlying asset value, K – strike price, g – Yield (divident, etc.), τ – expiration time, $N(..)$ – cumulative standard normal distribution

But the fundamental question we posed in Chapter 1 is: can we really measure financial risk by only the second moment of a distribution, in particular in a dynamic portfolio situation with global time dependence. The next section will provide some tentative, and, perhaps, discouraging, answers.

12.6 VaR and fractal pricing processes

12.6.1 *Concerns and doubts about VaR*

In this section we will formulate why we have deep concerns and doubts about the use of the VaR as an overall measure of the exposure to market risk, when VaR is based on assumed simple parametric distributions, like the Gaussian, and why we insist on measuring the stability of the empirical distributions of the rates of return $x(t)$, in addition to measuring their various forms of long-term time dependence in the various financial markets. We have observed, and reasoned throughout this book, that the Gaussian distribution is inadequate to describe financial market returns, since empirical financial market returns show skewed, leptokurtic, non-normal distributions and, most importantly, nonstationarity in the strict sense.[6] For example, from Chapter 3 we already know that some nonlinear market pricing systems may produce nonstationary distributions without a definable ("existing") mean or variance!

The classical Modern Portfolio Theory (MPT) of Markowitz and Sharpe is the basis for the VaR theory. It presupposes stationary (Gaussian) rates of return distributions. It will be the starting point for the following discussion. Gauss showed about two hundred years ago that the limiting distribution of a set of independent, identically distributed (i.i.d.) random variables is the normal distribution.[7] This is the classical Central Limit Theorem or CLT. But in Chapter 3, we noticed that there are instances where amplification occurs at extreme values and that may lead to heavy, long-tailed distributions, such as the Pareto income distribution. These long-tailed distributions led Lévy to formulate a generalized stable density function, of which the normal as well as the Gauchy distributions are special cases.

In Chapter 3, we also mentioned the Generalized Central Limit Theorem (GCLT) for stable distributions, properly parametrized by Zolotarev. We recall that the *stability exponent* α_Z determines the kurtosis of the distribution, i.e., the peakedness at its central location δ and the fatness of the tails. When $\alpha_Z = 2$, the distribution is normal with variance $\sigma^2 = 2\gamma^2$. However, when $\alpha_Z < 2$, the second moment, or (population) variance, becomes infinite or undefined. When $1 < \alpha_Z < 2$, the first moment exists, but when $0 < \alpha_Z \leq 1$, the theoretical (population) average becomes infinite or undefined too. For example, the Cauchy distribution has infinite, undefined mean and variance. This means that the Cauchy distribution has no limiting mean or variance!

Remark 481 *Of course, we can always compute the (sample) average over time or the variance over time of a finite data set. Undefined theoretical (population) averages and variances only mean that there is no convergence to fixed finite moment values, when we enlarge the data set. The sequential mean and variance of that data set, which calculate the mean and the variance respectively, as observations are added to the data set one at a time, will then never converge to a specific mean and variance, but will continue to "wander."*

Thus, if the distribution of rates of return is not Gaussian and $\alpha_Z < 2$, the variance of the finite data set can say nothing about the theoretical (population) variance, because it does not even exist in the limit! This is, of course, what is meant by a non-ergodic data set. The variances of our finite financial data sets are potentially unstable and don't tend to any value, even as the data set increases in size.

For example, we found that the rate of return series $x(t)$ of the S&P500 stock index shows $1 < \alpha_Z = 1/H = (1/0.6) = 1.67 < 2$. In that case $x(t)$ is fractal and globally dependent, and has infinite memory. It also has a stable mean, like a stable Lévy distribution, but it has an undefined or "infinite" variance.[8] This non-convergence or "wandering path" of the variance of stock and stock index returns has entered the finance literature under the scientific misnomer of "stochastic volatility" (cf. Hull and White, 1987, 1988, 1998a,b). There is no stochasticity involved in indefiniteness! Probability cannot be substituted for ignorance, as we discussed in detail in Chapter 1. In such a case it may not be prudent to base a risk measure, such as VaR on the computed standard deviation, since that standard deviation remains undefined over time. That is, the sequential variance, c.q., standard deviation will never converge! For some other distributions we may find that $0 < \alpha_Z \leq 1$, so that the average also does not converge, in addition to the non-convergence of the variance.

12.6.2 Fama–Samuelson MPT proposition

We learned in Chapter 3 that if two distributions are stable with the same value of α_Z, their sum also is stable with the same stability exponent α_Z. This mathematical result has applications in MPT, which is, or at least should be, rather disturbing for global portfolio managers (Lucas and Klaassen, 1998; Sornette, 1998).

Proposition 482 (Fama–Samuelson) *If the securities in a portfolio have rates of return $x(t)$ with the same stability exponent α_Z, then the portfolio itself has a rate of return $x(t)$ that is stable, with the same value of α_Z.*

Proof From Chapter 3 we have the logarithm of the characteristic function of the non-standardized stable distribution of the random variable $X \sim \mathbf{S}(\alpha, \beta, \gamma, \delta; 0)$

$$\ln[E\{e^{j\omega x}\}]$$

$$= \left(-\gamma^\alpha |\omega|^\alpha \left[1 + j\beta \tan \frac{\pi\alpha}{2} sign(\omega)(\gamma|\omega|^{1-\alpha} - 1)\right] + j\delta\omega \right) \quad \text{if } \alpha \neq 1$$

$$= \left(-\gamma|\omega| \left[1 + j\beta \frac{2}{\pi} sign(\omega)(\ln|\omega| + \ln\gamma)\right] + j\delta\omega \right) \quad \text{if } \alpha = 1$$

$$(12.25)$$

with the four parameters: (1) *stability exponent $\alpha_Z \in (0, 2]$*, (2) *skewness parameter $\beta \in [-1, 1]$*, (3) *scale parameter $\gamma > 0$*, and (4) *location parameter $\delta \in \mathbb{R}$.*

For simplicity, we'll discuss the case of symmetric distributions when $\beta = 0$, so that

$$\ln[E\{e^{jx\omega}\}] = j\delta\omega - \gamma^{\alpha_z}|\omega|^{\alpha_z} \tag{12.26}$$

For the stable distributions of two rates of return $x_i(t)$, $i = 1, 2$, the distribution of the weighted portfolio sum $x_p(t) = w_1 x_1(t) + w_2 x_2(t)$, with $w_1 + w_2 = 1$, has the characteristic function (cf. Chapter 1):

$$
\begin{aligned}
\ln E\{e^{jx_p\omega}\} &= \ln E\{e^{j(w_1 x_1 + w_2 x_2)\omega}\} \\
&= \ln[E\{e^{jw_1 x_1\omega}\}E\{e^{jw_2 x_2\omega}\}], \text{ i.e., stable distributions} \\
&= \ln E\{e^{jx_1 w_1\omega}\} + \ln E\{e^{jx_2 w_2\omega}\} \\
&= [j\delta_1 w_1\omega - \gamma_1^{\alpha_z}|w_1\omega|^{\alpha_z}] + [j\delta_2 w_2\omega - \gamma_2^{\alpha_z}|w_2\omega|^{\alpha_z}] \\
&= j(w_1\delta_1 + w_2\delta_2)\omega - [w_1^{\alpha_z}\gamma_1^{\alpha_z} + w_2^{\alpha_z}\gamma_2^{\alpha_z}]|\omega|^{\alpha_z} \\
&= j\delta_p\omega - \gamma_p^{\alpha_z}|\omega|^{\alpha_z}
\end{aligned}
\tag{12.27}
$$

so that the location parameter, or mean, of the stable portfolio distribution

$$\delta_p = w_1\delta_1 + w_2\delta_2 \tag{12.28}$$

and its scale parameter

$$\gamma_p^{\alpha_z} = w_1^{\alpha_z}\gamma_1^{\alpha_z} + w_2^{\alpha_z}\gamma_2^{\alpha_z} \tag{12.29}$$

It is easy to see that this bivariate return result generalizes, so that for stable distributions with the same stability parameter in general, for a portfolio with $i = 1, 2, \ldots, n$ assets, the portfolio location parameter or mean

$$\delta_p = \sum_{i=1}^{n} w_i\delta_i, \quad \text{where } \sum_{i=1}^{n} w_i = 1 \tag{12.30}$$

and the portfolio scale parameter

$$\gamma_p^{\alpha_z} = \sum_{i=1}^{n} w_i^{\alpha_z}\gamma_i^{\alpha_z} \tag{12.31}$$

or

$$\gamma_p = \left(\sum_{i=1}^{n} w_i^{\alpha_z}\gamma_i^{\alpha_z}\right)^{1/\alpha_z} \tag{12.32}$$

∎

Fama (1965) and Samuelson (1967) used this proposition to adapt the portfolio theory of Markowitz (1952) for infinite or undefined variance distributions of rates of return on investments. It is a peculiar fact of history that this Proposition of Fama and Samuelson has disappeared from the standard textbooks on investments and portfolio analysis and management, although it has considerable empirical value! S&P500 stock index is often used as the market index in the Capital Asset Pricing Model (CAPM). But, as we just saw, the S&P500 stock index has no finite limiting variance, and this fact alone undermines most if not all of the stock and bond pricing results from the CAPM.

Remark 483   *For Gaussian distributions, when $\alpha_Z = 2$, we have the familiar portfolio variance relationship from classical Markowitz mean – variance analysis, except that Markowitz' important diversifying correlation term is missing!*

$$\gamma_p^2 = w_1^2 \gamma_1^2 + w_2^2 \gamma_2^2 \tag{12.33}$$

For Gaussian distributions, the variance $\sigma_i^2 = 2\gamma_i^2$ (i.e., $\gamma_i^2 = \sigma_i^2/2$), so that for stable distributions with the same α_Z we have also

$$\sigma_p^2 = w_1^2 \sigma_1^2 + w_2^2 \sigma_2^2 \tag{12.34}$$

The Proposition implies that the distribution of the portfolio returns is *self-affine* and scales with stability exponent α_Z as scaling exponent. In other words, the shape of the stable distribution of portfolio returns is the same as that of the underlying asset returns, no matter what the scale of portfolio variance. Only the value of the location parameter changes.

How does the existence of stable non-Gaussian rates of return distributions affect portfolio diversification? For example, when we use uniform weights $w_i = 1/n$,

$$\gamma_p^{\alpha_Z} = \left(\frac{1}{n}\right)^{\alpha_Z} \sum_{i=1}^n \gamma_i^{\alpha_Z} \tag{12.35}$$

we can discern three important cases:

(1) When $1 < \alpha_Z \leq 2$, the portfolio risk, as measured by the scaling parameter

$$\gamma_p = \frac{1}{n} \left(\sum_{i=1}^n \gamma_i^{\alpha_Z} \right)^{(1/\alpha_Z)} \tag{12.36}$$

decreases, as the number of assets in the portfolio, n, increases. In other words, there is a diversification effect: including more assets in the portfolio reduces the portfolio risk, despite the empirically established fact that there exists no finite limiting variance.

Remark 484   *Since most (but not all!) empirical stocks appear to have a stability exponent of $\alpha_Z \approx 1.67$, diversification does reduce the non-market risk of an* *empirical stock investment portfolio, including that of the portfolio underlying the S&P500 Index. But this risk reduction through diversification has nothing to do with the covariances, as in Markowitz' (1952) original theory.*

(2) When $\alpha_Z = 1$

$$\gamma_p = \frac{1}{n} \sum_{i=1}^{n} \gamma_i \tag{12.37}$$

there is no diversification effect: adding more assets to the portfolio does not reduce the portfolio risk.

(3) When $0 < \alpha_Z < 1$, increasing the number of assets in the portfolio may actually increase the portfolio risk.[9] In this case, neither the means nor the variances of the rates of return of the assets in the portfolio exist. Neither their means nor their variances converge. In other words, when asset return rates behave like black noise, increasing the portfolio size only increases the portfolio risk!

Thus MPT-diversification to reduce non-market risk is still useful when the asset returns are non-Gaussian, but they have stable distributions with the same stability $1 < \alpha_Z \leq 2$, despite the fact that these stable distributions have undefined variances. However, when $\alpha_Z = 1$, there is no diversification and when $0 < \alpha_Z < 1$, the portfolio risk can actually increase when more assets are included in the portfolio. Thus, it is very important for portfolio managers to compute the homogeneous Zolotarev alpha $\alpha_Z = 1/\alpha_L$, to determine the degree of achievable diversification. Portfolio risk managers should also compute the multifractal spectrum of heterogeneous stock return stability exponents $\alpha_{Zi} = 1/\alpha_{Li}$, which lie outside the range of the usual measurement of the homogeneous Hurst exponent H, as we discussed in Chapter 8.

It is also very important to realize that, since there is no correlation under parametrized stable distributions, Markowitz-type portfolio diversification and optimization, which exploits such correlation among the assets, simply does not work. However, this does not necessarily mean that there does not exist a *Tobin liquidity preference theorem*. As we will see, we can still reduce the risk in a portfolio by including more risk-free cash, even when the distributions are nonstationary but stable. In other words, it is dynamic *liquidity management* that ultimately determines the investment portfolio risk exposure of a fund manager (Bawa *et al.*, 1979). That is, dynamic liquidity management should be similar to the dynamic risk management of the extreme values of high risk dams!

12.6.3   *Skewed–stable investment opportunity sets*

The Fama–Samuelson Proposition is an example of Mandelbrot's invariance of scaling under weighted mixture (= weighted linear combination; cf. Chapter 3). It shows why it is important to determine the stability parameters of the rates of return $x(t)$ for the assets in a portfolio and to see if they are the same. However, if the stability parameters are different, heterogeneous, α_{Zi}, this simple generalization of Markowitz mean-variance analysis, or MPT and its derivatives, does no longer hold true. Or, as Peters (1994, p. 208) states:

> ... different stocks can have different Hurst exponents and different values of α_Z. Currently, there is no theory on combining distributions with different alphas. The EMH, assuming normality for all distributions, assumed $\alpha_Z = 2.0$ for all stocks, which we know [now] to be incorrect.[10]

Huston McCulloch of Ohio State University has done some empirical work on what happens when the stability parameters α_{Z_i} for the rates of return of the assets in a portfolio are heterogeneous, i.e., they are different from each other. In particular, he has produced interesting 3-dimensional visualizations of the resulting Markowitz efficiency frontiers, which are no longer 2-dimensional (McCulloch, 1986, 1996). In accordance with his findings, McCulloch (1996) also developed an alternative to the Black–Scholes option pricing formula, using stable distributions.

12.7 Software

For the first exercise you need John Nolan's program STABLE.EXE (900 kb), obtained from his expert web site: http://www.cas.american.edu/˜jpnolan/ stable.html, which calculates stable densities, cumulative distribution functions and quantiles. STABLE.TXT (16 kb) provides the description of the STABLE.EXE program.

The other Exercises can be executed in Microsoft EXCEL spreadsheets or by using the Statistics Toolbox available from The MathWorks, Inc., 24 Prime Park Way Natick, MA 01760-1500, USA. Tel (508) 647-7000; Fax (508) 647-7001: http://www.mathworks.com/products/wavelettbx.shtml.

For pictures of McCulloch's skew–stable investment opportunity set see his web site: http://www.econ.ohio-state.edu/jhm/ios.html.

12.8 Exercises

Exercise 485 *Plot the cumulative density function (c.d.f.) of the S&P500 rates of total return, using Nolan's STABLE software. (Its instructions are in Nolan's User's Guide for STABLE Version 2.11, available in the Online Teaching Aids. All output generated by STABLE appears in the stable.out file).*

Exercise 486 *What would be your best VaR estimate at a 99 percent confidence level for this empirical distribution?*

Exercise 487 *Did you use the Zolotarev, or any other parametrization? If yes, how? If not, what did you do to derive a best VaR estimate?*

Exercise 488 *Would it have made a difference to your VaR estimate when you would have used simple stationary Gaussian distribution approximations* *and based your VaR estimate on the assumed constant standard deviations? Demonstrate your conclusion.*

Notes

1 At this moment there are not yet Hurst or Lipschitz exponent measurements of real estate investment returns available in the financial literature, but they will soon be published.
2 I agree with their conclusion that probability theory relates only to (Las Vegas type roulette, card, one-armed-bandit) game situations. But I disagree with their assumption that probability theory has anything to do with the empirical world. Nobody has ever proved that *probability* is an empirically observable real world phenomenon, in contrast to *randomness* or *uncertainty* (cf. Chapter 1). Probability theory does not explain any empirical phenomenon in the real world and is therefore not a *scientific* theory, but only a *philosophical* theory.
3 Even very recently, McDonald of Northwestern University still assumes in his new text book (McDonald, 2003) that the distribution is normal, so that the Hurst exponent is $H = 0.5$, despite all the empirical evidence to the contrary. Different financial markets exhibit different degrees of persistence, as I brought to his attention, when I reviewed six chapters of his book a few months before its publication.
4 The three gorges are called Qutang, Wu and Xiling. Information for this example was gathered from the Internet, in particular from http://21stcenturysciencetech.com/articles/Three_Gorges.html, and from http://www.chinaonline.co...er/ministry_profiles/threegorgesdam.asp.
5 EV theory, which was discovered by Stephan Resnick (1987), seems to have been first applied to VaR by François Longin in 1996, followed by Jon Danielson, Casper de Vries and their collaborators at the Tinbergen Institute in The Netherlands and at the London School of Economics (LSE) in London, by Paul Embrechts and Alexander McNeil at the ETH Zentrum in Zürich, and by Francis Diebold and his associates at the Wharton School in Pennsylvania, USA.
6 Because it is often implicitly assumed that the distributions are Gaussian, "stationarity" is often taken to mean "stationarity in the wide sense." (cf. Chapter 1).
7 Carl Friedrich Gauss (1777–1855), German mathematician and scientist is acknowledged to be one of the three leading scientists and mathematicians of all time (the other two are Archimedes and Newton). He was a child prodigy, who taught himself reading and arithmetic by the age of three. His outstanding works include the discovery of the method of least squares in 1795, the discovery of non-Euclidean geometry, and important contributions to the theory of numbers. During the 1820s, with the collaboration of the physicist Wilhelm Weber, he explored many areas of physics, including magnetism, mechanics, acoustics and optics.
8 Similarly, Fama (1965) and Peters (1994, pp. 210–212) compute an approximate value of $\alpha_Z = 1.66$ for the Dow Jones Industrial Index. Peters clearly demonstrates the non-convergence of the volatility of the DJIA, as we have done for the volatility of the S&P500 Index in Chapter 3.
9 This range of $\alpha_Z = 1/\alpha_L$ cannot be measured by the Hurst exponent H, but can be measured by the Lipschitz α_L.
10 EMH = Efficient Market Hypothesis (cf. Chapter 2).

Bibliography

Bassi, Franco, Paul Embrechts and Maria Kafetzaki (1998) "Risk Management and Quantile Estimation," in Adler, Robert J., Raisa E. Feldman and Murad S. Taqqu (Eds) (1998), *A Practical Guide to Heavy Tails: Statistical Techniques and Applications*, Birkhäuser, Boston, 111–130.

Bawa, V. S., E. J. Elton and M. J. Gruber (1979) "Simple Rules for Optimal Portfolio Selection in a Stable Paretian Market," *Journal of Finance*, **34**(4), 1041–1047.

Blum, Peter, and Michel M. Dacorogna (2002) "Extremal Moves in Daily Foreign Exchange Rates and Risk Limit Setting," Working Paper, August 5, Converium Re, Zürich, Switzerland.

Dacorogna, M. M., O. V. Pictet, U. A. Müller and C. G. de Vries (2001) "Extremal Forex Returns in Extremely Large Data Sets," Working Paper presented at the 2001 Annual Meeting of the European Finance Association at the University of Konstanz.

Dowd, K. (1998) *Beyond Value at Risk: The New Science of Risk Management*, John Wiley and Sons, New York, NY.

Duffie, D., and J. Pan (1997) "An Overview of Value at Risk," *Journal of Derivatives*, **4**(3), 7–49.

Elliott, Robert J., and John van den Hoek (2000) "A General Fractional White Noise Theory and Applications in Finance," *Quantitative Methods in Finance and Bernoulli Society 2000 Conference* (Program, Abstracts and Papers), 5–8 December, 2000, University of Technology, Sydney, pp. 327–345.

Embrechts, P., C. Kluppelberg and T. Mikosch (1997) *Modeling Extreme Events for Insurance and Finance*, Springer Verlag, New York, NY.

Embrechts, P., S. Resnick and G. Samorodnitzky (1998) "Living on the Edge," *RISK*, 96–100.

Fama, Eugene F. (1965) "Portfolio Analysis in a Stable Paretian Market," *Management Science*, A, **11**(3), 404–419.

Grau, Wolfdietrich (Ed.) (1999) *Guidelines on Market Risk*, Volume 5: Stress Testing, Österreichische Nationalbank (ÖNB), 62 pages.

Hanley, M. (1998) "A Catastrophe Too Far," *RISK Supplement on Insurance*, July.

Hendricks, D. (1996) "Evaluation of Value-at-Risk Models Using Historical Data," *Economic Policy Review*, Federal Reserve Bank of New York, **2**, 39–69.

Hopper, G. (1996) "Value at Risk: A New Methodology for Measuring Portfolio Risk," *Business Review*, Federal Reserve Bank of Philadelphia, July–August, 19–29.

Hua P., and P. Wilmott (1997) "Crash Courses," *RISK*, June, 64–67.

Hull, J. C., and A. White (1987) "The Pricing of Options on Assets with Stochastic Volatilities," *Journal of Finance*, **42**(2), 281–300.

Hull, J. C., and A. White (1988) "An Analysis of the Bias in Option Pricing Caused by Stochastic Volatility," *Advances in Futures and Options Research*, **3**, 27–61.

Hull, J. C., and A. White (1998a) "Value at Risk When Daily Changes in Market Variables Are Not Normally Distributed," *Journal of Derivatives*, **5**(3), 9–19.

Hull, J. C., and A. White (1998b) "Incorporating Volatility Updating Into the Historical Simulation Method for Value at Risk," *Journal of Risk*, **1**(1), 5–19.

Jorion, Philippe (1997) *Value at Risk: The New Benchmark for Controlling Market Risk*, McGraw-Hill, New York, NY.

Ju, X., and N. Pearson (1999) "Using Value-at-Risk to Control Risk Taking: How Wrong Can You Be?," *Journal of Risk*, **1**(2), 5–36.

Kindleberger, Charles P. (1996) *Manias, Panics, and Crashes: A History of Financial Crises*, John Wiley and Sons, New York, NY.

Koedijk, K. G., M. M. Schafgans and G. G. de Vries (1990) "The Tail Index of Exchange Rate Returns," *Journal of International Economics*, **29**(1/2), 93–108.

Lauridsen, Sarah (2000) "Estimation of Value at Risk by Extreme Value Methods," *Extremes*, **3**(2), 107–144.

Litzenberger, R. H., D. R. Beaglehole and C. R. Reynolds (1996) "Assessing Catastrophe Reinsurance – Linked Securities as a New Asset Class," *Journal of Portfolio Management*, **23**(2), 76–86.

Longin, F. M. (1996) "The Asymptotic Distribution of Extreme Value Returns," *Journal of Business*, **69**(3), 383–407.

Lucas, A., and P. Klaasen (1998) "Extreme Returns, Downside Risk, and Optimal Asset Allocation," *Journal of Portfolio Management*, **25**(1), 71–79.

Luciano, Elisa, and Marina Marena (2001) "Value at Risk Bounds for Portfolios of Non-normal Returns," Working Paper, April, University of Turin and International Center for Economic Research (ICER), Turin, Italy.

Mandelbrot, B. B., and J. R. Wallis (1969) "Some Long-Run Properties of Geophysical Records," *Water Resources Research*, **5**(2), 321–340.

Markowitz, Harry M. (1952) "Portfolio Selection," *Journal of Finance*, **7**(1), 77–91.

McCulloch, J. Huston (1986) "Simple Consistent Estimators of Stable Distribution Parameters," *Communications in Statistics – Computation and Simulation*, **15**, 1109–1136.

McCulloch, J. Huston (1996) "Financial Applications of Stable Distributions," in Maddala, G. S., and C. R. Rao (Eds), *Statistical Methods in Finance* (*Handbook of Statistics*), **14**, Elsevier, Amsterdam, The Netherlands, pp. 393–425.

McCulloch, J. Huston (1997) "Measuring Tail Thickness in Order to Estimate the Stable Index α: A Critique," *Journal of Business and Economic Statistics*, **15**(1), 74–81.

McDonald, Robert (2003) *Derivatives Markets*, Addison-Wesley, New York, NY.

McNeil, A. J. (1996), "Estimating the Tails of Loss Severity Distributions Using Extreme Value Theory," Mimeo, ETH Zentrum, Zürich, pp. 5–6.

McNeil, A. J. (1998), "Calculating Quantile Risk Measures for Financial Return Series Using Extreme Value Theory," Mimeo, ETH Zentrum, Zürich, Switzerland.

Peters, Edgar E. (1994) *Fractal Market Analysis*, John Wiley and Sons, New York, NY.

Rachev, Svetlozar, and Stefan Mittnik (2000) *Stable Paretian Models in Finance*, John Wiley and Sons, New York, NY.

Resnick, S. (1987) *Extreme Values, Regular Variation and Point Processes*, Springer Verlag, New York, NY.

Samuelson, Paul, A. (1967) "Efficient Portfolio Selection for Pareto-Lévy Investments," *Journal of Financial and Quantitative Analysis*, **2**(2), 107–122.

Shafer, Glenn, and Vladimir Vovk (2001) *Probability and Finance: It's Only A Game*, John Wiley and Sons, New York, NY.

Sornette, D. (1998) "Large Deviations and Portfolio Optimization," *Physica*, A, **256**, 251–283.

Sornette, D. (2003) *Why Stock Markets Crash: Critical Events in Complex Financial Systems*, Princeton University Press, Princeton, NJ.

Whitcher, B., S. D. Byers, P. Guttorp and D. B. Percival (2002) "Testing for Homogeneity of Variance in Time Series: Long Memory, Wavelets and the Nile River," *Water Resources Research*, **38**(5), 1029–1039.

Wilson, Thomas C. (1998) "Value at Risk," Chapter 3 in Alexander, Carol (Ed.) (1999), *Risk Management and Analysis*, Volume 1: *Measuring and Modelling Financial Risk*, John Wiley and Sons, New York, NY, 61–124.

Appendix A: original scaling in financial economics

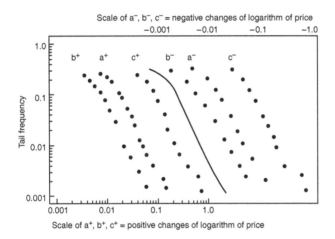

Figure A.1 Mandelbrot's original evidence for scaling in economic pricing processes.

Source: Reprinted from Mandelbrot 1963b by permission of The University of Chicago Press.
© 1963 by The University of Chicago Press.

The original evidence for scaling of the prices in the cotton market was produced by Mandelbrot (1963) and reproduced as Plate 340 in Mandelbrot (1982, p. 340), as in Figure A.1. Mandelbrot advanced the hypothesis of an underlying stable distribution on the basis of the observed invariance of the return distribution across different frequencies and the apparent heavy tails of the cotton price distributions.

Bibliography

Cootner, Paul H. (Ed.) (1964) *The Random Character of Stock Market Prices*, The MIT Press, Cambridge, MA.

Mandelbrot, Benoit B. (1963) "The Variation of Certain Speculative Prices," *The Journal of Business*, **36**, 394–419 and **45**, 1972, 542–543.

Mandelbrot, Benoit B. (1982) *The Fractal Geometry of Nature*, W. H. Freeman and Co., New York, NY (updated and augmented version, 18th printing, 1999).

Appendix B: S&P500 daily closing prices for 1988

The following time series of S&P500 daily closing prices are taken from table 2.7 in Sherry (1992), pp. 29–32. They form a test set of data to be used in some of the Chapter Exercises.

The Asian and Latin American FX and stock market data for Chapter 8 are available from the author on CD at cost.

Obs#	Daily	Obs#	Daily	Obs#	Daily	Obs#	Daily	Obs#	Daily	Obs#	Daily	Obs#	Daily	Obs#	Daily
1	255.940	33	257.910	65	258.510	97	252.570	129	272.020	161	260.240	193	271.860	225	266.470
2	258.630	34	261.610	66	265.490	98	253.020	130	271.780	162	256.980	194	272.390	226	266.220
3	258.890	35	265.640	67	266.160	99	250.830	131	270.020	163	257.090	195	278.070	227	267.210
4	261.070	36	265.020	68	269.430	100	253.510	132	270.550	164	261.130	196	278.240	228	269.000
5	243.400	37	264.430	69	270.160	101	253.760	133	267.850	165	259.180	197	277.930	229	267.230
6	247.490	38	261.580	70	271.370	102	254.630	134	269.320	166	259.680	198	273.980	230	268.640
7	245.420	39	262.460	71	271.570	103	253.420	135	270.260	167	262.330	199	275.220	231	270.910
8	245.810	40	267.820	72	259.750	104	262.160	136	272.050	168	262.510	200	275.500	232	273.700
9	245.880	41	267.220	73	259.770	105	266.690	137	270.510	169	261.520	201	276.410	233	272.490
10	252.050	42	267.980	74	259.210	106	265.330	138	268.470	170	258.350	202	279.380	234	271.810
11	251.880	43	267.880	75	257.920	107	266.450	139	270.000	171	264.480	203	276.970	235	274.930
12	249.320	44	267.300	76	256.130	108	267.050	140	266.660	172	265.590	204	282.880	236	277.590
13	242.630	45	267.380	77	256.420	109	265.170	141	263.500	173	265.870	205	283.660	237	278.130
14	243.140	46	269.430	78	260.140	110	271.520	142	264.680	174	265.880	206	282.280	238	276.590
15	246.500	47	269.060	79	262.460	111	270.200	143	265.190	175	266.840	207	282.380	239	277.030
16	252.170	48	263.840	80	263.930	112	271.260	144	262.500	176	266.470	208	281.380	240	276.520
17	249.570	49	264.940	81	263.800	113	271.430	145	266.020	177	267.430	209	277.288	241	276.310
18	249.380	50	266.370	82	262.610	114	274.300	146	272.020	178	269.310	210	278.530	242	275.310
19	252.290	51	266.130	83	261.330	115	274.450	147	272.210	179	268.130	211	278.970	243	274.280
20	257.070	52	268.650	84	261.560	116	269.770	148	272.060	180	270.650	212	279.060	244	276.290
21	255.040	53	271.220	85	263.000	117	270.680	149	272.980	181	268.820	213	279.060	245	278.910
22	255.570	54	271.120	86	260.320	118	268.940	150	271.930	182	269.730	214	279.200	246	277.470
23	252.210	55	268.740	87	258.790	119	271.670	151	271.150	183	270.160	215	276.310	247	277.380
24	252.210	56	268.840	88	257.480	120	275.660	152	269.980	184	269.180	216	273.930	248	276.870
25	250.960	57	268.910	89	256.540	121	274.820	153	266.490	185	269.760	217	275.150	249	277.870
26	249.100	58	263.350	90	257.620	122	273.780	154	261.900	186	268.880	218	273.330	250	276.830
27	251.720	59	258.510	91	253.310	123	269.060	155	262.750	187	268.260	219	273.690	251	277.088
28	256.660	60	258.060	92	253.850	124	272.310	156	262.550	188	269.080	220	267.920	252	279.400
29	255.950	61	260.070	93	256.780	125	270.980	157	258.690	189	272.590	221	267.720	253	277.720
30	257.630	62	258.070	94	258.710	126	273.500	158	260.560	190	271.910	222	268.340		
31	259.830	63	258.890	95	255.390	127	271.780	159	260.770	191	271.380	223	263.820		
32	259.210	64	260.140	96	251.350	128	275.810	160	261.030	192	270.620	224	264.600		

Figure B.1 S&P500 daily closing prices taken from table 2.7 in Sherry (1992), pp. 29–32.

Index

For Product Safety Concerns and Information please contact our EU
representative GPSR@taylorandfrancis.com Taylor & Francis Verlag GmbH,
Kaufingerstraße 24, 80331 München, Germany

Printed and bound by CPI Group (UK) Ltd, Croydon, CR0 4YY
01/05/2025
01858427-0001